Network Security, Administration and Management:

Advancing Technology and Practice

Dulal Chandra Kar
Texas A&M University–Corpus Christi, USA

Mahbubur Rahman Syed
Minnesota State University, Mankato, USA

Information Science
REFERENCE

Senior Editorial Director:	Kristin Klinger
Director of Book Publications:	Julia Mosemann
Editorial Director:	Lindsay Johnston
Acquisitions Editor:	Erika Carter
Development Editor:	Joel Gamon
Production Editor:	Sean Woznicki
Typesetters:	Natalie Pronio, Jennifer Romanchak, Milan Vracarich Jr
Print Coordinator:	Jamie Snavely
Cover Design:	Nick Newcomer

Published in the United States of America by
Information Science Reference (an imprint of IGI Global)
701 E. Chocolate Avenue
Hershey PA 17033
Tel: 717-533-8845
Fax: 717-533-8661
E-mail: cust@igi-global.com
Web site: http://www.igi-global.com/reference

Library of Congress Cataloging-in-Publication Data

Network security, administration and management: advancing technology and
practice / Dulal Chandra Kar and Mahbubur Rahman Syed, editors.
    p. cm.
  Includes bibliographical references and index.
  Summary: "This book identifies the latest technological solutions, practices
and principles on network security while exposing possible security threats
and vulnerabilities of contemporary software, hardware, and networked
systems"-- Provided by publisher.
  ISBN 978-1-60960-777-7 (hardcover) -- ISBN 978-1-60960-778-4 (ebook) -- ISBN
978-1-60960-779-1 (print & perpetual access) 1. Computer networks--
Management. 2. Computer networks--Security measures. I. Kar, Dulal Chandra,
1960- II. Syed, Mahbubur Rahman, 1952-
  TK5105.5.N466724 2011
  005.8--dc22
                                    2011010430

British Cataloguing in Publication Data
A Cataloguing in Publication record for this book is available from the British Library.

All work contributed to this book is new, previously-unpublished material. The views expressed in this book are those of the authors, but not necessarily of the publisher.

Table of Contents

Section 1
Network Systems Security

Chapter 1

Bruce Hartpence, Rochester Institute of Technology, USA

Chapter 2

Christophe Veltsos, Minnesota State University, Mankato, USA

Chapter 3

Christos Bouras, Research Academic Computer Technology Institute (CTI) &
University of Patras, Greece
Kostas Stamos, Research Academic Computer Technology Institute (CTI) &
University of Patras, Greece

Section 2
Authentication and Data Privacy: Passwords and Keys

Chapter 4

B. Dawn Medlin, Appalachian State University, USA
Douglas May, Appalachian State University, USA
Ken Corley, Appalachian State University, USA

Section 3
Network Security Auditing, Assessment, and Manageability Security

Section 4
Sensor Network Security

Section 5
Security Architectures, Algorithms, and Protocols

Detailed Table of Contents

Section 1
Network Systems Security

This is an introductory chapter that addresses security issues of all common networking devices such as hubs, switches, access points, and routers, as well as vulnerable network protocols such as ARP (Address Resolution Protocol), SRP (Spanning Tree Protocol), ICMP (Internet Control Message Protocol), and DHCP (Dynamic Host Configuration Protocol). In addition, the chapter critically examines security issues in common routing protocols such as RIP (Routing Information Protocol), BGP (Border Gateway Protocol), and OSPF (Open Shortest Path First), as well as some network management protocols such as SNMP (Simple Network Management Protocol) and CDP (Cisco Discovery Protocol). Later, the chapter suggests ways to ensure device security, as well as protocol security to mitigate possible attacks.

This chapter discusses current trend and evolution in security threats, in which attackers use multiple, persistent approaches to attack a target. Traditional security technologies and practices such as anti-virus software, firewalls, intrusion detection systems, cryptosystems, and automated patch delivery and installation mechanisms are shown to have limitations to mitigate such risks and attacks, known as blended threats. Accordingly, the author presents new security controls and strategies to mitigate such evolving risks. In addition, the chapter underscores the need for security awareness education and proposes organized training programs for common users.

Chapter 3

Christos Bouras, Research Academic Computer Technology Institute (CTI) &
University of Patras, Greece
Kostas Stamos, Research Academic Computer Technology Institute (CTI) &
University of Patras, Greece

This chapter addresses security issues of the components that are responsible for provisioning multi-domain network services, particularly for resource reservation and allocation of network services. The authors discuss the importance of inter-domain security during negotiation of resource reservations, as well as intra-domain security during initiation and realization of a resource reservation. Correspondingly, architectures and procedures to handle user authentication, trusted communications between modules or components, and multi-domain user authorization are provided in the context of a case study. Particularly, the chapter presents security requirements and procedures for protecting against various types of attacks on a networked system that supports differentiated services and bandwidth on demand services over multiple domains.

Section 2
Authentication and Data Privacy: Passwords and Keys

Chapter 4

B. Dawn Medlin, Appalachian State University, USA
Douglas May, Appalachian State University, USA
Ken Corley, Appalachian State University, USA

This chapter provides an account of security breaches in healthcare industry due to social engineering attacks and reported results of a simulated study of a social engineering attack on hospital employees to obtain authentication information such as passwords. The authors identify violations of HIPAA (Health Insurance Portability and Accountability Act) and HITECH (Health Information Technology and Clinical Health Act) regulations among healthcare employees who are supposed to protect the privacy and medical records of patients. The chapter also reports research results on the choice of passwords based on human psychology and memory, and exposes severe deficiencies in the choice of passwords by common users that can be exploited easily using social engineering techniques. The findings in the chapter underscore the need for stringent control and aggressive policy.

Chapter 5

Reed Petty, University of Arkansas at Little Rock, USA
Jiang Bian, University of Arkansas at Little Rock, USA
Remzi Seker, University of Arkansas at Little Rock, USA

Security of modern cryptography relies upon secrecy of keys. Public key infrastructure plays the crucial role in the storage management, distribution, and verification of such keys in cryptography. This chapter provides a comprehensive overview of popular public key algorithms, their applications in key exchange and digital signatures, and their vulnerabilities and weaknesses. The chapter identifies several management challenges based on the very basic foundation of trust upon which the public key infrastructure relies. In addition, the chapter highlights emerging technologies such as quantum computing that can make public key cryptographic techniques useless and accordingly discusses implications of quantum cryptography in cryptography in general.

Chapter 6

Chuan-Kun Wu, Chinese Academy of Sciences, China

This chapter describes key management schemes and issues under various application domains such as mobile ad hoc networks, wireless sensor networks, and mobile telecommunication systems. Topics on key management include key agreement, group-based key agreement and distribution, PKI (Public Key Infrastructure) mechanisms, secret sharing scheme based key management, key escrow, password associated key management, key management in PGP, and key management in UMTS (Universal Mobile Telecommunication System) systems. In addition, the chapter discusses limitations of different methods used in key management.

Section 3
Network Security Auditing, Assessment, and Manageability Security

Chapter 7

Aftab Ahmad, Norfolk State University, USA

The sheer complexity of network systems warrants a need for a framework that can be used to assess security in such systems. Specifically, this chapter shows how the ITU-T Network Security Framework (X.805) can be utilized in a performance model for assessing a security system. As an example, the chapter uses a model to assess the security of the popular sensor network standard IEEE 802.15.4. The model can be applied to assess security using security metrics addressing various vulnerabilities and threats, such as destruction of information, corruption of information, loss of information, information disclosure, and service interruption.

Chapter 8

Yin Pan, Rochester Institute of Technology, USA
Bo Yuan, Rochester Institute of Technology, USA
Sumita Mishra, Rochester Institute of Technology, USA

Network security auditing is a process to assess policies, procedures, and controls to identify security risks or vulnerabilities in network systems. This chapter describes network auditing process, procedure, standards, and frameworks. A detailed discussion of procedures and technologies to identify various network security threats and vulnerabilities is provided. State of the art techniques and procedures for determination and management of risks are also discussed. Through a series of procedural steps for a case study, the chapter illustrates different phases of network discovery, network penetration, network threat analysis, and audit reporting.

Chapter 9

Salvador Mandujano, Intel Corporation, USA

Network manageability deals with remote administration, management, and service of network devices and any other devices connected to a network, such as servers, laptop computers, PDAs, and cell phones. This chapter analyzes a number of manageability frameworks, protocols, and services for various platforms such as desktops, laptops, servers, and mobile devices for their vulnerabilities and misuses. Among the manageability protocols discussed, OMA (open mobile alliance) device management protocols for mobile devices to perform firmware updates for changing configurations is noteworthy. The chapter discusses IPMI (Intelligent Platform Management Interface) standard to monitor and reconfigure server platforms using AMT (Active Management Technology) solution on a chipset created by Intel Corporation for laptop and desktop systems.

Section 4
Sensor Network Security

Chapter 10

Murat Al, University of Arkansas at Little Rock, USA
Kenji Yoshigoe, University of Arkansas at Little Rock, USA

Wireless sensor networks belong to a class of ad hoc networks that are very vulnerable to various attacks due to unique characteristics of sensor devices of limited processing power, limited battery life, and limited memory capacity. Chapter 10 provides a general overview of vulnerabilities, attacks, and countermeasures in wireless sensor networks, compares salient characteristics and applications of common wireless technologies with those of wireless sensor networks, describes characteristics of attacks and corresponding countermeasures as proposed in literature, and qualitatively provides a comparative analysis of the attacks on wireless sensor networks. Identifying security vulnerabilities is an essential step towards devising a security solution. The chapter provides an exhaustive list of attacks and corresponding defense mechanisms to mitigate or prevent such attacks. Many of these attacks are found in wireless networks. However, additional attacks, such as denial of sleep attacks to drain battery life, attacks on data aggregation, node capturing, and tampering are very possible on sensor networks due to their characteristics. System constraints and security design issues using current security solutions using cryptographic techniques and other means are discussed in the chapter.

Chapter 11

Sumita Mishra, Rochester Institute of Technology, USA

This chapter provides an overview of emerging applications of wireless sensor networks, correspondingly addresses security concerns, and discusses existing and possible security solutions for such emerging applications of wireless sensor networks. Existing security solutions are found to be inadequate for many emerging sensor network applications that involve collection of highly sensitive data that requires stringent privacy. In particular, the chapter identifies security issues in Body Area Networks (BAN), Smart Grid Networks, and Area Surveillance Networks, and finally, addresses security requirements for such emerging sensor network applications as secure data storage, key establishment and management, access control, and link layer security.

Chapter 12

Md. Golam Kaosar, Victoria University, Australia
Xun Yi, Victoria University, Australia

This chapter presents a computational model as well as a protocol that can be used to maintain data privacy while performing data aggregation operations by intermediate nodes on data en route to the base station from a sensor node. According to the computational model, a sensor node perturbs its data, generates two fragments from the data, and uploads the fragments to two separate semi-trusted servers, from which a data collector or a base station can collect and combine them. Security proofs provided by the authors show that any of the servers or any intermediate sensor node neither can discover any individual data nor can associate any data to an individual. Beyond sensor networks, the scheme has many other content-privacy sensitive applications such as auction, voting and feedback collection, and privacy preserving data mining.

Section 5
Security Architectures, Algorithms, and Protocols

Chapter 13

Rajeev Agrawal, North Carolina A&T State University, USA
Chaoli Cai, Western Michigan University, USA
Ajay Gupta, Western Michigan University, USA
Rajib Paul, Western Michigan University, USA
Raed Salih, Western Michigan University, USA

This chapter proposes a new efficient algorithm to detect anomalous behavior among the mobile nodes of an ad hoc network. Based on belief networks of probabilistic graphical models, the algorithm builds a normal profile during training by utilizing data on relevant features such velocity, displacement, local computation and communication time, energy consumption, and response time of each node in the network. Using a specific Bayesian inference algorithm, the algorithm can distinguish abnormal behavior during testing. In a simulated study by the authors, the algorithm is shown to achieve high detection rates greater than 95%, and with low false alarm rates below 5%. According to the authors, the algorithm can detect anomalies even data is incomplete or missing. The algorithm has many applications, including intrusion detection in ad hoc networks.

Chapter 14

In this chapter, the authors propose a new data regulation protocol that utilizes packet filtering at the source end to mitigate distributed denial of service attacks. The protocol provides a target controlled traffic mechanism implemented at the source gateway. Underlying assumption of the protocol is that the gateway at the source as well as the target can be under attack, but not compromised. The security analysis of the protocol shows its robustness under various attack scenarios such as source address spoofing, distributed attacks, and spoofed acknowledgements. A proof of the concept implementation verifies the claims made by the authors in the chapter.

Chapter 15

Contrary to email and similar other systems, IM (Instant Messaging) systems face a different set of security challenges due to their real-time characteristics. This chapter describes architectures and protocols of today's IM systems, identifies threats to IM services, and offers various defense mechanisms. Particularly, the chapter focuses on the two most damaging attacks, IM spams and IM worms. For IM spams, new detection and spam filtering mechanisms are proposed. A new architecture for detection and defense against IM spams are also proposed.

Foreword

I had the opportunity to review the content of this book and I was very impressed with the quality and variety of interesting topics. The collection of these topics could be very useful as support material for any network security course or as a reference material. These topics cover cryptography (a blended threat approach by cyber attackers); potential security breaches in healthcare industry and need for better password management; use of anomaly detection algorithms in intrusion detection systems; security issues in allocation of network services over multiple federations of networks or services; vulnerability for network manageability; network security auditing; vulnerability of wireless sensor networks; vulnerability of Instant Messaging (IM) due to their real-time characteristics; security issues of all common networking devices as well as routing protocols; security assessment model for network systems; and a new data regulation protocol that utilizes packet filtering at the source end to mitigate distributed denial of service attacks.

Cyrus Azarbod
Minnesota State University, Mankato, USA

Cyrus Azarbod, *PhD, is currently a professor at the Information Systems and Technology department at Minnesota State University at Mankato since September of 1985. He has Ph.D. in computer science (databases). Database security, auditing, and disaster recovery areas are among his focus in teaching and research. Dr. Azarbod is also the founder and CEO of InfoGem which is an Information System consulting company since 1998. He has provided consulting to many companies such as IBM-Rochester, Schweser Study Program (A Kaplan Professional Company), General Electric, and Kato Engineering (a subsidiary of Emerson Company). His training courses and consulting also covers several other areas such as fuzzy relational databases, multi-level secure database systems, security in statistical databases, data modeling, database design and implementation, software engineering, data mining and data warehousing, distributed databases, SQL, Oracle database programming and administration, CASE tools, knowledge discovery, integration of heterogeneous databases, and online course development.*

Preface

The explosive growth and deployment of networking technology that supports connectivity to a diverse range of computing devices running many network systems and applications poses many complex security challenges to networking and computer security professionals. To cope with such ever-increasing security challenges, professionals are often trained with knowledge to handle security problems for specific hardware and software systems, which may be inadequate and inapplicable if a situation or system changes. Having a broad background particularly in the contemporary development of network and information security issues and their solutions would certainly enhance one's ability to adapt to a new situation quickly to handle security issues. However, contemporary research results on network and information security are not readily available in useful or comprehensible form to the people who need them in a timely manner. Accordingly, this book presents a body of literature based on the current research and trends in network and information security with contemporary security issues and solutions and preventive measures. This reference will be particularly useful for those who are in administration and Information Systems management, who are required to be up to date on the latest network and security concepts, protocols, algorithms, and issues relevant to modern network and Information Systems and services. This book presents a diverse set of viewpoints from diverse contributors, such as academics, researchers, and industry professionals.

OBJECTIVES OF THE BOOK

The main purpose of the book is to make current research results on network and information security available and coherent to networking and security professionals, managers, and administrators who often lack the necessary background to understand scholarly articles published in journals and conferences. The book is intended to bridge the gap in knowledge between research communities and security professionals. Specifically, the book aims to accomplish the following objectives:

- To identify, accumulate, and disseminate worldwide, the latest technological solutions, practices, and principles on network and information security for management, administrative, and research purposes
- To provide network security professionals and trainers, network systems designers and developers, and academicians with a book that can serve as a reference
- To provide undergraduate and graduate students in Information Technology, Management Information Systems, Computer Information Systems, and Information Assurance with a book containing theoretical as well practical details of current network and information security practices

- To highlight future security issues and challenges for ever-expanding and emerging network services and systems.

TARGET AUDIENCE

The book is a collection of chapters written by scholars/researchers and professionals well familiar with the state of the art in the area of computer and network security. The book provides a general coverage of network and information security issues, concerns, security protocols, architectures, and algorithms. Recent research results from existing literature on network and information security are reported in the book in a format understandable and usable by networking professionals including network administrators and Information Systems managers. The book will enable networking professionals grasp emerging technological developments in networking and to cope with the corresponding security challenges. In addition, students and educators in computer science, Information Systems, and Information Technology can use the book as a reference for network and information security. Network designers, network engineers, and network systems developers may use the book as a reference to design, develop, and deploy networking systems with appropriate considerations for security and ease of administration accordingly.

ORGANIZATION OF THE BOOK

The book is comprised of fifteen self-contained chapters and divided into the following five sections:

- Section 1: Network Systems Security
- Section 2: Authentication and Data Privacy: Passwords and Keys
- Section 3: Network Security Auditing, Assessment, and Manageability Security
- Section 4: Sensor Network Security
- Section 5: Security Architectures, Algorithms, and Protocols

Section 1: Network Systems Security

This section introduces the readers with basic device, protocol, network, system, and inter-domain security issues and solutions.

Networking devices are integral parts of a computer network and often become targets for attackers and if successful, can make the whole network vulnerable. Internet vulnerabilities of these devices arise from limited capacity of the devices in terms of memory and processing power, limitations of their operating protocols and principles, incorrect configurations, and flaws in hardware and software design and implementation. Chapter 1, "*Basic Device and Protocols Security*," by Bruce Hartpence, addresses security issues of all common networking devices such as hubs, switches, access points, and routers, as well as vulnerable protocols such as ARP (Address Resolution Protocol), SRP (Spanning Tree Protocol), ICMP(Internet Control Message Protocol), and DHCP (Dynamic Host Configuration Protocol). In addition, the chapter examines and exposes security issues in common routing protocols such as RIP (Routing Information Protocol), BGP (Border Gateway Protocol), and OSPF (Open Shortest Path First) protocols as well as network management protocols such as SNMP (Simple Network Management Protocol) and

CDP (Cisco Discovery Protocol) protocols. Finally, the chapter suggests ways to ensure device security, as well as protocol security, to mitigate possible attacks.

Recent technological development in security software, hardware, and mechanisms, such as anti-virus programs, firewalls, intrusion detection systems, cryptosystems, and automated patch delivery systems, have successfully mitigated risks and attacks on cyber based systems and services. However, cyber attackers are devising more sophisticated attacks to exploit new vulnerabilities that are often overlooked, as network or systems administrators are only concerned defending their networks, operating systems, and services on known vulnerabilities. Often such attacks use a blended threat approach in which an attacker uses a number of methods simultaneously to infect and take control of a target system. Chapter 2, by Dr. Christophe Veltsos, *"Mitigating the Blended Threat: Protecting and Educating Users,"* examines this evolving threat, discusses limitations of traditional security technologies and controls to mitigate this threat, and presents new security controls to mitigate this type of new evolving risks. In addition, the chapter proposes security awareness education and training programs for common users to mitigate the blended treat.

Multi-domain resource reservation involves provisioning and allocation of network services over multiple federations of networks or services. One such example is bandwidth and queue allocations at the network elements for providing QoS over multiple domains. Cooperating components that are responsible for provisioning services over multiple domains must ensure inter-domain security during negotiation of resource reservations, as well as intra-domain security during initiation and realization of a resource reservation. Chapter 3, *"Security Issues for Multi-Domain Resource Reservation,"* by Christos Bouras and Kostas Stamos addresses such security issues in this context and provides architectures and procedures to handle multi-domain user authentication, trusted communications between inter-domain modules or components, and multi-domain user authorization. Particularly, the chapter presents security requirements and procedures for protecting against various types of attacks on a networked system for differentiated services and "bandwidth on demand" services over multiple domains.

Section 2: Authentication and Data Privacy: Passwords and Keys

In this section, we present three chapters that deal with vulnerabilities of password-based authentication mechanisms due to social engineering attacks, as well as key management mechanisms and infrastructures currently used for data privacy and other cryptographic services.

Social engineering attacks exploit inherent human characteristics such as kindness, mutual trust, willingness to help, et cetera to gain access to unauthorized private information, systems, and services. A hospital or a healthcare facility is very susceptible to social engineering attacks as unauthorized attackers can easily befriend healthcare workers or providers in such an environment. Chapter 4, *"Healthcare Employees and Passwords: An Entry Point for Social Engineering Attacks,"* by Dawn Medlin, Douglas May, and Ken Corley provides an account of security breaches in healthcare industry and discusses violations of HIPAA (Health Insurance Portability and Accountability Act) regulations. In addition, the chapter provides an analysis of research results on the choice of passwords characteristically based on human psychological traits and memorization ability and exposes severe deficiencies in passwords used by common masses, as they are very predictable or obtainable easily by social engineering means. Specifically, the chapter focuses on research on the choice and usage of passwords by employees in five different hospitals and reports significant findings that employees are very likely to share their passwords with their family members and other healthcare employees. These findings underscore the need for stringent control and aggressive policy, not only in healthcare industry, but also in other similar industries as well.

Security of modern cryptography relies upon secrecy of keys. Public key infrastructure plays the crucial role in the storage management, distribution, and verification of such keys in cryptography. Chapter 5 by Reed Petty, Jiang Brian, and Remzi Seker entitled *"Public Key Infrastructure,"* presents a comprehensive overview of popular public key algorithms, their applications in key exchange and digital signatures, and their vulnerabilities and weaknesses. The chapter identifies several key management challenges based on the very basic foundation of trust upon which the public key infrastructure relies. In addition, emerging technologies such as quantum computing that can make public key cryptographic techniques useless are also discussed. However, quantum cryptography can offer new solutions to all of our cryptographic needs instead, as stated in the chapter.

Public key cryptography has eliminated the need for a separate secure channel for transmission of the secret key to be shared by the communicating entities. However, the straightforward application of public key cryptography for key exchange is vulnerable to man-in-the-middle attacks. The problem is solved with a public key infrastructure (PKI) that serves as a certifying authority for all public keys. But managing public key certificates is rather complex as it requires one or more certification authorities, and the process involves excessive computation and communication cost. Alternatively, identity based cryptography simplifies the process as it eliminates the need for public certificate verification. Chapter 6 by Chuan-Kun Wu, *"Key Management"* provides a survey of current key management schemes and discusses key management issues under various application domains such as mobile ad hoc networks, wireless sensor networks, and mobile telecommunication systems. Subsequently, the chapter covers in detail the mechanisms of public key infrastructure, key escrow systems, and the key management aspects in the PGP email system. In addition, the chapter covers password-based key management as well as secret sharing scheme based key management schemes. Finally, the author critically delineates limitations in various key management methodologies.

Section 3: Network Security Auditing, Assessment, and Manageability Security

This section deals with managerial aspects of network security such as standards, frameworks, and procedures for assessment and auditing of network security as well as security issues of manageability hardware and software technologies.

Network systems are complex, and hence, require a reference framework to account for all possible threats and for assessment of security with a good degree of confidence. Chapter 7, *"Security Assessment of Networks"* by Aftab Ahmad stresses the need for a framework for security assessment and proposes an assessment model for network systems. Particularly, the chapter shows how the ITU-T Network Security Framework (X.805) can be utilized in a performance model for assessing a security system. As an example, the chapter uses the model to assess the security of the popular sensor network standard IEEE 802.15.4. The model can be applied to assess security using security metrics addressing vulnerabilities and threats such as destruction of information, corruption of information, loss of information, information disclosure, and service interruption.

Existing security technologies such as firewalls, intrusion detection systems, and cryptography, though they have greatly boosted security for networks and computer systems, are often insufficient to deter and prevent certain types of attacks, such as Web-based attacks, hidden backdoors, et cetera. Network security auditing is a process to assess policies, procedures, and controls to identify security risks or vulnerabilities in network systems. Network security auditing can expose threats from such attacks by setting appropriate security policies, procedures, and controls. Chapter 8, "*Network Security Auditing*" by Yin Pan, Bo Yuan, and Sumita Mishra introduces network auditing process, procedure, standards, and frameworks. A detailed discussion of procedures and technologies to identify various network security threats and vulnerabilities is provided in this chapter. State of the art techniques and procedures for determination and management of risks are also discussed. Through a series of procedural steps for a case study, the chapter illustrates different phases of network discovery, network penetration, network threat analysis, and audit reporting.

Network manageability deals with remote administration, management, and service of network devices and any other devices connected to a network such as servers, laptop computers, PDAs, and cell phones. Manageability hardware and software technologies allow an administrator through an out of band channel to remotely access and troubleshoot a system regardless of the conditions or the power state of the system. Chapter 9, "*Network Manageability Security*" by Salvador Mandujano analyzes a number of manageability frameworks, protocols, and services for various platforms such as desktops, laptops, servers, and mobile devices. Manageability technologies are also vulnerable to attacks and misuses on the system such as firmware tampering, device tracking, device reconfiguration, loss of administrative control, and so on. Several manageability protocols are discussed in this chapter including the OMA (Open Mobile Alliance) device management protocol for mobile devices that can be used to perform firmware updates and change configurations. The chapter also discusses IPMI (Intelligent Platform Management Interface) standard to monitor and reconfigure server platforms such as AMT (Active Management Technology) solution on a chipset created by Intel Corporation for laptop and desktop systems and DASH (Desktop and Mobile Architecture for System Hardware) as a standard that makes remote administration of hardware over a TCP/IP network. Finally, it describes and discusses security issues of SNMP (Simple Network Management Protocol).

Section 4: Sensor Network Security

Wireless sensor networks belong to a class of ad hoc networks that are very vulnerable to various attacks due to unique characteristics of sensor devices of limited processing power, limited battery life, and limited memory capacity. Accordingly, this section provides a survey of security concerns, attacks, and solutions for existing, as well as emerging applications of wireless sensor networks. In addition, it includes a new data privacy protocol that allows in-network data aggregation.

Chapter 10 by Murat Al and Kenji Yoshigoe, "*Security and Attacks in Wireless Sensor Networks*," provides an overview of vulnerabilities, attacks, and countermeasures in wireless sensor networks, compares salient characteristics and applications of wireless sensor networks with those of common wireless technologies, describes characteristics of attacks and corresponding countermeasures as proposed in literature, and qualitatively provides a comparative analysis of the attacks on wireless sensor networks. Identifying security vulnerabilities is an essential step to devise a security solution. The chapter provides an exhaustive list of attacks and corresponding defense mechanisms to mitigate or prevent such attacks. Many of these attacks are found in wireless networks. However, additional attacks such as denial of sleep attacks just to drain battery life, attacks on data aggregation, and node capturing and tampering are very possible on sensor networks due to their characteristics. System constraints and security design issues using current security solutions such as cryptographic techniques and other means are also discussed in this chapter.

Wireless sensor networking technology has found extensive applications in many sectors. Despite wide applicability, security is a big concern as their environment of deployment is often easily accessible, making a wireless sensor network very vulnerable to attacks. Chapter 11: "*Wireless Sensor Networks: Emerging Applications and Security Solutions*" by Sumita Mishra addresses security concerns and discusses existing and possible security solutions particularly for emerging applications of wireless sensor networks. Existing security solutions are found to be inadequate for many emerging sensor network applications involving collection of highly sensitive data that requires stringent privacy. It is very challenging to design a robust and efficient security scheme for wireless sensor networks due to limited processing power and battery life of sensor nodes. In particular, the chapter exposes security issues in Body Area Networks (BAN), Smart Grid Networks, and Area Surveillance Networks, and finally, addresses security requirements for such emerging sensor network applications in terms of secure data storage, key establishment and management, key establishment and management, access control, and link layer security.

Communication activities are excessively more energy consuming than computation in wireless sensor networks. Data aggregation, or in-network processing of data in a wireless sensor network, is an attempt to reduce communication overhead to extend the life of the network for an application. However, data privacy is a big concern since a data aggregating node along a path to the base station can reveal the data in plaintext. Accordingly, Chapter 12: "*Privacy Preserving Data Gathering in Wireless Sensor Networks*" by Md. Golam Kaosar and Xun Yi presents a computational model as well as a protocol that can be used to maintain data privacy while performing data aggregation operations by intermediate nodes on data en route to the base station from a sensor node. According to the computational model, a sensor node perturbs its data, generates two fragments from the data, and uploads the fragments to two separate semi-trusted servers, from which a data collector or a base station can collect and combine them. Security proofs provided by the authors shows that any of the servers or any intermediate sensor node neither can discover any individual data nor can associate any data to an individual. Beyond sensor networks, the scheme has many other content-privacy sensitive applications such auction, voting and feedback collection, and privacy preserving data mining.

Section 5: Security Architectures, Algorithms, and Protocols

This final section presents new research results on security architectures, algorithms, and protocols for detection and prevention of intrusions and distributed denial of service attacks, as well as for controlling of spams and worms in instant messages.

Many Intrusion Detection Systems for traditional wired networks often use anomaly detection techniques in their core to detection intrusions by comparing an abnormal traffic behavior or pattern with the normal traffic behavior or pattern. In contrast, such comparison of traffic patterns becomes very challenging in an ad hoc networking environment due to node mobility and lack of a fixed infrastructure within the network. Chapter 13: "*BANBAD: A Centralized Anomaly Detection Technique for Ad Hoc Networks*" by Rajeev Agrawal, Chaoli Cai, Ajay Gupta, Rajib Paul, and Raed Salih proposes a new algorithm for anomaly detection that is found to be very suitable for ad hoc networks. The anomaly detection algorithm is based on statistical Belief Networks (BN) that builds a normal profile during training by using system features and checks deviation during testing. As ad hoc networks are very dynamic in nature due to mobility of their nodes, they may hinder any on-going data collection process for intrusion detection, which can in turn cause a great deal of difficulty in accurate profile generation by an intrusion detection scheme. As such, existing intrusion detection schemes will not work, due to constantly changing network configuration and/or incomplete information. As reported in the chapter, the proposed anomaly detection algorithm is found to detect anomalies even if data is incomplete or missing in such a dynamic environment.

Distributed Denial of Service (DDoS) attacks on a target host can be launched remotely by an adversary using freely available attacking tools. Categorically, three types of DDoS attacks are possible: 1) a master node recruits a multitude of agent nodes by exploiting their vulnerabilities and carries out a well-coordinated attack on the target simultaneously, 2) a single malicious node that launches the attack by spoofing its IP address, and 3) in a hybrid attack, a master node recruits and configures each agent machine for address spoofing for its outgoing packets.

Chapter 14: *"Data Regulation Protocol for Source-End Mitigation of Distributed Denial of Service Attacks"* by Nirav Shah and Dijiang Huang proposes a new data regulation protocol that utilizes packet filtering at the source end to mitigate distributed denial of service attacks. The protocol provides a target controlled traffic mechanism implemented at the source gateway in contrast with target-end filtering network using firewalls. The underlying assumption of the protocol is that the gateway at the source as well as the target can be under attack, but not compromised. The security analysis of the protocol shows its robustness under various attack scenarios such as source address spoofing, distributed attacks, and spoofed acknowledgements. A proof of the concept implementation verifies the claims made by the authors in the chapter. The proposed protocol holds the gateway of the source network accountable for all of the egress traffic leaving the network thus providing an incentive for source-end filtering.

Instant Messaging (IM) is a popular and efficient communication mechanism that allows users to chat from desktops to cellphones and hand held devices. Though simple and convenient, contrary to email and other similar systems, IM systems face a new security challenges due to their real-time characteristics. Chapter 15: *"Instant Messaging Security,"* by Zhijun Liu, Guoqiang Shu, and David Lee provides a review of the architectures and protocols of today's IM systems, identifies threats to IM services such as IM spam and IM worm, provides a survey of various defense methods, and eventually, proposes new, effective solutions for filtering IM spam and controlling IM worm, including smart worm. In this chapter, several spam detection, controlling, and filtering mechanisms such as challenge-response filtering, fingerprint vector based filtering, Bayesian filtering, and collaborative feedback based filtering are discussed and evaluated for IM systems. In addition, the authors provide a mathematical model for IM worm behavior and correspondingly propose defense mechanisms including a topology aware throttling scheme to slow down worm propagation.

The concept of computer networking started with the purposes of communication, sharing of hardware, data files, and software. The chapters in this book demonstrate how the increase in complexity of the nature of services provided by networking and rise in the malicious intent of some participants has made security issues and security management a very core area in communication. The readers will be familiar with network security administration, its current trends and issues, and find that as wonderful and useful as networking is for sharing resources and saving cost and time, it has to be secure to even be considered a solution. Else, it would be creating more problems than it is solving.

Dulal C. Kar
Texas A&M University-Corpus Christi, USA

Mahbubur Rahman Syed
Minnesota State University, Mankato, USA

Acknowledgment

We would like to thank all of our authors for their scholarly contributions that have made this book a resourceful document with the contemporary research results in network and information security. Without their contributions, this book would not be a reality. We thank our editorial advisory board members for their support in all phases of the book project such as dissemination of our invitation for book chapters, communicating with prospective authors, and review of book chapters. Our sincere thanks go to the book chapter reviewers, whose constructive and comprehensive reviews have helped to enhance the quality of the book in many respects. We acknowledge contributions of our graduate student assistants, Ms. Geetha Sanapala who assisted us in collecting email addresses and preparing email lists of prospective authors, and Mr. Clifton Mulkey who assisted us in last-minute reviewing of some chapters.

A special note of thanks goes to the staff members of IGI Global for their constant editorial assistance and professional support that helped to keep the project on schedule. Particularly, we would like to thank Ms. Erika Carter whose invitation for editorship offered us the opportunity for this editorial service and Mr. Joel Gamon who supported us with necessary guidance and documents to smoothly manage the project in all phases since its inception.

Finally, we hope that the readers will be greatly benefitted from the book.

Dulal C. Kar
Texas A&M University-Corpus Christi, USA

Mahbubur Rahman Syed
Minnesota State University, Mankato, USA

Section 1
Network Systems Security

Chapter 1
Basic Device and Protocol Security

Bruce Hartpence
Rochester Institute of Technology, USA

ABSTRACT

Security texts often focus on encryption techniques, firewalls and security for servers. Often missing are the inherent weaknesses in the very building blocks of modern local area networks. This chapter discusses the devices and protocols common to every single production network running today in terms of their basic security vulnerabilities and provides some techniques for reducing security threats. Specifically, this chapter will cover the operation of routers, switches and access points with a brief mention of hubs. Protocols covered will include the spanning tree, internet control message, address resolution, management, and routing protocols. Packet captures and screenshots will be used to illustrate some of the protocols.

INTRODUCTION

There is more to network security than encrypting user data, virtual private networks or installing firewalls. While these are very important, we must review every aspect of network communication to ensure that we are providing adequate protection to network resources. The reality is that every device and protocol has its own set of vulnerabilities.

DOI: 10.4018/978-1-60960-777-7.ch001

In addition, most network activities such as file transfer are simply implemented with the intent on accomplishing the end goal rather than being designed with security in mind.

As a result, we currently deploy networks that are plagued by security holes at all levels of the TCP/IP (or OSI) model and every type of networking device. These security holes are present not because a programmer didn't protect against buffer overflow or there was a flaw in the encryption algorithm, but because devices and protocols are operating exactly as intended. The good news is that with an understanding of basic behavior and some minor configuration changes, many of these weaknesses can be minimized or eliminated entirely. Lastly, by having insight into the network and understanding the baseline measurements, one can more easily respond to an attack in progress or deal with the aftermath. This chapter will examine some of the common elements deployed today and how the standard operation makes reconnaissance for an attacker simpler. We will also discuss some basic steps to help mitigate the security holes.

Sometimes understanding the nature of an attack or our vulnerabilities can give us an idea as to the vectors that might be used. The reverse is also true. Regardless of your point of view, it is difficult to defend against an attack if you do not understand nature of the attack. There are many reasons that an attacker may target a network and attacks are not always for material gain. Some of these reasons include but are not limited to;

- Spotting an easy target
- Access to user data
- Access to company resources especially bandwidth or storage
- Denial of service
- Settling a grudge
- Competition
- Fun

Underscoring the need to understand the threat is a series of polls from the Computer Security Institute. For more than a decade this organization has collected data on attack types, security deployments, personnel skills and many other aspects of computer crime. Consistently, the top threats or problems experienced by those responding to the poll are viruses, insider abuse and laptop theft or fraud (Richardson, 2008). Some insider threats result from poorly configured security that gave unauthorized personnel access to restricted

resources. No matter the cause, it is clear that a better firewall isn't the answer.

RECONNAISSANCE

Apart from the most obvious or brute force attacks, exploits usually begin with some sort of investigation or reconnaissance. Depending on the goal of the attack, the recon may be as simple as driving around looking for an open access point that is still using the default configuration or a much more in-depth analysis of network traffic, behavior and resources. The information gained during this phase of the attack can come from a wide variety of sources. Employees may be unwitting accomplices as they are tricked or social engineered into revealing information. Wireless scans can often be very fruitful and some companies even post a considerable amount of information on web pages in order to make employee resources easier to find. As an example, many organizations may electronically post the locations or even IP addresses of printers and servers. The intent is that employees will now be able to more easily connect to these devices without having to generate a troublecall to the helpdesk. Of course this also makes it easier on the bad guy.

Some methods of gaining information are passive in that the attacker is not actively running queries such as a port scan at a system on the network. The best example is probably eavesdropping or capturing packets. It is interesting that many companies do not report problems with eavesdropping but a very appropriate question is; "How do you know?" Recon can also be much more aggressive including configuration attempts or attacking a network element. Auditing companies even engage in dumpster diving and waiting for receptionist coffee breaks to get by security.

It is not always obvious what the target actually is. If the attacker takes advantage a switch weakness, we might say that the switch was under attack and assume this to be the target. In fact, this was simply a more active form of reconnaissance. The attacker was hoping to learn something from the traffic flowing out of the switch. Once the information has been obtained, the real attack may begin. One of our major goals with network security is to reduce the ability of the bad guys to complete their reconnaissance.

EQUIPMENT

Every network is comprised of the same basic equipment and capabilities. Each piece of equipment also comes with its own set of security vulnerabilities ranging from exposure of data to allowing control of the device. We'll start from the bottom of the TCP/IP protocol stack and work our way up, examining devices at layers one, two and three and the associated problems. Specifically we'll take a look at hubs, access points, switches and routers.

Hubs

While most organizations have moved away from hubs, we've included them as a reference point. As we know, hubs have some defining characteristics;

- They do not possess a great deal of intelligence
- They repeat traffic out all ports except the source port
- While fast, they do not scale well due to collisions
- They typically do not filter traffic

The obvious security problem is that hubs essentially broadcast traffic to any node connected which means that an attacker gaining access to a network port can see everything. However, it is worth noting that this particular behavior can vary between manufacturers. For example, some vendors isolate slower speed connections. As for access to live ports, it is not uncommon to see

jacks installed in conference rooms, seating areas or spare offices.

For these performance and security reasons, hubs have largely been replaced with switches. So, we're safe from prying eyes right? Wrong. It turns out that there are other network devices that either behave like a hub in certain situations or can be forced to act like a hub through some sort of attack.

Access Points

Another name for an access point is wireless hub. While this isn't exactly accurate, it is not too far off either. Like a hub, the access point (AP) broadcasts traffic to anyone capable of hearing it. The difference is that while an attacker had to get access to a physical port in order to see the hub traffic, when an AP is present you only need an antenna. It is like sprinkling ports everywhere. Let's take a little closer look at AP behavior. The AP has several major responsibilities;

- Notifying network users of its presence and negotiating connections
- Forwarding traffic between the wired and wireless sections of the network
- Handling traffic for all of the wireless nodes currently connected
- Encrypting or otherwise securing traffic if configured to do so

These are requirements of every AP being used and these standard functions introduce security holes into your network. For the moment we'll put aside the broadcast nature of the traffic and discuss these basic AP responsibilities.

An AP uses a special frame called a beacon to inform you of its presence and includes the wireless communication parameters. This same frame advertises the AP to potential attackers. The common approach to protect against this is to remove the SSID or network id from the beacon frame, so that the beacon does not broadcast the network name. The reality is that this doesn't actually hide the network because this same information is included in another frame called the probe response.

The probe response is the AP answer to a probe request sent from a node that already knows of the network. When a valid node wishes to join a network, it does not typically wait for a beacon frame. Instead it transmits a probe request to speed up the association process. So, an attacker wishing to learn about your network simply has to wait for the AP to issue a probe response. This is a process that can occur several times a second depending on how many nodes are present. In addition, because of roaming behavior and nodes going into sleep to conserve power, probe requests are a regular part of the network traffic. In fact, by removing the SSID from the beacon frame, you may actually be creating problems for the valid wireless

users and encouraging them to connect to rogue APs (Ciampa, 2007). A probe response with the exposed SSID of "teamJ" is shown in Figure 1.

APs also connect the wired and wireless segments together. Traffic flows between the two sides. This means that when nodes on either side of the AP communicate, the AP forwards everything. Let's take a couple of examples. When two wireless nodes communicate, as long as they are connected to the same AP, the transmission is limited to the wireless segment and does not cross to the wired side. The same can be said of two wired nodes communicating as these frames stay on their side of the network. However, when one node is wireless and one is wired, this traffic exists on both sides of the AP. The problem being introduced here is that an attacker listening in on wireless traffic can now determine not only the

Figure 1. 802.11 Probe Response

```
⊟ IEEE 802.11 MAC Protocol
    Function            Probe Response
  ⊞ PLCP Header
  ⊞ Frame Control Byte 0
  ⊞ Frame Control Byte 1
    Duration ID         14849
  ⊞ Destination Address
  ⊞ Source Address
  ⊟ BSSID
      Hex Address       00-0F-F8-58-1D-53
      Group Bit         [xxxxxxx0 xxxxxxxx xxxxxxxx xxxxxxxx xxxxxxxx]  off
      Local Bit         [xxxxxx0x xxxxxxxx xxxxxxxx xxxxxxxx xxxxxxxx]  off
    Fragment            [xxxxxxxx xxxx0000]  0
    Sequence            [00110111 0000xxxx]  880
    Time Stamp          3560575421038723072
    Beacon Interval     100
  ⊟ Capability Information
      Channel Agility   [0xxxxxxx xxxxxxxx]  Off
      PBCC              [x0xxxxxx xxxxxxxx]  Off
      Short Preamble    [xx1xxxxx xxxxxxxx]  On
      Privacy           [xxx0xxxx xxxxxxxx]  Off
      CF Poll Request   [xxxx0xxx xxxxxxxx]  Off
      CF Pollable       [xxxxx0xx xxxxxxxx]  Off
      IBSS              [xxxxxx0x xxxxxxxx]  Off
      ESS               [xxxxxxx1 xxxxxxxx]  On
      Reserved          [xxxxxxxx 00000000]  0
  ⊟ Information Element
      Identity          SSID
      Length            5
      SSID              teamJ
```

wireless nodes present, but the wired nodes and servers as well.

If we add broadcast traffic to the mix, we can see that it no longer matters where the node is because AP behavior in the presence of broadcast frames is to send broadcast frames everywhere. As an example, a wired node generates an address resolution protocol (ARP) request for a node on the same network. This type of message is necessarily a broadcast frame. If we assume that the wired node is connected to a switch, the switch forwards the ARP request everywhere, including the port used by the AP. Upon receipt of the ARP request, the AP waits for an opportunity to transmit and then broadcasts this ARP request to the wireless network.

Propagation distance for a particular wireless transmission between wireless hosts is limited by their surroundings, power level and antenna type. Often APs are equipped with improved transmission capabilities when compared to wireless nodes. By handling this traffic, the AP is usually increasing the distance that a transmission will travel. In fact, if we were to compare the network diameter of an ad hoc network to that of an infrastructure network using APs we would see that installing the AP can double the network footprint. If we add the signal improvement of an 802.11n network, this transmission distance is again pushed further out.

So an attacker can find an AP of a target network whether that AP is broadcasting the SSID or not. In addition, we can now see that the traffic in jeopardy is not just that of the wireless nodes but the wired nodes as well. The AP and nodes can be configured to encrypt the transmission which solves some of these problems. However, there are still many organizations and home users that have not taken this step. The percentage of wireless networks that are still unencrypted is astonishing. A recent study revealed that 25% of small companies running wireless networks do not password protect them (NCSA, 2009). In addition, those that have deployed encryption techniques often make mistakes on the implementation and

do not go far enough with their solutions. We have seen a shift to WiFi Protected Access with a Pre-Shared Key (WPA-PSK) instead of WEP, but these implementations often use short, easy to guess passphrases.

Attackers can also learn from non-data traffic on a wireless network. There is quite a bit more management traffic on a wireless network than on a wired Ethernet network because of the operation of 802.11. Beacon and probe request frames are just two examples. Others include association requests and authentication frames. In addition, this traffic is often not encrypted with the data traffic. It is very common to see unencrypted management even if the data is protected. An attacker wishing to learn MAC addresses or see the operation of the network with an eye towards breaking the encryption need only capture frames passively.

Lastly, 802.11 operations create other vulnerabilities because of the management frames. For example, hosts do not authenticate the management frames. In other words, hosts listen to or obey management frames that they receive, making them easy targets for hijacking or denial of service via the authentication and association conversations. If an attacker forges a disassociation message and sends it to a wireless host, the host will disconnect from the network. It will try to reconnect but this sort of forgery is often the beginning of a larger attack. To illustrate the problem, the node reconnecting goes through the WPA-PSK handshake process. This is precisely what the attacker wanted to see because the information contained in the handshake is part of the keying material and is required in order to perform certain attacks including breaking the encryption.

Switches

As a replacement for hubs, switches have done very well especially since the cost per port has come down, capabilities are greater and link speeds have improved. Switches also have many features that hubs never possessed. From a security standpoint, some key benefits to switches include changes to the forwarding behavior (no longer broadcasting all traffic), support for virtual local area networks (VLANs), basic port security and 802.1X.

Switches forward based on MAC address (at least for known devices) and consult a source address table before transmitting a frame to the destination. This means that for a significant portion of network traffic, only the proper destination receives the transmission. This is a major improvement over the method used by hubs, even if the forwarding decision and processing of the frame cyclical redundancy check (CRC) both introduce latency. This method of forwarding is not without its weaknesses. For unknown addresses, broadcast (a destination MAC address of ff-ff-ff-ff-ff-ff) and multicast (a destination typically beginning with a first octet of 01) traffic, the switch behaves just like a hub in that forwards these frames out all ports but the source. This process is called flooding. VLANs can reduce the effect of flooding because they can be used to segment the switch into smaller logical network segments. This means that this sort of traffic is only flooded to a particular VLAN.

In addition to flooding, switches have other vulnerabilities because of their basic operation. The source address table or SAT is an example of one place a switch can be attacked. The switch tries to populate the SAT with MAC addresses learned from the traffic seen on the network. A typical SAT has enough capacity to store the MAC addresses of thousands of network devices, and the switch consults and updates this table every time a frame is received. But what happens if the SAT table space is filled? In this case, the switch cannot place a new address into the SAT and so must flood any traffic not matching the addresses already in the SAT. A clever attacker will fill the SAT with addresses by sending extra traffic to the switch. This traffic has a different source MAC address in each frame. The result is that frames destined for the valid network nodes must be flooded everywhere, essentially turning

the switch into a hub (Paggen & Vyncke, 2007). A great tool for generating frames is *macof*.

As stated earlier, VLANs can be an effective tool for breaking up a network and make it more difficult for an attacker to discover valuable network resources. In a switch without VLANs, any network host connected to the switch is connected to the same logical domain as all other hosts. A VLAN boundary would prevent the host from seeing existing layer 2 traffic on the other VLANs, effectively breaking a switch into several smaller switches. This is an improvement but the use of VLANs still does not make the switch or traffic impervious to attack. In addition to the attacks previously mentioned, one of the side effects of placing more and more intelligence into switches is that they often try to configure ports automatically. The goal is to negotiate the connection parameters with the opposite end of the link. A simple example of this is the speed negotiation for a 10/100/1000 port. Many other parameters can be negotiated including the port mode of operation.

VLANs can span several switches. In order to convey VLAN membership information between switches, a trunking protocol is used. A trunk port understands the trunking protocol and is used by the switch to sort out traffic destined for the various VLANs. Every frame traveling on a trunk line between switches running VLANs will be encapsulated in a trunking protocol. The industry standard trunking protocol is 802.1q. To facilitate communication between switches, the ports are often allowed to dynamically determine the parameters for the link. A port that is permitted to dynamically configure itself can change to a trunk port as opposed to the normal "access" port operation and vice versa.

An attacker can take advantage of this by tricking the switch port into believing that another switch with a trunk port is present. The attacker sends a dynamic trunking protocol message to the switch and the switch, believing a neighbor switch to be present, changes the attackers port from access mode to trunk mode. Following basic operation, all broadcast or flooded traffic destined for any VLAN will also be sent out any trunk ports. The switch is simply trying to reach as many network nodes as possible. Unfortunately this also includes the attacker.

The other half of an attack like this is to not only see traffic, but transmit into the network. Once node VLAN membership is determined, the attacker can generate frames tagged for the proper VLAN and using the destination MAC address of the target. In this way traffic can be directed to any VLAN or destination known to the switch.

Lastly, switches participate in other protocols that have their own vulnerabilities. By exploiting either the structure or operation, an attacker can drastically affect network performance and completely disrupt traffic. We will discuss some of these in the protocol section of the chapter.

Routers

Stating the obvious, routers route. Send a packet to a router for forwarding and it will send it to the destination. Routers come in many shapes and sizes and while they all possess the same basic functionality, there is a big difference between what we call a router that might be used in a production network and a home gateway product. It is only when we start adding things like filter lists and policies do routers become a device that can contribute to network protection. A home gateway comes with built in firewall capability, network address translation, management interfaces and a dynamic host configuration protocol (DHCP) server. In many ways, the home gateway is a more secure device out of the box than an access router used in a company network.

Routers are also similar to network hosts. They require IP addresses in order to operate (switches and APs do not) and they use and respond to ARP messages. ARP messages can be used to exploit both host and router traffic through what is called a man in the middle attack. Man in the middle is

discussed in more detail in the section on ARP. Like switches, routers participate in protocols that can be exploited. Examples include ICMP, routing protocols and management. While not all of these escalate to ownership of the router itself, they can be used to easily disrupt network traffic and operation. A more thorough discussion of ARP, ICMP, routing protocols and management issues can be found later in the chapter.

A Word about Network Traffic

Our discussion to this point has focused on network devices and what they effectively give away due to their standard operation. Gaining access to traffic can be a big part of an attackers' reconnaissance. Almost all traffic on a network is what we call clear-text". This means that passive observers can the read the contents of a particular packet because by default, it is not encrypted. It turns out that if we were to capture a random series of packets on a network we would be able to read or see the following items;

- The layer 2 header including the MAC addresses
- The layer 3 header including the IP addresses
- The layer 4 header including the port numbers
- The application data

As for the application data, the amount that can be read varies from transaction to transaction but in many cases all of the content can be read. For example, an FTP conversation can be read in its entirety including the username and password. The same is also true for telnet. Many parts of a web page sent over the network via http can be read. An example of this is shown in Figure 2.

This particular packet was captured while browsing to the IP address of an unsecured router. As you can see, details regarding the device, telephone numbers and essentially any other text

Figure 2. HTTP packet

```
Hypertext Transfer Protocol
Line-based text data: text/html
    <HTML><HEAD><TITLE>Router Home Page</TITLE></HEAD>\r\n
    <BODY BGCOLOR=#FFFFFF><H1>Cisco Systems</H1><H2>Accessing Cisco 2651 "Router"</H2>\r\n
    <MENU><DL><H4></H4>\r\n
    <P>\r\n
    <DT><A HREF=telnet://192.168.1.254>Telnet</A> - to the router.<P>\r\n
    <DT><A HREF=/exec/show/interfaces/CR>Show interfaces</A> - display the status of the interfaces.\r\n
    <DT><A HREF=/exec/show/log/CR>Show diagnostic log</A> - display the diagnostic log.\r\n
    [truncated] <DT><A HREF=/level/15/exec/->Monitor the router</A> - HTML access to the command line interface at level <A HREF=/level/00/exec/->0,
    <P>\r\n
    <DT><A HREF=/exec/show/tech-support/cr>Show tech-support</A> - display information commonly needed by tech support.\r\n
    <P><DT><A HREF=/go/qdm>QoS Device Manager</A> - Configure and monitor QoS through the web interface.\r\n
    </DL></MENU>\r\n
    <HR>\r\n
    <H3>Help resources</H3>\r\n
    <OL>\r\n
    <LI><A HREF=http://www.cisco.com>CCO at www.cisco.com</A> - Cisco Connection Online, including the Technical Assistance Center (TAC).\r\n
    <LI><A HREF=mailto:tac@cisco.com>tac@cisco.com</A> - e-mail the TAC.\r\n
    <LI><B>1-800-553-2447 or +1-408-526-7209</B> - phone the TAC.\r\n
    <LI><A HREF=mailto:cs-html@cisco.com>cs-html@cisco.com</A> - e-mail the HTML interface development group.\r\n
    </OL>\r\n
    </BODY></HTML>\r\n
    \r\n
```

is visible. For space, this is actually a portion of the overall packet. Were the entire contents displayed here, we could see the MAC addresses, IP addresses, port numbers, type of transmission, browser used and the destination. This sort of information helps the attacker determine the best type of exploit to use on a particular target.

Some developers have taken a step towards security by encrypting the username and/or password before they are transmitted. However, this does not mean that the data is covered by the same encryption. For example, you may need a password to access a network share but once you access a file, we are back to clear text.

PROTOCOLS

IP based networks depend on the operation of a couple of basic protocols. No matter what organization is running the network, these protocols or their cousins are always present. Examples include the address resolution protocol, spanning tree, internet control message protocol and routing protocols. Each of these is critical, and all of these have inherent security flaws.

Address Resolution Protocol (ARP)

The purpose of ARP is to find the MAC address associated with an IP address. A node initiating the conversation issues an ARP request for a particular IP address. This is a broadcast frame and from our previous discussion we know that both switches and access points forward these everywhere. If the node matching the destination IP address is available, then it will return an ARP reply. All hosts use ARP messaging including routers. In addition, though not required for normal operation, if a switch or AP is given an IP address for management purposes, ARP will be used here as well.

Note that like many conversations, the ARP messages are easily read by an observer. Once a node receives a reply, the application traffic can now begin to flow because the Ethernet frames can be properly addressed. In addition, this newly acquired information is temporarily stored by the source host in an ARP table. If an attacker can corrupt the table, then the host (or the data sent from the host) may be able to be exploited. An example of the ARP table is shown in Figure 3.

Some operating systems are willing to accept unsolicited ARP replies. This means that even if a host never asks for the MAC address of a destination IP, the attacker may supply one in hopes

Figure 3. ARP Table

```
Interface: 192.168.1.2 --- 0xb
  Internet Address      Physical Address      Type
  192.168.1.1           00-e0-29-29-8a-8a     dynamic
  192.168.1.254         00-05-32-da-5a-a1     dynamic
  192.168.1.255         ff-ff-ff-ff-ff-ff     static
  224.0.0.9             01-00-5e-00-00-09     static
  224.0.0.22            01-00-5e-00-00-16     static
  224.0.0.252           01-00-5e-00-00-fc     static
  255.255.255.255       ff-ff-ff-ff-ff-ff     static
```

that the host will populate the ARP table with bad information. The idea is that the destination IP will be mapped to the MAC address of the attacker rather than the real destination. However, even if the host is not willing to listen to these unsolicited messages, it is possible for an attacker to simply wait for the questions to be asked and then try to beat the valid answer back to the host. Another approach is to simply fill the network with answers. The first answer received is assumed to be the correct one. It gets worse. Not only will an attacker poison the ARP table of a host, but of the router as well (Nachreiner, 2009).

At this point, the host believes that the attacker is the router and the router believes that the attacker is the host. Thus the attacker is the "man in the middle". Upon receiving traffic from either of these, the attacker simply forwards the traffic on after copying anything they desire. In this way, all traffic between the two devices is at risk. Finally, since ARP is part of normal operations, this traffic is never questioned and the attack is invisible to the nodes involved. Unfortunately, we rarely check our ARP tables for bad information. In fact, it's quite probable that even if we read the table, the bad information might not be recognized for what it is.

Spanning Tree Protocol (STP)

The spanning tree protocol (STP) defined by IEEE 802.1D runs between layer 2 bridges and switches. The primary mission of STP is to prevent loops from occurring in an Ethernet network. Were a loop to exist, traffic would have the potential to circulate endlessly to the point of preventing valid network traffic from flowing. This is because unlike IP, layer 2 frames do not possess a time to live field and are never removed from the network. In this regard, the protocol works very well, albeit slowly. For this reason, there have been improvements made to STP, namely rapid STP. However, the operational goals are essentially the same; eliminate logical loops through the election of a root bridge and the establishment of a tree like structure. This is accomplished via the exchange of special STP frames called bridge protocol data units or BPDUs. In a topology where loops are discovered, certain switch ports will be blocked preventing traffic from flowing in that direction. What is important to realize is that spanning tree automatically builds the layer 2 topology.

Part of the behavior during normal operation is to allow topology changes when a switch joins or leaves the network. At this point, the other switches listen to either new BPDUs or respond to the loss. Factors affecting the topology changes include the MAC addresses of the switches, path costs, port IDs and priority values.

The problem is that all of the switches listen to this information and must act on it. So, an attacker wishing to disrupt the operation of the network can inject BPDUs into the network which can trigger topology changes. If done often enough or at the right frequency, the network can become inoperable because of the constantly changing pathways (IEEE, 1998). For example, if a network has reached steady state such that the traffic flows in a particular direction, an attacker can inject BPDUs that will force the traffic to flow in the opposite direction. During a topology change, it is not uncommon for network nodes to experience a temporary loss of connectivity. Removing the injected traffic changes the traffic direction again. The effect can be devastating and is simply taking advantage of the basic behavior of a very common protocol.

Wireless networks can have additional problems because the speeds of the wireless links are slower than on the wired segments. If all of the network traffic was to be directed over the wireless links, severe bottlenecks or outages could occur as the links were overrun. In addition, many wireless devices can act as either access points or bridges. Configuration and wiring mistakes can create as many problems as attackers do.

Internet Control Message Protocol (ICMP)

The Internet Control Message Protocol (ICMP) defined in RFC 826, has two basic functions; error and information messaging. The protocol is designed to provide feedback in the event that a destination cannot be reached or a transmission is not allowed. It can also give us information regarding the presence of a particular IP address and aid in path discovery. There are several different types of ICMP messages, and several reasons for including ICMP in any discussion of security. The first is that like many network transmissions, these messages are clear text and can aid in network reconnaissance. Examples of important information might be addresses of routers on the network, addresses of MobileIP foreign agents or even information about the network settings.

The ICMP echo request also provides an attacker with a "known good" for many attacks since it usually carries the alphabet as can be seen in Figure 4. Traffic can be injected into an encrypted network which results in the bad guy having both the unencrypted and the encrypted version of the same traffic. This makes cracking the encryption much easier.

An attacker almost couldn't ask for an easier pattern to match. Once the attacker obtained the encrypted version of the same thing, working backwards using the same algorithm reveals the key used.

ICMP is also tool for the attacker to use while performing reconnaissance on your network or staging attacks. Almost all IP based devices are

Figure 4. ICMP Echo Request

```
Internet Control Message Protocol
   Type: 8 (Echo (ping) request)
   Code: 0 ()
   Checksum: 0x485c [correct]
   Identifier: 0x0400
   Sequence number: 256 (0x0100)
⊟ Data (32 bytes)
     Data: 6162636465666768696A6B6C6D6E6F707172737475767761...
     [Length: 32]

00 11 21 2c 16 21 00 05   32 da 5a a0 08 00 45 00    ..!,.!.. 2.Z...E.
00 3c 01 44 00 00 7f 01   b4 2a c0 a8 02 01 c0 a8    .<.D.... .*......
03 01 08 00 48 5c 04 00   01 00 61 62 63 64 65 66    ...H\.. ..abcdef
67 68 69 6a 6b 6c 6d 6e   6f 70 71 72 73 74 75 76    ghijklmn opqrstuv
77 61 62 63 64 65 66 67   68 69                      wabcdefg hi
```

programmed to listen and respond to ICMP messages. By using basic programs like PING and TRACERT which generate ICMP messages, a potential attacker can find out a great deal about your network.

PING sweeping is a method by which an entire address space is "pinged" one address at a time in order to see which addresses give answers. PING has many options, some of which can be used for path discovery. TRACERT is an excellent diagnostic tool but attackers can use this same tool to find their way through your network and gain the addresses of the router interfaces. Again, these are basic components of any IP based network and the devices are simply obeying their normal operation. In Figure 5 the output from a Windows tracert displays not only the router interfaces contacted, but the pathway used.

Lastly, ICMP messaging, most notably the ICMP redirect (see Figure 6) can be used by an attacker the poison the host routing table. This is another form of the man in the middle attack outlined in the ARP section.

The purpose of a redirect message is to inform the host of a better pathway to the destination. The better pathway is actually via a different router. Once the host learns of this, it updates the local routing table and uses that entry from that point on. But what if the new pathway was not a router at all but an attacking machine instead? The host is completely unaware of this because redirects are a part of the normal protocol operation. The attacker simply made it appear as though the redirect message came from a valid router. Once the attacker receives the redirected packets, they are copied and forwarded to the proper destination via the proper pathway (Mason & Newcomb, 2001). This is also a difficult attack to detect because it looks like standard traffic. Redirects are actually a normal part of networking. Like ARP tables, we rarely check our routing information unless there is a problem. If done correctly, the man in the middle attack leaves no

Figure 5. Tracing a Route

```
Tracing route to OZLAN041 [192.168.3.1]
over a maximum of 30 hops:

  1    1 ms    1 ms    1 ms  192.168.1.254
  2    2 ms    1 ms    1 ms  192.168.2.254
  3    1 ms    1 ms    1 ms  OZLAN041 [192.168.3.1]

Trace complete.
```

Figure 6. ICMP Redirect

```
Internet Control Message Protocol
  Type: 5 (Redirect)
  Code: 0 (Redirect for network)
  Checksum: 0xe1fc [correct]
  Gateway address: 192.168.2.254 (192.168.2.254)
⊞ Internet Protocol, Src: 192.168.2.1 (192.168.2.1), Dst: 192.168.3.1 (192.168.3.1)
⊟ Internet Control Message Protocol
    Type: 8 (Echo (ping) request)
    Code: 0 ()
    Checksum: 0x485c [incorrect, should be 0xf2ff]
    Identifier: 0x0400
    Sequence number: 256 (0x0100)
```

trace and does not disrupt traffic. *Ettercap* is another tool to add to the toolbox.

Routing Protocols

Most organizations run some sort of interior routing protocol to help ensure that all of their network segments are reachable and have some protection against failure. Static routing, while quick and reliable, requires management and the routes do not automatically failover upon loss. Routers running routing protocols exchange information (in clear text of course), and then decide whether or not to change their local routing tables based on the received information. Common interior routing protocols include the Routing Information Protocol (RIP) and Open Shortest Path First (OSPF).

In a RIP packet, information regarding some of the networks known by the router is clearly visible. But the real problem with routing protocols is that they are often designed with minimal security in mind. When a router shares information in the form of a RIP table exchange or an OSPF link state update, other routers participating in the same protocol will listen. This is fine if the information is valid. However, as with some of the scenarios already outlined, there is nothing to stop an attacker from sending a properly formatted but nonetheless false routing update. This can force all of the routers to change aspects of the routed topology just as we saw with spanning tree. At a minimum this causes disruption of service but in some cases a clever attacker can route traffic off-site and then route it right back to the valid routers. This was demonstrated at the 2008 DefCon conference where a small team of security researchers hijacked all of the traffic destined for the security conference (Zetter, 2008). While this particular attack was completed using the Border Gateway Protocol (BGP) which is designed for a different type of network, it serves to illustrate the problem.

Dynamic Host Configuration Protocol (DHCP)

The primary purpose of the Dynamic Host Configuration Protocol (DHCP) is to provide a network host with information required to operate on the network. Minimally this will include;

- IP address
- Network Mask
- Default Gateway

However, there are many options associated with DHCP and so a message can include much more information about the network including an indication of services available and the addresses of the computers offering the service. An example of a DHCP acknowledgement packet is shown in Figure 7.

In this case we can see that even a basic DHCP message will include such items as the IP address, DHCP server address, host name, mask, router and servers. This information can make DHCP messages very attractive to an attacker performing reconnaissance. Like all of the protocols and devices discussed in this chapter, DHCP is a part of almost every single network and therefore almost every single network has some level of exposure to attack if steps are not taken to secure the conversation.

Problems with DHCP extend well beyond our ability to see into the packet. Many servers are configured with a free pool of addresses so any host asking for an IP address will receive one, even if it doesn't belong on the network. This is true of most home networks as well since wireless home gateways come preconfigured as a DHCP server. Even if this free pool of addresses is minimized or removed, IP addresses can be stolen or spoofed by attackers impersonating valid nodes because the traffic can be captured and read if it is unencrypted. DHCP provides all of the information that an attacker requires in order to operate on your network.

Figure 7. DHCP ACK

```
Bootstrap Protocol
   Message type: Boot Reply (2)
   Hardware type: Ethernet
   Hardware address length: 6
   Hops: 0
   Transaction ID: 0xef203a67
   Seconds elapsed: 0
 ⊞ Bootp flags: 0x8000 (Broadcast)
   Client IP address: 0.0.0.0 (0.0.0.0)
   Your (client) IP address: 192.168.1.2 (192.168.1.2)
   Next server IP address: 0.0.0.0 (0.0.0.0)
   Relay agent IP address: 0.0.0.0 (0.0.0.0)
   Client MAC address: HonHaiPr_12:1c:a9 (00:1f:e2:12:1c:a9)
   Client hardware address padding: 00000000000000000000
   Server host name not given
   Boot file name not given
   Magic cookie: (OK)
 ⊞ Option: (t=53,l=1) DHCP Message Type = DHCP Offer
 ⊞ Option: (t=54,l=4) DHCP Server Identifier = 192.168.1.254
 ⊞ Option: (t=51,l=4) IP Address Lease Time = 23 hours, 54 minutes, 9 seconds
 ⊞ Option: (t=58,l=4) Renewal Time Value = 11 hours, 57 minutes, 4 seconds
 ⊞ Option: (t=59,l=4) Rebinding Time Value = 20 hours, 54 minutes, 52 seconds
 ⊞ Option: (t=1,l=4) Subnet Mask = 255.255.255.0
 ⊞ Option: (t=6,l=4) Domain Name Server = 192.168.1.99
 ⊞ Option: (t=44,l=4) NetBIOS over TCP/IP Name Server = 192.168.1.100
 ⊞ Option: (t=15,l=4) Domain Name = "test"
 ⊞ Option: (t=3,l=4) Router = 192.168.1.254
   End Option
   Padding
```

Industrious hackers can even insert a DHCP server of their own into a network and provide IP addresses to hosts. Hosts do not care where the address comes from, they just want one. In this way an attacker can direct host to whatever resources they want.

Management Protocols

Management protocols like the Simple Network Management Protocol (SNMP) and the Cisco Discovery Protocol (CDP) can be very helpful for either obtaining information or controlling network devices remotely. Used with care they are very powerful allies when trying to keep tabs on your network elements and performance. This is especially true of SNMP. SNMP uses what is

called a "community string" as a form of password when requesting data from a device or making configuration changes. The community string is sent in cleartext of course. While SNMPv3 provides increased security, many devices do not support this version or have capability issues. So it is much more typical to see previous versions deployed.

There are many web pages that list the default usernames, passwords and IP addresses for a wide variety of equipment. The same is true for SNMP community strings. Some vendors have early versions of SNMP enabled by default. When combined with the clear text nature of the protocol, SNMP can represent a significant security threat. Imagine losing control or your own network devices because they were using default

SNMP values or sending them in unencrypted and unauthenticated. SNMP is also a routable protocol which means that devices allowing queries or control via SNMP can be reached from anywhere.

While CDP is not used to control network elements, it does provide a great deal of information and is run by default on all Cisco equipment. An example of a CDP message is seen in Figure 8. In this case we can see a good deal of information about the device. With these details provided, an interloper can now tailor the attack to the device, looking up popular or successful exploits against this particular device and software combination (Vladimirov, 2006).

It is instructive to review how we actually connect to a network element when making configuration changes. When sitting in the same wiring closet it is common to connect to a device via the console or serial port. However, this connection has a limited physical distance and so does not scale well as we deploy devices across the company campus. Typically we perform some level of basic configuration using the console port and then move to an IP based method for communicating with the device. The most common protocols are telnet, SSH, HTTP or HTTPS.

Most security policies specify that telnet shall not be used because it transmits the username and password in clear text. In addition, HTTP is considered insecure because part of its transmission is also viewable. However, there is a lot of older equipment that lacks support for more advanced protocols. There may be an increased cost because HTTPS and SSH are packaged in an advanced feature set that may be beyond an organizations budget. If this is the case, a decision must be made to either find some way of making the connection more secure or disallowing remote access to the device.

One other notable problem is that many vendors enable the web interface by default. The usernames and default passwords are well known and an attacker need only browse to the correct IP address in order to gain control over the device. The http packet seen in Figure 2 was obtained in this way. This has been a problem for home gateway devices and much higher end production equipment.

ATTACK MITIGATION

Thus far we have discussed some of the security weaknesses introduced by the devices and protocols that are part of almost every single network. Often we see that many advanced attacks follow a simpler exploit against one of these weaknesses

Figure 8. CDP Packet

```
Cisco Discovery Protocol
  Version: 2
  TTL: 180 seconds
⊞ Checksum: 0xbf6f [correct]
⊞ Device ID: Switch
⊞ Addresses
⊞ Port ID: FastEthernet0/5
⊞ Capabilities
⊟ Software Version
    Type: Software version (0x0005)
    Length: 218
    Software Version: Cisco Internetwork Operating System Software
              IOS (tm) C2950 Software (C2950-I6Q4L2-M), Version 12.1(22)EA8, RELEASE SOFTWARE (fc1)
              Copyright (c) 1986-2006 by cisco Systems, Inc.
              Compiled Fri 12-May-06 17:19 by myl
⊟ Platform: cisco WS-C2950-24
    Type: Platform (0x0006)
    Length: 21
    Platform: cisco WS-C2950-24
```

and the intended target has little to do with the original harassment. Stated another way, the first attack is only a prelude to another larger, more dangerous attack. As an example, early reconnaissance may reveal the type of devices being used, their operating systems, patch level and any applications that might be running. Therefore, if we can make it more difficult for the bad guy to complete the first attack, the second more deadly attack may never occur.

Baselining

A visit to the doctor almost always results in a check of our weight and blood pressure regardless of the reason for going. These regular checks provide the background that assists in future diagnostics. Without this information we are shooting in the dark as to what normal is supposed to be. In the same way, regular checks on the health of your network make it much easier to solve problems or keep potential attackers out. The idea is to take a look at what is running on your network, how well the network currently operates and perform some level of testing on your own systems in order to discover potential weaknesses. The value of performing top to bottom intrusion tests against every single network asset has been debated with some questioning the time and money spent on the process. A sample of some of the key points can be found in an Information Security Magazine article in which security experts Bruce Schneier and Marcus Ranum outline the issue (Ranum & Schneier, 2007). No matter the side of the debate, few dispute the importance of having a good understanding of what is normal for network operation. While you may decide to limit the testing that is done against every system, sticking your head in the sand is asking for trouble. This is true for not only security, but optimization and troubleshooting as well.

There are several baseline tests that we might complete and many of them can be automated. These measurements should include items like protocol distribution and utilization numbers but also an evaluation of what type of traffic is actually running on the network, especially during changes and even when the organization is closed. Having a lot of nighttime traffic may indicate network intrusions. This includes the protocols discussed in this chapter and the applications that the network consumers are using. For example, what percentage of your traffic is specific to the Internet? How many TCP SYN messages (which indicate connection requests) do you see over a particular period of time? Changes to these values may indicate problems with services or a potential attack.

Protecting Network Devices

We know that each type of device has its own particular set of vulnerabilities. In many cases, the device also has a set of corresponding security techniques to help defend against threats. What follows is a discussion of some of these techniques for each device, except for hubs. The only recommendation that for hubs is to avoid using them.

Access points have another weakness that most other network devices do not have – they are often deployed where the users can see them, sometimes actually being within reach. This is a problem for theft and because most APs have hardware reset buttons. An attacker can simply push the button to put the AP back to the original factory settings or reconfigure it such that it looks like properly set up with the correct SSID, but with the attacker rather than the administrator in control. So access points should be deployed out of sight and perhaps with a locking mechanism. The only components that might be visible are the antennas. Even this isn't always necessary depending on the construction materials near the AP.

The following best practices should also be a part of the wireless configuration;

- Change the default configuration values.

- Encrypt the traffic. Minimally WPA2-PSK with a 20 character passphrase. However, this ties security to the device and not the user. For more robust security using 802.1X with EAP-TLS or PEAP.
- Filter traffic to/from the wireless segments
- Even with more robust encryption and authentication, wireless users can use VPNs for access if you believe the threat level sufficient.
- Make sure that you periodically survey your physical spaces for excessive coverage, rogue devices, unwanted traffic and the presence of other potentially harmful wireless signals.
- Send APs back to the switch in their own VLAN.

The protection for switches focuses primarily on the individual ports. The important ideas are limiting the traffic that can be sent out and the damage that an attacker can do (Castellini, 2005). Switch best practices include;

- Using VLANs to segment the network.
- All unused ports should be shut down and placed in a VLAN that is not routable and pruned from trunk lines.
- Remove dynamic configuration options from the ports.
- Use port security options. Port security tools typically control the number of MAC addresses associated with a particular port. A specific list of allowable MAC addresses can also be maintained. If an unknown MAC address or an excessive number of MAC addresses are seen on a particular port, the switch can opt to prevent the traffic or even shut the port down.

Router security primarily focuses on management and access to the device. The big problem for routers is that they are IP enabled and are often directly accessible from the public Internet. Re-gardless of the type of device (switch, AP, router, etc.) management best practices encompass;

- Creating accounts for users instead of allowing access without a password or community passwords for configuration.
- Disable telnet and http access to the device.
- The network used to manage the device should be different than the production network. It is not uncommon to use a specially addressed network that is only accessible via internal networks so the management IP addresses are not public.
- It is always a good idea to save your configurations off of the machine and log configuration changes or attempts.
- Limit the services that are run locally.

Network Protocols

In our protocol discussions, we have examined several potential vectors that may be used to compromise a network. Some of these can be addressed via configuration changes but many cannot. In the case of the latter, our primary defenses are either disallowing the traffic or vigilance.

ARP is an example of a protocol that is so pervasive and simple, it is difficult to modify the operation to make is more secure without creating problems for the network. Often we do not realize that a problem exists until connectivity problems have been reported. Fortunately, an attacker wishing to exploit ARP has to be on the same network as the target and so may be easier to spot. However, wireless segments remain a challenge but encryption can help. Our best defense may be knowing the values (or at least the vendor codes) and locations of the correct MAC addresses. In this way, when we see duplication in ARP tables or changing locations in source address tables we may be alerted to a potential problem. The hard part is that we have to look and these are not usually on the agenda for the network administrator.

Minimally network documentation should include an inventory of local MAC addresses.

ICMP has a profile that is similar to ARP in that it is part of every network. However, many of the ICMP message types are not used in today's networks and so it is possible to block most of this type of traffic without creating problems for your network. For example, most users do not use PING or TRACERT and so ICMP can easily be filtered out in these sections of the network. To prevent reconnaissance from outside, routers can be configured to ignore or filter out external requests using ICMP. Lastly, since ICMP is a handy diagnostic tool, filter rules can be written to allow only specific devices or users to transmit ICMP messages. We must be careful as complex networks occasionally make use of ICMP redirects or destination unreachable messages. Eliminating ICMP from the network would remove these tools. IPv6 may offer some hope with these protocols as ARP is no longer part of network operations. However our dependence on ICMP actually increases. But, IPv6 has encryption integrated into the protocol for greater privacy.

Spanning tree is a necessary part of the network and one that can be defended to a certain extent. First, it is possible that your network may not depend on STP everywhere and so some of the vectors can be shut down. Local spanning tree priorities can be set to low values so that an attacker may have a harder time forcing your topology to change. In addition, devices can be configured to ignore BPDUs that are received on particular ports or unauthorized configuration charges.

Routing protocols represent two basic problems for a security minded network administrator; exposure of routing information and the possibility for route manipulation. Fortunately there are features and practices that will help in securing this portion of the network traffic. Since almost any routing protocol will handle the basic functions required, it is prudent to consider all of capabilities during selection. For example, a protocol like RIP advertises routing information with every single packet. A protocol such as OSPF only sends this information during the initial configuration of the links. This alone reduces exposure of the data as the routers only generate simple "HELLO" packets the rest of the time. To help solve our other problem, OSPF messages can be authenticated with encrypted passwords so that routers need not react to false messages. The data itself is not encrypted.

When using DHCP there are some basic practices that can help with the security of the protocol. We know that DHCP can give away a lot of information about the network. According to WindowsSecurity.com, the first line of defense against such an inherently insecure protocol is solid physical security for the network. The free pool of addresses should be minimized or even eliminated. There is no reason to give out addresses to every node sending a request. DHCP also has the ability to use reservations. Hosts are given an IP address that has been set aside for them based on their MAC address. This server can also log all lease operations which provides a record of these transactions. To be clear, a clever attacker can get around these reservations by spoofing a valid MAC address but this often raises red flags. While it is beyond the scope of this chapter it is important to realize that the DHCP server is vulnerable and should be patched and hardened.

Management protocols such as SNMP and CDP should be disabled. More importantly, network traffic should be monitored in order to see what else is running on the network both intentionally and by accident. Shutting these protocols down will reduce the information given out and the ability of attackers to take control of network devices. There are occasions where remote management is desired and for these, SNMPv3 has the ability to not only authenticate the messaging but also encrypt the transmission.

To conclude this section we could say that some of our best tools for dealing with the network security issues discussed in this chapter might be our awareness of normal network behavior, our willingness to take a look at what might have changed and applying some basic techniques on network devices and protocols to control what attackers can learn about the network.

SUMMARY

This chapter has focused on devices and protocols that are part of almost every single IP based network. Both are more than willing to provide potential interlopers with information about your operations and architecture through their normal and expected behavior. By reviewing the basic performance we can get a greater understanding of the threat represented and take a few steps in mitigating some of the problems by providing less information to the attackers. Specifically we concerned ourselves with STP, ICMP, ARP, DHCP, routing and management protocols. Devices covered included hubs, switches, access points and routers.

REFERENCES

Castellini, M. J. (2005). *LAN switching first step* (pp. 205–215). Indianapolis, IN: Cisco Press.

Ciampa, M. (2007). *CWSP guide to wireless security* (pp. 49–53). Boston, MA: Thompson Course Technology.

IEEEComputer Society. (1998). IEEE standard for Information Technology–telecommunications and information exchange between systems–local and metropolitan area networks–common specifications part 3: Media Access Control (MAC).

Mason, A. G., & Newcomb, M. J. (2001). *Cisco secure Internet security solutions*. Indianapolis, IN: Cisco Press.

Nachreiner, C. (2009). Anatomy of an ARP poisoning attack. *WatchGuard Network Security Analyst*. Retrieved March 2010 from http://www.watchguard.com/infocenter/editorial/135324.asp

NCSA. (2009). *October 2009 NCSA / Symantec small business study*. Retrieved March 2010 from http://staysafeonline.mediaroom.com/index.php?s=43&item=51

Paggen, C., & Vyncke, E. (2007). *LAN switch security: What hackers know about your switches*. Indianapolis, IN: Cisco Press.

Ranum, M., & Schneier, B. (2007). Bruce Schneier and Marcus Ranum debate the necessity of penetration tests. *Information Security Magazine*. Retrieved March 2010 from http://searchsecurity.techtarget.com/magazineFeature/0,296894,sid14_gci1256987_mem1,00.html

Richardson, R. (2008). *2008 CSI computer crime and security survey* (pp. 14–15). Computer Security Institute.

Tulloch, M. (2006). *DHCP server security*. Retrieved March 2010 from http://www.windowsecurity.com/ articles/DHCP-Security-Part1.html

Vladimirov, A. A. (2006). *Hacking exposed Cisco Networks – Cisco security secrets and solutions*. Emeryville, CA: McGraw-Hill.

Zetter, K. (2008). Revealed: The Internet's biggest security hole. *Wired Magazine*. Retrieved March 2010 from http://www.wired.com/threatlevel/2008/ 08/revealed-the-in/

ADDITIONAL READING

Castellini, M. J. (2005). *LAN Switching First Step* (pp. 205–215). Indianapolis, IN: Cisco Press.

Ciampa, M. (2007). *CWSP Guide to Wireless Security* (pp. 49–53). Boston, MA: Thompson Course Technology.

Comer, D. (2008). *Computer Networks and Internets* (5th ed.). Upper Saddle River, NJ: Prentice Hall.

Deering, S. (1991). *RFC 1256 - ICMP Router Discovery Messages.*

Forouzan, B. (2003). *Data Communications and Networking*. New York, NY: McGraw-Hill.

Gupta, M. (2006). *RFC 4443 - Internet Control Message Protocol (ICMPv6) for the Internet Protocol Version 6 (IPv6)*. Specification.

Held, G. (2003). *Securing Wireless LANs*. Hoboken, NJ: John Wiley & Sons Inc. doi:10.1002/0470869690

IEEE Information technology Telecommunications and information exchange between systems - Local and metropolitan area networks - *Specific requirements - Part 11: Wireless LAN Medium Access Control (MAC) and Physical Layer (PHY) Specifications, 1999.*

IEEE Standard for Local and Metropolitan Area Networks. (2004). *Media Access Control (MAC)*. Bridges.

Johnson, A. (2008). *Routing Protocols and Concepts*. Indianapolis, IN: Cisco Press.

Plummer, D. C. (1982). *RFC 826 - Ethernet Address Resolution Protocol.*

Postel, J. (1981). *RFC 792 – Internet Control Message Protocol.*

Chapter 2
Mitigating the Blended Threat:
Protecting Data and Educating Users

Christophe Veltsos
Minnesota State University, Mankato, USA

ABSTRACT

While technological controls such as anti-virus, firewall, and intrusion detection, have been widely used to mitigate risk, cyber-attackers are able to outsmart many such controls by crafting new and more advanced malware and delivering them via planned attacks, a perfectly blended threat. This chapter explores this evolving threat and the failure of traditional controls. New strategies are presented to address this new threat landscape, including both human and technological approaches to mitigating risks of doing business in a Web 2.0 world.

INTRODUCTION

In early January 2010, Google shocked the world by revealing that it had been hacked. Just a month earlier, hackers had penetrated Google's systems to steal intellectual property as well as data about some of its Gmail service users, notably human rights activists (Google, 2010; Zetter, 2010). The event was not an isolated case, however, and reports quickly surfaced that as many as 20 other large U.S. companies had been similarly probed and breached, including some outside the technology sector such as companies in the finance and chemical sectors. The attacks were targeted with pinpoint accuracy and the attackers had successfully penetrated the technical defenses in place at some of the most technologically and security savvy companies.

Financial sector companies, a lucrative target for attackers, have also had their share of security incidents. In early 2009, Heartland Payment Systems announced that its computer systems had suffered one of the largest data breach ever, potentially exposing as many as one hundred and

DOI: 10.4018/978-1-60960-777-7.ch002

thirty million credit card transactions (Worthen, 2009; DatalossDB, 2010). The level of sophistication of the attack was termed "light-years more sophisticated" (Zetter, 2010) than commonly seen malevolent activity. The malware was so deeply rooted that an earlier investigation by internal employees and regular audits had not been able to detect its presence. In March 2010, one of the masterminds behind the attack was convicted to 20 years in jail for his role in the breach. Yet, this was only one in a string of massive breaches perpetrated by the same small group of attackers, who, according to the indictment, would "identify potential corporate victims, by, among other methods, reviewing a list of Fortune 500 companies" (US-DOJ, 2010, p. 6). The list of companies infiltrated by this group reads like a who's who of large businesses. For Heartland however, the costs of dealing with the aftermath of this incident are still mounting. According to the company's Q1-2010 SEC filings, it has spent upwards of 139 million dollars to deal with the "processing system intrusion" (US-SEC, 2010).

However, attackers are not solely focused on large, well-funded targets. Any business that has something of value—be it financial, intellectual, military or healthcare data—can find itself a target. Furthermore, the continued decentralization of IT infrastructure means that there are more systems to be secured and sensitive data is likely to flow all throughout the enterprise and beyond with the use of Web 2.0 technologies. Meanwhile, information security professionals have the arduous task of ensuring the confidentiality, integrity, and availability (CIA) of data across the enterprise, using a combination of physical, technical, and administrative controls. Yet, these professionals have come to realize that many of the technologies that work today to protect the company may no longer be effective tomorrow. The need to continuously adjust one's security measures is due not only to the rapid adoption of new technologies but also to the rapid rate of innovation shown by attackers. Attackers are able to exploit new vulnerabilities almost as soon as existing ones are being patched, creating a constant game of cat and mouse between security professionals and attackers.

As companies embrace the benefits of Web 2.0—a term used broadly to include rich Internet-based applications, Software As A Service, and Cloud Computing—new opportunities are created for attackers to try to acquire, modify, or destroy company data. As explained in more details in the sections that follow, current technological controls have so far proven quite ineffective in countering these new and rapidly evolving threats. Existing policies must be updated, or new ones created, and practices must be adjusted to ensure continued safety and privacy of sensitive data. To date, a company's best tactic in protecting sensitive data is the adoption of appropriate technical controls combined with the education of its workforce about the risks posed by a Web 2.0 world.

The failure of existing technical controls to provide adequate protection against these threats puts greater importance on hardening systems that handle sensitive data, developing an incident response capability to deal with incidents that are likely to arise, and developing more effective information security education, training, and awareness programs (SETAs). While SETAs need to be periodically revised in order to stay current with company policies and practices as well as the ever-changing nature of threats, management also needs to evaluate and validate the effectiveness of SETA programs, rather than simply counting the percentage of employees who have completed the annual awareness training.

CYBER-CRIME: A CLEAR AND PRESENT DANGER

In less than a decade, business executives, government leaders, and citizens everywhere have come to realize the rapid rise of a new problem, one with global actors and victims: cyber-crime.

While relatively new, cyber-crime knows no borders. Worse, attackers can choose to operate or relocate to areas that have weak legislative or judicial processes or to politically troubled areas where bribes may offer protection from law enforcement. The truly global nature of this business means that anyone, anywhere, can attack anyone else, whether they are within shouting distance or half a world away.

Recent reports from law enforcement, incident response companies, or security product vendors point to a thriving underground market for stolen electronic data (Richardson, 2008; Secunia, 2008a; Sophos, 2009a; Symantec, 2010; Verizon, 2009), one that has matured to the point that hackers can increase their profits by specializing in a given skill-set (e.g. browser hacks or PDF hacks). According to the FBI (2010), cyber-criminals can specialize in being malware coders, stolen data brokers, IT infrastructure administrators, hackers, social engineers, hosting providers, money launderers, as well as leaders or decision makers.

Much like a traditional marketplace, the underground market for stolen data sees varying volumes of leading market items and asking prices. A Symantec report (2010) showed that the most sought after item, a valid credit card number, actually dropped in price in 2009 to as low as $0.85 per card, down from about $4 in 2008. The second most sought after item was valid bank account credentials, priced as low as $15; prices are generally believed to be about 5% of an account's value. Unlike consumers who have to worry about credit card theft, checking or savings theft, or identity theft, businesses have the added burden of protecting custodial data – data about others that they need to or are required to handle – as well as protecting their own intellectual property, something that is often hard to accurately value.

Deloitte, a frequent advisor to large companies around the globe, called cyber-crime "the fastest growing cyber security threat" (2010, p. 1). The Organization for Economic Co-operation and Development warned businesses worldwide that "the onslaught of malware attacks is increasing, both in frequency and sophistication, thus posing a serious threat to the Internet economy and to national security" (OECD, 2009, p. 11) As early as 2006, security researchers called cybercrime "an epidemic" (Cymru, 2006, p. 1), and highlighted the lack of cooperation and enforcement as a growth enabler for cyber criminals. Geer (2006), also warned of what was then a visible trend, now a fait-accompli, that attackers would pounce if they could mount attacks at low cost and with little fear of being caught or prosecuted.

In short, the current level of demand for sensitive electronic data coupled with the ease by which attackers can operate has and continues to fuel a boom in criminal hacking activity. The presence of a global underground market means that anything that has value can be turned into monetary gain for the cyber criminals, thus virtually guaranteeing further attacks. To make matters worse, security professionals warn that as more companies decide to virtualize their systems and move them to the cloud, entirely new classes of attacks awaits us (Kellerman, 2010).

CURRENT ATTACK LANDSCAPE

Evolution of Attacks

As Bejtlich (2010) points out, early computer attacks were primarily the domain of government and military entities, often spying on each other or disrupting each other's capabilities. However, the threat moved towards the defense industrial base, and more recently to companies that have valuable financial or intellectual property that the attackers can harness and profit from.

While early hackers may have been after fame, the current crop of cyber criminals are firmly after electronic goods that have monetary value. A recent report issued by the United Nations Office on Drugs and Crime (UNODC, 2010) estimates that the figure for Internet-based identity crimes reaches one billion dollars annually. Global cybercrime estimates reach as high as one trillion dollars in "lost intellectual property and expenditures for repairing the damage" done in the previous year (Mills, 2009). A portion of this loot is being used to fund research into new attack methods and explore new targets.

Types of Attacks

As early as 2006, security researchers could see the rapid rate of progress that attackers were demonstrating (Holtz, 2006). The attack landscape evolved from what are now considered traditional attacks against the operating system or services to new applications and web-based services.

For decades, computer security administrators focused their defenses around the network, operating systems, and server-side applications. The aim was to prevent, or seriously hinder, any successful attacks against servers, either by attacking the operating system itself, or any of the services running on it. As operating system vendors improved their development and patching processes such attacks became harder to perpetrate, at least by non-privileged, remote, attackers. Similarly, while early networking services came configured in "open" modes (e.g. SMTP open relays), server applications are now developed and deployed with security in mind. Facing a reduced attack surface, attackers sought new vulnerable areas to exploits.

The attack landscape today is much more varied and sophisticated, giving rise to terms like Advanced Persistent Threat (APT) and Blended Threat (BT). The APT speaks to an adversary's level of dedication to achieving their goals – often believed to be state-sponsored – using a broad range of techniques at their disposal, from the mere virus to complex or never-before-seen malware. Even if detected and removed, the threat agents would seek to re-infect, most likely via other means, in order to maintain control (Bejtlich, 2010). The APT is much like a precision strike and the target is often unaware that their systems

have been compromised. The entity behind the APT is usually after intellectual property (IP) or military/government data.

By contrast, an attack using a Blended Threat approach can be a lot noisier, as it would use multiple methods to infect a target, behavior which often leaves a very detectable trace of activity in log files and can propagate to other systems under its own directive. While an APT attacker may choose to use a BT as a means of attack, he would very carefully control the rate and spread of the infection in order to avoid detection and maintain access (Chen, 2008). Such methods are often after data that can be quickly monetized, even if the breach is discovered, such as credit card information or bank account credentials.

For BTs, attackers can use management consoles in order to help them control both the rate of spread and how quickly the stolen information is reported back to them. The availability of a management console means that such attacks can be scaled from the initial small target set to reaching as many targets as possible on the Internet. In comparison, APTs are not easily scaled, and as such the attacker has to be highly selective in his choice of targets in order to achieve a sustainable cost/benefit ratio (Herley, 2010).

Third-Party Applications: An Easy Target

By taking aim at software applications, attackers are able to increase the attack surface and thus the number of exploitable vulnerabilities at their disposal. With the move to Web 2.0, more people use web browsers to do business. Not surprisingly, web browsers have become one of the targets of choice for attackers. Recent reports about the state of security of various web browsers should leave anyone uneasy about using these programs to do any kind of online financial transactions. A Secunia report (2008a) found that the four major browsers (Firefox, Internet Explorer, Opera, Safari) had a combined total of 208 known vulnerabilities; the combined number of vulnerabilities in browser plug-ins, also known as add-ons, was 470. A 2009 browser hacking contest held at CanSecWest, an annual security conference in Canada, appears to validate the frailty of web browsers. The contest winner was able to exploit one browser (Apple Safari) in under two minutes while another contestant was able to exploit three major browsers (Microsoft Internet Explorer 8, Apple Safari, and Mozilla Firefox) the same day (Goodin, 2009).

Investigations into the attack on Google in early 2010, dubbed Aurora, have pointed to one browser in particular as one of the primary means of infection into the company systems: Microsoft Internet Explorer 6, which has been superseded by versions 7 and 8 (NSS Labs, 2010). However, the attack vector was found to also apply to other browser versions across most flavors of the Windows operating system (CVE-database, 2010). While browsers are an easy means of compromise, many other exploitable applications are also available to attackers.

In 2010, Adobe PDF and Flash were singled out by various security firms for the large percentage of attacks that use flaws in the PDF Reader software or the Flash platform to infect machines (Keizer, 2010). In prior years, Microsoft products, notably its Office suite, had been a favorite target for attackers (Goodin, 2010). While these programs are often installed on home and business machines, they are by no means the only ones being targeted. A 2010 Secunia report put the number of vulnerabilities typically present on the average user's machine between 2007 and 2009 at 420; in the first half of 2010, that number had already reached 380. The report also contains a list of the top ten vendors with the most vulnerabilities; all are well-known software companies.

Reeling the User in

One of the biggest changes in attack methodology is that the attacker now often has to draw, or rather lure, the user to him or convince the user to open a file or web link. By combining social engineering factors into their methodology, attackers have been able to increase the likelihood that the user would help bring about the first stage of the infection. The recent growth of social networks has only amplified this opportunity as many are now having wide open conversations with perceived "friends" across the Internet, and clicking on links sent to them pretending to direct them to pictures, articles, movies, or songs of interest.

The post-event analysis of the attack on Google (operation Aurora) has revealed that attackers spent time carefully researching the online lives of several employees before sending the victims a link from what appeared a person they trusted in (Westervelt, 2010a). Such attacks blending technical exploits and social engineering have been on the increase and can often bypass existing controls (Westervelt, 2010b).

THE FAILURE OF TRADITIONAL CONTROLS

Over the past decade, improvements in network defenses and operating system defenses have resulted in attackers shifting their attack strategies away from network and operating systems to focus on exploiting software applications (such as browsers, word processors and digital formats like PDF) and social networks, often combining those attacks in a blended threat. This shift in attack methodology has allowed attackers to bypass many of the traditional administrative, physical and technical security controls, present in the enterprise today.

Administrative Controls

While most devices today log access and usage information, many companies have not provided proper administrative oversight, often allowing these logs to go unmonitored for months. The presence and thorough monitoring of such logs is critical in order to quickly detect and react to blended threats. Even though regular audits will often point to such weaknesses, the current pace of attacks render the annual audit ineffective at giving a true picture of one's risks.

A CyLab survey report (2010) found that executive leadership and boards of directors are often uninterested or unaware in the management or reporting of risks dealing with information security or privacy. As a result, many organizations lack any formal position tasked with oversight of security or privacy.

Finally, as companies scramble to provide often mandated information security awareness training to their employees, those programs are often relegated to IT or HR staff, with little time, training, or resources available to measure the impact and effectiveness of such training. As Leavitt warned, as early as 2005, tools like Instant Messaging (IM) can be a great vehicle for hackers to reach into enterprise networks. The presence of instant communication capabilities, i.e. social media, needs to be addressed as part of the security awareness training.

Physical Controls

While computing and storage capacities have exploded, physical security controls remain largely unchanged. Doors, windows, locks, gates and lighting fixtures still work in much the same way that they have for decades. What has changed is the amount of information available on small, portable devices that can easily be lost, stolen, duplicated, or damaged during shipment.

These devices, laptops, netbooks, personal digital assistants (PDAs), smart phones, can now contain spreadsheets full of custodial data or intellectual property. With smart phone memory sizes commonly reaching 16 or 32 gigabytes (GB) and laptop hard drives reaching near a half a terabyte (TB), it is all too easy to have to deal with a potential exposure of millions of dollars' worth of financial records or intellectual property. Proper

inventory of physical assets is a key component of the modern enterprise's umbrella of physical controls.

IT Controls

Traditional IT controls include password-protected access to resources, firewalls to block outside access to protected servers and networks, as well as host-based software controls such as anti-virus, intrusion detection/prevention suites, or blacklisting technologies.

While the use of single-factor authentication mechanisms like passwords has served IT security reasonably well until now, many factors make its continued use as a single point of control somewhat shaky. Reports of hackers breaking into a system by guessing or brute-forcing someone's password are frequent occurrences. While users deplore the inconvenience of stronger passwords or requirements for frequent changes, IT administrators themselves are often just as lax in their handling of privileged account credentials. MacLeod (2007) provides a series of auditing recommendations to control the level of privileged access enjoyed by IT insiders, including creating an inventory of privileged accounts, enforcing password aging as per policy, and providing secure storage mechanisms.

While enterprises can deploy specific identity management technologies, such controls are not usually found in Web 2.0 services. When Bonneau (2010) examined the password practices of 150 websites, the authors found that best practices are far from universal and only 14 sites checked a chosen password against a dictionary to root out entries such as "password."

While the password is often the gatekeeper for access to resources, the firewall is often the gatekeeper to access services on the network. Firewalls have evolved to provide solid protection against externally-sourced scans and obvious access attempts. However, firewalls do little to address the multitude of incoming and outgoing traffic that the average user might be exposed to (McDougal, 2009). By simply reading email with an embedded image, or by clicking on a link contained in a social network application or browser, a user's query would be allowed to traverse the firewall as it is considered a valid outbound request; the response would likely be a piece of malware ready to launch the next stage of the attack, a perfectly blended threat.

To defend against malware, a generic term that includes viruses, Trojans, and worms, security vendors promote their anti-malware technologies that are supposed to detect and prevent a majority of this unwanted and malevolent activity. As with other blacklisting-based technologies, the pace of innovation shown by attackers means that the anti-malware needs to be updated regularly in order to catch the latest threat. Yet, the software must detect an ever increasing array of threats, without impacting system resources beyond an acceptable level. Krebs (2010) mentions a recent NSS Labs report in which the average time to detect the latest threat was found to be 45 hours, ranging from as little as four hours to as many as four days. Another report found that the top anti-malware product caught only 22% of 300 known pieces of malware, while the second best only caught 2% (Secunia, 2008b).

Perhaps the most significant example of the failure of traditional controls against blended threats is a recent memo distributed by the Financial Services Information Sharing and Analysis Center (FS-ISAC) in 2009. The memo, entitled "Account Hijacking of Corporate Customers - Recommendations for Customer Education" highlights the need to establish better computer hygiene by using a dedicated computer or operating system, deploying strong authentication, as well as better implementing mechanisms for authorizing financial transactions.

NEW CONTROLS TO MITIGATE A NEW RISK REALITY

In order to effectively mitigate the risks posed by well-funded, innovative attackers, the enterprise must review and improve the controls it puts in place.

Administrative Controls

One of the key factors in providing adequate risk management is for the executive and board-level sphere to be fully cognizant of range of cyber threats, including blended threats, and provide adequate oversight and funding for such operations. ANSI (2010) released a report targeted at Chief Financial Officers to help them grasp of the realities of cyber risk. Similarly, the Association of Certified Fraud Examiners (ACFE, 2010), released a guide for executives on managing the risk of fraud, with several sections dedicated to IT controls. A CyLab (2010) survey report emphasized the need for management to establish a risk management function separate from the audit function, to ensure dedicated lines of responsibility for security and for privacy, to establish cross-organizational teams to deal with security and privacy issues, to regularly review the effectiveness of controls, and to review the annual funding levels for IT risk management.

In 2010, the ACM, an organization of computing professionals with strong ties with academia, convened a roundtable of Chief Technology Officers to discuss malware defenses, highlighting the need for greater cooperation between industry and academia to deal with the threat (Creeger, 2010). Emerging areas such as enterprise risk management (ERM) can greatly benefit from more research and will ultimately lead to a better educated new generation of executives. In the meantime, research such as Foley (2009) and can provide a starting point for establishing a new risk management framework.

One visible indication that top level executives have understood cyber risks can be found in the recent change to the SEC filings of companies such as Google, and others targeted in the same attack, as the latest filings now contain new language warning investors of cyber risks (McMillan, 2010). Another sign of progress is the change in the software requirements process; enterprises and even state government are demanding more secure software. The state of New York recently took the lead by proposing specific language about software security in its Request for Proposal process (NY-OCS, 2010). The document, entitled "Application Development Security Procurement Language" mandates adequate training, background checks, and supervision by security specialist for software developers.

Physical Controls

Physical controls play an important role in ensuring an overall security and privacy posture for the enterprise. This domain requires appropriate attention, funding, and regular review, especially following any incident in which physical security was compromised. While some other controls can help supplement the lack of physical controls (e.g. encryption helps balance the risk of exposure due to lost or stolen laptops), the overall controls must be balanced to prevent any gaps that an attacker could exploit.

While a majority of blended attacks are likely to originate from outside the enterprise, the physical security function has an important role to play in ensuring that access to data is properly guarded, that computing resources are properly accounted for, and that physical representations of data are properly handled and disposed of when no longer useful. The growing use of "documents to be shredded" containers within the corporation means little if those containers are not properly secured against access or theft. Similarly, plenum areas near data centers should be properly sealed to ensure that only authorized personnel can gain entry to tend the servers.

IT Controls Required to Deal with APTs and Blended Threats

Advanced Persistent Threats and Blended Threats require that the enterprise balance the new risks with appropriate controls. Instead of trying to secure every device or network route, the security function should focus on protecting sensitive data, where it resides, where it is processed, and while in transit.

While operating systems are more secure, the threat of attacks on third party software means that servers and workstations need to be hardened and regularly patched in order to offer a greater level of resistance against attackers. The availability of cheap storage and processing power also means that virtualization can be used not only to provide better resource utilization but also to help isolate or recover from an attack by freezing an infected system or restoring it from a known good state (McDougal, 2009). A new virtualization platform called QubesOS (2010) promises to deliver a seamless virtualized desktop experience for users by blending the windows of multiple virtual machines – each dedicated to a specific purpose such as work, banking, email, research – into one desktop. New research into virtualization seeks to hide the presence of the virtual machine from malware (Carpenter, 2007) or reduce the attack surface of the virtualization architecture (Steinberg, 2010).

As noted earlier, attackers are currently gaining access by successfully compromising third party applications, including the web browser platform. One alternative to full virtualization is to virtualize or sandbox each application so that an infected application cannot infect the rest of the computing environment. Sandboxie is a low-cost program that provides a security sandbox for a browser (or any other application program) so that any changes to the drive or the registry would be wiped when the application is closed. Sandboxie adds an icon on the desktop; clicking on it will open the default browser in a secure sandbox. Figure 1 shows the default browser loaded in the sandbox; note the extra "[#]" characters in the application window title bar. Figure 2 shows how one can delete any changes done to the sandboxed environment, including undoing a potential malware infection and associated registry or file changes.

Another alternative is to harden the browser, for example by using a combination of Mozilla Firefox with the NoScript plug-in. The NoScript plug-in disables JavaScript and other active content such as Adobe Flash, thereby providing a more robust browser with a reduced attack surface.

Figure 1. The sandboxed browser (note the extra "[#]" characters)

Figure 2. Deleting any changes to the Sandboxed program(s)

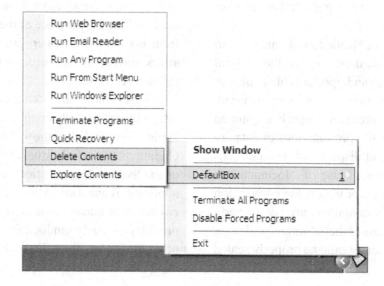

Figure 3 shows a web page as viewed with the default (i.e. more secure) settings with JavaScript disabled. Figure 4 shows how one can quickly enable rich browser features like JavaScript for trusted sites. Figure 5 shows the same web page now reloaded with JavaScript enabled, thus making the page more functional, but subject to potential JavaScript-based attack vectors.

Even stronger controls may be necessary in order to protect a company's financial assets. Recent advice from the banking sector recommends the use of special purpose or dedicated operating systems in order to deal with new, as-of-yet-unknown threats (FS-ISAC, 2009). Such a control could have helped a California business protect the $465,000 that went missing from its account almost overnight (McGlasson, 2010). The attackers stole the bank credentials but also disabled the alerting service provided by the business' bank. A Gartner report (Litan, 2009) raises the alarm about the ease by which attackers are defeating many of the commonly employed banking controls, including two-factor authentication, which was once thought to be the penultimate answer. The sophistication of IT controls must be

Figure 3. JavaScript secret – NoScript protection on

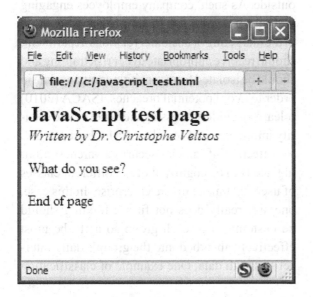

commensurate with the level of access granted and the risks posed.

Ultimately no amount of defenses may be sufficient to protect against a well-armed attacker. Strong enterprise security governance seeks to not only establish a strong defense but also a strong incident response capability (Potter, 2010). Malware detection and remediation requires a new set of skills that is only now becoming available through academic education and specialized training. However, new research shows a high level of interest and activity in this area (Jiang, 2010; Kolbitsch, 2009; Passerini, 2009).

USERS: A CRITICAL FIRST LINE OF DEFENSE

Information security is not a technical problem that can be addressed with a technical solution. Instead, it is a complex problem that must be addressed using an array of controls, including one that has been overlooked, or under-appreciated, for too long: the human element.

The Need for Security Awareness Education and Training

Bonneau (2010) surveyed the authentication mechanisms and policies of 150 websites and found that there were wide differences between the market leaders and average sites. Password length and complexity requirements varied greatly, thereby contributing to a lack of universality and cohesion as to what is a secure password. One of the signs that users need help with password management is when they acknowledge keeping their passwords "in-sync," i.e. using one master password for several different identities.

As users become more aware of the risks surrounding online access, banking credentials, and intellectual data, they can also be lured into a false sense of security. By now, most users are familiar with the need for and the benefits afforded

Figure 4. The NoScript dialog box

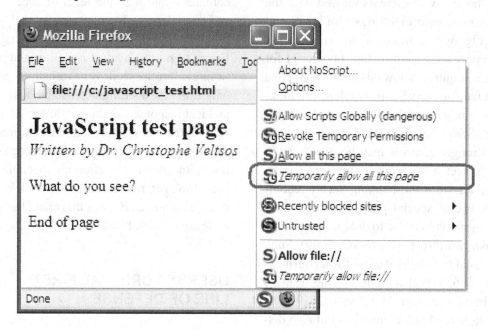

Figure 5. JavaScript secret – NoScript protection off

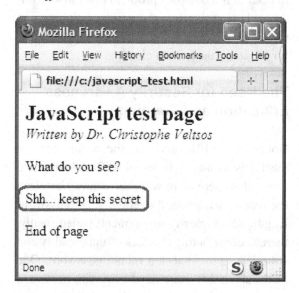

by technical solutions like antivirus programs and firewalls. However, as discussed previously, these controls are no longer sufficient to adequately protect against a determined attacker. By believing they are safe, users may engage in riskier behavior (i.e. clicking links without a second thought). This behavior, termed Risk Homeostasis by Wilde (2001) suggests that an individual will keep his/her overall level of risk almost constant: if a technical control helps reduce risk, users will compensate by engaging in more risky behavior.

Since 2008, the use of social media has skyrocketed for both individuals and corporations (Baker, 2010). But social media allows unfettered communications between insiders and those on the outside. As such, company employees engaging with customers through social media, such as those in the marketing or customer relations department, should receive appropriate cyber risk training and should be isolated from sensitive company data in order to avoid potential breaches. ISACA (2010) released a guide addressing the benefits and security implications of social media for business use.

Effective information security awareness training needs to be cognizant of the different classes of users that make up the enterprise. In this case, one size really does not fit all; training should be customized to each group so as to be most effectively absorbed into the group's daily interactions with data. One example of classification is to provide customized training for executives (high-level access privileges to large amounts of data, but very little time), IT professionals (better versed in technical controls and cyber risks, but often have privileged access into vast parts of the company's data or networks), and the average user (some access to data, but little training into the dangers they may be exposed to).

Running an Effective Security Awareness Program

As more research and best practices become available, companies should use this information to help measure and improve the effectiveness of their security awareness programs; the use of appropriate metrics is key to developing effective training. Jaquith (2007) provides several examples of both proven and failed security-related metrics. While items like percentage of the workforce having completed the training are useful, they do nothing to gauge the effectiveness of the program. If attendees forget to log out at the end of a computer-based information security awareness session, they have obviously not absorbed the material presented to them even though they attended the session.

Instead of generic statements such as "you should not do…" and "you should do…," some training programs show participants what can happen and how quickly they can be fooled. Others choose to test participants, often with a pre-training measurement and a post-training measurement (Kumaraguru, 2010; Smith, 2009). For example, by showing users a list of 200 passwords used by the Conficker/Downadup malware (Cluley, 2009) and asking them to identify any passwords that they have used recently, users will better appreciate that "password" and "secret" are not very secure passwords. Research into the psychology of security can help ensure that the training is designed, delivered, and evaluated to have maximum impact (Sternberg, 2010).

Ultimately, as the enterprise realizes that technical security controls are not foolproof, it is more likely to rely on its workforce as a first line of defense instead of a dumb interface between the screen and keyboard (PwC, 2010).

FUTURE RESEARCH AND CHALLENGES

If the past is any prediction of what we can expect from hackers and cyber criminals, it is likely that we will see additional targeted attacks against technical controls like virtualization or applications like Sandboxie and NoScript, especially if a large segment of the Internet population adopts these controls. Research into similar attacks has already begun in the case of virtual machines, and several vulnerabilities have been found and exploited to allow malware to escape the security of a virtual environment in order to compromise a host machine (Westervelt, 2008). Many pieces of malware today already modify their behavior when they are being run in a virtual environment, primarily to thwart the efforts of security researchers (Fitzgibbon, 2009).

Web 2.0 technologies promise to empower individual business units to take more control of their infrastructure needs. The net effect however is that IT is often left out of the loop, both in the procurement stage and in the operations stage, until an incident brings the matter to IT's attention. A corollary of not being dependent on the internal IT department is that it can no longer help protect and monitor the data once it leaves the confines of the enterprise. As businesses consider moving more of their infrastructure to managed cloud computing services, they often learn the hard way that simply outsourcing the responsibility does not mean that they have outsourced the risk.

The year 2010 also marks a turning point of sorts with a sharp jump in the research on and coverage of mobile malware. As cell phones are replaced by smart phones, the latter benefiting from many times more processing power and memory than the original personal computer, more sensitive data is making its way on those devices. In addition, always-on connectivity means easy access to the device and back to the attacker's servers. Unfortunately, the smart phone environment does not lend itself very easily to running anti-malware software (Lawton, 2008).

One area where significant progress is being made are the changes being discussed in academic circles about the evolution of software threats and whether students in various software-related disciplines are being taught the right concepts and skills (Stroustrup, 2010). Whether writing open-source or closed source software, there is a clear need to write better software with fewer bugs at the onset and to reduce the time needed to patch serious or critical bugs in deployed software. As to which is more secure, there is no clear consensus on whether open-source is safer than closed-source software; for now, we may have to settle on whichever is patched first (Härtig, 2010).

CONCLUSION

The underground economy has fueled a wave of hacker activity that threatens the privacy and security of data closely guarded by corporations, governments and individuals. The state of insecurity today demands a new paradigm; instead of hoping that one will not be attacked, one must prepare for such an attack so as to be able to quickly detect and respond to any security incidents. As more data interacts with or moves to Web 2.0 environments, the attack surface has shifted from the network and operating system to the realm of browsers and rich content applications. Technical controls such as hardened browsers and sandboxed environments do provide a safer computing environment for Web 2.0 users. However, technical controls alone are not sufficient to maintain adequate security. Information security education, training, and awareness programs will need to be continually adjusted to provide employees with

the knowledge needed to maintain the safety of the data entrusted to them in the face of advanced malware and blended threats.

REFERENCES

ACFE. (2008). Managing the Business Risk of Fraud - A Practical Guide. Retrieved from http://www.acfe.com/documents/managing-business-risk.pdf

ANSI. (2010). *The financial management of cyber risk: An implementation framework for CFOs*. Retrieved from http://webstore.ansi.org/cybersecurity.aspx

Baker, S., & Green, H. (2010). Social media will change your business. *BusinessWeek*. Retrieved from http://www.businessweek.com/bwdaily/dnflash/content/feb2008/db20080219_908252.htm

Bejtlich, R. (2010). Understanding the advanced persistent threat. *Information Security Magazine*. Retrieved from http://searchsecurity.techtarget.com/ magazineCurrent/0,296884,sid14,00.html

Bonneau, J., & Preibush, S. (2010). *The password thicket - technical and market failures in human authentication on the Web*. The Ninth Workshop on the Economics of Information Security (WEIS 2010), Cambridge, MA, June 7-8, 2010.

Carpenter, M., Liston, T., & Skoudis, E. (2007). Hiding virtualization from attackers and malware. *IEEE Security & Privacy, 5*(3), 62–65. doi:10.1109/MSP.2007.63

CERIAS. (2009). *Unsecured economies: Protecting vital information*. Retrieved from http://www.cerias.purdue.edu/site/blog/post/ unsecured_economies_and_overly_secured_reports/

Chen, T., & Peikari, C. (2008). Malicious software in mobile devices. In Zhang, Y., Zheng, J., & Ma, M. (Eds.), *Handbook of research on wireless security*. Hershey, PA: Idea Group Publishing. doi:10.4018/9781599048994.ch001

Cluley, G. (2009). *Passwords used by the Conficker worm*. Retrieved from http://www.sophos.com/blogs/gc/g/ 2009/01/16/passwords-conficker-worm/

Creeger, M. (2010). CTO roundtable - malware defense. *ACM Queue; Tomorrow's Computing Today, 8*(2), 40.

CSI. (2009). *CSI computer crime & security survey*. Retrieved from http://gocsi.com/survey

CVE-dataabase. (2010). Retrieved from http://web.nvd.nist.gov/view/ vuln/ detail?vulnId=CVE-2010-0249

CyLab. (2010). Governance of enterprise security. Retrieved from http://www.cylab.cmu.edu/outreach/governance.html

Cymru. (2006). Cybercrime - an epidemic. *ACM Queue, 4*(9), 25-28.

Dataloss, D. B. (2010). Largest incidents. *Data Loss Database*. Retrieved from http://datalossdb.org/index/largest

Deloite. (2010). *Cyber crime - a clear and present danger*. Retrieved from http://www.deloitte.com/assets/Dcom-UnitedStates/Local%20Assets/Documents/AERS/us_aers_Deloitte%20Cyber%20Crime%20POV%20Jan252010.pdf

FBI. (2010). *Speech remarks for Steven R. Chabinsky, Deputy Assistant Director, Cyber Division, FBI*. Federal Bureau of Investigations. Retrieved from http://www.fbi.gov/pressrel/ speeches/chabinsky032310.htm

Fitzgibbon, N., & Wood, M. (2009). *Conficker.C: A technical analysis*. Sophos Labs. Retrieved from http://www.sophos.com/sophos/docs/eng/marketing_material/conficker-analysis.pdf

Foley, S. (2009). *Security risk management using internal controls*. First ACM Workshop on Information Security Governance (WISG'09), November 13, 2009, Chicago, IL.

FS-ISAC. (2009). *FBI/FS-ISAC/NACHA joint alert - account hijacking of corporate customers: Recommendations for customer education*. Retrieved from http://www.nacha.org/c/riskTools.cfm

Geer. (2006). Playing for keeps. *ACM Queue, 4*(9), 42-48.

Goodin, D. (2009). A grim day for browser security at hacker contest: Safari, IE and Firefox all down for the count. *The Register*. Retrieved from http://www.theregister.co.uk/ 2009/03/19/pwn2own_day1/

Goodin, D. (2010). It's official: Adobe Reader is world's most-exploited app. *The Register*. Retrieved from http://www.theregister.co.uk/2010/03/09/adobe_reader_attacks/

Google. (2010). *A new approach to China*. Google Blog. Retrieved from http://googleblog.blogspot.com/2010/ 01/new-approach-to-china.html

Härtig, H., Hamann, C.-J., & Roitzsch, M. (2010). *The mathematics of obscurity - on the trustworthiness of open source*. The Ninth Workshop on the Economics of Information Security (WEIS 2010), Cambridge, MA, June 7-8, 2010.

Herley, C. (2010). *The plight of the targeted attacker in a world of scale*. The Ninth Workshop on the Economics of Information Security (WEIS 2010), Cambridge, MA, June 7-8, 2010.

Holz, T., Marechal, S., & Raynal, F. (2006). New threats and attacks on the World Wide Web. *IEEE Security and Privacy, 4*(2), 72–75. doi:10.1109/MSP.2006.46

ISACA. (2010). *Social media - business benefits and security, governance and assurance perspectives*. ISACA. Retrieved from https://www.isaca.org/Knowledge-Center/Research/ Documents/Social-Media-Wh-Paper-26-May10-Research.pdf

Jaquith, A. (2007). *Security metrics: Replacing fear, uncertainty, and doubt*. Upper Saddle River, NJ: Addison-Wesley Pearson Education.

Jiang, X., Wang, X., & Xu, D. (2010). Stealthy malware detection and monitoring. [TISSEC]. *ACM Transactions on Information and System Security, 13*(2).

Keizer, G. (2010). Adobe: We know we're hackers' favorite target. *NetworkWorld*. Retrieved from http://www.networkworld.com/news/2010/060410-adobe-we- know-were-hackers.html?hpg1=bn

Kellerman, T. (2010). Cyber-threat proliferation - today's truly pervasive global epidemic. *IEEE Security & Privacy, 8*(3), 70–73. doi:10.1109/MSP.2010.94

Kolbitsch, C., Comparetti, P., Kruegel, C., Kirda, E., Zhou, X., & Wang, X. (2009). *Effective and efficient malware detection at the end host*. 18th Usenix Security Symposium, Montreal Canada. August 10-14, 2009.

Krebs, B. (2010). *Krebs on security blog*. Retrieved from http://krebsonsecurity.com/2010/06/ anti-virus-is-a-poor-substitute-for-common-sense/

Kumaraguru, P., Sheng, S., Acquisti, A., Cranor, L., & Hong, J. (2010). Teaching Johnny not to fall for phish. *ACM Transactions on Internet Technology, 10*(2). doi:10.1145/1754393.1754396

Lawton, G. (2008). Is it finally time to worry about mobile malware. *IEEE Computer, 41*(5), 12–14.

Leavitt, N. (2005). Instant messaging - a new target for hackers. *IEEE Computer, 38*(7), 20–23.

Litan, A. (2009). *Where strong authentication fails and what you can do about it*. Gartner. Retrieved from http://www.gartner.com/DisplayDocument?ref=clientFriendlyUrl&id=1245013

MacLeod, C. (2007). One of today's most overlooked security threats—six ways auditors can fight it. *ISACA Journal, 5*. Retrieved from http://www.isaca.org/Journal/Past-Issues/2007/Volume-5/Pages/JOnline-One-of-Todays-Most-Overlooked-Security-Threats-Six-Ways-Auditors-Can-Fight-It.aspx

McDougal, M. (2009). *Castle warrior - redefining 21st century network defense*. 5th Annual Workshop on Cyber Security and Information Intelligence Research: Cyber Security and Information Intelligence Challenges and Strategies. Oak Ridge, Tennessee, April 13-15, 2009

McGlasson, L. (2010). *Account takeover: The new wrinkle - fraudsters disable email verification service in CA scam*. Retrieved from http://www.bankinfosecurity.com/ articles.php?art_id=2728

McMillan, R. (2010). After Google hack, warnings pop up in SEC filings. *ComputerWorld*. Retrieved from http://www.computerworld.com/s/article/9177845/ After_Google_hack_warnings_pop_up_in_SEC_filings

Mills, E. (2009). Cybercrime cost $1 trillion last year, study. *ZDNet*. Retrieved from http://www.zdnet.com/news/cybercrime-cost-1-trillion-last-year-study/264762

NoScript. (n.d.). *JavaScript/Java/Flash blocker for a safer Firefox*. Retrieved from http://noscript.net/

NSSLabs. (2010). *Vulnerability-based protection and the Google "Operation Aurora" attack*. Retrieved from http://nsslabs.com/test-reports/NSSLabs_Vulnerability-based%20Protection-Google-EPPv14.pdf

NY-OCS. (2010). *Application security procurement language*. Office of Cyber Security, State of New York. http://www.cscic.state.ny.us/ resources/aspl.cfm

OECD, Organization for Economic and Co-operative Development. (2009). *Computer viruses and other malicious software a threat to the Internet economy*. Retrieved from http://www.oecd.org/document/16/0,3343,en_2649 _34223_42276816_1_1_1_37441,00.html

Passerini, E., Paleari, R., & Martignoni, L. (2009). How good are malware detectors at remediating infected systems? In *Proceedings of the 6th Conference on Detection of Intrusions and Malware & Vulnerability Assessment, DIMVA*, Como, Italy, Lecture Notes in Computer Science. Springer, July 2009

Potter, B. (2010). Thinking operationally. *IEEE Security and Privacy*, *8*(3), 54–55. doi:10.1109/MSP.2010.109

PwC. (2010). *Protecting your business - security awareness - turning your people into your first line of defence*. Price Waterhouse Coopers. Retrieved from http://www.pwc.co.uk/eng/publications/protecting_your_business_security_awareness.html

Qubes, O. S. (2010). *The QubesOs Project*. Retrieved from http://qubes-os.org/Home.html

Richardson, R. (2008). *2008 CSI computer crime and security survey*. Retrieved from http://i.cmpnet.com/v2.gocsi.com/pdf/CSIsurvey2008.pdf

Sandboxie. (n.d.). *Sandbox security software for Windows*. Retrieved from www.sandboxie.com

Secunia. (2008a). *2008 report*. Secunia. Retrieved from http://secunia.com/gfx/Secunia2008Report.pdf

Secunia. (2008b). *Internet security suite test October 2008*. Secunia. Retrieved from http://secunia.com/gfx/Secunia_ Exploit-vs-AV_test-Oct-2008.pdf

Secunia. (2010). *Secunia half year report 2010*. Secunia. Retrieved from http://secunia.com/gfx/pdf/Secunia_ Half_Year_Report_2010.pdf

Smith, A., & Toppel, N. (2009). *Case study - using security awareness to combat the advanced persistent threat*. 13th Colloquium for Information Systems Security Education (CISSE), June 1-3, 2009.

Sophos. (2009a). *Security threat report: 2009*. Retrieved from http://www.sophos.com/sophos/docs/eng/ marketing_material/sophos-security-threat-report-jan-2009-na.pdf

Steinberg, U., & Kauer, B. (2010). *NOVA-a microhypervisor-based secure virtualization architecture*. EuroSys 2010 Conference. April 13–16, 2010, Paris, France.

Sternberg, G. (2010). The psychology behind security. *ISSA Journal*, April 2010. Retrieved from http://www.issa.org/Library/Journals/2010/April/ISSA%20Journal%20April%202010.pdf

Stroustrup, B. (2010). What should we teach new software developers & why. *Communications of the ACM*, *53*(1), 40–42. doi:10.1145/1629175.1629192

Symantec. (2010). *Internet security threat report*. Retrieved from http://www.symantec.com/business/ theme.jsp?themeid=threatreport

UNODC. (2010). *The globalization of crime: A transnational organized crime threat assessment*. United Nations Office on Drugs and Crime, 2010. Retrieved from http://www.unodc.org/unodc/en/data-and-analysis/tocta-2010.html

US-DOJ. (2010). *US v. Albert Gonzalez*. US Department of Justice. Retrieved from http://www.usdoj.gov/usao/nj/press/ press/files/pdffiles/GonzIndictment.pdf

US-SEC. (2010). *Heartland payment systems reports first quarter results*. US Securities and Exchange Commission. Retrieved from http://www.sec.gov/Archives/edgar/data/1144354/000119312510109892/dex991.htm

Verizon. (2009). *Data breach investigations report*. Verizon Business Security Solutions. Retrieved from http://www.verizonbusiness.com/resources/security/reports/2009_databreach_rp.pdf

Westervelt, R. (2008). *Exploit code released for critical VMware flaw*. Search Security. Retrieved from http://searchsecurity.techtarget.com/news/article/0,289142,sid14_gci1302293,00.html

Westervelt, R. (2010a). *For Google, DNS log analysis essential in Aurora attack investigation*. SearchSecurity.com. Retrieved from http://searchsecurity.techtarget.com/news/article/0,289142,sid14_gci1514965,00.html

Westervelt, R. (2010b). *More firms targeted by advanced persistent threats, study finds*. SearchSecurity.com. Retrieved from http://searchsecurity.techtarget.com/news/ article/0,289142,sid14_gci1516233,00.html

Wilde, G. J. S. (2001). *Target risk 2: A new psychology of safety and health*. Toronto, Canada: PDE Publications.

Worthen, B. (2009, January 20). Card data breached, firm says. *Wall Street Journal*, 2009. Retrieved from http://online.wsj.com/article/SB123249174099899837.html

Zetter, K. (2010). Google hack attack was ultra sophisticated, new details show. *Wired*. Retrieved from http://www.wired.com/threatlevel/2010/01/operation-aurora/

ADDITIONAL READING

Arnason, S. T., & Willett, K. D. (2007). *How to Achieve 27001 Certification: An Example of Applied Compliance Management*. Boca Raton, FL: CRC Press.

Baker, W. H., Hylender, C. D., & Valentine, J. A. (2008). 2008 data breach investigations report. Verizon Business Security Solutions. Retrieved from www.verizonbusiness.com/resources/security/databreachreport.pdf

Brooks, F. P. (1995). *The mythical man-month: Essays on software engineering*. Reading, MA: Addison-Wesley.

CERT. (2007). 2007 E-crime watch survey: Over Confidence Is Pervasive Amongst Security Professionals. Retrieved from http://www.cert.org/archive/pdf/ecrimesummary07.pdf

Cheang, A. (2009). *Guidelines for Cybersecurity*. Retrieved from www.itsc.org.sg/pdf/synthesis09/Two_Cybersecurity.pdf

Corp, S. (2008). Internet Security Threat Report Volume XIII. Retrieved from http://www.symantec.com/about/news/ resources/press_kits/detail.jsp?pkid=threat_report_13

Gordon, L. A., Loeb, M. P., Lucyshyn, W., & Richardson, R. (2005). *2005 CSI/FBI Computer Crime and Security Survey*. Computer Security Institute.

International Organization for Standardization and International Electrotechnical Commission (2005). ISO/IEC 27001:2005, Information Technology - Security Techniques - Information Security Management Systems – Requirements.

International Organization for Standardization and International Electrotechnical Commission (2005). ISO/IEC 27002:2005, Information technology. Security techniques. Code of practice for information security management.

Jaquith, A. (2007). *Security Metrics: Replacing Fear, Uncertainty, and Doubt*. Upper Saddle River, NJ: Addison-Wesley Professional.

McCumber, J. (2005). *Assessing and managing security risk in IT systems: A structured methodology*. Boca Raton, FL: Auerbach Publications.

National Institute of Standards and Technology. (2002). Special Publication Risk management guide for information technology systems (800-30). Washington, DC: U.S. Government Printing Office. Retrieved from http://csrc.nist.gov/publications/nistpubs/800-30/sp800-30.pdf

National Institute of Standards and Technology. (2006). NIST IR 7298: Glossary of Key Information Security Terms. Washington, DC: U.S. Government Printing Office. Retrieved from http://csrc.nist.gov/publications/nistir/NISTIR-7298_Glossary_Key_Infor_Security_Terms.pdf

Ponemon, L. (2009). Data loss risks during downsizing. Study sponsored by Symantec Corporation, and conducted by Ponemon Institute LLC. Retrieved from http://scm.symantec.com/DLP/en/resources.php

Schneier, B. (2004). *Secrets & lies: Digital security in a networked world*. Indianapolis, IN: Wiley Publishing.

Skoudis, E., & Liston, T. (2006). *Counter Hack Reloaded* (2nd ed.). Upper Saddle River, New Jersey: Prentice Hall.

Sophos (2009a). Security threat report: 2009. Retrieved from http://www.sophos.com/sophos/docs/eng/marketing_material/ sophos-security-threat-report-jan-2009-na.pdf

Sophos (2009b). Security at risk as one third of surfers admit they use the same password for all websites, Sophos reports [Press Release]. Retrieved from http://www.sophos.com/pressoffice/news/articles/2009/03/password-security.html

Whitman, M. E. (2003). Enemy at the gate: Threats to information security. *Communications of the ACM, 46*(8). doi:10.1145/859670.859675

Whitman, M. E., & Mattord, H. J. (2003). *Principles of information security*. Boston, MA: Thomson Course Technology.

KEY TERMS AND DEFINITIONS

Availability: Seeks to ensure that the data will be available, and usable, in a timely and reliable manner.

Awareness: Activities and materials used to focus one's attention on matters of information security.

Blended Attack: A type of malware that supports multiple methods to infect new targets. Often, blended attacks are used in conjunction with additional information about a victim, such as information gleaned from social networks or via phishing attacks, to increase it effectiveness.

Confidentiality: Ensuring that only those with proper authorization have access to the information.

Exploit: A software tool that enables a hacker to gain (unauthorized) access to data or a system.

Integrity: Seeks to prevent any unauthorized modification or destruction of data.

Malware: A piece of malicious software designed to impact confidentiality, integrity, or availability of a system or its data. Malware is a generic term used to include viruses, worms, Trojans, or spyware.

Password: A password is a form of authentication, consisting of a string of characters, presented by the user to authenticate him or her to a system. Passwords are considered "something you know," as opposed to other forms of authentication which may ask for "something you have" or "something you are."

Phishing: Uses deception to trick users into divulging sensitive information (credit card numbers, date of birth, social security numbers, etc).

Chapter 3
Security Issues for Multi–Domain Resource Reservation

Christos Bouras
Research Academic Computer Technology Institute (CTI) & University of Patras, Greece

Kostas Stamos
Research Academic Computer Technology Institute (CTI) & University of Patras, Greece

ABSTRACT

In this chapter, we deal with the issue of security regarding components that are responsible for provisioning multi-domain network services, either automatically or through some form of administrator interaction. It is evident that a malicious compromise of such a component would have far-reaching implications for the stability of the network. Furthermore, trust between cooperating domains is a delicate issue, and each partner in the multi-domain federation has to have some guarantees that peers in the service are not going to be security compromised. We enumerate some of the related dangers and propose ways to limit the attack surface, reduce the intrusion possibilities, and guarantee the quick resolution of any successful violations.

The issue of security is studied in two main parts: Inter-domain security, for the communication between domains and the successful negotiation of resource reservations, and intra-domain security, for the internal communications within a domain for the initiation of a resource reservation and its actual realization in the network devices. Resource reservation is studied both on the level of IP services based on Differentiated Services architectures, and on the level of dynamic circuit reservation based on Layer 2 technologies.

The chapter is completed with a case study on the authentication and authorization framework designed in the context of a Pan-European network resource reservation service, in the Geant academic and research network.

DOI: 10.4018/978-1-60960-777-7.ch003

INTRODUCTION

A specific example of automated network administration for resource provisioning is the Bandwidth Broker entity, which is the component responsible for providing QoS within a network domain and negotiating the realization of a service across peering domains. The Bandwidth Broker manages the resources within the specific domain by controlling the network load and by accepting or rejecting bandwidth requests. In this context, resources refer to bandwidth and queue allocation at the network elements in order to achieve better performance in terms of throughput, delay, jitter, packet loss and reordering. A user within the domain that is willing to use an amount of the network resources between two nodes, has to send a request to the Bandwidth Broker. The decision to accept or reject a request is made by the admission control module. In the case that the requested resource is managed by multiple domains, the Bandwidth Broker is also responsible for the inter-domain communication with Bandwidth Brokers of adjacent domains. This procedure requires communication between adjacent Bandwidth Brokers and also a special agreement between the domains. Several such automated systems have been proposed and implemented (Bouras et al. 2007, Campanella et al. 2006, Shigeo Urushidani et al. 2008). In this chapter, our focus is on the security aspects in the context of Bandwidth Broker interdomain and intradomain communication, on the past work that has been done in this area and on the theoretical challenges and proposed solutions.

In addition, several efforts have been made for the automated multi-domain provisioning of circuit services at layers below the IP layer. One such extensive effort has been taken over by the Geant pan-european research and academic network, using the name AutoBAHN (Automated Bandwidth Allocation across Heterogeneous Networks). In the framework of this activity, it has specified and is developing a Bandwidth on Demand (BoD) service intended to operate in a multi-domain environment using heterogeneous transmission technologies. The AutoBAHN system aims at providing a guaranteed capacity, connection-oriented service between two end points. In this context resources refer to the provisioning of the circuits themselves. The reservation of network resources by an end-user, an application or middleware software is automated to a large extent, as the AutoBAHN system, in cooperation with localized provisioning systems that may be available in various participating domains, takes care of the interdomain communication and orchestration of the pathfinding, resource checking, scheduling and low-level network configuration procedures. A user submits a reservation through a GUI while applications and middleware utilize a related API. The AutoBAHN service supports multi-domain point-to-point connectivity with symmetric capacity and paths. It is also capable of handling advance reservations and of providing protection to the service. In our discussion, a domain refers to an administrative entity that is responsible for the management of a set of network elements. A single domain may contain multiple technological domains, but in terms of authority and authentication, it is considered as a single entity.

The overall architecture of the AutoBAHN system, its goal and the network mechanisms it employs are thoroughly presented in Campanella et al. (2006). The core of the system is comprised of the following main modules: Inter-domain Manager (IDM), Domain Manager (DM), Technology Proxy, Reservation Request Handling, User access module, AAI module, Inter-domain Pathfinder, Intra-domain Pathfinder and Topology Abstraction module. This chapter highlights the architecture of the AAI system (Authentication and Authorization Infrastructure) of the AutoBAHN platform, for the purposes of a detailed case study that has wider applicability.

BACKGROUND

Dealing with sensitive information such as the network resources management has to increase the awareness of possible security problems. The Public Key Infrastructure model (PKI) has been developed in order to deal with a number of possible attacks and protect against security, privacy and authentication violations. It is generally understood as the set of policies and software that regulate or manipulate the use of certificates and of public and private keys. Asymmetric encryption is a basic component of the architecture, which is based on a public key that can be disclosed to anyone, and a private key that is known only to its holder.

Our discussion intends to identify the ways with which the resource provisioning system implementation can be guarded against the various types of attack. In general, network attacks can be summarized in the following broad categories:

- Integrity attacks: The attacker tries to compromise the correctness, timeliness, authenticity or quality of the information exchanged.
- Confidentiality attacks: The attacker tries to disclose sensitive information that should normally only be accessible for authenticated parties.
- Availability attacks: The attacker tries to make the service unavailable to legitimate users.

Furthermore, a robust implementation also has to be capable of recovering from situations that do not pose a direct security threat, but can nonetheless compromise the operation of the system. Such cases are:

- Equipment / software malfunction: One or more of the communicating peer modules do not operate as expected and, for whatever reason, produce invalid, unexpected or simply erroneous results.
- Users' misbehavior: Users that do not follow the rules that have been mutually agreed upon, by for example violating the SLAs and attempting to increase their network resource usage at the expense of other users. These users have to be identified and disciplined according to the policies that have been set in place for each case.

There are the following aspects of security that relate to possible users' misbehaviour:

- Non-repudiation: The intent here is to make it impossible for the user to credibly deny having performed an action, for example by refusing to acknowledge that that he/she is the sender of an exchanged message.
- Authentication: The intent is to only allow legitimate users to have access to the resource reservation service. The access may be used to perform any service-related activity, such as reservation request, reservation query, reservation administration and management, etc.
- Authorization: The intent is to differentiate between the actions that legitimate users are allowed to perform. This means that authentication is a prerequisite for authorization, but authorization goes a step further by restricting the level of access a user may have to the service.

WS-Security Standards

A multi-domain resource reservation infrastructure such as Bandwidth Brokers rely on the communication between multiple and often remote components. Communication over the HTTP protocol using XML messages following the SOAP standard have been a very popular way of constructing such multi-domain services, where interoperability and automated machine interaction is a primary objective. It is therefore important to also consider the implications of securing message exchanges through the WS-Security standards (WS-Security, 2010).

An alternative to Web Services Security in this context is also the usage of Transport Layer Security in order to exchange messages over HTTPS. This approach however, does not provide true end to end security, which is guaranteed by WS-Security from the moment an XML message is constructed to the point it is parsed. However, some researchers have also criticized aspects of WS-Security for possible exploitation weaknesses (Gruschka et al., 2009).

The purpose of WS-Security is to specify how technologies such as XML-Signature, XML-Encryption and SAML can be used for securing SOAP messages.

XML-Signature is the way to provide data integrity through the utilization of digital signatures. A digital signature is used in the context of asymmetric encryption, where the communicating parties own their secret private key and have announced the corresponding public keys.

A sender can then produce, using a hashing algorithm, a digest of the exchanged message, and then encrypt the digest using its own private key. The encrypted digest is called a digital signature, and the receiver of the message can decrypt the digest (using the sender's public key), be certain that only the specified sender may have produced the encrypted digest (since he is the only one holding the corresponding private key), and re-run the hashing algorithm in order to compare it with the decrypted digest and make sure that the exchanged message has not been tampered with. Figure 1 illustrates the digital signature concept as used in modern cryptography.

The purpose of XML Signature is to assure data integrity and it can also be considered in the context of authentication and non-repudiation. The WS-Security standard specifies how XML Signature can be used to bind the identity of a sender to a SOAP message.

XML-Encryption defines how the contents of an XML message should be encrypted using cryptography in order to convert plaintext into ciphertext. XML-Encryption is usually used in combination with XML-Signature, such as in a

Figure 1. Digital signature concept

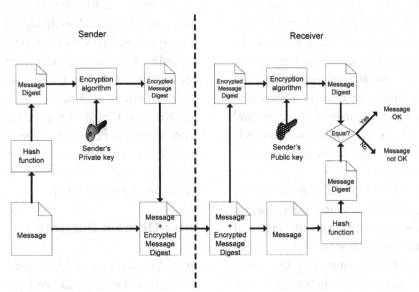

combination known as Sign-Encrypt-Sign, where the plaintext document is first signed, and then the signature is encrypted, along with the plaintext. Finally, the ciphertext is signed again in order to ensure that it can not be changed, either intentionally or by accident, without being noticed.

The Secure Assertion Markup Language (SAML) is a specification that aims at enabling portable trust, by specifying assertions using XML. These assertions are used for providing authentication of single persons or applications between multiple different domains, without requiring a central authentication registry, which often introduces problems of scalability, management and confidentiality.

SECURITY APPROACHES FOR DIFFERENTIATED SERVICES

The SIBBS protocol (Simple Inter-domain Bandwidth Broker Signaling) is proposed by the Internet2 community in order to implement the inter-domain communications of resource reservation between the Bandwidth Brokers. It exchanges two pairs of messages for QoS configuration purposes, the Resource Allocation Request (RAR) / Resource Allocation Answer (RAA) messages to request for a service, and the CANCEL / ACK messages to terminate the requested service. The transmitted information is sensitive and therefore has to be protected against possible security compromises. In Lee et al. (2004), the authors outline the main security threats that inter-domain Bandwidth Broker communication has to protect against, and explain how the Public Key Infrastructure (PKI) can be integrated in order to produce a secure SIBBS implementation.

In Bouras et al. (2008), an efficient algorithm for the Bandwidth Broker's admission control module has been proposed, with the intent of achieving satisfactory utilization of the network resources without heavily impacting the Bandwidth Broker's performance. In Bouras et al.

(2005) the architecture has been extended so that it can support a distributed Bandwidth Broker architecture as illustrated in Figure 2. In the case of a distributed Bandwidth Broker operation, the messages exchanged between the remotely positioned Bandwidth Broker modules have also to be secured, since in that case there is also a fair amount of intra-domain Bandwidth Broker communication that exchanges sensitive information related to the management of the network resources in the domain managed by the Bandwidth Broker.

The security for messages exchanged between the Bandwidth Broker components and messages directed to the Policy Enforcement Points (PEPs) can be enforced using the PKI model with lightweight certificates that do not have a large impact on the communication overhead imposed on the network.

Inter-Domain Security

Inter-domain security deals with the communications between Bandwidth Brokers that manage neighbouring domains. The effort on this area has concentrated on securing protocols such as the SIBBS protocol (Qbone, 2002, Sander, 2000), that deal with the Bandwidth Broker communication across domains.

A common certification authority or a common hierarchy of trust enables the signing of exchanged messages and their validation at the receiving end according to the digital certificates issued by the certification authority. Furthermore, the issue of authorization of user actions and requests (dealing with what level of access a user originating from a specific domain is allowed to have in the overall multi-domain service) can be dealt with the utilization of portable trust approaches such as the utilization of SAML.

Intra-Domain Security

Intra-domain security has to deal with the communication between the Policy Decision Point

Figure 2. Security-enhanced distributed architecture

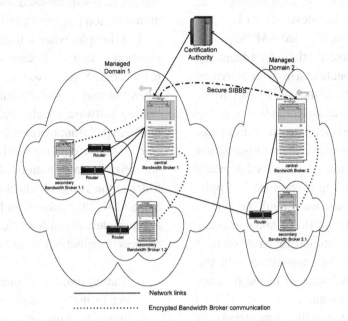

(PDP) that is the Bandwidth Broker, and the Policy Enforcement Points (PEPs) that are typically the network routers that are appropriately configured in order to enforce the Bandwidth Broker's decisions. Also, in the case of a distributed Bandwidth Broker implementation, a large amount of sensitive internal Bandwidth Broker information is likely to be transmitted over the network and is therefore, vulnerable if not properly protected. The overall internal design of the service determines the amount of intradomain information exchanged. For example, several approaches utilize multiple distributed components that coordinate in order to produce admission decisions. Distributed approaches gain in scalability, but introduce complexity, may not achieve optimal results and introduce increased level of information exchange. Their security requirements are therefore also more widespread. In any case, the actual configuration of network devices upon the execution of an accepted user reservation requires access to low level network functionality, which makes network administrators nervous. Therefore, a layered and modular approach is usually more successful, where domain may re-use already existing, tested and trusted components for network configuration, with a limited and well-defined interface towards the multi-domain provisioning service components.

CASE STUDY: POLICIES FOR AAI IN GEANT

The European project GN3 (GEANT, 2010) encompasses a range of research activities to advance both networking and user services in Europe. Central to this project, is the goal of providing high-quality services from one end user to another over multiple interconnected networks. GEANT has deployed services in two main areas: The provisioning of L3 QoS based on Differentiated Services (DiffServ) architecture, and the provisioning of Bandwidth on Demand (BoD) based on dynamic allocation of L2 circuits. The activity that has specified and prototyped a Bandwidth on Demand service intended to operate in a multi-domain environment using heterogeneous transmission technologies is called AutoBAHN, while the activity that has developed a L3 QoS provisioning framework is called AMPS.

In this section we describe the design decisions and implementation conclusion from the activities related to authentication and authorization for users of the service. After a user has been authenticated using the edugain infrastructure (Edugain, 2010) and is able to submit a resource reservation request, an authorization procedure takes place that determines, according to the specified policies, whether this specific user should be able to reserve resources. This decision is taken in every domain along the reservation path, based on user attributes that have to be transmitted with the reservation request and mapped to the policies implemented by each domain.

The AAI infrastructure is therefore comprised of three main areas, which are described in detail below: User authentication, trusted communications between modules and multi-domain user authorization.

User Authentication

When a user wants to make a reservation in a resource, eduGAIN SSO (Single Sign-On) in-

frastructure will be used for authentication and authorization purposes as illustrated in Figure 3.

In principle, when a user tries to make a reservation directly, the resource redirects the user to the Single Sign-On service of his/her federation. Then the user is authenticated through the federation software which sends the SSO response and SAML 2.0 authorization back to the resource. The response contains both authentication and authorization information as SAML 2.0 attributes. Finally, the resource checks the SSO response and SAML 2.0 attributes and responds to the user appropriately about his reservation request. The proposed attributes transmitted are the following:

- Name/Email: A unique id of the user wanting to make a reservation. This could be either the name or the email of the user, or a combination of both.
- Organization: The organization/domain/federation of which the user is a member.
- Project Membership: This attribute should contain a specified value (e.g. AUTOBAHN) that demonstrates that this user is an authorized AutoBAHN user.
- Project Role: This attribute offers granularity in terms of the subset of available

Figure 3. Message flow when a human user wants to make a reservation

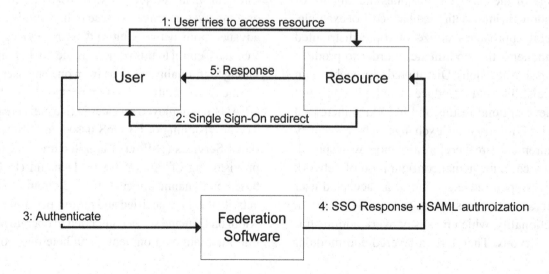

actions that the user is allowed to perform, and can contain values such as Administrator, Developer, User, etc.

The procedure takes place in the following steps as shown in Figure 4:

1. The user (through a web browser) tries to access the AutoBAHN service (the web-based User Interface) of the starting point of the required reservation.
2. The eduGAIN filter intercepts the request and sends to the web browser an http redirection to an Identity Provider (IdP). In order for this redirection to take place, eduGAIN has implemented a WFAYF (Which Federation Are You From) service, which allows the user to select the appropriate IdP for further processing.
3. The user's web browser sends an http request to the IdP server.
4. The IdP server sends to the web browser a page to authenticate the user.
5. The user sends his credentials (login and password, certificate, etc) to the IdP server.

6. The IdP authenticates the user using the credentials and the local database (such as LDAP). The user attributes concerning AutoBAHN are also retrieved.
7. The IdP server redirects the web browser to the AutoBAHN service.
8. The local AAI also sends the autoBAHN attributes to the IDM. The IDM stores these attributes.
9. The IDM sends the BoD request page.
10. The user fills in the page and sends it to the IDM. From then on, the reservation request procedure is initiated by the IDM.

Trusted Communications Between AutoBAHN Modules

In principle, when the client module wants to communicate with another module (the resource), it sends its request to the required resource along with its X.509 certificate through its eduGAIN filter as shown in Figure 5. The eduGAIN filter of the resource authenticates the client by validating its certificate. The certificate contains identification

Figure 4. AutoBAHN Single-Sign On authentication procedure

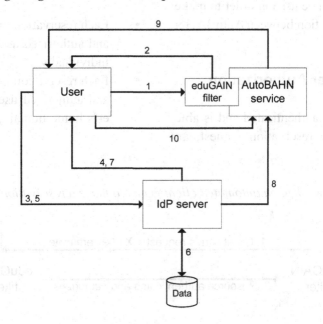

information that allows the resource to authenticate only designated clients.

Below is presented the detailed procedure in the context of the AutoBAHN system for the trusted communication between AutoBAHN modules.

1. The AutoBAHN module that wants to communicate (client) must have a certificate, so no interaction for credentials is needed. The X.509 certificate is issued by a Certificate Authority (CA) subordinated to one of the eduGAIN roots of trust.
2. The client module sends its request and the certificate to the resource.
3. The resource module performs trust validation by checking that the whole trust path of the certificate correctly resolves to the root(s) of trust defined by eduGAIN.
4. The resource checks that the client module is allowed to access it.
5. The resource provides the requested answer to the client module.

In the case of AutoBAHN, the support for eduGAIN means that the dedicated eduGAIN trust fabric (composed of a hierarchy of Certification Authorities) can be used in order to make the trusted communication between AutoBAHN modules possible.

Multi-Domain User Authorization

After a user has been authenticated and is able to submit a resource reservation request, an authorization procedure should take place that determines, according to the specified policies, whether this specific user should be able to reserve the resources. This decision has to be taken in every domain along the reservation path, based on user attributes that have to be transmitted with the reservation request and mapped to the policies implemented by each domain.

Figure 6 presents the detailed multi-domain authorization procedure in the context of the AutoBAHN system.

Steps 1-6 are the user authentication procedure. Steps 9-19 are the possible authorization procedure within the start domain of the reservation. When the reservation request has been authorized in its Home Domain and the IDM wants to propagate further down the selected reservation path, it has to send the request to the next domain. The attributes are sent in the same request. An eduGAIN module is planned to be used in order to concatenate these attributes in the AutoBAHN request (XML).

Upon arrival at the next domain, the possible authorization procedure is repeated there and at every subsequent domain.

Concerning the classification of users there are several different options:

*   Each reservation made by an authenticated and authorized user is credited to the user individually.
*   Each reservation made by an authenticated and authorized user is credited to the user's home domain, and counts against an

Figure 5. Message flow when an automated client wants to make a reservation

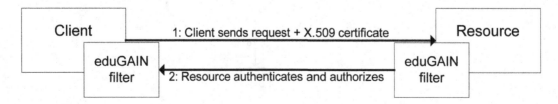

Figure 6. Multi-domain authorization procedure

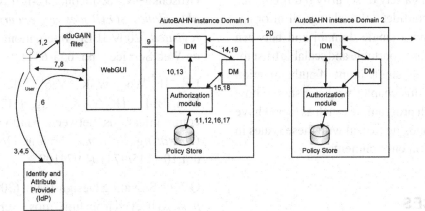

aggregate limit for all users from the same domain.

• Each reservation made by an authenticated and authorized user is credited to the total number of reservations and counts against an aggregate limit for all AutoBAHN users.

It is possible that each domain chooses its own policy regarding the classification of users, or that over time policies change. The authorization procedure should therefore be able to handle all of the above possibilities.

Furthermore, some sort of granularity in terms of authorization flexibility is required, so that for example users can perform a subset of the available actions through the AutoBAHN management interface (e.g. monitor service, use service, and administrate service). The structure of the subset of allowable actions can also be defined by each domain.

FUTURE RESEARCH DIRECTIONS

Multi-domain authentication and authorization infrastructures pose a new and significant challenge as federated services are being developed and deployed. Deployments have to maintain their security objectives in a potentially unfriendly environment, while simultaneously being practi-

cal and effective in terms of user experience and convenience. The widespread deployment of multi-domain reservation services, such as in the case of Geant, is going to provide valuable insight in the large scale characteristics of such services. Furthermore, as multi-domain resource reservation services are moving from the experimental to the production phase, which is also the case for the Geant BoD service, the effectiveness of the AAI infrastructure in the face of actual security challenges is going to be assessed.

CONCLUSION

Security for multi-domain resource reservation services is a subject that touches upon most of the building blocks of security: Confidentiality, integrity, non-repudiation, authentication, authorization, availability etc. It is a very important subject, as any security breach might have repercussions on the proper operation of the network and thus be a potential costly matter. In this chapter we have presented the security requirements and the proposed procedures for protecting against various types of attacks both for layer 3 services based on IETF Differentiated Services architectures, and for Bandwidth on Demand services exemplified by the Geant AutoBAHN service. Emerging multi-domain provisioning services have a variety of security requirements, ranging from confidential exchange of information both within a single domain and between peering domains, to portable and scalable trust for user requests, and single point of authentication procedures. In this chapter we have shown how current research programmes such as Geant have dealt or are proposing to deal with these issues in actual production environments.

REFERENCES

Bouras, C., Haniotakis, V., Primpas, D., Stamos, K., & Varvitsiotis, A. (2007). *AMPS - ANStool: Interoperability of automated tools for the provisioning of QoS services.* TERENA Networking Conference 2007, Lyngby, Denmark, 21 - 24 May 2007.

Bouras, C., & Stamos, K. (2004). *An adaptive admission control algorithm for bandwidth brokers.* 3rd IEEE International Symposium on Network Computing and Applications (NCA04), Cambridge, MA, USA, August 30 - September 1 2004, (pp. 243–250).

Bouras, C., & Stamos, K. (2005). *Examining the benefits of a hybrid distributed architecture for bandwidth brokers.* The First IEEE International Workshop on Multimedia Systems and Networking (WMSN'05).

Campanella, M., Krzywania, R., Reijs, V., Sevasti, A., Stamos, K., Tziouvaras, C., & Wilson, D. (2006). *Bandwidth on demand services for European research and education networks.* 1st IEEE International Workshop on Bandwidth on Demand, 27 Nov 2006, San Francisco (USA).

Edugain. (2010). Retrieved from www.edugain. org

GEANT network. (2010). Retrieved from http://www.geant.net/

Gruschka, N., & Iacono, L.-L. (2009). *Vulnerable cloud: SOAP message security validation revisited.* 2009 IEEE International Conference on Web Services (pp. 625-631).

Lee, B., Woo, W.-K., Yeo, C.-K., Lim, T.-M., Lim, B.-H., He, Y., & Song, J. (2004). Secure communications between bandwidth brokers. *Operating Systems Review*, *38*(1), 43–57. doi:10.1145/974104.974109

QBone Signaling Design Team. (2002). *Final report.* Retrieved from http://qos.internet2.edu/wg/documents-informational/ 20020709-chimento-etal-qbone-signaling/

Sander, V. (2000). *The security environment of SIBBS.* Retrieved from http://qbone.internet2.edu/bb/SIBBS-SEC.doc

Urushidani, S., Fukuda, K., Ji, Y., Abe, S., Koibuchi, M., Nakamura, M., et al. Shiomoto, K. (2008). *Resource allocation and provision for bandwidth/networks on demand in SINET3.* IEEE Network Operations and Management Symposium Workshops, April 2008, Salvador da Bahia, Brazil.

WS-Security Specification. (2010). *Library specification.* Retrieved from http://www.ibm.com/developerworks/ library/specification/ws-secure/

ADDITIONAL READING

Abdalla, M., Boyen, X., Chevalier, C., & Pointcheval, D. (2009). Distributed Public-Key Cryptography from Weak Secrets, Public Key Cryptography - PKC 2009, LNCS 5443, pp. 139-159, Springer, Stanislaw Jarecki and Gene Tsudik (Eds.), March 2009.

Adams, C. (2003). Understanding PKI: Concepts, Standards, and Deployment Considerations, (2nd Edition), Addison-Wesley Professional, 2002m ISBN-13: 978-0672323911.

Barak, B., Canetti, R., Lindell, Y., Pass, R., & Rabin, T. (2005). Secure computation without authentication. In V. Shoup, editor, CRYPTO 2005, volume 3621 of LNCS, pages 361-377. Springer, Aug. 2005.

Bellare, M., Pointcheval, D., & Rogaway, P. (2000). Authenticated Key Exchange Secure Against Dictionary Attack, Advances in Cryptology - EUROCRYPT 2000, Lecture Notes in Computer Science, vol. 1807, pp. 139-155, B. Preneel, ed., Springer-Verlag, May 2000.

Bertino, E., Martino, L., Paci, F., & Squicciarini, A. (2009). *Security for Web Services and Service-Oriented Architectures, Springer, ISBN-13,* 978–3540877417.

Blake, S., Black, D., Carlson, M., Davies, M., Wang, Z., & Weiss, W. (1998). An Architecture for Differentiated Services. *Internet RFC, 2475,* 1998.

Caffrey, L. (EDT) & Okot-Uma, R. (2001). Trusted Services and Public Key Infrastructure (PKI), ISBN: 0850926602.

Chang, C. C., Hwang, K. F., & Lin, I. C. (2003). Security Enhancement for a Modified Authenticated Key Agreement Protocol. *International Journal of Computational and Numerical Analysis and Applications, 3*(1), 1–7.

Dournaee, B. (2002). XML Security. *McGraw-Hill Osborne Media, ISBN-13,* 978–0072193992.

Fitzi, M., Gottesman, D., Hirt, M., Holenstein, T., & Smith, A. (2002). Detectable byzantine agreement secure against faulty majorities. In 21st ACM PODC, pages 118-126. ACM Press, July 2002.

Gennaro, R. & Lindell, (2003). Y. A framework for password-based authenticated key exchange. In E. Biham, editor, EURO-CRYPT 2003, volume 2656 of LNCS, pages 524-543. Springer, May 2003.

Gentry, C., MacKenzie, P., & Ramzan, Z. (2006). A Method for Making Password-Based Key Exchange Resilient to Server Compromise, Advances in Cryptology - CRYPTO 2006, pp. 142-159. Lecture Notes in Computer Science Volume 4117, Springer Berlin / Heidelberg September 24.

Grob, T. (2003). Security Analysis of the SAML Single Sign-On Browser/Artifact Profile.

Holtby, D., Kapron, B. M., & King, V. (2006). Lower bound for scalable Byzantine agreement. In E. Ruppert and D. Malkhi, editors, 25th ACM PODC, pages 285-291. ACM Press, July 2006.

Kanneganti, R., & Chodavarapu, P. (2008). SOA Security. *Manning Publications, ISBN-13,* 978–1932394689.

Katz, J., & Shin, J. S. (2005). Modeling insider attacks on group key-exchange protocols. In V. Atluri, C. Meadows, and A. Juels, editors, ACM CCS 05, pages 180-189. ACM Press, Nov. 2005.

Nichols, K., Jackobson, V., & Zhang, L. (1999). A Two-bit Differentiated Services Architecture for the Internet, Internet RFC 2638, July 1999.

O'Neill, M. (2003). Web Services Security. *McGraw-Hill Osborne Media, ISBN-13,* 978–0072224719.

Panko, R. (2003) *Corporate Computer and Network Security, Prentice Hall, ISBN-13,* 978–0130384713.

Pfitzmann, B., & Waidner, M. (2002). Privacy in Browser-Based Attribute Exchange, In Proceeding of the ACM Workshop on Privacy in the Electronic Society.

Raina, K. (2003). *PKI Security Solutions for the Enterprise: Solving HIPAA, E-Paper Act, and Other Compliance Issues* (1st ed.). Wiley.

Rosenberg, J., & Remy, D. (2004). Securing Web Services with WS-Security: Demystifying WS-Security, WS-Policy, SAML, XML Signature, and XML Encryption. *Sams, ISBN-13*, 978–0672326516.

Windley, P. J., & Media, O. (2005). *Digital Identity.*, *ISBN-13*, 978–0596008789.

Zhang, X., Park, J., & Sandhu, R. (1990). Schema Based XML Security: RBAC Approach, Machine Simulator, Third International Conference on Computer Assisted Learning

Zhang, Z., Duan, Z., & Hou, Y. (2001). On Scalable Design of Bandwidth Brokers", IEICE Transactions on Communications, Vol. E84-B, No.8, pp. 2011-2025, August 2001.

KEY TERMS AND DEFINITIONS

Authentication: The process of confirming that a principal (person or application) is the one that is claimed to be and has access to the provided service.

Authorization: The process of determining what operations a principal is allowed to perform.

Availability: The assurance that the service is up and running and can be accessed by its legitimate users.

Bandwidth Broker: As defined by the IETF, a Bandwidth Broker is an agent that has some knowledge of an organization's priorities and policies and allocates Quality of Service (QoS) resources with respect to those policies.

Bandwidth on Demand: The dynamic reservation of dedicated channels for data transport between varying locations with guaranteed levels of service.

Confidentiality: The assurance that exchanged information is available only to the parties that are intended to obtain it.

Integrity: The assurance that exchanged information has not been tampered with while on transit from the sender.

Non-Repudiation: The assurance that an action has been performed by a specific principal, who can not deny this action.

Quality of Service: The ability to guarantee a certain level of performance to a user, application or data flow.

Section 2
Authentication and Data Privacy:
Passwords and Keys

Chapter 4

Healthcare Employees and Passwords:
An Entry Point for Social Engineering Attacks

B. Dawn Medlin
Appalachian State University, USA

Douglas May
Appalachian State University, USA

Ken Corley
Appalachian State University, USA

ABSTRACT

The healthcare industry has benefitted from its employees' ability to view patient data, but at the same time, this access allows for patient's healthcare records to be easily captured or stolen. Although access to and transmission of patient data may improve care, increase delivery time of services, and reduce healthcare costs, security of that information may be jeopardized due to the innocent sharing of personal and non-personal data with the wrong person. Through the tactic of social engineering, hackers are able to obtain information from employees that may allow them access into the hospitals networked information system. In this study, we simulated a social engineering attack in hospitals of varying sizes with the goal of obtaining employees passwords. If employees are willing to share their passwords, serious questions and concerns about the state of employee security awareness within the healthcare system must be raised.

INTRODUCTION

Healthcare records generally include, but are not necessarily limited to, individual patient's health history, diagnosis, laboratory results, treatments, and the doctor's progress notes. A patient's personal information, such as address, phone number, and social security number, are all items that may be included and accessible to some or all health-

DOI: 10.4018/978-1-60960-777-7.ch004

care employees. These records are vulnerable to security breaches and theft. Both hackers and social engineers have successfully found ways to penetrate networked health data systems by simply asking for the information or by finding weaknesses within the system.

Unfortunately, the largest threat to a healthcare agency's security may not be outsiders, but rather their own employees. Inside employees actually can pose the largest threat to the security and privacy of information as they can exploit the trust of their co-workers, and they generally are the individuals who have or have had authorized access to the organization's network and who are familiar with its internal policies, procedures, and technologies. Additionally, internal employees can exploit that knowledge to facilitate attacks and even collude with external attackers (http://www.cert.org/insider_threat/).

Due to increased regulations and the increased opportunities for exploitation that exist in today's digital world, it is even more important for healthcare providers to keep healthcare records and the information held within, safe and private. Governmental agencies have adopted initiatives that specifically address the issues and rights of healthcare patients. More specifically, the security and privacy of healthcare information is protected by the Health Insurance Portability and Accountability Act (HIPAA), requiring healthcare agencies to do everything possible to protect their information.

There are many threats to the privacy of a patient's information, and one of the largest threats is social engineering. Social engineering is generally defined to include the use of trickery, personal relationships and trust to obtain information; more specifically, it is the art of deceiving people into giving confidential, private or privileged information or access to a hacker (Gragg, 2007).

In our study, we simulated how a social engineer might gather information from unsuspecting hospital employees. Healthcare employees must be especially vigilant in their efforts to guard their passwords, as many have access to personal and medical information. HIPAA regulations are very definitive and have specific standards related to security and privacy of information; infractions of those regulations can be costly to the organization and its reputation, as well as devastating to a patient.

BACKGROUND

The electronic accumulation and exchange of personal health information has been promoted as significant benefits to healthcare consumers and providers. Many healthcare policy experts believe that broader health information technology adoption may lead to the availability of more complete and transparent information, ultimately helping to contain healthcare costs while simultaneously improving healthcare quality.

But with this availability of information comes the opportunity for more fraudulent activity such as social engineering attacks. According to Thornburgh (2004) social engineering has gained profound acceptance in the information technology community as an effective social and psychological tool for exploiting the IT security mechanism of a target organization. For many social engineers the process of obtaining meaningful information may lead to the insight of the organization's security policy, the countermeasures the organization has put in place and specifics relating to personnel and their level of security privilege.

If the social engineer is attempting to find out about one particular patient, they may target that person's medical health record. A patient's medical record may include gender, race, family history, sexual history including types of birth control, sexual activity and treatment, any history or diagnosis of substance abuse, and diagnosis of mental illness. Other medical information, such as HIV status, may also be included. The accessibility of this confidential information may open the door to various forms of discrimination. For instance, chronic diseases such as HIV and AIDS may result in an increase in insurance rates or even denial of coverage, due to the extensive medical treatment usually needed by these patients. Individuals may even be ostracized or stigmatized because of their disease type. Patients expect the information contained in their records to remain secure and private, to be seen only by those individuals whose access is medically or administratively necessary.

Unfortunately, patient's medical records are being illegally accessed and often when a breach occurs, the incident is seen in the news. Table 1 represents security breaches of occurrences that affected individual patients, to an occurrence that wreaked havoc on thousands of patients.

One of the core aspects and a basic goal of the Health Insurance Portability and Accountability Act of 1996 (HIPAA) is to provide more electronic medical information, therefore resulting in more opportunities for cyberthreats. HIPAA

regulations were enacted to protect the privacy and security of patients and their medical records; simply put, they make it illegal for unauthorized personnel to access or release information from someone's medical records.

In relationship to password safety and protection, HIPAA addresses security and privacy measures, either directly or indirectly, in the following standards (http://www.hhs.gov/news/facts/privacy.html). These standards, as listed in Table 2, include management processes, user education and training, and access control.

Despite its legal requirements, however, HIPAA standards are not always followed. As an example, one well-publicized case involved a New Jersey hospital where movie actor George Clooney was treated for injuries following a motorcycle accident. After he was treated and released, the hospital reportedly suspended more than 20 employees who were not directly involved

Table 1. Examples of security breaches

DATE	ORGANIZATION	EVENT	RECORDS AFFECTED
2010	Comprehensive Care Management Corporation, New York	Theft, Unauthorized Access. Several items were stolen such as a Laptop, Desktop Computer, while other applications were used to access data such as email.	1,020 patients
2009	Memorial Medical's Lee Campus, Johnstown, PA.	Police found a red notebook in the purse of a female employee of the hospital with passwords from the hospital. She admitted using the passwords to gain access to personal information.	200 patients
2009	Cedars-Sinai Medical Center, Los Angeles, California	A male previously employed in the billing department was sentenced to prison after he pleaded guilty to stealing patient records and defrauding insurance companies of hundreds of thousands of dollars.	1005 patients
2009	Kaiser Permanente Hospital, Bellflower, California	Hospital workers improperly accessed the medical records of Nadya Suleman, the mother who gave birth to octuplets. The hospital has since fired 15 employees. California health regulators fined Kaiser Permanente's Bellflower hospital $250,000 on May 14 for failing to keep employees from snooping in the medical records of Nadya Suleman	Individual
2008	NY Presbyterian Hospital/Weill Cornell Medical Center, New York, New York	A man who worked in the admissions department at a Manhattan hospital was charged with stealing and selling information on nearly 50,000 patients. Prosecutors said the man exploited his access to the hospital's computer system to acquire lists of patient names, phone numbers and Social Security numbers over a two-year period.	50, 000 patients

Table 2.

Security Management Process [161.308(a)(1)] Healthcare organizations must show that they have a consistent set of internal processes, with implementation that is widespread and institutionalized. Processes range from establishing criteria for who has access to what, and who can request certain resources; to ensuring that access rights are revoked immediately upon employee termination.   **Security Awareness and Training [161.308(a)(5)]** HIPAA requires that staff members be trained and educated concerning the proper handling of PHI. This basic-level security training should include measures such as password management.   **Access Control [161.312(a)]** HIPAA security regulations require a definition of who has access to PHI within the organization, as well as the rules determining an individual's right of access, and the reasons for denying access to some individuals.

in his care but who looked at his medical records and possibly shared his personal information with others (Hupp, 2007).

In November 2007, ID Analytics, Inc. announced the results of a new study on the harm resulting from data breaches. Their study analyzed more than ten million identities spanning over a dozen data breaches. The organization found five separate cases where breached identity data was misused by fraudsters, with two of those cases resulting from internal employee theft or misuse of data (http://www.idanalytics.com/news_and_events/20071107.html).

Issues

Americans hold a strong belief in their right to privacy, and that belief has been served by the legal system of the United States. Privacy is also a constitutional concept, as found in the Fourth Amendment to the U.S. Constitution (Gostin, 2000). In fact, the preamble to the federal Privacy Rule, promulgated pursuant to HIPAA, notes that the existence of a generalized right to privacy as a matter of constitutional law suggests there are enduing values in American law related to privacy.

As required by HIPAA as well as other state laws, healthcare institutions are required to provide security methods in order to protect patient's information. One such method is through the authentication of the individual requesting access. Healthcare employees are generally subjected to some type of authentication process. Although there are different ways of authenticating em-

ployees, most systems are based on the use of a physical token (something one has), secret knowledge (something one knows) or biometrics (something one is) (Burnett & Kleiman, 2006). In today's healthcare institutions, the most common authentication mechanism is still the simple use of a password (something one knows or creates). This type of authentication method can offer to employees the ability to quickly enter into a system, but human practices such as using the same password on different systems and writing down a password may degrade the quality of password security (Pfleeger and Pfleeger, 2007).

Healthcare organizations as well as their employees must be made well aware of those factors related to password choice that may compromise password management. Essentially, there are two types of passwords – strong passwords and weak passwords. If the password is a strong password then it can offer momentous benefits, but a weak password can only offer significant risks.

The authentication method of individuals creating their own passwords is not atypical. For healthcare organizations the password functions like the key to a lock, anyone who has it can get in to see the patient's information. Toward that end, there have been recommendations from governmental agencies to hospitals on how to construct a password. One of the first guidelines in creating good passwords was published in 1985 by the Department of Defense and is still relevant today (http://www.alw.nih.gov/Security/FIRST/papers/password/dodpwman.txt). Their guidelines recommended the following: 1) passwords must be memorized; 2) passwords must be at least six characters long, 3) passwords must be replaced periodically, and 4) passwords must contain a mixture of letters (both upper- and lowercase), numbers, and punctuation characters.

Most networks administrators and security experts would concur with all of the above Department of Defense recommendations, however, that was in 1985 when the advice was given and when social engineering as well as other types of attacks were not as common as they are today. According to CERT (the Computer Emergency Response Team), the advice to use upper and lower case alpha characters for Novell and/or VMS systems is useless since both of these systems are case insensitive.

Suggestions concerning password creation are currently typified by web pages such as the Georgetown University Information Security Office web site http://security.georgetown.edu/passwords.html). Their password guidelines include the following:

"When selecting passwords, keep the following guidelines in mind:

- Choose a password that is at least eight characters in length.
- Create passwords that contain all of the following: uppercase and lowercase letters, numbers, and punctuation and symbol characters (e.g. !@#$%^&*()_+|~-=\`{} []:";'<>?,./).
- Avoid using dictionary words in your passwords. This includes foreign language words, slang, jargon, and proper names.
- Avoid using passwords that contain words associated with Georgetown University, such as *georgetown*, *hoyas*, *jesuit*, or *healy*.
- Avoid common misspellings and substitutions in your passwords (e.g. replacing "e" with *"3"* or *"i"* with *"1"*)
- Avoid using passwords that are based on your name, userid, birthdates, addresses, phone numbers, relatives' names, or other personal information."

Problems

Many of the deficiencies of password authentication systems arise from the limitations of human cognitive ability (Pond et al., 2000). If humans were not required to remember a password, a maximally secure password would be one with maximum length that could consist of a string of numbers, character, and symbols. In fact, the requirements to remember long and complicated passwords are contrary to the way the human memory functions. First, the capacity of human memory in its capacity to remember a sequence of items is temporally limited, with a short-term capacity of around seven items plus or minus two (Kanaley, R., 2001). Second, when humans remember a sequence of items, those items cannot be drawn from an arbitrary and unfamiliar rang, but must be familiar 'chunks' such as words or familiar symbols. Third, the human memory thrives on redundancy.

In fact, studies have shown that individuals' short term memory will retain a password for approximately 30 seconds thereby requiring individuals to attempt to immediately memorize their passwords. It has also been shown that if an individual is interrupted before they fully memorize the password; it will fall out of their working memory and most likely be lost.

Also, if an individual is in a hurry when the system demands a new password, individuals must sacrifice either the concentration of the critical task at hand or the recollection of the new password. Related to this issue is having to create the content for this new quickly demanded password. The pressure to choose creative and secure passwords quickly generally results in individuals failing in their attempt to memorize this new password. For healthcare organizations this can result in reset rates at one per reset per every four to five users per month (Brostoff and Sasse, 2001).

In order to combat the issue of having to remember so many different passwords some users have resorted to the selecting familiar terms such as a pet or family name, their own name, their phone number, or other common terms that could be found in a dictionary. British psychologist Helen Petrie, Ph.D., a professor of human/computer interaction at City University in London analyzed the passwords of 1,200 British office workers who participated in a survey funded by CentralNic, an Internet domain-name company in 2001. She found that most individuals' passwords fell into one of four distinct password categories which were family, fan, fantasists, and cryptic.

The first category of "family," comprised nearly half of the respondents. These individuals selected their own name, the name of a child, partner or pet, birth date, or significant number such as a social security number. Further, Dr. Petrie found that individuals also choose passwords that symbolized people or events with emotional value or ties.

One third of the survey participants were identified as "fans," using the names of athletes, singers, movie stars, fictional characters, or sports teams. Dr. Petrie also found that these individuals wanted to align themselves with the lifestyle represented by or surrounded around a celebrity status. Two of the most popular names were Madonna and Homer Simpson.

Fantasists made up eleven percent of survey responses. Dr. Petrie found that their passwords were comprised of sexual terms or topics. Some examples included in this category were terms such as "sexy," "stud" and "goddess."

The final ten percent of participants were identified as "cryptics." These users were seemingly the most security-conscious, but it should also be noted that they were also the smallest of all of the four identified categories. These individuals selected unintelligible passwords that included a random string of letters, numerals, and symbols such as Jxa+157.

Self-created computer passwords are generally personal, and they reflect the personalities of millions of people as they attempt to summarize their life through a few taps on the keyboard. As psychologists know, people and personalities are often very predictable in the aggregate, as may be their choices of passwords. Psychologists have found that humans can store only five to nine random bits of information in their short-term memory (Andrews, 2004), making it difficult to remember long and complicated passwords. Therefore, users have often chosen passwords with personal meanings that they can associate with something in their long-term memory.

Most social engineers rely on employees to unknowingly help them attack company networks and systems by simply answering a series of simple questions. Today, most healthcare agencies have intrusion detection/prevention systems such as firewalls that can be used to alert organizations in the event of a security breach, but these systems cannot prevent employees from inadvertently sharing information with others. Therefore, the question still remains, "how much information might an employee provide to a stranger or to a co-worker?"

In addition, social engineers can obtain information from the employee by pretending to innocently ask questions about hobbies, family members and pets, or the employee's birth location, and can then assume the legitimate employee's identity. Next, they are able to gain access to all of the information that the employee is authorized to view. It is therefore imperative that employees be taught about the need for strong passwords and the tactics of social engineers.

RESEARCH METHODOLOGY

Instrument

To simulate a real social engineering attack and to obtain a fair statistical representation of the security in relation to healthcare organizations, a survey was administered to employees of five hospitals. These hospitals consisted of varying sizes and were in different regions of the state. Hospital administration approval was obtained before administering the instrument, but the administration did not endorse the survey to respondents, nor did they ask them to participate.

Data was gathered to not only determine how many employees would disclose their passwords and other personal information such as their address, phone number and email, but also simulated the types of information individuals were willing to share with co-workers, colleagues, or friends of colleagues. The information that employees were willing to share, including their passwords and other personal information, would certainly make it easier to hack into a system instead of having to "guess" at the necessary authentication information.

Data Collection

The data set was comprised of 118 responses, with respondents working in small rural areas with approximately 5,000 people, to larger, more urban populations of 500,000. Fifty-three of the respondents filled out entry forms for a drawing, and thus provided the researchers with additional personal and identifiable information.

Analysis and Results

Interestingly, the findings noted in Table 3 indicate that most respondents were often required to use a password to access systems, but rarely changed their passwords. As further indicated, most of the respondents used the same password on multiple accounts. The practice of rarely changing passwords and/or using the same password for multiple accounts would assist social engineers, thus allowing them to easily attain access to one system and possibly more.

Table 3. Password Statistics

Variable Name	Question	Answers	N	Mean	Std Dev
Pass_Freq	How often do you use a password to access systems?	1 = Very Often 5 = Never	118	1.23	0.59
Pass_Change	How often do you change your passwords?	1 = Very Often 5 = Never	117	2.85	1.13
Reuse	Most people use the same password on multiple accounts. How often do you do this?	1 = Very Often 5 = Never	118	2.47	1.32
Choose_Pass	On average, do you choose your own password or have one assigned?	1 = Choose Own 0 = Assigned	117	0.89	0.32
Characters	How many characters are in your most commonly used password?	1 = 1-3, 2 = 4, 3 = 5, 4 = 6, 5 = 7, 6 = 8, 7 = 9, 8 = 10+	116	5.03	1.71
Numbers	Do your passwords contain any numbers?	1 = Yes, 0 = No	117	0.87	0.34
Special_Char	Do your passwords have any special characters in them (@, #, %, &, etc)	1 = Yes, 0 = No	118	0.16	0.37
Password	Please tell us your password	1 = Shared 0 = Did Not Share	118	0.73	0.45

Analyzing the results related to employees' other password practices found that eighty-nine percent (89%) were allowed to choose their own passwords, with the average password being about seven characters in length. In addition, only sixteen percent (16%) of the employees included special characters, adding to the problem of less than secure passwords.

Most interesting, of the 118 respondents, seventy-three percent (73%) of the employees shared their passwords with a co-worker or the friend of a co-worker through this survey instrument. It should be noted that one of the largest threats is that of the internal employee and again, the confidentiality of the password. Internal employees can also act as social engineers to gain access to additional resources.

As seen in Table 4, half of the respondents created passwords consisting of family names, including their own name or nickname, the name of a child, or significant other. It is obvious that a very small percentage of employees are using most of the best practices recommended by governmental, educational, and private organizations.

The category of "other," with forty-five percent (45%) of the respondents indicated that their passwords included a number. The choice to integrate a number is important, but just as important is the placement of that number and whether or not the number relates to meaningful and informative information such as a phone number or birth date.

Fifteen percent (15%) of the respondents self-reported the inclusion of "fan-based" words, which could include names of athletes, singers, movie stars, and fictional characters or sports teams. "Place" was the next highest category, with fourteen percent (14%), using another identifiable piece of information such as the city where the employee works or lives.

The smallest of all of the self-identified password categories was "fantasy," followed closely by the categories of school and faith. Five percent (5%) of the employees selected the "cryptic" category, suggesting that these employees are security-conscious since that category includes passwords that are unintelligible or include a random string of letters, numbers, and symbols. Unfortunately, as noted earlier, is it also the smallest of all of the eight self-reported categories.

A T-test was conducted to show see if there were significant differences between those that shared their password versus those that did not share their password in relation to the categories established by Petri and others. Those that used family as a part of their password were also more willing to share their password (see Table 5). A significant difference was found between those

Table 4. Password Categories

Variable Name	Question	Answers	N	Mean	Std Dev
Family	Does your password fit into this category?	1 = Yes, 0 = No	118	0.50	0.50
Cryptic	Does your password fit into this category?	1 = Yes, 0 = No	118	0.05	0.22
Number	Does your password fit into this category?	1 = Yes, 0 = No	118	0.45	0.50
Fan	Does your password fit into this category?	1 = Yes, 0 = No	118	0.15	0.95
Faith	Does your password fit into this category?	1 = Yes, 0 = No	118	0.03	0.18
School	Does your password fit into this category?	1 = Yes, 0 = No	118	0.02	0.13
Fantasy	Does your password fit into this category?	1 = Yes, 0 = No	118	0.00	0.00
Place	Does your password fit into this category?	1 = Yes, 0 = No	118	0.14	0.34
Other	Does your password fit into this category?	1 = Yes, 0 = No	118	0.51	0.50

Table 5. Employees willing to share or not share passwords

		Shared Password			Did Not Share Password		Difference	
	N	Mean	Std Dev	N	Mean	Std Dev	Mean Dif	Sig.
Pass_Freq	86	1.14	0.41	32	1.47	0.88	-0.33	0.01
Pass_Change	85	2.69	1.09	32	3.28	1.14	-0.59	0.01
Reuse	86	2.48	1.26	32	2.44	1.50	0.04	0.89
Pass_Train	84	0.51	0.50	31	0.61	0.50	0.10	0.34
Awar_Train	83	0.53	0.50	30	0.70	0.47	0.17	0.11
Current_Train	85	4.13	1.09	30	3.97	1.07	0.16	0.48
Choose_Pass	85	0.93	0.26	32	0.78	0.42	-0.15	0.02
Family	86	0.58	0.50	32	0.28	0.46	0.30	0.00
Cryptic	86	0.05	0.21	32	0.06	0.25	-0.02	0.73
Number	86	0.50	0.50	32	0.31	0.47	0.19	0.07
Fan	86	0.20	1.10	32	0.03	0.18	0.17	0.40
Faith	86	0.02	0.15	32	0.06	0.25	-0.04	0.30
School	86	0.01	0.11	32	0.03	0.18	-0.02	0.47
Fantasy	86	0.00	0.00	32	0.00	0.00	0.00	NA
Place	86	0.14	0.35	32	0.13	0.34	0.01	0.84
Other	86	0.55	0.50	32	0.41	0.50	0.14	0.18
Characters	86	5.26	1.62	30	4.37	1.81	0.89	0.01
Numbers	86	0.91	0.29	31	0.77	0.43	0.13	0.06
Special_Char	86	0.20	0.40	32	0.06	0.25	0.14	0.08

who shared their passwords in comparison to those who did not in relation to how often they changed their passwords.

Several findings were significant. Sixty-three percent of those who included family as a part of their passwords were willing to share it. Even more surprisingly, those individuals who included numbers in their passwords were willing to share their passwords at a rate of 50%; this seems counter intuitive, as one would assume that employees who have created stronger passwords by including numbers would be less likely to share their passwords. As expected by most security experts, those who were more security conscious with the inclusion of a special character were not as willing to share it.

DISCUSSION

This study reveals several interesting findings. As noted earlier, most employees used the same passwords on multiple accounts, even though they frequently changed them. The actions of repeatedly using the same password are contrary to suggested recommendations by most security experts, because a hacker who gained access to one account could more easily access other systems. Requiring individuals to maintain a new password for each system or application would obviously make systems more secure but is in conflict with humans' short-term human memory capabilities. Employees may consider it necessary to include familiar names, places, and numbers in their passwords so that they can easily recall them.

Though most employees indicated that their employers offered password security training either very often or often, it appears that either the types of training very not very effective or that the employees did not take it very seriously. As noted in Table 5 and on the positive side of good password practices, those employees offered password training were significantly more likely to NOT use a dictionary word as their password and were more likely to have a password that was at least 6 characters in length. On the negative side, however, those same employees were just as willing to share their passwords even after receiving the training as those that had not received training, suggesting that today's training is deficient in some way.

Other interesting findings emerged in relation to sharing or not sharing passwords. Employees who changed their password frequently were also more likely to share it. This action is contradictory in the fact that employees on one hand appear to be very security conscious while changing their password often and at the same time feeling secure enough to share it with others. Perhaps they were less concerned about sharing it because they thought it would be changed soon and so they perceived less risk.

In comparison, those individuals who were assigned passwords were less likely to share them, which may be a question of remembrance, where they don't share it because they don't remember it. Another possibility may be that if assigned a password, they considered it more sensitive and not to be shared. It may also be that those that are assigned passwords treat them with more respect due to the care the organization gives in giving it to them.

Last, those respondents who had longer passwords were more likely to share them, giving credence to the idea that, because most individuals do not retain information for more than 30 seconds, they would not remember a long password even if told to them by another. Whether or not this is the case, it is inconsistency that on one hand the employee has the awareness of good security practices to create a long password, but on the other hand offers it freely to others.

FUTURE TRENDS

Managers must be vigilant in their efforts to protect patient information as required by several laws. Most recently, on February 17th, 2009, President Obama signed into law the Health Information Technology and Clinical Health Act (HITECH) as part of the American Recovery and Reinvestment Act. The HITECH Act enhances the security and privacy provisions as well as the penalties contained in the Health Insurance Portability and Accountability Act of 1996 (http://www.nixonpeabody.com/publications_detail3.asp?ID=2621). This new law also requires patients be notified in the event of a security breach.

More specifically, the Federal Trade Commission (FTC) and the Department of Health and Human Services (HSS) have issued the first set of HIPAA privacy/security guidance under the new HITECH Act requirements. The new guidance relates to the security breach notification requirement, which is expected to go into effect September 2009 (http://compliance.utimaco.com/na/tag/hitech-act/). "Under this requirement, health plans and personal health record (PHR) vendors must provide individual notification if there has been a security breach of protected health information (PHI). Notification must be provided to individuals in writing within 60 days of discovery of the breach. If the breach involves more than 500 individuals, notice also must be made in prominent media outlets and to the Secretary of Housing and Health Services or to the FTC for PHR vendors (http://compliance.utimaco.com/na/tag/hitech-act/).

For healthcare administrators, security is enhanced by using systems tools that are already available, such as Active Directory and LDAP (Lightweight Directory Access Protocol). Most likely, one or the other, or a combination of both is already in use to help in the securing of information. Even when other front-end access management products, like IBM Tivoli, Citrix or Sun Microsystems' Java System Identity Manager are in use, the directory server on the back end is likely to be Active Directory, LDAP or both.

With LDAP, it's possible to set a minimum password length, minimum number of alphabetic and numeric characters, number of repeat characters and the number of characters which must be different from a user's previous passwords. Group Policy Objects (GPO) in Active Directory also allows for those settings, in addition to settings that prevent an employee from reusing up to 24 of his or her last passwords, force password resets after a set time frame and require passwords to be complex with a combination of numbers, uppercase and lowercase letters. Since both Active Directory and LDAP integrate with third-party access management provisioning tools, password compliance would no longer be a concern.

Other solutions include thin clients, which are low-cost, centrally managed computers with no CD-ROM players, disk drives, or expansion slots. These devices use a central system to store data, providing high levels of availability, reliability, and security. The idea is to limit the capabilities of these computers to only essential applications, which eliminates the need to store data on a desktop device. There is no local storage, no local processing, and no local opportunity to gain access to sensitive data other than in its displayed form.

Additionally, more healthcare agencies may consider adopting biometrics. Biometrics is the science of identifying people through physical characteristics. Usually not one technology but a cluster of several, biometrics uses fingerprints, handprints, retina scans, voice recognition, facial structure, and even hand motions while writing a signature-to identify individuals (Simpson, 2002).

HIPAA calls for a tiered approach to data access in which staff members only have access to the information they require to perform their jobs.

Biometrics makes possible such a tiered approach, while eliminating the security breaches that result from shared passwords or lost badges. Biometric applications are extremely limited even though they have been around for nearly two decades; however, that is changing, due to decreasing cost, increasing accuracy, emerging technology, public acceptance, and stricter compliance regulations.

Smart cards may also be used as these operate with a chip that includes stored memory, and an operating system. A patient's entire clinical history is stored on the smart card which can only be accessed via reading devices in a physician's office, primary care center, hospital, or other medical institution. Through the use of this device, exposed paper records will not be a concern. An added benefit of smart cards is the ability for users to electronically forward patient information to other healthcare authorities and insurers. Specifically, Java-based card technology emerges as a leading platform because of its ability to support multiple healthcare applications securely, while incorporating biometrics for positive identification and authentication.

As existing technological trends advance and new technology enters the marketplace, it is important to remember that both the employee and the patient must always be vigilant in protecting the information within the patient's record and on healthcare agency networks. Computerized systems and security methods cannot prevent individuals from talking or providing information to the shrewd, cunning and calculating social engineer.

CONCLUSION

Findings of the present study indicate that employees are willing to share personal information with co-workers and friends of co-workers. Seventy-three percent (73%) of the employees shared information that a social engineer could use to create a profile of an employee and gain access to the employer's network and other confidential patient information. It is imperative that employees understand the consequences of sharing information, as well as the importance of creating and maintaining strong passwords.

The simulation that was carried out during this study demonstrated that many employees may currently be in violation of HIPAA and HITECH regulations due to their willingness to share their information and their practice of creating weak passwords, thus allowing for easy access into a system. Hospitals and other healthcare agencies must identify ways to educate employees regarding HIPAA and HITECH regulations to protect patients and prevent penalties for sharing or misusing information.

REFERENCES

Analytics, I. D. (2007). *Data breach harm analysis from ID Analytics uncovers new patterns of misuse arising from breaches of identity data.* Retrieved on November 12, 2009, from http://www.idanalytics.com/ news_and_events/20071107.html

Andrews, L. W. (2004). *Passwords reveal your personality.* Retrieved March 13, 2007, from http://cms.psychologytoday.com/ articles/pto-20020101-000006.html

Brostoff, S., & Sasse, M. A. (2001). *Safe and sound: A safety-critical approach to security.* Position paper presented at the New Security Paradigms Workshop 2001, Cloudcroft, New Mexico.

Burnett, M., & Kleiman, D. (2006). *Perfect passwords. Selection, protection, authentication.* Syngress.

CERT. *(2009).* Insider threat research. Retrieved December 1, 2009 from http://www.cert.org/insider_threat

Department of Defense. (1985). *Password management guideline.* Retrieved September 2004, from http://www.alw.nih.gov/Security/ FIRST/papers/password/dodpwman.txt

Georgetown University. (2009). *Information security.* Retrieved November 12, 2009, from http://security.georgetown.edu/passwords.html

Gostin, L. O. (2000). *Public health law: Power, duty, restraint* (pp. 132–134). Berkeley, CA: University of California Press.

Gragg, D. (2007). *A multi-level defense against social engineering.* SANS. Retrieved July 1, 2009, from http://www.sans.org/reading_room/whitepapers/engineering/920.php

Hupp, M. *(2007).* Protecting patient medical records from the nosy. Retrieved on November 30, 2009 from http://www.bizjournals.com/milwaukee/ stories/2007/11/12/focus3.html?t=printable

Intelegen, Inc. (2008). *Human memory.* Retrieved on December 1, 2009 from http://brain.web-us.com/memory/human_memory.htm

Kanaley, R. (2001). Login error trouble keeping track of all your sign-ons? Here's a place to keep your electronic keys, but you better remember the password. *San Jose Mercury News*, 3G.

Nixon Peabody. (2009). *Health law alert.* Retrieved on November 15, 2009 from http://www.nixonpeabody.com/ publications_detail3.asp?ID=2621

Pfleeger, C. P., & Pfleeger, S. L. (2007). *Security in computing* (4th ed.). Prentice Hall.

Pond, R., Podd, J., Bunnell, J., & Henderson, R. (2000). Word association computer passwords: The effect of formulation techniques on recall and guessing rates. *Computers & Security, 19*, 645–656. doi:10.1016/S0167-4048(00)07023-1

Simpson, R. L. (2002). Chicago. *Nursing Management*, *33*(12), 46–48. doi:10.1097/00006247-200212000-00017

Thompson, S. T. (2006). Helping the Hacker? Library Information, Security, and Social Engineering. *Information Technology and Libraries*, *25*(4), 222–226.

Thornburgh, T. (2004). Social engineering: The dark art. *Proceedings of the 1st Annual Conference on Information Security Curriculum Development*, Kennesaw State University, Kennesaw, GA, September 2004.

US Department of Health and Human Services. (2009). *Protecting the privacy of patients' health information*. Retrieved on November 12, 2009 from http://www.hhs.gov/news/facts/privacy.html

Utimaco. (2009). *Health IT data breaches: No harm, no foul*. Retrieved on November 12, 2009 from http://compliance.utimaco.com/na/tag/hitech-act

KEY TERMS AND DEFINITIONS

Authentication: A method by which individuals can be identified to the network or other computer system.

HIPAA: A federal law that mandates how patient's healthcare information will be handled and protected.

Passwords: A common type of authentication method.

Privacy: Relates to the information that should not be seen by others.

Security: The protection of information/data from hackers.

Social Engineering: A nontechnical approach used by hackers to gain meaningful information.

Strong Passwords: Require the use of special characters or numbers or a combination of alpha characters and numbers in a random string that makes it difficult to crack.

Weak Passwords: Words that are in a common dictionary and could be easily cracked by a software program or is information that is readily available and accessible.

Chapter 5
Public Key Infrastructure

Reed H. Petty
University of Arkansas at Little Rock, USA

Jiang Bian
University of Arkansas at Little Rock, USA

Remzi Seker
University of Arkansas at Little Rock, USA

ABSTRACT

Electronic forms of communications are becoming increasingly pervasive. The Internet links not only senders and receivers of e-mail, but also consumers to suppliers, businesses to businesses, citizens to governments, and so forth. The potential for communications to be intercepted, hijacked, emulated, or otherwise manipulated for nefarious purposes is an area of grave concern. The security of message traffic relies heavily upon encryption. Encryption relies upon keys. Public key infrastructure (PKI) addresses keys – how they are used, how they are exchanged, and how they are validated. Furthermore, public key cryptography provides confidentiality, integrity, authentication, and non-repudiation. In general, PKI is a broad subject matter and is constantly evolving to meet the rapid growth in today's information world. This chapter is intended to reveal the mystery, and perhaps misconceptions, of the PKI as well as offering readers a broad high-level view of the PKI.

INTRODUCTION: WHY ARE WE HERE?

Just after midnight on December 7, 1941, on a tiny island situated between Seattle and Bremerton Washington, radio technicians snagged a message flying through the ether. Monitoring of message traffic flowing between Washington DC and Tokyo had become routine. The intended recipient was the Japanese Embassy. The transmission began at 1:28 a.m. and was complete by 1:37 a.m. At 7:58 a.m. an alert was raised, "Air Raid, Pearl Harbor. This is Not a Drill!" A few hours later, the American Pacific Fleet lay decimated (Kahn, 1967).

American code breakers, having gained technical skill while working in programs with distinctive code names, such as "Magic" and "Purple", were aware of the message content well before the bombs fell. What do we learn from this story?

DOI: 10.4018/978-1-60960-777-7.ch005

1. Codes can be broken. The Japanese government was stunned to learn that the Americans had been "reading their mail" for months.
2. Obtaining a technical advantage by exploiting a weakness in a crypto system does not necessarily translate into a strategic advantage. The officials in Washington DC had opportunity to respond and reduce the impact at Pearl Harbor but failed to do so.

In cryptography, it is helpful to assign names to the roles assumed by various players. Traditionally "Alice" and "Bob" refer to parties having a need to communicate with each other. "Eve the Eavesdropper" hopes to read Alice and Bob's secrets. "Mallory the Malevolent" hopes to modify or disrupt the messages sent by Alice to Bob.

In the case of the Pearl Harbor embassy message, Alice was an official located in Tokyo. Bob was the Japanese embassy in Washington, and Eve was the naval intercept station located near Seattle. Mallory was not yet active.

More than 50 years has passed since the events described above occurred at Pearl Harbor. Communication and computer technology have progressed at an astonishing rate. The risk that communications may be compromised now reaches directly into the lives of billions of people. This chapter explores technology intended to manage and, hopefully, reduce such risk.

THE THREE-FOLD MISSION OF ENCRYPTION

Encryption systems serve a three-fold mission: (1) protect the message content, (2) authenticate sender and receiver, and (3) prevent the repudiation after transmission. Alice, Bob, and Eve are active players. Their roles will be explored as we explore each area.

Privacy

The Greek word *kryptos* means "secret, hidden". The first and most fundamental objective of cryptography is the keeping of secrets secret. Alice and Bob are strongly motivated to prevent Eve from learning of the message content. Alice and Bob also are strongly motivated to protect against Mallory's desire to tweak individual words, or entire paragraphs, within their messages. Alice and Bob consider their message to be a private matter not to be read by others, and certainly not to be altered by others. Alice and Bob may be generals in a military campaign, captains in an industry, a lawyer and a client, a doctor and a patient, a political candidate and a campaign chairman, and so forth.

Authentication

The industry refers to the process of verifying player identities as authentication. Assume for a moment that you, the reader, have a need to withdraw cash from your local automatic teller machine. Let us, for the moment, designate the teller machine as Alice. The bank to which Alice communicates we will designate here as "Bob the Banker".

For this discussion, we will designate Alice with a title, "Alice the ATM" to help us remember her role in the current scenario. Before Alice the ATM hands you your cash, she checks with Bob the Banker to ensure that your account exists, has sufficient cash to cover your withdrawal, and so forth. Both Alice and Bob are strongly motivated to ensure that each is who they say they are. Furthermore, both Alice and Bob are interested in ensuring that "you are who you are you are". Both Alice and Bob believe that you would be unhappy if "Mallory the Malevolent" were to withdraw some or all of your cash. Similarly, both you and Bob would be unhappy if Mallory were to replace Alice with a fake ATM that increased each of your requests for cash by $100 and pocketed the difference. The question becomes how Alice verifies that you are who you say you are. And more significantly, how does Bob verify that Alice is who she says she is? For this particular example, the solution to the first part of the question usually involves account numbers, passwords, and/or PIN numbers. The solution to the second portion involves cryptography.

Non-Repudiation

Suppose that you, Alice, have been doing business with your friend "Bob the Broker" for years and have grown accustomed to providing stock orders via e-mail. Today you notice that the stock market is diving. Frantically you, Alice, prepare an e-mail directing that Bob initiate a "sell everything right now!" order. Bob gets to work.

Just as Bob presses the "commit key" Alice notices that the stock market has suddenly and dramatically reversed its free fall. Alice recognizes that a buying opportunity such as this has not existed for years. Alice sends a second message, "Buy more of everything right now!".

A few days later Alice, stinging from the substantial losses (including margin calls) arising from both the sell and buy transactions, argues that she never sent the second buy order. Bob, not being familiar with the finer points of technology, is unable to prove that he acted at Alice's direction. He has retained a copy of the message, but it is not enough. Alice successfully argues that the buy order was placed by Mallory the Malevolent, and that Bob should have known the difference.

The remainder of this chapter will focus upon the cryptographic methods by which Alice and Bob implement cryptographic solutions to protect the content of their messages, authenticate that the message sender and receiver are who they say they are, and prevent repudiation after the message has been sent.

MAIN-FOCUS: PUBLIC KEY INFRASTRUCTURE

Key Management

A fundamental design goal of encryption systems is to base the security of the system upon the key, and only the key. Publishing the details of the implementation, including the source code which implements the encryption algorithm selected, would have no impact on the security of messages encrypted by that implementation. The key, only the key, unlocks the content.

As keys, by definition, are the fundamental elements required to expose message content, the management of keys becomes an important problem. Before we explore the management of keys, it is appropriate to consider the role that keys place in symmetric encryption systems.

Symmetric Encryption Systems

Here we use the term "door" to refer to a barrier. A door bars entry. In the case of the physical world, unauthorized access to sensitive places is protected via a door that can only be opened with an appropriate key. In the message security world, access to sensitive message content is protected by a door that can only be opened with an appropriate key. The door has a name. It is called "Symmetric Encryption".

Symmetric Encryption is directly analogous to a physical lock. As is true with physical locks, many varieties of symmetric encryption "locks" also exist. The characteristics may vary; but the fundamental objective is the same: bar access to message content from everyone excepting those who have the key.

In symmetric encryption systems, the key that locks the door is the same key that unlocks the door. Locking and unlocking the door to one's home, garage, car, and office is not much of a problem when the hand that locks is the same hand that unlocks. Only one key is necessary.

There is no need to clone the key and share a copy with a trusted friend. Its whereabouts is always known, and there is little likelihood that the key will silently disappear from its owner's pocket. Assuming that the lock associated with the key is tamper and pick resistant, the lock cannot be opened without the key even by those who have a perfect knowledge of its inner workings.

Challenges quickly accumulate once Alice has a need to allow Bob access. She must give Bob the key or a duplicate of the key. Allowing another, such as Eve or Mallory, to deliver the key to Bob raises new risks. They may create a copy for themselves. Alice has a problem: She must deliver the key to Bob herself, face to face, or employ expensive alternatives such as Carol's (Bonded) Courier Company. Not too many years ago, the military equivalent to Carol's Courier Company was a government diplomat carrying a red passport issued only to government officials and traveling with a pouch containing encryption keys chained to his wrist.

Many varieties of locks implemented via symmetric encryption systems exist. Such locks are not new. Julius Caesar (Bob) locked the content of secret battle plans by shifting the letters of his message up or down a few characters in the alphabet. The extent of the shift is the key. The original text is referred to as "plain-text" and the scrambled text is called "cipher-text". Eventually the cipher-text was delivered by a runner to the intended recipient, Alice. Assuming that Alice was aware of the key used by Bob, the original message could quickly be recovered allowing the empire to continue to prosper.

The inner workings of very good symmetric encryption algorithms, like good locks, tend to be published openly allowing scrutiny by all who have an interest. Once design of the encryption system is sufficiently resistant to the tools and methods used by lock pickers, the security provided by the lock is said to rely entirely upon the key. Given sufficient time and scrutiny, Alice and Bob can be reasonably assured that the only way to open the lock is to utilize the key, which significantly reduces Eve's options.

A factor of grave importance to the designers of encryption systems is the extent that an adversary, such as Mallory, may be able to discover ways to recover message content without having the key. In the world of encryption, the tools and methods utilized by lock-pickers is broadly referred to as "cryptanalysis". Mallory understands very well the intricate details of encryption algorithms that have been published openly. She may also encrypt her own plain-text with her own key in her efforts to identify and understand patterns produced in the cipher-text.

Symmetric key encryption algorithms tend to be much faster than their public key cousins. Implementations vary, some are stream ciphers which encrypt/decrypt one bit at a time, others are block ciphers which encrypt many characters (often 16) at a time. Implementations include DES and Triple DES (NIST, 1999), RC2 and RC5 (Rivest, 1994) from RSA Data Security, IDEA (Lai & Massey, 1991) from Ascom, Cast (Adams, 1997) from Entrust, Safer (Biryukov, 2003) from Cylink, Blowfish (Schneier, 1994) from Counterpane Systems, and AES (Furguson, Kelsey, Schneier, Stay, Wagner, & Whiting, 2000), adopted by the NIST as a replacement for DES (Bulman, 2000).

Catch-22. Secret Keys Lead to Secret Messages?

The sender and receiver of secret messages via symmetric encryption systems have a dilemma. They must share a secret key with each other in order to communicate. If Alice and Bob utilize a secret message to share their secret key, then they must first arrange a second secret key to protect the secret message that contains the secret key, ad infinitum, a "Catch-22" (Heller, 1955). If sharing a secret requires a secret, how do they share the initial secret? A paradox exists. It cannot be done without Alice first whispering a secret key into Bob's ear, or by utilizing Carol's (Bonded) Courier Company (the reputation of Eve's Escrow Enterprise having been compromised previously).

The Catch-22 described here is a fundamental characteristic of symmetric encryption algorithms. A private key, after all, must remain private in order to be effective. This issue is key management.

Public Key Infrastructure Addresses the Key Management Challenge

Methods have been discovered which quickly discern that a number consisting of hundreds of digits is arguably prime without requiring that the number be factored! What do large prime numbers have to do with encryption? The answer involves trapdoor functions.

Imagine that Alice, being predisposed to developing relationships with handy people, has previously befriended Larry the Locksmith. For all of his life Larry has been fascinated by a special variety of locks having a very special property: one key to lock and another entirely different key to unlock. For the purposes of this example, Larry designated his invention as a "PublikeyLock". While fascinating to locksmiths, the PublikeyLock did not enjoy very much commercial success because it did not address the key management issue. Somehow a cost effective means was needed to get the unlock key into the receiver's hands.

The mathematical equivalent of a Larry's PublikeyLock is called a trapdoor function (described in detail later). For now, given two very large prime numbers and a carefully constructed trapdoor function, Alice is able to construct a Public key that she gives to Bob and all the world (allowing anyone to lock) as well as a private key, which she retains to herself (only Alice can unlock).

An encryption system having two related keys, one private and the other published to the public, significantly alleviates (but does not eliminate entirely) the key management issue.

A BRIEF HISTORY

In the Beginning: Whitfield Diffie and Martin Hellman

Public key cryptosystems were first publicly noted in 1976 by Whitfield Diffie and Martin Hellman of Stanford University and independently by R.C. Merkle of the University of California (Hellman, 2004). In 1978 Ron Rivest, Adi Shamir, and Leonard Adleman of MIT published the RSA algorithm (Rivest, Shamir, & Adleman, 1978). Few companies initially realized the importance of the work of these pioneers.

In 1983 MIT was granted patent number 4,405,829 for a work titled "Cryptographic Communications System and Method". That same year, in a Timonium, Maryland basement, two U.S. National Security Agency (NSA) engineers founded Industrial Resource Engineering (IRE). IRE made a name for itself by selling enterprise network security solutions, using encryption technology to protect the public and private networks of financial institutions. Later they expanded into the federal government sector. Acquisitions of Securealink, Cylink Corporation, Raqia Networks, Inc., and SSH followed (SafeNet, 2009).

The pioneering work of Whitfield Diffie and Martin Hellman has become ubiquitous in the security industry.

MIT Produces RSA: Rivest, Shamir, and Adleman

It is critical to understand that the scheme developed by Whitfield Diffie and Martin Hellman (DH) solves a key sharing problem. Using the DH algorithm, Alice and Bob can negotiate a secret key through an insecure channel.

Ron Rivest, Adi Shamir, and Leonard Adleman were intrigued with the work of Diffie and Hellman. They recognized that integrating public key algorithms and symmetric encryption algorithms represented an area of tremendous opportunity. In

1978, this group of three extraordinary individuals published an algorithm known as RSA, the name deriving from the initials of Rivest, Shamir, and Adleman (Burnett, 2001).

Ron Rivest's interests are not narrowly focused in Public key areas. He is also the inventor of symmetric encryption algorithms RC2, RC4, RC5, and co-inventor of RC6 (along with Matt Robshaw, Ray Sydney, and Yiqun Lisa Yin as an entry in the NIST AES competition intended to identify a suitable replacement for DES (Rivest, 1998).

PGP: Pretty Good Privacy and Phil Zimmerman

In 1991 the very foundation of the glass temples where cryptographic knowledge was safely kept from the eyes of other than government mathematicians was shaken to the core. Someone dared to publish an implementation of strong crypto, available to everyone, for any reason, for free! Phil Zimmerman had unleashed Pretty Good Privacy (PGP).

Pretty Good Privacy is best described by Zimmerman himself. From the documentation supplied by the free distribution we see:

"Pretty Good(tm) Privacy (PGP), from Phil's Pretty Good Software, is a high security cryptographic software application for MSDOS, Unix, VAX/VMS, and other computers. PGP allows people to exchange files or messages with privacy, authentication, and convenience. Privacy means that only those intended to receive a message can read it. Authentication means that messages that appear to be from a particular person can only have originated from that person. Convenience means that privacy and authentication are provided without the hassles of managing keys associated with conventional cryptographic software. No secure channels are needed to exchange keys between users, which makes PGP much easier to use. This is because PGP is based on a powerful new technology called "Public key" cryptography.

PGP combines the convenience of the Rivest-Shamir-Adleman (RSA) Public key cryptosystem with the speed of conventional cryptography, message digests for digital signatures, data compression before encryption, good ergonomic design, and sophisticated key management. And PGP performs the Public key functions faster than most other software implementations. PGP is Public key cryptography for the masses." (Zimmerman, 1991)

At the time of the release of PGP, Cryptosystems using keys larger than 40 bits were classified as munitions within the definition of the US export regulations. Penalties involved prison sentences. Fortunately, after a few years the government quietly closed the investigation against PGP's author without filing charges.

PKI Adoption in Business

The astonishing rate of infrastructure technical development during the 1990's and the decade that followed is driving phenomenal data exchange rates, methods, and reasons between both businesses and individuals. Cloud computing, meshed networks, RFID, VPN, innovative hand-held wireless devices, new cellular applications, social networks, and so forth have increased the ability of anyone to connect with anyone anywhere at any time. The challenges faced by network security are at least equal. Traditional centralized authority-based mechanisms more often than not fail to adequately address emerging networking patterns. New network topologies require new security methods, which in turn often require that one consider how to decentralize trust within the entire security architecture (Meiyuan, 2009).

Business usage of PKI falls primarily within three areas: (1) HTTP/SSL, (2) Electronic Data Interchange (EDI ANSI-X12) with other business trading partners, and (3) E-mail. All rely upon a trusted, and often a third-party, certificate authority that bind Public keys and related properties with respective user identities. Digital signatures allow companies to share data without the fear of disclosing sensitive information to unintended recipients. The certificate authority (CA) is usually involved in the exchange of keys and enables the entire process. CAs certify Public keys by issuing users a digital certificate that contains the user's identity, Public key, and key expiration date. The technology is also favored by the federal government and large state governments (Grupe, 2003). The user identity must be unique within each certificate authority. For each user, the user identity, the Public key, their binding, validity conditions and other attributes are persistent. This has led to wide acceptance within banking, other financial institutions, government, and large enterprises.

Businesses and governments advocate digital signatures in order to minimize processing costs. Whether companies move to adopt the technology now, or wait and be forced by customers and suppliers to adopt it later, digital signatures will soon be a reality for every organization having a need to exchange data with others.

A PEEK INSIDE

Most commonly used cryptographic systems cannot be proven to be secure because often the security they provide is conditional and based on various mathematical assumptions. A simple example is the factorization problem of natural numbers. It is hardly feasibly to factor the product of two large primes or to compute discrete logarithms using limited computational resources. However, obviously it is easy enough to compute the product of two large prime numbers. Cryptographists often craft their security schemes based on the difficulty of solving such mathematical problems.

Trap Door One-Way Functions

We have a name for such problems in computer science. A trapdoor function, as an extension of one-way functions, is a function that is easy to compute one way, yet believed to be hard to invert in the opposite direction. The sense of "easy" and "hard" here are relative and often understood in the sense of computational complexity. A good interpretation of the terms "easy" and "hard" is "cheap enough for the legitimate users", yet "computationally expensive for any unauthorized adversaries".

The notion of a trapdoor permutation was first introduced by Whitfield Diffie and Martin Hellman in their famous journal "New Directions in Cryptography" (Diffie & Hellman, 1976) published in 1976's IEEE transactions on information theory. Mathematically, a permutation $f()$ is said to be a one-way function if it is computationally easy to conduct, but computationally intractable to invert. In another words, given $f()$ and input x, it is computationally easy to evaluate. Let's assume that the product of $f(x)$ is y. So that,

$$y = f(x)$$

$f()$ is a one-way function if it is hardly possible to reverse the function to get x given only y and $f()$. As an extension of one-way function, a trapdoor function $t()$ has the same characteristic, which is easy to compute one-way, yet hard to invert. However, $t()$ is said to be a trapdoor function if there exists a secret parameter s, such that given $y=t(x)$ and s, it is computationally feasible to compute x. Here the secret information s is the trapdoor.

In cryptography, trapdoor functions are the fundamental tools of all sorts of encryption and authentication crypto systems. The reason is obvious. Let's consider the example of a door lock and its key. It is considerably difficult to open the door without using the key (however, this is not impossible as a skilled person can still pick the door lock without using the original key). On the other hand, it is piece of cake to unlock the door with the key. Here the key is the trapdoor.

Trapdoor/one-way functions are known to be hard to find. Following are several candidates:

- Multiplication and factoring problems are the basis on which several Public key schemes are based, including the well-known RSA algorithm (Rivest, Shamir, & Adleman, 1978). Factoring is the process by which a large integer is split into a set of smaller integers (factors) such that when the factors are multiplied together the original larger integer is the result. Prime factorization restricts the products of factoring to a set of prime numbers. Every integer has a distinctive prime factorization set. The multiplication of two prime numbers is easy, but so far, extensive research has failed to identify an efficient method to factor the product of large prime numbers.

- Rabin function (Extracting Square Roots) has been demonstrated to be as difficult computationally as is factoring the product of large prime numbers (Rabin, 1979). In general, a Rabin function $E()$ takes two positive integer m and n, where $n = pq$ and p and q are two primes, and computes the remainder of $m^2 mod\ n$. Let's define:

$$E_m = m^2 mod\ n$$

Inversion of this function, that is, given o and n, find the m such that $m^2 mod\ n=0$, which requires extracting the square roots modulo n, is hard without the extra information (p and q).

Discrete exponential and logarithmic problems are the fundamental basis of both the Diffie-Hellman and the elliptic curve cryptosystems. Let's keep it simple and focus on the Diffie-Hellman problem. The encoding function $f()$ raises a number g to x and modulo a large prime number p to produce y.

$$f(x)=y=g^x mod\ p$$

The discrete logarithm problem is simply finding x given only y, g and p, which is extraordinarily difficult to do.

Nevertheless, none of the one-way functions described above have been proven to be indeed one-way. However, reiterating the earlier claim, a computationally inexpensive way to inverse any of these functions has yet to be discovered.

The Notion of Private and Public keys

If one grasps the concept of trapdoor functions, the notion of private and public keys is straightforward. Presumably, in any Public key cryptosystems, the cipher-text is generated by encrypting the plain-text message with a recipient's public key. And the cipher-text cannot be read (decrypted) unless one can provide a matching private key. Private keys are not intended to be disclosed to others. A widely used analog of such schemes is the postal service. In this analogy, the public key is one's home address. And anyone who knows the address can send a letter to that address through the postal service. However, assume that one's mailbox is locked using a padlock, and only the owner has the key. The key to the mailbox padlock is the physical equivalent to a private key. The letters sent to you are presumably safe as long as the padlock key is protected.

Public and private key pairs are mathematically related. The relationship must be computationally impossible to reverse, that is to generate the private key given only the corresponding public key and, perhaps, the cipher text. Trapdoor functions are perfectly suited to such a scheme. For example, let's consider the discrete logarithm problem (Menezes, Vanstone, & Oorschot, 1996). First, one chooses a random integer x and a generator g. It is easy to compute $h = g^x$ and publish it and g as your public key. One can retain x as the private key, taking care to keep it secret. As discussed, it is hardly possible to compute x from (g, g^x), since its underlying mathematic problem-discrete logarithm-cannot be solved with reasonably available computational resources and time (reasonable is considered by many to span many hundreds of years).

But, how does one use the public/private key pair to exchange secret messages with an associate? Let's introduce a public key encryption, the ElGamal encryption cryptosystem that relies upon the keys generated above. To keep it simple, this illustration removes the constraints of how to choose g and x. However, in real life, poorly selected values of g and x will certainly lead to information leakage.

Assume that Alice wishes to send to Bob a private message. Alice generates a public key (g, g^x) which she makes available to Bob while retaining x as her private key. To encrypt a message m using the public key (g, g^x), Bob must first choose a random y and calculate his own public key (g, g^y) which he makes available to Alice while retaining y as his private key. Alice then computes a shared secret $s = (g^x)^y$ and encrypts her message m by calculating the cipher-text $c = m \cdot s$. Alice then sends to Bob both the cipher-text c and his public key g^y.

So, how does Bob decrypt? The objective of decryption is to compute m given (x, g^x, g^y, g, c). First, Bob calculates the shared secret $s = (g^y)^x = (g^x)^y = g^{xy}$. Then Bob computes m by $m = c \cdot s^{-1}$ which converts the cipher-text c into the original message m. This works because:

$$c \cdot s^{-1} = (m \cdot s) \cdot s^{-1}$$
$$= (m \cdot (g^y)^x) \cdot (g^{xy})^{-1}$$
$$= m \cdot g^{yx} \cdot g^{-xy}$$
$$= M$$

The process is very clever and straightforward!

HASHES AND DIGITAL SIGNATURES

When considering trapdoor/one-way functions and public/private key pairs, one inevitably encounters the well known one-way functions-hash functions which form the basis of digital signatures.

Hashes

Hashes are implementations of one-way functions which do not necessarily qualify as trapdoor functions. A hash differs from a trap-door in that it does not require an inversion procedure. A hash function is a well defined and deterministic procedure that maps larger domains to smaller ranges. Strictly speaking, a hash function h maps a large, possibly arbitrary length of data into a small and fixed length datum. One can think of a hash function as the postman who delivers mail to an apartment building. He stands in front of the mail boxes in the apartment building. He looks at the destination addresses on each of the envelopes and puts them into the correct mailbox. The number of letters is certainly larger than the number of mailboxes. The address on the envelope can be considered as a small amount of well defined values that uniquely represent a unique mailbox based on its location. Similarly, a *hash value* can be considered to be a well defined value that uniquely represents a much larger message based on its content. The outputs of a hash function are usually referred as *hash values*, *hash codes* or simply *hashes*.

Hash function implies a many-to-one relationship between a large and possibly variable domain and a smaller fixed domain. Hence, the possibility of a *collision* exists, which means the hash function may map the contents of two or more input arguments to the same hash value. A good hash function should spread out the input to the output mapping as evenly as possible. In a perfect world, a "perfect hash function" should map distinct input elements to distinctive outputs with no collisions. Obviously, a perfect case is not possible to archive, since the input domain is often million times larger than the output range. An example is the birthday paradox. In probability theory, the birthday problem is to guess the probability that in a group of randomly chosen people, some (two or more) people will have the same birthday. No matter how random and even the distribution is, the population of the world (6.69B) is much larger than the number of days (365 days, non-leap year) per year. Collisions are inevitable. Actually, the number of people needed to achieve a high probability of collision is very small. Studies by Mckinney (1966), Mathis (1991), Sayrafiezadeh (1994) show that in a group of 23 randomly chosen people, the probability of two people having the same birthday is 50.74%. For a group of 57 or more people, the probability approaches 100%.

Although, collisions in hash function are theoretically unavoidable, it is certainly manageable depending on the input domain. There exists a set of hash functions that are characterized as cryptographic strength hash functions. These are designed such that the probability of a collision is minimized. By definition, a cryptographic hash function takes an arbitrary block of data and returns a fixed-size bit string. The input data is called "message" and the output hash value is often called "message digest". As a type of one-way function, a cryptographic hash function can easily compute the hash value of a given message. However, it is not feasible to invert the process and identify the message input given only the hash value. In addition, cryptographic hash functions are designed such that it is not possible to modify a message without changing its message digest (hash). In other words, it is not feasible to find two different messages with the same hash values. This property defines the essence of collision resistant.

Cryptographic hash functions have been used widely in various security applications. Because it is infeasible to change a message without also changing the resulting hash value, hash functions are perfectly suited for use in roles requiring message authentication codes (MACs) or other forms of authentication. Cryptographic hash functions are an important component in various digital signature schemes as digital fingerprints and checksums essential to detection of data corruption or unauthorized data modification.

Digital Signatures

Digital signing of messages is a branch of public key cryptography. A digital signature is a well defined process that can prove the authenticity of an electronic document or message. As in ordinary handwritten signatures, a properly implemented digital signature provides to the message receiver a high degree of assurance that the document was created and signed by the owner of the key required to produce the digital signature. Moreover, a verified digital signature can prove that the document or message received has not been altered in transit.

The concept of digital signatures was first described by Whitfield Diffie and Martin Hellman (Diffie & Hellman, 1976), however they did not provide an implementation. Not long afterwards, Ronald Rivest, Adi Shamir, and Len Adleman, who invented the RSA algorithm, provided a digital signature proof of concept implementation using their RSA encryption algorithm.

If one grasps the notion of public/private key, one can quickly make sense of the digital signatures utilizing a public key infrastructure. A solid digital signature schema consists of three different algorithms: 1) a key generation algorithm to generate public/private key pairs, 2) a signing procedure that produces a signature given an input message and a private key, and 3) a verification function, that verifies that a digital signature is valid and thus proves the authenticity of a message or document.

A simple example utilizing ElGamal (Menezes, Vanstone, & Oorschot, 1996) demonstrates how a digital signature can be produced and verified:

Choose a random number x as the private key, where $1 < x < p-1$. p is a large prime. Compute $y=g^x mod\ p$, where g is a random integer of the multiplicative group of integers modulo p, Z_p^* (i.e. just consider it as a special group of integers). Therefore, the Public key is (p, g, y).

To sign a message m:

- Step 1: Select a random integer k, where $0 < k < p-1$ and $gcd(k, p-1) = 1$.
- Step 2: Compute $r = g^k mod\ p$.
- Step 3: Produce $s = (h(m) - xr)k^{-1}mod(p-1)$

The (r,s) is a signature of message m.

To verify the correctness of signature (r,s), one must test the following equation.

$$g^{h(m)} = y^r r^s\ mod\ p$$

The equation above is true for valid signatures when:

$$h(m) = xr + sk\,mod\ (p - 1)$$

and

$$
\begin{aligned}
g^{h(m)} &= g^{xr}g^{ks}\\
&= (g^x)^r(g^k)^s\\
&= (y)^r(r)^s\,mod\,p
\end{aligned}
$$

Since, x is the private key, which holds the fact that it is known only to the signer. Therefore, the authenticity of the message can be proven in cases where the signature satisfies the equation.

A QUESTION OF TRUST

Is public key cryptography perfectly safe? The answer is certainly not. While amused by the beauty and cleverness of the public key infrastructure and its applications, in the back of one's mind lingers another question—how to break them.

The Role of Signatures

Forgery of signatures often happens in the paper world. Imagine this scenario: an aged individual is requested to place his/her signature on a crucial document that transfers all of his or her valuable belongings to an unrelated person. Perhaps this might be his or her housekeeper, or someone else entirely. The scenario now moves into an attorney's office. A very angry relative angrily confronts the attorney, "I know my uncle's handwriting. That is NOT his signature." How does one verify the signature on a piece of paper? Perhaps by questioning witnesses? Suppose that there are no witnesses? One must then locate a qualified document examiner to check the document. Suppose the document is prepared digitally and signed electronically? Can one prove the authenticity of the document? Yes. One may assert that this is true by employing a PKI digital signature. But, is it safe? Can a digital signature be forged?

In the ElGamal signature scheme discussed above, the security of the digital signature relies on the difficulty of solving discrete logarithm problem in the multiplicative group Z_p^*. An adversary must either find the signer's secret key x or be lucky enough to identify a hash input that collides with the original message content. Both of these are believed to be hard problems. However, it is not impossible. The security of the ElGamal signature scheme relies heavily on the parameters p and g. Choosing k carefully is required. Various research efforts (Bleichenbacher, 1996; Liu, Cheng, & Wang, 2006) have shown that it is possible to forge ElGamal signatures when additional information on these two parameters is available.

Even though technology is producing digital signatures that are increasingly secure, adoption of digital signatures has not been fully realized. Digital signature applications are still in an early stage of development. The market for digital signature software and services remains young and small. Many businesses consider the security of digital signatures to be uncertain even given that Electronic Signatures in Global and National Commerce Act (ESIGN) was enacted by the U.S. Congress in 2000. The law permits the use of digital signatures in various areas, and most notably assures that contracts and agreements signed electronically will withstand scrutiny by the courts. However, digital signatures are increasingly utilized by consumers, especially when engaging in electronic commerce involving the Internet. The security concerns are real. The security of all public key based digital signatures relies heavily on the secrecy of the private key. However, there is no physical connection between the key and the key owner. How does one guarantee that the person who is holding a private key is its true owner?

Impersonation, the Exchange of Keys

Impersonation is a common attack against digital signatures and also secured communications which rely upon public keys. One step back, the beauty of PKI systems is that it allows two entities to communicate over an unsecured channel without having to meet physically in order to exchange keys. Alice can openly send Bob a message encrypted with Bob's Public key, and no one other than Bob can read the message, since it can only be decrypted by Bob's private key. But, how does Bob know the message is truly from Alice, but not from their evil friend—Mallory? Unless the key exchange involves some type of authentication authority, he cannot know with an assurance than an interloper is not involved.

In unauthenticated public key based message exchange protocols, impersonation is possible.

One steps forward, returning to the famous Diffie-Hellman (Diffie & Hellman, 1976) key agreement protocol that allows two people to agree on a shared secret exchanged via an unsecured channel. In order to agree on a shared secret, first Alice and Bob agree to generate a value g derived from a finite cyclic group G.

- Step One: Alice picks a random number x as her private key and sends Bob g^x.
- Step Two: Bob picks a random number y as his private key, computes the shared secret $s=(g^x)^y=g^{xy}$ and sends g^y back to Alice.
- Step Three: Alice then can compute the same shared secret $s=(g^y)^x=g^{xy}$.

Alice and Bob can use this shared secret to secure all consequent communications using a symmetric encryption algorithm and g^{xy} as key. It looks secure as long as no one else can get hold of either party's private keys. However, let's take a look at how an adversary can defeat the system without obtaining the private keys.

As usual, Alice initiates the Diffie-Hellman key exchange protocol. She picks x as her private key and then sends Bob g^x. However, an eavesdropper, Eve, intercepts Alice's Public key and sends her own Public key g^z to Bob without anyone's notice. When Bob replies, Eve gets Bob's Public key g^y, substitutes it with hers again and replies Alice with g^z. Both Alice and Bob, think they are sharing a private secret with each other and their communication encrypted by this secret is safe. But in fact, the shared secret Alice holds is g^{xz}, and the secret Bob holds is g^{yz}. Both of them are actually sharing secrets with Eve, and they are unknowingly communicating via a third party. This vulnerability is called a man-in-the-middle attack, and it occurs because no authentication scheme is used in the Diffie-Hellman key agreement protocol. One possible solution is to use public key certificates.

Certification, the Role of Certificate Authorities, X.509

A Public Key Certificate binds a public key to an entity (such as an individual) using digital signatures. The certificate can then be used to verify that a public key belongs to that individual. Typically, the certificate is signed by a well-known certificate authority (CA). A CA is similar to a Notary Public. Suppose you have an important legal document that you must deliver to another who must be absolutely certain that it was you, and only you, who signed the document. You appear before a notary public and sign the documents in front of him/her. The notary will check photo IDs, and perhaps other documents as necessary, to assure that you are whom you claim to be. The notary then adds his/her signature to your own. This asserts that your signature was produced by your hand while physically present before the notary. Once notarized, the signatures on the documents that you signed gain a great deal of credibility. A public key certificate serves a role similar to that of a notary. Certificates are necessary to assure others that your digital signature was not forged.

Many similarities exist between notaries and certificate authorities. To obtain a certificate, one must first present identity information to a well-known CA. The CA then binds this identity information to your public key and signs the entire package with the CA's key. When being questioned, the challenger needs only to verify the CA's signature to ensure its authenticity. As the individual's identity document is attached to the public key, and the public key has been signed by a well-known CA, the challenger should have no doubts about the authenticity of the individual's signature.

X.509 (ITU-T, 2005) is an ITU-T (Telecommunication Standardization Sector) standard for PKI. It defines specific formats for public key certificates and the algorithms that verify that a given certificate path is valid under a given PKI. In the X.509 system, a CA issues a certificate that binds a public key to a specific Distinguished Name (DN) or to an Alternative Name such as a DNS entry. Distinguished Name is a naming convention standard that has been widely used in Lightweight Directory Access Protocol (LDAP) to refer an LDAP object. A DN is a sequence of relative distinguished names (RDNs) connected by commas. An RDN is a key-value pair in the form of "attribute=value". For example, my identity can be expressed as: CN=Jiang Bian, OU=Info Tech, O=U7AMS.

Continuing the first person dialogue, the next question becomes: How do I use it? First, I must generate a public key pair and send the public key to a well-known CA such as VeriSign or Thawte (now owned by VeriSign). Of course, they will ask me to present my IDs (driver license, passport, etc) to verify my identity in order to make sure that I am who I claim to be. If they find my credentials to be in order, they will then sign my public key and generate a public key certificate, which binds my identity to my public key. From that point forward, all of the documents signed with my private key can be trusted, or at least verified.

There are many secure communication protocols and standards that support X.509 style certificates. Examples include Secure Shell (SSH), Transport Layer Security (TLS/SSL), Hypertext Transfer Protocol Secure (HTTPS), Lightweight Directory Access Protocol, etc.

The Web, SSL/TLS, HTTPS

With the growth of the Internet and the World Wide Web over the last two decades, many people have become familiar with the Hypertext Transfer Protocol (HTTP). HTTP is an application layer protocol for distributed hypermedia information systems (Fielding, et al., 1999). However, broad use of HTTP for transferring sensitive data has exposed a need for stronger security measures. TLS and its predecessor, SSL are cryptographic protocols that provide security at the Transport Layer enabling secured communications over unsecured networks such as the Internet. Researchers have given considerable attention to a new standard, HTTPS (Rescorla, 2000). HTTPS is built upon HTTP and SSL/TLS protocols. It provides encryption services and assures the identity of the server that hosts the web application.

The main idea of HTTPS is to create a secure channel that passes over an insecure network. There are two parts of the HTTPS protocol. First, the trust of the web server is established by verifying the site's certificate which was signed by a well-known CA. This is equivalent to saying that "I trust the CA, so I will also trust the entities that the CA has certified". The second part is to create a secure communication channel through a series of handshakes between the client and the server using PKIs to establish a shared secret, and to secure all subsequent communications encrypted via the shared key. HTTPS provides reasonable protection from eavesdroppers and man-in-the-middle attacks, since the adversary can't provide a valid certificate to perform an impersonation attack. All communications between the client and server are encrypted with a key that is unknown to the adversary.

VULNERABILITIES AND WEAKNESSES

The security of most encryption algorithms depends on mathematical assumptions, such as computational impracticalities of factoring n as pq, if p and q are large enough. However, the rapidly developing computer technology is increasing computational power available to launch an attack. Much of the public key infrastructure would be completely broken if quantum computers become a reality. Furthermore, while the design of the whole public key infrastructure may be mathematically sound, the security of a system relies upon users to protect their keys.

Security Design, Hidden Risks

In 2000, Carl Ellison and Bruce Schneier published a paper in the Computer Security Journal that discusses "Ten Risks of PKI" (Ellison & Schneier, 2000). They raise a number of questions regarding the security design of the PKI and CA architecture. The points raised have some measure of merit and sparked a heated discussion. As is true in all heated discussions, two points of view exist. On the other side of this discussion, Aram Perez authored a counter-response (Perez, 2000). To be fair and objective, a few key points representing both points of view are summarized:

- Risk #1: "Who do we trust, and for what?" Ellison and Schneier are questioning the authority of the CAs that issue public key certificates. However, this writer agrees with Perez on this question. In the "real world", we all rely on third-parties to provide proof of our identities. We often use our driver license, which issued by a third-party, the government, to prove that we are who we said we are. As in the "real world", fake certificates exist as do fake driver licenses. Sure, we need to be cautious when verifying a certificate signed by a CA in case it is fake. However, it is not a problem of PKI + CA system itself, but rather reflects the discipline with which keys are managed.

- Risk #2: "Who is using my key?" The most significant risk in PKI + CA systems is the user's private signing key. It is true that loss of one's private key, like the loss of a credit card or a house key, is cause for grave concern that warrants an immediate response. However, this is a problem of any key-based encryption system and is not unique to PKI.

- Risk #4: "Which John Robinson is he?" Both sides agree that public key certificates only bind a public key with a name, but few people have ever raised the question of what should be done when the name itself is ambiguous.

- Risk #6: "Is the user part of the security design?" The SSL protocol does create a web of trust. However, as a user, we should be careful to understand exactly what it is that SSL assures and what it does not. SSL security only binds the website's domain name or its DNS address to its public key identity. It answers the question: Is this person who he says he is? It cannot claim that this person will never do bad things. Likewise, SSL security has no control over the information content that a website may deliver.

PKI is not a perfect security system. It is a security methodology. Automobiles are not perfect transportation devices. Automobiles are a transportation methodology. As Schneier and Ellison have argued in their paper, "Security is a chain; it is only as strong as the weakest link." However, the weakest link of a PKI based security system is rarely the PKI itself. How does one make sure the root certificate (CA's certificate) on one's computer has not been compromised? If an adversary has hacked into a computer, and added himself as a CA into the root certificate trust list, what may happen? All of his malicious websites, perhaps including some that emulate the touch and feel of your bank, will appear to be authentic and without any certificate warnings. Is this bad? Yes. An adversary can simply build a clone of your bank site, and you will be entering your bank account and password with no indication that something is amiss. After all, the site's certificate has been verified! Is this a risk that exists when PKI is in use? Yes. Is PKI at fault? Probably not.

Attacks: Man-in-the-Middle, Side channel, Certificate Collisions

Setting human factors aside for a moment and examining the question: is PKI framework mathematically perfect or technically sound? The answer, unfortunately, is that it is not. As we have demonstrated in a previous section, a well-educated adversary can defeat the system without breaking the private keys. A PKI + CA system itself can prevent man-in-the-middle (MITM) attacks, since both parties in the communication are expected to have been verified by a CA. However, it is still possible to perform such an attack if one party does not verify the other's certificate carefully, or not at all. For example, Clients using SSL-encrypted web sessions (HTTPS) authenticate the server using a PKI X.509 certificate. Suppose that the server does not authenticate the client (i.e., it is not practical and meaningful to do so, since not all users will have certificates and the server doesn't really care who the user is on the transport layer). The HTTPS protocol inherently subjects users to MITM attacks. An SSL web session begins with the client challenging the server identity when presented with a server certificate. If the client is unable to confirm that the server's certificate has been signed by a trusted CA, the client browser raises a warning. If the client is able to confirm that the certificate has been signed by a trusted CA, the authenticated certificate is retained for future reference. However, most of the browsers in use today (e.g. Internet Explorer, Firefox, Safari, etc.) present a very generic warning and do not properly state the risks of accepting certificates whose authenticity cannot be confirmed. Should a naive user accept a flawed certificate without taking appropriate precautions, it is easy for a well-educated adversary to prepare a self-signed certificate and initiate MITM attacks. When the adversary has access to the target users' Local Area Network (LAN) the attack becomes trivial (Esser, 2001) (Callegati, Cerroni, & Ramilli, 2009).

Traditional attacks mounted against security systems in general, and encryption algorithms in particular, focus primarily on inputs and outputs—the plaintext and/or the ciphertext is manipulated in an attempt to identify the key. Many variations of this process, known as cryptanalysis, exist. Varieties include cipher text only attacks, known plaintext attacks, chosen-plaintext attacks, chosen-ciphertext attacks, and so forth.

Non-traditional attacks may exploit areas often considered to be well beyond the reach of conventional encryption. For example, encryption routines take time to execute. The timing is measured. The timing may provide clues such as the volume of data being encrypted, the size of the key, and so forth. Another "side-channel" that may provide information useful to an attacker is the rate of power consumption, how frequently faults are occurring, or even the sound produced by a disk drive. The underlying principal is that any effects caused by the execution of the cryptosystem may yield useful information about the system.

An example of a timing attack is based on the measurements of the time an encryption routine requires to perform operations. This information can lead to information about the secret keys. Such as in Diffie-Hellman protocol, private-key operations consist of computing $y^{x_0} mod^0 n$, where n is public and y can be found by eavesdropping. The victim computes $y^{x_0} mod^0 n$ for different values of y, where y, n and the computation time are known to the attacker (i.e. through statistical modeling). We assume that x is w bits long. Because of the differences in time of computing the exponent bit k ($0<k<w-1$), the adversary can determine that whether the k bit is set or not (i.e. from statistical data, the time of the operation when bit k is set or not will be consistently different. Then we can say, if it is slow, bit k is 0, otherwise it is 1 or vice verse.) (Kocher, 1996).

X.509 certificates are too large to sign directly. Therefore, the CA uses a cryptographic hash function to generate a certificate digest and then signs the digest. A well-designed cryptographic hash function can transform arbitrary-length data into a fixed-length message digest. The probability that a modification of the message will result in a totally different message digest is a measure of "collision resistance". A message digest is often used to represent the whole message. A very popular cryptographic hash function is MD5 (Message-Digest algorithm 5) (Rivest, 1992) introduced by Ron Rivest in 1991, which produces a 128-bit hash value. In 2004, some Chinese researchers, Wang et al., discovered the possibility of engineered collisions in MD5 (Wang, Feng, Lai, & Yu, 2004). In 2005, they published a paper entitled "How to Break MD5 and Other Hash Functions" (Wang & Yu, How to Break MD5 and Other Hash Functions, 2005). The paper demonstrated an efficient way of finding collisions. This development was very damaging for CAs using MD5 hash functions. An adversary could construct a certificate that produced a hash identical to a valid certificate belonging to someone else. As CAs sign the hash, the adversary could use his own certificate to impersonate that signed by the CA. As both certificates produce an identical hash value, web browsers have difficulty discriminating between the two.

MANAGEMENT CHALLENGES

The entire Public Key Infrastructure rests upon a foundation of trust. Organizations seeking to enjoy the benefits of PKI must consider and overcome a number of challenges, many of which require considerable institutional and technical discipline. It is difficult to overstate the emphasis, commitment, and attention required to achieve a successful PKI implementation.

Speaking frankly and candidly, organizations that adopt a casual approach to PKI implementation risk compromising sensitive data and inflicting very tangible harm upon their organizations.

PKI management challenges fall into three general areas:

1. Creation and disposal of "Trust". Objects representing "trust", including keys, are often created by the parties external to the certification authority. Care must be taken to ensure that trusted objects truly represent the entity intended and not an impersonator, that the generation environment is secure, and that the newly created key is not compromised.

The communications channel used to pass the key on to the certificate authority <u>must</u> be secured. Confidence in an organization's Certificate Authority will be irreparably lost should the keys that it certifies be modified to suit the needs of a motivated adversary (Mallory the Malevolent) while en route from the creator to the CA.

The reverse case, revocation of trust, is similar. Revocation of keys must be accomplished quickly and accurately, but only after verification that the revocation requestor is legitimate.

2. Maintenance of "Trust". Objects representing "trust", including private keys, signatures, delegated certificates provided by other CA's (appropriately verified), and similar objects are retained by organizations as needed to facilitate the CA's mission. Such data, as is true of all data, resides in environments that will fail in time. The question is not if, but when, a media failure will occur. Media failure is a certainty, only the timing is unknown.

Organizations establish policies and practices that protect against data loss arising from media failure. These involve some form of replication to alternative media. The replication may be in the form of backups, file system and/or database journal entries, or similar. Often the backups are created in clear text and stored in readily accessible locations in order to facilitate rapid recovery when disaster strikes.

Much of the data retained by CA's, by definition, is extraordinarily sensitive. For example, exposure of the private key portion of a public key pair warrants immediate key revocation, and a far more costly damage control initiative to limit the effects of sensitive information previously encrypted that now must be assumed to be compromised.. Among the favorite techniques of "Mallory the Malevolent" involve gaining access to backup media that is casually stored within inadequately protected physical locations.

3. Exceptional access to "Trust". It is not uncommon that organizations be faced with circumstances requiring that encrypted materials be recovered by other than the intended parties. Employees may leave their organizations seeking opportunities elsewhere, courts may demand access to encrypted records, regulatory policies may demand copies of keys be placed into some type of escrow arrangement enabling inspection and compliance with defined audit controls (such as those spawned by the Sarbanes-Oxley Act of 2002).

An argument can be made that the risk of failure of a security system is directly related to the extent that sensitive materials are replicated. A colloquial equivalent often cited is the phrase, "The strength of the chain is determined by its weakest link" followed closely by its cousin, "the more links, the greater the likelihood that a link somewhere will fail".

Organizations must carefully craft policies and practices that effectively balance the needs of key security against needs to recover data under exceptional conditions.

Organizations seeking to implement Public Key Infrastructures may find it appropriate to carefully review both past and current PKI developments occurring in industry and elsewhere.

Journal archives similar to the "Privacy Law and Policy Reporter Archive" (PLPR) (accessible via http://www.austlii.edu.au/au/journals/PLPR/) can also be helpful. PLPR provides a monthly review and analysis of privacy laws, policies and practices.

Lastly, software systems supporting Public Key Infrastructures are available via a number of well established sources, including several for-profit vendors. A query directed at common internet search engines is sufficient to generate a representative list of commercial options.

EMERGING TECHNOLOGIES

Quantum computing, an emerging technology based on the principles of quantum mechanics, is posing new challenges. Quantum computers must be highly parallel given the principles underlying their operation. Parallel computation is an important consideration for many cryptographic attacks, such as factoring of large integers. For example, Shor's algorithm could solve prime factorization and discrete logarithms, problems in polynomial time on quantum computers (Shor, 1999). Much of the public key infrastructure would be completely broken should quantum computing become a reality.

One of the exciting application areas of quantum computation is quantum cryptography. The main difference between quantum communication and classical communication is that it enables Alice and Bob to sense if Eve is trying to eavesdrop on communications. This property of quantum communications makes sniffing of traffic and therefore man-in-the-middle attacks impractical. Unlike traditional PKI systems, which rely on the computational difficulty of factoring large prime numbers or solving discrete logarithm problems, the security of quantum cryptography rests on the foundations of quantum physics. Initially, quantum cryptography was impractical as it was not possible to store a single polarized photon or spin-1/2 particle for days without significant

loss of polarization (Wiesner, 1983). However, Bennett and Brassard realized that quantum objects are meant to transmit information rather than store information, and presented their arguments in their 1984 paper addressing the BB84 protocol (Bennett & Brassard, 1984). Information transmitted in quantum communication is first encoded to quantum bits or qubits—a quantum analogue of the classical two-state bit. As in a bit system, a qubit can have two possible values, 0 or 1. However, unlike the classical bit whereas a bit must be either 0 or 1, a qubit can be 0, 1 or a superposition of both. This characteristic enables the quantum communication to be more secure and attack resistant. Much research has been directed in the area of theoretical quantum cryptography and its practical extension as quantum communication protocols (Bennett & Brassard, 1989) (Bennett, Bessette, Brassard, Salvail, & Smolin, 1992) (Schumacher, 1995) (Schmitt-Manderbach, et al., 2007) (Huang, Chen, Guo, & Lee, 2007).

CONCLUSION

The November 2009 edition of the journal *Communications of the ACM* opens a discussion with:

Security is about economics. Users, administrators, organizations, and vendors respond to the incentives they perceive. Users just want to get their work done; they don't have good reasons to value security, and view it as a burden. If it is hard or opaque, they will ignore it or work around it; given today's poor usability they are probably doing the right thing. If you force them, less useful work will get done. Tight security usually leads first to paralysis and then to weak security, which no one complains about until there is a crisis (Lampson, 2009).

Public Key Infrastructure seeks to address the key management challenge: exchanging keys between two parties without compromising the key. While the future will undoubtedly bring new methods to scramble data, authenticate the owners of keys, and prevent repudiation of past communications, the most significant gains will likely involve infrastructures supporting the exchange of key material.

Current State of the Art

Matt Blaze correctly summarizes in his afterward included in Bruce Schneier's Applied Cryptography:

High-quality ciphers and protocols are important tools, but by themselves make poor substitutes for realistic, critical thinking about what is actually being protected and how various defenses might fail (attackers, after all, rarely restrict themselves to the clean, well-defined threat models of the academic world) (Schneier, 1995).

The state of the art currently relies heavily upon certificate authorities to address key distribution challenges. Security of public-key algorithms rests on the assumption that the result obtained by multiplying a pair of very large prime numbers will remain difficult to factor. Should an efficient (in terms of time) method be discovered to factor large numbers, the Public Key Infrastructure will collapse. Fortunately efficient factoring methods remain elusive.

REFERENCES

Adams, C. M. (1997). *Constructing symmetric ciphers using the CAST design procedure.* Retrieved December 12, 2009, from http://cryptome.org/jya/cast.html

Bennett, C. H., Bessette, F., Brassard, G., Salvail, L., & Smolin, J. (1992). Experimental quantum cryptography. *Journal of Cryptology*, 3-28.

Bennett, C. H., & Brassard, G. (1984). Quantum cryptography: Public key distribution and coin tossing. *IEEE International Conference on Computers, Systems, and Signal Processing*, 175. Bangalore, India: IEEE.

Bennett, C. H., & Brassard, G. (1989). The dawn of a new era for quantum cryptography: The experimental prototype is working! *Sigact News*, 78-82.

Biham, E., & Shamir, A. (1991, February). Differential cryptanlysis of DES-like cryptosystems. *Journal of Cryptology*, 3-72.

Biryukov, A. (2003). Cryptanalysis of SAFER++. *CRYPTO, 2003*, 195–211.

Bleichenbacher, D. (1996). *Generating ElGamal signatures without knowing the secret key. Advances in Cryptology --- EUROCRYPT~'96* (pp. 10–18). Springer-Verlag.

Bulman, P. (2000, October 2). *Commerce Department announces winner of global information security competition.* Retrieved December 11, 2009, from http://www.nist.gov/public_affairs/releases/g00-176.htm

Burnett, S. (2001). *RSA security's official guide to cryptography*. McGraw-Hill.

Callegati, F., Cerroni, W., & Ramilli, M. (2009). Man-in-the-middle attack to the HTTPS protocol. *IEEE Security and Privacy*, 78-81.

Diffie, W., & Hellman, M. (1976). New directions in cryptography. *IEEE Transactions on Information Theory, 22*(6), 644–654. doi:10.1109/TIT.1976.1055638

Ellison, C., & Schneier, B. (2000). *Ten risks of PKI: What you're not being told about public key infrastructure*. Computer Security Journal.

Esser, S. (2001). *IE https certificate attack*. Retrieved December 1, 2009, from http://security.e-matters.de/ advisories/012001.html

Fielding, R., Gettys, J., Mogul, J., Frystyk, H., Masinter, L., Leach, P., et al. (1999). *Hypertext Transfer Protocol -- HTTP*. Retrieved December 1, 2009, from http://www.w3.org/Protocols/HTTP/1.1/diff-v11-Rev0

Furguson, N., Kelsey, J., Schneier, B., Stay, M., Wagner, D., & Whiting, D. (2000). *Improved cryptanalysis of Rijndael*. Seventh Fast Software Encryption Workshop. Springer-Vertag.

Grupe, F. (2003). Understanding digital signatures. *The CPA Journal, 73*(6).

Heller, J. (1955). *Catch-22*. New York, NY: Simon and Schuster.

Hellman, M. (2004, November 22). *Oral history inverview with Martin Hellman*. Transcript, 58pp. (J. R. Yost, Interviewer).

Huang, D., Chen, Z., Guo, Y., & Lee, M. (2007). Quantum secure direct communication based on chaos with authentication. *Journal of the Physical Society of Japan*.

ITU-T. (2005). *ITU-T recommendation X.509: Information Technology - open systems interconnection - the directory: Public key and attribute certificate frameworks*. Retrieved December 1, 2009, from http://www.itu.int/rec/T-REC-X.509-200508-I

Kahn, D. (1967). *The codebreakers, the story of secret writing*. New York, NY: Scribner.

Kocher, P. C. (1996). Timing attacks on implementations of Diffie-Hellman, RSA, DSS, and other systems. *CRYPTO '96: Proceedings of the 16th Annual International Cryptology Conference on Advances in Cryptology* (pp. 104-113). London, UK: Springer-Verlag.

Lai, X., & Massey, J. L. (1991). *A proposal for a new block encryption standard*. Springer-Verlag.

Lampson, B. (2009). Usable security: How to get it. *Communications of the ACM, 52*(11). doi:10.1145/1592761.1592773

Liu, J., Cheng, X.-G., & Wang, X.-M. (2006). *Methods to forge ElGamal signatures and determine secret key*. 20th International Conference on Advanced Information Networking and Applications, 2006. AINA 2006 (pp. 859-862).

Mathis, F. H. (1991). A generalized birthday problem. *SIAM Review*, 265–270. doi:10.1137/1033051

Mckinney, E. H. (1966). Generalized birthday problem. *The American Mathematical Monthly*, 385–387. doi:10.2307/2315408

Meiyuan, Z. (2009). Centralized trust management for securing community networks. *Intel Technology Journal, 13*(2).

Menezes, A. J., Vanstone, S. A., & Oorschot, P. C. (1996). *Handbook of applied cryptography*. Boca Raton, FL: CRC Press, Inc.

NIST. (1999, October 25). Data encryption standard. *FIPS PUB 46-3*.

Perez, A. (2000). *Response to ten risks of PKI*. Retrieved December 1, 2009, from http://homepage.mac.com/aramperez/ responsetenrisks.html

Rabin, M. O. (1979). *Digitalized signatures and public key function as intractable as factorizations*. Cambridge, MA: Massachusetts Institute of Technology Press.

Rescorla, E. (2000). *HTTP over TLS*. Retrieved December 1, 2009, from http://www.ietf.org/rfc/rfc2818.txt

Rivest, R. (1992). *The MD5 message-digest algorithm*. United States: RFC Editor.

Rivest, R., Shamir, A., & Adleman, L. (1978). A method for obtaining digital signatures and public key cryptosystems. *Communications of the ACM, 21*(2), 120–126. doi:10.1145/359340.359342

Rivest, R. L. (1994). The RC5 encryption algorithm. *Proceedings of the Second International Workshop on Fast Software Encryption*, (pp. 86-96).

Rivest, R. L. (1998, August). The RC6 block cipher. *MIT Laboratory for Computer Science*.

SafeNet. (2009). *History*. Retrieved October 20, 2009, from http://www.safenet-inc.com/About_SafeNet/ The_Company/History.aspx

Sayrafiezadeh, M. (1994). The birthday problem revisited. *Mathematics Magazine*, 220–223. doi:10.2307/2690615

Schmitt-Manderbach, T., Weier, H., Furst, M., Ursin, R., Tiefenbacher, F., & Scheidl, T. (2007). Experimental demonstration of free-space decoy-state quantum key distribution over 144 km. *Physical Review Letters*, 98.

Schneier, B. (1994). *Description of a new variable-length key, 64-bit block cipher (Blowfish)*. Retrieved December 11, 2009, from http://www.schneier.com/paper-blowfish-fse.html

Schneier, B. (1995). *Applied cryptography*. New York, NY: John Wiley & Sons, Inc.

Schumacher, B. (1995). Quantum coding. *Physical Review A.*, 2738–2747. doi:10.1103/PhysRevA.51.2738

Shor, P. W. (1999). Polynomial-time algorithms for prime factorization and discrete logarithms on a quantum computer. *SIAM Journal on Computing*, 303–332.

Wang, X., Feng, D., Lai, X., & Yu, H. (2004). *Collisions for hash functions MD4, MD5, HAVAL-128 and RIPEMD*. Cryptology ePrint Archive, Report 2004/199.

Wang, X., & Yu, H. (2005). *How to break MD5 and other hash functions. EUROCRYPT* (pp. 19–35). Berlin/Heidelberg, Germany: Springer.

Wiesner, S. (1983). Conjugate coding. *SIGACT News*, 78-88.

Zimmerman, P. (1991). *Phil's pretty good privacy*. Retrieved December 1, 2009, from ftp://ftp.pgpi.org/pub/pgp/2.x/doc/pgpdoc1.txt

ADDITIONAL READING

Beauchemin, P., & Brassard, G. (1988). A Generalization of Hellman's Extension to Shannon's Approach to Cryptography. *Journal of Cryptology*, *1*, 129–131. doi:10.1007/BF02252870

Bennett, C. H., Bessette, F., Brassard, G., Salvail, L., & Smolin, J. (1992). Experimental Quantum Cryptography. *Journal of Cryptology*, 3-28.

Bennett, C. H., & Brassard, G. (1984). Quantum Cryptography: Public key distribution and coin tossing. *IEEE International Conference on Computers, Systems, and Signal Processing* (p. 175). Bangalore: IEEE.

Bennett, C. H., & Brassard, G. (1989). The dawn of a new era for quantum cryptography: The experimental prototype is working! *Sigact News*, 78-82.

Beth, T., Jungnickel, D., & Lenz, H. (1985). *Design Theory*. Zurich: Bibliographisches Institut.

E. Biham & A. Shamir. (1993). *Differential Cryptanlysis of the Full 16-Round DES*. Lecture Notes in Computer Science. 494-502. (Advancances in Cryptology – CRYPTO '92).

Bishop, M. (2005). *Introduction to Computer Security*. New York: Addison-Wesley.

Blakley, G. R. (1979). *Safeguarding Cryptographic Keys*. AFIPS Conference Proceedings, 48, 313-317.

Buetulspacher. (1994). *Cryptology*. Mathematical Association of America.

Catalano, D. (2005). *Contemporary Cryptology*. Berlin: Birhauser Verlag.

Coutinho, S. (1999). *The Mathematics of Ciphers, Number Theory and RSA Cryptography*. Natick, MA: A.K. Peters.

Diffie, W. (1992). The First Ten Years of Public key Cryptography. *Contemporary Cryptology, The Science of Information Integrity*, IEEE Press, 135-175.

Diffie, W., & Hellman, M. (1976). New Directions in Cryptography. *IEEE Transactions on Information Theory*, 22(6), 644–654. doi:10.1109/TIT.1976.1055638

Diffie, W., & Landau, S. (1998). *Privacy on the Line, The Politics of Wiretapping and Encryption*. Cambridge, MA: The MIT Press.

Diffie, W, Van Oorschot, P.C., & Wiener, M. J. Authentication and Authenticated Key Exchanges. Designs, codes and Cryptograpy, 2, 107-125.

Gaines, H. (1939). *Cryptanalysis, A Study of Ciphers and their Solution*. New York: Dover Publications.

Huang, D., Chen, Z., Guo, Y., & Lee, M. (2007). Quantum Secure Direct Communication Based on Chaos with Authentication. *Journal of the Physical Society of Japan*.

Kohneim, A. G. (1981). *Cryptography, A Primer*. New York: John Wiley and Sons.

Menezes, A. J., Vanstone, S. A., & Oorschot, P. C. (1996). *Handbook of Applied Cryptography*. Boca Raton, FL, USA: CRC Press, Inc.

Patterson, W. (1987). *Mathematical Cryptology for Computer Scientists and Mathematicians*. Lanham, MD: Rowman and Littlefield.

Rivest, R., Shamir, A., & Adleman, L. (1978). A Method for Obtaining Digital Signatures and Public key Cryptosystems. *Communications of the ACM*, 21(2), 120–126. doi:10.1145/359340.359342

Schneier, B. (1996). *Applied Cryptography*. New York: John Wiley & Sons.

St. Denis, T., & Johnson, S. (2007). *Cryptography for Developers*. Rockland, MA: Syngress Publishing, Inc.

Stallings, W. (2006). *Cryptography and Network Security, Principles and Practices*. Upper Saddle River, NJ: Pearson Prentice Hall.

Stamp, M. (2007). *Applied Cryptography, Breaking Ciphers in the Real World*. New York: John Wiley and Sons.

Stinson, D. (1995). *Cryptography: Theory and Practice*. New York: CRC Press.

Tanenbaum, A. (1981). *Computer Networks*. Englewood Cliffs, NJ: Prentice-Hall.

Van Heyst E. & Pederen, T.P. (1993). How to Make Efficient Fail-Stop Signatures. *Lecture Notes in Computer Science*, 658, 366-377. (Advances in Cryptology – EUROCRYPT '92).

Van Tilborg, H. (2005). *Encyclopedia of Cryptography and Security*. New York: Springer Science + Business Media, Inc.

Yao, A. (1982). Theory and Applications of Trapdoor Functions. *Proceedings of the 234d Annual Symposium on the Foundations of Computer Science*. 80-91. IEEE Press.

KEY TERMS AND DEFINITIONS

CA (Certificate Authority): An organization that creates and verifies digital certificates.

Certificate: A packet of data that includes a Public key and information about the key owner.

Hash: A function which converts a relatively large volume of data into a small fixed sized block of data, usually 128 to 512 bits. Hash data is an important component of digital signatures.

PKI (Public key Infrastructure): Consisting of a certificate authority (CA), registration authority (RA), and a certificate management system.

Public Key: A published key. Public key cryptography relies upon key-pairs, one of which is the Public key which is published, and the other being a private key whose distribution is restricted to the key owner. One of the keys encrypts, the other decrypts.

RA (Registration Authority): Acts as an agent that verifies the legitimacy of certificate authorities.

Signature: A document is considered to be signed when the hash of the document has been encrypted by the private key of the key owner. The document may be verified as authentic and unchanged by anyone having access to the owner's Public key.

Single Key: Also known as a Symmetric key. A secret shared between both the originator and the receiver of a message that is used to encrypt and decrypt the message.

Chapter 6
Key Management

Chuan-Kun Wu
Chinese Academy of Sciences, China

ABSTRACT

In secure communications, key management is not as simple as metal key management which is supposed to be in a key ring or simply put in a pocket. Suppose Alice wants to transmit some confidential information to Bob over the public networks such as the Internet, Alice could simply encrypt the message using a known cipher such as AES, and then transmit the ciphertext to Bob. However, in order to enable Bob to decrypt the ciphertext to get the original message, in traditional cipher system, Bob needs to have the encryption key. How to let Alice securely and efficiently transmit the encryption key to Bob is a problem of key management. An intuitive approach would be to use a secure channel for the key transmission; this worked in earlier years, but is not a desirable solution in today's electronic world. Since the invention of public key cryptography, the key management problem with respect to secret key transmission has been solved, which can either employ the Diffie-Hellman key agreement scheme or to use a public key cryptographic algorithm to encrypt the encryption key (which is often known as a session key). This approach is secure against passive attacks, but is vulnerable against active attacks (more precisely the man-in-the-middle attacks). So there must be a way to authenticate the identity of

DOI: 10.4018/978-1-60960-777-7.ch006

the communication entities. This leads to public key management where the public key infrastructure (PKI) is a typical set of practical protocols, and there is also a set of international standards about PKI. With respect to private key management, it is to prevent keys to be lost or stolen. To prevent a key from being lost, one way is to use the secret sharing, and another is to use the key escrow technique. Both aspects have many research outcomes and practical solutions. With respect to keys being stolen, another practical solution is to use a password to encrypt the key. Hence, there are many password-based security protocols in different applications. This chapter presents a comprehensive description about how each aspect of the key management works. Topics on key management covered by this chapter include key agreement, group-based key agreement and key distribution, the PKI mechanisms, secret sharing, key escrow, password associated key management, and key management in PGP and UMTS systems.

1. INTRODUCTION

In the world of secure communications, a key is usually something used to encapsulate a message, just like our metal keys which are used to secure locks. An electronic key can also be used for the purpose of authentication, and a metal key sometimes plays the same role. So from the application point of view, an electronic key has much similarity with a metal key. Note that the way to manage metal keys can be quite simple: simply put the metal keys in a pocket, or in a key ring attached in one's belt, or put them in a handbag. This simple way of metal key management has been proved to be fairly secure in most of the cases in our normal life. One may naturally think about the possibility of electronic key management simply by memorizing in human brains. Unfortunately our brains are neither reliable no secure, and our memory has been proved to be a bad way of managing electronic keys.

It is noted that the electronic world is very different from the real one, and the electronic key management is much more complicated than the metal key management. With respect to the electronic key management, there are sophisticated theories and methodologies. This chapter tends to give a comprehensive introduction of the fundamental techniques in key management

issues, where without confusion, a key means an electronic key.

To commence the introduction, let's make a scenario. Let Alice be someone in the world who wants to communicate securely with Bob, who is also someone somewhere in the world, on the earth or even in the space yet reachable via electronic signals. In order to provide confidentiality of their communications, Alice uses an encryption algorithm which can be publicly available, e.g. the advanced encryption standard (AES). Alice can do the encryption easily, and send the encrypted message (called ciphertext) to Bob. Now the problem is how does Bob decrypt the ciphertext? Here we do not care about the reliability of the communication, and we assume that Bob does not have problems in correctly receiving the ciphertext. Obviously there should be a way for Alice to send the encryption key to Bob, or equivalently there should be a way for letting Alice and Bob share a common encryption key, so that Alice's encryption can be decrypted by Bob, but not anyone else. In 1976, Diffie and Hellman presented a way for letting secrets to be shared over the public channels, where even if all the communications over the public channels are eavesdropped by an attacker, the attacker is not able to guess/compute the shared key between Alice and Bob (Diffie & Hellman, 1976). This is the well-known Diffie-Hellman key agreement scheme, which is introduced in Section 2.

A natural generalization of the key agreement between two communication parties is the key agreement problem for a group of members, and an alternative key management for a group of members is called key distribution, where a trusted third party playing the role as a key distribution center is needed. This problem is discussed in Section 3. This chapter then further introduces some practical key management solutions for Ad Hoc and sensor networks. This can be found in Section 4.

Now Alice can find a way to agree/share on a common key with Bob whenever they want to establish a secure communication. However, in the commercial world, Alice may not exactly know who Bob is, she knows Bob by some publicly available information such as name, email addresses, or even IP addresses. However all these kinds of information can be faked. How does Alice know that the one at the other end of the communication network is really the Bob that she intends to communicate with? Even with a Diffie-Hellman key agreement protocol, there can be a man-in-the-middle attack. This problem is actually a problem of trust, here by trust we mean that one is convinced that the information being trusted is genuine, and not having been faked. There does not seem to have a solution to this problem unless a path of trust between the communication parties can be made, this leads to the involvement of a trusted third party (TTP). An alternative solution to the key agreement very much similar to Diffie-Hellman key agreement is to employ the public key cryptosystem, where the public key of the recipient is used to encrypt a random session key that is then used to encrypt the communication data, which can be proved to be a secure solution provided that the public key of Bob is not faked. This problem can be solved using a public key infrastructure (PKI), where the most well-known one is the international standard

X.509 protocol set. A detailed introduction of PKI is given in Section 5.

In secure communication systems, an encryption key is used to transmit data securely from a sender to a receiver. Once the secure communication is complete and the receiver has successfully recovered the original data, the life of the encryption key comes to the end. However, as introduced above, the secret key agreement process needs to employ a public key cryptosystem (note that the Diffie-Hellman key agreement can be viewed as a public key cryptosystem, where the lifetime of the public keys is relatively short), and in a public key cryptosystem, a public key always has a corresponding private key, and the private key is meant to be a long time key which should be kept for some time, practically from a few hours to a few years depending on the application environments. Then it turns out how to manage the private keys. These private keys (as in public key cryptographic systems) could get lost (e.g. due to lost from memory or recording media), or be stolen. Fortunately some techniques are available to prevent the loss of such kind of secrets. One of the approaches is the secret sharing techniques, which are introduced in Section 6, and another approach is key escrow for key backup which is introduced in Section 7. There can be some other approaches but are out of the scope of this chapter due to rich content in the key management issues and the space limitation of such a chapter.

In real information systems, access is controlled by account names and passwords. Some of the secrets in computer systems are also protected/encrypted by a password, and there are even some password-based cryptosystems. However the choice of password seems to have a conflict between memorability and randomness. In Section 8, some security issues with respect to password related key management are discussed.

Although there is a large amount of different scientific research about the key management problems with different application constraints, in many industry applications, however, there can

Figure 1. Diffie-Hellman key agreement protocol

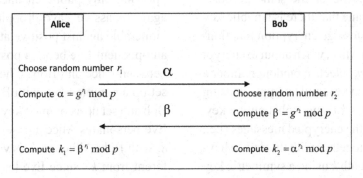

be very different and yet practical key management schemes being used. To show how some of the practically used key management schemes are different from what have been studied by academics, this chapter also briefly introduces two typical examples, i.e., key management techniques in mobile telecommunication systems as in Section 9, and that in the pretty good privacy (PGP) system as in Section 10.

Finally, Section 11 of this chapter points out some of the limitations of the key management in protecting the security of information systems, and Section 12 makes a brief conclusion.

2. KEY AGREEMENT

In traditional communication systems, there is a sender and a receiver, so the secure communication requires both the sender and the receiver have a same secret (the encryption as well as the decryption key). How to make a secret known between a sender and a receiver had been a difficult problem. In 1976, Diffie and Hellman proposed a key agreement scheme using public channels (Diffie & Hellman, 1976). Assume that user Alice and user Bob want to establish a common secret using the available public channels, they may first agree on some parameters: a large prime number p, a random number $g<p$. These parameters can be discussed over the public channels and should be assumed to be publicly available. Then Alice

chooses a random number r_1, and Bob chooses a random number r_2. Alice computes $\alpha = g^{r_1} \bmod p$ and sends the result α to Bob, and Bob computes $\beta = g^{r_2} \bmod p$ and sends the result β to Alice. Based on the received messages, both Alice and Bob can compute $k_1 = \beta^{r_1} \bmod p = g^{r_1 r_2} \bmod p$ and $k_2 = \alpha^{r_2} \bmod p = g^{r_1 r_2} \bmod p$ respectively. It is easy to verify that $k_1 = k_1$ holds, which means that Alice and Bob now know a common secret. This is the well known Diffie-Hellman key agreement protocol. The process of the Diffie-Hellman key agreement protocol can be illustrated in Figure 1.

The Diffie-Hellman scheme can be viewed as a public key cryptosystem. In a public key cryptosystem, any user has a private/public key pair, where the public key, as its name indicates, can be made public, with which it is computationally infeasible to compute the corresponding private key, where the private key is used only by the owner. In the Diffie-Hellman scheme, the random number r_i chosen by a user can be viewed as a private key of the user, and $y_i = g^{r_i} \bmod p$ can be viewed as the corresponding public key. This public key cryptosystem however is meant to be used for secret key agreement. In 1978, Rivest, Shamir, and Adleman invented a real public key cryptosystem, known as RSA (Shamir, Rivest, & Adleman, 1978) public key cryptosystem, which can be used for message encryption as well as for digital signatures. The encryption feature can be used for key agreement, or the same purpose. More precisely, assume that there is a public key cryptosystem with message encryption functionality available. Then Alice, when about to encrypt a confidential data m, selects a random number k as the data encryption key, and encrypts m using k. Alice then encrypts k using Bob's public key. Alice sends both of the encrypted messages (i.e., the encrypted key k together with the data m having been encrypted with k using a symmetric key encryption algorithm) to Bob. When Bob receives the message, Bob is able to extract k by decrypting the corresponding ciphertext of k using his own private key, and then is able to decrypt the data m encrypted with k. This mechanism of secure communication is used by many practical security systems, including the PGP system as introduced in Section 5. This mechanism is believed to provide the same security as using the Diffie-Hellman key agreement scheme, as long as both the public key systems are secure.

It should be noted that, in practical implementations, there is usually a message telling the recipient who the sender of the message is, i.e., the identity information is usually associated with a requesting or responding message, this is particularly the case in the key agreement process. In the Diffie-Hellman key agreement protocol, what an attacker can possibly get are the system parameters and the information transmitted over the public channels. More precisely, to an attacker, the values of p, g, α, and β can be made available (although practically to get these values it takes some effort, but that effort is far less than breaking a normal cryptographic algorithm), and the goal of the attacker is to guess the common key $k_1 = k_2$. This problem has been analyzed by researchers for decades, and to date it is believed that the problem (known as computational Diffie-Hellman problem) is as hard as the discrete logarithm problem[1], although the two problems have not been proved to be equivalently difficult.

The Diffie-Hellman key agreement looks like a perfect solution for a common secret to be set up using only public channels, which is secure against passive eavesdropping. However it is vulnerable against positive attacks. Assume that an opponent Eve being a positive attacker hides between Alice and Bob. When Alice requests to set up a common key with Bob, Eve personates Bob and set up a common key k_1 with Alice. Then Eve personates Alice and set up a common key k_2 with Bob. Although k_1 is very likely to be different from k_2, since Eve knows both k_1 and k_2, Eve can effectively "observe" all the "secure" communications between Alice and Bob. More precisely, when Alice sends a message which is encrypted using k_1, which Alice believes to be a common secret known by both Alice and Bob, Eve intercepts the message and decrypts it using k_1, then Eve encrypts the decrypted result (a plaintext) with k_2 and sends the result to Bob. When Bob receives the message, he can decrypt the message using k_2 successively, hence Bob believes that k_2 is the common secret known by Alice and Bob. As a result, both Alice and Bob communicate "securely" by encrypting/decrypting the messages using a key which is supposed to be commonly known between them, however in fact they use two different keys for the encryption and decryption due to the active involvement of Eve, where Eve is able to see all the communication messages. This scenario of attack is known as a kind of *man-in-the-middle attack*, and can be illustrated in Figure 2.

The reason why the man-in-the-middle attack can be successful is because the lack of authentication in the original Diffie-Hellman key agreement protocol, as can be seen from figure 2, when Alice is supposed to tell Bob that she is Alice, the message is intercepted by Eve, and Eve creates a new message sending to Bob. In the new message, it tells that the message came from Alice which in fact comes from Eve, and Bob is assumed to believe. When Eve replies Alice, a wrong identity message is also used. If there is a way to confirm the actual sender of the messages, then the man-in-the-middle attack can be detected and

Figure 2. The Man-in-the-middle attack of Diffie-Hellman key agreement protocol

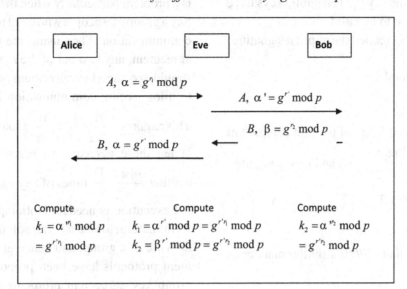

hence the attack cannot be successful. After the proposal of many practical digital signature schemes that provide good mechanism of authentication, and alternative solutions for key management including the public key infrastructure (PKI, see Section 5), it seems that to add the feature of authentication in Diffie-Hellman like key agreement is possible. In 1992, Diffie et. al. studied the problem of authenticated key agreement, which is followed by many studies on authenticated key agreement protocols (Diffie, Oorschot, & Wiener, 1992).

Among many good authenticated key agreement protocols, the MQV (Menezes-Qu-Vanstone) protocol has demonstrated a great efficiency and hence is very practical, this also leads the MQV key agreement protocol to be incorporated in the public-key standard IEEE P1363 (Menezes, Qu, & Vanstone, 1995). Basically, the MQV key agreement employs a static key and an ephemeral key, and it uses an elliptic curve over a finite field. Let P be an element of large prime order of an elliptic curve E, denote the order of P be n. Another parameter used in the protocol is h, the cofactor, defined as $h = \dfrac{|E|}{n}$, where $|E|$ is the

order of the elliptic curve E. For technical reasons it is required that $\gcd(n, h)=1$.

Given the above preparation, then the MQV protocol can be described as follows: in the setup process, each user is given a public key and private key pair, where there is a way to verify the validity of the public key (say via public key certificate). To distinguish the keys of different users, we will use (x_A, y_A) to denote the private/public key pair of Alice, and similarly (x_B, y_B) to denote the private/public key pair of Bob. In the case when an elliptic curve is used, the private/public key pairs satisfy that $y_A = x_A \cdot P$ and $y_B = x_B \cdot P$. When Alice and Bob want to establish a common key, they follow the steps below:

1. Alice chooses a random integer a as her ephemeral private key, and generates her ephemeral public key as $\alpha = a \cdot P$;

2. Similarly, Bob chooses a random integer b as his ephemeral private key, and generates his ephemeral public key as $\beta = b \cdot P$;

3. Alice sends her ephemeral public key α to Bob, and Bob sends his ephemeral public key β to Alice. It is assumed that Alice already has Bob's public key y_B and Bob already has

Alice's public key y_A. The public keys have been verified to be valid.

Alice calculates SA (called the implicit signature)

$$SA = (a + a' x_A) \bmod n$$

where a' is the first L bits of the first component of α, here $L = \left\lceil \dfrac{\log_2 n + 1}{2} \right\rceil$, and then compute

$$K_{AB} = h \cdot SA(\beta + b' y_B)$$

Bob calculates SB in a similar manner as

$$SB = (b + b' x_B) \bmod n$$

where b' is the first L bits of the first component of β, and then compute

$$K_{BA} = h \cdot SB(\alpha + a' y_A)$$

If Alice and Bob follow the protocol, they will compute the same shared secret key $k = K_{AB} = K_{BA}$.

3. KEY MANAGEMENT IN GROUP ORIENTED ENVIRONMENTS

With the development of computer networks, secure communications become common in many commercial applications, and more and more applications involve multiple participants. This lead to the need of secure group communication, and hence group key agreement become necessary in a secure group communication system. In theory, it is possible to enable secure group communications using the traditional key agreement (whether the original or authenticated key agreement is subject to what the actual application environment), however the efficiency diminution

is a problem particularly when the group is large. Say a group of n people who want to enable secure communication. Then using the traditional key agreement, any two out of the n group members should execute a key agreement protocol in order to allow secure communication between them. This requires $\dfrac{n(n-1)}{2} \approx \dfrac{n^2}{2}$ protocol executions. When these agreed keys reach their lifetime, another $\dfrac{n(n-1)}{2}$ times of key agreement protocol execution is needed. Noticing this problem, it was natural to find a better solution suitable for the case of a group, and hence group key agreement protocols have been proposed. Since the group key agreement protocols are a practical consideration, the man-in-the-middle attack is naturally taken into consideration.

Typical applications in group-oriented communications include broadcast (one-to-many), Internet voting (many-to-one), and multiparty conferences (many-to-many). Apart from those applications where human are the main participants, there are applications where electronic devices are important participants, these include communications in Ad Hoc and sensor networks. In the group-oriented communications, the security requirements are no longer for two parties, but more parties. The difference between two and more parties are that, in the two party communication model, once a party is not active in the communication (e.g. leaving), then the communication is terminated. However in the multiparty model, a user may leave a communication while the communication needs to be actively continue, and a new user may join a communication group when the communication is continuously going on.

With the new features of group-oriented communications, the security requirements are not just protecting man-in-the-middle eavesdropping and active attacks, but also some of the group members who once are legitimate users. For example, when a member leaves a communication group, regardless whether this leaving is his own choice or being forced to (e.g., suspected to be a comprised node), the member who was a legitimate member will no longer be a legitimate member after the leave action. On the other hand, a new user may join a communication group and become a legitimate member, in that case the member was not a legitimate user before the joining action. In both of the cases, a user can become a legitimate group member at a specific period of time, and can become an illegible member at some other time. Once one is not treated to be a legitimate group member, the security mechanism should apply to prevent him from being able to "hear" the communication. This requires forward security and backward security to be satisfied. By forward security, we mean that when a member leaves a communication group, the member is no longer able to intercept the group communications due to the encryption key having been changed. By backward security, we mean that, for a new member joining a group, he is unable to decrypt the communications that could have been recorded before his joining.

The goal of securing group communications is to establish a common key to be shared by the communication group members. It should be noted that before a group key is to be established, the authenticity of the group members should be verified. From the key infrastructure section we know that, the fundamental point for the entity authentication to be done is an initial trust, i.e., there must be some trust. In wide network applications, this trust normally comes from a third party, so there should be a trusted third party (TTP), such as key distribution center, or public key certification center. Here we will call it a TTP in general. This TTP may or may not be actively involved in the communication when it needs to initiate a group communication.

3.1 Group Communications with an Active TTP

Assume that all the communication members trust a TTP, and this TTP also participate in the group communication, then group key management can become quite simple, one of practical and efficient solutions is to let the TTP securely distribute a group key to the group members. Since the TTP is being trusted by the group members, the TTP is able to find a secure and authenticated way to send messages to the group members. This model is called *key distribution*, where the TTP is often called the *key distribution center* (KDC).

There are different ways for the TTP to be trusted. One is the symmetric key cryptography based, where all the group members share an unique key with the TTP, and when a group key is to be established, the TTP generates a random number as the group key (a temporary session key), which is to be encrypted using the keys shared with each of the group members. So the key update process can be the same as key establishment.

Another way for the TTP to be trusted is asymmetric key cryptography based, where all of the group members have the valid public key of the TTP, and the TTP also has a valid public key of each of the group members. There is no need for the group members to trust each other when the KDC is actively involved in the communications, hence the use of public key certificate is not necessary.

Note that in the case of key distribution, if every time when a group key is to be updated, the KDC needs to distribute n messages to the n group members each is an encrypted message of the new group key. This approach is not efficient. In group-oriented communications, it is expected that the key update process (due to group member leave or joining) should be simpler than the initial key establishment. Fortunately this is possible in certain circumstances for the KDC model. Considering a scenario when the communication is wireless where all the communication has to be broadcasted, then the following is an improvement on the key update cost but only for the case of new user joining a communication group. Let the current group key be k. When a new user joins the communication group, the KDC generates another random number k' as the new group key. Instead of sending the k' securely to each individual group members, the KDC encrypts k' using k and broadcast the message, which enables all the existing group members to get the new key, and the KDC encrypts k' using a key owned by the new user (a shared symmetric key or a public key), and broadcasts the message. The message can only be decrypted correctly by the new user, hence the key update is successful with traditional security (against external attacks) as well as backward security (against the new user to access the previous communications) being provided. The cost saving here is mainly because that sending a message to a single user and to all the group members makes no different as it has to be broadcasted, and hence it only applies to this special case.

There have been of course many good key distribution schemes designed, which have taken into consideration the communication and computation cost particularly for key update. Some of the research can be found in the contemporary literature (Canettii, Garay, Itkis, Micciancio, Naor, & Pinkas, 1999; Chiou & Chen, 1989; Chu, Qiao, & Nahrstedt, 2002; Perrig, Song, & Tygar, 2001; Waldvogel, Caronni, Sun, Weiler, & Plattner, 1999; Wong, Gouda, & Lam, 2000; Wang & Wu, 2006). Here we give a brief description of the work of Wong et. al. to show how the efficiency can be improved (Wong & Gouda, 2000).

In 2000, Wong et. al. proposed a logical key hierarchy (LKH) scheme. In the LKH scheme, user keys are shared with the KDC, and they are mapped into the leaf nodes of a logical key tree, where each of the intermediate (no-leaf) nodes represents a key encryption key (KEK) (Wong & Gouda, 2000). The top root key will be the group session key. Each user knows his leaf node key as well as all the intermediate node keys along

the path from his corresponding leaf node to the top root node. Since the intermediate nodes do not represent any of the real entities, the key tree is called a logical key tree, and the structure is called a logical key hierarchy. In the process of communication, the KDC needs to maintain the key tree which may have to be updated due to member leave or joining. It is noted that in the LKH structure, when a member leaves the group, or when a new user joins the group, only the node keys along the path from the leaf node to be changed (removed or added) to the top root node need to be updated, and the number of such keys is $O(\log n)$. When n is fairly large, this number is much smaller than n and hence the scheme is a big improvement.

3.2 Group Communications without an Active TTP

Although a TTP may not actively involved in group communications, the existence of the TTP is still necessary, as this is where the trust can be established. In this case, there must be something issued by the TTP as evidence for authentication purposes. This certificate is often a public key certificate, and the TTP is often the certificate issuing authority who doesn't have to be actively involved in a group communication session.

Although the public key infrastructure gives a good solution in managing public key certificates, its application and management however are rather complicated. Recall that in the public key infrastructure, one or more certification authorities (CA) are needed, and each time a public key certificate is to be verified, the validity of the certificate is to be checked first. When the scope of group communication is fairly small, e.g. within an organization, where the security threat is not so serious, then the use of public key infrastructure will undoubtedly brings unnecessary computation and communication cost. Therefore, a more convenient key management mechanism suitable for small scale applications is proposed, this is identity based key management.

The concept of identity based cryptography was first introduced by Shamir in 1984 (Shamir, 1984), and have attracted much interest (see for example: Jeong, Kwon, & Lee, 2008; S. Wang, Cao, Choo, & L. Wang, 2009; Huang, & Cao, 2009). The main technical issue in identity based cryptography is the key management problem. More specifically, in an identity based cryptography scheme, there is a key generation center (KGC) whose role is to generate a private key for each of the group members in the system based on their identity information. Technically, the process of generating a private key of a specific group member is to apply the private key of the KGC onto the identity of the member using certain algorithm. This process will allow that only the owner of a specific identity will be able to decrypt the messages encrypted using his identity information as the public key. It is noted that, due to that the private key generation process makes use of the private key of the KGC, the encryption using a user's identity as public key will have to use the KGC's public key as well. Therefore, in an identity based cryptography, the key management is not an independent issue, but has to be incorporated into the actual encryption/decryption process. Once the private keys for the users have been generated and securely sent to the users, the KGC is no more needed to be on-line during group communications.

Compared with the public key infrastructure, the use of identity-based cryptography brings much simplicity, at least the public key certificate verification process is not needed. However it also brings inconvenience and risks as well. First of all, user public key update becomes more difficult, because the user identity information is used as the public key of the user, and the identity information of a user is usually assumed to be widely known among the group members, and change of identity information will cause confusion. Second, due to the user private keys being generated by

the KGC, the security of the system hence is highly relied on the KGC. If there is a security vulnerability of the KGC, for example internal attacks from hostile managing staff members of the KGC which can become inevitable, then the whole system becomes very weak or the security can be totally lost. Therefore, there are different options with respect to the practicality of the identity based cryptography.

There is a tradeoff between the public key infrastructure and the identity based cryptography, which is called *certificateless cryptography* (Al-Riami & Paterson, 2003). The basic idea of a certificateless cryptography is a combination of an identity based cryptography and the use of public key mechanism. More precisely, a user's actual public key is composed of the identity of the user, which is the same as in identity based cryptography, and a public key chosen by the user at discretion. The KGC is no longer able to forge the user due to the lack possession of the user private key, and the public key does not need a certificate due to the use of identity based mechanism. When a user's public key is to be updated, only the public key part chosen by the user needs to be updated. Although there are different arguments about the certificateless cryptography, however, it can be treated as a practical solution in many applications, irrespective of the fact that it still has some security vulnerabilities.

Regardless whether the identity based cryptography or the public key certificate is used, the purpose of using the public keys is for user authentication. However how to let the group members share a group session key is not yet solved. When no trusted third party actively participates in the communication, the generation of a group session key needs the cooperation of all the group members. This manner of key generation is called *group key agreement*.

As for the case of key distribution, in order to improve the efficiency of group key agreement, the idea of logical key tree structure is also adoptable. First, a logical key tree is established according to the number of group members, where each leaf node represents the key of a group member, each parent node represents a key shared by its children nodes. Apart from the leaf nodes which represent the keys owned by the group members, all the intermediate nodes of the key tree are only logically defined. In order for the key agreement process to work, all the group members are supposed to know the structure of the logical key tree.

It is noted that, before the logical key tree is structured, only the structure of the key tree is known to the group members, while the keys represented by the tree nodes are unknown which are to be generated during the key agreement process. For the simplicity of description, we consider a case of binary key tree. It is noted that, since the key tree may not be perfectly balanced, a parent node may have one child node being a leaf node, while the other child node being an intermediate node.

In order for such a logical key tree to be established, each group member generate a random number as his leaf node key. Then every pair of children nodes agree on a key using the mechanism of traditional two-user key agreement (e.g. Diffie-Hellman key agreement), and the process of agreeing on a parent node key goes up from bottom, and eventually reaches the top root node, which is the group session key that is agreed and shared by all the group members.

When a user leaves the group, only the node keys along the leaf node representing the user's key to the top root node need to be updated. Since the depth of the logical key tree is log n, where n is the number of total group members, the number of keys to be updated is hence log n.

When a new user joins the group, there are different ways to add the user to the tree. Naturally the joining process should try to keep the key tree as balanced as possible, and with this principle, a new leaf node is added to the tree (the position of the new leaf node may not be unique, but has to be made known to all the group members). Then the new user generates a random number

as his leaf node key, and applies key agreement techniques as in the traditional two-user case to update all the ancestor node keys. Similar to the case of user leave, the number of node keys to be updated is also log n.

The above logical key tree structure can be implemented with different approaches. Since there are many sub-process of two-user key agreement, how the users authenticate each other can be of many different means. Some of the authenticated key agreements such as authenticated Diffie-Hellman and pairing-based key agreement are all possible. More detail about the group key agreement can be found in the works of Perrig et al. and Song et al. (Perrig, Song, Tygar, 2001; Wang & Wu, 2006).

4. KEY MANAGEMENT IN MOBILE AD HOC NETWORKS AND WIRELESS SENSOR NETWORKS

Apart from the group-oriented communications, where a group of participants actively participate in a communication and need to share a same encryption session key. However there is another group communication model where not all the group members actively participate in a same communication at a same time, but need to be connected together, i.e., any two of the group members should be able to communicate. It is different from the traditional two-party communication where no other parties need to be considered. A typical application environment of this group communication model is in mobile Ad Hoc networks (MANETs) and wireless sensor networks (WSN).

The features of a MANET and a WSN have much similarity in the sense that, both kinds of networks can be of very large scale, there is no infrastructure and no public service. However they are also different particularly in the sense of resource constraint (including limited energy consumption, computation and storage capability, limited distance of transmission). In general, nodes in a MANET may have less constraint than those in a WSN, but is more dynamic due to its mobile feature. The mobile feature makes the network structure more dynamic, which results in different approaches in routing and many security features. Here we mainly consider the key management issues in wireless sensor networks.

It is known that in order to enable a secure communication between two network nodes, there should be a common key established between these two nodes. Given the limited computation and storage capability, public key algorithms are usually not used in WSN. If a key is to be given to any pair of sensor nodes (pre-distribution or established using a key agreement scheme), each sensor node will have to store $N-1$ different keys, where N is the total number of sensor nodes. This approach obviously requires a relatively large storage of the sensor nodes, and would eliminate the scalability of the network. Another intuitive and energy-saving approach of key management is to set a same key (initial key) to all the sensor nodes before the sensor network is to be established. However the vulnerability for this setting is that, once a node is captured by an attacker, the attacker is able to know all the communications in the network, i.e., no security remains once a node is compromised. Considering the dynamic feature of node leave and node joining (in some cases, no network nodes can be added), there is no forward and backward security.

The limited resource of WSN makes the key management difficult. The key pre-distribution is still a good idea, but the common key is only used for authentication and key agreement, and not directly used in data encryption. A recent work by Eschenauer and Gligor proposes that, in the key pre-distribution process, a number of pre-defined keys are defined, and each node is given a random subset of these keys, hoping to have a common key with its neighbor nodes. When the number of keys in each node increases, the possibility for any two neighbour nodes to have a common

key also increases. Practically there should be a tradeoff between the number of keys that each node has and the probability that two neighbour nodes have a common key from their collections. In some cases, there is a chance that two neighbour nodes do not have a common key, then they may be able to find a short path, along the path, each two neighbour nodes have a common key, so that key agreement can be made along the path. When two nodes have a common key or can establish a common session key, then we call that the two nodes are connected. The goal of key management in WSN is to improve the network connectivity with small amount of numbers of keys each sensor node has to hold. This problem is studied by Chakrabarti et al, and Camtepe et al. (Chakrabarti, Maitra, & Roy, 2006; Camtepe, & Yener; 2007). Also Kawamura et al. studies possible attacks to the key pre-distribution scheme (Kawamura, M. Zhang, & L. Zhang, 2008).

In their work, Eschenaur and Gligor assume that the sensor nodes are distributed at random (e.g. dropped from the air), then no knowledge about the distribution of the sensor nodes is assumed in the process of key pre-distribution (Eschenaur & Gligor, 2002). However in practice, the distribution can be controlled in some degree, so the knowledge of distribution can be taken into account in key pre-distribution, which could largely improve the network connectivity with the same number of keys each node has, or equivalently reduces the number of key that each node has without sacrifice the network connectivity. There are some studies on this, for examples, Liu, Ning, and Du (2005) propose a group-based key pre-distribution scheme, Yu and Guan (2008) and Du, Deng, Han, and Varshney (2006) propose a key pre-distribution scheme based on deployment knowledge, and Younis, Ghumman, and Eltoweissy (2006) and Anjum (2006) propose key pre-distribution schemes based on knowledge of location.

A good overview about the key management schemes in WSN and MANET are provided by

Xiao, Rayi, Sun, Du, Hu, & Galloway (2007) and Merwe, Dawoud, McDonald (2007) respectively.

5. PUBLIC KEY INFRASTRUCTURE

In public communications when the two communicating parties A and B do not trust each other, in order for B to trust that some public key is really owned by A, there must be a trusted third party (PPT) involved. Let the PPT be T, then the responsibility of T is to show to B that something is really the public key owned by A, and in this case, T should be able to judge whether something is really owned by A. The involvement of the TTP is better to be offline, otherwise the communication load from communication parties to the PPT can be a bottleneck when the PPT serves a large number of users. A proven good way of allowing the PPT to work offline is the use of public key certificates. More precisely, a public key certificate is something issued by a certification authority (CA) proving the ownership of a public key. A public key certificate typically includes the information about the user identity (e.g. the IP address of the user), the public key to be issued, the issuing date and the expiration date of the certificate. This information is to be signed by the CA, so that users can verify the validity of the certificates, and hence trust the ownership of a particular public key.

In order to verify the signature of the CA, the public key certificate issuing authority, users are supposed to know the valid public key of the CA. How about when a user does not know (or cannot trust) the public key of the CA? this is considered as an external user which is not considered to be valid to use the public key certificate system. It is a fundamental assumption about the trust that users in the system know the valid public key of the CA, and without this assumption, no real trust among users can be established. Readers may have a number of questions, for example, why does the CA issue public key certificates for users? the

answer to this question is rather simple: because CA is an organization for such service, who may or may not make profits, and users are its customers. How does the CA know that the public key provided by a user for public key certificate is a valid one? This question is out of the question, since no one would apply for a certificate using someone else's public key, as this would provide chances for others to attack the user, and gives no benefit to the user. Another question is about how the CA knows the identity of a user being valid? This depends on the application and is subject to be handled by the CA. In many applications, the CA needs to confirm the identity information of the users by alternative means, such as phone call confirmation, or to allow an offline registration.

The last question is about who can be the CA. Again the answer depends. Regardless in which case, today the whole world is connected by the Internet, apart from the world wide voice network connection. So no one is able to be the CA serving world wide users. However there are some needs in large scale, such as country wide applications. In order to provide a practical solution to such cases, the public key infrastructure (PKI) is put forward.

The PKI is a standard system for public key certification issuing and management. It seems to be an easy task, but have many detailed considerations when becomes a standard, factors to be considered include the format of public key certificates, the process of certificate revocation and update, storage and enquiry of the certificates, and how the public key certificates can be verified across domains. Hence, in July of 1988, the public key certificate standards, X.509, become an ITU-T standard for a public key infrastructure (PKI). X.509 specifies standard formats for public key certificates, certificate revocation lists, attribute certificates, and how the certificate validation can be done in the case of single CA as well as multiple CAs.

Standards about the X.509 include the follow specifications:

- **RFC 1422:** Privacy Enhancement for Internet Electronic Mail: Part II Certificate-Based Key Management.
- **RFC 1424:** Privacy Enhancement for Internet Electronic Mail: Part IV: Key Certification and Related Services.
- **RFC 1704:** On Internet Authentication.
- **RFC 2535:** Domain Name System Security Extensions.
- **RFC 2459:** Internet X.509 Public Key Infrastructure: Certificate and CRL Profile (A new draft is being prepared to replace this RFC.).
- **RFC 2510:** Internet X.509 Public Key Infrastructure: Certificate Management Protocols.
- **RFC 2511:** Internet X.509 Public Key Infrastructure: Certificate Request Message Format.
- **RFC 2527:** Internet X.509 Public Key Infrastructure: Certificate Policy and Certification Practices Framework.
- **RFC 2559:** Internet X.509 Public Key Infrastructure: Operational Protocols - LDAPv2.
- **RFC 2560:** Internet X.509 Public Key Infrastructure: Online Certificate Status Protocol - OCSP.
- **RFC 2587:** Internet X.509 Public Key Infrastructure: LDAPv2 Schema.
- **RFC 2692:** Simple Public Key Infrastructure Requirements.
- **RFC 2693:** Simple Public Key Infrastructure Certificate Theory

Irrespective of so many specifications, we can describe the principle of the PKI in X.509 in a simple way. Assume there is a certification center CA, a registration authority RA, and a sophisticated database for storing the public key certificates. Then the PKI in X.509 has the following processes.

Issuing a certificate: A user proves his valid identity to the CA and provides a public key, CA then issues a public key certificate for the given public key. The user can verify the validity of the public key certificate. Note that the purpose of a public key certificate is to prove the ownership of a particular public key, any other user who needs to use the public key should be able to verify the validity of the public key certificate, and hence trust the validity and the ownership of the public key.

Storage of a certificate: Once public key certificates are issued, another question is how to let other users know where to get the public key certificate of a particular user? An intuitive way of doing that is to ask for such a certificate directly from the user. However, in the case of electronic commerce, the user may not always be on-line. Even if on-line, the user may not be able to reply such queries promptly. Even if an automatic means for providing public key certificate on request is available, other users may not be able to find how to contact the user so that such a query can be made. Therefore, there is a big need for the public key certificates to be kept by a trusted and publicly known directory so that query for a certificate can be made easier. For this sake, new public key certificates need to register at the registration authority (RA), so that the certificate can be stored by the RA together with user information once the RA verification on the certificate is passed.

Certificate revocation and update: Although a public key certificate normally has an expiry date, for all sakes, revocation of a public key certificate may become necessary before its expiry date.

When a user requests for the revocation of a public key certificate, it requires the user to sign a message in specific format using the private key corresponding to the public key of the certificate. On successful verification of the signature on a certificate revocation, the certification information is revoked from the database, and in the mean time, the certificate information is added into a database called certification revocation list (CRL).

When a user requests for the update of a public key certificate, the user choose a new public key, use the previous private key (corresponding to the existing public key certificate) to sign a specific message containing the information of the new public key. This signed message is sent to CA. When CA verifies the signature to be valid, the CA will issue a new public key certificate for the new public key. Then the user needs to send the new public key certificate together with certificate update a request that is signed using the previous private key to the RA. On successful verification of the request and the new public key certificate, RA will update the previous public key certificate with the new one, and in the mean time, the removed public key certificate information is added to the CRL.

Obtaining a certificate: When a user needs to obtain a public key certificate of some other user, a request is to be sent to the RA. The RA then searches a public key certificate for the nominated user information (normally user ID). Once such a certificate is found, it is sent back to the user on request. There are circumstances when a request is not about a public key certificate, it is only about the validity of a specific public key certificate, then the RA only needs to check the CRL for possible inclusion of the certificate. Being a standard, it requires that every public key certificate has an unique label or identity, so that for a validity enquiry, it only needs to send the label or identity of the public key certificate instead of the whole certificate.

Certificate verification: Once a user obtains a public key certificate of another user, the validity of the certificate is to be verified. The verification process is necessary as this is when a public key is confirmed to be a valid one belonging to someone. When the verifier (the user who requested for the public key certificate) has the same CA as who issued the public key certificate to be verified, the verification process is simply to check the validity of the signature made by the CA, since the verifier has the public key information of the

CA. However for a large scale application, there can be cases when multiple CAs are involved, this is why the X.509 standard is in place. When the verifier does not trust the CA who issued the certificate, the process of verification becomes more complicated. In fact, the process of public key certificate verification is to find a path of trust so that verification can be done step by step. There are different certification structures for certification authorities as well as normal users: a top-down tree structure, a bidirectional tree structure, and a bridge CA structure. They are briefly introduced as follows.

- **Top-down certification structure:** In this structure, there is a root certification authority CA_0 who issues public key certificates to its child CA's, denoting them as CA_1, CA_2, ..., CA_n. Each of the child CA, for example CA_k, issues public key certificates to its own children CA's (such as $CA_{k,1}$, $CA_{k,2}$). After certain number of levels, the last descendant CAs will issue public key certificates to their own users. This structure can be depicted in Figure 3.

In the structure shown in figure 3, the arrow directs how a public key certificate is issued. For example, the arrow starting from CA_0 pointing at CA_2 means that CA_0 issues a public key certificate for CA_2.

With this structure of certification, assume that all the users know the public key of CA_0, then when a user obtains a public key certificate of another user, the user who requested the public key certificate being as a verifier can perform a reverse path according to the top-down structure to find a certification path (also known as path of trust), and then perform the verification according to the top-down certification structure. For example, let's see how user A verifies a public key certificate of user C. Assume that A has got a public key certificate of user C, then from the public key certificate, A can find who the issuing

Figure 3. A top-down tree structure of certification

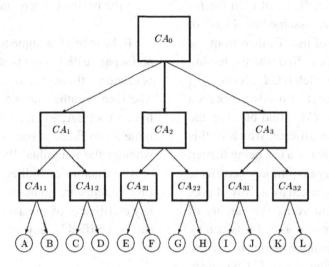

CA of the certificate is, which is CA_{12}, as in the case of what figure 3 depicts. Since CA_{12} is not a valid CA of user A, A needs to obtain a public key certificate of CA_{12}, find out who the issuing CA is for this certificate, which in this case is CA_1. Again CA_1 is not a CA being trusted by A, A then needs to obtain a public key certificate of CA_1, find out who the issuing CA is for this certificate, which in this case is CA_0. Since CA_0 is the root CA, whose public key is supposed to be known to all the users, and user A has a valid public key of CA_0, hence is able to verify the validity of the public key certificate of CA_1 issued by CA_0. When this verification is successful, A then has a valid public key of CA_1, with which A is able to verify the validity of the public key certificate of CA_{12} issued by CA_1. When this verification is successful, A then has a valid public key of CA_{12}, with which A is able to verify the validity of the public key certificate of C issued by CA_{12}.

The top-down certification tree structure has some disadvantages. First of all, all the users in the system are assumed to have the valid public key of the root certification authority CA_0. When such a system is large, say national wide, then this assumption is hard to be implemented, not only technically, but also has many other factors including political ones. Second, the verification has to go through the to-down process from the very root CA, regardless how close the two users may be neighboured. Hence the following bi-directional tree structure of certification is more practical.

- **Bidirectional tree structure:** The bidirectional tree structure looks very much like figure 3, but the difference is that the arrows are bidirectional. A bidirectional arrow means that both of the arrowed CAs issue a certificate to each other: a parent CA issues public key certificate to all of its children CAs, and and each child CA issues a certificate to its father CA. This means that a CA may have different public key certificates issued by different children CAs, even if the public key is the same. It seems to have many more certificates than the top-down tree structure, and as a consequence, the certificate verification can become much simpler in certain circumstances.

Now we give an example to show how the user A can verify the certificate of C in the bi-directional tree structure. Assume that A has got a public key certificate of user C, then from the public key certificate, A can find who the issuing CA of the certificate is, which is CA_{12}. Since CA_{12} is not a valid CA of user A, A needs to obtain a public key certificate of CA_{12}, find out who the issuing CA is for this certificate, which in this case is CA_1. Again CA_1 is not a CA being trusted by A, fortunately CA_1 has a public key certificate issued by CA_{11} which is trusted by A. Now A uses the public key of CA_{11} to verify the validity of the public key certificate of CA_1 that is issued by CA_{11}, and after the verification being successful, A is able to use the public key of CA_1 to verify the validity of the public key certificate of CA_{12} that is issued by CA_1, and after the verification being successful, A is able to verify the validity of the public key certificate of C that is issued by CA_{12}. Note that the verification process does not need the involvement of CA_0, and the path of verification is shorter than the case of top-down tree structure. In practice, this can be a big saving on computation and communication cost for the certificate verification, because in most of the cases the public key certificates are being verified by close neighbours, which is far away from the root CA.

- **Bridge CA structure:** The above bidirectional tree structure of certification is more efficient than the top-down structure in terms of certification verification. However its scalability is not good. Once a PKI system is established, it is hard to change its scale to a large extend, particularly difficult to change the number of levels of CAs. Note that it may not be practical to establish a PKI system in very large scale, and different organizations may have their own PKI systems. In order to merge those existing PKI systems into a larger one, so that secure and authenticated communication

can be possible across those organizations, the bridge CA structure is a good solution.

To be in brief, assume that there are n existing and separate PKI systems, the bridge CA structure is to merge these PKI systems into a larger one. The idea is rather simple: let each PKI system have a root CA, and let these root CA's pairwise issue a certificate to each other. Then regardless whether the individual PKI systems are of top-down structure or bidirectional structure, these PKI systems are connected together, and public key certificates of any user in the big PKI system can be verified by any other user in the system.

6. SECRET SHARING

In key management, one important scope is to ensure the security and availability of a secret key. By the security it means that the chances for the secret to get lost (leaked in purpose or by accident, or stolen) are to be minimized, and by availability it means that the chances for the secret to be correctly recovered are maximized. However these two security goals seem to be in conflict in some sense. In order to increase the chances to ensure the secret to be recovered whenever in need, an intuitive way is to let more people to hold the same secret, however this approach will naturally increase the chances for the secret to get lost. This problem was solved by a smart idea due to Shamir (1979) and Blakley (1979). For simplicity of description, we use the Shamir secret sharing scheme to demonstrate the solution.

For the sake of preventing key loss, Shamir proposed the concept of secret sharing and proposed a concrete secret sharing scheme (Shamir, 1979). The basic idea of Shamir's secret sharing is that, given a secret message x that is to be shared, it is split into n different parts, each part is called a *share* (or called a *shadow* in some literatures) of the secret, and these shares are to be hold by n people with anyone holding a different share. It also satisfies the property that, when any k ($k \leq n$) of these shares are put together, the original secret can be recovered easily. However when less than k shares are put together, it is computationally infeasible to recover the original secret. Such a secret sharing scheme is called a $[k, n]$ threshold scheme. In Shamir's secret sharing scheme, it also satisfies that any less than k shares provide no information about the original secret. Such a secret sharing scheme is called to have *perfect security*.

In most secret sharing schemes, it assumes that there is a super user who creates the shares to the share holders. Given that, Shamir's secret sharing scheme works as follows: first let s_0 be the original secret to be shared, and security parameters k and n are all set (usually $k < n$). Let $GF(p)$ be a finite field with p elements, where p is a large prime number. The super user of the system chooses k-1 random numbers $s_1, s_1, s_2, \ldots, s_{k-1}$ over $GF(p)$, and construct a polynomial

$$f(x) = s_0 + s_1 x + s_2 x^2 + \ldots + s_{k-1} x^{k-1}.$$

On share creation, the super user chooses n random numbers $x_1, x_2, \ldots, x_n$ over $GF(p)$, and compute $y_i = f(x_i)$, $i = 1, 2 \ldots, n$, then (x_i, y_i), $i = 1, 2 \ldots, n$ are n shares. It is known that when any k of these shares are provided, the polynomial $f(x)$ can uniquely be determined, and hence the original secret s_0 is recovered. In fact, it is not necessary to reconstruct $f(x)$ for the purpose of recovering s_0, the famous Lagrange interpolating method can be used to compute s_0 given k pairs of (x_i, y_i). For simplicity, let these k pairs be (x_i, y_i), $i = 1, 2 \ldots, k$, then we have

$$s_0 = \sum_{i=1}^{k} y_i \sum_{j \leq i} \frac{x_j}{x_j - x_i}$$

Note that in practical implementations, x_i doesn't have to be a random number, it can be the identification code of the user indexed by i, or simply the index i, by doing this, the implementation of the scheme can become simpler.

Shamir's secret sharing scheme is a $[k, n]$ threshold scheme. As a generalization of secret sharing schemes, those with a general access structure have been proposed. More precisely, assume that there is a set M of participants who will hold some shares of a secret s. However due to different roles of the members in M, some of the members may have the secret s by themselves (e.g. the super user of the system), in which case there is no need for secret sharing and will not be considered in secret sharing schemes, and a small group of some of the members may be able to recover the original secret, while other members may need a larger group in order to be able to recover the secret. Any group of members (a subset of M) who are able to recover the original secret is called an *authorized set*, otherwise it is called an *unauthorized set*. Therefore the goal of secret sharing is to design a suitable scheme given a particular access structure (the subsets of M being defined as authorized sets). Naturally the authorized sets should be monotone, i.e., if a subset A_1 of M is an authorized set of a secret sharing scheme, then any of the subsets of M containing that subset A_1 is also an authorized set of the scheme. In case of $[k, n]$ threshold secret sharing scheme, any k and more members become an authorized set, while any less than k members form an unauthorized set. The study of secret sharing with general access structure can be found in (Xu, &Zha, 2007; Marti-Farre, 2007; Tartary, Pieprzyk, & Wang, 2008).

Another problem with respect to secret sharing is cheating. The goal of secret sharing is to allow a group of participants each holding a piece of information about the secret to be able to recover the secret, so that the risk of the secret being lost or stolen becomes minimized. It is noted that once the secret is recovered using some of the shares from an authorized set, the original secret becomes no longer a secret at all to those who participated in the secret recovery, this includes the revealing of all the shares used in the secret recovery process. Note that if one of the participants provides a piece of wrong information (a false share) by purpose or otherwise, then what is recovered is not the original secret and hence becomes useless, however since the one providing the false information is able to get all the other shares, and hence is able to recover the true original secret by himself, while all the others are fooled. Given that, there can be cases where more than one participant tends to provide false information intending to steal the secret afterwards. Therefore in practical applications, cheating detection and prevention becomes an interesting and important topic. Cheating detection and prevention was not considered in Shamir's original scheme, but has been studied extensively in literatures. Some of the related research can be found in (Tartary, Pieprzyk, & Wang, 2008; Fitzi, Garay, Gollakota, Rangan, & Srinathan, 2006; Araki, 2007).

Another problem associated with secret sharing is that there must be a super user in the system who can create the shares. Since the super user must know the secret in order to be able to set up the system, which is not desired in many circumstances, there are studies about threshold cryptography, where there is no need in such a super user. The study of threshold cryptography is beyond this topic about key management, and interested readers are referred to (Desmedt & Holloway, 1997).

As a different kind of secret sharing, the visual cryptography has experienced a big development in recent years. The basic mechanism of visual cryptography is to make an original secret image into a number of shares, and when some of the shares are stacked together, the original image appears. Due to the visual quality and the pixel expansion problem, the methods of visual cryptography are very different from normal secret sharing schemes. Some of the recent results about visual cryptography can be found in (Wang, Li, & Yi, 2008; Yang, & Chen, 2006; Chen, Chan, Huang, Tsai, & Chu, 2007; Liu, Wu, & Lin, 2010).

7. KEY ESCROW SYSTEMS

Although secret sharing provides good solutions to preventing key loss and secret leaking, they have limitations in many practical applications due to the key recovery process being no duplicable. For example, in electronic commerce applications, some secret information (e.g. a private key used for signature) can hardly be managed via secret sharing, because this kind of keys are used so often. However even those keys used frequently can get lost, e.g. lost from a hard disk failure or caused due to no recoverable forgotten password. Therefore there should be some means to protect the loss of this kind of secrets. It seems to be a paradox that the more careful you take to secure something, sometimes the more chances to get it lost due to unreliable memory, and key management has the same problems. In order to enable key recovery in case it gets lost, in 1993, the White House announced the use of key escrow schemes, and in July of the same year, an algorithm called SKIPJACK is adopted as the official key escrow algorithm.

The principle of key escrow is that, users make a copy of their secrets to be kept by a key escrow center, and once the key is lost for any reason, the users can request key recovery from the escrow center. Hence the key escrow center has to be a trustworthy organization. Due to the privacy legislation in US, it is difficult for the key escrow scheme to be widely accepted, the main concern is the trustworthy of the key escrow center. Nevertheless, the idea of key escrow does provide a practical solution for key backups. In order to tradeoff the use of key escrow services and the privacy concerns, one of the proposals is that the keys to be escrowed are those less 48 bits of the original, so that when a key recovery is requested, an exclusive search of the 48 unknown bits has to be performed. This much of effort is affordable at key recovery service, and can provide some prevention of the key escrow center from manipulating the user keys by discretion without any cost. So, the key escrow is rather a policy in key management than a technical solution, although there are some techniques involved.

8. PASSWORD BASED KEY MANAGEMENT

In many practical applications, security setting is primarily based on a password. One such scenario is that user accounts in a computer system are accessed using a user name (essentially no security) and a password. Due to the nature of the passwords being memorized by human, they are often not so random, and many of them are often quite weak and have high chances of being included in a password dictionary which could be used by an attacker in a dictionary attack. A high risk comes from the fact that many people can access to different systems (e.g. desktop computer, laptop computer, server in work environment, email accounts including multiple free such accounts), and often use a single password to access to different accounts. This means that if one of the accounts is being compromised (e.g. the administrator of a free email provider), then other accounts that use the same password can be accessed easily.

The weakness of choosing passwords can hardly be improved due to the nature of human memory being limited. So we can only hope that the dictionary attack can be made harder. A password dictionary is a collection of some possible passwords that could have been used. The principle of password dictionary attack is that, the attacker has a way to test whether a guessed password is correct. Such a guessed password is chosen from a password dictionary, each at a time, until a suspected password is found and an attack is likely to be successful, or to the end of the dictionary which means that the attack fails. If this test has to be done on-line, then a mechanism can be applied to eliminate the attack, say the maximum number of guesses, in that case the

chances of a guess to be successful are very small or negligible. If such a mechanism is not possible, then a delayed response for any access request with a password will also effectively eliminate the chances of dictionary attacks. For example, if there is a two seconds delay in access request which is acceptable, and a password dictionary typically has tens of millions (or more) items, then it may take years to complete an exhaustive dictionary attack.

However, if an off-line dictionary attack can be performed, then the time to complete an exhaustive dictionary attack can be only a few seconds or even less. So the objective of password based cryptography (here we only consider the key management problem) is to avoid the possibility of applying an off-line password dictionary attack. Unfortunately this simple security goal seems not so easy to achieve, many of the password based key management schemes claimed to be secure against off-line dictionary attack (apart from many other possible security threats) are later found to be not the case. Some of the recent studies on password based key management schemes, designs and security analysis, can be found in (Nam, et al., 2007; Lu & Cao, 2007; Huang, 2009; Guo, Li, Mu, & Zhang, 2008; Chung & Ku, 2008; Phan, Yau, & Gol, 2008).

9. KEY MANAGEMENT IN PGP SYSTEMS

Pretty Good Privacy (PGP) (Atkins, Stallings, & Zimmermann, 1996) is a self-contained security protocol stack designed for protecting email security. It was initially designed and largely developed by Zimmermann, and with some industry enhancement later on.

PGP employs symmetric key ciphers as well as public key cryptographic algorithms. Here we only look at the key management issues. The public keys and their corresponding private keys are long-term user keys, while when a symmetric key cipher is used for data encryption, a symmetric session key is created. This key is generated at random by the party who needs the encryption, and it is then encrypted using the public key of the intended recipient. This kind of hybrid use of symmetric and asymmetric key cryptography is widely used in practical applications. However the management of public keys and of private keys can be quite different in different applications. In PGP, user public keys are stored in a database called the *public key ring*. When a user public key is needed for session key encryption or for signature verification, the user ID is to be provided, and the system takes the user ID as an index, to find from the public key database what the corresponding public key is. Once a public key is found, it is returned to the requester. It is noted that there is no confident way of verifying whether a public key really belongs to a specific user, and the system has security risk due to its low level of trust (the trust of the genuineness of the public keys). However, since the PGP is designed for personal email security, and most of the public key owners are assumed to be known to the database (more precisely, known to whoever added the public key information to the public key ring), so the level of trust depends on the actual users.

With respect to the private key management for which most of the security system do not have a clear solution, PGP has a concrete way of managing the user private keys. In PGP, user private keys are also stored in a database, called the *private key ring*. Different from the public key ring, what is stored in the private key ring is not plain data of private keys, the private keys are encrypted using each user's password before being stored in the private key ring. When a private key is extracted from the private key ring (for creating a signature or decrypting a symmetric session key), the owner user needs to provide a user name and a password, the user name is used as an index to search from the database what the encrypted private key is, and the password is used to decrypted the searched

data to retrieve the private key. Once the system is quit, the private key information will be removed from the computer system which will reduce the chances of the private keys to be compromised. It is also noted from the private key management in the PGP systems how important the passwords need to be properly protected, including a good mechanism of choosing good passwords.

It should be noted that, the public key ring contains public keys of remote users, while the private key ring contains private keys of local users.

The key management in PGP is simple and practical, however the security is limited, and hence is not recommended to encrypt very confidential emails. For those with commercial transactions, the Security Multi-Purpose Internet Mail Extension (S/MIME) protocol should be used, which is also a security protocol for email security, but with enhanced key management than PGP and hence has higher level of security, and as a return, it is less convenient to use for normal users. For example, the use of PKI in S/MIME makes the public key verification process more complicated.

10. KEY MANAGEMENT IN MOBILE TELECOMMUNICATION SYSTEMS

The Universal Mobile Telecommunications System (UMTS) defines many protocols for mobile communications, for example the Global System for Mobile (GSM) and protocols in the Third Generation Partnership Project (3GPP). Ignoring the differences from the underlying physical layers in different systems, the security mechanisms are quite similar, especially the authentication and key agreement (AKA) architecture.

In UMTS system, the communication mobility comes from the wireless communications from a mobile device to the base station that serves it. From the base station to the central part of the service network, there can be sophisticated authentication and confidentiality services involved, since this part of communication is conducted with wired lines, there are many mature security solutions that can be used. Of course the UMTS uses a specially designed authentication and encryption mechanism for the wired part of communications, however for the UMTS security, it is more concerned with the wireless part of communications, assuming that the wired part has no security problems.

In studying the security of UMTS, there are three components considered: a mobile user equipment (UE), a visitor location register (VLR), and a home location register (HLR). The HLR also plays the role of an authentication center. When such a system is being setup, the authentication center (located in the HLR) sets up a common symmetric key K as the seed key with each user UE, and the consequent encryption and authentication keys are all deducted from this seed key. This seed key is burned in the SIM card (or USIM card) and cannot be read by external devices.

The algorithms for the authentication key and encryption key deduction from K can be made public[2], and they are available both in the mobile device and the authentication center. The authentication center passes some authentication parameters together with encryption keys to VLR for user authentication and data encryption purposes.

Forgetting about the authentication process in UMTS which can be complicated in different systems, if we only look at the key management issue, it is rather simple: a long-term symmetric key shared by UE and HLR, and some temporary authentication and encryption keys are generated from the long-term key. There will be a random number involved in the authentication process which is to thwart replay attacks.

11. THE LIMITATIONS OF KEY MANAGEMENT

If we treat a cryptographic algorithm as a lock, then the keys used by the algorithms are keys to the lock. The security measure of a cryptographic algorithm is about how hard it is to crack the lock, however an opponent may try to steal the keys instead of trying to crack the lock. In many cases, the former attempt of attack can be much easier than the latter. So when we talk about security of a system, it is not about the security of the cryptographic algorithms being employed, it is about the weakest link in the whole security processes.

We have discussed different methods in key management, some of those key management schemes are secure or even perfect (e.g. Shamir's secret sharing) in some sense, however the security measure in real information systems can be quite different. Compared with the encryption and digital signature algorithms which can be of very high security, both in theory and in practice, the security in an information system can be very low, where the key management problem can be the weakest link. This is because that the characteristics of human have to be taken into account. For example, in the X.509 public key infrastructure, as long as the digital signature algorithm in the system is secure, the system seems to be secure. However the security vulnerability may come from the management of private keys. A normal user may have less experience about how to protect his/her private keys, usually people tend to store the information (confidential or otherwise) in a computer hard disk, which can be stolen by a Trojan horse, even if the hard disk or the file is protected with a password. The effort in getting a user's private key can be much less than that in breaking a digital signature algorithm.

Practically, the security requirements on cryptographic algorithms become higher and higher, this is because once a cryptographic algorithm is commercially used, it will stay for long time, and will have to undergo different cryptanalysis.

Once a security weakness is found, with the help of developed hardware and software technology, and even developed algorithms, a cryptographic algorithm can be broken easier than it was supposed to be. The fact in the real world is that, we can safely use many of the well known cryptographic algorithms without having to worry about their security, and more network security protocols are available than before, however the cases of successful network attacks do not seem to reduce. One of the important reasons is that user passwords are not becoming stronger. Regardless how secure the cryptographic algorithms and the security protocols are, once a user password is compromised, access to the network is as easy as an authorized user. Therefore, when considering the security level of a information system, the characteristics of human have to be taken into account. This means that the information security is not just a technical issue, it has something to do with business management as well as social, political, and even psychological issues.

12. CONCLUSION

Key management is an important part in secure communication systems, many self-contained security system have their own key management schemes. Apart from PGP that has its own key management schemes, another widely approach of key protection is to store a key in a hardware that cannot be read from external devices, and can be read only through an internal interface. The UMTS system uses this way to protect user keys. Of course the new applications of mobile communication will not only use the secret keys, but will also need the support of PKI, which should follow the X.509 standard for scalability purposes. However as for the management of user private keys, there are still no good solutions, particularly in the commercial applications. Although hardware seems to be able provide a good protection against reading, but once the hardware

is lost, e.g. together with a mobile device, then little security will remain. In order to minimize the loss due to hardware loss, the combination of a hardware plus password protection seems to be very effective in practice. However this kind of protection is only for commercial purposes as it still has limited security.

There have been many key management schemes, this doesn't mean that we do not need more. In fact, whenever there is a new application, many new key management candidate schemes will be designed, and the key management is an endless topic of research.

REFERENCES

Al-Riyami, S. S., & Paterson, K. G. (2003). Certificateless public key cryptography. *Proceedings ASIACRYPT 2003*, (LNCS 2894), (pp.452-473). Springer-Verlag, Anjum, F. (2006). *Location dependent key management using random key predistribution in sensor networks*. ACM Workshop on Wireless Security (WiSE'06), (pp. 21-30).

Araki, T. (2007). *Efficient (k, n) threshold secret sharing schemes secure against cheating from n-1 cheaters*. Australasian Conference on Information Security and Privacy (ACISP 2007), (LNCS 4586, pp. 133-142).

Atkins, D., Stallings, W., & Zimmermann, P. (1996). *PGP message exchange formats*.

Blakley, G. R. (1979). Safeguarding cryptographic keys. *Proceedings of the National Computer Conference*, *48*, 313–317.

Camtepe, S. A., & Yener, B. (2007). Combinatorial design of key distribution mechanisms for wireless sensor networks. *IEEE/ACM Transactions on Networking*, *15*(2), 346–358. doi:10.1109/TNET.2007.892879

Canetti, R., Garay, J., Itkis, G., Micciancio, D., Naor, M., & Pinkas, B. (1999). Multicast security: A taxonomy and some efficient constructions. *Proceedings - IEEE INFOCOM, 2,* 708–716.

Chakrabarti, D., Maitra, S., & Roy, B. (2006). A key pre-distribution scheme for wireless sensor networks: Merging blocks in combinatorial design. *Journal of Information Security, 5*(2), 105–114. doi:10.1007/s10207-006-0085-4

Chen, Y.-F., Chan, Y.-K., Huang, C.-C., Tsai, M.-H., & Chu, Y.-P. (2007). A multiple-level visual secret-sharing scheme without image size expansion. *Information Sciences, 177*(21), 4696–4710. doi:10.1016/j.ins.2007.05.011

Chiou, C. H., & Chen, W. T. (1989). Secure broadcast using secure lock. *IEEE Transactions on Software Engineering, 15*(8), 929–934. doi:10.1109/32.31350

Chu, H. H., Qiao, L., & Nahrstedt, K. (2002). A secure multicast protocol with copyright protection. *ACM SIGCOMM Computer Communications Review, 32*(2), 42–60. doi:10.1145/568567.568570

Chung, H.-R., & Ku, W.-C. (2008). Three weaknesses in a simple three-party key exchange protocol. *Information Science, 178,* 220–229. doi:10.1016/j.ins.2007.08.004

Desmedt, Y., & Holloway, R. (1997). Some recent research aspects of threshold cryptography. In *Proceedings of the 1st Intl. Information Security Workshop,* (pp. 158-173). Springer-Verlag.

Diffie, W., & Hellman, M. E. (1976). New directions in cryptography. *IEEE Transactions on Information Theory, 22,* 644–654. doi:10.1109/TIT.1976.1055638

Diffie, W., Van Oorschot, P. C., & Wiener, M. J. (1992). Authentication and authenticated key exchanges. *Designs, Codes and Cryptography, 2*(2), 107–125. doi:10.1007/BF00124891

Du, W., Deng, J., Han, Y. S., & Varshney, P. K. (2006). A key pre-distribution scheme for sensor networks using deployment knowledge. *IEEE Transactions on Dependable and Secure Computing, 3*(1), 62–77. doi:10.1109/TDSC.2006.2

Eschenauer, L., & Gligor, V. (2002). A key-management scheme for distributed sensor networks. In *Proceedings of the 9th ACM Conference on Computer and Communications Security,* (pp. 41-47).

Fitzi, M., Garay, J., Gollakota, S., Rangan, C. P., & Srinathan, K. (2006). *Round-optimal and efficient verifiable secret sharing.* Theory of Cryptography Conference (TCC 2006), (LNCS 3876, pp. 329-342).

Fu, H., Kawamura, S., Zhang, M., & Zhang, L. (2008). Replication attack on random key pre-distribution schemes for wireless sensor networks. *Computer Communications, 31*(4), 842–857. doi:10.1016/j.comcom.2007.10.026

Guo, H., Li, Z., Mu, Y., & Zhang, X. (2008). Cryptanalysis of simple three-party key exchange protocol. *Computers & Security, 27,* 16–21. doi:10.1016/j.cose.2008.03.001

Huang, H., & Cao, Z. (2009). *An ID-based authenticated key exchange protocol based on bilinear Diffie-Hellman problem.* ACM Symposium on Information, Computer & Communication Security (ASIACCS'09), (pp. 333-342).

Huang, H.-F. (2009). A simple three-party password-based key exchange protocol. *International Journal of Communications and Systems.* John Wiley & Sons.

Jeong, I. R., Kwon, J. O., & Lee, D. H. (2008). Strong ID-based key distribution. *IEICE Transactions on Communications. E91-B*(1), 306–308.

Kim, H.-S., & Choi, J.-Y. (2009). Enhanced password-based simple three-party key exchange protocol. *Computers & Electrical Engineering, 35,* 107–114. doi:10.1016/j.compeleceng.2008.05.007

Liu, D., Ning, P., & Du, W. (2005). Group-based key predistribution in wireless sensor networks. *Proceedings of the 4th ACM Workshop on Wireless security (WiSE '05)*, (pp. 11-20).

Liu, F., Wu, C., & Lin, X. (2010). Some extensions on threshold visual cryptography schemes. *The Computer Journal, 53*(1), 107–119. doi:10.1093/comjnl/bxn072

Lu, R., & Cao, Z. (2007). Simple three-party key exchange protocol. *Computers & Security, 26,* 94–97. doi:10.1016/j.cose.2006.08.005

Marti-Farre, J. (2007). A note on secret sharing schemes with three homogeneous access structure. *Information Processing Letters, 102*(4), 133–137. doi:10.1016/j.ipl.2006.08.016

Menezes, A., Qu, M., & Vanstone, S. (1995). *Some new key agreement protocols providing mutual implicit authentication.* Second Workshop on Selected Areas in Cryptography (SAC 95), (pp. 22-32).

Merwe, J., Dawoud, D., & McDonald, S. (2007). A survey on peer-to-peer key management for mobile ad hoc networks. *ACM Computing Surveys, 39*(1), 1–45. doi:10.1145/1216370.1216371

Nam, J. (2007). Security weakness in a three-party pairing-based protocol for password authenticated key exchange. *Information Sciences, 177*(6), 1364–1375. doi:10.1016/j.ins.2006.09.001

Perrig, A., Song, D., & Tygar, J. D. (2001). ELK: A new protocol for efficient large group key distribution. *Proceedings of the 2001 IEEE Symposium on Security and Privacy*, (p. 247).

Phan, R. C. W., Yau, W.-C., & Gol, B. M. (2008). Cryptanalysis of simple three-party key exchange protocol (S-3PAKE). *Information Science, 178,* 2849–2856. doi:10.1016/j.ins.2008.02.008

Shamir, A. (1979). How to share a secret. *Communications of the ACM, 22,* 612–613. doi:10.1145/359168.359176

Shamir, A. (1984). Identity-based cryptosystems and signature schemes. *Advances in Cryptology: Proceedings of CRYPTO 84*, (LNCS 196, pp. 47-53). Springer-Verlag.

Shamir, A., Rivest, R. L., & Adleman, L. (1978). A method for obtaining digital signatures. *Communications of the ACM, 21*(2), 120–126. doi:10.1145/359340.359342

Tartary, C., Pieprzyk, J., & Wang, H. (2008). Verifiable multi-secret sharing schemes for multiple threshold access structures. *International Conference on Information Security and Cryptology (Inscrypt 2007)*, (LNCS 4990, pp. 167-181).

Waldvogel, M., Caronni, G., Sun, D., Weiler, N., & Plattner, B. (1999). The VersaKey framework: Versatile group key management. [Special Issue on Middleware]. *IEEE Journal on Selected Areas in Communications, 17*(9), 1614–1631. doi:10.1109/49.790485

Wang, D., Li, X., & Yi, F. (2008). *Probabilistic (n, n) visual secret sharing scheme for grayscale images.* International Conference on Information Security and Cryptology (Inscrypt 2007), (LNCS 4990, pp. 192-200).

Wang, L., & Wu, C. (2006). *Authenticated group key agreement for multicast.* Cryptology and Network Security (CANS2006), ([). Springer-Verlag.]. *LNCS, 4301,* 55–72.

Wang, S., Cao, Z., Choo, K.-K. R., & Wang, L. (2009). An improved identity-based key agreement protocol and its security proof. *Information Sciences, 179*(3), 307–318. doi:10.1016/j.ins.2008.09.020

Wong, C. K., Gouda, M., & Lam, S. (2000). Secure group communications using key graphs. *IEEE/ACM Transactions on Networking, 8*(1), 16–30. doi:10.1109/90.836475

Xiao, Y., Rayi, V. K., Sun, B., Du, X., Hu, F., & Galloway, M. (2007). A survey of key management schemes in wireless sensor networks. *Computer Communications, 30*(11-12), 2314–2341. doi:10.1016/j.comcom.2007.04.009

Xu, J., & Zha, X. (2007). Secret sharing schemes with general access structure based on MSPs. *The Journal of Communication, 2*(1), 52–55.

Yang, C.-N., & Chen, T.-S. (2006). Reduce shadow size in aspect ratio invariant visual secret sharing schemes using a square block-wise operation. *Pattern Recognition, 39*(7), 1300–1314. doi:10.1016/j.patcog.2006.01.013

Younis, M., Ghumman, K., & Eltoweissy, M. (2006). Location-aware combinatorial key management scheme for clustered sensor networks. *IEEE Transactions on Parallel and Distributed Systems, 17*(8), 865–882. doi:10.1109/TPDS.2006.106

Yu, Z., & Guan, Y. (2008). A key management scheme using deployment knowledge for wireless sensor networks. *IEEE Transactions on Parallel and Distributed Systems, 19*(10), 1411–1425. doi:10.1109/TPDS.2008.23

ENDNOTES

[1] The discrete logarithm problem is to compute x given a prime p, an integer $g < p$, and $y = g^x$ mod p. This problem is known to be NP hard.

[2] In GSM system, those deduction algorithms were originally assumed to be confidential as a commercial secret, however it was incidentally made available from the Internet, and hence became publicly known, and some security vulnerabilities are found. The history has shown that, protecting an algorithm as part of security requirement is no longer applicable to contemporary secure communications. Hence in 3G systems, all the cryptographic algorithms are made publicly known from the very beginning of design, meant to ensure the security under some public security analysis.

Section 3
Network Security Auditing, Assessment, and Manageability Security

Chapter 7
Security Assessment of Networks

Aftab Ahmad
Norfolk State University, USA

ABSTRACT

In this chapter, a novel performance model for assessing security of a layered network has been proposed. The work is motivated by the fact that there is a need for a reference framework to account for all threats to a networked system. There are few such models available, and one of them is recommended by the International Telecommunications Union (ITU). The proposed assessment model is based on the ITU security framework, recommended in the ITU-T Recommendation X.805. We employ this model to quantify network security against five threat categories mentioned in the recommendations. The quantification has been done based on the recommended measures against all threats. A threat vector has been proposed that defines required measures for a particular threat category. Other vectors, such as the security implementation vector define how effectively these measures are implemented in a given device, system, or network. As a simple application of the proposed model, the security provided by the IEEE 802.15.4 standard is analyzed, viewing it as an 'end-to-end' system (e.g., for ad hoc sensor network applications). The proposed security assessment model can be applied to any type of network (wireless, wired, optical, service oriented, transport, etc.). The model can be employed to obtain security assessment in the form of five security metrics, one for each threat category (destruction, corruption, removal, disclosure, and interruption). An expression for the overall security against all threats has also been derived.

DOI: 10.4018/978-1-60960-777-7.ch007

1. INTRODUCTION

Security provisioning has become an essential part of network architecture standardization process. Every new standard in networking, be it an interface standard, link level, routing level or end-to-end level, has some features to secure the exchange of information. This has resulted in a boost of user confidence in using network infrastructure for sensitive data, such as business plans, credit cards and other ecommerce applications. The open competition staged by NIST to decide the Rijndael algorithm for the Advanced Encryption System (AES) is a testimony to the international cooperation for securing information in computers. Standardization of SHA Hash algorithm has strengthened the data integrity solutions. The public key infrastructure (PKI), perhaps not as well-defined as we might like it to be, is gearing towards as secure a communications between a business and its customers as there can be. Third party Digital Certificates (DC) are used quite commonly, making non-repudiation a thing of the present rather than future. There are, in fact, measures for all security threats and usually it is the human error that results in successful attacks rather than a breaking of encryption algorithms. In the midst of all these developments, we have forgotten a fundamental concept of comparing commodities – security being the commodity in this case. The fundamental concept in question is the measurement of security. If we could measure security, we could shop for it and quantify our level of confidence in the security system that we install. While fundamental breakthroughs are needed to define security measurement systems, the next best thing is to have assessment solutions for comparative analysis of security systems in networks. This Chapter addresses the same issue for networked systems. The main goals of this chapter relate to underlining the need for security assessment as well as proposing an assessment model for networkable systems. The proposed system gets as close to measuring the security as current state-of-research allows and provides a direction to designing full-fledged security performance models, as more research becomes available.

We show in this Chapter that the ITU-T Network Security Framework (X.805) can also be employed in deriving a performance model for assessing a security system. The Chapter is organized as follows: in the next section, the problem background is discussed along with current research. Following the background discussion, an account of security components is presented that also includes the basic structure of the ITU-T X.805 recommendation. This is followed by the proposed usage of X.805 in developing a security assessment model. An application of the model is included to assess the security provided by the popular sensor network standard IEEE 802.15.4. Following this example are Future Research Directions, Conclusions and References.

2. BACKGROUND

Information assurance systems have evolved into highly complex systems, based on a large number of sub-systems and components. There are too many factors that influence the performance of a security system. Even a small part of it can be quite complex to analyze. For example, an encryption algorithm has to be complex enough so that it can't be reverse-engineered even if publicized, such as what happened with RC4. There are many ways in which an encryption algorithm can be compromised; it could have weak key generation, distribution or/and regeneration mechanisms, weak random number generation mechanism, or simply could allow one of the several attacks (Heys, 2010). In networked systems, information assurance can be even more challenging as the sources of compromise multiply due to a number of protocol layers and types of activities (user data exchange, signaling information exchange or management data). Consequently, each activity on each layer has to be protected, as any layer can be the source of attack as shown in Figure 1. Additionally, the types and numbers of attacks are increasing all the time as reported in a recent survey paper by Igure and Williams (Igure & Williams, 2008). A comprehensive security system will protect not only against the known threats, but also the threats that are yet to be designed and discovered. One way to design such a system is to first define threat categories that could account for all attacks and then define security measures against these categories (instead of individual attacks). This is essentially the approach taken by the Lucent Network Security Framework (LNSF) (McGee , 2004). The ITU-T Security Framework (ITU-T, 2003) is a result of Lucent Network Security Framework, developed by Bell Labs. The ITU-T X.805 differs only slightly from the original LNSF framework in that X.805 defines five threat categories as against four defined by LNSF.

Due to the versatile and complex nature of vulnerabilities of networked systems, work to secure them has been following the trail of attacks. As such, there is still no 'science' of designing a security system for networks, albeit having secure encryption and integrity solutions. The topic of security is as old as the information itself, but arguably has remained elusive to openly sharable research. It should not be surprising then that work on measuring security is rather limited and unorganized. Part of the problem is the lack of attack models. In some areas, such as network worm spreading, some progress has been made, e.g., as reported in (Chen, 2007). The authors of this paper present a way of quantitatively measuring the spreading ability of network-aware worms. They have derived a few metrics, including an 'infection rate' with which a worm can spread. The main strength of their work is that it is based on actual datasets collected over a period of time (7 days) and the model has been verified by comparison to simulation. Their main limitation is that it is applicable only to active attacks, specifically worms. In (Frigualt, 2008) the authors use an ap-

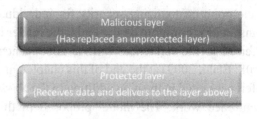

Figure 1. Even a single compromised layer in a network can be a point of vulnerability

proach based on Bayesian Networks to model the temporal evolution of network vulnerabilities and their consequential impact on the overall network security. Even though the Common Vulnerability Scoring System (CVSS) available at http://www.first.org/cvss/ provides a temporal impact measure of vulnerabilities, the paper considers it insufficient due to the inability of CVSS to relate vulnerabilities to the overall security impact on the network. The paper uses an attack-graph-based metrics system and interprets an attack graph as a special case of a Dynamic Bayesian Network. Their work is a valuable addition, especially if CVSS score are assigned such that they reflect the probabilities of vulnerabilities. The use of attack graphs is explained in (Wang, 2007). The attack graphs show the relationship among vulnerabilities that can have a cumulative effect to assist an attack type. The ITU X.805 has a set of security dimensions to thwart each threat types. Looking from this direction, the attack graphs could be used to design a system like the X.805 by creating attack graphs for a threat category and then taking care of each vulnerability in an attack graph for a particular threat category. The work in (Wang, 2007) presents a security framework that is inclusive of resource significance of the security apparatus, system reconfiguration cost and attack resistance. The paper however falls short of applying the framework on an example system (even though an example system is employed in deriving the framework).

There is in fact a major effort among the academic and industry professionals to come up with a way of creating security metrics that could be used not only for assessing the security but at some point customizing security for individual transactions. For more on the topic, the reader is referred to the references (NIST, 2007; Chen, 2008; Elahi, 2009) at the end of this chapter, and references cited in them, in addition to the above mentioned work. The model proposed in this chapter is based on ITU X.805 framework, which is a comprehensive framework tested by Lucent, who is also its proponent.

3. COMPONENTS OF A SECURITY SYSTEM

There are generally two types of threats faced by information systems, natural and man-made. Reliability measures are employed generally against natural threats. An information assurance or security system is a set of protection mechanisms against man-made threats to the information. These threats arise from internal as well as external factors to an organization. The threats materialize in the forms of attacks on the system due to vulnerabilities. Security mechanisms should provide protection against all known and possibly unknown attacks. This calls for classifying attacks into threat categories and defining security measures to thwart each of these categories. In layered networking systems, such as the Internet, Intranet, IEEE LANs, MANs, etc. the protection has to be provided for all activities, such as user data, signaling data and system management data, and at various modular network components, such as the infrastructure, the services provided and network applications that are used by customers and service providers, including application service providers (ASPs). X.805 views a security system in the above context, that is, it defines threat categories, security measures (called security dimensions), security planes and security layers.

Security threat categories define how attacks can be classified into the effects they might have.

Also, classifying attacks into threat categories should result in incorporating future attacks into one of the existing categories. If security measures are available for each threat category, and if a future attack can be classified as belonging to one of the categories, then the security system will be future-proof. Security dimensions are the measures recommended by X.805. A specific group of these dimensions/measures provides protection against a given threat category, as will be seen in the following paragraphs. The same dimension can be included in more than one group, thus providing protection against multiple threat categories. Security plans relate to the type of activity to be protected, whether user data, control data or management data. *Security layers* define the types of network resources that must be secured.

The job of a security system is to provide protection against all threats on all security levels on all security planes for each protocol layer. X.805 visualizes three security layers and three security planes for each layer of the Open System Interconnection Reference Model (OSI-RM), with eight dimensions providing security against five threats. For the OSI network with seven layers, this corresponds to $3 \times 3 \times 8 \times 7 = 504$ security measures to protect all layers against all threats to user data, signaling data and management data. Moreover, the framework recommends the protection mechanisms to be implemented during three phases of the security program, namely, (i) definition and planning, (ii) implementation and (iii) maintenance. Figure 2 shows the components of a security system as provided by X.805. Following is a description of these components.

3.1 Threats

The security apparatus is designed around meeting security concerns caused by system vulnerabilities and threats. In X.805, five threat categories are defined that can be the cause for security concerns. A successful attack results in a security breach. The expectation from the Framework is that when

Figure 2. The ITU-T X.805 Framework

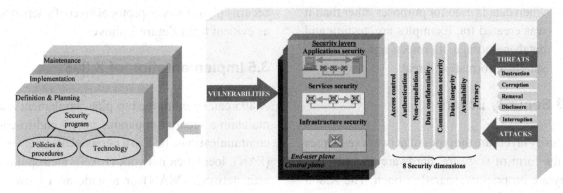

implemented to thwart all these threats, all existing and future attacks will be taken care of. The threat categories are:

1. Destruction of information/resources (DI)
2. Corruption/modification of information (CI)
3. Theft/removal/loss of information/resources (RI)
4. Information disclosure (ID)
5. Service interruption (SI)

Protection against each of the above threats requires one or more security measures. The security measures are called dimensions in the X.805 terminology.

3.2 Security Dimensions

Eight security dimensions have been defined in X.805. These are:

1. *Access control* provides protection against unauthorized use of network resources. A weakness in this dimension can expose the network to destruction of information/resources, corruption/modification of information, theft/removal of information and information disclosure. This makes it a highly sensitive dimension.

2. *Authentication* relates to confirming the identities used by a user or device for gaining access. Its lack can expose the network to theft/removal of information and information disclosure.

3. *Non-repudiation* is the capability of identifying the actual sender of data. Its absence can result in attacks classified under all the five threat categories. This makes it the most crucial dimension in terms of the number of attacks it can protect against.

4. *Data confidentiality* is a measure against unauthorized disclosure of information. It protects against theft, removal or loss of information and/or resources.

5. *Communication security* is a measure to make sure that information does not take an unwanted route or destination, and therefore provides protection against information disclosure and theft, removal or loss of information and/or resources, just like data confidentiality.

6. *Data integrity* is a protection measure against tampering of data, and thus it can thwart attacks that can be classified under destruction of information and/or network resources as well as data corruption.

7. *Availability* is a measure against destruction of information and/or network resources and service interruption.

8. *Privacy* relates to protecting user information when data is used for purposes other than it was created for. Examples are, testing and database storage. It protects against disclosure of information threat.

3.3 Security Layers

Security layers are the types of network resources in the form of software, hardware and whether they are proprietary, shared or open. The X.805 framework divides a protocol layer into three security layers.

1. *Infrastructure security layer* consists of security of devices and their interconnections.
2. *Services security layer* consists of the security of services provided by a network or a particular layer, including transmission, value-added and third-party services.
3. *Application security layer* consists of the security of network applications that devices, users or services may use.

3.4 Security Planes

The security system envisioned by X.805 provides security not only for end-user data, but also for signaling and configuration information. Accordingly, the

1. *End-user security plane* has security dimensions to provide the security layers for user data, the
2. *Control security plane* provides security dimensions for protecting against threats to the information relating to efficient transmission of information (machine-to-machine information) and the
3. *Management security plane* must have its own eight dimensions to provide security for management data. Sometimes it is user-to-machine data, such as for device configuration.

The three security layers are provided for each security plane for each protocol layer of a network, as evident from Figure 2 above.

3.5 Implementation of X.805

X.805 can be employed to plan, implement and maintain a security apparatus in any end-to-end communications, be it in a personal area network (PAN), local area network (LAN), metropolitan area network (MAN) or a wide area network (WAN). A complete implementation of X.805 framework calls for all eight dimensions to be implemented on each security layer of each security plane for each protocol layer. For example, access control to infrastructure security layer for end-user data is different from access control in the application security layer for end-user data. Therefore, on an OSI network, access control needs to be implemented separately $7 \times 3 \times 3 = 63$ times, each time to protect against threats for a different activity type (defined by security planes), for different security layer at different OSI layer. One access control mechanism can't be used by everyone, as it will expose system to unauthorized users. That does not mean, however, that the algorithms and mechanisms used to implement access are also different for different instances of implementation. Different keys can be used for algorithms, different packet types can be used for different security layers and different access permissions can be used for different activities.

In this subsection, we briefly describe typical generic mechanisms used to implement each dimension.

Access Control is needed whenever a restricted access policy is to be implemented. Restricted access is as against open access. In open access, any request to access network resources is accepted. In restricted access mechanisms, a minimum of two levels of communications are needed. First, an access mechanism is needed for communication of the request and response, which is usually open access. Once the requester has been identified as a legitimate entity, an access mechanism is enforced to determine the eligibility of the requested resource. During the first phase of communications, information that uniquely identifies the requester and access server as a user or user group is exchanged. On successful exchange of this identifying information, a trust relation is established between the requester and responder of the access control system. As a result of this trust, certain type and amount of network resources are made available to the requester depending on role or request. The *authentication* is in fact one phase of the access control mechanism. *Authentication* is completed when information uniquely identifying the requester is received and verified by the responder. However, *access control* completes only when a determination has been made as to what resources can be allowed to be used and to what extent. This can be done by a simple user classification, such as in role-based access control (Ferraiolo, 2001) in many operating systems, or by using a subscription database such as home location register (HLR) used in cell phone networks (Heien, 1999).

Non-repudiation is implemented by requiring a user entity to perform an action that can't be performed by any other entity and can be verified by a receiving entity. For example, using a secret key to generate a hash fingerprint of the data. Third party services can also be used to verify the identity of the sending entity where applicable. Such third party, usually referred to as certification authority (CA) uses digital certificates containing verified information about the user.

Data confidentiality is implemented by encrypting the data so that only the intended recipient has the information about how to decrypt it.

Communications security is typically implemented by using static routes. In dynamic routing it can be provided by including as route metrics the security related features of the routers and intermediate networks. In wireless communications systems anti-jamming techniques, such as spread spectrum modulation, also provide some communications security at the physical layer of the OSI Reference Model.

Data integrity is implemented by transmitting the finger prints of unencrypted data along with the encrypted data (assuming that the encryption can't be broken). The recipient, after decrypting the received data, generates its finger print by employing the same algorithm as the sender. By comparing the two finger prints, recipient can determine whether the data has been altered or not.

Availability can be implemented by continuously monitoring links between any two end points, such as by exchanging periodic text messages, and denying the ability of a denial of service (DOS) attacks, for which access control and authentication methods could be used to allow only the eligible entities on the network. At PHY layer, some sort of physical security of the infrastructure (in wired networks) and anti-jamming techniques (in wireless) can also be employed.

Privacy can best be implemented by requiring by law its non-disclosure for the legitimate recipients. Confidentiality techniques also apply to privacy to some extent but it does not provide protection against the unauthorized exposure of information by the legitimate recipient.

4. X.805 FRAMEWORK FOR SECURITY ASSESSMENT

Security can't be measured. There is the absence of theoretical framework for this purpose. A theoretical framework would allow us to define a unit of security and how it can be applied to various mechanisms to realize it. For example, if we define the amount of security as the probability that a certain minimum number of attempts k are required, each attempt costing d amount of resources and t time, then we could possibly design a system that is secure with a certain probability for a given length of time and number of attempts if the attacker has certain amount of resources. This kind of system would be helpful in avoiding spending

Figure 3. Steps of security assessment
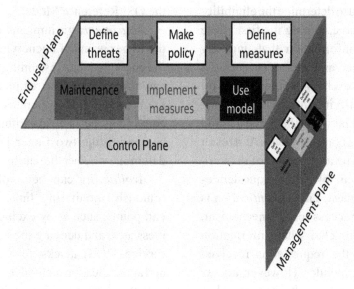

too much for security on each computer, network or transaction. Ultimately, such a system would help apply security on a per transaction basis, making networks run a lot more efficiently. Such a framework is largely absent. Even if it were to be available for existing threats, we would need a different model for unforeseen threats.

The next option to estimating the security of a network is to assess security. Security assessment would, too, result in only labeling a system as one of the subjective grades of security rather than objectively assigning a number that describes security. Additionally it requires a reference to view the security system as compared to the reference system. ITU-X.805 provides such a reference. Bell Labs has used this approach in analyzing the security of actual systems (see for example (McGee, 2004) for VPN).

Our approach is one step further from the Bell Labs approach, that is, to devise a number system to ascribe to a security vector to the security system. Such a security vector can be used to extract information about various threats. In this Chapter, we present preliminary model in which we define the vector and demonstrate its use for

a simple personal area network standard, IEEE 802.15.4. A more rigorous model is being investigated and will be presented in future, in which the security vector will have a value contingent upon the *amount* of security it provides. Figure 3 shows some steps required to design a security assessment model for a layered system.

In the next section we present the model.

4.1 Proposed Security Model

Figure 4 shows a map of security dimensions and their relation to threat categories as per the X.805. From this figure, we can represent security against each threat as an eight-element vector showing the need of each dimension or lack of it (a more rigorous discussion is given later). For example, the security vector for *Disclosure* would be (1,1,1,1,1, 0, 1,0), where the left-most '1' means that *access control* is required from Figure 4 and the right most '0' means that the *privacy* dimension is not required.

These vectors together with the corresponding implementation vectors (see Figure 5 and discussion later) determine the raw security system. In

Figure 4. Dependence of threats on dimensions

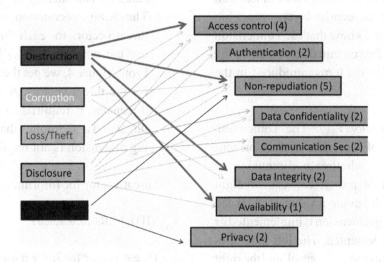

Figure 5. Conceptual security assessment model

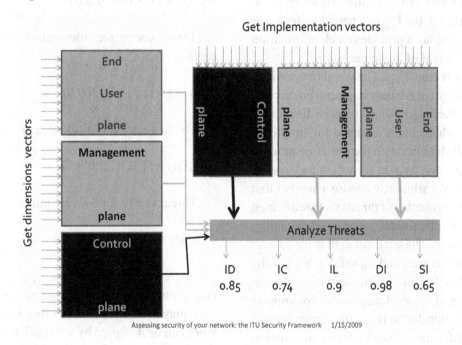

order to determine a single number representing the assessed amount of security, each threat needs to be analyzed in terms of the impact of the implementation on the corresponding threats. Figure 5 shows this concept in which the security assessment system comes up with numbers for each threat type depending on the dimension vectors and the implementation vectors (see below the definitions). In current systems, the dimension vectors can be traced (effectively what Lucent approach does). There is not a substantial amount of work available in allocating implementation vectors. The implementation vector would actually be a measurement of how secure a dimension is on each of the three security layers.

From Figure 4, we know that each dimension affects security against certain threat types. In the following, we define the terns introduced in the model.

A. *Dimension Vector(V_{DV})*. The Dimension Vector (V_{DV}) of a security system in general indicates whether a dimension is implemented or not. It consists of eight elements, each having a value of '1' if the corresponding dimension is implemented or '0' if not implemented. The left-most element represents 'access control' and the right most 'privacy'. The order between 'access control' and 'privacy' follows from Figure 4. At a glance, the V_{DV} of a network, device or a protocol layer provides quick information of the extent of implementation.

B. *Weight Vector (V_{WV})*. The Weight Vector is an eight-digit (non-binary in general) vector that shows the security impact of each dimension. In this chapter it is assumed for simplicity that all dimensions have the same amount of impact on a threat for which they are required. We arbitrarily choose a number that shows the number of threats that are affected by the implementation of the corresponding dimension. The left most digit is for 'access control' (corresponding to DV). We use the notation V_{WV} to denote the weight vector. As sees in Figure 4, access control impacts information destruction, information corruption, information loss/theft and information disclosure. So, it's assumed to have a weight of 4. More research is required in defining and determining the weight vectors for a given implementation of each dimension. With the assumptions of this chapter, the V_{WV} should be {4,2,5,2,2,2,1,2} or a fully secure system, as seen from Figure 4.

C. *Threat Vector (V_{TH})*. Threat vectors show the dependence of protection against a threat

category considering all eight dimensions. The X.805 recommendation defines the threat vectors for each threat category. We use the notation V_{TH} (.) for threat vector. From Figure 4, we get the following values for the threat vectors. A '1' implies that a dimension is required to protect against a threat and a '0' implies that the corresponding dimension is not required.

Threat vector for Information destruction:

$$V_{TH} (ID): (1,0,1,0,0,1,1,0)$$

Threat vector for Information corruption

$$V_{TH} (IC): (1,0,1,0,0,1,0,0)$$

Threat vector for Information removal/loss/theft:

$$V_{TH} (IR) = (1,1,1,1,1,0,0,0)$$

Threat vector for Disclosure of information:

$$V_{TH} (DI) = (1,1,1,1,1,0,0,1)$$

Threat vector for Service interruption:

$$V_{TH} (SI) = (0,0,1,0,0,0,0,1)$$

The left-most value shows dependence on 'access control' and the right-most on 'privacy', etc.

It may be pointed out here, that another framework can be designed by appropriately changing the threat vectors for the same implementation of dimensions.

D. *Security Implementation Vector* (V_{SIV}). Finally, the security implementation vector (V_{SIV}) shows the security provided by actual implementation of dimensions in a system, layer or a device. For example, a value of (1,1,1,1,1,1,1,1) shows that all the eight security dimensions have been implemented to provide an impact of 100%, while a value of (0,0,0,0,0,0,0,0) shows that none of them is implemented. The left-most value is for 'access control; while the right-most for 'privacy' according to Figure 4. For this Chapter, the security implementation vector is the same as the dimension vector. Once research about the comparative strengths of various implementations (or algorithm) of a dimension is matured, V_{SIV} will represent the strength of implementation of a dimension. For example $V_{SIV} = \{\alpha_1, \alpha_2, \alpha_3, \alpha_4, \alpha_5, \alpha_6, \alpha_7, \alpha_8\}$ means that access control implementation provides a security impact equal to α_1 and privacy implementation provides a security equal to α_8 and so on. The values of α_k's are assumed to vary between 0 and 1 inclusive. It may be noted that every plane on every layer will have a different value of V_{SIV} in general. Additionally, each threat category can have its own V_{SIV} value. The difference between the weight vector and implementation vector is that the former relates to the impact of a dimension on the overall system security while the later relates to its implementation strength in comparison with other implementations. For examples, the weight vector for data confidentiality tells us how many threats will the system be exposed to in the absence of data confidentiality, while its implementation vector will tell how good is the algorithm used in implementing it. This is another open area for research.

E. *Security Assessment Model.* Let S_i be the security against a threat 'i' and ω_i denote the impact of this threat on the overall system security, where i has a value from among (ID, IC, IR, DI, SI) depending on threat category.

Then, following from the above definitions of various vectors, we define the security against threat 'i' by the following relations:

Let us define $P(a,b) = \{a_i b_i\}$ as a vector consisting of elements that are product of corresponding elements of vectors a and b (all vectors are *row vectors*). In the following, we show that:

$$P(a,b) = [\delta_{ij}\{[a^Tb][1^T]\}]^T \qquad (1)$$

where,

δ_{ij} is the Kronecker's delta function defined as:

$\delta_{lm} = \{l = m\}$ meaning that $\delta_{lm} = 1$ when $l = m$ and zero otherwise,

is a row vector of eight 1's, and [1]

x^T is the transpose of x.

Proof: $P(a,b) = [\delta_{ij}\{[a^Tb][1^T]\}]^T$

For simplicity, we assume that a and b have eight elements to remain within the context of this chapter.

Accordingly:

$a = \{a_1, a_2, a_3, a_4, a_5, a_6, a_7, a_8\}$, (1 x 8 *matrix*)

$b = \{b_1, b_2, b_3, b_4, b_5, b_6, b_7, b_8\}$, (1 x 8 *matrix*)

$[a^Tb] = c$, $\{c_{ij}\} = \{a_i b_j\}$, $i, j = 1, 2, ...8$. (8 x 8 *matrix*)

$\delta_{ij}[a^Tb] = d = \{c_{jj}\} = \{a_j b_j\}$, $j = 1, 2, ...$

(8 x 8 *diagonal matrix*)

$[d1^T] = e = \{e_j\} = \{c_{jj}\} = \{a_j b_j\}$, $j = 1, 2, ...$

(8 x 1 *column matrix*)

$[d1^T]^T = f = \{f_j\} = \{c_{jj}\} = \{a_j b_j\}$, $j = 1, 2, ...$

(1 x 8 *row matrix*)

$$= [\delta_{ij}\{[a^{\mathrm{T}}b][1^{\mathrm{T}}]\}]^{\mathrm{T}}$$

$$= P(a,b)$$

Using the definitions of various vectors, we define the security S_i provided against the threat '*i*' as follows:

$$S_i = \frac{P(V_{SIV}, V_{TH}).V_{WV}}{V_{TH}.V_{WV}} i \qquad (2)$$

A dot '.' between two vectors denotes the dot product or scalar product and without a dot it's a matrix multiplication.

Interpretation of Equation (2). Equation (2) is the ratio of the total weights implemented in all dimensions relating to thwarting threat *i*, to the total weights necessary to thwart threat *i* in order to conform to ITU X.805. As a check, we see that for a full implementation of dimensions against a threat, the numerator is equal to the denominator providing 100% protection in accordance with the X.805 standard. If we define $S = \{S_i\}$ as consisting of the security against each of the five threats and $\omega = \{\omega_i\}$ the impact vector whose elements are the impact of each of the threat category on the overall system security, then the overall system security S can be defined as

$$S = \omega.S \qquad (3)$$

$$\omega = (\omega_{ID}, \omega_{IC}, \omega_{IR}, \omega_{DI}, \omega_{SI})$$

$$S = (S_{ID}, S_{IC}, S_{IR}, S_{DI}, S_{SI})$$

The dot product of Equation (3) can be expanded to the following:

$$S = \omega_{ID} S_{ID} + \omega_{IC} S_{IC} + \omega_{IR} S_{IR} + \omega_{DI} S_{DI} + \omega_{SI} S_{SI}$$

Ideal Case Scenario. Equation (2) defines the security measure against a threat category. For an ideal case, we will have the following values of various vectors for ID.

V_{TH} (ID): {1,0,1,0,0,1,1,0}

V_{WV} (ID): {4,2,5,2,2,2,1,2}

V_{SIV}:{1,1,1,1,1,1,1,1}

$V_{WV}(ID . V_{TH} (ID) = 4 + 5 + 2 + 1 = 12$

$P(V_{SIV}, V_{TH}) = \{1,0,1,0,0,1,1,0\}$

$P(V_{SIV}, V_{TH}).V_{WV}(ID) = 4+5+2+1 = 12$

From Equation (2) for this case:

$$S_{ID} = S_i = \frac{P(V_{SIV}, V_{TH}).V_{WV}}{V_{TH}.V_{WV}}\bigg|_{ID} = 1.0 = 100\%$$

Similarly, it is easily shown that for an ideal case, the overall security is 100% from Equation (3).

Equations (1)-(3) provide a model for labeling a system in terms of security on the footsteps of X.805.

Until the writing of this chapter, work on ω and weight vector is required. For application of the model in this Chapter we assume that $\omega = (1/5, 1/5, 1/5, 1/5, 1/5)$ and the weight vector simply reflects the number of threat categories that each dimension affects. It must be noted that the weight vector requires analysis of each dimension and the assumption that its components are equal to the number of threats it thwarts is rather simplistic (*Note: the lack of availability of research for ω and V_{WV} shows how much lacking the research in security really is*).

Figure 6. Protocol architecture of IEEE 802.15.4

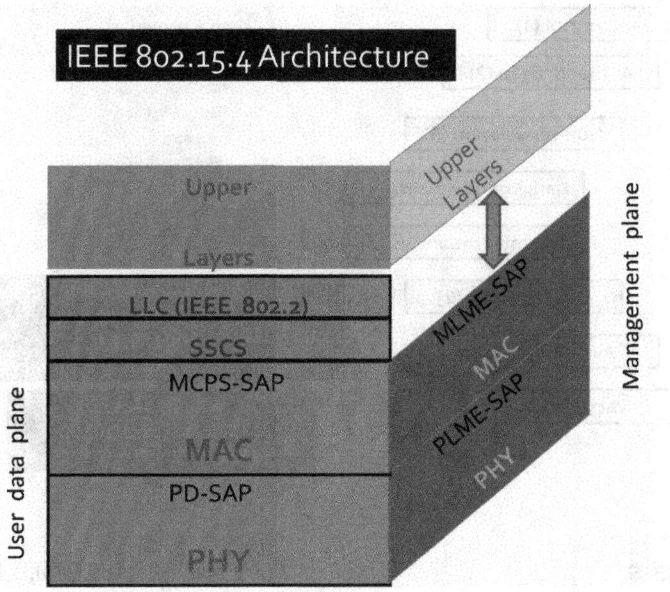

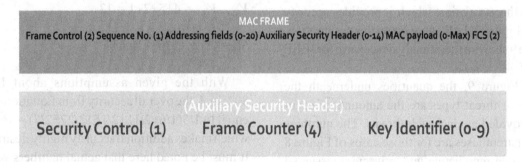

Figure 7. IEEE 802.15.4 MAC frame

5. SECURITY ASSESSMENT OF IEEE 802.15.4

Figure 6 shows a protocol plane for the IEEE 802.15.4. The standard has been designed for ultra-low power, low-data rate devices and one of the objectives of the standard is to have low protocol overhead.

The standard specifies PHY and MAC layer protocols and interfaces and defines a MAC frame shown in Figure 7.

Among other things, the MAC frame has an auxiliary security header consisting of 5-14 octets.

This frame is used for security for the user plane. According to the specifications, the security provisioning is not mandatory and could be provided on a scale of eight levels (level 0 being no security). Figure 8 shows which dimensions are explicitly provided in the standards.

As seen from Figure 8, the standard does not have access control, authentication, communications security and privacy security.

Figure 8. Security dimensions in IEEE 802.15.4

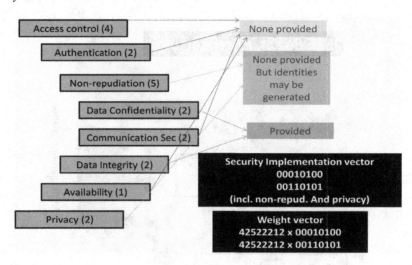

5.1 Threat Analysis

In the simplest threat analysis model presented above, a dimension's weight is based on the number of threats against which it provides security as per Figure 4. Following up on this assumption, Figure 9 shows a threat analysis scenario for IEEE 802.15.4.

In Figure 9, the quantities underneath the boxes for threat types are the amounts of security provided against such threats. The numbers in the parentheses are for those cases of Figure 8 where 'non-repudiation' and 'privacy' are assumed to be provided.

The values in Figure 9 are calculated by using Equations (1)-(3), with:

$$S_i = \frac{P\left(V_{SIV}, V_{TH}\right) \cdot V_{WV}}{V_{TH} \cdot V_{WV}}$$

For example, with i = ID, we have:

$$V_{SIV} = (0,0,0,1,0,1,0,0)$$

$$V_{TH} = (1,0,1,0,0,1,1,0)$$

$$V_{WV} = (4,2,5,2,2,2,1,2)$$

$$P(V_{SIV} \cdot V_{TH}) = (0,0,0,0,0,1,0,0)$$

$$P(V_{SIV} \cdot V_{TH}) \cdot V_{WV} = 2$$

$$V_{TH} \cdot V_{WV} = 4+5+2+1 = 12$$

$$S_{ID} = 2/12 = 1/6 = 16.6\%$$

With the given assumptions about IEEE 802.15.4, the overall security from Equation (3) is equal to $1/5(1/6+2/11+2/15+2/27+2/7) = 16.8\%$, which makes additional security highly desirable. It must be noted here that actual numbers would vary widely depending on the levels of security (from the 7 levels defined in the standard). If we need to define security weights for encryption algorithms and message integrity codes to be less than 1, thus incorporating some meaningful implementation vector, the numbers will fall further. Work on obtaining weights of individual algorithms and mechanisms is still not available. The model is good for at least comparative analysis, in the absence of such representative weights. In future, once we can define ω's and V_{SIV}'s, we can get numbers that reflect a measure of absolute security for a given layer, system or device. We may be able to label systems with a number to reflect its security.

Figure 9. IEEE 802.15.4 threat analysis

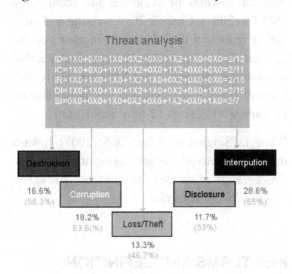

security will not be defined at each layer separately, as we do today (TSL, IPsec, EAP are configured separately). We should be able to design security protocols that will talk to each other so that if the security requirements of a packet are known at the application layer, the lower layers automatically configure themselves accordingly.

7. CONCLUSION

The Chapter presents a model for performance assessment of the security of a networked system. The model is derived from the definitions of security dimensions and threat categories of the ITU-T X.805 Recommendation, and can easily and appropriately be customized to incorporate other security frameworks. We successfully show by applying the model that IEEE 802.15.4 is a low security standard, as expected. An indirect contribution of the model is that one can design sound security systems by appropriately designing the security implementation vectors. Also, we have pointed out areas that need more research in order to design measureable security systems for layered, networked systems, thus providing a useful direction for future research in network security.

6. FUTURE RESEARCH DIRECTIONS

Security is finally getting recognition. Every network standard includes a component of securing the exchange of data between communicating nodes. However, this is not considered sufficient, as every organization that wants to protect its data uses security as a value added service. This can change once we have a way of measuring our trust in security. The work reported in this chapter is a direction to achieving such a trust, by being able to assess the amount of security provided by a security apparatus. As outlined in the chapter, there are unanswered questions in identifying algorithms with a performance metric that can be used to label each security measure implementation with a strength or impact factor. More research is needed for this purpose. Even though the availability of such research results will complete the model presented in this chapter, a more fundamental issue of proving that the X.805 framework can comprehensively take care of all future attacks, is still open. We may get another framework and then another one until we create a theory of designing one. The obstacle to such a work is that attacks are done by humans, and it is not easy to model human intentions. It is still projected here that we will be able to select security on a per transaction basis in future. Additionally,

REFERENCES

Chen, Z., & Ji, C. (2007). Measuring network-aware worm spreading ability. *Proceedings of the IEEE INFOCOM 2007*, Anchorage AK.

Chen, Z., Ji, C., & Barford, P. (2008). *Spatial-temporal characteristics of Internet malicious sources. Proceedings of IEEE INFOCOM*. Mini-Conference.

Elahi, G., Yu, E., & Zannone, N. (2009). *A modeling ontology for integrating vulnerabilities into security requirements conceptual foundations*. 28th International Conference on Conceptual Modeling, Gramado, Brazil.

Ferraiolo, D. F., Sandhu, R., Gavrila, S., Kuhn, D. R., & Chandramouli, R. (2001). Proposed NIST standards for role-based access control. [TISSEC]. *ACM Transactions on Information and System Security, 4*(3). doi:10.1145/501978.501980

Frigault, M., Wang, L., Singhal, A., & Jajodia, S. (2008). Measuring network security using dynamic Bayesian network. In *Proceedings of 4th ACM Workshop on Quality of Protection*, (pp. 23–30).

Guttman, P. (2010). *The convergence of Internet security threats* (spam, viruses, Trojans, phishing). Retrieved July 10, 2010, from http://www.cs.auckland.ac.nz/ ~pgut001/pubs/blended.pdf

Heien, G., & Horrer, M. (1999). *GSM networks, protocols, terminology and implementation*. Norwood, MA: Artech House Inc.

Heys, H. M. (2010). *A tutorial on linear and differential cryptanalysis*. Memorial University of Newfoundland. Retrieved on July 10, 2010, from http://www.engr.mun.ca/~howard/ PAPERS/ldc_tutorial.pdf

IEEE802 Committee. (2006). Part 15.4: Wireless Medium Access Control (MAC) and Physical Layer (PHY) specifications for low-rate Wireless Personal Area Networks (WPANs).

Igure, V., & Williams, R. (2008). Taxonomies of attacks and vulnerabilities in computer systems. *IEEE Communications Surveys and Tutorials, 10*(1), 6–19. doi:10.1109/COMST.2008.4483667

ITU-T. (2003). *Security architecture for systems providing end-to-end communications*. (Recommendation X.805).

McGee, A. R., Vasireddy, S. R., Xie, C., Picklesimer, D. D., Chandrashekhar, U., & Richman, S. H. (2004). A framework for ensuring network security. *Bell Labs Technical Journal, 8*(4), 7–27. doi:10.1002/bltj.10083

National Institute of Standards and Technology (NIST). (2007). Chapter 20: Assessing and mitigating risks to a hypothetical computer system. *Special Publication 800-12 – an introduction to computer security – the NIST handbook*. Retrieved from http://csrc.nist.gov/publications/nistpubs/800-12/800-12-html/index.html

Wang, L., Singhal, A., & Jajodia, S. (2007). Toward measuring network security using attack graphs. *Proceedings of the 3rd International Workshop on Quality of Protection*.

KEY TERMS AND DEFINITIONS

Advanced Encryption Algorithm (AES): An symmetric block encryption and decryption system using rijn-dael algorithm as specified in Federal Information Processing Standards 197 (FIPS-197).

AES: Same as Advanced Encryption Algorithm.

Security Dimensions: The eight security measures specified in X.805.

Security Layers: The types of network resources that need to be protected, namely, infrastructure, services and applications.

Security Planes: The types of activities or data that need protection, namely, the user data, the control and signaling data, and management data.

SHA: A set of four Secure Hash Algorithms (SHA-1, SHA-256, SHA-384, SHA-512) specified by NIST for data fingerprinting.

Threat Categories: General categorization of what can go wrong as a result of attacks on computer or network. X.805 defines five threat categories.

X.805: The ITU document specifying recommendations for security architecture for end-to-end systems.

Chapter 8
Network Security Auditing

Yin Pan
Rochester Institute of Technology, USA

Bo Yuan
Rochester Institute of Technology, USA

Sumita Mishra
Rochester Institute of Technology, USA

ABSTRACT

As people increasingly rely on computer systems and networks for services such as online banking, online shopping, and socialization, information security for identity protection and privacy has become more important today than ever. Businesses and organizations are also obligated to provide such security to comply with state and federal laws and regulations. Managing security risks and ensuring compliance with information security regulations and industry standards have become important for businesses and organizations. Security auditing is an effective process to assess policies, procedures, and controls in identifying risks associated with networks and various operating systems. This chapter emphasizes network security audits and discusses various auditing procedures and technologies to identify and examine threats and vulnerabilities in computer networks, and to determine how to assess and manage risk posed to a network.

INTRODUCTION

We live in a connected world, increasingly dependent on computer systems and networks for news, business, social networking, and daily life activities. However, over the past decades, very little has changed in the computer system and network architectures and communications protocols, which were not initially designed for

the magnitude of current networks and usages. By taking advantage of existing vulnerabilities and flaws in protocol designs and implementations, adversaries with various motives have launched cyber-attacks against businesses and organizations to steal intellectual property and personal records, which results in financial losses, damaged reputations, serious degradations of critical services, and reduced public confidence (Kraemer et al, 2009; McClure et al, 2009; Wilson, 2009). Network security is a prime concern for governments,

DOI: 10.4018/978-1-60960-777-7.ch008

businesses and citizens. Maintaining network and systems integrity, availability and security is imperative for protecting data and ensuring normal operations.

A combination of technologies such as firewalls, intrusion detection systems (IDS), and encryption, has greatly increased network security, but these are insufficient to prevent web-based attacks, social engineering attacks, social networks attacks, hidden backdoors, etc. To counter these types of attacks, security policies, procedures and controls must be set and checked regularly. Security auditing, through penetration tests (He & Body, 2005), active scanning, passive sniffing and analysis, is an effective process to measure policies, procedures and controls in identifying risks associated with networks and various operating systems (Buchanan & Gibb; Longley et al, 2008; Sayana, 2003; Wright et al, 2008; Zhang et al, 2009). Auditing creates roadmaps for organizations to build defenses and countermeasures against cyber attacks and threats. As Westcott (2007) stated, "A comprehensive security audit may not cure all of a security manager's data woes, but it should go a long way toward reducing the risk of exposing negative consequences" (p. 8). Audits will uncover security holes that expose organizations to malicious acts.

Information system audits include auditing corporation policies, framework, operating systems and database, application software, physical security, network security, etc. Although most companies are confident about the physical security of their offices and facilities, little is known about the security of their computer networks. This chapter emphasizes on an important component of overall information systems auditing -- network security audits. Procedures and technologies to identify various network threats and vulnerabilities, and determine how to assess and manage risks posed to a network are discussed. This chapter also demonstrates the state of art techniques, through a case study, used in different phases of network auditing including network discovery, penetration, and network threat analysis and control.

BACKGROUND KNOWLEDGE FOR AUDITING

Assets, Vulnerabilities, Threats, and Risk Analysis

Information security includes activities that provide protection for information assets against risks of unauthorized access, misuse, disclosure, modification, or destruction. Information security essentially focuses on four major areas: asset, threat, vulnerability and risk (Alberts, 2003). An *asset* is any valuable information such as intellectual property, business intelligence, personal identities, and other mission critical data for businesses and organizations. *Risk* refers to the likelihood of a negative impact or consequence such as financial loss and/or reputation damages. A *threat* is any deliberate or accidental action that individuals, either internal or external, take to potentially harm an asset, for example, stealing personal identification and bank account information, intellectual property theft, and sabotage. *Vulnerability* is a defect or weakness in software or computer systems, and human nature that allows a threat to exploit and penetrate security protections. For example, a buffer-overflow vulnerability in an application may allow an attacker to seize control of a system. A social engineering attack takes advantages of weaknesses of human nature such as kindness, greedy, etc. to circumvent security protections. Asset, threat, vulnerability and risk are intertwined such that when threats and vulnerabilities occur at the same time, security can be breached, in which case the asset is harmed, and the risk is realized.

To ensure information security and reduce risks, an organization must identify critical assets and find out how susceptible the assets are to attack by exploiting known vulnerabilities. This is where security audits come to play.

Basic vulnerabilities associated with a network include, but are not limited to, the following categories:

1. Unsecure/plain text data transfer – services such as Telnet, ftp, http, SMTP v2 (and below) pass data including usernames and passwords in clear text. Passwords and other sensitive data, when passing through the public medium, can be stolen or modified.
2. Misconfiguration, such as weak passwords or vulnerable services cause unauthorized access to the network and systems on the network.
3. Malicious attacks on vulnerable applications render the network and services unavailable (Denial of Service) for legitimate users and businesses.
4. Misconfiguration of the networks and systems or vulnerable services cause the network to be accessible and controlled by an adversary from anywhere at anytime.
5. Insider information or virus payload

Before discussing network security auditing, it is important to know what security audits are about and how they can be used to help information security.

Introduction to Security Auditing

Auditing is not a new concept; auditing of financial statements, or financial audits, has quite a long history and can be traced back as early as the sixteenth century (History of Financial Audit, 2010). Auditing is a methodical examination and review of measurements against a standard/ policy and reporting on the areas that failed to meet the standards. It not only answers questions about what works and what does not, but also demonstrates how an auditor finds problems and how to fix them. Recently, auditing has become

a standard practice for information security in industry (Westcott, 2007). A conformance audit, for example, focuses on measuring how well a system or process conforms to policies and procedures that have been defined in an organization. Payment Card Industry (PCI) conformance ensures that all Web-facing applications are protected against known attacks. A security audit, on the other hand, is a more general audit that can be used to measure policy, procedure, systems, and applications against industry best practice in order to determine if there is a need for improvement. A security-team will carry out a comprehensive risk evaluation and analyze the identified risks to compile a priority list for risks to be addressed accordingly.

Network Auditing Process and Procedure

SANS Institute (SANs, 2010) defines a six-step audit process in the audit course of Auditing Networks, Perimeters, and Systems (Audit 507, 2010).

- Audit Planning
- Discussing the plan with relevant people
- Measuring the systems
- Preparing the report
- Presenting results
- Report to management

During the Audit planning stage, the auditor works with the organization to determine audit objectives and scope. The objectives are what goals the organization is trying to achieve, and the scope defines what the audit is going to cover in terms of the time period and the population of the organization involved in the audit. Once the objective and scope are determined, the auditor will research and create an audit strategy – a detailed step-by-step audit to-do checklist. The checklist is the audit procedure that the auditor will follow to measure the systems.

After the planning stage, the auditor will meet the relevant people including the top-level personnel to layout his/her auditing plan and get the approval and feedback from them. After reaching an agreement, the auditor starts the fieldwork to measure the systems and infrastructures based on the checklist. Finally, the auditor prepares for a report detailing the findings and recommendations and presents to the management.

Auditing Standards, Framework and Regulatory Compliance

As mentioned earlier, auditing is the process of measuring computer systems and networks against a standard/policy. Security policies, guidelines, standards, and procedures provide a mandate and basis for maintaining network security (Westcott, 2007). At present, many federal regulations, security frameworks, and standards exist in an effort to enforce protection of information, privacy, and transparency of information.

ISO 17799, a collection of statements defining good practice for managing information security, is widely regarded as a broad and comprehensive standard for information security best practices (Lai & Tai, 2007; Ohki et al, 2009; Solms, 2005; and Westcott, 2007).

Other effective and widely used standards and frameworks include *IT Infrastructure Library* (ITIL, 2010) and Control OBjectives for Information and related Technology (COBIT, 2010). ITIL, developed in UK, provides a comprehensive checklist, practices, and procedures in IT Services Management, IT development and IT operation. ITIL v3 library, the latest version of ITIL published in 2007, comprises five volumes that cover concepts and practices in service strategy, service design, service transition, service operation and continual service improvement. COBIT from ISACA, on the other hand, is a worldwide governance framework addressing not only information security, but also information technology governance, information systems and technology control, compliance, and auditing. It also provides supporting toolsets that help decision-makers to implement controls, address technical issues, and reduce business ris[REMOVED HYPERLINK FIELD]ks.

Organizations may use multiple of frameworks such as COBIT and ISO 17799 as reference frameworks for Information Security governance (Ohki et al, 2009; Solms, 2005).

Continuous Monitoring

In order to effectively identify vulnerabilities and reduce risks, auditing has to be performed periodically, normally every 3 or 6 months. However, organizations that are constantly at risk of errors and fraud resulting in financial losses, require an ongoing monitoring in addition to periodic audits to effectively manage security risks in highly dynamic environments. To achieve this goal, the National Institute of Standards and Technology (NIST) released a new Risk Management Framework (RMF) that includes *Continuous Monitoring* as one of the major steps of the framework. This new RMF is included in NIST Special Publication (SP) 800-53 and SP 800-37, Revision 1, *Applying the Risk Management Framework to Federal Information Systems,* in February 2010. (NIST, 2010; NIST continuous monitoring, 2010). The concept of Continuous-Auditing was first introduced by Vasarhelyi and Halper in 1991 (Vasarhelyi & Halper, 1991; IIA, 2005) as a process that automatically performs control and risk assessments in real time using automated data extraction and analytical tools. NIST defined a continuous monitoring strategy in the new RMF to help support near real-time risk management to manage IT security risks in highly dynamic environments. *RedSeal Network Advisor* and *RedSeal Vulnerability Advisor* (RedSeal, 2010) from *RedSeal Systems In*c. support continuous monitoring and analysis of network controls and automatically determine the risk of each identified vulnerability.

Virtualization Auditing

Virtualization is widely being adopted by businesses and organizations (Kroeker, 2009). Some of the benefits of virtualization include reduction in hardware, operation and energy costs, cutting down on server provisioning time, and elimination of planned down time. However, with the benefits of virtualization, we need to be aware of the increase in auditing and compliance costs (Berman, 2009; Phan & Yao, 2009). Virtual machines introduce some unique security challenges. The existing IT security policies, procedures and technologies for non-virtual setup are not designed to protect the virtual infrastructure. In (Berman, 2009), the author lists the five challenges introduced by virtualization.

1.   With the introduction of a new operating system and management layer, new threats can arise. Hence the auditor and the security team of the company need to be aware of the virtualization structure and the security needs arising due to virtualization. The security deployment plan needs to be designed and verified.
2.   The threat surface of the data center increases with virtualization. Hence, the risk of attacks including denial of service increases. The defense has to be extended to the host OS as well as the virtual infrastructure. This virtualization-aware security mechanism can protect the environment against attacks and also reduce compliance and management costs.
3.   Virtualization can lead to abuse of privileges due to the merger and overlap of roles of network, system and security administrators. The combined role of virtual administration can lead to a total compromise of all aspects

should the privileges be breached. Hence critical tasks should be protected with dual controls enforced by processes and tools. These processes should monitor for unauthorized behavior, enforce segmentation, prevent unauthorized access and limit the spreading of malicious code and malware (Berman, 2009). Hence the auditing costs will be reduced if these preventive measures are in place.
4.   The virtual environment can change very fast compared to the physical deployment. Hence accidental or deliberate changes can lead to the introduction of new threats and vulnerabilities. Policies related to configuration and change management should be in place to avoid this problem.
5.   Virtual infrastructure is accessible by the adversary from anywhere in the network, regardless of the physical security methods in use. Hence audit and monitor tools should be in place for the data paths leading to the virtual infrastructure. Every virtualization host and storage network should be protected by these tools.

NETWORK AUDITING TECHNIQUES AND PROCEDURES

While the Internet has made it possible for businesses and people to be connected constantly, it has also exposed them to potential data breaches, identity theft, and other information security issues.

With many open source hacking tools available online, even script kiddies are capable of breaking into one's network and systems that are not appropriately secured. How does one know whether a network is vulnerable to attacks? One common practice is to regularly conduct security audits for vulnerability assessment and close security holes before hackers reach them. To address network security concerns, many security-auditing solutions have been developed, either commercially or open source (Skoudis and Liston, 2006). In this section, we follow the auditing procedure and utilize both hacking and security techniques to audit networks. It is important to note that the only difference between a hacker and a security auditor lies in the person's motivation and whether he has the permission to perform the task.

Information security auditing involves checking systems and perimeter security, firewall rule sets, router access control lists, port scanning, and intrusion detection setting. An auditor should scan both internal and external connections. Scanning from the outside to inside of a network allows the auditor to see what a hacker can see and therefore eliminate externally accessible vulnerabilities; scanning from the inside to outside of the network allows the auditor to locate potential inside threats, so as to discover internally accessible vulnerabilities, especially when a backdoor has been placed in the network.

The overall auditing procedure includes, but is not limited to:

- Physical security audits
- Wired and wireless network security audits
- Perimeter security audits to find out whether routers, firewalls and IDS configurations, settings, and rule sets are well defined and configured.
- DMZ servers and services security
- Internal systems security
- Scan network from the outside to find out what a hacker can exploit
- Scan network from the inside to eliminate internal threats

This chapter only focuses on the procedure and techniques used in a wired network audit as wireless network auditing is a topic by itself. A case study will follow to demonstration the details of the audit.

Audit Preparation and Infrastructure Audit

Network audits start with audit preparation. At this very early stage, the auditor must have a clear picture of

- What are the critical assets in the network to be protected?
- Where do the assets reside?
- Which servers and applications have access to the critical information?
- Who has access to the critical systems and how do they access them, local or remote? If remote access is allowed, which protocols are allowed?

The goal of auditing is to identify vulnerabilities imposed on the assets as well as surrounding applications, servers, and networks.

The first step for an auditor is to determine the responsibility and audit scope – systems, servers, perimeters and subnets within the scanning range. The auditor will start with the company's network diagram and study the company's business plan and policy/procedure to see whether the network meets the business plan and whether the policy is updated based on best practices and regulations.

The auditor has to ensure the accuracy of the network design, i.e., whether the servers, routers, and firewall are placed at the right locations. For example, critical systems with databases are placed inside the internal network, with an additional firewall between the inside network and the DMZ. The Intrusion detection systems (IDS) are deployed in the right spots to capture attacks at the border and more importantly, the attacks that have managed to pass through.

The next step is to research potential vulnerabilities and risks associated with the software and operating systems running on servers, systems and perimeters that participate in network activities. The final step of the audit planning is to create a checklist detailing the strategy and plan to conduct the audit. A security audit should be based on existing, well-known strategies of IT governance. COBIT, ITIL, and ISO17799 discussed in the previous section define good practices for managing information security. Here are some examples that may be included in a network-auditing checklist:

- Is the network susceptible to reconnaissance attack and network discovery, i.e., how much information on the network, such as a network diagram including live systems, routers, OS types, open services, employee list, etc are available to hackers?
- Are there any vulnerable services on the network that allow hackers to exploit the vulnerabilities to gain access to systems on the network?
- Are there any Trojans, backdoors or rootkits on the network?
- Are there services that allow users to send sensitive information in clear-text?
- Are there any services that reveal useful information such as service type, version, and instructional error messages, either through banner or insecure configurations that could be used by unauthorized users to attack the system?
- Are security patches up-to-date? Have the systems been set up to receive auto updates for patches/vulnerabilities to the software used in the network environment?
- Is management traffic separated from user traffic?
- Are there sufficient logs including router ids and system logs of the network activity? How often are the logs analyzed in order to identify unauthorized access and attacks? Is any backup policy for the logs in place?
- Is encryption applied to sensitive data that is transferred over the network?
- Who is allowed to access internal systems via a shell or command line access? What is the authentication/authorization control?

- What is the strength of the encryption algorithm employed in the network? Is there a strong password policy for user access?
- What is the effective modem policy and wireless security policy? (This is not covered in this chapter)

Identify the Exposure to Reconnaissance

Since the usual first step to launch an attack is to discover as much information as possible about the target network, a penetration test for low-technology reconnaissance should be conducted to find out how much information is publicly available to others, including hackers. The Counter Hack Reload (Skoudis & Liston, 2006) is an excellent book describing the techniques for reconnaissance and network discovery.

Low-Technology Reconnaissance

Low-technology reconnaissance includes, but is not limited to, social engineering, physical breakins and dumpster diving. Social Engineering takes advantage of people's good nature to be helpful and friendly to garner resources including sensitive information, such as password. For example, an attacker may call company employees through a stolen internal voice service, possibly using a fake caller ID, to trick victims into revealing sensitive information by pretending to be a manager, a system administrator, a new employee, a customer, or a contractor.

Physical breakins (or piggybacks) intend to physically access the targeted internal network or systems by directly plugging into an open Ethernet jack or access unguarded systems via keyboard to steal or tamper with sensitive information, and even plant backdoors.

Skoukis points out in Counter Hack Reload (Skoukis and Liston, 2006) that "this type of attack is devastating since it bypasses perfectly configured firewalls; defeats super strong crypto; and evades even most finely tuned IPS tools".

War Dialing: Searching for Unsecured Modems

There are various ways to connect a computer to a network – via a wireless link through an Access Point, through an Ethernet jack, or via a modem through telephone lines. War dialing aims to search for accessible modems with weak access control in a targeted telephone exchange, hoping to connect to a computer on a targeted network. Even though it is not as popular as war driving today, war dialing is still an easy and effective way for hackers to gain access to a targeted network. Many companies are not aware of abandoned modems that are still connected to their networks with weak or no passwords for authentication.

War Driving: Searching for Accessible and Unsecured Wireless Local Area Networks

Wireless networks are widely used by organizations and individuals. In recent years, there have been increasing threats of adversaries entering a targeted organization via an unsecured wireless access point, bypassing expensive firewalls and intrusion detection/prevention systems. War driving is a common technique used by hackers to discover accessible Wi-Fi wireless access points (APs) in a moving vehicle, with a portable computer or PDA. If a corporate wireless network is not configured properly with sufficient strength in encryption and authentication, the wireless network may become the weakest link in the overall security of the whole network.

Exercising war driving or wireless spectrum analysis is an importance step of network security audits, even for businesses and organizations that do not have wireless networks. Rogue wireless access points can be inserted easily into a wired network by employees or attackers.

Table 1.

Domain Name: RIT.EDU
Registrant:
Rochester Institute of Technology
103 Lomb Memorial Drive
Rochester, NY 14623-5608
UNITED STATES
(585) 475-4357
abuse@rit.edu
Technical Contact:
helpdesk@rit.edu
Name Servers:
NS1.RIT.EDU 129.21.3.17
NS2.RIT.EDU 129.21.4.18
CCUVAX.NORTHWESTERN.EDU
Domain record activated: 21-Apr-1988
Domain record last updated: 13-Aug-2009
Domain expires: 31-Jul-2010

Note that some basic concepts of war driving and war dialing are included here for the completion of the Reconnaissance list of an auditing process. The details of these are beyond the scope of this chapter.

Web-Based and Whois Database Reconnaissance

Internet search engines such as Google and Yahoo, organizations' web sites and newsgroups, and social networking sites such as Facebook and mySpace can provide a wealth of information about a potential target. Information including an organization's contacts, news, emails and even name servers' IP addresses are often publically available.

Whois databases are official databases used to determine domain name registrants' information via a TCP-based query/response protocol. Given a target's domain name, one can simply get all the information using InterNIC at www.internic.net/whois.html. Table 1 is the partial result of searching the domain name of rit.edu from InterNIC.

The information revealed through this search includes the organization administrator's name, phone number, email, the organization's address, and also the Domain Name Server (DNS) IP ad-

Figure 1. Sam Spade features

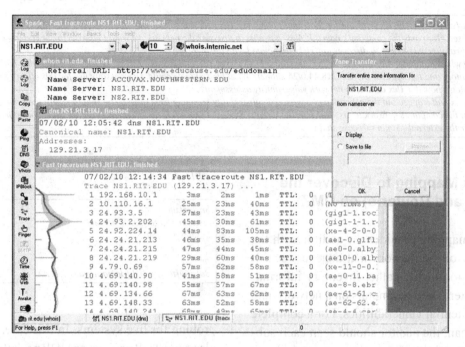

dresses. When this information falls into a hacker's hand, the employee's name can be used potentially for a social engineering attack, the phone number is valuable information for a war-dialing attack, and the address reveals the physical location for a war-driving exercise, dumpster-diving or even a physical break-in. Since a DNS server contains records of mapping between systems' human-friendly names and their IP addresses, if the DNS is not configured appropriately, systems IP addresses and names will be uncovered via a zone transfer attack (covered in the next section).

Sam Spade: An Automated Reconnaissance Tool

Sam Spade (Atkins S., 2010) is a free general-purpose network utility package for Windows systems with features for both reconnaissance and network mapping purposes.

Figure 1 shows Sam Spade's search result for *rit.edu* as well as other network exploit features (covered in next section) such as *zone transfer*, *DNS query*, *traceroute*, *ping*, etc.

If a targeted network cannot survive some of these reconnaissance exercises, an attacker at this point may have already acquired access to the inside of the network. In most scenarios, by then the attacker will have at least gained the information about the company's website, location, IP address ranges, as well as the IP addresses of the DNS name servers.

We start our case study (Table 2) assuming the only available information is the target's name. Various techniques for network mapping, port scanning, and vulnerability assessment are introduced and demonstrated throughout the case study.

Given the IP address range or DNS name server's IP address, will the network survive further scanning to discover devices on a network and exploiting vulnerabilities for intrusion?

Table 2. Case study

> *Alex was hired as an assistant security auditor for a small company. His task was to map out the company's network to find out what a hacker could see given only the company's name. If Alex was able to discover the network, he would move to the next step - conducting a network vulnerability assessment to discover any risks associated with this network.*
>
> *By searching whois database, Alex discovered the company's DNS server's IP address as 123.218.44.100. Was Alex able to develop a network inventory and topology for the 123.218.44.0/24 subnet? What kind of tools could Alex possibly use for this effort? Knowing the network topology, how did Alex conduct a network vulnerability assessment?*
>
> *Note: After Alex had mapped out the network and conducted vulnerability scanning from outside, he should repeat the same exercises from inside of the company's network to discover internal threats. Since the procedure and techniques are the same for both directions, we only cover the external scan in this case study.*

Network Mapping to Discover the Servers and Router(s) on DMZ

Network mapping provides the auditor with the same view of the network that attackers see. It also helps to quickly gather inventory information of systems and perimeters on a network and identify potential vulnerabilities. For a complete network scan, the auditor should scan each subnet, one at a time. There are many techniques to identify live hosts. The most efficient way to get this information is by exploiting a DNS zone transfer vulnerability. DNS contains IP-hostname mapping information that can only be accessed from authorized servers. If the DNS name server is not configured correctly to restrict this sensitive information to only authorized servers, the DNS name server has a zone transfer vulnerability. If the name server discovered during reconnaissance has this vulnerability, it will reveal all the IP-hostname information upon receiving a zone transfer request resulting in a loss of confidentiality.

Both *nslookup* and *dig*, the primary diagnostic tools for querying the Domain Name Service information, can be used to exploit the zone transfer vulnerability. The syntax for using both these tools is given in Tables 3 and 4.

Besides using DNS zone transfer, the common technique used to identify live hosts is sending ICMP packets to the target, for example, *ping target-IP* or *nmap –sP targetIP*. If any responses from the target returns, it means that the target machine exists. However, the target may block incoming ICMP messages to prevent outside

Table 3.

```
$nslookup
>server [target_DNS_server]
> set type=any
> ls –d [target_domain]
or
$dig @[target_IP] [domain_name] –t AXFR
```

probing for live systems. In this case, one could also send TCP packets or UDP packets to certain known services or ports and wait for the services responses from live hosts.

Knowing the live systems, the next step is to find out their operating system types and how these live systems are connected through routers.

The primary technique to map a network is *traceroute*, a program that shows the number of hops between a source system to its destination as well as the list of intermediate routers that connect two systems. *Traceroute* helps people to understand how systems are connected to each other, and also reveals how the target system is connected.

To understand how *traceroute* works, one must first understand the "time-to-live" (TTL) field of an IP packet, an integer value. When a packet passes through a router, the router determines the next hop and also decrements the TTL value by one; if the value of TTL>0, the router forwards the packet to the next hop. If TTL = 0, the router discards the packet and sends an *ICMP time exceeded* packet to the sender. As a result, the packet will not be forwarded to the next hop, either because TTL reaches 0 or the packet reaches

Table 4. Case study continued

Knowing the DNS name sever of 123.218.44.100, Alex used nslookup from his machine in 12.1.1.0/24 subnet to find the company's domain name of lemon.corp
[root@localhost root]# nslookup
> server 123.218.44.100
Default server: 123.218.44.100
Address: 123.218.44.100#53
> 123.218.44.100
Server: 123.218.44.100
Address: 123.218.44.100#53
100.44.218.123.in-addr.arpa name = dmz-earth.lemon.corp.
Then dig is used for testing whether this name server has zone transfer vulnerability.
[root@localhost root]# dig @123.218.44.100 -t axfr lemon.corp any
; some results are omitted.
dmz-earth.lemon.corp. 3600 IN A 123.218.44.100
dmz-fire.lemon.corp. 3600 IN A 123.218.44.101
dmz-water.lemon.corp. 0 IN A 123.218.44.103
dmz-wind.lemon.corp. 3600 IN A 123.218.44.102
; some results are omitted.
Alex found four live systems, 123.218.44.100-103, along with their full names with nslookup and dig.

---

the destination. *Traceroute* works by incrementing the "time-to-live" (TTL) value of consecutive packets by 1 with initial TTL value of 1. Since the first round of packets sent have TTL=1, so they will only reach the first router. The second round of packets set have TTL=2, they will reach the second router and so on until the packets hit the destination or TTL exceeded a threshold value, which means that the destination is unreachable.

OS fingerprinting is the process of determining what operating system is running on a detected live system. Based on the known responses from different operating systems, OS fingerprinting tools are able to predict the type of the OS on the target device. Two types of fingerprinting tools are commonly used – active OS fingerprinting and passive OS fingerprint tools.

Active OS fingerprinting tools, such as *nmap* (nmap, 2010) and *xprobe2* (xprobe2, 2010), actively send a number of probing packets and analyze the responses of these packages. *Nmap*, when the fingerprinting argument (-O) is set, always sends out a fixed number of pre-defined crafted packets in a fixed order. It then detects the OS type based on the responses to these probe packets. *Xprobe2*, on the other hand, sends out some packets, relying on fuzzy signature matching and probabilistic

guesses to draw a conclusion, or sends out more crafted packets for further probing. While both tools have their own strengths and weaknesses, an auditor usually uses multiple tools in order to reduce false positives and false negatives.

Passive fingerprinting tools such as *P0f* (Zalewski, 2010) only sniff packets from the network and make OS identifications based on differences of the TCP implementations. *P0f* analyzes TCP packets such as *SYN, SYN/ACK, RST, Stray ACK*, etc, to match the signatures predefined in its fingerprinting database for a specific OS type.

Passive OS identification has recently caught the interest of researchers due to its stealthy nature and the fact that it does not inject any traffic into the network.

Some automated tools combine both OS fingerprinting and network mapping techniques. *Cheops-ng* (cheops-ng, 2010) is a free tool that can not only draw a network diagram, but also support remote operating system identification. *Nmap* is also capable of identifying live hosts, showing the network diagram (fe3d, 2010) and performing OS fingerprinting.

Figure 3 illustrates the network topology that was determined by Cheops-ng. Obviously, the Cisco router had two interfaces, 123.218.44.1 and 12.1.1.1.

Table 5. Case study continued: Network mapping

To continue to exploit the systems and network, Alex used nmap to ping (-sP) the subnet of 123.218.44.0/24 to identify live systems on this subnet. The result is consistent with the zone transfer result. Obviously, the targeted company did not block ICMP incoming messages.
[root@localhost root]# nmap -sP -v -n 123.218.44.0/24
Host 123.218.44.1 appears to be up.
Host 123.218.44.100 appears to be up.
Host 123.218.44.101 appears to be up.
Host 123.218.44.102 appears to be up.
Host 123.218.44.103 appears to be up.
Read data files from: /usr/share/nmap
Nmap done at Wed Mar 23 12:54:41 2010 -- 256 IP addresses (5 hosts up) scanned in 22.26 seconds
Next, Alex tried traceroute from the source, his machine resided in 12.1.1.0/24, to the destination, 123.218.44.100. The result shows that one router routes the traffic between 12.1.1.0/24subnetand123.210.44.0/24 subnet. Alex found out from this test that the target does not filter ICMP Time Exceeded messages. As a result, this network was exposed to network topology mapping.
[root@localhost root]# traceroute -I 123.218.44.100
traceroute to 123.218.44.100 (123.218.44.100), 30 hops max, 40 byte packets
1 (12.1.1.1) 1.478 ms 1.224 ms 1.204 ms
2 (123.218.44.100) 2.783 ms 2.852 ms 2.809 ms
Both the command line nmap and GUI based nmap -- ZenMap were used to identify live systems' operating system types.
Alex ran nmap –sT –O 123.218.44.1 to identify its OS type.
[root@localhost root]# nmap –sT –O 123.218.4.1
... ...
Device type: firewall\storage-misc\VoIP phone\general purpose\WAP\specialized
Running Fortinet embedded, Linksys Linux 2.4.X, Netgear embedded, Secure Computing Linux 2.4.X, Adaptec embedded, Linux 2.4.X\2.6.X, Netgear Linux 2.4.X, VMware ESX Server 3.0.X
... ...
Based on nmap's result, Alex predicted that 123.218.44.1 was an interface of a router.
Figure 2shows live hosts as well as their OS types by running ZenMap, which was launched from Alex's machine with the target to be set to 123.218.44.0/24. ZenMap predicted 123.210.44.100 was running FreeBSD version 6.2-RELEASE, both 123.218.44.101 and .103 were Windows Systems, and 123.218.44.102 was a Linux system.

Figure 2. ZenMap showing live hosts and OS fingerprinting

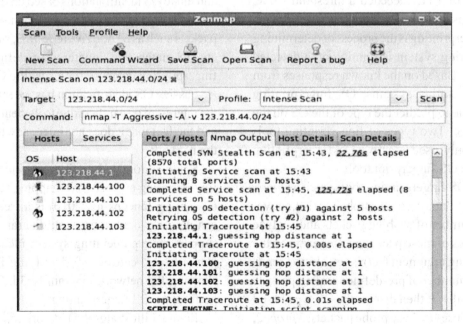

Table 6. Case study continued: Network mapping

Alex also performed an Xprobe2 scan to verify nmap's results. The xprobe2 result for 123.218.44.101 was shown below. Xprobe2 detected this system to be a Windows system, but was not so sure about the type of the system. The rest of the xprobe2 results is also included in Table 81.

[root@localhost root]# xprobe2 123.218.44.101
[+] Primary guess:
[+] Host 123.218.44.101 Running OS: "Microsoft Windows 2003 Server Enterprise Edition"
(Guess probability: 91%)
[+] Other guesses:
[+] Host 123.218.44.101 Running OS: "Microsoft Windows 2000 Workstation SP1" (Guess
probability: 91%)
[+] Host 123.218.44.101 Running OS: "Microsoft Windows NT 4 Server Service Pack 4"
(Guess probability: 91%)

P0f, the passive fingerprinting tool was also launched to determine the OS types relying on monitoring traffic from/to 123.218.44.0/24 subnet. '-A' option uses SYN+ACK to determine the OS types. Note that Alex's machine could be plugged in 123.218.44.0/24 to match traffic involved with these four live systems, or in other subnets that have traffic to/from 123.218.44.0/24 subnet. P0f was able to detect OS types for three live systems, but could not predict system 123.218.44.102's type. Table 8 below showed the detailed result from p0f.

[root@localhost root]# p0f –A
… … ….
<Fri Apr 10 00:10:25 2010> 123.218.44.100:21 – FreeBSD 5.0
-> 12.1.1.2:60090 (distance 1, link: Ethernet/modem)
… … … ..
<Fri Apr 10 00:10:27 2010> 123.218.44.101:80 – Windows XP SP1
-> 12.1.1.2:43002 (distance 1, link: Ethernet/modem)
<Fri Apr 10 00:10:27 2010> 123.218.44.101:3389 – Windows XP SP1
-> 12.1.1.2:54394 (distance 1, link: Ethernet/modem)
<Fri Apr 10 00:10:27 2010> 123.218.44.101:443 – Windows XP SP1
… … … ..

Next, the automated tool, cheops-ng, was launched to map out the entire network. Alex started cheops-agent& in his terminal window running as a background process, he then launched cheops-client and set the viewspace to 123.218.44.0/24.

Table 7. Case study continued: Network mapping

At this point, Alex used p0f, cheops-ng, nmap and xprobe2 for operating system fingerprinting. Below is the comparison of the results using each one. Due to potential false positives and false negatives, the auditor must NOT rely on only one tool to draw a conclusion.

Identifying Vulnerable Services through Port Scanning and Vulnerability Assessment

Knowing the network topology, specifically the live systems and routers, a hacker's next step is to knock on each device in an attempt to learn the purpose of each system and search for weaknesses to allow him/her to enter the system and network. Since every open port is a potential doorway for malicious attacks, the auditor should first identify all open ports, then thoroughly study the purpose of each open port against the organization's policy for open-port and best practices, and ensure that they are necessary to the business. The network administration should always be aware of the open port list and quarantine the corresponding services.

Port Scanning Tools

Among all the available commercial and free port scanning tools, *nmap* is the most popular one aside from its other uses such as identifying live hosts and OS fingerprinting mentioned in the previous section. *Nmap* was originally written by network security expert Gordon Lyon (also by his pseudonym Fyodor Vaskovish). It runs on Linux, Windows and some varieties of UNIX.

To accomplish the goal of identifying open ports, *nmap* sends specially crafted packets to

Table 8. Operating system fingerprinting using multiple tools

Device/IP	Operating System Fingerprinting			
	P0f	**Cheops-ng**	**Nmap**	**Xprobe2**
Router interface 1 **12.1.1.1**	No information	Cisco Aironet 1100 or 1242G WAP (IOS 12.3 - 12.4)	Cisco CatOS, Cisco IOS 11.X|12.X	
Router interface 2 123.218.44.1	No Information	No Information	Embedded Linux OS fromNetgear, Linksys VMware ESX	Foundry Networks Iron-Ware Version 3.0.01eTc1 Linux Kernel 2.4.X
System 1 123.218.44.100	FreeBSD 5.0	FreeBSD 6.1-RELEASE - 6.2-RELEASE	FreeBSD 6.1-RELEASE - 6.2-RELEASE	FreeBSD 4.6 FreeBSD 5.X/4.X
System 2 123.218.44.101	Microsoft Windows XP SP1	Microsoft Windows XP SP1	Microsoft Windows 2000 SP0/SP1/SP2 or Windows XP SP1	Microsoft Windows 2000 Workstation Microsoft Windows NT 4 Workstation
System 3 123.218.44.102	UNKNOWN	Linux 2.6.9 - 2.6.21	Linux 2.6.9 - 2.6.21	Linux 2.4.29 Linux 2.4.21-2.4.24
System 4 123.218.44.103	Microsoft Windows XP SP1	Microsoft Windows Server 2003 SP1 or SP2	Microsoft Windows Server 2003 SP1 or SP2	Microsoft Windows Server 2003 Microsoft Windows Server 2000 SP2

Figure 3. Network topology determined by cheops-ng

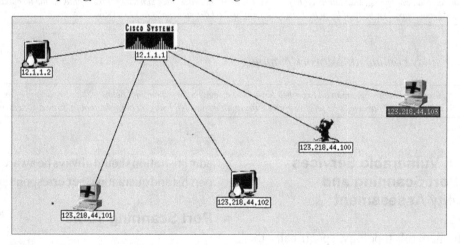

the target host to interact with each port and then analyzes the responses. For example, according to TCP protocol specification, if one sends a TCP packet to a closed port, a RESET packet or an ICMP Port Unreachable packet will be returned. If a TCP port is open, a TCP three-way handshake will follow. If a crafted User Datagram Protocol (UDP) packet is sent, since UDP is a connectionless protocol that provides no guarantees for delivery,

the receiver may not send an acknowledgement back even thought it successfully receives packets. As a result, the sender will not receive any responses from the target for a successful delivery to an existing port. If the target returns an ICMP port unreachable, that means the port is closed. Therefore, UDP scans help to identify closed ports. If no UDP responses return from the target, it could mean that the port is open, a firewall filtered out

Table 9. Case study continued: Port scanning

In previous scans, Alex found 4 live systems, 123.218.44.100-103, in the target network. Here Alex tried nmap to find all open ports for these four systems.
[root@localhost root]# nmap -sS -sV -O -T5 -v --reason 123.218.44.100-103
where -sS specifies TCP SYN scan; -sV specifies version scan detecting version number of the service; -O specifies OS fingerprinting; -T5 sets scan timing to be aggressive; -v is verbosity; --reason shows the reason a port is in a particular state.
Here was the result for scanning 123.218.44.100 with information of all detected open and closed ports, correspondent services and version number (if nmap can determine), and OS type.
 # Nmap 4.68 scan initiated Mar 23 20:54:41 2010 as: nmap -sS -sV -O -T5 -v --reason 123.218.44.100-103
#... ... ...skip some results... ... ...
Interesting ports on 123.218.44.100:
Not shown: 1823 filtered ports
Reason: 1803 no-responses and 20 admin-prohibited
PORT STATE SERVICE REASON VERSION
20/tcp closed ftp-data reset
21/tcp open ftp? syn-ack
53/tcp open domain syn-ack ISC BIND 9.3.2
113/tcp closed auth reset
Device type: general purpose
Running: FreeBSD 6.X
OS details: FreeBSD 6.1-RELEASE - 6.2-RELEASE
#... ... ...skip some results... ... ...
ZenMap provides a nice GUI front-end to nmap. The use of color and a graphical layout makes the data gathered in an nmap scan much easier to read. Alex also used ZenMap for the port scan as illustrated inFigure 4. He simply typed in the target systems and chose a Profile of Operating System Detection, which will not only run port scan, but also detect OS type. The command is interpreted by ZenMap and shown on the GUI. However, it could be modified to add in more arguments if a user chooses to.

Figure 4. ZenMap showing live system, Operating Systems, and open ports

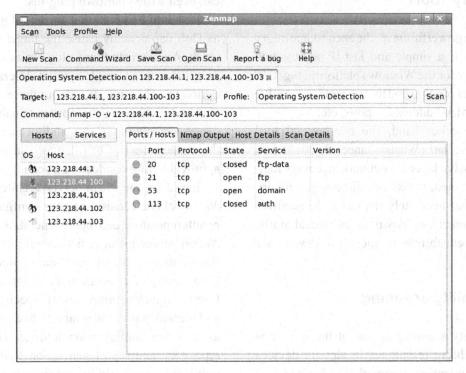

the response, a packet is lost, or a closed port's response has not returned. In this case, further probing is required.

Nmap supports many types of scanning including ping sweeping (-sP), UDP Scanning (-sU), various TCP scanning (-sT, -sS, -sF, -sX –sN, -sA), FTP bounce scans (-b), Idle Scanning (-sI), and many more (McClure, Scambray & Kurz, 2009; Skoudis & Liston, 2006).

It is important to note that the timing of sending packets is crucial for the scanning process. An attacker might send packets very slowly to a target in a stealthy way to prevent detection. Alternatively, an attack might aggressively send packets that could potentially flood or even crash the target system. *Nmap* supports different timing options such as paranoid, sneaky, polite, normal, aggressive and insane from the slowest to the highest speeds.

Other Port Scanning and Network Discovery Tools

Besides the powerful *nmap*, the open source *angry IP scanner* is a simple and fast IP address and port scanner for the Windows platform. *Angry IP scanner* uses pings to find live systems and resolve hostname MAC addresses, ports, etc.

On the other hand, the commercial tool *WhatsConnected* (WhatsConnected, 2010) is a comprehensive layer 2/3 network discovery tool. Its features include network discovery, network mapping that accurately depicts and visualizes device connectivity down to individual ports, and search capabilities to query how devices are connected.

Vulnerability Scanning

Vulnerability scanning is one of the most important auditing techniques to identify devices on the organization's network that have known vulnerabilities, so that these weaknesses can be

fixed to prevent the bad guys from exploiting them against these devices. Various vulnerability-scanning tools are available to not only identify the vulnerabilities, but also provide recommendations to fix them. Among all the available tools, *Nessus* (Nessus, 2010) is the most comprehensive free vulnerability-scanning tool.

Nessus is often used to remotely scan specified systems and subnets searching for known vulnerabilities. It actively sends out vulnerability checks to the target and analyzes the responses received. The vulnerability checks/attacks are based on small programs, called plug-ins, written in C or *Nessus Attack-Scripting Language (NASL)*. For example, backdoor plug-ins check for signs of backdoors installed on the target system and remotely controlled by a hacker. DoS plug-ins look for vulnerable services that could be crashed or halted under DoS attacks. When a new vulnerability is out, a new plug-in will be developed to load into the *Nessus* vulnerability database. You can even write your own plug-ins!

It should be noted that certain plug-ins such as DoS can actually cause the target system to crash. *Nessus* lists these plug-ins as dangerous plug-ins with a triangle symbol. Users have the option to only run tests without these dangerous checks by choosing the option "Enable all but dangerous plug-ins." An auditor must inform the management of this danger and get written approval before conducting a scan.

Based on the client-server architecture, the *Nessus* client consists of user configuration, a results repository, and report generation, while the *Nessus* server includes a vulnerability database that contains a list of up-to-date vulnerabilities for a variety of systems, and a scanning engine. User configuration allows user to specify the target and identify which vulnerability to check as well as the other configuration settings. The results repository and report generation tool generate vulnerable reports with recommendations for remedial actions. The scanning engine, the key

Table 10. Case study continued: Vulnerability assessment using Nessus

> *After discovering the target network topology, live systems, and identifying the services running on each system, Alex used Nessus to look for vulnerable services that allows an attacker to gain access to the systems and network.*
> *Alex started the Nessus daemon followed by the Nessus client. Alex also ran nessus-update-plugins to make sure that all plug-ins are up to date including latest vulnerabilities checks. Then Alex setup targets of 123.218.44.100-103 in Target selection, leaving other configuration value as default and started a scan. The Nessus result is organized based on subnet, host and port. In this case study, vulnerabilities are collected for each live host and depicted inFigure 5.*

Figure 5. Nessus report for the case study

Table 11. Case study continued: Vulnerability assessment using Nessus

> *Clicking on the system, 123.218.44.101, you will see the number of open port and the vulnerabilities from this system, sorted according to their severities as illustrated inFigure 6.*

Figure 6. Nessus vulnerability report for host 123.218.44.101

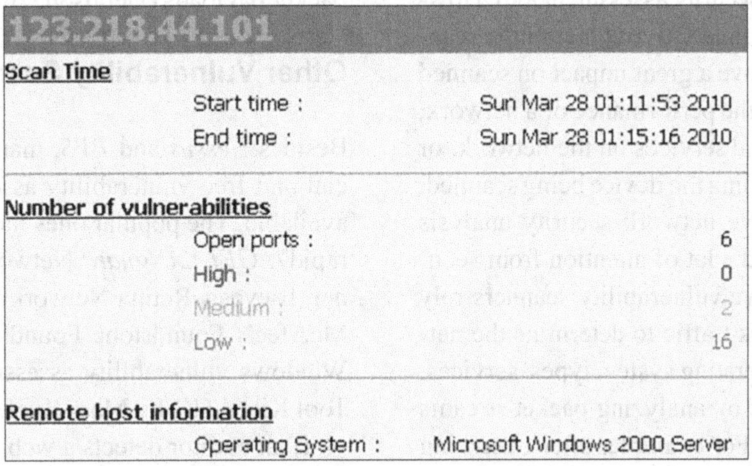

component of the *Nessus* server, crafts packets based on user inputs and the database, and sends them to the target to determine vulnerabilities.

Nessus also includes a great reporting tool that allows users to quickly review and analyze the list of vulnerabilities. Each vulnerability is labeled with a unique *Nessus* plug-in ID that links to the plug-in and the vulnerability description, and each finding is color-coded so that users can prioritize the problems and focus first on the highest server problems found, which are shown in red. Finally, solutions and security advisories with external links are also provided to help users to fix the problems.

Table 12. Case study continued: Vulnerability assessment using Nessus

If you further study the vulnerabilities, one of the Medium vulnerabilities is Microsoft Windows Remote Desktop Protocol Server Private Key Disclosure Vulnerability. ***Synopsis:*** *It may be possible to get access to the remote host.* ***Description:*** *The remote version of Remote Desktop Protocol Server (Terminal Service) is vulnerable to a man in the middle attack.* *An attacker may exploit this flaw to decrypt communications between client and server and obtain sensitive information (passwords, ...).* ***Solution:*** *Force the use of SSL as a transport layer for this service.* *See also:* http://www.oxid.it/downloads/rdp-gbu.pdf http://www.nessus.org/u?c544b1fa ***Risk factor:*** *Medium / CVSS Base Score: 6* *(AV:R/AC:H/Au:NR/C:P/A:P/I:P/B:N)* *CVE: CVE-2005-1794* *BID: 13818* *Other references: OSVDB:17131* **Nessus ID: 18405**

Passive Vulnerability Scanning

There is no doubt that *Nessus* is a powerful and effective network security assessment tool. However, as an intrusive and active vulnerability scanner, *Nessus* may have a great impact on scanned devices: affecting the performance of a network, disturbing hosts and services on the network, or even possibly crashing the device being scanned. As a result, passive network security analysis recently has gained a lot of attention from security experts. Passive vulnerability scanners rely on sniffing network traffic to determine the network topology, operating system types, services, and vulnerabilities by analyzing packet streams (Deraison, 2009). For example, after observing a SYN-ACK packet to/from TCP port 25 of one of the monitored devices, the passive scanner can determine that the device hosts a Simple Mail Transfer Protocol (SMTP) service.

Passive Vulnerability Scanner (PVS, 2010) is a commercial tool from Tenable Network. It passively monitors network traffic in real-time without sending any probing traffic. It uses its own plug-ins with a plug-in language that includes multiple regular expression styles of pattern matching to recognize vulnerable service banners and to match vulnerability signatures from the packet payloads (Deraison, 2009).

Other Vulnerability Scanning Tools

Besides *Nessus* and *PVS*, many other commercial and free vulnerability assessment tools are available. The popular ones include *NeXpose* by rapid7, *GFI LANguard* Network security Scanner, E-eyes's Retina Network Security Scanner, McAfee's Foundstone Foundscan, and the free Windows vulnerability assessment tool, Attack Tool Kit (ATK) by Marc Ruef.

If an auditor detects a web server on the network, additional web vulnerability scanning tools such as IBM's *AppScan*, Cenzic *Hailstorm*, *Nikto*, and *WebScarab* should be used. These tools are designed particularly for web server scanning to identify various common Web vulnerabilities such as SQL injection, remote code execution, broken authentication, cross site scripting, invalidated input, buffer overflow, etc.

Table 13. Case study continued: Web vulnerability assessment using Nikto

Alex detected 123.218.44.101 had port 80 open. Alex used Nikto, an open source web server scanner to perform a comprehensive test against the web server. Nikto determined that the server was running MS IIS 5.0 web server and has the following vulnerabilities:
HTTP methods allowed:
TRACE which could be used for fingerprinting the web server
DELETE which could be used for removing files from the web server
PUT which allowed clients to save files on the web server
PROPFIND/PROPPATCH that revealed WebDAV was installed with potential WebDAV vulnerabilities exist.
SEARCH that could be used to search directory listing
Also the IIS 5.0 was outdated and the TARCE method made the server vulnerable to cross site scripting and credential theft.

Figure 7. Nikto partial results for 123.218.44.101

```
- ------------------------------------------------------------------
- Nikto 1.36/1.37      -      www.cirt.net
+ Target IP:        123.218.44.101
+ Target Hostname:  123.218.44.101
+ Target Port:      80
+ Start Time:       Wed Apr  7 17:54:46 2010
- ------------------------------------------------------------------
- Scan is dependent on "Server" string which can be faked, use -g to override
+ Server: Microsoft-IIS/5.0
- Retrieved X-Powered-By header: ASP.NET
+ Allowed HTTP Methods: OPTIONS, TRACE, GET, HEAD, COPY, PROPFIND, SEARCH, LOCK, UNLOCK
+ HTTP method ('Allow' Header): 'TRACE' is typically only used for debugging--it should be disabled. Note, this does not mean
 the server is vulnerable to XST. OSVDB-877.
+ HTTP method ('Allow' Header): 'PROPFIND' may indicate DAV/WebDAV is installed. This may be used to get directory listings i
f indexing is allowed but a default page exists. OSVDB-13431.
+ HTTP method ('Allow' Header): 'SEARCH' may be used to get directory listings if Index Server is running. OSVDB-425.
+ Public HTTP Methods: OPTIONS, TRACE, GET, HEAD, DELETE, PUT, POST, COPY, MOVE, MKCOL, PROPFIND, PROPPATCH, LOCK, UNLOCK, SE
ARCH
+ HTTP method ('Public' Header): 'TRACE' is typically only used for debugging--it should be disabled. Note, this does not mea
n the server is vulnerable to XST. OSVDB-877.
+ HTTP method ('Public' Header): 'DELETE' may allow clients to remove files on the web server.
+ HTTP method ('Public' Header): 'PUT' method may allow clients to save files on the web server.
+ HTTP method ('Public' Header): 'PROPFIND' may indicate DAV/WebDAV is installed. This may be used to get directory listings
if indexing is allowed but a default page exists. OSVDB-13431.
+ HTTP method ('Public' Header): 'PROPPATCH' may indicate DAV/WebDAV is installed.
+ HTTP method ('Public' Header): 'SEARCH' may be used to get directory listings if Index Server is running. OSVDB-425.
+ Microsoft-IIS/5.0 appears to be outdated (4.0 for NT 4, 5.0 for Win2k)
+ / - Appears to be a default IIS install. (GET)
+ / - TRACE option appears to allow XSS or credential theft. See http://www.cgisecurity.com/whitehat-mirror/WhitePaper_screen
.pdf for details (TRACE)
+ / - TRACK option ('TRACE' alias) appears to allow XSS or credential theft. See http://www.cgisecurity.com/whitehat-mirror/W
hitePaper_screen.pdf for details (TRACK)
```

NETWORK SNIFFING AND ANALYSIS

Network sniffing and analysis is an important step in network auditing to detect internal and external attacks. *Wireshark*, *tcpdump*, and *WinDump* are the most popular sniffing and analysis tools used by auditors in a hub connected network environment or via a mirror port from a switched network. These tools are capable of capturing all the traffic sources or destinations in the same subnet using the *libpcap/WinPcap* library. They use the same syntax to filter specific traffic based on IP addresses, MAC address, ports and protocols.

ngrep

ngrep (ngrep, 2010) is another useful network sniffing and inspection tool. Similar to the tools mentioned above, it uses the *pcap* library to capture packets. However, *ngrep* allows users to specify extended regular or hexadecimal expressions for matching against payloads of packets at the network layer. *ngrep* displays only the information that matches the specified regular expression within a packet. The information *ngrep* prints can be specified through its augments. It is important to note that *ngrep* is only capable of capturing clear-text content. As a result, if data encryption

Table 14. Case study continued: Network traffic inspection using ngrep

---

Alex plugs in his machine to 123.218.44.0 subnet with interface of eth0, set 123.218.44.100 as its DNS.
*Alex ran**ngrep -d eth0 port 53***to monitor network interfaces eth0 (-d eth0) for the activities crossing source or destination port 53 (DNS).*
When 123.218.44.101 made a DNS request for resolving IP address of cnn.com, the following result was printed by ngrep:
Interface: eth0 (123.218.44.2/255.255.255.0)
filter: (ip or ip6) and (port 53)
#
U 123.218.44.101:46470 -> 123.218.44.100:53
.F1...........cnn.com.....
#
U 123.218.44.100:53 -> 123.218.44.101:46470
.F1............cnn.com..
... ...
#
Alex also used ngrep to identify unencrypted sensitive or critical information passing through the subnet of 123.218.44.0 as indicated below.
[root@localhost root]# ngrep -d eth0 'error' port syslog
ngrep first converted service name syslog to its correspondent port number. In UNIX, the configuration file is /etc/services.
Monitoring the network interfaces eth0, ngrep displayed network-based syslog packets containing the word of "error".
[root@localhost root]# ngrep -wi -d eth0 'user|pass' port 21
Monitoring eth0 interface, ngrep displayed traffic crossing source or destination port 21 (FTP) that matches for the words (-w) "user" or "pass" with looking case-insensitively (-i).

---

techniques were in use, *ngrep* would fail to match the encrypted patterns from packets.

NetworkMiner

All the tools covered above are great packet sniffing tools that are capable of effectively capturing all the traffic and storing the traffic to a *pcap* file which can be processed later. However, they have a limited capability to perform comprehensive analyses on the captured data. *NetworkMiner* (Hjelmvik, 2010), developed by Erik Hjelmvik, is an open-source passive network forensic analysis tool. Besides performing live sniffing of network traffic, *NetworkMiner* is primarily used to perform comprehensive offline analyses based on the captured *pcap* file(s). This tool groups all the traffic as incoming and outgoing sessions under each host (host centric) in the network. Based on the captured traffic, it interprets each host's hostname and its operating system and gathers detailed information such as server banners, open ports, and the domain name under each node.

By monitoring the network traffic to and from each system on the network, one can not only identify systems' abnormal behaviors to detect compromised nodes, but also examine whether sensitive data is passing through the network without one's knowledge.

Network and System Logging and Analysis

Network and system logs provide valuable information to troubleshoot hardware and software problems, trace events occurred on a server and network, and identify unauthorized access and break-ins. However, logging may not be automatically turned on and the log files may not be analyzed and archived appropriately. Therefore, an auditor should verify that sufficient logs are enabled and configured, log management and policies are in place for analyzing and consolidating the logs when the logs are full, and the log entries are consistent without signs of deletion and modification.

Table 15.

```
#Configure the Cisco router to enable logging and send message to a specified syslog server
conf t #configure terminal
logging IP_address_of_syslog_server #Provide the ip address of the syslog server
logging trap level #limit what messages are sent to the syslog server, emergencies, alert, etc.
logging facility local7 # use local7 as a facility
logging on #enable logging
#Configure the syslog server
touch /var/log/cisco #create the log file in /var/log directory
#Adding the following line to /etc/syslog.conf to send Cisco messages to the file /var/log/cisco
local7.level /var/log/cisco
```

Logging in Unix/Linux Systems

Syslog, a comprehensive event logging system, is commonly used in Unix and Linux systems. It consists of three parts, a logging daemon called *syslogd*, library routines to submit messages to syslogd (for example, *openlog* or *syslog*), and a user-level command to submit log entries from a shell. Syslogd collects log information from kernel, system and user processes, and dispatches these messages to appropriate locations either in a local or a remote system based on the configuration file, */etc/syslog.conf*. In Linux, by default, the log files are located in /var/log directory. For example, /var/log/messages contains general messages including authentication failure, hardware and configuration issues, and system booting and shutdown information.

The basic syntax for /etc/syslog.conf is:

Facility(s).level action

where *facility* identifies the source of a message, for example, *kern, user, mail, local0* through *local7*, etc. *Level* implies the urgency and severity level of the message, for example, *emerg, alert, crit, error, warning, notice, info*, and *debug* in the order of importance. Levels also indicate the minimum importance that a message must have in order to be logged. Action specifies where the message should be forwarded, for example, to a file in local machine or to the *syslogd* of a remote system.

The line "*mail.alert /var/log/mailalerts*" tells *syslogd* to send any mail alert and emergency message to the file */var/log/mailalerts*.

The line "*kern.* * *@129.21.3.41*" would allow *syslogd* to send all kernel messages to *syslogd* of a remote system with IP address of 129.21.3.41.

The common practices for maintaining logs include:

- Periodically compress and archive logs to tapes or other permanent media
- Keep logs for a certain period of time before deletion by rotating the log files. Various utility programs/scripts exist in Unix and Linux to rotate the log files so that only the oldest log file will be deleted in every rotation period.

When the rotation method is chosen for maintaining logs, one should be aware that an attacker could purposefully inject many bogus log entries to erase his/her malicious activities from the logs via rotation.

Logging in Cisco Router

By default, a Cisco router logs anything at the level of debugging and above, and sends them to its console. However, one can configure the router to send logs to an internal buffer or an external *syslog* server. The following example shows the steps to send the log messages to an external Linux server:

Table 16.

Here is one example of the outline of an audit report. Cover page includes Title, date, To, Attn, From, subject
TABLE OF CONTENTS
EXECUTIVE SUMMARY
INTRODUCTION
Background
Scope & Objectives
NOTABLE STRENGTHS
AREAS FOR IMPROVEMENT
Section 1 Primary Findings
Finding 1 xxxxxxxxx
Recommendation 1
Recommendation 2
......
Ramifications/implications (if any)
Finding 2 xxxxxxxxx
Recommendation 1
Recommendation 2
......
Ramifications/implications (if any)
Section 2 Other Findings
Finding 1 xxxxxxxxx
Recommendation 1
Recommendation 2
......
Ramifications/implications (if any)
Finding 2 xxxxxxxxx
Recommendation 1
Recommendation 2
......
Ramifications/implications (if any)
AUDITEE RESPONSES
EXHIBITS/ APPENDIX

Logging in Windows Systems

Windows Log Service includes the application log, system log and security log in *Windows Event Viewer*. The application log logs events selected by applications and programs while the system log contains events such as driver failures and hardware issues that are logged by system components. Therefore, users cannot decide what entries to be logged in application and system logs. The security log, the most important log for auditing, records valid and invalid logon attempts as well as activities such as creating, opening/closing, or deleting files or other objects. Windows Event Log service automatically starts when the system

starts. However, Security logging is, by default, turned off. It is the administrator's responsibility to specify which events are logged in the security log.

To ensure windows log system is configured correctly, an auditor should verify the following:

- Sufficient events are logged in security log
  ○ Security log should at least include events of *failed logons, changes to security settings,* and *access to critical files.*
- Parameters in Event Viewer are configured correctly according to corporation's policy
  ○ Logfile's location and permission
  ○ Maximum size of the log file
  ○ The method to wrap and archive the configuration file when its maximum log size reaches.

As the goal of performing an audit is to identify vulnerabilities so that an organization can address these issues, e.g., by applying patches or updates to mitigate the threats, the final stage of an audit is to write an audit report.

Auditing Report

The audit report is a formal report written by an auditor to provide the user with an assessment of a network and its host systems including recommendations to fix any problems discovered (Audit Report Sample, 2010). The audit report usually includes the areas in which the organization performed well and the areas in which it failed to meet the criteria, why they are potential risks, what the impact of the failure could be, why they fail, and how to correct them.

The executive summary provides the auditor's perspective and highlights of major findings discovered through the audit. It also includes the auditor's recommendations in brief. As a sum-

Table 17. Case study continued: Alex's audit report

Note that this report is for illustrative purposes only and is not a complete audit report.
<u>A Segment of EXECUTIVE SUMMARY</u>
This exercise was to find out how much information that can be readily obtained by auditors or attackers using common network and security assessment tools starting with no existing prior knowledge of the topology. Using common tools, the auditor was able to identify active systems on the network along with their operating systems, and depict the network topology that they were resided. In addition, the auditor was able to determine the services on these systems that were publically accessible, some of which were unnecessary, while others were vulnerable and could potentially allow an adversary to gain access and control of the system.
To fix the problems detailed in this report, the auditor recommended taking the following actions: *• Block incoming ICMP messages, except for the hosts that you want the public to ping, to prevent from identifying live systems.* *• Filter ICMP Time Exceeded messages to thwart network mapping* *• Update software and operating systems to the newest possible versions, and patch all the vulnerable services.* *• Disable all unnecessary and dangerous network services and programs.* *• Install Intrusion Detection Systems to monitor traffic internally and externally.* *• Perform system and network security audits regularly.* *The auditor recommended the company to make immediate actions in order to protect the information assets of the organization.*
<u>A Segment of AREAS FOR IMPROVEMENT</u>
Section 1 Primary Findings *Finding 1 Network and systems are exposed to network discovery* *Recommendation 1* *Block incoming ICMP messages, except the hosts that you want the public to ping, to prevent from identifying live systems.* *Recommendation 2* *Filter ICMP Time Exceeded messages to thwart network mapping* *Ramifications/implications (if any)* *Network topology is wide open to outside that allows attacks to exploit your services vulnerabilities and can potentially allow an attacker to gain control over your systems* *Finding 2 The remote version of Remote Desktop Protocol Server (Terminal Service) is* *vulnerable to a man in the middle attack.* *Recommendation 1* *Force to use SSL as a transport layer for this service* *Ramifications/implications (if any)* *An attacker may exploit this flaw to decrypt communications between client and server and obtain sensitive information.*

mary of the audit, the executive summary usually is written at the end.

The scope of the audit covers the purpose and goal of an audit, the standards/regulations used, and the time duration of the audit.

NOTABLE STRENGTHS lists the areas in which the organization performed well.

AREAS FOR IMPROVEMENT is the main body of the report that provides details on specific findings resulting from auditor's tests. The findings presented in each section are prioritized based on the significance of ramifications and implications of each finding. The findings with significant impacts to an organization are listed in the section of *primary findings* while others that are not a high priority to be fixed, but also require attentions are included in *the section of*

other findings. Recommendations for fixing each identified problem are included in both sections.

CONCLUSION

This chapter presents the auditing process and technologies to identify and examine various networking threats and vulnerabilities. The state-of-the-art auditing techniques as well as security solutions for reconnaissance, network discovery, port scanning and vulnerability assessment have been discussed at different phases of network auditing. A case study was created to help demonstrate the auditing process and techniques throughout the chapter.

REFERENCES

Alberts, C., & Dorofee, A. (2003). *Managing information security risks, the OCTAVE approach.* Addison-Wesley.

Atkins, S. (2009). *Sam Spade download.* Retrieved February 30, 2010, from http://www.softpedia.com/get/Network-Tools/Network-Tools-Suites/Sam-Spade.shtml

AUDIT. 507 (2009). *Auditing networks, perimeters, and systems.* Retrieved March 30, 2010, from http://www.sans.org/security-training/auditing-networks-perimeters-systems-6-mid

Audit Report Sample. (2003). *APHIS animal care program – inspection and enforcement activities.* Retrieved May 30, 2010, from www.usda.gov/oig/webdocs/33002-03-SF.pdf

Berman, M. (2009). Virtualization audit 101: The top 5 risks and recommendations for protecting your virtual IT. *Computer Technology Review.*

Buchanan, S., & Forbes Gibb, F. (2007). The information audit: Role and scope. *International Journal of Information Management, 27*(3), 159–172. doi:10.1016/j.ijinfomgt.2007.01.002

Cheops-ng. (n.d.). Retrieved March 30, 2010, from http://cheops-ng.sourceforge.net/

COBIT. (2010). *Official site.* Retrieved March 30, 2010, from http://www.isaca.org/Knowledge-Center/COBIT/Pages/Overview.aspx

Deraison, R., Gula, R., & Hayton, T. (2009). *Passive vulnerability scanning introduction.* Retrieved May 13, 2010, from http://www.nessus.org

Fe3d. (2010). Received March 15, 2010, from http://nmap.org/book/zenmap-topology.html

He, L., & Bode, N. (2005). Network penetration testing. *EC2ND 2005, Proceedings of the First European Conference on Computer Network Defense,* (pp. 3-12). UK.

Hjelmvik, E. (2008). Passive network security analysis with NetworkMiner. *Insecure Magazine, 18,* 18-21. Retrieved May 13, 2010, from http://www.net-security.org/dl/insecure/INSECURE-Mag-18.pdf

ITIL. (2010). *Official site.* Retrieved March 30, 2010, from http://www.itil-officialsite.com/

Kraemer, S., Carayon, P., & Clem, J. (2009). Human and organizational factors in computer and information security: Pathways to vulnerabilities. *Computers & Security, 28,* 509–520. doi:10.1016/j.cose.2009.04.006

Kroeker, K. L. (2009). The evolution of virtualization. *Communications of the ACM, 52*(3). doi:10.1145/1467247.1467253

Lai, Y. P., & Tai, J. H. (2007). Network security improvement with isolation implementation based on ISO-17799 standard. In *Network-based Information Systems* (pp. 69–78). Springer. doi:10.1007/978-3-540-74573-0_8

Longley, D., Branagan, M., Caelli, W. J., & Kwok, L. F. (2008). Feasibility of automated information security compliance auditing. *Proceedings of the IFIP TC 11 23rd International Information Security Conference,* (pp. 493–507).

McClure, S., Scambray, J., & Kurz, G. (2009). *Hacking exposed: Network security secrets and solutions* (6th ed.). New York, NY: McGraw Hill.

Nessus. (n.d.). *Website.* Retrieved March 30, 2010, from http://www.nessus.org/nessus/

NIST-Continuous Monitoring. (2010). *Frequently asked questions.*

NIST SP 800-37. (2010). *Major revisions.* Retrieved July 27, 2010, from www.onpointcorp.com/documents/NIST_SP_800-37.pdf

Nmap. (n.d.). *Website.* Retrieved March 30, 2010, from http://nmap.org/

Ohki, E., Harada, Y., Kawaguchi, S., et al. (2009). Information security governance framework. *WISG '09, Proceedings of the first ACM workshop on Information Security governance*, Chicago, Illinois, USA.

Phan, T., & Yao, D. F. (2009). *SelectAudit: A secure and efficient audit framework for networked virtual environments. Lecture Notes of the Institute for Computer Sciences, Social Informatics and Telecommunications Engineering LNICST 10, Collaborative Computing: Networking*. Applications and Worksharing.

RedSeal. (2010). *FISMA, continuous monitoring and near real-time risk management, complying with the new NIST risk management framework.* Retrieved July 28, 2010, from http://www.redseal. net/documents/RedSeal_and_the_NIST_Risk_ Management_Framework.pdf

SANs Institute. (n.d.). *Website*. Retrieved March 30, 2010, from http://www.sans.org

Sayana, S. A. (2003). Approach to auditing network security. *Information Systems Control Journal, 5*.

Skoudis, E., & Liston, T. (2006). *Counter hack reloaded, a step-by-step guide to computer attacks and effective defenses*. Prentice Hall.

Solms, B. V. (2005). Information security governance: COBIT or ISO 17799 or both? *Computers & Security, 24*, 99–104. doi:10.1016/j. cose.2005.02.002

Telenable Security. (2010). *PVS - Passive Vulnerability Scanner*. Retrieved March 30, 2010, from http://www.tenablesecurity.com/products/pvs/

The Institute of Internal Auditor (IIA). (2005). *Continuous auditing: Implications for assurance, monitoring, and risk assessment*. Retrieved July 25, 2010, from www.acl.com/pdfs/wp_gtag_ may05.pdf

Vasarhelyi, M. A., & Halper, F. B. (1991). The continuous audit of online systems. *Auditing: A Journal of Practice and Theory, 10*(1), 110-125.

Westcott, R. (2007). Maximizing the ROI of a security audit. *Network Security*, (March): 8–11. doi:10.1016/S1353-4858(07)70026-0

WhatsConnected. (n.d.). Retrieved May 15, 2010, from http://www.whatsupgold.com/products/ whatsup-gold-plugins/whatsconnected/index. aspx

Wikipedia. (n.d.). *History of financial audit*. Received May 20, 2010, from http://en.wikipedia. org/wiki/Financial_audit

Wilson, T. (2009). *ITRC report: Malicious attacks increased in first half of 2009*. Retrieved March 23, 2010, from http://www.darkreading. com/insiderthreat/security/privacy/showArticle. jhtml?articleID=218000187

Wright, C., Freedman, B., & Liu, D. (2008). An introduction to network audit. In *The IT regulatory and standards compliance handbook* (pp. 195–227). Syngress. doi:10.1016/B978-1-59749-266-9.00009-6

Xprobe2. (2010). Received March 30, 2010, from http://xprobe.sourceforge.net/

Zalewski, M. (n.d.). *p0f*. Retrieved from http:// lcamtuf.coredump.cx/p0f.shtml

Zhang, J., Fang, D., & Liu, L. (2009). Intelligent content filtering model for network security audit system. *Proceedings of Second International Workshop on Knowledge Discovery and Data Mining*, (pp. 546-548).

ADDITIONAL READING

Andrews, M., & Whittaker, J. (2006). *How to Break Web Software: Functional and Security Testing of Web Applications and Web services*. Addison Wesley.

Angry IP scanner. http://www.soft32.com/download_572.html

Barnett, R. (2006). *Preventing Web Attacks with Apache*. Addison-Wesley.

Forte, D. et al (2009). Security audits in mixed environments. *Network Security, Volume 2009, Issue 3*, pp. 17-19

Forte, D. et al (2009). The importance of log files in security incident prevention. *Network Security, Volume 2009, Issue 7*, pp. 18-20.

Jiang, X. F., Ly, M. V., Taneja, J., Dutta, P., & Culler, D. (2009). Experiences with a high-fidelity wireless building energy auditing network, *SenSys '09: Proceedings of the 7th ACM Conference on Embedded Networked Sensor Systems*.

Kroeker, K. L. (2009). The evolution of virtualization. *Communications of the ACM, 52*(Issue 3), doi:10.1145/1467247.1467253

Lincke, S. J. (2007) Network security auditing as a community-based learning project,

Lu, H. YingjLi, Y. J., Atluri, V. Jaideep Vaidya, J. (2009). An efficient online auditing approach to limit private data disclosure, *EDBT '09: Proceedings of the 12th International Conference on Extending Database Technology: Advances in Database Technology*.

Naous, J., Stutsman, R., Mazieres, D., McKeown, N., & Zeldovich, N. (2009). Delegating network security with more information, *WREN '09: Proceedings of the 1st ACM workshop on Research on enterprise networking*.

Natan, R. (2005). *Implementing Database Security and Auditing*. Elsevier Digital Press.

Pipkin, D. (2002). *Halting the Hacker: a practical guide to computer security* (2nd ed.). NJ: Prentice Hall.

Premaratne, U., Samarabandu, J., Sidhu, T., Beresh, B. & Jian-Cheng Tan (2008). Application of Security Metrics in Auditing Computer Network Security: A Case Study. *Proceedings of 4th International Conference on Information and Automation for Sustainability. ICIAFS 2008*, pp. 200-205

Rehman, R. (2003). *Intrusion Detection with SNORT: Advanced IDS Techniques Using SNORT, Apache, MySQL, PHP, and ACID*. NJ: Prentice Hall.

Router Audit Tool (RAT). Received May 30, 2010, from http://ncat.sourceforge.net/

Schultz, E. Shumway, R.(2002). *Incident Response: A Strategic Guide to Handling System and Network Security Breaches*. New Riders, Boston.

SIGCSE '07: Proceedings of the 38th SIGCSE technical symposium on Computer science education.

The website for Open Web Application Security Project. Received May 30, 2010, from http://www.owasp.org/index.php/Main_Page.

VULNERABILITY ASSESSMENT TOOLS

Cenzic's Hailstorm. http://www.cenzic.com/

E-eyes's Retina Network Security Scanner. www.eeye.com

GFI LANguard Network security Scanner, www.gfi.com/lannetscan

IBM's AppScan. http://www-01.ibm.com/software/awdtools/appscan/

McAfee's Foundstone Foundscan. www.foundstone.cm/products/ondemandservice.htm

NeXpose. http://www.rapid7.com/vulnerability-assessment.jsp

Nikto, http://cirt.net/nikto2

OWASP's WebScarab. http://www.owasp.org/index.php/Category:OWASP_WebScarab_Project

Windows' vulnerability assessment tool, Attack Tool Kit (ATK), www.computec.ch/projekte/atk

Chapter 9
Network Manageability Security

Salvador Mandujano
Intel Corporation, USA

ABSTRACT

As the number of devices connected to computer networks increases, so does the need for algorithms, protocols, and tools to manage these devices and their communications infrastructure. Manageability solutions allow Information Technology administrators to keep control over such resources in order to identify, configure, and repair network devices remotely in a way that reduces desk visits and maximizes service availability for customers. This chapter studies the security and privacy aspects of different manageability technologies. It describes the protection mechanisms built into standard protocols and highlights some of the basic risks they face when deployed in an enterprise environment. Solutions for desktop, laptop, server, and cell phone platforms are discussed and compared in the context of common threats to managed devices, as well as the control consoles that monitor them. Secure enablement and configuration guidelines are provided for implementers and designers to develop effective threat models when integrating manageability software and hardware inside a computer network. The analysis presented in this chapter will help the reader understand how network manageability solutions work and what their strengths and weaknesses are from the security standpoint.

INTRODUCTION

Network manageability encompasses a wide range of remote administration activities that help minimize downtime and accelerate the control and repair of devices connected to a network, from multi-core servers and laptop computers, to PDAs and cell phones. IT shops as well as Manageability Service Providers (MSPs) use these solutions to remotely access a variety of systems connected to enterprise and home networks in order to reconfigure software, apply patches, and monitor performance and security. Manageability technologies can decrease cost of ownership by

DOI: 10.4018/978-1-60960-777-7.ch009

limiting the number of systems that need to be taken to the shop for repair and by reducing the number of desk visits an IT shop needs to cover to support its users.

One of the most powerful capabilities that manageability systems offer is access to a device regardless of health level or power state. That is, even though applications or the operating system may not be operational, an out-of-band channel implemented on the manageability framework is available to remotely troubleshoot the computer, printer, or whatever the device may be. Similarly, if the system is executing in power-saving mode (e.g., standby, hibernate), manageability solutions often support discovery and wakeup functionality that will allow administrators to locate the device on the network, reboot it, and take a look at it, for instance, by establishing a keyboard-video-mouse (KVM) session.

Due to the nature of manageability tasks, access to administration consoles must be carefully controlled, and failure to do so could result in significant network disruption, privacy violations and other security breaches. As we will see, the interfaces made available by the device for administration consoles to connect to them must be secured with strong authentication, and the traffic encrypted in order to prevent unauthorized parties from abusing secondary interfaces. For instance, if the firmware update function on a managed device is not properly protected, an attacker could try to corrupt the firmware on multiple PCs or servers inside the enterprise and prevent them from booting – a costly problem to repair, especially if physical access to the system is necessary.

This chapter analyzes a number of frameworks and protocols that have been developed to support network manageability. New as well as proven technologies that combine hardware, firmware and software components are available today to make manageability more effective, scalable and secure. Protecting this support infrastructure, however, requires clear separation of duties, sound implementations, as well as comprehensive audit-

ing that allow network administrators to preserve their control over the managed devices at all times. Depending on the type of device, the implications of having insufficient protection coverage may vary. For instance, if a manageability protocol is deployed to troubleshoot laptop systems in the enterprise but the protocol standard does not offer a security bar that is high enough to adequately match the value of the information stored on those systems, the manageability solution may in fact add risk and reduce the security of the network.

Recent research (Bojinov, 2009; Wojtczuk, 2009) has shown an increased interest in the security of manageability products, in part, due to the OS-agnostic nature of some solutions and their privileges over platform resources. We will discuss the protection properties of a number of well known network manageability technologies for servers, desktop computers, laptops and mobile devices. These solutions will be analyzed and compared highlighting their security strengths, limitations as well as their applicability to different classes of networks and devices.

BASIC MANAGEABILITY FUNCTIONS

Manageability technologies support a number of fundamental functions that allow administrators to anticipate potential problems and maintain devices operating as expected. From the analysis of different solutions (Campbell, 2007; Sheldon, 2001; Kumar, 2009; Blair, 2007; Berlin, 2009), we can identify some common capabilities offered by them:

- Discovery. Ability to find and identify devices connected to the network.
- Inventory collection. Software, firmware and hardware on the device can be inventoried for tracking and update purposes.
- Eventing. Manageability solutions offer a number of notification mechanisms

to communicate anomalous conditions to management consoles. (Notice that reaction to those conditions is typically out of the scope of a manageability solution.)

- Power transitions. Allow administrators to power up, reset, shutdown and power-cycle the device and, in some cases, transition it into a power-saving mode (e.g., hibernate, standby).
- Code updates. Administrators using manageability solutions can remotely update two basic code components of a platform:
  - Software (OS and applications typically stored on hard drives and solid state drives).
  - Firmware (boot executables and drivers stored on small non-volatile memories typically built into the system that control basic flows).
- Reconfiguration. Ability to change configuration settings such as boot options, feature availability, and user accounts (i.e., manageability accounts).
- User data removal. Some systems offer the ability to remotely erase user data (e.g., contact lists, private files) from the device once it has been identified as lost or stolen, or before recycling it and reassigning it to a new owner.

These operations can be frequently performed over two interfaces: **local** interfaces and **remote** interfaces. Access to local interfaces often requires logging into the system, first as a system user (either, over the network or on the device itself), and then issuing a manageability command from that account over the local interface to reach a Service Processor (e.g., an embedded controller) that may be in charge of supporting manageability functions and that may require further authentication by the users. In some cases, the main processor is itself responsible for running manageability software

and no separate interface is used. Remote operation, on the other hand, does not require a local system account. Remote interfaces allow direct connectivity to the device for purposes of repair and inventory collection and the accounts and privileges needed to manage the system are part of a separate domain inside de device.

When the system is not operational (for example, when the OS has been corrupted but the device is still booting), manageability technologies utilize a secondary, out-of-band interface supported by an embedded network stack that runs on top of a small SP (e.g., ARM, 8051, PIC, H8). This stack allows administrators to locate the damaged device and establish Serial Over LAN (SOL) or KVM sessions to troubleshoot and repair the problem. Out-of-band interfaces must be considered high-availability interfaces and constitute a fundamental component of a manageability solution. Access over out-of-band ports, however, may be seen by some as a backdoor into the system as they effectively create a new access vector in the system in addition to the primary interfaces (Wojtczuk, 2009). These communication channels must undergo careful scrutiny when designed and implemented in order to reduce risk and guarantee the privacy and security properties that manageability solutions must always preserve.

There are some threats that are common to many manageability technologies and that we will mention in this chapter. Although some security risks are only applicable to certain platforms (e.g., 3G-enabled smart phones, SOL-capable computers), the following threats are significantly broad and can be used to compare protection levels among manageability solutions (Table 1).

The following sections will explore manageability solutions in the context of the above threats. We will discuss how they implement basic manageability functions and what devices are supported best by each technology.

Table 1. Threats to manageability technologies

	Threat	Description
1	Loss of administration control	Administrators cannot access a managed device and are unable to recover control over it
2	Code injection into SP	Code injected at runtime into a service processor
3	Firmware tampering	Unauthorized modification or update of the firmware on the device that supports manageability functions
4	Privacy breach	Private information is compromised using manageability capabilities (this includes abuse by system administrators themselves)
5	Device tracking	A device is uniquely identified and tracked using a serial number or similar identifier needed by the manageability solution
6	Management console compromise	Management console is compromised by attackers, typically via a remote exploit; may expose multiple managed devices
7	Extended Denial of Service	Corruption of the device caused through the use of manageability functions; the device is not operational for an extended period of time and physical access if often required to repair the system
8	Data removal	Information stored on a managed device is deleted by an attacker; this includes audit logs
9	Access to the main OS through the out-of-band capability	A user with access to the out-of-band interface bypasses protections and gets access to the main OS (i.e., privilege escalation)
10	Device reconfiguration	A managed device is misconfigured by an attacker in order to lower the protection bar or plant a back door

OMA DEVICE MANAGEMENT

OMA Device Management (DM) is a manageability protocol created by the Open Mobile Alliance to support firmware updates, change configuration settings and check the status of smaller devices such as smart phones and cell phones (Campbell, 2007). What makes the OMA DM standard different to other manageability protocols is its awareness of the limitations small devices have in terms of amount of memory, persistent storage capacity, processor speed, bandwidth, and battery life.

XML (Extensible Markup Language) is used to format the OMA DM messages exchanged between management consoles and devices at various transport levels that encapsulate the XML and transmit it over local and remote interfaces:

- Local interfaces. OMA DM communications over a wired interface can be implemented over RS-232 and USB (for instance, to transfer data between a PC and the device). This type of interface has been used by attackers in the past to probe the

device and try to access protected data. For this reason, it must be considered an access vector that should be secured (see Table 1, Threat 9).

- Remote interfaces. Over-the-network OMA DM manageability can be implemented using two types of transmission means:
  - Wireless: Bluetooth, GSM, CDMA, IrDA
  - Wired: HTTP, SMS, WSP (WAP) and OBEX

Remote interfaces are always a priority to security researchers and architects. The challenges of combining manageability solutions like OMA DM with modern protocols like CDMA or OBEX often results in solutions that have not been tested as much and that could be consider weaker than older protocols like TCP, UDP and IP, which have been around for a while and have been improved over the years. New standards may contain vulnerabilities at the unit and interoperability levels and therefore must be implemented following

Figure 1. OMA Device Management and Description Tree

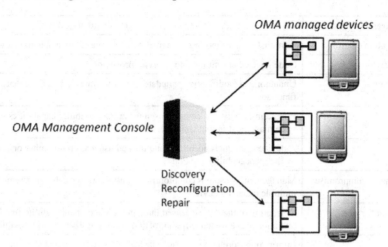

secure-by-design principles that ensure that new technologies are free from most vulnerabilities and cannot be easily defeated by known attacks.

OMA DM supports authentication mechanisms to guarantee that all request-response interactions in the manageability session occur only between authorized parties. A series of messages to verify the identity of console and device need to be transmitted before a manageability operation can be established and the device is securely accessed. When implementing OMA DM, always remember that the authentication support offered by the standard will help create a more secure manageability channel within your network.

Version 1.0 of the OMA DM specification had some limitations in terms of security that subsequent versions have fixed. Version 1.2, for instance, incorporated enhanced security, nonce synchronization and XML encryption (Campbell, 2007). Version 1.3 added functionality for the discovery of the managed devices, which accelerated the process of determining what functions are available on the device. Some of the early shortcomings of the protocol could not be fixed without breaking backward compatibility, so version 2.0 of the standard was released to correct important coordination issues when separate management consoles supported the same devices concurrently.

It also added support for virtualization on mobile devices, which allows remote administrators to access any of the operating runtimes that may be in execution on the device at any given time.

Each managed devices in OMA DM contains an OMA DM Tree (Figure 1). This data structure stores references to objects inside the device (i.e., configuration variables, updatable storage elements on the system) and provides a structured way to query and change system objects while maintaining a single reference repository whose organization can be customized by the manufacturer. Each node or object in the tree has a set of fields that a management console can change according to the permissions specified by the Access Control List of the node. This ACL defines who has the privilege to add children to the node, replace them, delete them, or modify their properties.

The core protocol commands supported by OMA DM are: *Add, Atomic, Copy, Delete, Exec, Get, Replace, Sequence, Alerts and Results*. Of these, the following operations are considered security sensitive: *Add, Copy, Delete, Exec, and Replace*, as they may allow a user to alter the integrity of the data on the device, or remove information pieces (see Table 1, Threat 8, Threat 10). For instance, the following XML will remove the account identified by the account GUID (Global Unique Identifier):

```
<Delete>
   <CmdID>1600</CmdID>
   <Item>
        <Target><LocURI>./Account/
Local/(the account GUID)</LocURI> </
Target>
   </Item>
</Delete>
```

Before issuing a sensitive operation like the one above, it is necessary to verify authorizations on the specific device and confirm the user has the right privileges to request the desired operation on the target.

When an OMA DM session is not protected with integrity algorithms, it may be possible to modify the command that is being requested by a console (e.g., replacing a *Copy* with a *Delete*). Similarly, if XML encryption is not used, or if the channel is not encrypted at the transport level, traffic in the clear may be modified before it reaches its destination.

The *Exec* command is used to invoke long running operations such as a firmware update or a file download. Once *Exec* completes, the device must send a status message reporting the result of the operation. Blocking or tampering with status messages may result in the automatic reinitialization of the operation, which could degrade the device's performance or, if an audit log is used to track manageability operations, it could exhaust the number of memory writes supported by the device's non-volatile memory repository (e.g., flash memory).

In order for an OMA DM server to connect to the client, it needs to complete a setup phase and a management phase:

- **Phase 1: Setup.** Initialization takes place during this phase on both sides of the connection, on the client and on the server side. They prepare the session to exchange data over OMA DM by authenticating one another and reserving resources for the session (memory, descriptors and ports). Since this is the phase in which systems can be contacted by malicious users in the vicinity of the device, it is likely that compromise attempts will appear at this point before a protected channel is established.

- **Phase 2: Management.** Once the setup phase is complete, the client receives a stream of commands from the server, executes them sends back status messages. The protected channel created before the management phase constitutes a fundamental protection mechanisms offered by OMA DM for data in transit. Vulnerabilities at this point are more likely to be at the implementation level (e.g., programming errors implementing one of the two phases).

As you see, establishing trust and verifying identities are crucial parts of any modern manageability protocol and require several steps (e.g., issuing a challenge, validating proper hashing, refreshing nonces, and authorizing manageability operations). These steps must be carefully implemented as coding flaws at either end of the connection could result in limited protection and a false sense of security.

FUNCTIONS AND THEIR SECURITY

Bootstrap

The OMA DM provisioning process is called 'bootstrap' and allows a server to prepare a clean device and make it ready for communication with the console. This is done during manufacturing or when the system needs to be refurbished or repaired from a critical failure. Notice that there are attacks that attempt to remove all information on the device using software or abusing the bootstrap API (Table 1, Threat 8). It is recommended that OMA DM bootstrap functionality be restricted to local interfaces in order to prevent any potential denial-of-service attacks launched remotely (Table 1, Threat 7) that may be targeting more than one device.

Notification Initiated Sessions

For security and performance reasons, OMA DM-managed devices do not follow a pulling mechanism that continuously listens for messages from the management console (Campbell, 2007). Instead, communication with clients systems is based on notifications received from the server that ask the device to establish a full session first in order to exchange manageability information. Identification and authentication of these notifications must always rely on persistent, strong information elements. Spoofing attacks, in which the identity of a management console is stolen, must be prevented by adhering to OMA DM's hashing-based identification method. For example, SMS (Short Message Service) notifications being received from the server must be authenticated with an HMAC code. MD5 and server credentials can be used, although more recent algorithms like SHA-256 are recommended (Hardaker, 2006).

TLS/SSL

Transport Level Security (TLS) and Secure Sockets Layer (SSL) are mandatory protocols for the protection of traffic in OMA DM (Dierks, 1999). A best-practice in network manageability is to authenticate clients and servers for all levels of operation using protocols like TLS/SSL, which will offer integrity and authenticity verification for simple status notification messages as well as complete firmware upgrade flows. HTTP Basic and Digest authentication can both be used to complement TLS with password-based access control. Although these methods are considered weak, they can complement the protection scheme

when an encrypted channel has been already established at the transport level. (Notice that encryption algorithms protect the integrity and confidentiality of data, so once the payload of a TCP packet is encrypted, the HTTP credentials traveling inside it will also be protected).

Nonce Synchronization

In OMA DM, MD5 nonces must be refreshed for each session. In order to do this, the client sends a new nonce to the server every time a new session is established. This value will be in use for the duration of the next session, but is exchanged in advance. Version 1.2 of the DM specification supports nonce resynchronization. It is recommended to enable this feature during the bootstrapping of any device to avoid exploitable race conditions. Nonces must be implemented in such a way that they are difficult to predict. They should be sufficiently random in order to prevent impersonation attacks using digest databases (e.g., rainbow tables) by making sure that the distribution of nonce values from session to session does not follow a pattern that is easy distinguishable.

Password and Cipher Suites

t is recommended that OMA DM passwords and nonces are 16 bytes in length or longer. Since the handling of these values is automated, the user does not have to type them in directly onto the device. Regarding the selection of cipher suites, servers and clients must support the following three TLS encryption schemes:

- TLS_RSA_WITH_AES_128_CBC_SHA-1
- TLS_RSA_WITH_3DES_EDE_CBC_SHA
- TLS_RSA_WITH_RC4_128_SHA

If SSL 3.0 is used (SSL 2.0 or below is not acceptable by the OMA standard), the following cipher suites will have to be used in order to provide confidentiality, integrity and authentication to the communication between devices and consoles:

- SSL_RSA_WITH_RC4_128_SHA
- SSL_RSA_WITH_3DES_EDE_CBC_ SHA

XML Signature and XML Encryption

Starting with 1.2 of the OMA DM specification, XML Signature and Encryption are supported. This provides implementers with an additional option to encapsulate message signatures within the XML using RSA encryption and SHA1 hashing to produce a signature. This eliminates the need to rely on transport level protection which may require more computing power, infrastructure, and bandwidth to secure XML data transfers. Notice that if a different algorithm is used for electronic signatures (for instance, SHA-256 for hashing, or ECC for encryption), compatibility with XML Signature and XML Encryption-supporting products may be broken. The solution will have to be customized in order to handle these different data blocks, but this is a tradeoff that may result in heightened security that could be justified if the value of information if high.

Encryption at the XML-message level is also supported (i.e., RSA and AES128). In the event a signature is generated and message encryption is also necessary, XML Signature must be used first and then XML Encryption, which will be applied to the message and the signature together. This will prevent hash collision attacks by forcing decryption of the message before hash values are exposed.

INTELLIGENT PLATFORM MANAGEMENT INTERFACE (IPMI)

We now review IMPI, a manageability solution for servers. The Intelligent Platform Management Interface (IPMI) is a manageability standard that allows administrators to monitor and reconfigure server platforms remotely (Sheldon, 2001). IPMI is OS-agnostic, which makes it possible for an administrator to manage the system when there is no OS, when the OS is down, and even when there is a functional problem that prevents the platform OS from running as expected. In addition to out-of-band access, IPMI supports inventory collection, eventing and BIOS reconfiguration, among other features. Version 2.0 of the specification incorporates several enhancements over versions 1.0 and 1.5 and security in particular has been improved by offering more options to create a robust interface to the managed server in terms of encryption and authentication mechanisms.

IPMI's main component is the Baseboard Management Controller or BMC, which is a hardware board connected to other internal controllers on the server via the IPMB (Intelligent Platform Management Bus) and to other BMCs on a different device through the IPMC (Intelligent Platform Management Chassis) bus. At the core of many BMC architectures lays the Service Processor (SP) responsible for receiving service requests and channeling them to the corresponding entity inside the server. Internally, the BMC has a direct link to the network card that allows remote administrators to access the system without having to go through the software stack supported by the OS. These two components, the BMC and the network card, are connected over the System Management Bus (SMBus). From the security standpoint, this bus can be driven through CPU code and also through other devices connected to it. Vendors implementing IPMI must include all active (i.e., programmable) entities connected to SMBus in their threat models in order to prevent unauthorized parties on this bus to capture data transmitted over the interface.

The SP represents an important attack target in IPMI (Table 1, Threat 2). The very nature of a separate, secondary processor may represent a threat to the OS and its applications as it constitutes and independent runtime capable of executing code that is not directly accessible to the CPU and antivirus software. If code is injected into the SP, it may be difficult to regain control and, given the privileges a SP often has, a compromised BMC may become a threat to the rest of the network.

BMCs can be accessed remotely using protocols like RMCP (Remote Management Control Protocol) which create a separate link in the connection from administrator to the system. This connection has two segments: 1) the one created by using RMCP to reach the BMC from a console, and 2) the one established by using IPMI to reach server internals from the BMC. From the exposure perspective, these links need to be protected in order to prevent traffic sniffing and replay attacks.

FUNCTIONS AND THEIR SECURITY

Platform Data

IPMI information is kept on two main storage areas, the SDR and the FRU. The IPMI SDR (Sensor Data Record) contains information about the different sensors connected to the system – temperature sensors, fault sensors, voltage sensors and fan speed control sensors. The current thresholds for such sensors and the latest values read from them are stored on the SDR and need to be protected from tampering, which could trigger unnecessary platform resets and even prevent the execution of event handlers to react to anomalous conditions. The IPMI FRU (Field Replaceable Unit) stores information regarding the different devices connected to the server, their type, manufacturer ID, etc., and constitutes a database for hardware inventory that can be queried through IPMI.

Regarding sensitive data, the System Event Log (SEL) maintains a record of system events and must be protected against tampering: If the SEL does not contain accurate information or if permissions to modify or remove data are not

properly controlled (Table 1, Threat 8), it will not be possible to reconstruct the system's access history when trying to detect potential abuse by outsiders, or even insiders. Also, alert systems built around IPMI rely on SEL information in order to communicate events to remote consoles. Vulnerabilities in the SEL implementation may significantly limit the efficacy of such support tools.

Eventing

An IPMI administrator can configure a number of alerts that will be triggered when the specified conditions appear and administrators need to be notified about potential problems to investigate. Alert configuration can be done by sending Platform Event Trap (PET) messages over Simple Network Management Protocol (SNMP) to the management console, which can also query manageability audit logs maintained on the device to help review the system's history and perform system diagnostics.

Tools

There are a number of open-source code bases that help implement IPMI firmware. Although it may be possible to integrate this code into an IPMI solution (e.g., a production version for a server), there are no guarantees regarding the security of the code. In general, open-source components close to the Linux kernel and some services used in dozens of Linux distributions around the world receive significant scrutiny by developers with regards to the quality of the code (for instance, they will detect and repair security problems such as buffer overflows, format string vulnerabilities and arithmetic errors). In the case of IPMI code available on the Internet, it is unknown how much attention has been given to the security of the code. For that reason, it would be convenient to review the code before incorporating it into the firmware of any production server.

Tools like IPMItool are also accessible online and help validate compliance to the standard. IPMI itself offers a test suite to verify functionality. Implementers should consider using it in order to review the correct implementation of security-relevant features such as authentication, the command firewall module, and the encryption flows. The IPMI Conformance Test Suite is available online and also offers reference drivers, test code and guidance on how to avoid common mistakes when implementing the IPMI standard.

RMCP+

In order to transmit IPMI messages over a TCP/IP connection, the Remote Management Control Protocol+ (RMCP+) is used. RMCP+ adds extensions to the RMCP packet format to perform encryption, authentication and enhanced discovery. RMCP is a wired protocol defined in the IPMI documentation that did not originally contemplate many attacks and protections in its first specification. Manageability traffic transferred in the clear as well as limited authentication options made necessary the definition of extensions that would make IPMI more secure. These are some improvements to the security of RMCP+:

- Encryption. Encryption of IPMI messages is possible with RMCP+ and can be applied selectively. In order to provide flexibility with regards to encryption overhead and improve performance, message encryption can be used only with some types of message that are considered sensitive while the rest can remain unencrypted. In order to define the sensitivity of IPMI traffic exchanged via RMCP+, six privilege levels are available:
  - 0h = Unspecified (returned with error completion code)
  - 1h = CALLBACK level
  - 2h = USER level
  - 3h = OPERATOR level

  - 4h = ADMINISTRATOR level
  - 5h = OEM Proprietary level

Levels 3h, 4h, and 5h carry most of the information that could be of interest to attackers trying to gain access to an IPMI-managed server. Implementers should always consider those three levels and assign them to command messages, connection control messages, and credential update messages. Proper level assignment along with encryption will give enhanced security to IPMI and will reduce the potential for attack.

The encryption algorithms supported by the protocol are the following and reduce the risk of traffic sniffing and data tampering to which LAN and WLAN systems are often exposed:

- 00h none
- 01h AES-CBC-128
- 02h RC4-128
- 03h RC4-40
  - Authentication. Similarly, key exchange authentication codes can be defined for IPMI messages using the RMCP+ Authenticated Key-Exchange Protocol (RAKP). The options are:
- 00h RAKP-none
- 01h RAKP-HMAC-SHA1
- 02h RAKP-HMAC-MD5

Notice that although MD5 is considered a weaker algorithm, it requires fewer computational steps and is therefore an alternative to SHA-1 and SHA-2 if session activation on the server has specific time constraints to consider, or if the management controller implementing IPMI has limited computational resources. RAKP+ uses pre-shared symmetric keys to mutually authenticate a managed server and the console connecting to it. Implementers must review how these keys are generated and stored on the device in order to avoid key predictability and key-extraction attacks.

- Integrity. Although MD5 and SHA-1 are popular hashing algorithms still in use today, collision vulnerabilities have been reported in both systems. ISVs and developers implementing IPMI may expect to see support for SHA-2 (e.g., SHA-256) in the future but, due to backward compatibility, MD5 and SHA-1 are likely to continue to be supported. These are the suites in RMCP+ that can be used to protect the integrity of IPMI messages in RMCP+:
- 00h None
- 01h HMAC-SHA1-96
- 02h HMAC-MD5-128
- 03h MD5-128
- Random number generation (RNG). A word of caution when following the IPMI 2.0 specification with regards to random number generation. At any given time, a managed server system maintains two counters, P and Q. P reports the total number of power cycles that have been performed on the server, and Q the number of RNG requests per power cycle. The specification recommends generating a random number by doing: $HMAC(P\|Q)$. Although these are two 32-bit numbers and the hashing algorithm may be strong (e.g., SHA-256), the counters being used may not be difficult to infer, especially on new or recently deployed systems. When using RNG functionality in IPMI, always consider alternative sources of entropy provided by the hardware that could increase the randomness of the values produced by the RNG. These sources could include voltage, temperature and system noise read-accessible to the BMC.
- Command firewall. The command firewall was an important feature added to IPMI after its original specification. An IPMI-managed device can receive a number of commands over the network and send alarms to the management console. If an

attacker tries to spoof the identity of a system and sends fake alerts to a console reporting problems, it may be possible to misconfigure the system and bring it down (Table 1, Threat 7 and Threat 10). It is therefore important to follow a defense-in-depth approach by creating several layers of protection, from identification to traffic filtering. In addition to the encryption and authentication features we have mentioned, IPMI offers the Command Firewall capability that allows administrators to disable specific commands that could be abused by attackers in the event that an account is compromised:

- Cold Reset
- Warm Reset
- Manufacturing Test On
- Set ACPI Power State
- Broadcast Commands

These are all candidates for a command firewall policy in IPMI and must be considered security-sensitive in all IPMI threat models.

- Serial Over LAN (SOL). Once a remote console establishes a connection to the BMC over IPMI, it can enable the SOL feature to exchange data between the console and the device over a serial link. Serial communications are encapsulated in UDP packets and transferred over the network using IP. Notice that SOL implements sequence numbers in order to enable synchronization between client and server. If predictable, these numbers could produce SOL session hijacking and availability problems. Reviewing the initialization and maintenance of these sequence numbers is necessary in order to prevent known attacks on session establishment and data transport.

ACTIVE MANAGEMENT TECHNOLOGY (AMT)

Active Management Technology (Kumar, 2009) is a manageability solution created by Intel that is embedded into the chipset of laptop and desktop systems. AMT offers out-of-band access over LAN and WLAN connections and supports functions such as inventory collection, remote boot and network filter definition. A number of memory controller hubs (MCH) and platform controller hubs (PCH) contain a service processor called Manageability Engine (ME), which is the subsystem at the core of AMT that enables the execution of firmware on the platform (Figure 2). The ME supports a runtime real-time OS as well as an embedded network stack featuring protocols like TCP/IP, HTTP, TLS and 802.11 (WiFi) that are used to make manageability modules reachable through a WS-Management (Cabrera, 2005) API and a proprietary SOAP-based interface.

AMT allows administrators to access a system even though the OS may be down or damaged. This is done via out-of-band connections over TCP/IP ports that bind to the ME (port 16992 for unencrypted traffic, port 16993 for TLS-protected traffic).

The manageability functions AMT offers are powerful and their utilization can be configured using access control lists, or ACLs. The most salient features of AMT include:

- Hardware inventory collection. Remote retrieval of data regarding the amount of DRAM available on the system, processor type, system name, network MAC address, etc.
- Third-party data storage (3PDS). Allows registered software applications to store information on a non-volatile memory repository (i.e., flash) rather than on the hard drive. Version information, keys or any other data element can be stored by registered software on the AMT 3PDS store.

- Remote power control. When an AMT administrator is logged into the system, he can request power control functions such as platform shutdown, platform reset and platform boot over in-band or out-of-band connections.
- Keyboard-video-mouse (KVM). Through the AMT KVM feature, it is possible to establish an interactive session with the managed device and accelerate system diagnostics and repair.
- IDE Redirection. This capability allows a remote administrator to boot the laptop or desktop system from a remote hard drive, floppy disk or CD-ROM image.
- Serial Over LAN (SOL). Similarly to its IPMI counterpart, it is possible to redirect input and output communications to a remote location via a serial connection – for instance, to establish a text-based session using a remote keyboard and display on the management console.
- System Defense. This is hardware-supported packet filtering feature that uses the embedded network card to accept or reject TCP, IPv4, IPv6 and UDP packets based on a policy defined by the administrator. The policy is enforced by registers in the MCH or PCH chipset.
- Application watchdog. A heart-beat algorithm allows AMT to monitor applications executing in the OS in such a way that administrators can react to anomalous conditions observed on the system (e.g., the antivirus software stops responding or the personal firewall gets disabled).
- Wake on LAN (WOL). Systems in standby or hibernate mode may be powered-on remotely by a console via a magic packet. Since pushing OS and application patches typically requires the system to be fully operational, WOL allows the administrator to wake up the system so that more system resources are available.

Figure 2. Active Management Technology architecture

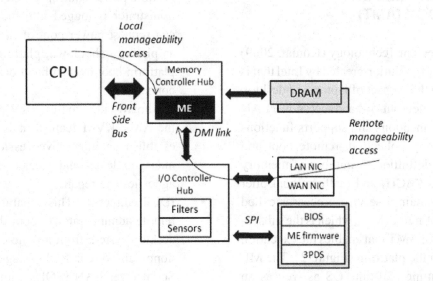

AMT offers communication over HTTP 1.0/1.1 between devices and consoles. AMT WS-Management messages traveling over HTTP are encapsulated in SOAP/XML and, since the traffic travels as part the HTTP payload (every transaction is independently authenticated), enabling transport-level encryption is recommended by using TLS/SSL on all interfaces. In the case of wireless, AMT supports a combination of authentication methods including EAPFAST TLS, PEAP MS-CHAP v2, EAPFAST MS-CHAP v2, EAP GTC and EAPFAST GTC that can be used to secure the communication with systems managed over a WLAN connection.

AMT supports local interfaces too. Code running on the CPU can communicate with the ME via the HECI interface (Kumar, 2009). In this case, a management console can connect to the OS network stack and request AMT manageability services over this local interface without having to access the embedded stack on the ME, which would be slower. The interface is used, for instance, by the Watchdog feature in order to monitor software applications. It also allows for regular applications to access the ME and request configuration changes, or to store information on the 3PDS. All interfaces, local and remote, must be secured with equivalent security levels. In the case of the remote interfaces, the concern is a potential attack coming from inside or outside the enterprise via a network connection. In the case of local interfaces, malware already operating on the host could try compromise the ME sub-environment, which hosts a processor independent from the CPU and that could be targeted to inject code (Table 1, Threat 2). If all interfaces are not aligned in terms of protection level, one of them could become the weaker link that could expose the platform as a whole.

Communication between management consoles and AMT devices travels over TCP/IP and can be protected with transport level encryption. TLS server authentication is supported in combination with password-based user authentication (e.g., HTTP Digest). TLS Mutual Authentication is also included and certificates must be provisioned on the device as well as on the management console for this stronger mode to operate. In large deployments, existing Public Key Infrastructure (PKI) for the enterprise can be leveraged to configure AMT systems. In small and medium businesses where PKI may not be readily available, it may be necessary to generate self-signed certificates in order to encrypt traffic traveling between systems in this TLS mode.

FUNCTIONS AND THEIR SECURITY

Local and Remote Interfaces

AMT executes firmware that implements remote interfaces such as TCP/IP and HTTP. These interfaces constitute attack vectors and must be secured in home and enterprise environments. Enabling TLS 1.0/SSL 3.0 is always recommended. Similarly, the local interface that uses HECI buffers can be protected by enabling TLS/SSL. Even though exposure of internal interfaces is limited, enabling transport-layer encryption is a good protection to activate in AMT as spying applications could be trying to sniff on local connections to AMT's TCP sockets.

Stealth Compromise

If an AMT administrator account is compromised, the system could be accessed in a very stealthy way (i.e., via the out-of-band channel; Table 1, Threats 3). This is true for all manageability technologies that support out-of-band functionality and administrator ACLs. It is recommended that full auditing is enabled in AMT in order to increase the probability of detecting such abuse. Also, privileges should be granted based on role by carefully creating administrator and user accounts on the system that selectively assign rights to the different AMT features and the resources available.

Privacy

AMT uses a Privacy Icon to report to the user whether the technology is enabled or disabled (Table 1, Threat 4) and the OS event log also captures the status of the AMT boot flow. Inside AMT,

another audit log is offered for IT administrators to review access history and detect abuse. This log helps protect one of the most powerful features of AMT and similar technologies: The in-band and out-of-band channels that allow authorized IT personnel to connect to the system without having an OS user account. By monitoring account activity in the event log and by implementing a sound password update policy, it is possible to increase the privacy of users whose systems use AMT.

Third-Party Data Storage (3PDS)

AMT offers flash storage to software applications that can keep version control information or keys on flash memory. AMT does not guarantee the confidentiality of data in the 3PDS. It is important for implementers to understand that no 3PDS encryption is offered by AMT and that they should protect (e.g., encrypt) any sensitive data before storing it on this repository.

Firmware Authentication

The firmware executed on the ME service processor is signed by the manufacturer in order to prevent unsigned code from executing on this subsystem. This protection mechanism also prevents malware from overwriting ME code and guarantees that the image loaded from the flash is clean – if the firmware image is somehow corrupted or not signed, the secure boot process will fail hereby signaling a potential integrity problem with ME code.

Remote BIOS Reconfiguration and Update

Some manageability functions may be very sensitive and this is the case of BIOS and software updates over AMT (Table 1, Threat 3). It is recommended to always password-protect BIOS screens with a string that is different to the AMT administration password. This will prevent

Figure 3. Simple Network Management Protocol connectivity

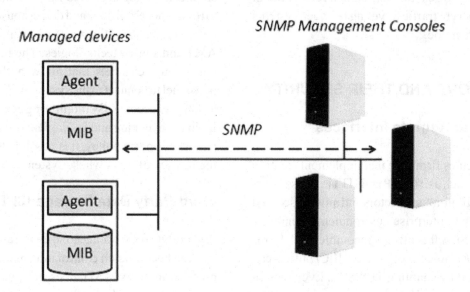

an attacker from touching BIOS configuration even if an AMT account has been compromised. Firmware updates are distributed along with BIOS update images by different manufacturers. AMT administrators must check the availability of new firmware patches and apply them as necessary as part of regular patching procedures for software applications and OSs.

SIMPLE NETWORK MANAGEMENT PROTOCOL (SNMP)

Simple Network Management Protocol (SNMP) is a widely deployed network standard to monitor devices on a computer network including PCs, printers, servers, bridges and routers (Blair, 2007). SNMP is composed of an agent, a management information base, or MIB, which is composed of a series of objects stored on the device, and an application layer protocol to access the MIB from an administration console, also known as NMS (Network Management System; Figure 3). Although SNMP is a software-based manageability solution and does not offer out-of-band

access, the configuration privileges granted to the SNMP agent are significant and must be restricted in order to avoid system disruption and other remote abuse scenarios.

SNMP-managed devices contain a software agent that uses UDP port 161 to receive requests from management consoles, and sends alerts to the consoles using UDP port 162. This read-only status reporting capability is not the only function of SNMP. The protocol can modify the configuration of devices connected to the network and this is the feature that must be considered sensitive (Table 1, Threat 10).

Given the number of enterprise systems that support SNMP these days, it is important to assess the security of this manageability protocol and understand its virtues and limitations. If compromised, an SNMP console could, at the very least, impede the identification and repair of systems (Table 1, Threat 1), but it could also create extended availability problems (Table 1, Threat 7) if tampering with SNMP reconfiguration functions derive, by mistake or intentionally, in the corruption of one or more systems.

SNMP version 1.0 and version 2.0 of the standard contemplate a small number of protections mechanisms. In fact, the access code used in SNMP known as the 'community string' used to be transmitted in the clear and this vulnerability was used in many exploits that were made public several years ago. An SNMP community string in the clear effectively exposes the authentication value shared among several systems hereby exposing them to devices that could be reading all the traffic on a network segment (for instance, devices operating in promiscuous mode). This flaw made the protocol vulnerable to sniffing attacks, and the lack of a challenge-response mechanism to validate the identity of managed systems made it vulnerable to brute-force (i.e., attack in which all different combinations of the string are tried till finding a match) and dictionary attacks (i.e., using dictionary words to derive message digests directly comparable to an authentication string).

Security issues limited the deployment of SNMP for a while. The protocol was later found to be prone to traffic sniffing and spoofing on TCP/IP networks where alerts could be modified to fake the identity of the originator and trick management consoles into reconfiguring, and sometimes disabling, routers, servers, printers, and other electronic systems connected to the LAN.

SNMP's weak configuration defaults were also quickly spotted by security researchers who found they could access devices whose default credentials had not been changed after deployment. This granted immediate access to network resources to unauthorized users. Similarly, systems configured with a null community string gave attackers a chance to freely access devices without having to pass any authentication round. Implementers of SNMP must remember that community strings must always be used and that default values must be promptly replaced upon first access.

FUNCTIONS AND THEIR SECURITY

SNMP privileges

Granting proper privileges to query specific objects on the device over SNMP has proven challenging. The first versions of the protocol did not offer the ability to give limited access rights to each user, but in more recent releases read and write permissions can be granted through ACLs to reduce the exposure of the multiple configuration variables accessible on the MIB databases. By carefully separating administration privileges it is possible to prevent single-administrator attacks (Table 1, Threat 4) and network topology attacks in which a user may be collecting information about the systems on the network in order to infer attack paths and even vulnerabilities based on information such as device type, connection speeds, vendor name and version numbers.

SNMP version 3.0 added security features that can be used to further protect traffic exchanged between devices and consoles: With stronger authentication it is possible to better control how systems are viewed on the network and by what users; with encryption SNMP traffic can be protected against unauthorized disclosure and modification; and with the integrity mechanisms offered by version 3.0 (e.g., secure hashing), information that does not need to be encrypted can still be protected against unauthorized modification while in transit.

Security Model

SNMP version 3.0 (Blair, 2007) incorporates two security models: 1) a user-based security model (USM) and, 2) a view-based access control model (VACM) that protects the MIB and the objects stored on the device. The former supports data encryption and authentication of traffic between all devices and management consoles, whereas the latter safeguards actual access to the MIB.

User Security Model

USM protects SNMP against data modification, disclosure and reordering attacks by incorporating authentication and encryption – HMAC-MD5 and HMAC-SHA for authentication, and CBC-DES for encryption. The standard also allows users to define other cryptographic algorithms to use, which makes adoption more flexible.

The MIB is the repository that stores manageability information on each device. Internally, it is designed as a tree structure that links a collection of objects together encoded under ASN.1 to describe different system properties. SNMP does not specify what information to store on the MIB, but rather offers the data types needed to describe a system. These data types include: counters, network addresses, strings and time ticks. MIB information is considered an asset from the threat modeling perspective and therefore access control to it must be tightened during deployment.

In the past, SNMP has been affected by a questionable security model. Although it offered strong capabilities to query and troubleshoot a device, ISVs were reluctant to use the reconfiguration features shipped with the protocol due to the low security bar it offered. All new security features in SNMP, including encryption and authentication, must be consistently implemented in order to create a solid SNMP network that keeps attackers out and still makes possible the remote administration of PCs, servers and other electronic devices.

The following are additional security relevant aspects of SNMP's USM:

- **USM discovery and authentication**. In order to discover an SNMP agent, two transactions need to occur:
    1. A packet with a bogus ID (msgAuthoritativeEngineID) needs to be sent to the device. When the packet is received by the device agent, the ID will be identified as incorrect and the device will send back a discovery packet with the correct ID in response.
    2. As a second step, an authenticated packet is sent specifying bogus values for the Time and Number of Boots fields (msgAuthoritativeEngineboots, msgAuthoritativeEngineTime, respectively). This packet will be discarded by the agent that will reply with an SNMP message indicating the correct values for Time and Number of Boots.

These numbers returned by the agent must be maintained by the SNMP console for subsequent interactions as they constitute authentication material. In addition to the user credentials being verified when contacting a device, these additional fields must be properly populated in the packets in order for the SNMP exchange to proceed. In the case of the *Time* field, the console must increment this value every second in order to maintain synchronization with the agent. This check is an interesting part of SNMP version 3.0's authentication model and is a different way to keep the security of a manageability connection protected.

- **Privacy.** Although the SNMP ID used to distinguish a device from the rest may be predictable by combining data pieces such as enterprise number, IP or MAC address, and an administratively assigned string, IDs can be updated at any time by administrators in the event they are compromised (Table 1, Threat 4). As long as SNMP IDs can be modified by authenticated and authorized users, it is a good practice to support them as they will not add significant exposure to tracking attacks.
- **Security levels.** Three protection levels are defined in SNMP: noAuthNoPriv (no authentication and no Privacy required), authNoPriv (authentication required, but no privacy) and authPriv (authentication and privacy protections required). Depending

on the sensitivity of the device and the configurable variables it makes available through SNMP, the security level necessary to access the device must be adequately chosen. Variables that control power state should always require 'authNoPriv' mode. All manageability exchanges to update credentials must carry an 'authPriv' protection level.

- **User tables.** In order to determine what users have access to the device, a User Table is maintained. This table contains user names, authentication protocols, authentication keys, privacy protocols, and privacy keys. A particularity of the SNMP version 3.0 standard is that it maintains separate keys to support authentication and privacy. Although the use of a common key for authentication and confidentiality is not rare in many other manageability systems, USM offers enhanced security by maintaining two distinct keys (if one of them is compromised, authentication or encryption might be affected, but not necessarily both).

View-Based Access Control Model

VACM provides access control in SNMP using the concept of a 'view'. Views control access to a subset of data elements. For instance, if access must be restricted to a number of objects, a view that groups a few of those objects can be created and privileges can be assigned over the group or 'view', rather than over each object individually; this simplifies permissions maintenance considerably. A view in SNMP is in fact an object subtree in the MIB to which access privileges are attached. Administration of views and object permissions is a basic component of SNMP's security scheme and requires an understanding of the specific data stored on the MIB repository as information and its value varies from implementation to implementation.

VACM is responsible for verifying requests submitted from the consoles and ensuring that the requested objects are only made available to authorized parties. The primary entry point to consider in VACM is the *isAccessAllowed()* gate which controls information from four different tables that contain the authorization information of the device:

1. **Context table.** The context table defines groups of objects or contexts to which a common privilege mask is assigned. An object can belong to more than one context, and an entity requesting access to the MIB can be given permissions for one or more contexts.

2. **Group table.** This table captures the control policy for groups of users. A number of role-based groups are defined via VACM and common security privileges can be assigned to all members of the group collectively.

3. **Access table.** This table stores the permissions for all groups and is an important attack target as it stores group names, permissions and view information. When multiple permission levels are specified on the Access table for a single group, SNMP implements a protection mechanism though which the level considered highest security will be selected, hereby preventing the problem of having two overlapping privilege levels trying to guard a single object. (If both were available for verification, an attacker could choose to focus on the weaker level thinking that it might be an easier garget to compromise).

4. **View Tree Family table.** This table stores the MIB views referenced by other tables.

The VACM algorithm to grant or deny access uses: a) the security name field (i.e., user name) to obtain group information from the Group table; b) the Context table to find context name, and c) the Access table to identify the view over which

Read, Write and Notify privileges will be granted. Due to this multi-link access evaluation, SNMP version 3.0 VACM must be carefully configured. Even when the security model offers sufficient modularity and granularity to control variables and users, the view-based model may be overly complex to maintain, especially for smaller IT departments. It is this type of reduced deployment where SNMP security becomes a challenge if sufficient resources are not devoted to creating and maintaining solid manageability infrastructure.

DESKTOP AND MOBILE ARCHITECTURE FOR SYSTEM HARDWARE (DASH)

Desktop and mobile Architecture for System Hardware (DASH) is a group of specifications based on WS-Management (Cabrera, 2005) that provide standards for the implementation of out-of-band and remote manageability interfaces on desktop and mobile systems (Blair, 2007). DASH makes possible the remote administration of hardware over a TCP/IP network in the enterprise by defining profiles and protocols that can be used to characterize a system and control access to it.

The main functions that DASH offers include:

1. **Boot and power control.** An administrator can force system reboot, shutdown or power cycle when repairing a system. This is considered a security sensitive function as compromise of this module may result in loss of the control over the most basic configuration settings and operations of the system (Table 1, Threat 1).
2. **Alerts.** Temperature alerts, voltage alerts, etc. can be communicated to a management console using DASH alerts.
3. **Software and hardware inventory.** Inventory collection is one of the most fundamental manageability tasks. DASH allows a remote system to retrieve a list of

software and hardware components installed on the system in order to identify upgrades that may be needed.

4. **Account management.** This function enables the configuration of DASH manageability accounts.
5. **Device redirection (USB, serial, KVM).** The DASH specification includes the ability to mount remote devices on the system that is being managed. The security of this function must be guaranteed though strong authentication and authorization (Table 1, Threat 1 and Threat 4) as well as a sound implementation of the protocols.
6. **BIOS management.** Modern laptop and desktop systems have numerous configuration settings that can be modified at boot time by BIOS. This includes boot device precedence, password protection and feature enablement. Several researchers have recently focused on the security of system BIOS, and a DASH-enabled system could represent an opportunity to compromise BIOS remotely (Wojtczuk, 2009). Some systems implement BIOS extensions that appended to BIOS code extend its reach into chipset-based technologies. This type of functionality increases the risk that a compromised BIOS represents on the platform and, therefore, this feature must be considered security sensitive (Table 1, Threat 10).
7. **Software and firmware installation and update.** Modification of code on the platform is always a primary security threat that must be always addressed (Table 1, Threat 3 and Threat 10).
8. **NIC management.** DASH offers the ability to let traffic trough or block it. Since remote manageability is the primary objective of DASH, compromising NIC management may mean a system on the network cannot be accessed or repaired (Table 1, Threat 1 and Threat 7).

DASH aims at standardizing manageability for client systems (i.e., desktop and laptop) and is based on the Common Information Model (CIM) schema. CIM offers standard definitions for the elements of an IT environment. It describes them as objects and stipulates the interactions among them as relationships, just the way database schemas do. The primary objective of CIM is to characterize the key players that participate in manageability flows in order to provide a single interpretation of these components among vendors that will allow them to create technologies that can interoperate.

CIM defines concepts like computer system, operating system, network, service, and storage unit, as some of the most basic elements on the network and provides the means to, from a conceptual standpoint, access and monitor them. The standard is extensible and allows implementers to define new components and new relationships. For instance, in the case of security technology, firewalls, intrusion detection systems and antivirus software can be modeled by abstracting the communication link between basic IT-managed components and these new components using CIM. DASH uses a map created with CIM to enable standard manageability to reach all relevant systems on the network.

DASH provides these standard manageability functions to manage systems and enables access to systems regardless of their power and health state. The following section describes some of its most relevant features.

FUNCTIONS AND THEIR SECURITY

Standard Manageability Model

DASH defines three layers of components in a manageability system: clients, manageability access points or MAPs, and managed systems. Clients actually represent administrators with the permissions to access a managed system via a DASH-defined management protocol. It is the MAP layer the one that implements security functionality (i.e., authentication, authorization, and audit capabilities) and which can become an attack target.

The three layers are exposed on the network but the access points, which handle session establishment between clients and managed systems, are the most critical component. Access points also store local account data and ACLs that make possible the establishment of manageability channels. Interfaces connected to the access point must be evaluated from the security standpoint in order to detect implementation flaws before releasing a DASH-enabled system into production.

An external authorization, authentication and audit service is defined by DASH which is not part of the access point internals. This external service is an abstraction that allows developers to compose support systems for handling keying material, certificates and user privileges (for instance, a directory system like LDAP or a distributed authentication system like Kerberos).

Access in All System States

The MAP layer is responsible for controlling access to the devices and also for determining whether the device is in a mode in which the requested task is permitted. Although the MAP needs to make sure that requests are properly formed, that the client has permissions, and that the device can service the request in its current state, it does so by using information received from the managed elements themselves. If the data being sent from the device can be modified (e.g., no integrity protection is enabled), or if an attacker can influence the state in which the device is, it may be possible to trick the MAP into approving an illegal access request.

Active Capabilities

DASH uses the SOAP/XML-based WS-Management API to format and transmit messages taking advantage of the following function classes:

- **Discovery of managed elements.** Allows administrators to identify DASH-managed devices. Security violations include preventing a device from being discovered, identifying a device as DASH-managed when it is not, and impersonating a device.
- **Creation, destruction and redefinition of managed elements.** This function class is security sensitive as it can be used to alter the manageability layout presented to the consoles.
- **Access to audit logs and inventory tables.** Removal or alteration of audit logs is an important security violation which must be prevented by using integrity protections and two-person controls (i.e., a single administrator cannot modify or clear the audit log). Inventory information is not typically a security asset per-se, but alteration of the software information on the system (for instance, version numbers) could prevent a system from being repaired or patched.
- **Transmission of configuration commands.** This is the most significant function class in DASH from the security standpoint. Strong privilege separation, integrity and authentication must be implemented if the implementer wants to prevent the DASH from being abused by remote attackers.

DASH can be understood also as a network protocol stack in which TCP packets transport HTTP 1.0/1.1 data between console and device (if TLS is used, DASH traffic is protected at the transport level). HTTP packets in turn transport SOAP/XML code that defines the WS-Management directives summarized in the above classes. It is through the combination of these directives that in-band and out-of-band manageability happens. There are a number of add-on cards in the market that support DASH. These can be installed on different desktop and laptop hardware and constitute a scalable way to implement manageability when the chipset does not have this support already built in.

DASH SECURITY CLASSES

There are two security levels or classes defined by DASH, Class A, which is weaker, and Class B, which is stronger:

- **Class A security.** Although HTTP 1.1, which is recommended by DASH to transport traffic, provides authentication to client and server, the algorithms it supports are weak and therefore TLS/SSL must be used. The Basic and Digest authentication mechanisms that HTTP implements do not provide strong data integrity and do not support data confidentiality. In Class A, the traffic travels in the clear, although integrity attacks could be detected with the use of the MD5-based Digest authentication system.
- **Class B security.** DASH offers a higher security level in which all data transmitted between client and server is encrypted. There are three modes through which Class B security may be achieved:
  a. **HTTP_TLS_1 mode.** Uses TLS 1.0 for authentication and encryption. Administrators connecting from a console are authenticated using HTTP Digest and X.509 certificates are provisioned on each managed device to authenticate them (optionally, TLS Mutual Authentication can be implemented). The TLS cipher suite required for this mode is TLS_RSA_ WITH_AES_128_CBC_SHA (RSA

key exchange with AES bulk encryption and SHA hashing).

b. **HTTP_TLS_2 mode.** Is the same as HTTP_TLS_1 but instead of using HTTP Digest authentication, HTTP Basic authentication is used. Although Basic authentication is not as strong as Digest, all the traffic in both modes is secured with the same protection strength (same TLS cipher suite).

c. **HTTP_IPSEC mode.** Unlike the other two previous modes in which traffic is protected at the transport layer, this mode combines HTTP 1.1 Digest authentication with IPSec to provide managed device authentication at the IP level. ESP transport mode is required for IPSec and one of the following two cipher suites are necessary:

- AES-GCM (key size: 128 bits, ICV or Digest length: 16 bytes)
- AES-CBC (Key size: 128 bits) with HMAC-SHA1-96

It is important to notice that DASH uses role-based authorization with three operational roles: User, Operator, and Administrator. A User account only has read-only capabilities and cannot modify settings or data properties on managed devices. It is often not an obvious attack target as privilege escalation would be necessary in order to compromise more powerful DASH functions. An Operator, on the other hand, can issue read, write and execute operations and is able to change properties and settings on devices. The Administrator role is the one with the most privileges and can do everything an Operator can, plus it can also create and delete objects as well as accounts.

Eventing

In DASH, the eventing capability is a subscription-based model that leverages the CIM schema to define how to create and deliver alerts. Compared to SNMP, DASH eventing provides better granularity for alert definition and more robust event delivery. DASH also utilizes the WS-Eventing subscription system in order to define how alerts need to be routed on the network. Indication filters are created to monitor specific system conditions and DASH users subscribe to those filters. Once a condition triggers an indication, all users and applications subscribed to the filter received an alert generated by the DASH-managed device. By using the HTTP and TLS/SSL configuration combinations previously mentioned, it is possible to guarantee secure delivery and non-repudiation in DASH eventing.

CONCLUSION

Manageability technologies accelerate systems administration and allow Information Technology personnel to repair network devices from a remote location, often regardless of power or operational state. The out-of-band capabilities some of these solutions support represent a concern to security analysts as this interfaces create parallel access vectors into the managed infrastructure that are outside the reach of security software installed on the operating system such as antivirus and firewall packages. Most manageability technologies, however, include sufficient protections that implementers can use to secure the perimeter of any deployment, from a large enterprise network, to home systems that are accessed remotely by commercial service provider. There is no single manageability solution that is applicable to all platform types (i.e., server, smart phone, and laptop) and each technology has its strengths and weaknesses. It is necessary to carefully select the most adequate manageability protocol(s) based on the type of device that will be managed, the value of the information handled by them, and the overall exposure these systems will have to the Internet. By following the recommendations outlined in this chapter, it is possible to minimize the attack surface and maintain reliable remote access, accurate inventory collection, and effective systems troubleshooting using many of the network manageability solutions available today.

REFERENCES

Berlin, K., Cepulis, D., Chan, R., Lowell, D., Duke, J., Jair, F., ... Vincent, P. (2009). *SMBIOS reference specification version 2.6.* Standard specification. Distributed Management Task Force, Inc.

Blair, B., Hass, J., Hilland, J., Hines, D., & Shah, H. (2007). *Systems management architecture for mobile and desktop hardware – DASH.* White paper. Distributed Management Task Force, Inc.

Bojinov, H., Bursztein, E., Lovett, E., & Boneh, D. (2009). *Embedded management interfaces: Emerging massive insecurity.* Paper presented at Blackhat 2009, Las Vegas, NV.

Bumpus, W., Sweitzer, J., Thompson, P., Westerinen, A., & Williams, R. (1999). *Common information model: Implementing the object model for enterprise management.* John Wiley & Sons, Inc.

Cabrera, F., & Kurt, C. (2005). *Web services architecture and its specifications: Essentials for understanding WS.* Redmond, WA: Microsoft Press.

Campbell, I. (2007). *Symbian OS communications programming* (2nd ed.). West Sussex, UK: John Wiley & Sons, Ltd.

Dierks, T., & Allen, C. (1999). *The TLS protocol, version 1.0. Request for Comments RFC-2246.* Internet Engineering Task Force, Network Working Group. ·

Frye, R., Levy, D., Routhier, S., & Wijnen, B. (2003). *Coexistence between version 1, version 2, and version 3 of the Internet-standard network management framework.* Request for Comments RFC-3584.

Hardaker, W. (2006). *Use of SHA-256 in DNSSEC Delegation Signer (DS) Resource Records (RRs). Request for Comments RFC-4509.* Internet Engineering Task Force, Network Working Group.

Kumar, A., Goel, P., & Saint-Hilaire, Y. (2009). *Active platform management demystified.* Intel Press.

Sheldon, T. (2001). *Encyclopedia of networking and communications.* Osborne/McGraw-Hill.

Wojtczuk, R., & Tereshkin, A. (2009). *Ring -3 rootkits.* Paper presented at Blackhat 2009, Las Vegas, NV.

ADDITIONAL READING

Clemm, A. (2006). *Network Management Fundamentals.* Indianapolis, IN: Cisco Press.

Cole, E. (2009). *Network Security Bible* (2nd ed.). Indianapolis, IN: Wiley Publishing, Inc.

Limonchelli, C., Hogan, C., & Chalup, S. (2007). *The Practice of System and Network Administration* (2nd ed.). Boston, MA: Addison-Wesley.

Pfleeger, C., & Pfleeger, L. (2006). *Security in Computing* (4th ed.). Saddle River, NJ: Prentice Hall.

Wang, J. (2009). *Computer Network Security: Theory and Practice. Beijing, China: Higher Education Press.* Heidelberg, NY: Springer.

KEY TERMS AND DEFINITIONS

Discovery: Identification of a managed device connected to the network for purposes of inventory collection, system repair and software update.

Eventing: Alert and notification capabilities built into a manageability protocol to keep administrators informed about the state of managed devices and network infrastructure.

In-Band Interface: Manageability interface available when the system is in full-operation mode. This interface is often supported by the main processor.

Manageability: Tools and functions to remotely administer network resources that often support out-of-band functionality.

Management Console: Control station from which network devices can be located and managed by Information Technology personnel.

Out-of-Band Interface: Manageability interface available when the system is not in full-operation mode (e.g., when operating system is down, or when the file system is corrupted). This interface is typically served by a Service Processor.

Service Processor: Secondary processor, often a microcontroller, which supports the main processor with manageability tasks that need to be performed over an out-of-band interface.

Section 4
Sensor Network Security

Chapter 10
Security and Attacks in Wireless Sensor Networks

Murat Al
University of Arkansas at Little Rock, USA

Kenji Yoshigoe
University of Arkansas at Little Rock, USA

ABSTRACT

Understanding data security is crucial to the daily operation of Wireless Sensor Networks (WSNs) as well as to the further advancement of security solutions in the research community. Unlike many surveys in literature that handle the topic in close relationship to a particular communication protocol, we provide a general view of vulnerabilities, attacks, and countermeasures in WSNs, enabling a broader audience to benefit from the presented material. We compare salient characteristics and applications of common wireless technologies to those of WSNs. As the main focus of the chapter, we thoroughly describe the characteristics of attacks and their countermeasures in WSNs. In addition, we qualitatively illustrate the multi-dimensional relationship among various properties including the effectiveness of these attacks (i.e., caused damage), the resources needed by adversaries to accomplish their intended attacks (i.e., consumed energy and time), and the resources required to defend against these attacks (i.e., energy overhead).

INTRODUCTION

First version of the current generation sensor devices was introduced in mid 1990s with Wireless Integrated Network Sensors (WINS) at the University of California, Los Angeles UCLA). As computation power, communication range,

and lifetime of the devices have increased, the node sizes have significantly decreased. These changes have led to better performance of WSN devices resulting in better performance of existing applications as well as possible exploration of new application areas. In 2003, MIT's Technology Review had included Wireless Sensor Network (WSN) technology in its annual list of the ten most important technologies that will change the world

DOI: 10.4018/978-1-60960-777-7.ch010

(Huang, 2003). With new application areas and developments in wireless technologies, WSNs will gain more popularity and take more roles in our everyday lives.

WSNs are often deployed in areas where constant power is not available and recharging of batteries is not an option. Hence, the most important design aspect of a sensor network is its energy efficient operation to provide a long network lifetime. At present, with a pair of AA batteries a sensor node can operate several years. This comes at the cost of very constrained resources. Protocol designs in WSNs have to consider many constraints of the sensing devices such as limited battery power, memory size, and computing capacity. This makes a WSN more vulnerable to attacks than a wired or less energy constraint wireless network such as a Wireless Local Area Network (WLAN) or a Mobile Ad-hoc Network (MANET). On the other hand, the ever-increasing computational power of personal computers and laptops along with better performing decryption algorithms pose greater threats to wireless communication. For instance, various sniffing and wireless key hacking software is freely available on the Internet.

The objective of this book chapter is to make practical information on security in resource constrained wireless sensor networks available to a wide audience, ranging from practitioners to academic researchers. We explain security associated terms with respect to WSNs and present security relevant services. As the focus of the chapter, we thoroughly describe the characteristics of attacks and their countermeasures in WSNs. We qualitatively analyze and illustrate the multidimensional relationship of the discussed attacks. This allows a simplified comparison of relevant properties such as the effectiveness of a particular attack, the resources needed by the adversary to mount it, and the cost for the network to counter this attack.

BACKGROUND

Common Wireless Technologies and Their Typical Characteristics

This section provides an overview of common wireless technologies with their typical characteristics for a quick comparison. It does not attempt to cover all aspects of wireless technologies, nor does it give an exhaustive list of devices, protocols and applications that can be used with a particular wireless technology. Rather it helps broach the subject of wireless sensor networks by comparing it to prevalent technologies, such as WLAN and MANET.

Table 1 lists general properties of WLANs, MANETs, and WSNs for a comparison. WLANs and MANETs have many properties in common; hence, they are listed together in one column.

For the sake of completeness, we will briefly describe Wireless Mesh Networks (WMNs) that can be implemented using one or a combination of various technologies such as IEEE 802.11 (Wireless Local Area Network), 802.15 (Wireless Personal Area Network), 802.16 (Wireless Metropolitan Area Networks, also called WiMAX), cellular networks such as GSM (Global System for Mobile Communications) or CDMA (Code Division Multiple Access). Network components usually include end nodes or mesh clients, routers, and gateways. If the same type of hardware is used, mesh clients can be configured to act as routers or end nodes. Routers and gateways serve as access points for end nodes to the network, whereas the gateway additionally is a bridge between the mesh network and an external network such as the Internet. While in traditional networks the small number of access points or hotspots needs a wired connection to an external network, in a wireless mesh network access points themselves are wirelessly connected to each other forming a mesh. The advantages of WMNs include

Table 1. Comparison of WLAN and MANET with WSN

Property	WLAN, MANET	WSN
Node cost	Expensive	Inexpensive
Node type	Laptop, PDA, Printer	Mote
Battery	Rechargeable	Usually not rechargeable
Recourses	High processing power and memory	Very low processing power and memory
Bandwidth	1 to 54 Mbps	1 to 250 kbps
Operation	Usually human controlled	Autonomous
Function	Designed for communication	Primarily sensing
Node density	Few devices in network	High node density
Network type	WLAN: Infrastructure, Ad-Hoc MANET: Ad-Hoc	Ad-Hoc
Range	1 to 350 m	1 to 100 m

- operation with existing wireless standards such as 802.11a,b,g, 802.15, and 802.16,
- self configuring in terms of automatically adding nodes into the existing structure,
- self healing in terms of finding alternate paths,
- easy to install and expand

A mesh may serve as the underlying topology for the compared network types.

Another prevalent technology is the WPAN, standardized by the IEEE 802.15 working group. The IEEE 802.15.1 standard for personal area networks is based on the Bluetooth specifications.

Although it falls under the category of Ad-Hoc networks, it is possible to connect up to seven slave devices to a master device, and mostly it is used for cable replacement between two devices. While earlier devices used Infrared and RF, newer devices on the market use preferably Bluetooth. Table 2 lists main characteristics of WLANs, WPANs, and WSNs; most common usage, devices, operation mode, and network topology are presented.

In Tables 1 and 2, we have mentioned network types or modes as "Infrastructure", "Ad-hoc", "Ad-hoc (hierarchical)", and "Ad-hoc (Flat)". Most WLANs found in homes and small offices operate in infrastructure mode. Users connect to

Table 2. Main characteristics of WLANs, WPANs, and WSNs

WLAN	WPAN (Bluetooth)	WSN
• For communication with higher data rates • Processing, Communication • Laptop, PDA, Printer • Supportive devices: Router, Switch • Infrastructure • Mostly single hop	• For mobile devices planned to work within close proximity • Communication (Cable replacement) • PDA, Mouse, Headset • Supportive devices: Router, Switch • Ad-hoc • Mostly single hop	• Designed for remote monitoring and controlling • Sensing, Processing, Communication • Sensor, Actuator • Supportive devices: PDA, Embedded systems • Ad-hoc • Multi-hop
WLAN - Infrastructure • Dedicated gateway • Dedicated router	WPAN - Ad-hoc • Any node can be a gateway • Any node can route	WSN - Ad-hoc (Hierarchical) • Star, Mesh, Cluster Tree • Dedicated device categories • Some devices can route WSN - Ad-hoc (Flat) • Any node can route

the network via an access point, which in turn is connected to a wired Local Area Network (LAN) to provide access for users to services available through devices such as printers or file servers. Users cannot communicate directly with each other, but their traffic needs to go through the access point. In the ad-hoc mode, users spontaneously form a WLAN (self configuring) by directly communicating to each other. In a flat ad-hoc routing scheme all nodes are on the same level, i.e., each node performs routing function. All nodes maintain global information such as distance and route information to the destination, which is flooded through the network to all nodes. While being a simple and cost effective way of building a network, this mode is not scalable due to shared bandwidth problems and produces a large amount of overhead due to flooding of a large number of control packets. In a hierarchical ad-hoc network, end nodes are gathered into clusters following some clustering method where each cluster has a cluster head that serves as the main communication partner for end nodes within a cluster. Routing is performed between clusters, for which multiple routes may be available. This increases the robustness of routes and makes this network type scalable for large network sizes.

Worthwhile to mention is also the IEEE 802.15.4 standard and its task group, which species the physical and media access control for low-rate wireless personal area networks (LR-WPANs). The standard focuses only on physical (PHY) and medium access control (MAC) layers; the upper layers of the protocol stack are defined by the ZigBee Alliance (ZigBee, 2010). The PHY layer operates at two frequencies: one covering the operational frequencies of countries like the United States and Australia and the other covering the European band. The tasks of the MAC layer include synchronization and access control typically using the Carrier Sense Multiple Access with Collision Avoidance (CSMA-CA) mechanism. The network (NWK) layer enables

the sensor node to associate with or disassociate from the network. The set of ZigBee communication protocols is based upon the specification of this task group. It provides important features that optimize the functionality of a WSN, like fast and easy deployment, various security settings, and vendor independence. ZigBee uses the Advanced Encryption Standard (AES) block cipher. The ZigBee stack is designed with the paradigm of data and management entities, which provide respective services. Layers are designed with this paradigm in view and each layer is exposed to a service entity via a service access point (SAP). It is also responsible, when suitable, to commence a fresh network and assign addresses to devices associated with this fresh network. The ZigBee stack is comparatively smaller than stacks used in other wireless standards, sometimes needing as little as 4 KB of memory to function. However, full implementation of the ZigBee stack may take up to 32 KB of memory. Application specific deployments, requiring node databases and transactions for pairing tables, may require extra memory space for optimized operations. At present, ZigBee is the only standardized protocol set suited for WSNs and is maintained and published by a group of companies.

WSN ARCHITECTURE AND ORGANIZATION

Sensor nodes allow cost-effective sensing especially in applications where human observation would be inefficient, expensive, undesirable, or dangerous. Monitoring of phenomena is among the main applications of a WSN. It includes monitoring of physical or environmental conditions like magnetism, temperature, sound, motion, vibration, pressure, and chemical elements. WSNs provide ground for military, industrial, scientific, civilian and commercial applications (Sabbah, Majeed, Kang, Liu, & Abu-Ghazaleh, 2006). A military application includes the detection of biological

Figure 1. Main components of a sensor node

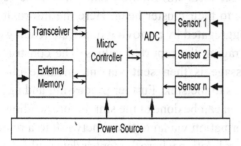

and chemical weapons (Hills, 2001). Some of the civil applications are habitat monitoring, structure monitoring, traffic monitoring, object tracking, and fire detection. WSNs mainly have been used in small scale by the military and academics for scientific purposes. With the miniaturization, growing capabilities, and decreasing production cost of sensing devices, the technology is becoming more practical for use in commercial applications and large-scale networks.

A simplified schema representing the essential components of the physical architecture of a wireless sensor is shown in Figure 1. It essentially depicts the sensor in a setting with the processing unit (Micro-Controller), the radio unit (Transceiver), External Memory, the analog-to-digital converter (ADC) and the Power Source.

Each WSN design aspect, i.e., hardware, software, topology, communication protocol, and encryption method faces the given rigid constraints with power as a primary limitation. When a WSN is deployed in a terrain where nodes cannot be retrieved for charging and maintenance, the lon-

gevity of the network becomes a crucial factor. This is the case with many WSN applications where nodes are deployed in uncontrolled environments including hostile areas, toxic regions or disaster sites (Park & Blake, 2007). A WSN device consumes significantly more energy for radio transmission than for computation (Intanagonwiwat, Estrin et al. 2002; Krishnamachari, Estrin et al. 2002; Madden, Franklin et al. 2002; Ali, Saif et al. 2006), thus reducing communication overhead will have a great impact on the overall energy savings of the network.

The topology of a WSN can be either distributed, also called flat, or hierarchical. A flat topology consists of devices of the same type that communicate directly with each other. The base station, also called a sink can be reached via multiple routes. A sink is the most powerful device in a WSN with an abundance of resources, which serves as the interface to the WSN and acts as a coordinator in charge of key management, node authentication and other management related tasks. A remote control station (e.g. located in an office or lab) can connect to the sink using an external network, in most cases the Internet. Queries, management instructions to, and data from the WSN are exchanged through the sink. A typical network is depicted in Figure 2. While this robustness in route availability is an advantage in small networks, keeping track of topology changes in a large network is very difficult. Due to nodes that run out of battery and nodes that are later added to the network the connectivity structure

Figure 2. Typical WSN

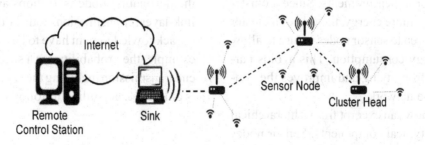

can constantly change. Every node is informed of these changes by flooding the network. This maintenance issue makes a flat topology inefficient when used for large scale networks.

A clustered hierarchical network is more energy efficient than a flat network topology (Akkaya & Younis, 2005; Chengfa, Mao, Guihai, & Jie, 2005; Choi, Shah, & Das, 2004). By clustering, a large network is partitioned into small areas with varying number of sensor nodes that can be administered autonomously. Every cluster has a head node called a cluster head that collects and aggregates sensed data from sensor nodes in its cluster. Cluster heads then send the aggregated data via either a single-path (Intanagonwiwat, Govindan, Estrin, Heidemann, & Silva, 2003; Karp & Kung, 2000) or multi-path (Budhaditya Deb, Sudeept Bhatnagar, & Badri Nath, 2003; B. Deb, S. Bhatnagar, & B. Nath, 2003; Deng, Han, & Mishra, 2006; Dulman, Nieberg, Wu, & Havinga, 2003; Jing, Han, & Mishra, 2004; Lee & Gerla, 2000; Loh & Tan, 2007; Xun, Yu, & Hong Ge, 2006; Ye, Zhong, Lu, & Zhang, 2005; Yibin & Midkiff, 2005) routing to a sink. Reaching the sink is the task of the cluster head. Hence, regular sensor nodes do not need to keep track of routing changes in the network and can keep their receivers off to save energy. This reduces the overall energy cost by eliminating network wide flooding for topology control packets and data packets. Cluster heads on the other hand always have to be awake so they can relay data from other locations to the base station. Although shown with a different symbol in Figure 2 for clarity purposes, sensor nodes and cluster heads can be devices of the same hardware type. In both configurations, they can perform measurements. Since a cluster head consumes more energy, the role of a cluster head can be given to sensor nodes in turn to allow balanced energy consumption. This avoids particular nodes from dying and improves the connectivity in the network.

Figure 2 shows an excerpt from a hierarchical WSN and its typical components. Sensor nodes collect local information and send these readings to their cluster head. Here the information is aggregated by removing duplicate readings or averaging the reported values. The constructed message is then sent via intermediate cluster heads to the sink. Further processing and aggregation can be done at the sink before sending the information via an external network to a remote control station where the sensor data is ultimately required. Network management data and queries for sensed data follow the reverse route.

The longer the path from source to destination is the higher is the probability that a message on this path will be intercepted. Having more than one sink in a given network shortens this distance and therefore decreases the capture probability on average. However, sinks are expensive devices and therefore not many of them can be deployed. Figure 3 shows how data can be collected in a WSN. In a network of Type I with one sink, which represents the vast majority of the works in the area of WSNs, or multiple (in most cases a few) sinks (Ciciriello, Mottola, & Picco, 2007; Egorova-Forster & Murphy, 2007; Intanagonwiwat, et al., 2003; Jing, et al., 2004; Kinalis & Nikoletseas, 2007; Sooyeon, Son, Stankovic, & Yanghee, 2004; Wan, Eisenman, & Campbell, 2003; Xiaoyan, Pu, Jiejun, Qunwei, & jun, 2005; Ye, Luo, Cheng, Lu, & Zhang, 2002), a message needs to travel a long distance to reach a sink. Here, the probability of a message being intercepted is very high. Another drawback of this network type is that the packet loss rate and energy consumption due to retransmissions increase with growing distance between source and destination. Let us assume the average loss rate per link is 10% and the destination node is 10 hops away. To avoid link-layer retransmission, both the data packet and the acknowledgement have to be received. In this example, the probability for a successful end-to-end transmission including the acknowledgement is only 12%, according to following calculation:

Figure 3. Number and location of super nodes

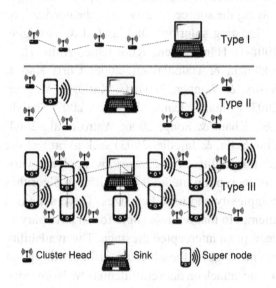

$$p_{Total} = p_{Link1} * p_{Link2} * \ldots * p_{Link20} = (p_{Link})^{20} = 0.9^{20} = 0.12 \tag{1}$$

Since neither the data packet nor the acknowledgement (ACK) must be dropped, the total number of hops is 20. Using forward error correction schemes decreases the number of retransmissions but adds overhead to the packet size.

In addition to sinks, powerful devices referred to as super nodes can be utilized that act as local sinks in the sense of collecting data from the network. Figure 3 shows three types of networks. Type I depicts a flat multihop network with one sink. Type II shows a hierarchical network with a reasonable number of super nodes. Type III illustrates a hierarchical network with a large number of super nodes. Super nodes are more powerful than sensor nodes but less powerful and less expensive than sinks and they are not intended to replace the sinks. With the presence of more powerful devices in addition to sensing nodes, more information can be aggregated and processed in the network. This is a desired feature for wireless sensor networks since the more data is processed in the network the less data must be transmitted to the sink, which reduces the energy

consumption and extends the longevity of the network (Pottie & Kaiser, 2000). The presence of super nodes means adding another tier to the network. Due to the abundance of resources, the super nodes themselves and their communication is considered to be secure against attacks aiming data confidentiality. Having many super nodes (Type III) would shorten the communication path between a source node that wants to transmit sensed data and a super node. This would significantly decrease the communication overhead and capture probability of a data packet. However, the price for having a large number of super nodes would be tremendous and therefore make this solution for a large-scale network impractical.

Network Type II with a reasonable number of super nodes offers the best balance between hardware cost, communication overhead, and security. The works described in (Ciciriello, et al., 2007; Egorova-Forster & Murphy, 2007; Intanagonwiwat, et al., 2003; Jing, et al., 2004; Kinalis & Nikoletseas, 2007; Sooyeon, et al., 2004; Wan, et al., 2003; Xiaoyan, et al., 2005; Ye, et al., 2002) resemble this network type in the sense that they use multiple sinks. Multipath approaches that transmit multiple copies of a message via multiple paths to the same destination aim to increase the communication reliability against packet loss due to bad channel conditions (Seah & Tan, 2006). However, in consequence these solutions have a most unpleasant effect on the confidentiality. The more copies of the same message travel through the network the higher is the probability that this message could be captured by an attacker. Multipath also refers to routing protocols where multiple paths between a source and destination are discovered but not used at the same time (Kai, Kui, & Wenjing, 2005; Lee & Gerla, 2000). The alternative paths can be used when the transmission via the main path is not preferable due to many reasons such as jamming, existence of a known attacker at that path, congestion, interference, topology changes, or dead nodes along the path. There also exist multipath routing protocols that improve data security by transforming a message into multiple shares by secret sharing schemes and sending these fragments of the message via multiple paths to the destination. A small number of compromised nodes along the path will not lead to compromise of the whole message (Kotzanikolaou, Mavropodi, & Douligeris, 2005; Lou, Liu, & Fang, 2004).

RELATED WORK

Raymond et al. (Raymond, Marchany, Brownfield, & Midkiff, 2006) proposed a framework for mitigating or defending against Denial of Sleep attacks. The paper presents a study of the impact of the attacks on the S-MAC, T-MAC, and the G-MAC protocols. To defend against Denial of Sleep attacks, a framework consisting of five key components is proposed. The components are Strong Link-layer Authentication, Anti-replay Protection, Jamming Identification and Mitigation, Broadcast Attack Protection, and Resilience against Compromised Nodes.

Multipath solutions in literature (Budhaditya Deb, et al., 2003; B. Deb, et al., 2003; Deng, et al., 2006; Kai, et al., 2005; Lee & Gerla, 2000; Loh & Tan, 2007; Seah & Tan, 2006; Ye, et al., 2005) are mainly used to improve data reliability by sending multiple copies of the same message via a number of paths or by using the existing paths alternatively one at a time. However, the transmission of multiple copies of the same message results in a large overhead, which defeats the goal of energy efficient operation. Using alternative paths can ensure that an attacker placed on the path from source to destination can only intercept packets that use this particular path. For a message consisting of multiple packets, this means that only a part of the message would be intercepted. However, one drawback of this solution is that the paths lead from one source to one destination. An eavesdropper located near the source or near the destination node can intercept all messages leaving the source or arriving at the destination.

Existing solutions such as (Al & Yoshigoe, 2008-1; Hämäläinen, Kuorilehto, Alho, Hännikäinen, & Hämäläinen, 2006; Chris Karlof, Sastry, & Wagner, 2004; C. Karlof & Wagner, 2003; Roman, Alcaraz, & Lopez, 2007; Shaikh, Lee, Khan, & Song, 2006; Watro et al., 2004; Zhu, Setia, & Jajodia, 2003) seek to protect the confidentiality of messages by applying various encryption methods that differ in algorithm complexity and used key sizes. These solutions attempt to make it infeasible for an adversary to decrypt an intercepted message. The availability of a message for the adversary is the starting point for any attack on data confidentiality. To improve communication confidentiality, (Al & Yoshigoe, 2008-2) introduces an end-to-end Adaptive Confidentiality Mechanism (ACM), which decreases the probability that an adversary can intercept a message in the first place. ACM is based on a multiple sink multiple path topology. The most apparent difference of ACM to existing works that use multiple sinks (Ciciriello, et al., 2007; Egorova-Forster & Murphy, 2007; Intanagonwiwat, et al., 2003; Jing, et al., 2004; Kinalis & Nikoletseas, 2007; Sooyeon, et al., 2004; Wan, et al., 2003; Xiaoyan, et al., 2005; Ye, et al., 2002) is "that" and "how" ACM uses super nodes, devices with an abundance of resources that serve as local data collection points. By incorporating a small number of super nodes to the large number of sensor devices, ACM effectively and efficiently can protect messages at a network level where resources are scarce. The multiple paths in ACM carry portions of a message rather than duplicates of the same. In addition, the multiple paths in ACM lead from a source node to "n" different destinations rather than to one destination. A resource constrained sensor device divides a message into several segments, encrypts them and sends them to a pre-defined set of "n" super nodes. Each super node encrypts and forwards the segments to the super node set leader. Upon receiving all segments, the super node set leader reconstructs the original message and sends it via a secure channel to a sink. This mechanism is vulnerable to the before mentioned eavesdropping attack at the source node. In contrast to the multipath solutions in literature, it is secure against an eavesdropping attack at the destination, since the packets arrive at different nodes, and hereafter are forwarded using secure channels.

SECURITY IN WIRELESS SENSOR NETWORKS

As WSNs find their way into new applications, the amount of sensible data and the need for undisturbed operation do increase. For a WSN designer or administrator it is crucial to understand security related vulnerabilities, attacks and their countermeasures.

This section focuses on challenging security issues in WSNs. First, the relevant security related terms and security requirements such as confidentiality, integrity, and others are discussed. The discussion includes definition and importance of each security requirement as well as how these requirements can be met.

SECURITY RELATED TERMS

Risk is the likelihood of a successful attack against a critical component or service that executes an existing threat by exploiting given vulnerabilities. Vulnerability is a weakness of the network that may be exploited. In this context, the term network includes all elements the network is built of, such as hardware, software, topology, and communication protocols. An attack is an action against the network with the intention of harming it. A threat is a potential attack that has not taken place yet.

As early as in the design phase one has to correlate these security related terms with the

particular network. When examined carefully in most cases one can find vulnerabilities in all these elements. While these definitions are related to WSN security, note that sensor nodes might be vulnerable to damage caused by dirt, weather or other environmental conditions if not properly protected. One would hardly call it an attack if nodes were damaged by rain for example. This shows that a threat can be executed without being exploited by an attack. Hence, all threats must be identified and considered in the planning phase.

Risk

In addition to the likelihood of a successful attack, risk also includes the degree of harm a given network element may suffer. Risk also depends on the quantifiable value of the device or service that is to be protected. For instance, a certain attack may have devastating effects on a valuable network component, and protection against this threat may entail a large overhead. However, if the likelihood of the occurrence of this attack were miniscule, one could decide to live with this risk to avoid the large overhead. We can see that the explained terms are interdependent. Therefore, risk analysis and the design of security depend very much on the case in hand. Different communication protocols have distinctive vulnerabilities. Depending on the application of the planned network, the vulnerability of a particular protocol might be very well acceptable because attacks exploiting that vulnerability might have no effect on the application, hence, would not constitute a risk. For example, if delay is not an issue for the application, an attack causing delays in the message delivery can be accepted. Installing expensive countermeasures to defend against this type of attacks for this application would be unnecessary. Consequently, protocols showing some weaknesses may be viable for a particular application, supporting that other characteristics make them suitable.

Vulnerability

Nodes and sinks (and thus the whole network) are vulnerable to energy exhaustion. If some nodes die due to depletion of their batteries, this could partition the network and isolate large numbers of sensor nodes from the rest of the network. Therefore, nodes should try to reach the average life expectancy across the network. Other vulnerabilities of nodes include breakable and insecure packaging, limited memory, and their proneness to failure. Sinks are usually powerful devices with sufficient memory and processing power. Usually they are connected to a constant power source. When this is not possible and they run on batteries, they are vulnerable to energy exhaustion. In densely populated areas as in towns, they might be protected, monitored, and maintained easily. However, in a scenario where the sink is remotely deployed with the other nodes, its packaging may be vulnerable to destruction. The wireless link, which is in most cases a radio signal using 916 MHz or 2.4 GHz is vulnerable to obstacles, fading, and interference. The network vulnerability is a collection and interaction of the vulnerabilities of the network elements, including the topology, communication protocols, average energy exhaustion, fault tolerance, and self organization.

Threat

Malfunctioning of a node can result in creating wrong data. A defect in the sensing device may influence the readings of that node only. On the other hand a malfunctioning of the circuitry can impact the aggregation and forwarding, hereby causing even greater damage. A captured node can be analyzed to reveal the installed algorithms, security mechanisms, and encryption keys. An adversary could then tamper with the node to make it an insider attacker and use the gained knowledge to form other attacks. False nodes created after compromising a legitimate node could be added into the system. A major threat

against the sink is the disclosure of its location. Once the location is known, it could be destructed. Various attacks such as Eavesdropping, Selective Forwarding, and Stealthy attacks are more effective when performed on packets near the sink. Node capture and unauthorized access are further threats against a sink. Among the threats against the communication link are obstacles, interference, and channel noise. Link failures may also be caused by transceiver malfunctioning of the nodes. A dense node deployment resulting in a large collision domain combined with high traffic density can decrease the accessibility of the channel resulting in high delays. Delays in channel access have also an adverse impact on the network performance. Further network threats are low scalability, large overhead, and network partitioning possibly caused by topology changes due to dead nodes.

Attack

There are a variety of Denial of Service (DoS) attacks against a sensor node, e.g. Interrogation, Flooding, Selective Forwarding, and Node Compromise. A sink could be isolated from the network by diverting the messages to a malicious device that acts as a sink after mounting a Sinkhole attack. One of the most direct ways to attack a link is to jam it; this includes Collision attacks. The availability of the link can be indirectly affected by other attacks. For instance, a Denial of Sleep attack that aims energy exhaustion by keeping the victim node's receiver busy. Here, the random bytes transmitted to the victim not only waste the victim's energy but also make the channel inaccessible to other nodes. Attacks against the network usually aim its communication mechanisms and services. Preferable targets are aggregation nodes, aggregated messages, and management information like synchronization packets, acknowledgements, RTS/CTS (Request To Send, Clear To Send), and data request packets. Note that many of the attacks formed against other components, i.e. nodes, links, and sinks have an impact on the general network performance.

Attackers are often categorized as mote class and laptop class attackers (C. Karlof & Wagner, 2003; See, Abd-Alhameed, Hu, & Horoshenkov, 2008; L. Wang & Kulkarni, 2006). Mote class attackers have capabilities comparable to sensor nodes and the damage they can cause is seen as more limited than potential damage induced by a laptop class attacker. While this is mostly true, there are cases that a few mote class attackers can degrade the network performance considerably. Selective Forwarding on single sensor node readings can be handled easier than the same mote class attack performed on aggregated data with high information density. Also for management and request packets coming from the base station; tampering with these packets can lead to great damage since many nodes rely on this information. Therefore, one has to consider the details of a given system. In the mentioned case, one could think of applying more resiliencies to aggregated messages by transmitting multiple copies via multiple paths.

SECURITY REQUIREMENTS

Security measures are very much dependent on the aimed, existing, and possible conditions, i.e. they have to consider various factors that change dramatically from case to case. Hence, in WSNs they have to be tailored for a narrow range of applications. In the following, we discuss services required to assure data security in a WSN.

Confidentiality

In wireless communications, messages can be intercepted by eavesdropping. Confidentiality is essential in a WSN environment to protect sensitive information. To maintain confidentiality data must be protected from unauthorized access, use, or disclosure while in storage, in process, and in transit. A sensor should not leak its readings to its neighbors and should transmit them via a secure channel to authorized receivers only. This is achieved by encrypting the messages, which prevents unauthorized users from accessing it.

Integrity

Data integrity is the assurance that the received data has not been changed after leaving the sender. The sender applies a publicly known one-way hash function to the message and appends this hash to the message. The receiver uses the same function to create the hash of the received message and compares it to the received hash. An altered message would result in a different hash.

Authentication

The problem with creating a one-way hash is that an adversary can still intercept the message, change it, create a hash of the changed message, and send the packet to the destination. To overcome this problem the sender and the receiver share a secret key to compute the message authentication code (MAC) of all communicated data. A MAC is an encrypted hash that is created by taking the message and the symmetric key as input values. After changing the intercepted message, the adversary cannot create a new MAC without having the key. This provides message integrity and authenticates the sender. Note that the message does not need to be encrypted to provide these two services. The message has to be encrypted in order to offer confidentiality.

Availability

Availability ensures that services and information are accessible to authorized users when requested. Various attacks entirely or partly can threaten their availability. If an intermediate node is attacked, or fails due to other reasons, the network should be able to maintain its function. This resiliency

Table 3. List of defense mechanisms

Defense Mechanism	Attack
Prevent Signal Detection with Low Probability of Detection/ Interception (LPD/I) such as Direct Sequence Spread Spectrum (DSSS), Frequency Hopping Spread Spectrum (FHSS), and Ultra-wideband (UWB)	Jamming, Collision, Eavesdropping
Tamper Resistant Packaging, Hiding Nodes;	Tampering, Node Compromise
Error Correcting Codes	Collision
Rate Limiting	Spoofed Request Packets, Interrogation, HELLO Flood, Flooding
Authentication (source verification)	Flooding, Wormhole, Impersonation, Sybil
Authentication (message verification)	Information Disclosure, Traffic Analysis
Authentication (source and message)	Denial of Sleep, Selective Forwarding, Bogus Routing, Sinkhole, De-synchronization
Confidentiality and Integrity (encryption and hashing)	Denial of Sleep, Information Disclosure, Traffic Analysis, Selective Forwarding, Replay, Bogus Routing (if protection applied to routing information packets), Sinkhole, Impersonation, Sybil, Node Compromise
Packet Leashes (Hu et al.) (limited distance)	Wormhole
Location Verification	Sybil
Stateless Connection	Flooding
Source Verification (cryptographic puzzle)	HELLO Flood, Flooding
Data Freshness (counter)	Replay
Geo Routing (location information), Multiple Disjoint Paths, Monitor Neighbor (hear it forwarding), Periodic End-to-End Probing	Sinkhole, Black Hole, Selective Forwarding

can be achieved e.g., by rerouting traffic or reassigning tasks to other nodes.

Data Freshness

An attacker can replay intercepted messages without the need to decrypt them. Even with provided confidentiality and integrity there is the need to ensure the freshness of messages. Although the secret keys may be updated, it takes time for the new keys to be distributed to all nodes. For the life span of the current key plus the time until the new key arrives Replay attacks can take place. One solution to this problem is including a counter into the packet. To keep the message overhead low, in another solution the communicating nodes keep local counters that need to be synchronized infrequently.

ATTACKS IN WIRELESS SENSOR NETWORKS

The chapter starts with a list of defense mechanisms against common attacks. Here after, the attacks are explained with all their facets; what the motive for an attack is, what vulnerability can lead to such an attack, which layers are affected, how it affects the node, how it can be detected, what preventive measures are, what countermeasures can be employed when attacked. The questions may vary for different attacks according their relevance. After discussing the attacks and security measures, we illustrate the comparison of relevant attack attributes.

The following table provides a list of defense mechanisms effective for various attacks. The attacks are explained in detail hereafter.

Many of the examined attacks can be found in wireless networks such as WLAN, MANET, and WSN. Their common vulnerability is the use of wireless communication. However, the differences in these technologies make it necessary to examine the attacks closely related to the unique characteristics of a given network technology. Within this area, the evaluation of attacks depends on additional traits, such as the capabilities of the devices, communication protocols, network size, and the importance of various security services. In literature, attacks have been categorized in various ways. Existing classifications include distinction between passive and active attacks (Padmavathi & Shanmugapriya, 2009; Stallings, 2006), attack location (Uluagac, Lee, Beyah, & Copeland, 2008), and communication protocol layer (Kavitha & Sridharan, 2010; Y. Wang, Attebury, & Ramamurthy, 2006). Each of these classification methods are useful and help to see the threats and attacks from different perspectives. Usually the attacks fall in multiple categories. The same attack can target different devices, such as sink, aggregator node, and regular sensor node and take place at various locations of the network with different results. In addition, the same attack can have an impact on multiple layers.

We categorize the attacks according to an adversary's primary intention. Many attacks can serve multiple purposes. For example, following its main purpose an attack can disturb the communication among various nodes. As a side effect, it could simultaneously exhaust the energy resources of a subset of these nodes. While the attacks are grouped according their main function, the explanations point out their extended use and further potential damages.

A Denial of Service (DoS) attack is aimed to prevent legitimate users from using services. A user in this context is any legitimate entity such as people or devices that require the service. The use of a service can be prevented partly or completely; even without preventing it, introducing large delays is another method of denying

service. In traditional computer networks, denial of service often describes the case that users are refused access to certain data located on a server. However, in a WSN it can apply to a broader range of conditions. Services can be the availability of nodes, sensed data, and a functioning communication among the nodes. Any disturbance in the operation of the network components can result in DoS. Some examples in a WSN include manipulating sensor readings with fake events, injecting false data, falsifying existing data, routing attacks and Denial of Sleep attacks. Nearly all attacks in which an attacker (i) actively interacts with a node or the packet, (ii) is included in the routing path, are DoS attacks. This is true for all the listed attacks, except the ones in the first group (Gain Information).

1 GAIN INFORMATION

Before an intruder can cause major harm, he needs to collect and analyze information about the network. The selection and realization of the attacks will depend on the vulnerabilities revealed by the analysis.

Eavesdropping, Passive Monitoring, Traffic Analysis, Information Disclosure

The terms eavesdropping and passive monitoring refer to the same attack. Eavesdropping is seldom described as a separate attack. It is rather a necessary first step for many attacks. Wireless signals can be received by any device in communication range. An attacker listens to ongoing communications in the targeted area and collects communication packets. Eavesdropping is also commonly used with the assumption that the intercepted message is disclosed. In this chapter, we describe Eavesdropping as the act of listening to the channel and intercepting packets. Whether the adversary is able to disclose any information from intercepted packets depends on the applied protection mechanisms. If no encryption and authentication mechanisms were used the packet content is immediately available as clear text. On the other hand, if the packet was protected, then the adversary has to penetrate the protection mechanism(s) first to disclose the information. Hence, we keep this operation separate from Eavesdropping and refer to it as Information Disclosure. Traffic Analysis attack aims to reveal as much as possible information about the network, e.g. the topology, MAC protocol, routing protocol, authentication mechanism, integrity mechanism, and the encryption keys. By analyzing the contents of many packets from various communication partners, the attacker can draw conclusions on these points. With a rate monitoring attack (Deng, Han, & Mishra, 2005) an adversary can determine which nodes are most active. The conclusion is that a highly active node must have some key roles in the network, i.e. it could be a cluster head, an aggregation node, a gateway node or even a base station. A time correlation attack monitors when a node receives and transmits packets. When this time is short, it can be assumed that this node is a relay node that immediately forwards the received packet. On the other hand, if a node's radio is inactive after receiving a packet, the conclusions could be that either this node was not the intended receiver of the packet, or it is an aggregator node that waits for more messages to arrive. The real strength of a time correlation attack is its ability to reveal the physical location of the base station. Due to the asymmetric communication pattern found in WSNs, i.e., traffic flows from sensor nodes to base station; the attacker knows that a packet eventually will go to a base station. An attacker can inject own packets into the network that can be easily distinguished from regular packets. Following these packets by monitoring the activities of nodes that handle them, the attacker can find the location of a base station. Destruction of the base station is one of the biggest threats a network faces. Such attack would be detected at once and

technicians and possibly some security personnel would shortly arrive on the premises. A new base station would be installed at another location that is more difficult to access. First, the adversary would need to leave the premise immediately upon destroying the base station to avoid being caught. Secondly, he would need to start from the beginning with his attacks to find the new base station; probably by having to overcome some improved security mechanisms. Placing a powerful attacking node near the base station would be more advantageous for the adversary. Messages arriving at the base station are very valuable. In most cases, they contain aggregated sensor readings many nodes have spent energy for sensing, processing, and forwarding. Intercepting such a message could reveal sensor readings of a whole region in condensed form, making the eavesdropping extremely efficient. With an attacking device near the base station, the described attacks will be more energy efficient for the attacker and more destructive for the network. Traffic analysis is an ongoing process. Once the attacker has discovered certain vulnerability, he can exploit it to gain knowledge about new vulnerabilities.

Data encryption is the most common technique employed to protect information content from disclosure. Various confidentiality mechanisms have been referred to in the discussion of related work. Ultra-wideband (UWB) communications systems have an inherent resistance to detection and intercept, due to their low average transmission power. The transmission power is so low that the eavesdropper has to be as close as a few yards to the transmitter to be able to detect the transmitted information. Furthermore, UWB pulses are time modulated with codes known to each transmitter and receiver pair. For an attacker it is next to impossible to detect these extremely narrow pulses, in the order of picoseconds, without knowing when they will arrive.

Deng et al. (Deng, et al., 2005, 2006; Jing, et al., 2004) focused on protecting the data traffic from aggregator nodes to base station through multi hop routing. The authors introduced countermeasures for defending the base station against traffic analysis attacks that include randomization of data paths from a sensor node to the base station and a random selection from multiple parent nodes for forwarding a packet. Since the network is still vulnerable to a time correlation attack even after applying these two methods, a fractal propagation technique is used in which fake packets are created and propagated in the network to achieve further randomness in the communication pattern. Evenly creating hot spots in the network to pretend the location of the base station to be in one of those high traffic areas, further helps in disguising the location of the base station and makes a traffic analysis attack more difficult.

2 DISTURB COMMUNICATION

The intention in interfering is to disturb the communication and drain the batteries of legitimate nodes. An Interference Attack can be mounted as a Jamming or Collision attack. For many of the attacks in the network layer, such as Worm Hole, Black Hole, and Selective Forwarding typically an attacker needs to be on the path of the data flow.

Jamming, Interference, Collision

Jamming occurs primarily in the physical layer and it can be accomplished in different ways. Near the source of the jamming signal where the signal is strong nodes cannot receive any packets since they are overshadowed by the jamming signal. At a greater distance where the jamming signal is about the same strength as the communication signal, they will interfere with each other and the received packet will be corrupted. Xu et al (Xu, Trappe, Zhang, & Wood, 2005) puts jamming attacks into four categories: constant, deceptive, reactive, and random jamming. A constant jammer sends continuously random data into the channel. Legitimate packets that are transmitted during this time will be corrupted. Other nodes that have packets to send cannot access the channel since it is constantly busy. In the case of deceptive jamming, instead of random bits the jammer blocks the channel by constantly transmitting regular packets to make it look like regular traffic. For example, if the jammer sends out preamble bits every receiving node will stay in receive mode to receive the data packet after the preamble. Staying in receiving mode over a long period of time will drain their batteries very soon. These two attacks are relatively easy to detect. The reactive jamming attack overcomes this shortcoming for the adversary by sending a jamming signal when sensing activity on the channel. This type of jamming is very costly for the attacker since the radio must continuously be on. In random jamming, the attacker's goal is to save energy. According to some schedule, the attacking node switches between sleeping and jamming mode. In literature, the last two types of attack are often referred to as Collision Attack. Since the jamming signal consists of short random signals or pulses, this attack is more energy efficient for the attacker. The communication in the network may not be entirely disabled but the packets that even partly have collided with the interfering signal are corrupted and therefore need to be retransmitted. Causing collisions in only one byte is enough to create a Cyclic Redundancy Check (CRC) error and to cripple the message (Znaidi, Minier, & Babau, 2008).

Detecting a collision attack is difficult since the attack time is short. In addition, network nodes may assume their packet has collided with other legitimate packets. However, receiving of many corrupted packets or receiving of many retransmission requests can suggest a collision attack. Jamming attacks can be detected by monitoring the connection quality, using techniques such as Packet Delivery Ratio (PDR)(Broustis, Pelechrinis, Syrivelis, Krishnamurthy, & Tassiulas, 2009) and statistical analysis of Received Signal Strength Indicator (RSSI). Applying a single technique may not be sufficient to identify jamming; however, if both techniques used together jamming attacks can clearly be identified. For example, a node can perform a consistency check between PDR and RSSI (Xu, et al., 2005). If the PDR shows a poor link quality (i.e., PDR value is almost zero) while the RSSI shows a strong signal, the node is regarded as being jammed. In addition, a node that is not located in the jammed area but sends packets that need to go through such an area can infer that the path is jammed by not receiving acknowledgements. More to detecting of jamming attacks can be found in (Broustis, et al., 2009; Çakiro lu & Özcerit, 2008; Muraleedharan & Osadciw, 2006; Sun, Hsu, & Chen, 2007). In the case of a collision attack, in most cases the whole packet is not lost but partly corrupted. Therefore, the use of error correcting codes can mitigate this attack (Lu, Krishnamachari, & Raghavendra, 2007).

Upon detection of a jamming signal, nodes should switch to a lower duty cycle and conserve as much power as possible. If the application were not time critical, a practical solution would be that a node refrains from transmitting until the jamming has ended. Another solution is re-routing the packets, after collaboratively identifying the jammed region, if redundant paths are available or can be established. Nodes located on the edge of the jammed region can report the jamming to unaffected nodes outside the region (Wood & Stankovic, 2002). Unaffected nodes will cease forwarding traffic to attacked nodes, hereby avoiding the jammed area. If the source node has sufficient power, it can increase its transmission power in an attempt to suppress the jamming signal. Using UWB radio communication is highly resistant to jamming; very short pulses (in the order of nanoseconds) are transmitted simultaneously on a large frequency band. Frequency Hopping Spread Spectrum (FHSS) and Direct Sequence Spread Spectrum (DSSS) are two of the most effective countermeasures against jamming. A hybrid of these solutions has been proposed by (Mpitziopoulos & Gavalas, 2009). Assuming

that the attacking device is a mobile device with limited battery power, it cannot afford to jam multiple channels or a relatively wide frequency band for a long time. However, the low cost and low power sensor nodes are usually not equipped with radios capable of using these techniques. In literature the wideband systems, such as FHSS, DSSS, and UWB are referred to as Low Probability of Detection (LPD) and Low Probability of Intercept (LPI) systems.

Wormhole

A wormhole is a high quality and low latency link between two malicious nodes located at two separate regions of a network. This low latency link can be a high bandwidth out of band or even a wired link. While the malicious device on one end of the wormhole is far away, the device on the other end is usually very close to a base station. Let "A" denote the region and the node at the far end side of the wormhole. Respectively, let "B" denote the region and the node that is close to a base station. The wormhole makes both nodes A and B attractive as forwarding nodes once it has carried traffic back and forth between the two regions. Nodes in region A will see that their transmission can reach the base station quickly and without collisions. The nodes in region B including the base station will experience the same advantages when trying to reach region A. Once nodes A and B are integrated in the routing tables of the nodes in the respective areas, the adversary can start mounting various attacks.

A simple attack formed using a wormhole can affect a huge number of nodes at both sides of the wormhole. Network management packets such as HELLO packets, requests and acknowledgments that are received at one side (A) can be replayed at the other side (B) of the wormhole. Nodes in region B will waste energy receiving packets that are irrelevant for them. Furthermore, since they are able to receive these packets they will assume that the senders of these packets are in one hop distance. Hence, nodes in region B will perceive the nodes in region A as their neighbors and include them into their routing tables. In an attempt to directly communicate to them they will waste energy. The same attack can be mounted on nodes in region A reversing the attack direction. It is difficult to detect and defend against wormhole attacks. However, geographic routing and clustering based routing protocols such as LEACH and TEEN are robust against this attack.

Sinkhole, Black Hole, Grey Hole, Selective Forwarding

A malicious node, this may be a device injected to the network or an existing but compromised node, distributes spoofed advertisement messages showing it has a high quality link to a data aggregation point or to the base station. Depending on criteria like the adversary's intentions, the existing communication protocol, and the type of the attacking device the malicious node could also advertise itself as a base station. An advertisement could include a very low packet drop statistic or a very low hop count to a base station. As a result, receivers of this advertisement will decide to use this malicious node as their next hop. In addition, the receivers of the spoofed advertisement will promote this supposedly high quality link to their neighbors hereby extending the attacked area or the number of attacked nodes. A malicious device that has become a preferred node as described is referred to as sinkhole node. Some protocols could require a node to build its own statistics about the end-to-end communication quality to a base station. In this case, the adversary would need to provide a real high quality link to a base station to be included in other nodes' routing tables. This can be accomplished with a Wormhole attack. Devices on both ends of a wormhole are sinkholes.

Among the DoS attacks in literature, we find the terms "Black Hole" and "Grey Hole". A sinkhole node acts as a black hole when it drops all packets it receives. In fact, any malicious device that is in

the routing loop could be a black hole, i.e., it does not have to be a sinkhole node. However, this is not an advisable move, considering the fact that soon none of the neighbors will send any messages through this node. A grey hole node selectively forwards packets. Here too, technically it is not necessary that this node is a sinkhole node.

In order to maximize energy efficiency in WSNs routing decisions are often based on parameters like minimum hop count, smallest end-to-end delay or end-to-end reliability. When luring traffic, wormhole and Sinkhole attacks exploit this property by offering seemingly the best paths that satisfy these requirements. Since nodes have to rely on the advertised link properties, it is very difficult to detect these attacks. Routing protocols using geographical location of nodes, referred to as geographic routing protocols are resilient to such attacks. GPSR (Greedy Perimeter Stateless Routing) (Karp & Kung, 2000) and GEAR (Geographic and Energy Aware Routing) (Yu, Govindan, & Estrin, 2001) are known examples in this category.

A multi-hop network requires intermediate nodes to route packets. A malicious node in the routing path can drop packets randomly or systematically. It could drop messages destined to a certain node; or the victim could be an important source node that usually transmits aggregated data. In another scenario, only management or control packets could be forwarded but data packets would be dropped. A Selective Forwarding attack is mostly combined with a Sinkhole attack to maximize its efficiency. Imagine an adversary who physically breaks into a certain area of a network that is monitored with motion sensors. A sinkhole in this region would drop messages coming from sensor nodes that have detected the intrusion but pass messages originating from other nodes. The sinkhole node would send an acknowledgement for the received packet and the sender of the message would assume that its message has been forwarded correctly.

To alleviate the effect of these attacks, after sending a message to its neighbor, the source node can listen whether the neighbor transmits the received message (Marti, Giuli, Lai, & Baker, 2000). With this mechanism, called Watchdog, nodes can rate their neighbors according to the forwarding ratio of their packets. This quality metric can be considered when choosing next hop nodes and updating the routing table. In a scarcely deployed network where nodes do not have sufficient neighbors to choose from this mechanism would not be effective. In (Ganesan, Govindan, Shenker, & Estrin, 2001) the authors demonstrate that using braided and disjoint paths can mitigate the effect of this attack. In (Al & Yoshigoe, 2008-2) the proposed Adaptive Confidentiality Mechanism divides the message into multiple portions and sends them through disjoint paths to multiple sinks. In this scheme, the adversary would need to intercept the segments on each path. However, this probability is very small. If at least one of the segments of the message arrives, the destination node will request the missing segments. The source node will come to know which of the used paths are unreliable and will use different paths for the retransmission.

Bogus or Spoofed Routing Information, Misdirection, Routing Loops, Flooding

By manipulating the routing process in a network, an attacker can cause havoc among the nodes. An attacker may spoof, alter, or replay routing information to disrupt traffic in the network (C. Karlof & Wagner, 2003). Random manipulation of routing information can cause confusions about the reliability of paths and location of nodes. Replayed transmission request packages will lead to retransmissions, hereby wasting the battery power of all nodes along the communication path. Certain nodes can be denied service by sending their packets into endless routing loops that are created by misdirecting packets. In the

same manner, a receiver could be the victim when traffic is constantly diverted from the node. Hence, these attacks can be used to exclude certain nodes from the network. Spoofed routing information is also used when promoting a sinkhole in a certain region. In a Flooding attack, an attacker can forge the source address when sending a request, so that the response(s) will return to the victim. Among further implications are extended source routes, network partitioning, and increased end-to-end delays. There is no one protocol or mechanism that can address all of these attacks. Clustering based protocols such as LEACH, PEGASIS, TEEN, and APTEEN are effective against routing related attacks. However, they are vulnerable to selective forwarding and flooding type of attacks. Rumor routing on the other hand is effective against HELLO flood attacks.

3 EXHAUST RESOURCES

Depending on the network topology, energy exhaustion can lead to partitioning of the network into segments that are isolated from the rest of the network. By selectively cancelling the availability of critical nodes an adversary can hamper or even disable the intended function of an entire network. Therefore, attacks leading nodes to total starvation of their power are very common.

Denial of Sleep

The link layer coordinates the access to the shared physical medium. The access can be schedule based or as in many cases contention based. Especially time critical and event driven applications require quick access to the channel without a node having to wait for its time slot. In any case, MAC protocols have characteristic communication patterns. This makes them vulnerable to Traffic Analysis attacks. An observing attacker can determine the utilized MAC protocol easily by analyzing the communication pattern in the network. In addition, the link layer is a preferred target of Denial of Sleep attacks because it also controls the radio of a sensor node. The radio consumes the most energy among the components of a sensor node device. Maximum energy is consumed in transmission mode. Depending on the used wireless sensor platform the receiving energy ranges between thirty and sixty percent of the transmission energy. It is comprehensible that an adversary is interested in mounting attacks that target abundant radio usage in order to shorten the lifetime of a sensor node effectively. When topologically critical nodes exhaust their power, it can lead to isolation of whole network segments from the rest of the network. This could lead to an abrupt degradation of network services.

To save energy sensor nodes spend most of their lifetime in sleep mode. With the intention of shortening the life time of the network an attacker can mount a Denial of Sleep attack to multiple sensor nodes. Originally, this attack was introduced by (Stajano & Anderson, 2000) and was called "sleep deprivation torture". The idea is to keep the attacked node busy with regard to power consumption to exhaust its battery. In literature, some attacks can be found that describe this procedure while having different names, as preferred by each author. Exhaustion and Starvation are among those names. There is no specific way to mount this attack; Denial of Sleep can be achieved in various ways. A plethora of distinctive DoS attacks can be employed to reach this goal: Node Compromise, Continuous Channel Access, Interrogation, Replay, HELLO Flood, Collision, Routing Loops, Flooding, RTS, Acknowledgement Spoofing, and Broadcast attack. Furthermore, an attacker can mount a Denial of Sleep attack without the need of breaking the link layer encryption.

Many of these attacks are subtle, i.e., the network behavior appears to be normal although the network is under attack. We explain detection and countermeasures when discussing the related attacks. However, attacks like Collision/ Interference, Continuous Channel Access, Routing Loops, Acknowledgement Spoofing, Sinkhole, and Selective Forwarding have a common aspect; in most cases they lead to packet loss. To reduce packet loss the random back-off mechanism is applied in many wireless communications protocols. After a collision, the transmitting node will assume that the channel is busy and will wait for a randomly determined time before attempting to retransmit. Each time a retransmission attempt fails an internal counter is incremented, which leads to increase of the back-off time. Since this mechanism is designed for inadvertent collisions, after several trials the sender should succeed transmitting the message. When on the other hand the collisions are deliberately caused by an attacker, we find the back-off mechanism a great hindrance. Due to the ever-increasing back-off times, attacked nodes defer from transmitting for a very long time. As a result, the attacker has abolished the availability of information, which is one of the three pillars of information security.

Interrogation

Many MAC protocols use the RTS/CTS handshake to mitigate the hidden node problem in wireless networks. By sending an RTS message, a sender expresses its intention to enter the channel. Nodes in communication distance that have not reserved the channel for themselves reply with a CTS message, stating that the channel is not occupied. In an Interrogation attack, the adversary repeatedly sends out RTS messages to elicit responses by listening nodes. Since the nodes are constantly preoccupied with sending CTS messages they cannot go into sleep mode, which leads to exhaustion of their battery power. Also, if they have own sensor data to transmit they defer from transmitting since another node already expressed its intention to use the channel. Hence, an Interrogation attack can lead to Denial of Service at multiple nodes.

With link layer authentication receivers of RTS messages can ensure that the messages originate from a legitimate node. TinySec (Chris Karlof, et al., 2004) is one of the secure communication protocols that provide authentication and it is implemented into the common sensor node operating system TinyOS (TinyOS, 2010). On the other hand, has the intruder been able to compromise a legitimate node and is using it to perform its attack, authenticating this node would not help preventing such an attack. A rate monitoring mechanism ensures that certain nodes cannot occupy the channel exhaustively. Of course, the attacker is not interested in the fairness that this mechanism imposes and therefore would mount the Interrogation attack never the less. However, in this case the neighboring nodes would discard the request messages and would not reply with CTS responses.

SYN Flooding

The transport layer manages end-to-end connections that are established after receiving a connection request. A device can simultaneously have multiple end-to-end connections; however, the number of open connections is limited. In this attack, an adversary sends multiple connection requests without sending the related acknowledgements to establish the connections. The victim node has to assign buffer space to the half open connections, cannot go into sleep mode, and cannot accept connection requests from legitimate nodes.

As a defense Znaidi, et al. (2008) proposes the use of a client puzzle; only after its solution is presented a connection will be accepted. The solution of such a cryptographic puzzle is computationally expensive and is therefore used to foil an adversary from mounting a SYN Flood attack with the interest of to preserving its own energy. Varying the complexity of the puzzles can serve as a tuning parameter. For instance, when the number of connections is getting too high the puzzle could become more complex. The disadvantage is that legitimate nodes requesting a connection are subject to the challenge with the puzzles as

well. Another strategy is to keep a low limit for number of open connections. The drawback of this method is that legitimate traffic is limited as well. Connection-less transport layer protocols are not affected by this attack.

De-Synchronization

Transport layer protocols that rely on sequence numbers are vulnerable to De-synchronization attacks. An adversary changes the sequence number of a packet when forwarding it or creates packets with higher than expected sequence numbers on behalf of a victim and sends them to the receiver. When seeing the unexpectedly high sequence number on the received packet the receiver assumes that many messages must have been lost and requests retransmission for these messages. A solution is to use authentication for all packets including control fields, which include sequence numbers.

4 ATTACK DATA AGGREGATION

Given a large-scale sensor network, in most cases it is not necessary to have the sensor readings of every sensor node available at the base station. It is sufficient or even necessary to aggregate the sensed data to create a concise report. First transmitting all the readings to the base station and aggregating them would be a waste of energy for the sensor nodes. Aggregating the data as soon as possible decreases the size of transmitted bytes and extends the lifetime of the network. Due to this fact, most network topologies have aggregator nodes on the paths to the base station. These could be a special type of device with more computation capabilities and battery power. In protocols that involve local trust centers or cluster heads, it is likely that such nodes also perform data aggregation. Another setting could be that the role of cluster heads or aggregating nodes can be given to any sensor node. A node with special tasks consumes more energy and its battery would deplete rapidly. To ensure an even battery consumption among the nodes the special tasks can be assigned following a random rotation scheme (Heinzelman, Chandrakasan, & Balakrishnan, 2000). In general, attacks have a greater impact when performed on aggregated data.

Stealthy

While packets containing aggregated data are equally vulnerable to attacks like Misdirection, Black Hole, Grey Hole and others; a Stealthy attack specifically targets such packets. Here, the attacker's goal is to make the user accept falsified aggregation results (Chan, Perrig, Przydatek, & Song, 2007). In this context, the user is the node that receives aggregated messages. For example, after mounting a successful Node Compromise attack on an aggregator node, the intruder can manipulate the aggregated data or even manufacture some fictitious data. With the "aggregate-commit-prove" approach proposed by (Chan, et al., 2007) the aggregator has to prove that is has performed the aggregation task correctly. With the help of cryptographic techniques of commitment, efficient random sampling mechanisms and interactive proofs, a user can verify that the received data is a good approximation of the true value. The authors also claim that this approach not only works with subverted aggregators but also with a fraction of corrupted sensor nodes in the network.

Sybil, Impersonation

In a Sybil attack, a malicious node presents itself with multiple identities to its neighbors. The node can have multiple identities at the same time. The Sybil attack can cause harm to distributed data storage, data aggregation, fair resource allocation, and voting systems. It can also affect geographic routing protocols (C. Karlof & Wagner, 2003), where coordinate information needs to be exchanged among neighboring nodes. In a routing protocol that requires disjoint paths a source node would be sending packets to the same malicious node while assuming it has used different neighbors. Depending on the number of his identities, an intruder may be able to decide on the outcome of a voting. This could be a vote on the legitimacy of one of the adversary's identities, which he would win participating on the voting with a sufficient number of forged identities (Newsome, Shi, Song, & Perrig, 2004). Furthermore, the Sybil nodes can lead to wrong data aggregation results by providing falsified sensor readings.

In an Impersonation attack, a malicious node impersonates another node by using its identity. For the victim node whose identity was stolen, the implications can be severe. The attacker can mount a flooding attack by sending many requests on behalf of the victim node. The victim would be flooded with the responses, which it would receive and discard. Such Denial of Service attack does not only keep the involved nodes from performing their default tasks, but the excessive radio usage shortens their lifetime immensely. In localization algorithms (Srinivasan & Wu, 2007) that involve reputation and trust mechanisms or some voting system, both, Sybil and Impersonation attacks can be very effective.

Public key cryptography could be used to verify the identity of a neighboring node. However, generating and verifying digital signatures are operations that are too costly for sensor nodes. (C. Karlof & Wagner, 2003) suggests that every node shares a unique symmetric key with a trusted base station that in turn provides two neighboring nodes with a pair-wise key, which they can use to implement an authenticated, encrypted link between them. In (Douceur, 2002) the author claims that it is always possible for an unfamiliar entity to present multiple identities except under conditions that are not practically realizable for large-scale distributed systems. After demonstrating that under realistic assumptions, without a logically centralized authority Sybil attacks are always possible, he then presents his solutions of direct and indirect validation.

5 PHYSICAL NODE CAPTURE

Many of the listed attacks serve multiple purposes. Following attacks have in common that the adversary needs to capture the victim nodes physically. Since the attacks have this common starting point it makes sense to discuss them together.

Node Destruction, Tampering, Compromise

One of the intrinsic characteristics of WSNs is its unattended operation. Once deployed, nodes are capable of building an Ad-Hoc network by establishing neighborhood connections and routing paths. In addition, changes in neighborhood relations and routing paths happen without external intervention. Hence a WSN is meant to operate autonomously and unattended. As with any unprotected asset, this vulnerability attracts attackers. In a densely populated area, we can assume that everyone can have access to network components.

Once an attacker has access to nodes, the damage he can cause may depend on many factors. One limiting factor is his recourses, e.g. whether he has the time and appropriate technical equipment and the required knowledge to perform the intended attack. Assuming that the attacker does not have the mentioned limitations the attack will depend on his intention. Stealing or destruction of nodes is one of the easiest attacks. When only a few nodes are destructed, this attack might go undetected. If network administrators do not go and physically check what happened to the nodes they could assume that the nodes failed due to environmental hazards or some unexpected technical issues. However, the destruction of many nodes would easily reveal the attack. If the attacker wants to harm the system without being detected,

he would choose to tamper with hardware or software of the devices. Light or moderate tampering can cause malfunctioning, e.g. incorrect sensor readings, limited communication capability, and limited operation times. Since the nodes have not completely quit their operation, it would take much longer to detect such an attack. The network administrator could analyze the sensor data to find inconsistencies or otherwise suspicious or unexpected behavior. The most subtle and yet the most comprehensive attack in the physical layer is the Node Compromise attack, which also has the highest demands on the attackers recourses. Here, the attacker obtains full control over the device's hardware and software. By modifying the existing or injecting new code, the attacker can convert the node to an attacking device. After extracting the code and cryptographic keys, he can run the stolen code on a laptop where he emulates the architecture of the compromised node. With his laptop, he would have a fully authorized node that has many advantages like more processing power, more memory and higher transmission range over a sensor node. After a successful Node Compromise attack the intruder is now capable of mounting various insider attacks.

A tamper proof hardware (packaging) can overcome the tampering and compromise problem. For example, when trying to open the packaging a mechanism would immediately erase the memory. As it is generally the case with added security, such hardware is expensive and imperfect. The fact is that tamper proof hardware does not exist (Schneier, 2000); Hence, all mechanisms in this category can be considered as relatively tamper resistant. A device may be resistant to tampering by most people or a given technology. However, the device may not stand against a determined attack in a well-funded electronics lab. Therefore, when planning to invest on tamper resistant hardware one should have an attacker profile and the likelihood of such attacks in mind. Going one-step back from tamper proof hardware, we can find approaches that are technically less sophisticated yet expensive. For instance, camouflaging and hiding nodes can help in minimizing unauthorized access to nodes, with the drawback of investing in extra labor in the network deployment phase. Furthermore, in certain network scenarios or applications it might not be possible to hide the nodes. Low Probability of Detection/Intercept communication techniques such as spread spectrum and UWB should be utilized that make it difficult to locate the signal source.

SYSTEM CONSTRAINTS

We would like to describe the characteristics and operation of a typical device in a non-resource constraint environment first, before viewing the system constraints of WSNs. The comparison of the attributes listed here with the attributes of WSN components will help in understanding the rigid design constraints for WSNs.

Standardization in wireless technologies such as Wi-Fi (Wi-Fi-Alliance, 2010) and MANET allows a multifaceted comparison of related products. Devices in these networks follow a modular building architecture, i.e. the building blocks are interchangeable. Let us think of a laptop as a member of a Wi-Fi network. Among the hardware components we can list motherboard, processor, memory, hard disk drive, NIC, and wireless network card. It is possible to build a laptop with components available from various vendors. In most cases, it is also possible to run various operating systems on the same set of hardware provided the hardware drivers are available for the particular operating system. Furthermore, the communication among the networked products including security services is seamless. Given this high degree of compatibility in hardware, software, communication protocols, and security services, it is possible to compare these components in various aspects such as performance, vulnerabilities, energy efficiency, and scalability. Although specific applications can be carried out

using distributed computing, the main objective of devices like laptops and PDAs is their personal use or their autonomous operation. The purpose is to provide users a wide range of services ranging from professional and multimedia applications to games. Communication among the devices usually takes place to provide web services or to accommodate the interaction between their users.

In contrast, the nature of applications in a WSN usually requires the nodes to carry out a given task collectively. Especially in large scale sensor networks, which may consist of thousands of nodes the readings of multiple sensors are required. The other crucial difference is that once deployed, sensor nodes are usually not accessible for recharging, maintenance, and reuse, which makes an energy efficient operation and low cost hardware imperative. These demands combined with the sheer number of devices form the design constraints for WSN products and protocols. Although network components in a WSN may provide very similar functionalities, each component such as hardware, software, communication protocol, and cryptographic algorithm found in one network may be unlike any of the components found in another network. To achieve the design goals it is necessary to build the devices as embedded systems that provide energy and performance optimized interaction. Furthermore, the communication protocols have to provide low computational complexity, low transmission overhead, and high scalability while accommodating application specific security requirements. Hence, the design of network components in a WSN does not follow a modular architecture to accommodate a wide range of applications but is tightly bound to a specific purpose.

The low degree of standardization in WSN technology makes a comparison of various architectures exceptionally difficult due to their dissimilarities. It is the same reason that makes the evaluation of security attributes extremely difficult. Because of the large variety of application scenarios, a myriad of secure communication protocols specifically designed for WSNs were proposed. A secure communication among sensor nodes is essential, especially if sensitive information is exchanged in a network deployed in a public or hostile area. A significant amount of study in WSNs is conducted to achieve secrecy, (Al & Yoshigoe, 2008-1, 2008-2; Perrig, Szewczyk, Tygar, Wen, & Culler, 2002; Pietro, Mancini, & Mei, 2006), authentication (Kausar & Masood, 2006; Perrig, et al., 2002; Pietro, et al., 2006; Yanchao, Wei, Wenjing, & Yuguang, 2006), and message integrity (Bo, Shrestha, Yan, & Yang, 2008; Chris Karlof, et al., 2004; C. Karlof & Wagner, 2003; Kausar & Masood, 2006; Madden, Franklin, Hellerstein, & Hong, 2002; Perrig, et al., 2002; Shaikh, et al., 2006; Watro, et al., 2004).

A work presented by (Guimaraes, Souto, Sadok, & Kelner, 2005) evaluates the power consumption of the CPU and radio for the encryption algorithms RC5, RC6, TEA SkipJack, and DES implemented in a sensor network platform. While the four algorithms listed first are designed and well suited for resource constraint devices, DES is a widely used algorithm in less constraint devices.

The energy consumption of a device is expressed as

$$E = V \times I \times \Delta T \qquad (2)$$

In this equation E is the spent energy in Joules, V the voltage in Volts, I the current in Amperes, and T the time in seconds. The values for V and I are taken from the MICA2 data sheet (MICA2, 2010). For the CPU we have the values V=3V, and I=8 mA. The radio has a voltage of 3V and a current of 27 mA. Since the voltage and the current are constant, the energy consumption can be calculated by measuring the CPU time for performing the cryptographic operations or the radio time for transmitting the link layer packet. Measurements were made on a MICA2 mote running TinyOS with B-MAC as the MAC layer protocol. The energy necessary to encrypt a payload of 29 bytes varies between 36 μJ for RC5 and 259 μJ

for the RC6 algorithm. The energy consumption for SkipJack and TEA lies between these values. In contrast, the DES algorithm, which is one of the most commonly used algorithms in wired or not energy constraints networks has an energy consumption of 14.6 mJ. On the other hand, the energy required for calculating the MAC for a 29 byte packet reveals energy consumption between 50 μJ for RC5 and 380 μJ for RC6. Here again, SkipJack and TEA lie with their values in between. In addition, here the DES algorithm with a consumption of 29 mJ is at best questionable for use in energy constraint devices.

We have mentioned that protocol designs for WSNs have to consider special design and resource constraints. From the work discussed above, we can see that encryption algorithms specifically designed for resource-limited devices can operate with power consumptions that are about 50 to 500 times smaller than an algorithm that is commonly used in traditional networks.

The energy consumed by the radio is measured for three security modes, which are default mode, authentication only, and encryption with authentication. In the default mode, the sent message has 36 bytes and the spent energy is 1215 mJ. The authenticated message with 37 Bytes requires 1247 mJ. When encryption and authentication is provided, the packet has a size of 41 Bytes and consumes 1385 mJ of energy. The increase of 3% for the authentication mode and 14% for authentication and encryption mode is due to the packet overhead of 1 or 5 Bytes respectively.

In contrast to the CPU, we see that the energy consumption of the radio unit for the discussed case is about 3 to 4 orders of magnitudes higher for the RC5, RC6, TEA, and SkipJack algorithms, and 1 to 2 orders of magnitudes higher for the DES algorithm. In the design of new protocols, we see that minimizing the use of the radio unit will have the greatest effect on the energy savings. This means reducing the number of topology control and other management packets, and reducing the packet overhead for data packets.

On the other hand, energy efficiency and security are inversely proportional in terms of overhead. Hence, the most energy efficient protocol might not be the best suited for applications with higher need for security, robustness against node failures, reliable message delivery or other application specific requirements.

QUALITATIVE ANALYSIS

Analyses on the impact of attacks on specific routing protocols exist in literature (C. Karlof & Wagner, 2003; Kong et al., 2005). Rather than investigating particular cases, our study considers WSNs in general and seeks to make simplified statements about the attacks. We base our statements on existing knowledge, techniques, results, and accepted practices in WSN research. After thoroughly studying a vast collection of existing work and putting the results into relation, we present a comparative analysis of attacks in WSNs. Although we use graphs to compare attributes of various attacks, this analysis should be perceived as a qualitative comparison.

WSNs are usually designed for certain tasks; therefore, they widely differ in many aspects. Among these aspects are their security requirements, vulnerability to various attacks, and the degree of damage various attacks can cause in a certain scenario. To obtain quantified data, it would either be necessary to probe a large number of different network types with varying security relevant properties and produce average values of the attack attributes, or to analyze only specific network scenarios. Hence, to make a comparison of attack attributes possible, we need to generalize the network and the threat model. It is clear that such an immense generalization cannot reflect the real circumstances in every possible network. The diversity in WSNs would make such a claim void. As an example, let us consider a network in which the privacy of messages is not required but achieving message integrity is a concern. In this case, message encryption and the computationally more intensive process of decryption are not necessary. Instead, the message could be sent in clear-text accompanied by a hash of the message that is used to detect message modification during the end-to-end transmission. Here, the defense cost needed to thwart a cryptanalysis attack that is targeting the message confidentiality would be zero. A case on the other extreme could be that the secrecy of messages is a great concern, such that a strong encryption mechanism with long encryption keys is required. The caused overhead in delay, processing energy, and transmission energy would result in higher defense cost for the same attack in this case. Hence, the assumptions for the network and the threats can be generalized as follows: The analysis envisions a large scale WSN with balanced security requirements and therefore is equally vulnerable to the discussed attacks. Furthermore, the envisioned network does not have any protection mechanisms already installed, so a comparison of the cost and effectiveness of attacks and defense mechanisms can be made.

The values in the graphs are subjective approximations and they are averaged since they may vary for short-term and long-term view. For example, a Collision attack disturbs communication and also leads to energy exhaustion of nodes due to retransmission of lost packets. While the first mentioned purpose is achieved right upon mounting the attack, the draining of batteries will take some time. This time may depend on many factors such as the frequency packets are generated and whether the routing protocol is able of avoiding attacked regions. We considered such characteristics when providing a single average value e.g. for the Attack Effect Time.

In Figure 4, Attack Preparation Time is the time the adversary spends with groundwork required to form the intended attack. This may include the positioning of attacking devices at certain locations, observing the network by recording all overheard traffic, and sending advertisement packets to be included in routing paths. The At-

Figure 4. Attack preparation time and attack effect time

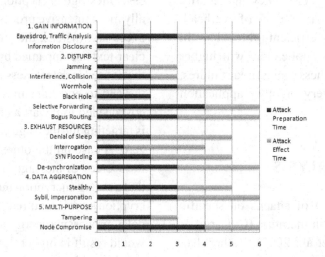

tack Effect Time is the period of time it takes an attack to achieve its intended goal.

We see that Information Disclosure has a short preparation time and a short effect time. This is true for our envisioned network that has no protection mechanism already in place. The strength of the chosen encryption mechanism will determine how secure the information is against disclosure.

The Black Hole attack differs from the others in that it has no bar for Attack Effect Time. For

the attacking node it takes some time to establish itself as a legitimate node and receive packets from its neighbors, which is expressed by the Attack Preparation Time. Once this is done, it takes no time to drop the received packets.

In Figure 5, the depicted bars for Average Attack Cost indicate the required cost for an attack on an unprotected system. The Attack Cost differs for short-term and long-term view. Most DoS attacks such as Denial of Sleep, Interrogation, Continuous Channel Access, Collision, and

Figure 5. Average attack cost and total time

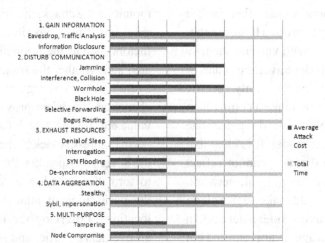

Figure 6. Average attack cost, damage, defense cost

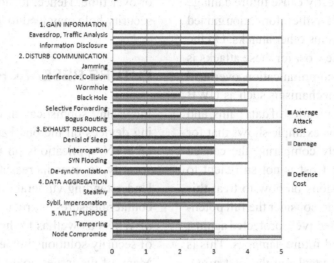

Flooding attacks, require more energy over time to maintain the attacks. The Total Time is the sum of Attack Preparation Time and Attack Effect Time.

For example, the Wormhole, Black Hole, Tampering, and Node Compromise attacks are costly in short-term since most effort is required at the beginning. Once the black hole is established or the node is physically tampered with, further activities performed for causing damage to the network require only little or no amount of energy. In this case it would be the dropping of packets and e.g. breaking a node's antenna, respectively. On the other hand, a Wormhole attack is costlier since the adversary uses it to tunnel packets over long distances. Similarly for the Node Compromise attack, to maintain attacks with a compromised node, the attacker will use it to send packets resulting in energy consumption.

For the Black Hole, Selective Forwarding, and the Bogus Routing attacks, the malicious node needs to be accepted by the network as a trusted node to be able to receive and send packets to neighboring nodes. Once this is accomplished, Black Hole and Bogus Routing attacks can be performed immediately. The longer bar for Average Attack Cost for the Selective Forwarding attack shows that this attack is more challenging

and costlier for the adversary. In contrast to the Black Hole attack, here, the attacker decides which packets to forward. For example, he could decide to drop certain type of packets or all packets originating from a certain node. Hence, such an attack needs more intelligence and planning and is therefore costlier.

In Figure 6, the adversary and the network administrator have a common interest on the attack attribute "Damage" to maximize the effect of their actions. The adversary is interested in attacks that have the least Average Attack Cost but at the same time lead to greatest potential damage. The network administrator on the other hand will try to defend the network against attacks that have a low Defense Cost and great potential damage. In this sense, the attribute Damage in the figure is a measure for the effectiveness of a defense mechanism used for this attack; the greater the damage it can prevent, the more effective it is. Damage describes any harm to the network, such as lost or delayed packets, increased energy consumption, and physical destruction.

For instance, none of the described types of harm is a direct consequence of Eavesdrop and Traffic Analysis attacks; hence, these attacks have no bar showing the caused damage. However, these attacks will indirectly cause future damage when the adversary exploits the information gained from those to form various other attacks. On the other hand, the Defense Cost for these attacks is very high due to the communication overhead caused by protection mechanisms such as UWB communication, randomization of data paths, and using fake packets. This example shows that for a certain attack, merely comparing the caused Damage with Defense Cost is not sufficient to make conclusive decisions on how to treat this attack. Rather, one has to consider the full potential of an attack to be effectively protected against its possible indirect and future damages. This is especially true for the attacks in the first group "GAIN INFORMATION". Hence, attacks in this group have special importance for the network administrator as well as for the adversary.

We envisioned a WSN with an average need for security requirements such as confidentiality, integrity, and authentication but no defense mechanisms installed or in place in the network. This allowed us to provide a qualitative comparison of attack attributes. A generalized view of WSNs was necessary to put various attacks and defense mechanisms, in terms of their attack attributes such as cost and effectiveness into relation. However, throughout the text we also gave many examples of specific applications and drew conclusions for these cases.

To take the most advantage of this study, network designers should know the peculiarities of their application to determine how the evaluated attack attributes would change when reflected on their network. For example, if the network components are inaccessible to intruders, the network designer does not need to invest in expensive tamper resistant hardware. Consequently for such network, the value for Defense Cost can be adjusted accordingly. However, we suggest that the selection of protection mechanisms should not exclusively depend on the primary security requirements of the application since most attacks do serve multiple purposes, either immediately

or over time. Hence, it should be noted that one security hole may lead to another.

FUTURE RESEARCH DIRECTIONS

Increasing sophistication of attacks and attacking devices on the one hand and the expansion of WSN applications on the other hand, make security an ever increasing demand of WSNs. Understanding vulnerabilities, attacks, and their countermeasures, is crucial to the daily operation of WSNs as well as to the further advancement of security solutions in the research community. Many of the issues could be solved with asymmetric key cryptography that usually requires long keys and computationally intensive algorithms. However, components in WSNs do not have the resources required to make efficient use of this paradigm. Due to resource limitations, existing routing protocols in WSNs have hardly reached the security level traditional communication networks offer. Thus, there is still need for energy efficient, secure and scalable solutions that consider the unique constraints and requirements of WSNs.

CONCLUSION

Starting from the physical layer and going up to the application layer, vulnerabilities exist in all the layers of the wireless networking protocol stack. These vulnerabilities vary with the utilized hardware, software, and the network topology. Furthermore, the same vulnerability may pose different types of threats and different degrees of risks depending on the security requirements of the application. The defenses for relevant attacks may involve certain encryption techniques, communication protocols, hardware specifications, and network deployment techniques. It follows that for ensuring security, one has to consider not only all layers of the protocol stack, but also the selection of hardware components. For example, the defense for Jamming and Collision attacks includes the use of frequency hopping or UWB; both are techniques that need to be supported by the selected hardware. Furthermore, we have seen that security is not only essential for messages in transit. Information being processed and stored needs to be protected as well. For example, a node compromise attack can lead to disclosure of non-encrypted information in storage and allow manipulation of the node's software.

A thorough assessment of the system vulnerabilities and threats requires a sound understanding of existing attacks. To foster the understanding of attacks and defense mechanisms, we first explained security related terms and security requirements in consideration of their relevance to WSNs. We then discussed the most significant attacks and defenses in all their facets. For a large scale WSN with balanced security requirements, we have compared the attributes of the discussed attacks, which include the time and cost for mounting various attacks and the cost required to defend against these attacks.

REFERENCES

Akkaya, K., & Younis, M. (2005). A survey on routing protocols for wireless sensor networks. *Elsevir Ad Hoc Networks, 3*(3), 325–349. doi:10.1016/j. adhoc.2003.09.010

Al, M., & Yoshigoe, K. (2008-1, July 14-17, 2008). *A secure and energy-efficient key generation mechanism for wireless sensor networks.* Paper presented at the International Conference on Parallel and Distributed Techniques and Applications, PDPTA 2008, Las Vegas, Nevada, USA.

Al, M., & Yoshigoe, K. (2008-2). *Adaptive confidentiality mechanism for hierarchical wireless sensor networks.* Paper presented at the GLOBE-COM Workshops, 2008 IEEE.

Bo, S., Shrestha, D., Yan, G., & Yang, X. (2008). *Self-propagate mal-packets in wireless sensor networks: Dynamics and defense implications.* Paper presented at the Global Telecommunications Conference, 2008. IEEE GLOBECOM 2008. IEEE.

Broustis, I., Pelechrinis, K., Syrivelis, D., Krishnamurthy, S., & Tassiulas, L. (2009). *FIJI: Fighting Implicit Jamming in 802.11 WLANs.*

Çakiro lu, M., & Özcerit, A. (2008). *Jamming detection mechanisms for wireless sensor networks.*

Chan, H., Perrig, A., Przydatek, B., & Song, D. (2007). SIA: Secure information aggregation in sensor networks. *Journal of Computer Security, 15*(1), 69–102.

Chengfa, L., Mao, Y., Guihai, C., & Jie, W. (2005). *An energy-efficient unequal clustering mechanism for wireless sensor networks.* Paper presented at the Mobile Adhoc and Sensor Systems Conference, 2005. IEEE International Conference on.

Choi, W., Shah, P., & Das, S. K. (2004). *A framework for energy-saving data gathering using two-phase clustering in wireless sensor networks.* Paper presented at The First Annual International Conference on Mobile and Ubiquitous Systems: Networking and Services, 2004. MOBIQUITOUS 2004.

Ciciriello, P., Mottola, L., & Picco, G. (2007). Efficient routing from multiple sources to multiple sinks in wireless sensor networks *Wireless Sensor Networks,* 34-50.

Deb, B., Bhatnagar, S., & Nath, B. (2003). *Information assurance in sensor networks.* Paper presented at the 2nd ACM International Conference on Wireless sensor networks and applications.

Deb, B., Bhatnagar, S., & Nath, B. (2003). *Re-InForM: Reliable information forwarding using multiple paths in sensor networks.* Paper presented at the 28th Annual IEEE International Conference on Local Computer Networks, 2003. LCN '03.

Deng, J., Han, R., & Mishra, S. (2005). *Countermeasures against traffic analysis attacks in wireless sensor networks.* Paper presented at the First International Conference on Security and Privacy for Emerging Areas in Communications Networks, 2005. SecureComm 2005.

Deng, J., Han, R., & Mishra, S. (2006). Insens: Intrusion-tolerant routing for wireless sensor networks. *Computer Communications, 29*(2), 216–230. doi:10.1016/j.comcom.2005.05.018

Douceur, J. (2002). *The sybil attack.* Paper presented at the First International Workshop on Peer-to-Peer Systems (IPTPS '02), Cambridge, MA.

Dulman, S., Nieberg, T., Wu, J., & Havinga, P. (2003). *Trade-off between traffic overhead and reliability in multipath routing for wireless sensor networks.* Paper presented at the Wireless Communications and Networking, 2003. WCNC 2003. 2003 IEEE.

Egorova-Forster, A., & Murphy, A. L. (2007). *Exploiting reinforcement learning for multiple sink routing in WSNs.* Paper presented at the IEEE Internatonal Conference on Mobile Adhoc and Sensor Systems, 2007. MASS 2007.

Ganesan, D., Govindan, R., Shenker, S., & Estrin, D. (2001). Highly-resilient, energy-efficient multipath routing in wireless sensor networks. *ACM SIGMOBILE Mobile Computing and Communications Review, 5*(4), 11–25. doi:10.1145/509506.509514

Guimaraes, G., Souto, E., Sadok, D., & Kelner, J. (2005). Evaluation of security mechanisms in wireless sensor networks. *ICW, 5*, 428–433.

Hämäläinen, P., Kuorilehto, M., Alho, T., Hännikäinen, M., & Hämäläinen, T. D. (2006). Security in wireless sensor networks: Considerations and experiments. In *Embedded computer systems: Architectures, modeling, and simulation* (pp. 167–177). Berlin / Heidelberg, Germany: Springer. doi:10.1007/11796435_18

Heinzelman, W. R., Chandrakasan, A., & Balakrishnan, H. (2000). *Energy-efficient communication protocol for wireless microsensor networks.* Paper presented at the 33rd Annual Hawaii International Conference on System Sciences, 2000.

Hills, R. (2001). Sensing for danger. *Science Technology Review*. Retrieved from http://www.llnl.gov/str/JulAug01/Hills.html

Huang, G. (2003). Casting the wireless sensor net. *Technology Review, 106*(6), 50–57.

Intanagonwiwat, C., Govindan, R., Estrin, D., Heidemann, J., & Silva, F. (2003). Directed diffusion for wireless sensor networking. *IEEE/ACM Transactions on Networking, 11*(1), 2–16. doi:10.1109/TNET.2002.808417

Jing, D., Han, R., & Mishra, S. (2004). *Intrusion tolerance and anti-traffic analysis strategies for wireless sensor networks.* Paper presented at the 2004 International Conference on Dependable Systems and Networks.

Kai, Z., Kui, R., & Wenjing, L. (2005). *Geographic on-demand disjoint multipath routing in wireless ad hoc networks.* Paper presented at the Military Communications Conference, 2005. MILCOM 2005. IEEE.

Karlof, C., Sastry, N., & Wagner, D. (2004). *TinySec: A link layer security architecture for wireless sensor networks.* Paper presented at the 2nd International Conference on Embedded networked sensor systems.

Karlof, C., & Wagner, D. (2003). *Secure routing in wireless sensor networks: Attacks and countermeasures.* Paper presented at the 2003 IEEE International Workshop on Sensor Network Protocols and Applications, 2003.

Karp, B., & Kung, H. T. (2000). *GPSR: Greedy perimeter stateless routing for wireless networks.* Paper presented at the 6th Annual International Conference on Mobile computing and networking.

Kausar, F., & Masood, A. (2006). *A random key distribution scheme for securing wireless sensor network.* Paper presented at the Multitopic Conference, 2006. INMIC '06. IEEE.

Kavitha, T., & Sridharan, D. (2010). Security vulnerabilities in wireless sensor networks: A survey. *Journal of Information Assurance and Security, 5,* 31–44.

Kinalis, A., & Nikoletseas, S. (2007). *Scalable data collection protocols for wireless sensor networks with multiple mobile sinks.* Paper presented at the 40th Annual Simulation Symposium, 2007. ANSS '07.

Kong, J., Ji, Z., Wang, W., Gerla, M., Bagrodia, R., & Bhargava, B. (2005). *Low-cost attacks against packet delivery, localization and time synchronization services in under-water sensor networks.*

Kotzanikolaou, P., Mavropodi, R., & Douligeris, C. (2005, 19-21 January). *Secure multipath routing for mobile ad hoc networks.* Paper presented at the Second Annual Conference on Wireless On-demand Network Systems and Services, 2005. WONS 2005.

Lee, S. J., & Gerla, M. (2000). *AODV-BR: Backup routing in ad hoc networks.* Paper presented at the Wireless Communications and Networking Conference, 2000. WCNC. 2000 IEEE.

Loh, P., & Tan, Y. (2007). A constrained multipath routing protocol for wireless sensor networks. *Embedded and Ubiquitous Computing,* 661-670.

Lou, W., Liu, W., & Fang, Y. (2004). *SPREAD: Enhancing data confidentiality in mobile ad hoc networks.*

Lu, G., Krishnamachari, B., & Raghavendra, C. (2007). An adaptive energy-efficient and low-latency MAC for tree-based data gathering in sensor networks. *Wireless Communications and Mobile Computing, 7*(7), 863–876. doi:10.1002/wcm.503

Madden, S., Franklin, M., Hellerstein, J., & Hong, W. (2002). *Tag: A tiny aggregation service for ad-hoc sensor networks.*

Marti, S., Giuli, T., Lai, K., & Baker, M. (2000). *Mitigating routing misbehavior in mobile ad hoc networks.*

MICA2. (2010). *Crossbow MICA2 wireless measurement system data sheet.* Retrieved from http://www.xbow.com/products/Product_pdf_files/Wireless_pdf/MICA2_Datasheet.pdf

Mpitziopoulos, A., & Gavalas, D. (2009). An effective defensive node against jamming attacks in sensor networks. *Security and Communication Networks, 2*(2), 145–163. doi:10.1002/sec.81

Muraleedharan, R., & Osadciw, L. (2006). *Jamming attack detection and countermeasures in wireless sensor network using ant system.* Orlando: SPIE Defence and Security.

Newsome, J., Shi, E., Song, D., & Perrig, A. (2004). *The sybil attack in sensor networks: Analysis & defenses.* Paper presented at the P3rd International Symposium on Information processing in sensor networks.

Padmavathi, G., & Shanmugapriya, M. (2009). *A survey of attacks, security mechanisms and challenges in wireless sensor networks.*

Park, E. C., & Blake, I. F. (2007). *Reducing communication overhead of key distribution schemes for wireless sensor networks.* Paper presented at the 16th International Conference on Computer Communications and Networks, 2007. ICCCN 2007.

Perrig, A., Szewczyk, R., Tygar, J. D., Wen, V., & Culler, D. E. (2002). SPINS: Security Protocols for Sensor Networks. *Wireless Networks, 8*(5), 521–534. doi:10.1023/A:1016598314198

Pietro, R. D., Mancini, L. V., & Mei, A. (2006). Energy efficient node-to-node authentication and communication confidentiality in wireless sensor networks. *Wireless Networks, 12*(6), 709–721. doi:10.1007/s11276-006-6530-5

Pottie, G. J., & Kaiser, W. J. (2000). Wireless integrated network sensors. *Communications of the ACM, 43*(5), 51–58. doi:10.1145/332833.332838

Raymond, D., Marchany, R., Brownfield, M., & Midkiff, S. (2006). *Effects of denial of sleep attacks on wireless sensor network MAC protocols.* Paper presented at the Information Assurance Workshop, 2006 IEEE.

Roman, R., Alcaraz, C., & Lopez, J. (2007). A survey of cryptographic primitives and implementations for hardware-constrained sensor network nodes. *Mobile Networks and Applications, 12*(4), 231–244. doi:10.1007/s11036-007-0024-2

Sabbah, E., Majeed, A., Kang, K., Liu, K., & Abu-Ghazaleh, N. (2006). *An application-driven perspective on wireless sensor network security.*

Schneier, B. (2000). *Secrets & lies: Digital security in a networked world.* John Wiley & Sons, Inc.

Seah, W., & Tan, H. (2006). *Multipath virtual sink architecture for wireless sensor networks in harsh environments.*

See, C. H., Abd-Alhameed, R. A., Hu, Y. F., & Horoshenkov, K. V. (2008). *Wireless sensor transmission range measurement within the ground level.* Paper presented at the Antennas and Propagation Conference, 2008. LAPC 2008. Loughborough.

Shaikh, R., Lee, S., Khan, M., & Song, Y. (2006). LSec: Lightweight Security Protocol for Distributed Wireless Sensor Network. *Personal Wireless Communications,* 367-377.

Sooyeon, K., Son, S. H., Stankovic, J. A., & Yanghee, C. (2004). Data dissemination over wireless sensor networks. *Communications Letters, IEEE, 8*(9), 561–563. doi:10.1109/LCOMM.2004.833810

Srinivasan, A., & Wu, J. (2007). A survey on secure localization in wireless sensor networks. In *Encyclopedia of wireless and mobile communications.*

Stajano, F., & Anderson, R. (2000). *The resurrecting duckling: Security issues for ad-hoc wireless networks.* (*LNCS, 1796,* 172–182).

Stallings, W. (2006). *Cryptography and network security: Principles and practice.* Prentice Hall.

Sun, H., Hsu, S., & Chen, C. (2007). *Mobile jamming attack and its countermeasure in wireless sensor networks.*

Tiny, O. S. (2010). *TinyOS is an open-source operating system designed for wireless embedded sensor networks.* Retrieved from http://www.tinyos.net

Uluagac, A., Lee, C., Beyah, R., & Copeland, J. (2008). Designing secure protocols for wireless sensor networks. In *Wireless algorithms, systems, and applications* (pp. 503-514).

Wan, C.-Y., Eisenman, S. B., & Campbell, A. T. (2003). *CODA: Congestion detection and avoidance in sensor networks.* Paper presented at the 1st International Conference on Embedded networked sensor systems.

Wang, L., & Kulkarni, S. (2006). *Authentication in reprogramming of sensor networks for mote class adversaries.*

Wang, Y., Attebury, G., & Ramamurthy, B. (2006). A survey of security issues in wireless sensor networks. *IEEE Communications Surveys and Tutorials, 8*(2), 2–23. doi:10.1109/COMST.2006.315852

Watro, R., Kong, D., Cuti, S.-f., Gardiner, C., Lynn, C., & Kruus, P. (2004). *TinyPK: Securing sensor networks with public key technology*. Paper presented at the 2nd ACM Workshop on Security of ad hoc and sensor networks.

Wi-Fi-Alliance. (2010). *Wi-Fi Alliance*. Retrieved from http://www.wi-fi.org

Wood, A., & Stankovic, J. (2002). Denial of service in sensor networks. *Computer*, 54–62. doi:10.1109/MC.2002.1039518

Xiaoyan, H., Pu, W., Jiejun, K., Qunwei, Z., & jun, L. (2005). *Effective probabilistic approach protecting sensor traffic*. Paper presented at the Military Communications Conference, 2005. MILCOM 2005. IEEE.

Xu, W., Trappe, W., Zhang, Y., & Wood, T. (2005). *The feasibility of launching and detecting jamming attacks in wireless networks*.

Xun, Z., Yu, L., & Hong Ge, M. (2006). *Node-disjointness-based multipath routing for mobile wireless ad hoc networks*. Paper presented at the Information and Communication Technologies, 2006. ICTTA '06.

Yanchao, Z., Wei, L., Wenjing, L., & Yuguang, F. (2006). Location-based compromise-tolerant security mechanisms for wireless sensor networks. *IEEE Journal on Selected Areas in Communications*, 24(2), 247–260. doi:10.1109/JSAC.2005.861382

Ye, F., Luo, H., Cheng, J., Lu, S., & Zhang, L. (2002). *A two-tier data dissemination model for large-scale wireless sensor networks*. Paper presented at the 8th Annual International Conference on Mobile computing and networking.

Ye, F., Zhong, G., Lu, S., & Zhang, L. (2005). GRAdient broadcast: A robust data delivery protocol for large scale sensor networks. *Wireless Networks*, *11*(3), 285–298. doi:10.1007/s11276-005-6612-9

Yibin, L., & Midkiff, S. F. (2005). *Multipath Fresnel zone routing for wireless ad hoc networks*. Paper presented at the 2005 IEEE Wireless Communications and Networking Conference.

Yu, Y., Govindan, R., & Estrin, D. (2001). *Geographical and energy aware routing: A recursive data dissemination protocol for wireless sensor networks*. (UCLA Computer Science Department Technical Report, UCLA-CSD TR-01-0023).

Zhu, S., Setia, S., & Jajodia, S. (2003). *LEAP: Efficient security mechanisms for large-scale distributed sensor networks*. Paper presented at the ACM CCS.

ZigBee. (2010). *ZigBee Alliance webpage*. Retrieved from http://www.zigbee.org

Znaidi, W., Minier, M., & Babau, J. (2008). *An ontology for attacks in wireless sensor networks*.

APPENDIX

Glossary of Acronyms

Table 4. Glossary of Acronyms

ACK	Acknowledgement
AES	Advanced Encryption Standard
CDMA	Code Division Multiple Access
CRC	Cyclic Redundancy Check
CSMA/CA	Carrier Sense Multiple Access with Collision Avoidance
CTS	Clear to Send
DES	Data Encryption Standard
DoS	Denial of Service
DSSS	Direct Sequence Spread Spectrum
FHSS	Frequency Hopping Spread Spectrum
GEAR	Geographic and Energy Aware Routing
GPSR	Greedy Perimeter Stateless Routing
GSM	Global System for Mobile Communications
LPD	Low Probability of Detection
LPI	Low Probability of Intercept
MAC	Medium Access Control; Message Authentication Code
MANET	Mobile Ad-Hoc Network
NWK	Network Layer
PDA	Personal Digital Assistant
PDR	Packet Delivery Ratio
PHY	Physical Layer
RC5	Block cipher designed by Ronald Rivest in 1994
RC6	Block cipher derived from RC5
RF	Radio Frequency
RSSI	Received Signal Strength Indicator
RTS	Request to Send
SAP	Service Access Point
SkipJack	Block cipher developed by the U.S. National Security Agency
TEA	Tiny Encryption Algorithm
UWB	Ultra-wideband modulation
Wi-Fi	Used synonymously for IEEE 802.11 technology (Alliance formed in 1999 to certify interoperability of WLAN products)
WINS	Wireless Integrated Network Sensors
WLAN	Wireless Local Area Network
WPAN	Wireless Personal Area Network
WSN	Wireless Sensor Network

Chapter 11
Wireless Sensor Networks:
Emerging Applications and Security Solutions

Sumita Mishra
Rochester Institute of Technology, USA

ABSTRACT

Wireless sensor networking technology has been used extensively by both commercial and military applications for sensing and data collection purposes. The self-configuring, self-healing nature and the ease of deployment of these networks make them an attractive option to other centralized approaches. Most of the existing networking solutions for sensor networks focus on the communication aspects and do not address the data security concerns of these networks. Since sensor networks are being deployed for emerging applications involving sensitive data and are envisioned to be integrated with the cyber space, it is essential to address the security needs of wireless sensor networks. Designing security solutions for Wireless Sensor Networks is an extremely challenging task due to the resource constraints of sensor nodes and the distributed nature of network design. This chapter provides an overview of emerging sensor networks involving sensitive data and a discussion of some of the proposed security solutions.

INTRODUCTION

Wireless Sensor Networks (WSNs) are not only being used for conventional applications such as environment monitoring and habitat monitoring but also for applications such as border and battle-field surveillance, homeland security, medical

applications and home appliance management that involve communication of sensitive information. For example, tactical surveillance data collected by unattended sensor networks or patient data collected by body area networks have a much higher level of sensitivity compared to the data collected by sensors deployed for environment monitoring. Moreover, most of these emerging applications involve connectivity of the WSN

DOI: 10.4018/978-1-60960-777-7.ch011

with the Internet for ubiquitous access of data collected by these networks. Some of the threats to sensor networks are similar to those for other wireless networks, yet others are quite different and unique (Undercoffer, 2002). For example, just like other wireless networks, sensor networks have security risks due to the openness of the wireless medium. Since a wireless channel is a broadcast channel, sensor data can be sniffed and attacked by simply tuning to the frequency band used for communication. The lack of infrastructure and centralized control is similar to MANETs. However, for military applications, WSNs are typically deployed in a hostile environment and remain unmonitored after deployment. Hence they are subject to node captures and compromises as well. There are very frequent topology changes due to node failures, which can lead to exploitation of network vulnerabilities by the attackers. Loss of data confidentiality, integrity and availability along with various threats such as routing disruption attacks and resource consumption attacks are major risks associated with wireless communications in sensor networks. The security requirements vary with the type of application supported by different WSNs. For example, some applications may only require that the data from the source to the sink has not been modified, i.e. the data integrity is preserved while others might have much more stringent data confidentiality needs, necessitating some kind of encryption. Some others may have the requirement of ensuring that the data is coming from the source that is trusted, i.e. some authentication mechanism should be in place.

In this chapter, some of the emerging sensor network applications and their security challenges and requirements are discussed. A step by step guide of configuring TinySec, a link layer security solution for sensor networks, is also included. The remainder of the chapter is organized as follows. The necessary background for the topic is presented in the next section. The emerging sensor network applications that involve collection of sensitive data are presented and discussed. The security requirements of these applications are analyzed followed by the configuration steps for TinySec. The conclusions and references are included at the end of the chapter.

BACKGROUND

There have been significant advances in the sensor hardware and software technology, making wireless sensor networking an attractive option for many emerging wireless applications. WSNs are formed by sensor nodes that are low-cost wireless devices having on-board sensing, processing and communication capabilities (Akyildiz, 2002; Pottie, 2000; Yick, 2008; Shi, 2004 and Hu, 2005). For some applications, a large number of sensor nodes are deployed in a designated area in a random fashion. Sensor nodes form a network automatically, i.e., they configure to form a self-organized distributed wireless network for sensing and data collection purposes. Some of the characteristics of WSNs are similar to those of mobile wireless ad hoc networks (MANET). For example, nodes in both mobile ad hoc networks and wireless sensor networks act as hosts as well as routers. Both of these networks are self-healing, i.e., the network automatically reconfigures in case of link failures due to mobility in MANETs or depletion of node energy in WSNs. However, there are some major differences between the two network types (Lopez, 2008).

Sensor networks are typically more energy and resource constrained than ad hoc networks. Most of the sensors are battery powered and are limited by the lifetime of the battery. Since the size of sensor is relatively small compared to the size of an ad hoc network node, the battery is also limited in size. Also, the data traffic pattern for ad hoc networks in usually from any node of the network to any other node, i.e., peer-peer. On the other hand, for sensor networks, it is generally from a group of sensors to a data collection point

Figure 1. Wireless Sensor Network deployment with several sensor nodes and a sink

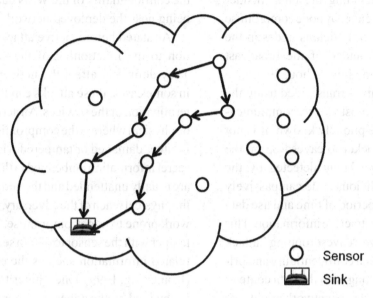

○ **Sensor**

⬛ **Sink**

(known as the sink), i.e., many-one. This type of traffic pattern is known as convergecast. The data travels from the sensors to the sink via multihop wireless links formed between the intermediate sensor nodes. Note that the sink has the capability to broadcast traffic for a part or the entire sensor network.

Compared to ad hoc networks, most sensor networks are deployed for a similar purpose and specific applications. For example, sensor nodes deployed for monitoring the temperature and other environmental characteristics of a region measure similar type of data and report back to the sink(s) in the network. Similarly, sensors deployed on a human body (body area network) measure data corresponding to vital signs or movement of the user and report it back to a personal data collection point. This is usually not the case for ad hoc networks where the network nodes can communicate peer to peer while supporting different types of applications.

The goal of a sensor network is to collect the data corresponding to the application that the network has been designed for. Hence fairness is not important as far as access of network by the nodes is concerned. This is typically not the case

for ad hoc networks. Another important difference is that in order to conserve energy and extend the battery life, sensor networks are usually a lot more delay tolerant than ad hoc networks. Hence these two types of wireless networks have a lot of similarities, yet have very different characteristics. A typical sensor network deployment is shown in Figure 1.

Before we talk about the security needs and solutions designed for sensor networks, it is important to discuss the vulnerabilities existing in this setup. Due to their nature, WSNs are vulnerable against both insider as well as outsider threats. Since sensor networks are usually deployed and managed by a single governing entity, all genuine network nodes are assumed to be cooperative and working towards the network goals. The malicious nodes can be external (not part of the network) and launch attacks to disrupt the functioning of the network or they can be internal (become a part of the network) and can cause major security breaches as well as hamper the network operation. Typically, internal attacks cause more damage to the network as the malicious node is misjudged to be an authorized and legitimate entity and is allowed to gain access to all the network resources, including the data. Insider attacks can be launched either by node compromise or by the deployment of malicious nodes in the network that take advantage of the broadcast nature of the wireless medium (Zhou, 2008).

Since the sensor data is transmitted using the wireless medium and most of the communication protocols used are publicly known, it is not too difficult for an attacker to eavesdrop on the communication without being detected by the network. Thus the malicious node can passively collect the data over a period of time and use data analysis techniques to extract the information. This is known as the passive "eavesdropping" attack which mainly affects data confidentiality and privacy (Lopez, 2008). Along with the data content, the traffic pattern of the sensor network might also lead to useful information for the attacker. This is known as the "Traffic Analysis" type of passive attack. For example, based on the type of traffic on the network, the position of the sink could be estimated. Typically, when sending data to the sink, the sensors communicate in a convergecast fashion, i.e., they support a many-to-one type of traffic pattern. The sensor nodes around the sink are the most critical part of the WSN as they participate in the relaying of information from distant nodes to the sink. The information obtained from this traffic analysis can be later used to launch more disruptive active attacks such as denial of service attacks on the sink.

It is very difficult to detect passive attacks as the attackers do not participate in the communication and their presence is not obvious in any manner. It is important to consider that traditionally, most sensor networks, consisting of low power nodes participating in short range communications, formed isolated networks that terminated at the data collection points or the sinks. Hence the adversary had to be in close proximity of the deployed WSN in order to launch eavesdropping attacks. However, with the emerging sensor networks being integrated with the cyber space, this might not be case and it might be possible to compromise on the confidentiality of the WSN data even without being near the deployed network.

As stated before, active attacks cause disruption to the functioning of the sensor network. They definitely affect the network services and in some cases, these attacks can lead to complete termination of the services. An active attack could be physical wherein the compromised sensor node is either damaged or tampered with, to obtain the secret information embedded in the sensor. WSNs are usually unattended and the nodes can be within the physical reach of the adversary, making the network prone to node compromise. The enemy can tamper with the sensor to obtain security protocols related information such as the encryption keys (Komerling, 1999). Once this critical information is obtained by the adversary, more severe attacks using this information can be launched, leading to complete network compromise in some cases. Also, with the physical access, the enemy can cause damage to the sensor hardware, rendering the node useless for participation in the WSN functioning. Fault tolerance, i.e., the ability of the network to maintain network functionalities in the event of node failures is extremely important for the successful operation of sensor networks. Hence resilience to these physical attacks is critical for WSNs that are deployed in a hostile environment.

Besides physical attacks, other active attacks that could be launched on WSNs include Denial of Service (DoS) attacks that mainly affect the availability of the network. DoS attacks are not accidental. They are malicious and disruptive and typically cause much more damage compared to the effort put forth by the adversary in launching the attack (Wood, 2002). These DoS attacks can be launched at the physical layer when the wireless medium is jammed by the adversary by transmitting at the same frequency as the sensor nodes or can be launched at higher layers of the protocol stack when the medium access and the routing functionalities of the WSN is disrupted (Perrig, 2004). Other active attacks include masquerading (when a malicious node behaves as a genuine node), message replaying (when the data obtained by a malicious node via eavesdropping or otherwise is relayed in the WSN at a later time), message modification (when the data obtained by a malicious node is changed before it is forwarded in the WSN), and packet injection (when spurious information is injected in the WSN by the malicious node). Some common active attacks launched on WSNs are creation of false control packets during the WSN deployment (hello flood attacks), capturing information from one part of the WSN and replaying in another part (wormhole attacks), capturing information in one part of WSN and tampering with the information (sinkhole attacks) and presenting multiple identities of the malicious node in different parts of the network (sybil attacks) (Karlof, 2003; Newsome, 2004; Parno, 2005; Chan, 2003; Cayirci, 2009).

Since a sensor network is a special type of computer network with its unique requirements and limitations described in the previous sections, the security considerations in this environment have to be addressed accordingly. Any security solution should achieve one or more of the security goals. Maintaining the secrecy (confidentiality) of sensitive data transmitted by sensor nodes is one of the most important security goals for WSNs (Walters, 2006). This goal is typically achieved by data encryption. Depending on the application, the entire data packet (the header and the payload) or just the payload may be encrypted to prevent unauthorized access of data by malicious nodes. Although data confidentiality prevents the enemy from accessing the information, it does not ensure that the transmitted messages are not altered by malicious nodes (integrity). For example, certain bits of the packets that are being transmitted may be modified by the adversary so that the content of the message is changed before it reaches the intended receiver. The message authentication code attached to the sent message can be used to check the integrity of data.

For most WSN applications, it is extremely important to ascertain that the received information is coming from a genuine sensor node and not a malicious node (authenticity). If authentication mechanisms are not in place, attackers can easily spoof the identity of a sensor node and launch any kind of insider attack in the network. Most of the existing solutions use the message authentication code (MAC) attached to a message to provide authentication. Also, the services provided by the WSN should be available whenever there is a requirement to transmit the sensed data. However due to active attacks launched by adversaries, the network availability can be severely affected. In particular, DoS attacks seriously hamper the availability of a WSN. Hence prevention and detection mechanisms for DoS attacks should be in place to ensure the availability of the network. Due to ease of executing replay attacks described earlier, it is important to ensure that the data being transmitted is genuine and valid. For example, if the session keys shared by the WSN nodes are refreshed and exchanged within the network, a replay of old information by an adversary could disrupt the functioning of the network. One of the ways to maintain freshness is to maintain a counter on the packet.

Designing a robust and efficient security framework for WSNs is difficult primarily due to the hardware limitations of the sensor nodes as well as the distributed nature of network design. Most of the security solutions for wired networks rely on either a trusted third party or computationally intense algorithms. Both of these options are not feasible for WSNs because the sensor nodes are battery powered and have extremely limited energy. Also, they are self-configuring networks that operate without any centralized control. Since some WSNs consist of a very large number of nodes, the security protocols need to address the scalability requirements of these networks. An ideal security solution for WSNs should be simple, flexible and scalable (Zhou, 2008). Since most MANET security protocols are designed with mobility constraint without any energy limitations, they are not suited for the WSN environment.

Since wireless sensor networks are being deployed for applications that involve sensitive data and are vulnerable to so many different types of threats, it is extremely important to address their security needs along with their communication and networking requirements. Some of these applications are discussed in the next section.

EMERGING SENSOR NETWORK TECHNOLOGIES AND THEIR SECURITY REQUIREMENTS

Body Area Networks

Wireless Body Area Network (BAN) is an emerging sensor networking technology that has shown a great potential for healthcare applications. Besides their usage in the medical field, they are also being proposed for fitness and entertainment industries (Hanson, 2009). Wearable or implantable sensors can be used to collect one or more vital signs (heart rate, blood pressure, Electro Cardiogram, oxygen saturation) and movement related data (Otto, 2006). During the past few years, several types of wearable health monitoring devices have been developed. Ranging from simple pulse monitoring devices to activity monitors and sophisticated implantable sensors, there is a wide range in the variety of these sensing devices. These devices can form a short-range communication network on the human body. The collected data is then transferred to a gateway/sink/data collection point via short range wireless communications.

Each BAN thus comprises several interconnected sensors on or near the human body. For healthcare applications, the data can be monitored remotely as well as in real time before being transferred for processing and storage in medical databases (Li M. and Lou W., 2010). This can be accomplished by connecting several of these BANs through a wide area networking technology (Internet or Cellular Network) to a medical server tier. The sensors on the human body connect to a personal server (e.g. a PDA, laptop, cell phone or a desktop computer) using a personal area networking technology, i.e., Zigbee or Bluetooth (Otto, 2006). This personal server controls the individual BAN and also provides the gateway functionality for the BAN to the Internet or the cellular phone network. The sensors collect patient-related data (vital signs and patient profile) and transmit to the personal server, which in turn relays the information to the medical server via wide area networking. Note that the personal server may process the data before relaying to avoid redundancy. Patient-related data can be accessed remotely from the medical server or queried locally from the personal server, depending on the application.

The centralized collection of data by the medical server facilitates uniform access by various healthcare entities, insurance companies as well as emergency response teams, thus increasing the overall efficiency of patient data management. Novel applications such as ubiquitous health monitoring, computer-assisted rehabilitation, emergency medical response system are possible due to this centralized data collection and access methodology (Li, 2010). This technology promises to reduce subjective data interpretation due to qualitative observation techniques and overcomes the barriers of infrequent data collection due to undersampling. Medical care can now be extended beyond the geographical boundaries of hospitals and provider offices and it facilitates the provision of individual care rather than generalized care to patients. One of the deployment scenarios of a body area network is shown in Figure 2.

Even though the BAN technology is primarily presented for the healthcare industry, the same network architecture can be used for an athlete or a person playing a videogame with interactive wearable devices. However, for the widescale adoption of this emerging sensor networking technology, several challenges have to be overcome. The user has to be convinced that BAN can contribute in enhancing the quality of his/her life. Since some of the proposed BAN sensors are

Figure 2. Wireless Body Area Network deployment scenario

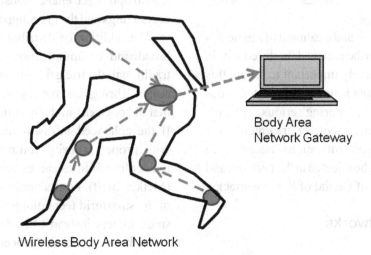

Body Area
Network Gateway

Wireless Body Area Network

implantable and wearable (Ashok, 2003; Jurik, 2008), the users need to be assured of their ease of use and safety. They should not be obtrusive and should have easy to understand and easy to use controls.

Besides these challenges, Body Area Networks pose several data security and privacy challenges. These concerns have to be addressed while the data is stored in the BAN or while it is being transmitted outside the BAN to the medical server. Also, privacy concerns govern that the user data be viewed and accessed by authorized entities only. Because of the requirements of ease of use and simplicity of BAN nodes, these sensors are typically very tiny with very small batteries. Hence they are extremely energy constrained, which makes the balance between addressing the security needs and practicality of these devices a very difficult problem to solve.

Besides eavesdropping, data modification and injection, wireless body area networks are susceptible to node compromise as they are usually not tamper-proof. Even if the data is encrypted and stored on the sensor, if the encryption key is also stored on the device (which is typically the case for most sensors in the market today), the original data can be easily recovered by the ad-

versary tampering with the node. The local server can also be physically or remotely compromised, thus leading to the compromise of the entire BAN controlled by the server. Node masquerade is also possible as authentic sensors can be easily replaced by malicious ones, which can gain access to the network data if proper authentication methods are not in place.

Besides confidentiality and integrity, data dependability is also an important security goal for BANs. Even under adverse conditions of node failure due to compromise or other reasons, user data should be accessible as it might become life-threatening for the patient otherwise. In order to address the privacy concerns, access control needs to be implemented. The access control should be fine-grained to provide different levels of access for different entities (Li, 2010). For example, the access for nurses, doctors and pharmacies should be different from that given to insurance carriers. Also, medical practitioners should have access to data corresponding to their patients only and not others. The patient should have the flexibility to provide this access to different groups of people based on factors such as time, location, incidents etc. There should be a provision for temporary access (authorized by the patient or a designated third party) to address the needs of data access in emergency situations.

Since the diagnosis and treatment of a patient is highly dependent on the patient data stored within the BAN, it is extremely important to secure this stored data. If the data is not authenticated properly, it might result in ignoring serious problems or mis-diagnosis and incorrect treatment of a medical condition. Authentication is necessary to prevent false data to be injected in the network and also for prevention of Denial of Service attacks.

Smart Grid Networks

Due to the changing climatic conditions and population increase on a global basis, there has been a tremendous increase in the demand for electric energy (DoE, 2002). The over-stressed and over-aged electricity supply infrastructure is unable to bear the burden of this demand, which has led to frequent blackouts and grid failures in many countries in the past few years. The age of most power transmission lines in the United States is approximately 50-60 years (Yang, 2007). The current grid lacks automation, fault tolerance and communication capability between the different components. This necessitates the upgrade of the electric grid in order to increase the reliability and efficiency of the end-to-end electric supply system.

The concept of smart grid was introduced to address the needs of the aging electric supply infrastructure. One of the key features of this emerging technology is the overlay of a digital two-way data communications system on top of the electricity distribution infrastructure. Smart grid technology can be considered as the modernization of the electric grid with the addition of bi-directional communication links between the supplier and the consumer. This enhancement will provide the capability of monitoring electricity consumption at coarse (per-home) as well as granular (per electrical appliance) levels. Hence a successful realization of smartgrid networking will lead to optimized energy consumption and usage, cost savings and the greening of our environment.

The addition of distributed intelligence and broadband communication capabilities to the traditional electric grid infrastructure poses new risks and brings in some unique security challenges that did not exist in the traditional infrastructure. If the enhanced infrastructure is not deployed with proper security controls in place, many new vulnerabilities can be created in the system (Metke, 2010). For example, one of the features of the smartgrid technology is the installation of smart meters instead of traditional electric meters at homes. These advanced meters, equipped with real-time sensors, are expected to measure the energy usage at a coarse as well as granular level and communicate the information securely back to the utility company. Every device in the consumer's home will be equipped with sensors monitoring the electricity usage in real-time and will also have wireless communication links to the smart meter. A typical deployment of a smart grid sensor network within the home of consumers is shown in Figure 3.

According to the research firm Chartwell, many of the North American utility companies are considering Zigbee and mesh networking as their choice for connecting smart meters and smart devices (Chartwell, 2010). Zigbee and mesh networking are wireless sensor technologies that rely on cooperative communications between neighboring smart meters and smart devices, which raises several security concerns (Metke, 2010). It is essential to protect the data collected via smartgrid due to privacy, confidentiality and authentication requirements of user data. The availability of the grid control systems affects the availability of electric power. Due to the sophisticated nature of the smart grid control systems, the connectivity between the systems has to increase. This enhancement in connectivity increases reliability but opens up many new vulnerabilities. Now the attacker has the capability of launching remote attacks due to the ease of access

Figure 3. Smart Meters communicating with the smart devices within a consumer's home using wireless sensor networking technology

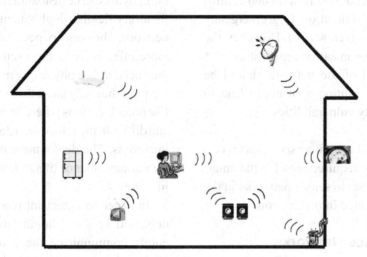

to the system. The attacker can not only penetrate the network, passively monitor the network but also launch active attacks to destabilize the network.

According to NIST (2010), "Cyber security is one of the key technical areas where the state of the art falls short of meeting the envisioned functional, reliability, and scalability requirements of the Smart Grid"(p. 142). The document also describes the key security challenges that are expected to be faced by Smart Grid designers. Some of them that pertain to sensors in the smart grid are listed below.

1. New device architectures that are cost effective and tamper resistant are desired. The architecture should be scalable, resilient and should have the capability of secure remote recovery. This will help in limiting the impact of attacks to a local level.

Suggested mitigation measures: "NIST crypto tamper evident requirements;

Mitigating (limiting) the value of attacks at end points (containment regions in the Smart Grid architecture); and expiring lightweight keys." (NIST, 2010, pp. 143)

2. With the distributed network of various embedded processors in smart grid devices, an intrusion detection mechanism should be in place. The data collected by sensors embedded in smart meters will be integrated with the cyber domain which enhances the possibilities of anomalous or malicious activity. Timely detection of these anomalies is required for the grid to function properly.

3. Design of an efficient key management scheme is essential. With tens of thousands of smart meters with embedded sensors participating in data communication, large scale key management along with efficient cryptography techniques is desired. The limitations of storage and computation still hold for these smart grid sensors.

4. Besides addressing the availability, confidentiality, authentication and privacy issues for wireless sensor data communications over the smart grid network, a fine-grained access control system needs to be in place for user/utility company/other authorized entities to gain access to the electricity usage data. Also the capabilities provided to the users should be different from those of the utility company. For example, broadcast communications

could be enabled from the electricity supplier to the users for communication and control in certain special situations (e.g. emergency shutdown of a given sector). However, the broadcast communication capabilities from the user's end of the network should be provided with caution as it might lead to several security vulnerabilities.

Note that the NIST document specifies several other cyber security requirements for the smart grid. The ones relevant to sensor networks in the smart grid are presented in this section.

Area Surveillance Networks

Perimeter/Area surveillance is one of the emerging applications of sensor networks in homeland security. Sensors are deployed strategically to monitor and detect intrusions in the target region. Malls, railroads, borders and even private properties can be monitored using the sensor networking technology. Low cost deployment and infrastructureless operation of wireless sensor networks make them a very attractive option for this application domain (Grilo, 2009). Sensor networks can be deployed very quickly for monitoring the perimeter of high

risk event locations. Once the task is completed, the network can be dismantled in no time, allowing for a very flexible deployment of the surveillance network. The security personnel can be managed more effectively in the event of breaches since they need not be physically monitoring all access locations but only those that are easily penetrable. For other locations where breaches are less likely and difficult, the sensors can do the job of detecting intrusions. The deployment of a sensor network for the surveillance of a railroad section is shown in Figure 4.

In order to detect intrusions effectively, the deployed sensors should have a means to securely communicate the detection information back to the control center, which is typically not part of the sensor network. Also, the differentiation between malicious and non-malicious intruders is very important since the detection mechanism will report all kinds of intruders. Detecting the trespassers trajectory could help in determining the intentions of the intruder (Dudek, 2009). The communication links within the deployed sensor network should be secured to prevent spurious data injection in the network. Another challenge of surveillance networks is physical security of the nodes, since the sensors are typi-

Figure 4. Surveillance of railroads by sensor networks

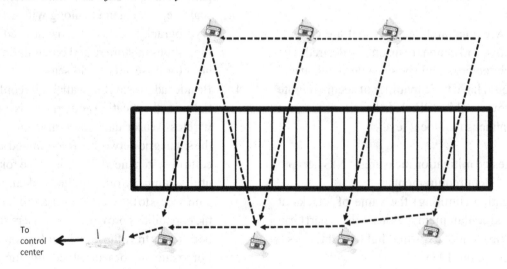

cally not monitored after deployment. Hence they should be tamper-resistant and node compromise detection protocols should be in place.

Even though several papers exist in the literature for energy-efficient intrusion detection protocols for surveillance, securing the sensor networks links has been not addressed by most of them. Hence this is still an open research problem.

ADDRESSING THE SECURITY REQUIREMENTS FOR EMERGING SENSOR NETWORK APPLICATIONS

Due to the limitations and unique characteristics of wireless sensor networks discussed in previous sections, the design and deployment of efficient data security solutions is extremely challenging. In this section, some of the existing work in literature that address security challenges and requirements of the emerging sensor networking applications are presented.

Secure Data Storage

One of the requirements of all the applications discussed in this chapter is that of secure and distributed data storage. The stored data in the sensor network should maintain confidentiality, integrity and dependability. In (Wang, 2009), a distributed data storage scheme is proposed. The encrypted data is broken down into several shares which are distributed and stored among neighbor nodes for storage. Threshold cryptography is applied to recover the original data and the integrity of data is checked by comparing the signatures generated by the neighboring nodes. Hence the goals of integrity, confidentiality and dependability are met by this distributed storage scheme. Small signature sizes ensure low overhead in terms of processing and storage. However, one of the drawbacks of this scheme is that the integrity check can be done by participating nodes in the sensor network and not a third party. Hence the personal server in a

body area network cannot check for the integrity of data received from the sensors.

In (Di Pietro, 2008), the authors address the issue of data survivability in sensor networks in the event of an intentional attack launched by adversaries to destroy the data stored in the network. For example, the attacker could attempt to erase all medical information stored in the sensors of a body area network. The main idea presented in this work is to constantly change the storage location of the data so that the probability of the adversary attacking a sensor which currently possesses the stored data is minimized. However, the assumption is that the enemy can only target a subset of the total sensors in the network and not the entire network at the same time. Also, movement of data involves a high processing and communication overhead, which could lead to many other issues in the resource-constrained applications.

Key Establishment and Management

Of the different security measures, establishment of cryptographic keys is critical as encryption as well as authentication mechanisms rely on these keys for their operation. Some of the existing and proposed key management solutions for sensor networks are described in this section. Cryptographic key management is one of the most challenging aspects of WSN security design (Camtepe, 2008). Security protocols rely on encryption mechanisms for ensuring data confidentiality. Also, for authentication purposes, the sender computes a Message Authentication Code (MAC) for each packet and appends to the sent message. Both the encryption algorithm and the MAC computation require cryptographic keys as inputs. Private Key cryptosystems are difficult to incorporate, as they depend on a central authority for key creation and distribution and are not scalable. A Public key cryptosystem could be computationally intensive and will be difficult to incorporate in situations where limited power and computer resources are available. TinySec, the security framework included in TinyOS (operating system standard for WSNs developed by U.C. Berkley) relies on pre-deployed network wide cryptographic keys (Karlof, 2004). Hence every node of the WSN uses the same key for encryption and decryption. Although this approach does ensure data privacy and integrity, it is extremely vulnerable to node compromise. It has been shown that TinySec keys can be obtained from a compromised node in less than a minute. The security of the cryptographic system is dependent on the secrecy of the crypto-graphic key. Since the entire WSN uses the same TinySec key, a single node compromise can lead to the complete network compromise. Hence secure management of cryptographic keys between the sender and receiver is a very important problem and should be addressed for successful wide scale deployment of WSNs.

When the sender and the receiver share a common key for cryptographic purposes, the mechanism is termed as symmetric key or private key cryptosystem. The sender uses the key to con-vert plaintext to ciphertext using the encryption algorithm. The receiver obtains the plaintext from ciphertext using the same key and the decryption algorithm. On the other hand, an asymmetric key or a public key cryptosystem uses a unique (public, private) key pair for each communicating node. The public key of the node is used for encrypt-ing data sent to the node. Since the private key is known only to the node, the data can be decrypted by the intended recipient only.

Symmetric key systems are computationally less intensive but do not scale well as each node requires a unique symmetric key with every other node in the network for successfully encrypting data between any two participating nodes. On the other hand, asymmetric key systems scale better but are more computationally intense. For resource constrained devices such as sensor nodes, symmetric key cryptosystem is more attractive and most of the existing work in the literature is based on this methodology. For large distributed networks like WSNs, the simplest way to setup

symmetric keys is to use network-wide key for encryption and decryption purposes (Karlof, 2004). However, since the sensor nodes are unat-tended for many applications, they are susceptible to node tampering and compromise. Hence, even though this approach provides data privacy and is simple to implement, it certainly is not optimal for networks like WSNs. The other extreme is to have pairwise symmetric keys preloaded for all sensor nodes in the network. However the number of unique symmetric keys loaded in each sensor becomes unacceptably large as the size of the WSN increases. It has been proposed to use the sink (data collection node for WSN) as the key distribution center for setting up pairwise sym-metric keys for the participating sensor nodes (Perrig, 2002). However, the sink becomes a single point of failure for the protocol. Also, it may lead to large communication overhead for the resource-constrained sensors due to the key exchange process.

Most recent approaches consider the key management problem for WSNs as a 2-step process (Zhou, 2008). Prior to the deployment of the WSN, each sensor node is loaded with the initial keying material. This is known as the key pre-distribution phase. The memory resources of the sensor nodes and the resilience of the nodes to compromise should be considered when the key-ing material is distributed. In other words, a node compromise should impact a minimum number of nodes based on the information obtained from the pre-distributed material. Once the network is deployed, the nodes communicate with each other and establish either pairwise symmetric keys or asymmetric keys, based on the algorithms used. This is the key agreement phase. Based on the communication pattern of the WSNs, a group key may also be established instead of pairwise keys (Zhu, 2003).

The distribution of keying material can be probabilistic, deterministic or hybrid (Camtepe, 2008). In the probabilistic approach, each node is preloaded with set of keys (key ring), randomly selected from a global key pool (Chan, 2006; Eschenauer, 2002). Hence the neighboring nodes share at least one key with a certain probability depending on several factors including the size of the key ring, which is dependent on the memory resources available. The challenge is to achieve a balance between the available resources and the desired key connectivity. On the other hand, deterministic approaches for key distribution define the global key pool and the key assignment to each node non-randomly to increase the key connectivity between neighboring nodes (Gong, 1990). Instead of uniformly distributing the keying material across the entire network, some schemes use location-based key material distribution to optimize one-hop key connectivity (Liu, 2003).

Asymmetric key cryptosystems are computationally intensive. However, they are more scalable and resilient to node compromise. Due to advances in the sensor hardware technology, some research groups have investigated the feasibility of adopting asymmetric key based schemes for WSNs (Gaubatz, 2005; Watro, 2004). The challenge is to adapt the asymmetric key computation algorithms or the hardware design so that the computations can be supported by the resources available to the sensor nodes. In (Gaubatz, 2005), the authors demonstrated that asymmetric key cryptosystems can be designed for sensor nodes with power consumption as low as 20 microwatts using optimized low-power techniques. The future of public key encryption architectures for sensor networks looks promising with advances in sensor energy harvesting techniques. Elliptic Curve Cryptography (ECC) based approaches are also being investigated for sensor networks. In (Malan, 2004), it was shown that TinyOS can be modified to support a public-key infrastructure based on ECC.

Access Control

Another security requirement for all the emerging sensor networking applications is some type of access control for the data in the network. This is important for maintaining the privacy of user data. For example, the smart grid data should be accessible by a particular user and not by any other entity in the network. Also, the type of data that can be accessed by the utility company should also be controlled at a granular level. Similarity, for body area networks, the patient data accessible by the doctors and medical practitioners should be different from the data available to the insurance companies. In (Venkatasubramanian, 2007), a role-based access scheme is proposed. The mapping between the users and their roles and the roles and corresponding privileges are defined. The level of control and granularity can be achieved by defining the roles and designating them to users appropriately. The authors also propose a criticality-aware access control in order to provide emergency access to data. This can be applied for Body area Networks in medical emergency situations. The challenge is to design access control methodologies that work with cryptography controlled data access.

An attribute-based encryption scheme is presented in (Bethencourt, 2007) which achieves fine-grained access control along with a one-to-many encryption methodology. In identity-based encryption, there is a single public key, and there is a master private key that can be used to make more limited private keys based on the user identity. The attribute-based encryption scheme presented in this work provides more flexibility than simple identity-based encryption, in that it allows complex rules specifying which private keys can decrypt which ciphertexts. Specifically, the private keys are associated with sets of attributes or labels. When data is encrypted, the key used for encryption depends on the access policy which also defines the appropriate decryption key.

Although an ideal sensor security solution should be able to satisfy all the above-mentioned requirements, it is an extremely challenging implementation problem due to the resource limitations of sensors. Most of the existing solutions address one or the other requirement based on the type of application. Two of the implemented solutions are discussed in the following section as case studies.

LINK LAYER SECURITY

Due to the energy constraints of the WSN environment, several link-layer security solutions have been proposed in order to conserve node energy (Karlof, 2004; Sastry, 2004; Li, 2005; Luk, 2007; Osanacek, 2009; Wood, 2006; Xue, 2003; Healy, 2009). These solutions are based on encryption mechanisms that work on a sensor-to-sensor or a sensor-to-sink link rather than end-to-end from the sender to the final destination. This enables the sensed data to be processed and aggregated at each intermediate node so that unnecessary transmissions can be avoided. Note that a lot less energy is expended in processing compared to every bit of information that is transmitted and received by sensors. Also, end-to-end security solutions can be subjected to certain DoS attacks which can be prevented by link layer security architectures that can detect spurious packets injected in the network at an early stage.

TinySec was the first fully-implemented link layer security framework proposed for the TinyOS operating system. The protocol design considers the WSN limitations of weak processing capabilities, small memory sizes, and limited energy resources of sensor nodes. Since TinyOS packets are very small (about 30 bytes), any security scheme cannot afford to add another 20-30 bytes as overhead, which is typically the case for security solutions for wireless local area networks and cellular networks (Karlof, 2004). TinySec leverages the low bandwidth of sensor network channels and the fact that messages in WSNs are transmitted for a very short range and hence need to be secured for a relatively short period of time. The authors assume that the amount of information that can be injected in the network

or that can be eavesdropped per unit time is very limited due to these inherent features.

TinySec solution is implemented entirely in software with no requirement for special hardware. It offers the users two modes of operation, depending on the requirements of the application. For some sensor applications, the only requirement is to authenticate the sending node. In that case, the optimal choice would be to use TinySec in the TinySec-Auth mode. On the other hand, if the application requires authentication as well as data confidentiality, TinySec-AE (authenticated encryption) mode should be chosen. In the TinySec-Auth mode, a message authentication code (MAC) is computed on the entire packet (unencrypted data and header) and attached to the packet whereas in the TinySec-AE mode, the data is encrypted and the MAC is computed over the packet header and the encrypted data. Since the TinySec solution is implemented at a lower layer of the protocol stack, it is transparent and can be very easily integrated with higher layer protocols. The packet formats for TinyOS, TinySec-Auth and TinySec-AE are shown in Figure 5.

SECURITY ADMINISTRATION OF SENSOR NETWORKS: CONFIGURING TINYSEC ON SENSOR MOTES

This exercise will assist in gaining hands-on experience with the implementation of TinySec in TinyOS. For details on the operating system, refer to TinyOS documentation (TinyOS, 2010). Note that this guideline is for the popular Mica2 motes. However, other motes can also be configured with TinySec (TinySec for MicaZ, 2008).

Through this exercise, the user can learn:

- TinySec capabilities and attributes.
- TinySec cryptographic key mechanisms and distribution.

Figure 5. Packet formats demonstrating the low overhead added by TinySec in both modes of operation

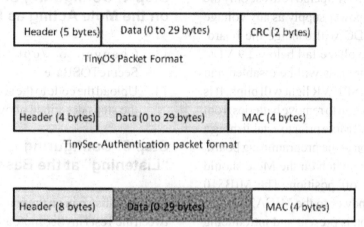

- Communicating encrypted data across wireless sensor networks.

  Equipment needed:

- Crossbow Mica2 motes sensor kit – Mica2 motes, MIB510 Serial Interface Programming board, MTS310 Multi-sensor module (Crossbow,2010)
- Serial cable (Straight-through RS-232 or USB-Serial Converter)
- A Windows based system

Step 1: Setup TinyOS Environment

1. Download the stable TinyOS 1.1.0 installation: http://www.tinyos.net/windows-1_1_0.html
   NOTE: TinyOS 1 is used due to the integration of TinySec. Currently, TinyOS 2, the latest version of the OS, does not integrate TinySec or similar security packages for use.
2. Install the TinyOS 1.1.0 package (Complete Installation). This will install Cygwin with the correct environment and tools.
3. Open Cygwin. Run toscheck to ensure the environment is correctly configured.

Step 2: Hardware Setup

4. The MIB 510 programming board serves a dual purpose, acting as a main programming tool for all Motes as well as being the gateway between the PC and a particular sensor network. The MICA2 Mote is the communication device which can be programmed to perform specific tasks. The Sensor Module is responsible for gathering requested data.
5. Connect the board to the PC's serial port via a standard straight-through RS-232 cable or a USB to serial converter.
   NOTE: The in-system-processor (ISP) on the MIB510 communicates with the PC through the serial port connection and runs at a constant baud rate of 115.2. It is important to note that some USB to serial port adapters cannot operate at 115 baud. Therefore, if you are experiencing problems uploading code to the motes, ensure that the converter is capable of such transmissions.
6. Supply power to your MIB510 by connecting it to an external source via the supplied power adapter. The green LED labeled ISP PWR should now be lit.

IMPORTANT: It is imperative to use only the provided power supply as any voltage over 7 VDC will damage the board. Shall the voltage fall below 2.9 VDC all code uploads will be disabled and the green ISP PWR light will blink. It is also important to remove batteries from the MICA2 Mote prior to establishing a connection to the programming board, the power switch on the Mote should be in the off position. The MIB510 supplies power to the MICA2 while a connection is present and introducing another power source will damage both components.

7. Pick one of the MICA2 Motes and attach it firmly to the MIB510 programming board via the 51-pin male to female connector.

Step 3: Configuring TestTinySec on the Mote:

This program is an example of data authenticated and encrypted through a wireless sensor network using TinySec.

8. Change directory to /opt/tinyos-1.x/apps/ TestTinySec
9. Upload the TestTinySec to a mote. To upload the code, type the following command while in the TestTinySec directory:

MIB510=COM <x> make mica2 reinstall

Where <x> corresponds to the COM port assigned to the serial connection.

10. Upon the first time compiling an application requiring TinySec you will notice: Generating default TinySec Key...
11. Once the program is loaded on the mote turn it off and remove the mote from the programming board.
12. Connect another mote to the programming board and turn it on.

Step 4: Configuring SecureTOSBase on the Mote Acting as Base

13. Change to /opt/tinyos-1.x/apps/ SecureTOSBase
14. Upload the code to the secondary mote using the steps described above.

Step 5: Configuring "Listening" at the Base

In order to listen in on the communication link between the TestTinySec mote and SecureTOSBase:

15. Change directory to /opt/tinyos-1.x/tools/ java
16. Type "make". This will compile the necessary java utilities.
17. An environmental variable must be set before you execute the Listen utility. Type the command:

export MOTECOM=serial@COM<x>:<baudrate>

Where <x> corresponds to the COM port assigned to the serial connection. Use the "mica2" constant in place of the baudrate parameter.

18. Execute the Listen utility
java net.tinyos.tools. Listen
NOTE: The listen utility will show raw data as TinySec is a link layer protocol where data is encrypted and decrypted at each node.

Every mote in the network can be programmed by repeating Step 3 for each mote.

CONCLUSION

Based on the above discussion, it is clear that most of the security needs of the emerging sensor networking applications are still being developed at this point in time. It is challenging to implement security solutions for these networks due to the size limitation of sensors in terms of resources and storage space. Most cryptographic solutions for these sensors should be lightweight in terms of computation speed and data storage requirements. Although wireless body area network prototypes are being developed and implemented, very few studies have been done to address the security and privacy needs of patient-related data (Li, 2010). Smart grid networking using sensors is a very nascent technology and the security challenges in these networks still need to be addressed. Similarly, the secure transmission of sensed data in surveillance networks is also an interesting problem. TinySec is a link layer security framework that could address some of the needs of these emerging applications. A step-by-step configuration guideline for TinySec is provided as a reference for sensor network professionals.

ACKNOWLEDGMENT

The authors would like to acknowledge Mr. Kristian Stokes and Dr. Yin Pan, who contributed to the steps for practical implementation for TinySec.

REFERENCES

Akyildiz, I. (2002). A survey on sensor networks. *IEEE Communications Magazine*, 102–114. doi:10.1109/MCOM.2002.1024422

Ashok, R., & Agrawal, D. (2003). Next-generation wearable networks. *Computer*, 31–39. doi:10.1109/MC.2003.1244532

Bethencourt, J., Sahai, A., & Waters, B. (2007). *Ciphertext-policy attribute-based encryption*. Proceedings of IEEE Symposium on Security and Privacy.

Camtepe, S., et al. (2008). Key management in wireless sensor networks. In J. Lopez & J. Zhou (Eds.), Wireless sensor network security. IOS Press.

Cayirci, E., & Rong, C. (2009). *Security in wireless ad hoc and sensor networks*. West Sussex, UK: John Wiley and Sons. doi:10.1002/9780470516782

Chan, H., et al. (2006). Random key predistribution schemes for sensor networks. IEEE International Conference on Communication, (pp. 2262-2267).

Chan, H., & Perrig, A. (2003). Security and privacy in sensor networks. IEEE Computer Magazine, 103-105.

Chartwell. (2010). Energy library. Retrieved from http://www.energylibrary.com/index.cfm/ID/7/iNewsID/197/

Crossbow Mica2 Motes. (2010). Retrieved from http://www.xbow.com

Di Pietro, R., et al. (2008). Catch me (If you can): Data survival in unattended sensor networks. Proceedings of IEEE PERCOM, (pp. 185-194).

DoE. (2002). National transmission grid study. Washington DC: US Department of Energy. Retrieved from http://www.ferc.gov/industries/electric/indus-act/transmission-grid.pdf

Eschenauer, L., & Gligor, V. (2002). A key management scheme for distributed sensor networks. Proceedings of 9th ACM Conference on Computer and Communications Security (CCS'02), (pp. 41-47).

Gaubatz, G., Kaps, J., & Sunar, B. (2005). *Public key cryptography in sensor networks – revisited*. Springer Inc.

Gong, L., & Wheeler, D. J. (1990). A matrix key distribution scheme. *Journal of Cryptology*, 2(1), 51–59. doi:10.1007/BF02252869

Grilo, A., Piotrowski, K., Langendoerfer, P., & Casaca, A. (2009). A wireless sensor network architecture for homeland security epplication. In Ruiz & Garcia-Luna-Aceves (Eds.) ADHOC-NOW 2009, (pp. 397-402). Berlin/Heidelberg, Germany: Springer-Verlag.

Hanson, et al. (2009). Body area sensor networks: Challenges and opportunities. IEEE Computer, 58-65.

Healy, M., Newe, T., & Lewis, E. (2009). Security for wireless sensor networks: A review. IEEE Sensors Applications Symposium, New Orleans, LA.

Hu, F., & Sharma, N. K. (2005). Security considerations in ad hoc sensor networks. Elsevier . *Ad Hoc Networks*, *3*(1), 69–89. doi:10.1016/j.adhoc.2003.09.009

Jurik, A., & Weaver, A. (2008). Remote medical monitoring. *Computer,* 96–99. doi:10.1109/MC.2008.133

Karlof, C., et al. (2004). TinySec: A link layer security architecture for wireless sensor networks. Proceedings of 2nd International Conference on Embedded Networked Sensor Systems (SenSys '04), (pp. 162-175).

Karlof, C., & Wagner, D. (2003). Secure routing in wireless sensor networks: Attacks and counter-measures. Ad Hoc and Sensor Networks, 293-315.

Komerling, O., & Kuhn, M. G. (1999). Design principles for tamper resistant smartcard processors. Paper presented at USENIX Workshop on Smartcard Technology, Chicago, IL.

Li, M., Lou, W., & Ren, K. (2010). Data security and privacy in wireless body area networks. IEEE Wireless Communications, 51-58.

Li, T., Wu, H., Wang, X., & Bao, F. (2005). SenSec: Sensor security framework for TinyOS. Proceedings of 2nd International Workshop on Networked Sensing Systems (INSS'05), San Diego, CA.

Liu, D., & Ning, P. (2003). Location-based pairwise key establishments for relatively static sensor networks. Proceedings of 2003 ACM Workshop Security of Ad Hoc and sensor networks (SASN'03), Fairfax, USA.

Lopez, J., & Zhou, J. (2008). *Wireless sensor network security*. Amsterdam, The Netherlands: IOS press.

Luk, M., Mezzour, G., Perrig, A., & Gligor, V. (2007). MiniSec: A secure sensor network communication architecture. IEEE International Conference on Information Processing in sensor networks (IPSN'07), Cambridge, MA.

Malan, D. J., et al. (2004). A public-key infrastructure for key distribution in TinyOS based on elliptic curve cryptography. Proceedings of 1st IEEE International Conference on Sensor and Ad Hoc Communication Networks (SECON'04), Santa Clara, CA.

Metke, A. R., & Ekl, R. L. (2010). Security technology for smart Grid networks. IEEE Transactions on smart grid, 1(1), 99-107.

Newsome, J., et al. (2004). The Sybil attack in sensor networks: Analysis and defenses. Proceedings of 3rd International Symposium on Information processing in sensor networks, ACM Press.

NIST. (2010). Report to NIST on smart Grid cyber security strategy and requirements. Retrieved from http://csrc.nist.gov/publications/drafts/nistir-7628/draft-nistir-7628_2nd-public-draft.pdf

Osanacek, P. (2009). *Towards security issues in ZigBee architecture*. Springer.

Otto, C., Milenkovic, A., Sanders, C., & Jovanov, E. (2006). System architecture of a wireless body area sensor network for ubiquitous health monitoring. *Journal of Mobile Multimedia*, *1*(4), 307–326.

Parno, B., Perrig, A., & Gligor, V. (2005). Distributed detection of node replication attacks in sensor networks. Proceedings of IEEE Symposium on Security and Privacy, Oakland, CA.

Perrig, A. (2002). SPINS: Security Protocols for Sensor Networks. *ACM Wireless Networks, 8*(5), 521–534. doi:10.1023/A:1016598314198

Perrig, A., Stankovic, J., & Wagner, D. (2004). Security in wireless sensor networks. *Communications of the ACM, 47*(6), 53–57. doi:10.1145/990680.990707

Pottie, G., & Kaiser, W. (2000). Wireless integrated network sensors. *Communications of the ACM, 43*(5), 51–58. doi:10.1145/332833.332838

Sastry, N., & Wagner, D. (2004). Security considerations for IEEE 802.15.4 networks. ACM Workshop on Wireless Security (Wise'04), (pp. 32-42).

Shi, E., & Perrig, A. (2004). Designing secure sensor networks. *IEEE Wireless Communications Magazine, 11*(6), 38–43. doi:10.1109/MWC.2004.1368895

TinyOS documentation. (2010). Retrieved from http://docs.tinyos.net

TinySec on MicaZ. (2008). Retrieved from http://www.cl.cam.ac.uk/research/security/sensornets/tinysec/

Undercoffer, J., et al. (2002). Security for sensor networks. Paper presented at CADIP Research Symposium, Baltimore, MD.

Venkatasubramanian, K. K., & Gupta, S. K. S. (2007). Security solutions for pervasive healthcare . In Xiao, Y. (Ed.), *Security in distributed, Grid, mobile, and pervasive computing* (pp. 443–464).

Walters, J. (2006). Wireless sensor network security: A survey . In Xiao, Y. (Ed.), *Security in distributed, Grid, mobile, and pervasive computing*. CRC Press.

Wang, Q. (2009). Dependable and secure sensor data storage with dynamic integrity assurance. *Proceedings - IEEE INFOCOM, 09*, 954–962.

Watro, R., et al. (2004). TinyPK: Securing sensor networks with public key technology. Proceedings of 2nd ACM Workshop on Security of Ad Hoc and Sensor Networks (SASN'04), Washington, D.C.

Wood, A. D., & Stankovic, J. A. (2002). Denial of service in sensor networks. *Computer, 35*(10), 54–62. doi:10.1109/MC.2002.1039518

Wood, A. D., & Stankovic, J. A. (2006). AMSecure: Secure link-layer communication in TinyOS for IEEE 802.15.4-based wireless sensor networks. Proceedings of 4th International Conference on Embedded Networked Sensor Systems (SenSys'06), (pp. 395-396).

Xue, Q., & Ganz, A. (2009). Runtime security composition for sensor networks (secure sense). IEEE 58th Vehicular Technology Conference (VTC'03), (pp. 2976-2980).

Yang, G. Z. (Ed.). (2006). *Body sensor networks*. Springer-Verlag. doi:10.1007/1-84628-484-8

Yang, Y., et al. (2007). A survey on technologies for implementing sensor networks for power delivery systems. Proceedings of IEEE Power Engineering Society General Meeting, (pp. 1-8).

Yick, J. (2008). Wireless sensor network survey. *Elsevier Computer Networks, 52*(12), 2292–2330. doi:10.1016/j.comnet.2008.04.002

Zhou, Y., & Fang, Y. (2008). *Securing wireless sensor networks: A survey* (pp. 6–28). IEEE Communications Surveys & Tutorials.

Zhu, S., et al. (2003). LEAP: Efficient security mechanism for large scale distributed sensor networks. Proceedings of 10th ACM Conference on Computer and Communications Security (CCS'03), (pp. 62-72).

KEY TERMS AND DEFINITIONS

Body Area Network: A wireless network formed by sensors attached on the human body for monitoring vital signs or movement.

Link Layer Security: Hop by hop encryption mechanism. Used for sensor networks to facilitate in-network data processing.

Sensor Security: Protection mechanisms for data exchange in sensor networks.

Sensor Surveillance: Use of sensors for monitoring activity and changes in a surreptitious fashion.

Smart Grid: Future electric grid design involving two-way electricity flow and two-way data flow from the supplier to the consumer.

TinyOS: Event based operating system designed for sensor networks.

TinySec: A hop by hop encryption mechanism developed for sensor networks.

Wireless Sensor Network: Sensing devices having the capability of sending and receiving data using wireless communication links.

Chapter 12
Privacy Preserving Data Gathering in Wireless Sensor Networks

Md. Golam Kaosar
Victoria University, Australia

Xun Yi
Victoria University, Australia

ABSTRACT

Sensor devices provide sophisticated services in collecting data in various applications, some of which are privacy sensitive; others are ordinary. This chapter emphasizes the necessity and some mechanisms of privacy preserving data gathering techniques in wireless sensor network communication. It also introduces a new solution for privacy preserving data gathering in wireless sensor networks. By using perturbation technique in a semi-trusted server model, this new solution is capable of reducing a significant amount of computation in data collection process. In this technique, data of a sensor is perturbed into two components which are unified into two semi-trusted servers. Servers are assumed not to collude each other. Neither of them have possession of any individual data. Therefore, they cannot discover individual data. There are many real life applications in which the proposed model can be applied. Moreover, this chapter also shows a technique to collect grouped data from distributed sources keeping the privacy preserved. Security proofs show that any of the servers or any individual sensor neither can discover any individual data nor can associate any data to an individual sensor. Thus, the privacy of individual data is preserved.

1. INTRODUCTION

Wireless sensor network (WSN) consists of sensors scattered in the environment to monitor, sense and control the environment. Each sensor is equipped with reasonable computational and communicational capability. A sensor node consists of a radio transceiver, a small microcontroller and an energy source, usually a battery. Size of a sensor may vary from a shoebox down to a microscopically small particle (Romer, Mattern, and Zurich, 2004). Cost of a single sensor also

DOI: 10.4018/978-1-60960-777-7.ch012

Figure 1. Sensor device components' block diagram and the data flow in a wireless sensor network (WSN)

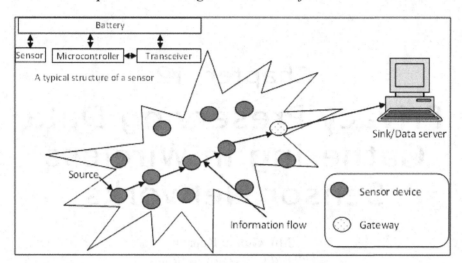

may vary from hundreds of dollar to few cents (Romer, Mattern, and Zurich, 2004). A typical sensor network with basic anatomy of a sensor device is depicted in Figure 1.

Sensor network can be applied in various applications including but not limited to: environment monitoring, waste water monitoring, vehicle monitoring, agricultural applications, greenhouse monitoring, enemy detection, wild animal monitoring, weather forecasting, scientific research, product tagging in supermarkets, smartcards etc. Ubiquitous computing which connects objects around human is based on the wireless sensor network. Objects in the environment would be equipped with sensors using which they would exchange information with their neighbors. Therefore, development of information gathering techniques in ubiquitous computing depends on the development of data gathering techniques in WSN.

One of the major obstacles observed in data aggregation is the preservation of privacy. Most individuals disagree to share their information if privacy is not preserved. Therefore, benefits of gathered data cannot be achieved unless the privacy of data is not preserved in a well acceptable manner. Privacy is a fundamental right of human

which guarantees other rights such as freedom of association, freedom of expression etc. According to The American Heritage Dictionary privacy means "The quality or condition of being secluded from the presence or view of others". Definition of privacy varies from literature to literature. Governmental privacy commission such as Office of Privacy Commission, Australian Government (Office of Privacy Commissioner) define privacy in a legislative point of view such as personal privacy, location privacy, sensitive information privacy etc. A technical definition might be found in the work of Vaidya, Clifton, and Zhu (2006) which states a privacy-preserving system must ensure: "any information disclosed cannot be traced back to an individual" and "any information disclosed does not constitute an intrusion". Most organizations in most countries are restricted and observed by active privacy acts which provide very strict guidelines to handle public data. In spite of possessing enormous amount of data, the data collectors cannot use the data unless they comply with the regulations enforced by privacy commission. Regulations might include according to Public Sector Information Sheets of Australian Government (2008): manner and purpose of collection of personal information, solicitation of personal information, storage and security of personal information, information relating to records kept by record-keeper, access to records containing personal information, alteration of records containing personal information, record-keeper to check accuracy etc of personal information before use, personal information to be used only for relevant purposes, limits on use of personal information, limits on disclosure of personal information etc.

Therefore, privacy preservation during data collection is a big challenge to meet. In a wireless sensor network it is more difficult due to its dynamic nature which will be discussed later in this section.

1.1. Wireless Sensor Network Privacy Issues

Wireless sensor network may deal with communication data, location data, biometric data, other personal sensitive data such as religious or philosophical belief, health information, political opinion, ethnic origin etc. Preserving privacy of these sensitive data is extremely important. Privacy in wireless sensor network can be troubled mainly due to two reasons: outsider attackers (replay attack, passive eavesdropper, denial of service etc) and inside attackers (nodes compromise each other, run malicious code etc). Privacy of data can be hampered by both content and context of the communication (Kamat, Zhang, Trappe, and Ozturk, 2005). Therefore privacy threat of wireless sensor network can be of two types too: content privacy and contextual privacy.

Content Privacy

This kind of privacy is considered preserved if the privacy of the data itself is preserved in the communication. In other words the information of an individual cannot be used for adversary that might go against his will. Information collected from individuals must be processed in such a way

that, no information can be attributed or associated to any individual. Example of content-privacy sensitive applications could be: auction, voting and feedback collections system, distributed privacy preserving data mining applications, military applications etc. Basically in these types of applications a trace of an involvement of an individual is not important. Rather the privacy of the data or message itself is the most important issue. Majority of the content privacy solutions are solved by cryptographic approaches. Others are solved using perturbation and randomization techniques. This chapter proposes a content privacy preservation protocol for gathering data in later sections.

Context Privacy

This kind of privacy is considered preserved if the privacy of the context associated with the transmission of an individual is preserved. Context privacy issue includes but not limited to: source and destination location, network identity, transmitted message length, time and duration of the transmission, frequency of the transmission etc. Example of context privacy sensitive applications could be: endangered animal activity monitoring system, mineral exploration applications, crime detection applications etc. Basically in these types of applications, the source, destination and other relevant information of a message is more sensitive than the actual data or message itself. To preserve this type of privacy the communication mechanism and routing protocols themselves are devised such that any kind of adversary gains as less information as possible about the transmissions.

1.2. Wireless Sensor Network Constraints

In a wireless sensor network every node is required to play an important role in establishing communication between different components in the network since there is no pre-defined infrastructure to support the network. Each node is free to roam and move while communicating with others. Routing is very important to transmit data since there might be single as well as multiple links in a path between same source and the destination. A node is also required to operate as a router to keep the communication process active. There are many challenging issues in wireless sensor network which include but not limited to:

Mobility

Opposed to the regular computer network, nodes in a wireless sensor network are not stationary. They are allowed changing their location at random speed without prior notification. At the same time, they require seamless service while moving. Therefore it is evident that mobility management in such networks would be very difficult and challenging to implement. More detail in mobility management in wireless sensor network can be found in the work of Ali, Voigt, and Uzmi (2006).

Power

Nodes in a wireless sensor network are operated by their tiny built-in batteries with limited capacity. All nodes are required to co-operate each other for the survival of the whole network for longer period. Failure of a single node might tear down an established path consequently it might degrade the performance of the whole network. To ensure efficient power mechanism and to enhance network lifetime, all algorithms and techniques must consume energy as less as possible.

Bandwidth

Due to the high bit error rate, re-transmission and link failure, it is difficult to acquire satisfactory amount of bandwidth in wireless communication system. The available bandwidth of the link also goes down further in the wireless sensor network due to other dynamic circumstances.

Scalability and Robustness

Since the number of nodes in the network is irregular, i.e. any number of users may shut down or start up arbitrarily, such infrastructure-less network design should be highly scalable and robust so that it could accommodate any number of nodes in the network and the effect of change of topology should also be dynamic.

More design issues of wireless sensor networks may be found in the works of Blumenthal, Handy, Golatowski, Haase, and Timmermann (2003); Lopez and Zhou (2008); and Phoha, LaPorta, and Griffin (2007). These sensitive and challenging issues in a wireless sensor network make the privacy preserving data gathering extremely difficult and lead the research on this area very hot.

1.3. Existing Solutions

Privacy issues were not considered from the earliest stages of wireless sensor networks. Later circumstances led to the necessity of privacy solutions. Primitive privacy solutions in wireless sensor network adopted some of the approaches such as MIX-Net by Chaum (1981), DC-Net by Chaum (1988), Onion-Routing Reed, Syverson and Goldschlag(1998), Crowds by Reiter and Rubin (1998) etc, with some required modifications proposed by Xiong, Zhang, and Shen (2008). Some of the research works of that direction are: Kong and Hong (2003); Boukerche, El-Khatib, Xu and Korba (2004); and Zhu, Wan, Kankanhalli, Bao, and Deng (2004) which provide weak location privacy in wireless sensor networks. In a wireless sensor network, an adversary can easily overhear a packet's direction and can guess the sink or source of the packet. In many applications preservation of contextual privacy is very important. Therefore there are good amount of research contribution available on this area too. Protection techniques against packet-tracing are proposed in the work of Kamat, Zhang, Trappe, and Ozturk (2005) as well as in the work of Ozturk, Zhang, and Trappe

(2004). Other location privacy mechanisms are proposed by Chaum (1981), Reed, Syverson, and Goldschlag (1998), Gruteser and Grunwald (2003) and Kang (2009).

Content-privacy solutions are provided in number of research works too. Regardless of the consideration of the infrastructure of the network, some randomization techniques have been proposed to preserve privacy such as by Agrawal and Srikant (2000), Evfimievski (2002), and Evfimievski, Ramakrishnan, Agrawal, and Gehrke (2002). Senders randomize their data before sharing and the receiver re-assembles them to generate resultant data close to the original data as accurately as possible. These techniques are not implementable in many applications since precision of re-assembly decreases as privacy constraints increased (Kargupta, Datta, Wang and Sivakumar, 2003). Another approach uses cryptographic techniques in which the data is encrypted before it is being shared. The collector (or miner in case of data mining applications) cannot decrypt individual inputs separately rather it can only decrypt the unified encrypted data together. This kind of encryption is known as homomorphic encryption detail of which may be found in the work of Katz and Lindell (2008). If x_1 and x_2 are two plaintext and E and D denotes encryption and decryption function respectively. Let us also assume y_1 and y_2 are two cipher-texts such that: $y_1 = E_k(x_1)$ and $y_2 = E_k(x_2)$ where, k is the encryption key. This encryption will be considered homomorphic if the following condition is held: $y_1 + y_2 = E_k(x_1 + x_2)$. Therefore these solutions do not let the data collector associate any information to a particular individual. An example of such approach is Secure Multiparty Computation (SMC) proposed by Yao (1986). Another cryptography based privacy preservation technique is proposed by Kantarcioglu and Clifton (2004), which involves enormous amount of mathematical computation and communication between data sites. Among other privacy preserving data mining solutions provided by

Lindell and Pinkas (2002) and Yang, Zhong and Wright (2005) are the ones which also involve huge amount of computation due to cryptographic computations. Eschenaur and Gligor (2002) and Perrig, Szewczyk, Tygar, Wen and Culler (2002) propose cryptographic solution to preserve privacy in wireless sensor networks. Yao and Wen (2008) propose a privacy protection for aggregate data collection in wireless sensor network called Data Aggregation Different Privacy-Levels Protection (DADPP). Here the privacy of an individual is protected against similar group members. Kundur, Luh, Okorafor, and Zourntos (2008) introduce a security and privacy in heterogeneous distributed multimedia wireless sensor network which also require large computation.

In some research works, lightweight privacy preserving authentication techniques are proposed. Otsuka, Shigetomi, and Imai (2006) propose a lightweight privacy preserving node identification technique, which requires only some random bit generation, bit-wise operation and small storage for keys. In this paper a linear parity with noise (LPN) technique is utilized and enhanced for radio-frequency identification (RFID) equipped devices. An asymmetric privacy preserving authentication protocol is proposed by Cui, Kobara, Matsuura and Imai (2007) which avoids exhaustive search in the database and thus increases efficiency.

Most of the cryptography based privacy preservation may not be suitable for very small and tiny sensor nodes due to their complexity involved in key management and mathematical computations etc. To achieve lightweight content-privacy preservation for wireless sensor network, we envision a non-cryptographic solution. Use of semi-trusted server based privacy preservation techniques proposed by Yi and Zhang (2007) and Yi and Zhang (2009) are interesting but still those use cryptographic approaches which were targeted for regular wired networks. Further research on this issue revealed that a data perturbation approach could be applied in semi-trusted model to preserve privacy which would be suitable for wired networks as well as wireless sensor networks. In this chapter we propose such a privacy preserving data gathering protocol which can be adopted in many applications.

2. PRIVACY PRESERVING DATA GATHERING IN WIRELESS SENSOR NETWORK

This section introduces a perturbation and semi-trusted server based privacy preserving data gathering technique for wireless sensor networks. In data gathering many operations such as addition, subtraction, multiplication, comparison etc. are needed to be performed on the actual data. Our proposed solution should be applicable for all of these basic functions with some minor modifications. However in this section summation has been taken as an example operation for simplicity. Data for a set of attributes are to be summed from a set of sensors such that none of the individual data will be revealed to other, not even to the servers. Moreover, this section also provides a solution for privacy preserving data gathering for grouped data. Unlike other privacy preserving techniques, this proposed protocol reduces lot of mathematical computation which would maximize the performance particularly for sensor devices.

Semi-Trusted Servers

Scattered data in the environment must be collected before being analyzed. Feedback collection or aggregation of data in wireless sensor network is infeasible in many applications unless privacy of data is ensured. It is practically impossible to find a centralized server to preserve privacy on which everybody can put legitimate trust. In other words, it is infeasible to assume a trusted third party in a solution, which might collect and deal such sensitive data. Therefore two semi-trusted server based system may be introduced to preserve the privacy

of user feedback. Two servers are semi-trusted if they correctly follow the protocol specification and never collude each other to discover any data. However, they individually are allowed to try to break privacy with the help of other users. It is also assumed that there exists private channel between each user and those servers using a standard private key encryption system such as DES (NBS FIPS PUB 46 (1977)) or AES (FIPS PUB 197 (2001)). The semi-trusted server concept was first introduced by Franklin and Reiter (1997 and Yi (2004) in exchanging documents and message respectively so that sharing entities know nothing but the final result. Similar idea is used by Yi and Zhang (2007, 2009) to provide cryptography based privacy preserved data mining solution. Semi-trusted server based privacy solution is very much realistic for applications where multiple authorities are involved with their mutual interest. As for example: in an aged care feedback system the government tries to ensure the quality of service provided by the aged care centers. In such circumstance, the governmental authority and the aged care center can own two semi-trusted servers. They must help each other for the proper operation of the application to ensure their mutual interest. At the same time neither of the servers would agree to collude with other party which might lead to the loss of their own interest.

2.1. Model

Let us assume there are N sensor devices S_1, S_2, ... S_N operating in an environment within a sensor network. They upload their data to the servers periodically or as required by the system. Data is relevant to n number of attributes: a_1, a_2, ... and a_n. S_1 needs to transmit values f_{i1}, f_{i2}, ... f_{in} for attributes a_1, a_2, ... a_n respectively. Table 1 can be formed for clarification:

Let us say there exist two semi-trusted servers M and K. There also exist private channels from all sensors to two servers which are secured by private key crypto system.

Table 1. Data to be delivered from sensors against all attributes

Sensors/Attributes	Data to be delivered by sensors			
	a_1	a_2	...	a_n
S_1	f_{11}	f_{12}	...	f_{1n}
S_2	f_{21}	f_{22}	...	f_{2n}
...	...	...	...	...
S_N	f_{N1}	f_{N2}	...	f_{Nn}
Total	$\sum_{i=1}^{N} f_{i1}$	$\sum_{i=1}^{N} f_{i2}$	...	$\sum_{i=1}^{N} f_{in}$

The protocol should be capable of retrieving the aggregated data for all the attributes while preserving the privacy of the data. That is, the data collector should be able to compute any or all of the values from $\sum_{i=1}^{N} f_{i1}, \sum_{i=1}^{N} f_{in}, \dots \sum_{i=1}^{N} f_{in}$, with the help of M and K without violating the privacy of the data of the sensors.

2.2. Our Protocol

A sensor perturbs its data and generates two fragments before uploading to the servers. Then it uploads one fragment of the data to M and other fragment to K for a particular attribute. None of the servers can have access to the information uploaded separately. To compute the final feedback, data collector needs to combine data together from the servers. Figure2 illustrates the proposed model in brief:

Let us say all N independent sensor devices are scattered in the environment having their communication capabilities with two semi trusted servers, M and K. There are n different attributes, a_1, a_2, ... a_n on which N parties provide their privacy preserved data. A big number B is shared to everybody in the network such that $B > \sum_{i=1}^{N} (data\, for\, any\, attribute)$. M and K accumulates and stores only one fraction of the attribute values provided by any sensor. Storage area for M and K are $M[a_1]$, $M[a_2]$, ... $M[a_n]$ and $K[a_1]$, $K[a_2]$, ... $K[a_n]$ respectively for attributes a_1, a_2, ... a_n respectively.

Necessary notations and pseudo code of the algorithm are shown in Box 1.

2.3. Flow Diagram

The flow of message in the protocol may be due to the following actions:

1. Sensors want to upload data due to periodic updates or a request from the server whenever required.
2. If the data collector or authority (either of the servers may work as a collector too) needs to

Figure 2. Semi-trusted server based privacy preserving data gathering model

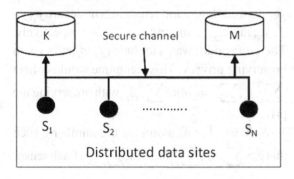

Box 1.

```
Notations:
A←[b,c]: pair of data/command 'b' and 'c' is transmitted to A through secured private channel. 'b' and 'c' are kept next to each other
to carry their relationship. This also shows that A successfully receives [b,c].
// or /*…*/: comment / explanation (not part of the algorithm)
Pseudo code:
send_data(sensor S, attribute a, value v)
// S_i uploads value v for attribute a,
{
Random_generator(v, r_1, r_2)
M←[a, r_1]
K←[a, r_2]
}
Receive_data(attribute a)
/*This function can be executed by both M and K to receive data about an attribute a, from any sensor.*/
{
If code runs in M then // Servers updates their database
M calculates: M[a]=M[a]+ r_1
Else
K calculates: K[a]= K[a]+ r_2
}
Calculate_aggregated_data(attribute a)
/*This function is executed by the data collector. Data collector can calculate aggregated data on a particular attribute a, anytime.*/
{
M←[send, a] //asks M to return data of a,
K←[send, a] //asks K to return data of a,
//M and K returns M[a] and K[a] respectively
If receives from both the servers
Calculates (K[a]+M[a]) mod B // this is the real value of v,
}
Random_generator(value v, number r_1, number r_2)
{
r_1= random_number() // generates a random number
r_2= random_number() such that v=(r_1+r_2) mod B
}
```

collect data for a particular attribute, it can ask the servers to return the corresponding accumulated data.

3. In response to the request of the collector, servers return the data for the relevant attribute.

Figure 3 depicts some of the communication steps in the protocol clearly.

2.4. Group Data Collection

To make data easier to understand, store and analyse, it is broken into groups. The proposed protocol can be used in group data collection too. This section depicts an instance of how grouped data can be collected from distributed data sources or sensor devices with preservation of privacy.

Let us say, each sensor (or any data source) has age information of some people which is grouped into three categories 'young', 'middle age' and 'senior'. Now all the sensors want to combine their total data without revealing their individual privacy. Let us assume number of people in group young, middle age and senior in N nodes are $y_1, y_2,$ ... $y_N, m_1, m_2, ... m_N$ and $s_1, s_2, ... s_N$ respectively. Therefore node i wants to share (y_i, m_i and s_i) with preserving privacy. This technique would collect $\sum_i^N y_i, \sum_i^N m_i, and \sum_i^N s_i$ with preserving the privacy.

Solution: Let us assume a big number g such that $g > \sum_i^N y_i, \sum_i^N m_i, and \sum_i^N s_i$. Each sensor

Figure 3. Communication flow diagram

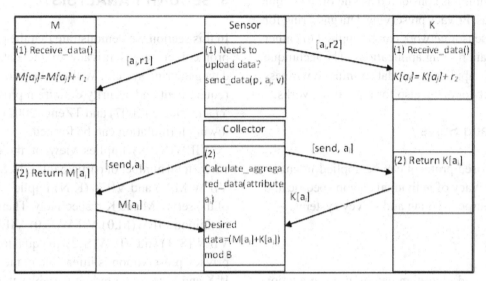

S_i computes $\left(y_i + m_i g + s_i g^2\right)$ and shares it to the servers according to the proposed protocol described in sub-section 2.3. After sharing these data according to the proposed protocol, the collector will retain

$V = (\sum_i^N y_i + g\sum_i^N m_i + g^2 \sum_i^N s_i)$. Collector receives V as a whole number from which it cannot reveal any data or associate any data to any individual. Collector now performs following operations to discover the sum for each group.

$$\sum_i^N y_i = V \ (mod\ g)$$

$$\sum_i^N m_i = \frac{(V - \sum_i^N y_i)}{g} \ (mod\ g)$$

and

$$\sum_i^N s_i = \frac{V - \sum_i^N y_i - \sum_i^N m_i}{g^2}$$

The solution can be extended for any number of groups. In the solution each party is required to send his data at least once. If we want to eliminate this restriction i.e. any party can update any number of times, then N should be considered as the number of total updates by all parties instead of the number of parties.

2.5. Applications of the Protocol

The protocol can be applied in many wireless sensor network oriented data gathering applications in which privacy preservation becomes a major concern. Example applications includes but not limited to:

Data Mining

Data mining is one of the means to utilize information by discovering underlying hidden useful knowledge from information. Data mining can be applied in many applications including advertisements, bioinformatics, database marketing, fraud detection, E-commerce, health care, security, sports, telecommunication, web, weather forecasting, financial forecasting, etc. Privacy preservation in data mining is considered as one of the major challenges. Privacy preserving data gathering for wireless sensor network can be applied to gather data in data mining applications. The technique is not only applicable for data mining in wireless sensor networks but also for regular networks.

Voting and Survey

The proposed protocol can be applied in ensuring the privacy of individual data in specific and general purpose voting and survey systems.

Auction

The proposed algorithm can be used in auction protocols too which might be suitable for regular network as well as sensor network. Participants in the auction would be able to bid their values for an item keeping their data private.

Multi-Authoritative Data Collection

Let us assume multiple authorities deploy their own sensors in a common environment to perform their own operations. Examples could be integrated security system composed of all security departments (e.g. police, military, criminal investigation department etc.), meteorological data collectors etc. If the authorities want to gather some data together to achieve their common interest, then the proposed technique can be applied to gather data.

Road Service Application

Proposed protocol may be applied to preserve the privacy of individuals in a system which calculates traffic status in roads based on the current location of vehicles.

3. SECURITY ANALYSIS

In this section we demonstrate that the proposed protocol preserves privacy of the data in the data gathering system. With the basis of privacy requirement and security definition provided by Yi and Zhang (2007) and TZeng (2002), the following formulation can be formed.

VIEW(S_i, N) implies view of the party S_i where total number of participants is N. Similarly VIEW(M,N) and VIEW(K,N) implies the view of the server M and K respectively. Therefore by definition VIEW(M,0), VIEW(K,0), VIEW(S_i,0), VIEW(S_i,1) and VIEW(S_i,2) all equal to Φ since privacy preservation is infeasible in these cases. If X and Y are two random variables then,

$X \approx_{poly} Y$ = (the probability of distinguishing X and Y) $\leq \dfrac{1}{2} + \dfrac{1}{Q(l)}$ for all polynomials Q(l) (X. Yi, Y. Zhang.(2007)). N parties want to unify their data v_1, v_2 ... v_N for a particular attribute in the servers. For simplicity the privacy definition and proof are provided for a single attribute which can be applied for all other attributes too. The privacy will be preserved if following conditions are satisfied (X. Yi, Y. Zhang.(2007)).

Two random variables

$$A_{N,j} = (VIEW\left(M, N\right), \sum_{i=1}^{j} r_{1i})\ \text{and}$$

$$B_{N,j} = (VIEW\left(M, N\right), R)\ \text{are polynomially}$$

indistinguishable ($A_{N,j} \approx_{poly} B_{N,j}$) for $1 \leq j \leq N$ and $0 \leq R < B$.

Similarly for K, two random variables

$$E_{N,j} = (VIEW\left(K, N\right), \sum_{i=1}^{j} r_{2i})\ \text{and}$$

$$F_{N,j} = (VIEW\left(K, N\right), R)\ \text{are polynomially}$$

indistinguishable ($E_{N,j} \approx_{poly} F_{N,j}$) for $1 \leq j \leq N$ and $0 \leq R < \sum v_i$.

Two random variables

$$C_{N,j} = (\bigcup_{i=1}^{j} VIEW\left(S_i, N\right), v_{j+1})\ \text{and}$$

$$D_{N,j} = (\bigcup_{i=1}^{j} VIEW\left(S_i, N\right), R)\ \text{are polynomi-}$$

ally indistinguishable ($C_{N,j} \approx_{poly} D_{N,j}$) for $n \geq 3$, $1 \leq j \leq n-2$ and $0 \leq R < \rho$.

Since all sensors generate identical random numbers r_1 and r_2, $(VIEW(M,N), \sum_{i=1}^{j} r_{1i})$,

$(VIEW(M,N), \sum_{i=2}^{j} r_{1i}) \cdots$

$(VIEW(M,N), \sum_{i=N-j+1}^{N} r_{1i})$ and

$(VIEW(M,N), \sum_{i=1}^{j} r_{2i})$, $(VIEW(M,N), \sum_{i=2}^{j} r_{2i})$

$\cdots (VIEW(M,N), \sum_{i=N-j+1}^{N} r_{2i})$ are the same.

Theorem: The proposed protocol preserves privacy based on the above mentioned privacy definition.

Proof:

(a) When N=1, then j=1 and
$A_{1,1} = (VIEW(M,1), r_1) = (r_1)$.

Since M does not have access to r_2, it cannot reveal the value of v_1. Therefore

$A_{1,1} = r_1 \approx_{poly} = (VIEW(M,1), r) = B_{1,1}$

When N>1 and $1 \leq j \leq N$

$A_{N,j} = \left(VIEW(M,N), \sum_{i=1}^{j} r_{1i}\right)$

$= \left(VIEW(M,N-j), VIEW(M,j), \sum_{i=1}^{j} r_{1i}\right)$

$= (VIEW(M,N-j), E\left(\sum_{i=1}^{j} r_{1i}\right), \sum_{i=1}^{j} r_{1i})$

$\approx_{poly} (VIEW(M,N), E\left(\sum_{i=1}^{j} r_{1i}\right), R)$

[Since $A_{1,1} \approx_{poly} B_{1,1}$]

$= (VIEW(M,N-j), R) = B_{N,j}$ [E indicates expected value]

Similarly for K, $E_{N,j} \approx_{poly} F_{N,j}$

(b) When N=3, j=1. Therefore

$C_{3,1} = (VIEW(S_1,3), v_2) = \left(\left(v_1, \sum_{i=1}^{3} v_i\right), v_2\right)$

With given v_1 and $\sum_{i=1}^{3} v_i$, sensor S_1 cannot be certain about v_2. Therefore,

$C_{3,1} \approx_{poly} \left(v_1, \sum_{i=1}^{3} v_i, R\right) = (VIEW(S_1,3), R) = D_{3,1}$

When N>3 and $1 \leq j \leq N-2$,

$C_{N,j} = \left(U_{i=1}^{j} VIEW(S_i,N), v_{m+1}\right) = \left(\left(\sum_{i=1}^{j} v_i, \sum_{i=1}^{N} v_i\right), v_{m+1}\right)$

Let us assume

$v_1' = \sum_{i=1}^{j} v_i$, $v_2' = v_{j+1}$, $v_3' = \sum_{i=1}^{N} v_i - \sum_{i=1}^{2} v_i$

Since $C_{3,1} \approx_{ploy} D_{3,1}$

$C_{N,j} = \left(v_1', \sum_{i=1}^{3} v_i', v_2'\right) \approx_{poly} \left(v_1', \sum_{i=1}^{3} v_i', R\right)$

$= \left(\sum_{i=1}^{j} v_i, \sum_{i=1}^{N} v_i, R\right) = \left(U_{i=1}^{m} VIEW(S_i,N), R\right) = D_{N,j}$

The protocol still preserves privacy if the data collector is allowed to collude one server and m other sensor nodes where m<n-1 in order to determine input from one of other nodes. Therefore none of the collectors or semi-trusted servers or any individual sensor can reveal or associate any data to any other individual sensor.

4. CONCLUSION

The proposed privacy preserving data gathering protocol focuses on the capability and nature of sensor network as well as the privacy issues in gathering distributed data. Very simple and light features of the technique would allow it run in tiny devices in sensor network. The technique is implementable for general purpose networks too. Realistic assumptions about the semi-trusted servers and the environment strengthen the feasibility of the solution. Moreover the security proof of the system shows the appropriateness of the proposed privacy preserving data gathering system.

To keep the scope of discussion relevant, the whole privacy issue in communication system of the wireless sensor network is not widely covered in the chapter, rather some useful references are hinted which might be a source of knowledge for those who are further interested. Though the protocol is suitable for most linear functions, in this chapter only summation is considered for simplicity. With some relevant modifications, other functions can be implemented too. A grouped data gathering technique is also proposed which can be extended for many applications.

The data gathering technique proposed in this chapter is a general solution which can be utilized in many areas some of which have been mentioned in this chapter. Therefore it is expected that this chapter would open a door towards further research and implementation to improve the privacy preserving data gathering scheme in general. Further implementation and comparison with other solutions might provide more confidence to the proposed protocol.

REFERENCES

Agrawal, R., & Srikant, R. (2000). Privacy-preserving data mining. *Proceedings of ACM SIGMOD International Conference on Management of Data*, (pp. 439–450).

Ali, M., Voigt, T., & Uzmi, Z. A. (2006). *Mobility management in sensor networks*. Mobility and Scalability in Wireless Sensor Networks, San Francisco, USA, June 2006.

Blumenthal, J., Handy, M., Golatowski, F., Haase, M., & Timmermann, D. (2003). Wireless sensor networks - new challenges in software engineering. *Proceedings of ETFA '03, IEEE Conference*, 16-19 Sept. 2003, vol 1, (pp. 551- 556). ISBN: 0-7803-7937-3

Boukerche, A., El-Khatib, K., Xu, L., & Korba, L. (2004a). *SDAR: A secure distributed anonymous routing protocol for wireless and mobile ad hoc networks*. In 29th Annual IEEE International Conference on Local Computer Networks, 16-18 Nov. 2004, (pp. 618– 624).

Boukerche, A., El-Khatib, K., Xu, L., & Korba, L. (2004b). *Anonymity enabling scheme for wireless ad hoc networks*. In Global Telecommunications Conference Workshops. GlobeCom Workshops 2004, (pp. 136–140).

Boukerche, A., El-Khatib, K., Xu, L., & Korba, L. (2004c). *A novel solution for achieving anonymity in wireless ad hoc networks*. The 1st ACM international workshop on Performance evaluation of wireless ad hoc, sensor, and ubiquitous, October 2004.

Chaum, D. (1981). Untraceable electronic mail, return addresses, and digital pseudonyms. *Communications of the ACM, 24*(2), 84–88. doi:10.1145/358549.358563

Chaum, D. (1988). The dining cryptographers problem: Unconditional sender and recipient untraceability. *Journal of Cryptography, 1*(1), 65–75.

Cui, Y., Kobara, K., Matsuura, K., & Imai, H. (2007). *Lightweight asymmetric privacy-preserving authentication protocols secure against active attac*. Fifth Annual IEEE International Conference on Pervasive Computing and Communications Workshops, 2007, (pp. 223-228). ISBN: 0-7695-2788-4

Eschenaur, L., & Gligor, V. (2002). A key-management scheme for distributed sensor networks. *Proc. of 9th ACM conference on Computer and Communications Security*, 2002.

Evfimievski, A. (2002). Randomization in privacy preserving data mining. *ACM SIG-KDD Explorations Newsletter*, *4*(2), 43–48. doi:10.1145/772862.772869

Evfimievski, A., Ramakrishnan, S., Agrawal, R., & Gehrke, J. (2002). *Privacy-preserving mining of association rules*. 8th ACM SIGKDD International Conference on Knowledge Discovery and Data Mining, (pp. 217–228). ACM Press.

FIPS PUB 197. (2001). *Advanced encryption standard*. Federal Information Processing Standards Publications, US Department of Commerce/N.I.S.T., National Technical Information Service, 2001.

Franklin, M. K., & Reiter, M. K. (1997). Fair exchange with a semi-trusted party. In *Proceedings of CCS'97*.

Gruteser, M., & Grunwald, D. (2003). *Anonymous usage of location-based services through spatial and temporal cloaking*. In *Proceedings of the International Conference on Mobile Systems, Applications, and Services* (MobiSys).

Kamat, P., Zhang, Y., Trappe, W., & Ozturk, C. (2004). Source-location privacy in energy constrained sensor network routing. *Proceedings of the 2004 ACM Workshop on Security of Ad Hoc and Sensor Networks* (SASN).

Kamat, P., Zhang, Y., Trappe, W., & Ozturk, C. (2005). Enhancing source location privacy in sensor network routing. *Proc. of 25th (ICDCS)*, 2005.

Kang, L. (2009). *Protecting location privacy in large-scale wireless sensor networks*, IEEE International Conference on Communications, 2009, (pp. 1–6). DOI: 10.1109/ICC.2009.5199372

Kantarcioglu, M., & Clifton, C. (2004). Privacy-preserving distributed mining of association rules on horizontally partitioned data. *Knowledge and Data Engineering IEEE Transaction*, *16*(9), 1026–1037. doi:10.1109/TKDE.2004.45

Kargupta, H., Datta, S., Wang, Q., & Sivakumar, K. (2003). *On the privacy preserving properties of random data perturbation techniques*. 3rd Int'l Conference on Data Mining, 2003, (pp. 99–106).

Katz, J., & Lindell, Y. (2008). *Introduction to modern cryptography*. *Taylor & Francis Group*. LLC.

Kong, J., & Hong, X. (2003). *ANODR: Anonymous On Demand Routing with Untraceable Routes for Mobile Ad-hoc Networks*. The 4th ACM international symposium on Mobile ad hoc networking & computing, June 2003.

Kundur, D., Luh, W., Okorafor, U. N., & Zourntos, T. (2008). Security and privacy for distributed multimedia sensor networks. *Proceedings of the IEEE*, *96*(1), 112–130..doi:10.1109/JPROC.2007.909914

Lindell, Y., & Pinkas, B. (2002). Privacy preserving data mining. *Journal of Cryptology*, *15*(3). doi:10.1007/s00145-001-0019-2

Lopez, J., & Zhou, J. (2008). *Wireless sensor network security*. IOS Press.

NBS FIPS PUB 46. (1977). *Data encryption standard*. National Bureau of Standards, US Department of Commerce, 1977.

Office of Privacy Commissioner. Australian Government. (n.d.). *Privacy information*. Retrieved from http://www.privacy.gov.au/ index.php

Otsuka, A., Shigetomi, R., & Imai, H. (2006). *Lightweight privacy for ubiquitous devices*. IEEE International Conference on Systems, Man and Cybernetics, 2006 (SMC '06), vol. 2, (pp. 1233-1237). ISBN: 1-4244-0099-6

Perrig, A., Szewczyk, R., Tygar, D., Wen, V., & Culler, D. (2002). SPINS: Security protocols for sensor networks. *Wireless Networks, 8*(5), 521–534. doi:10.1023/A:1016598314198

Phoha, S., LaPorta, T., & Griffin, C. (2007). *Sensor network operations*. John Wiley & Sons, Inc.

Public Sector Information Sheets. (2008). *Information privacy principles*. Office of Privacy Commissioner, Australian Government.

Reed, M. G., Syverson, P. F., & Goldschlag, D. M. (1998). Anonymous connections and onion routing. *IEEE Journal on Selected Areas in Communications, 16*(4), 482–494. doi:10.1109/49.668972

Reiter, M. K., & Rubin, A. D. (1998). Crowds anonymity for Web transactions. *ACM Transactions on Information and System Security, 1*(1), 66–92. doi:10.1145/290163.290168

Romer, K., Mattern, F., & Zurich, E. (2004). The design space of wireless sensor networks. *Wireless Communications, 11*(6), 54–61. doi:10.1109/MWC.2004.1368897

Vaidya, J., Clifton, C., & Zhu, M. (2006). *Privacy preserving data mining*. Springer. Xiong, P., Zhang, W., & Shen, F. (2008). *A novel solution for protecting privacy in ad hoc network*. International Conference on Advanced Language Processing and Web Information Technology, 2008. ALPIT '08, 23-25, (pp. 404–411).

Yang, Z., Zhon, S., & Wright, R. N. (2005). Privacy-preserving classification of customer data without loss of accuracy. *Proceedings of the Fifth SIAM International Conference on Data Mining,* Newport Beach, CA, April 21-23, 2005.

Yao, A. C. (1986). *How to generate and exchange secrets*. 27th IEEE Symposium on Foundations of Computer Science, 1986, (pp. 162–167).

Yao, J., & Wen, G. (2008). *Protecting classification privacy data aggregation in wireless sensor networks*. 4th International Conference on Wireless Communications, Networking and Mobile Computing, 2008. WiCOM '08, 12-14 Oct. 2008 (pp. 1–5). DOI 10.1109/WiCom.2008.951

Yi, X. (2004). Identity-based fault-tolerant conference key agreement. *IEEE Transactions on Dependable and Secure Computing, 1*(3), 170–178. doi:10.1109/TDSC.2004.31

Yi, X., & Zhang, Y. (2007). Privacy-preserving distributed association rule mining via semi-trusted mixer. *Data & Knowledge Engineering, 63*(2). doi:10.1016/j.datak.2007.04.001

Yi, X., & Zhang, Y. (2009). Privacy-preserving naive Bayes classification on distributed data via semi-trusted mixers. *Information Systems, 34*(3), 371–380.

Zeng, W. G. (2002). A secure fault-tolerant conference key agreement protocol. *IEEE Transactions on Computers, 51*(4), 373–379. doi:10.1109/12.995447

Zhu, B., Wan, Z., Kankanhalli, M. S., Bao, F., & Deng, R. H. (2004). *Anonymous secure routing in mobile ad-hoc networks*. The 29th Annual IEEE International Conference on Local Computer Networks, Nov. 2004, (pp. 102–108).

KEY TERMS AND DEFINITIONS

Adversary: Any third party tries to perform any malicious activity in security protocol. Adversary can be active as well as passive. **VIEW:** This parameter is used to measure the privacy achieved by a protocol. It implies the possible amount of information accessible by an entity. VIEW(S, N) implies view of a party S where total number of participants is N.

Content Privacy: Content privacy in a distributed environment is considered preserved if the privacy of data itself of the communication is preserved. In content privacy sensitive applications a trace of involvement of an entity is immaterial. Majority of the content privacy solutions are solved by cryptographic approaches.

Context Privacy: This kind of privacy is considered preserved if the privacy of the context associated with the transmission of an entity is preserved. In context sensitive applications, the source, destination and other relevant information of a message is more sensitive than the actual data or message itself. To preserve this type of privacy the communication mechanism and routing protocols themselves are devised such that any kind of adversary gains as less information as possible about the transmission.

Data Gathering: In broader sense data gathering means the collection of data into a server. For WSN, number of sensors may be scattered in the environment to collect some data about the environment. These sensors are managed in such a way that they are capable to upload the data to the server periodically or as necessary basis.

Semi-Trusted Server: A semi-trusted server is assumed not to collude with any of the participants. In semi-trusted server model, all participants sends data to the server and the server mixes / unifies all the data and transmits back the result to all the participants. Such model is known as semi-trusted mixer too.

WSN: Wireless sensor network (WSN) consists of a group of self configuring wireless sensor nodes, which are randomly distributed. Nodes operate without infrastructure support and do not require a base station or access point. They rely on each other to establish temporary network peers to communicate another node which is beyond the radio frequency (RF) range by routing packets through some intermediate nodes.

Section 5
Security Architectures, Algorithms, and Protocols

Chapter 13
BANBAD:
A Centralized Anomaly Detection Technique for Ad Hoc Networks

Rajeev Agrawal
North Carolina A & T State University, USA

Chaoli Cai
Western Michigan University, USA

Ajay Gupta
Western Michigan University, USA

Rajib Paul
Western Michigan University, USA

Raed Salih
Western Michigan University, USA

ABSTRACT

Anomaly detection is an important aspect of any security mechanism. We present an efficient anomaly detection algorithm, named. Using Belief Networks (BNs), the algorithm identifies abnormal behavior of a feature, like inappropriate energy consumption of a node in a network. By applying structure learning techniques to training dataset, BANBAD establishes a joint probability distribution among relevant features, such as average velocity, displacement, local computation and communication time, energy consumption, and response time of a node of the network. A directed acyclic graph (DAG) is used to represent the features and their dependencies. Using a training process, BANBAD maintains dynamic, updated profiles of network node behaviors and uses specific Bayesian inference algorithm to distinguish abnormal behavior during testing. BANBAD works especially well in ad hoc networks. Extensive simulation results demonstrate that a centralized BANBAD achieves low false alarm rates, below 5%, and high detection rates, greater than 95%. We also show that BANBAD detects anomaly efficiently and accurately in two real datasets. The key for achieving such high performance is bounding the false alarm rate at certain predefined threshold value. By fine-tuning at the threshold, we can achieve high detection rate as well.

DOI: 10.4018/978-1-60960-777-7.ch013

INTRODUCTION

Ad hoc network consists of a number of peer mobile nodes that are capable of communicating with each other without a priori fixed infrastructure. However, arbitrary node movements and lack of centralized control make ad hoc networks vulnerable to a wide variety of attacks from inside as well as from outside. It is very difficult to narrow down a single node that has been attacked in a large ad hoc network. Therefore, providing effective security protection is important to ensure the continued viability of these networks in a variety of pursuits.

In general, two complementary approaches exist to protect a system: prevention and detection. Intrusion prevention techniques, such as encryption and authentication, attempt to deter and block attackers. Unfortunately, prevention techniques can only reduce intrusions, not completely eliminate them (Gollmann 1999; Schneier, 2000). Despite the amount or quality of intrusion prevention measures, an intelligent attacker can exploit a single security hole to break into a system. Nothing is absolutely secure. Therefore, intrusion detection systems (IDSs) are indispensable for a reliable system. They serve as the important secondary line of defense.

Intrusion detection can be based either on detecting misuses or detecting anomalies. A misuse-based detection technique checks potential security breaches against known attack signatures and system vulnerabilities. If it finds a match, an alarm is generated. Since it is impossible to know all future attacks-or attack patterns in advance, misuse detection techniques are not effective in detecting new or unknown attacks. Given the constantly evolving nature of security breaches, anomaly-based techniques are needed. An anomaly-based detection technique models normal behavior by creating profiles of system and node states during the training process. During the testing process, it compares deviations from the normal profiles to determine whether a deviation is significant. If so, an alarm is triggered. Therefore, anomaly detection can check a whole host of different and new types of attacks. While misuse detection may be more efficient, anomaly detection is more comprehensive. In a dynamic security environment, a comprehensive technique is highly desirable and considered best. Anything less leaves systems open for attack. Unfortunately, the mobility of nodes inherent in ad hoc network makes profile generation difficult. Therefore, efficiently establishing and maintaining profiles for mobile nodes is crucial. Because of the ad hoc nature of the network, often availability of complete data is not possible; therefore a technique handling incomplete data is desired. The proposed BANBAD technique addresses these issues.

Intrusion Prevention Systems

Data encryption and authentication are two primary methods, and play an important role for intrusion prevention techniques. The basic idea behind such techniques relies on key management. Li, He, & Fu (2006) propose a static key management strategy, in which a key pre-distribution scheme is designed using the bivariate t-degree polynomial in a hexagonal coordinate system for the expected locations of the sensor nodes. By comparing with the square-based polynomial pre-distribution scheme, Liu & Ning, (2003) show that their scheme can improve the effectiveness of key management in terms of the probability of key establishment, and can extract appropriate security threshold with different polynomial degrees in sensor networks. In addition to static key management scheme (KMS), another type of KMS is the dynamic KMS in which keys can be updated periodically or on demand as a response to node capture. By performing key update, the compromised nodes are segregated and the network security can be enhanced. Li, He, & Fu (2007) propose a group-based dynamic key management scheme in wireless sensor networks without the requirement for a fixed infrastructure such as base stations and cluster heads. Their scheme ensures the network security without tampering the compromised sensor nodes with an acceptable overhead, when $k=l$, the overhead is minimum where k is the number of key polynomials known to each node and l is the number of polynomials unknown to each node.

Ma, Cheng, Liu, Rivera, & An (2007) propose an In Situ Pairwise Key (IPAK) bootstrapping algorithm for shared-key establishment between neighboring sensors. They introduce two sensor types, service sensors and worker sensors. The simulation study shows their work can achieve high key-sharing probability with low storage in *worker sensors*. Ren, Lou, & Zhang (2006) propose a location-aware multi-functional key management framework, which ensures both node-to-sink and node-to-node authentication along report forwarding routes, to guarantee end-to-end security in wireless sensor networks. The proposed BANBAD algorithm is designed for detection and not prevention.

Intrusion Detection Systems

Intrusion detection technique serves as the second line of defense, and is an important component of the defense in depth or layered network security mechanism. The two main intrusion detection techniques are misuse (abuse) detection and anomaly detection.

As to misuse detection techniques, Yang, Huang, & Qin (2009) propose a network misuse detection mechanism based on traffic log, combining the payload independent traffic classification technology. Through observation and comparisons over extensive experiments, the authors complete the selection of behavior features, and by using collaborative learning method (Kyriakopoulou, 2007), they overcome the problems of both sample in sufficiency and adaptability.

Anomaly detection approach was first proposed by Denning in (Denning, 1987). These algorithms can detect new types of intrusions by comparing the abnormal behavior with the normal behavior. One of the advantages of this approach is that it can detect the intrusions, which have not occurred so far or the system is not aware of them. But, these techniques also suffer from a high false alarm rate due to previously unseen behavior identified as anomaly, even though it is legitimate.

Most of the network intrusion detection techniques rely on labeled training data, but the training data is expensive to produce and manually classify. In addition, there is no guarantee that there are no intrusions when data is collected. An unsupervised anomaly detection technique has been proposed using density-based and grid-based clustering algorithm (Ingham & Somayaji, 2007). The algorithm discovers the characteristics of the connections from records of network traffic and uses the results to classify future connections.

Another type of detection technique is called Specification-based Detection technique, which is very similar to anomaly detection techniques, as intrusions are identified by comparing normal behavior. These methods use manually developed specifications of the expected behavior of system rather than previously seen behavior. Whenever system behaves outside of these specifications, this will be flagged as anomaly. The high rate of false alarms is avoided using these techniques, but still are not effective in detecting novel attacks, for example network probing and denial-of-service attacks. In addition to this, the development of detailed specifications depend on the complexity of network, more complex network would require a very detailed set of specifications of network, applications running, user behavior etc. In Sekar et al. (2002), specifications-based approach is combined with anomaly detection based approach to take the advantage of both the approaches. The state-machine specifications of network protocols are augmented with information about statistics that need to be maintained to detect anomalies. The state-machine model is used to map behaviors to transitions of the state machine and unusual behavior is detected by learning how frequently a transition has taken place. The following attacks targeted on lower layers of protocols such as IP and TCP are detected using this approach; *Apache2, Back, IP Sweep, Mailbomb, Mscan, Neptune, Ping-of-Death, Smurf, Queso, Satan, Portsweep*.

Our technique is based on statistical hypothesis testing approach. By comparing with the previous work, we achieve good performance: first, in terms of both the false alarm rate and the detection rate; second, BANBAD is applied to many different statistical distributions -- symmetric and skewed; third, it is widely applicable under different network scenarios, not limited to a specific network, e.g., ad hoc network, wireless sensor network, wireless network, etc.; fourth, BANBAD can handle incomplete dataset during testing. Application of our method to two real datasets strongly supports the effectiveness of BANBAD.

Background/Related Work

Zhang & Lee (2000) present an anomaly detection technique in which each node locally analyzes available network data for anomalies. Intrusion attempts are detected by employing a distributed cooperative mechanism in which all participating nodes cast votes according to data they have previously analyzed. Results of this work are incomplete. First, trace data-feature or audit data source-design is not complete. It is not clear what information a routing protocol should include to make the IDS effective. Second, the detection model design does not indicate when to initiate intrusion response. Finally, their technique suffers from performance penalties and high false alarm rates. Our work is an attempt to address these deficiencies.

Sun, Wu, Yu, & Leung (2006) describe another technique by using (a) the high-order Markov model to specify the mobility pattern of a user; (b) EWMA (exponentially weighted moving average) for fading in order to maintain an updated profile of each user; and (c) distance, a metric for indicating how closely a mobile user follows her routines. As they themselves address, the algorithm has high false alarm rates and low, dependent detection rates. Moreover, it is not easy to tell whether an anomaly exists when the speed ranges of nodes are fairly low.

Other work on anomaly detection (Cai, Ci, Guizani, & Al-Fuqaha, 2006; Sun, Yu, Wu, Xiao, & Leung, 2006), also suffers from major shortcomings. Many methods only achieve good performance when strong assumptions are met, like high velocity ranges (Cai et al., 2006; Sun et al, 2004; Sun et al., 2006). In addition, sometimes methods creating and updating dynamic profiles are very expensive (Zhang & Lee, 2000). TCM-KNN (Transductive Confidence Machines for K-Nearest Neighbors) algorithm is proposed in (Li & Guo, 2008) as a lightweight and on-line anomaly detection technique. First, a filter-based method – Information Gain (IG) is used for feature selection and then Support Vector Machine (SVM) is applied for feature weight optimization. This results into reduced computational cost and boosting its performance.

For anomaly detection techniques, two main approaches exist: Statistical-based and Rule-based. For Rule-based approaches, Silva et al. (2005) define multiple rules by taking into account data messages in wireless sensor networks. These rules can be used to determine if a specific type of network failure has occurred and to raise an intrusion alarm if accumulative network failures exceed a predefined threshold. Hilas presents a rule-based expert system that aims to detect superimposed fraud cases in the telecommunications network of a large organization (Silva, 2009). The expert system incorporates the network administrator's knowledge along with observations and knowledge derived from the application of data mining techniques on historical data. The knowledge is expressed in the form of rules implemented by C4.5 algorithm to classify calls into two classes, normal or anomaly (Witten & Frank, 2005).

For statistical-based approach, Chatzigiannakis, Androulidakis, Pelechrinis, Papavassiliou, &

Maglaris (2007) present a review and classification of data fusion algorithms, specifically addressing the anomaly detection problem. By comparing two different representative approaches, one based on the Demster-Shafer Theory of Evidence (Siaterlis & Maglaris, 2005), and the other based on Principal Component Analysis (Chatzigiannakis, Papavassiliou, Androulidakis, & Maglaris, 2006), under different attack scenarios, they identify which of these two approaches operates more efficiently, and could be used to detect a wide range of attacks in an integrated way. However, the crucial performance of anomaly detection, false alarm rate and detection rate are not exhibited in the paper. Liu, Cheng, & Chen (2007) propose the insider attacker scheme. By exploiting the spatial correlation among networking behaviors of sensor in close proximity, the scheme takes into consideration multiple attributes simultaneously without requiring prior knowledge about normal or malicious sensor activities.

Li & Fu (2008) propose the group-based anomaly detection scheme for wireless sensor networks. They use Mahalanobis distance measurement and the OGK estimators (Maronna, Martin, & Yohai, 2006) in the intrusion detection algorithm to consider multiple attributes (features) of the sensor nodes to detect malicious network attack behaviors. By conducting real data (http://db.csail.mit.edu) experiments and comparing with other intrusion detection schemes of Liu et al. (2007), lower false alarm rate and higher detection rate are achieved. However, all the features are assumed to be normally distributed, and handling missing or incomplete data is not clearly addressed.

Alves, Ferreira, Belo, & Lopes (2006), and Ferreira, Alves, Belo, & Cortesão (2006) propose two anomaly detection methods based on the concept of profiles for detecting telecom fraud situations. Some deficiencies are: first, it's not clear how to efficiently extract the threshold; second, they argue the profile should be always updated to avoid loss of information without considering the possibility of introducing error due to profile update; third, no false alarm rate

and detection rate are demonstrated to evaluate the proposed methods.

Statistical machine learning (SML) techniques have recently been used for anomaly detection. These techniques build a model for normal behavior and attacks are detected whenever system deviates from normal behavior. There is a possibility of manipulating the training data in such a way that learned model cannot detect future attacks. During the learning phase, typically the data are collected over one or two weeks of period only. Now, the adversary can take advantage of this and malicious data can be injected in this period and SML algorithms will learn the wrong model, therefore, detectors would not be able to trace any abnormality in the system. This process is known as poisoning. The adversary needs to have some information about the network to inject additional traffic, chaff, into the network without being detected. These attacks can be classified based on the amount of information available with the attacker. If attacker has no information at all, the attack is classified as uninformed attack and chaff is added randomly. If attacker has only the partial information about network, e.g. current volume of traffic, before poisoning it, this type of attack is called locally-informed. One unlikely but not impossible scenario is when the attacker knows everything about the network; this scenario is classified as globally-informed attack. All the above-mentioned poisoning techniques have been evaluated and an antidote based on techniques from robust statistics is presented in the context of PCA-subspace method in (Rubinstein et al., 2009).

One challenge, which model-based anomaly detection system faces is if it over generalizes the behavior of the network, it is likely to miss many attacks. On the other hand, under generalization produces too many false positives. It is important to develop a model that considers appropriate trade-offs between model and generalization. A design methodology, which addresses this issue is proposed in Ingham & Somayaji (2007), which starts out with an under generalized model and then looks for evidences of positions of specific input instances such as nodes with a large number of outbound edges, each with a low usage. It then uses heuristics-based input filters to replace highly variable portions of the input with more constrained inputs and retrain the model to verify that the targeted model portions no longer encode specific inputs.

In (Nychis, Sekar, Andersen, Kim, & Zhang, 2008), entropy-based methods for anomaly detection have been studied, since they provide more fine-grained insights than traditional traffic volume analysis. The flow-header features such as IP addresses, ports, and flow-sizes, and behavioral features such as the number of distinct destination/source IPs that each host communicates with, have been explored. It has been found that the time series of entropy values of the address and port distributions are strongly correlated with each other and provide very similar anomaly detection capabilities, whereas, behavioral and flow size distributions are less correlated and detect incidents that do not show up as anomalies in the port and address distributions. This study is useful in determining the feature selection criteria for anomaly detection.

The purpose of our research is to address the shortcomings in current anomaly detection methods to create an affordable, efficient, and effective anomaly detection method for ad hoc networks. The key improvements of the proposed BANBAD are the ability to obtain high detection rate (DR) while decreasing false alarm rate (FAR), be able to bound FAR, and handle incomplete samples.

OUR APPROACH: CENTRALIZED BANBAD ANOMALY DETECTION ALGORITHM

BANBAD Technique

In this section, we describe an efficient anomaly detection technique that can handle incomplete or missing data. The proposed detection algorithm depends on Belief Networks (BNs) to identify abnormal behavior of a target feature, such as energy consumption or response time, in a computer system. Our algorithm, referred to as BANBAD (Belief network Based Anomaly Detection), builds a normal profile during training by keeping track of various system features, and checks for deviation from this normal profile during testing. Data used during training is called the training sample and the one used during testing is called the testing sample.

Consider a BN that is used to detect anomalies in ad hoc networks, such as, a network of mobile hosts communicating wirelessly. In an ad hoc network, there is no priory fixed infrastructure such as base stations or mobile switching centers. Mobile nodes that are within each other's radio range communicate directly via wireless links, while those that are far apart rely on other nodes to relay messages as routers (Lidong & Zygmunt, 1999).

Suppose we keep track of energy consumption, average velocity, displacement, and response time of nodes in an ad-hoc network. The dependencies among these features can be represented, in a simplified scenario, by a chain model of the belief networks as in Figure 1.

Figure 1. The chain application model displaying the dependencies of various features of a mobile node

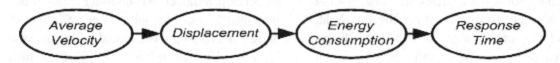

In this example, energy consumption is affected by Displacement (D) and it affects Response Time (R). Displacement is affected by Average Velocity. Note that for brevity we do not display all the factors that may affect energy consumption (E). In general, when all the major features that may affect a target feature are incorporated, a directed acyclic graph represents the dependencies among these features.

The continuous raw datasets in the training and testing samples are first categorized or discretized to decrease computational complexity. For example, Average Velocity (V) may be partitioned into two states $\{V_1, V_2\}$ where $V_1 \equiv \left[v_{min}, v_1\right)$ and $V_2 \equiv \left[v_1, v_{max}\right]$. Similarly, there are two states $\{D_1, D_2\}$ for Displacement (D), where $D_1 \equiv \left[d_{min}, d_1\right)$ and $D_2 \equiv \left[d_1, d_{max}\right]$; three states $\{E_1, E_2, E_3\}$ for Energy Consumption (E), where $E_1 \equiv \left[e_{min}, e_1\right)$, $E_2 \equiv \left[e_1, e_2\right)$, and $E_3 \equiv \left[e_2, e_{max}\right]$; and three states $\{R_1, R_2, R_3\}$ for Response Time (R), where $R_1 \equiv \left[r_{min}, r_1\right)$, $R_2 \equiv \left[r_1, r_2\right)$, and $R_3 \equiv \left[r_2, r_{max}\right]$.

To illustrate BANBAD, we will use energy consumption (E) with three states as our target feature. The belief is computed for each of the states in the training and testing samples. (Belief computation will be defined in the next section.)

Anomalies can then be detected using a distance function which is the difference of the beliefs between the training and testing samples. For example, the distance for a state of a feature can be defined as:

$$\text{Distance (S)} = \left| Bel_{tr}(S) - Bel_{te}(S) \right|. \qquad (1)$$

Where: S is a state of the target feature $Bel_{tr}(S)$ is the belief of S in the training data $Bel_{te}(S)$ is the belief of S in the testing data.

Let τ be the threshold tolerance. If the Distance (S) $\leq \tau$, S is considered normal; otherwise S depicts an anomalous behavior.

Figure 2 illustrates the general structure of the training and the testing processes of BANBAD, where both processes first consist of data and feature collection.

BANBAD uses BNs to learn causal relationship among features and handle incomplete datasets using that established causal relation (Cai, 2009; Pearl, 1988). In addition, we detect anomalies not just by using the direct belief computation, but also indirect belief computation that relies on the evidence from other features. The following sections will discuss these processes in details.

Figure 2. (a) The training process, (b) the testing process of BANBAD

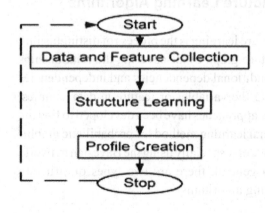

a.

b.

Belief Network (BN)

Bayesian and belief networks are examples of probabilistic graphical models. Basically, these models consist of random variables referred as nodes, and probabilistic dependencies referred as links (arcs) among them. These models are represented by direct acyclic graph (DAG).

There are several benefits of using these models. First, these models easily can cover missing or incomplete data. Second, the statistical technique behind these models has the ability to combine between the prior knowledge and the current input knowledge. This is very important especially when the prior knowledge is barely available or very expensive. For example, Bayesian network has a causal semantics that makes the encoding of causal prior knowledge particularly straightforward. Knowledge about relationships between structure variables provides inductive constraints that allow Bayesian networks to be learned from much less data than would otherwise be possible. Finally, these models allow us to express the causal relationship. Understanding the causal relationship helps us to know more about the problem domain. In addition, the causal relationship allows us to predict and be more certain about diagnostic event. For example, the physician attempts to look for symptoms as he can be sure that the patient has a particular kind of disease (Heckerman, 1996).

The causal reasoning is directly retrieved from two parts of network model, the conditional probabilities (lines) and the structure variables (nodes). These two parts keep changing with continuous inputs that enter the model. The process that happens between these two parts is called learning.

The learning process in these models is divided into sub processes. First, the *structure learning* that refers to the topology of the network (graph), and *parameter learning* that refers to the conditional probabilities for the network topology (parameters). The purpose of the structure learning is to finalize an optimal (best) network structure according to given random variables and conditional probabilities. Structure learning is very efficient for generating models in the form of directed graphical models.

Learning the model structure from the data by considering all possible structures exhaustively is infeasible as the number of possible structures grows exponentially with the number of nodes. According to Robinson (1977) who has proved that *r(n)*, the number of different structures for a Bayesian network with *n* nodes, is given by the following formula.

$$r(n) = \sum_{i=1}^{n} (-1)^{i+1} \binom{n}{i} 2^{i(n-1)} r(n-1) = n^{2^{o(n)}}$$

For example:

$$r(2) = 3, \ r(3) = 25, \ r(5) = 29281, \ r(10) \cong 4.2 \times 10^{18}$$

From these results, it seems impossible to perform an exhaustive search in a decent time as soon as the numbers of nodes exceed 7 or 8. Therefore, structure learning methods often use heuristic search. In other words, structure learning requires either sub-optimal heuristic search algorithms or algorithms which are efficient under certain assumptions. We will discuss structure learning algorithms in the next section.

Structure Learning Algorithms

Structure learning is the process of distinguishing structure graph by discovering the relationships as conditional dependencies and independencies among the variables or feature in data samples. Many approaches have been developed to find the optimal learning method for probabilistic graphical models especially using the Bayesian network.

In general, there are two types of structure learning algorithms:

- Constrained-based learning
- Score-based learning

Constrained-based learning performs a statistical test on the given rational variables to identify the structure graph. One of the most known algorithms under this category is called PC named after its developers in (Spirtes, Glymour, & Scheines, 2000). The basic hypothesis of PC algorithm is: the independence relationships have a perfect representation by DAG; we have a very large database; and statistical tests have no error. Under these conditions, the algorithm will discover an equivalent belief network. Computing p-value is usually used to determine whether there is independence for two variables. However, sometimes the direction of links needs to be selected with user interaction to keep the DAG structure because PC algorithm cannot necessarily finish complete arc orientation. Since, we have very large dataset, therefore, we apply PC algorithm mainly in our BANBAD work. The following are the important steps of the PC structure learning algorithm:

- **Assign initial graph**

Discover any pair of nodes that have dependencies and draw direct edge between them. For example, check whether X and Y are in the same set Z, if so draw edge between them.

- **Assign the unpaired nodes**

Discover the unidirectional independencies among the remaining nodes. Find node that has edge between two nodes. For example, find new node W such that $\left(X \longrightarrow W \longleftarrow Y \right)$

- **Finalize the unidirectional edge**

Point the remaining unidirectional edges such that no cycle appears in the final graph.

K2 algorithm is a score-based greedy search algorithm commonly used in belief structure learning. The performance of the K2 algorithm is greatly affected by the order of input nodes. If all the parents in the node ordering occur prior to their children in the node ordering, the algorithm will perform optimally and consequently the results are very accurate (Cooper & Herskovits, 1992). The K2 algorithm is very efficient as the node-ordering information reduces the search space of DAG, thus making the search non-exhaustive. However, the performance of the algorithm may be poor when using wrong orderings in which many children nodes appear prior to their parents and for orderings that are random in nature. Unfortunately, in most cases, the input node ordering is usually unknown. Hence, BANBAD uses PC algorithm to create the belief network.

Belief Computation

BNs allow us to learn causal relationship among features (Lidong & Zygmunt, 1999). BN technique tracks single target feature or many features by using Bayes' rule. Let $Bel(X_i)$ denote the belief of state X_i of a feature, then

$$Bel(X_i) = \frac{\pi(x_i) \times \lambda(x_i)}{\sum_i \pi(x_i) \times \lambda(x_i)} \qquad (2)$$

Where $\pi(x_i)$ is the causal reasoning value of X_i and $\lambda(x_i)$ is the diagnostic reasoning value of X_i.

Above definition of belief is a good metric for anomaly detection since it is assigned when the relevant evidence is taken into account. For example, consider the example of Figure 1. Suppose we observe the probability vector {0.7, 0.1, 0.2} for the energy consumption, where 0.7, 0.1 and 0.2 are the probabilities of E_1, E_2, and E_3, respectively. Here, 0.7 is the causal reasoning of E_1 (probability inferred from the parent node, D, that E_1 occurs) and is denoted as π (E_1), i.e., there is 70% chance that E_1 occurs in the training sample available to us. Let us now assume that we obtain two probability vectors {0.5, 0.2, 0.3} and {0.65, 0.21, 0.14} for E within the same time period from two different testing samples. Then, we evaluate the differences between the training sample and the two testing samples using distance function from equation 1.

Belief combines causal reasoning and diagnostic reasoning, where diagnostic reasoning of E_I is the probability inferred from the child node, R, that E_I occurs and is denoted as $\lambda(E_I)$. Here, R is a childless node, and initially we arbitrarily set $\lambda(R_i) = 1.0$.

We can compute the diagnostic reasoning of E_I given R in the training data by applying

$$\lambda(E_1) = \sum_i \lambda(R_i) * P(E_1|R_i),$$

i.e., $\lambda(E_{1-training}) = 1.0$ where, $P(E_1|R_i)$ is the probability that E_I occurs given R_i. Then, we obtain $Bel(E_{1-training}) = 0.7$. Since we have complete datasets for E and to account for several training samples, we can use

$$\lambda(E_{i-}) = \frac{\pi(E_{i-})}{\overline{\pi}(E_{i-training})} \qquad (3)$$

E_{i-} refers to individual training or testing sample and $\overline{\pi}(E_{i-training})$ refers to the weighted mean of all causal reasoning values of $E_{i-training}$. Thus, the diagnostic reasoning of the two testing data are $\lambda(E_{1-testing\ 1}) = 0.5\ /\ 0.7$ and $\lambda(E_{1-testing\ 2}) = 0.65\ /\ 0.7,$, respectively.

So, $Bel(E_{1-testing1}) \approx 0.30$ and $Bel(E_{1-testing2}) \approx 0.53.$. This implies that the first state, E_I, of the second testing sample {0.65, 0.21, 0.14} is closer to the training sample than the first testing sample. That leads us to the fact that each state of a feature may have its own true (normal occurrence) and false (does not occur) ranges, for example for D_I,

$$\underbrace{[0, \overline{\pi}(D_1) - \varepsilon)}_{False} \quad \underbrace{[\overline{\pi}(D_1) - \varepsilon, \overline{\pi}(D_1) + \varepsilon]}_{True} \quad \underbrace{(\overline{\pi}(D_1) + \varepsilon, 1]}_{False}$$

$$(4)$$

For some ε, $0 < \varepsilon < 1$. $\overline{\pi}(D_1)$ is the weighted mean of the causal reasoning of the first state D_I of feature D when multiple training samples exist. $\overline{\pi}(D_1) - \varepsilon$ is the lower bound of the true range of D_I and $\overline{\pi}(D_1) + \varepsilon$ is the upper bound of the true range of D_I. These true and false range settings above allow us to observe which evidences we have at the beginning of the testing process (Cai, Gupta, & Paul, 2009).

When we have incomplete testing sample due to some missing information, Bayesian inference techniques need to be incorporated in BANBAD using a belief propagation algorithm (Cai, 2009 ; Cai, Gupta, & Paul, 2009). The belief propagation algorithm is used to update the belief of E given evidence from its related features. The parent D transmits the causal reasoning (π message) and its child R transmits the diagnostic reasoning (λ message) to E for computing the belief of E.

1. Belief Computing for the Training Sample

As we mentioned before, we assume that the feature E is the target feature for anomaly detection. The following three steps summarize the belief computation of the feature E:

Step 1: Compute the causal reasoning (π)

Given complete raw dataset, the causal reasoning of each state of all the features can be observed. Let us say the causal reasoning of state X_i is π_{xi}, for $1 \leq i \leq 4$, and X= D, E or R.

The individual training data represents one sample, so after constant learning with multiple samples, a range around $\overline{\pi}_{xi}$ can be defined to account for normal occurrence.

This result is associating the range $[\overline{\pi}_{xi}-, \overline{\pi}_{xi}+]$ to the normal occurrence of X_i. Let $N=$ total size of n samples. By applying the weighted rule:

$$\overline{\pi}_{xi} = \sum_{j=1}^{n} \overline{\pi}_{xij} \frac{size \ of \ sample \ j}{N} \qquad (5)$$

We adapt our predefined range accordingly (i.e., weighted mean if sample sizes are different). Hence, for each additional sample (say n^{th}) of training, the updated causal reasoning is simply

$(n^{th}$ sample size $* \pi(n^{th}) +$ size of $(n-1)$ samples $* \pi_{(n-1)}) /N$

All the conditional probability distributions (CPDs) are computed as well, for example, the updated $P(E|D)$ is:

$$\frac{n^{th} sample \ size}{N} P(E|D)(n^{th}) + \frac{size \ of (n-1) samples}{N} P(E|D)_{(n-1)} \qquad (6)$$

And used in the testing process. Note that CPDs are fairly stable since we exclude totally random behavior.

Step 2: Compute the diagnostic reasoning (λ)

We can compute the diagnostic range of each feature by using one-to-one mapping from π to λ as $\lambda_{xi} = \dfrac{\pi_{xi}}{\overline{\pi}_{x_i}}$ for each individual sample, where $\overline{\pi}_{x_i}$ is the weighted mean of all π values of x_i.

- Belief computation:

Given both causal reasoning (π) and diagnostic reasoning (λ) from step 1 and 2, we can compute belief of the target feature E and/or all features by applying Bayes' rule as mentioned in equation 2.

2. Belief Computing for the Testing Sample

We use steps similar to the training sample. If we have complete testing sample, the belief computation is straightforward. Otherwise, when we have incomplete testing sample, Bayesian inference is used in a belief propagation algorithm to update the range of the causal and diagnostic reasoning of the target feature in a number of iterations. Each iteration propagates the belief to partially fill the gap created from the missing data. The following algorithm describes the testing process of BANBAD for a chain (say $D \rightarrow E \rightarrow R$) in a belief network when incomplete sample exists (Cai, 2009).

An anomaly is detected using the combined target feature rather than considering each individual state independently. Suppose the target feature has m states. Using the training data, we compute the belief probabilities of these m states. In order to bound the false alarm rate to 5%, the lower bound of each interval is set to the $(5/m)^{th}$ percentile and the upper bound is $(100-5/m)^{th}$ percentile. Then, for a testing sample, if the computed probabilities of all the states fall into their own normal (belief) range, we conclude that there is no evidence of anomaly; otherwise, an anomaly is detected.

EXPERIMENTS AND RESULTS

The key aspect of any anomaly detection technique is the nature of the input data. Dataset input is generally a collection of data instances (also referred as object, record, point, vector, pattern, event, case, sample, observation, or entity). Each data instance can be described using a set of attributes (also referred to as variable, characteristic, feature, field, or dimension). The attributes can be of different types such as binary, categorical, or continuous (Chandola, Banerjee, & Kumar, 2009). We conducted a detailed study of false alarm rate (FAR) and detection rate (DR) for BANBAD on different datasets. FAR represents the number of times an anomaly alert is issued but anomaly does not exist (Barnes, Schultz, Gruntfest, Hayden, &

Algorithm: Anomaly detection for incomplete sample

```
1: iteration = 1;
2: anomaly = false;
```
3: $Compute\ the\ ranges \left[\pi_{di}^-\ ,\ \pi_{di}^+\right], \left[\pi_{ei}^-\ ,\ \pi_{ei}^+\right],\ and \left[\lambda_{ri}^-\ ,\ \lambda_{ri}^+\right];$
```
4: while (iteration < max Iterations && anomaly == false){
5: Bayesian inference with π message passing from D to target feature E;
```
6: $if\, (\exists i \left[\pi_{ei}^-\ ,\ \pi_{ei}^+\right]_{line5} \cap (\left[\pi_{ei}^-\ ,\ \pi_{ei}^+\right]_{line3}\ or \left[\pi_{ei}^-\ ,\ \pi_{ei}^+\right]_{line21}) == \phi)\ \{$
```
7: anomaly = true;
8: break; }
9: else {
```
10: $Update\ ranges\ of\ \pi(E);$
11: $Compute\ \lambda(E)\ from\ \pi(E);\ \}$
```
12: Bayesian inference with π message passing from target feature E to R;
```
13: $if\, (\left[\pi_{ri}^-\ ,\ \pi_{ri}^+\right] \cap \left[\lambda_{ri}^-\ ,\ \lambda_{ri}^+\right] \neq \phi)$
14: $Update\ ranges\ of\ \lambda(R_i);$
```
15: Bayesian inference with λ message passing from R to target feature E;
```
16: $if\, (\exists i \left[\lambda_{ei}^-\ ,\ \lambda_{ei}^+\right]_{line11} \cap \left[\lambda_{ei}^-\ ,\ \lambda_{ei}^+\right]_{line15} == \phi)\ \{$
```
17: anomaly = true;
18: break; }
19: else {
```
20: $Update\ ranges\ of\ \lambda(E);$
21: $Compute\ \pi(E)\ from\ \lambda(E);\ \}$
```
22: Bayesian inference with λ message passing from target feature E to D;
```
23: $if\, (\left[\pi_{di}^-\ ,\ \pi_{di}^+\right] \cap \left[\lambda_{di}^-\ ,\ \lambda_{di}^+\right] \neq \phi)$
24: $Update\ ranges\ of\ \lambda(D_i);$
```
25: iteration++;}
26: if (anomaly == true) generate alert;
27: else rationCompute belief of target feature E;
28: End of Algorithm
```

Benight, 2009). On the other hand, DR is usually defined as the percentage of given abnormal changes that can be detected by an algorithm (Luo & Wang, 2004). FAR and DR are used to measure the performance of BANBAD for different types of datasets.

Using Synthetic Dataset

We generated a synthetic dataset of different dimensions, in which the features follow normal distribution with linear relationship among them. The dataset consists of six features for 100 days (replicates). The dimension of each dataset is $r *$ 6 * 100. Three different values for r have been chosen, namely 1000, 2000, and 5000. Without

Table 1. Categories of 6 features for Scheme 1

$f1$	$f2$	$f3$	$f4$	$f5$	$f6$
<30	<15	<25	<55	<45	<18
>=30	>=15	[25, 35)	[55, 81)	[45, 65)	>=18
		>=35	[81, 93)	>=65	
			[93, 99)		
			[99, 115)		
			[115, 130)		
			>=130		

loss in generality, we assume that the first feature, *f1* follows normal \distribution with mean, μ=30 and variance, $\sigma^2 = \left(\dfrac{20}{3}\right)$; other features *f2* to *f6* are generated using the following scheme (we intend to have some linear relations among the features), Scheme 1:

$$f2 : \frac{1}{2} \times f1 + \delta 1$$

$$f3 : 2 \times f2 + \delta 2$$

$$f4 : 3 \times f1 + \delta 3$$

$$f5 : \frac{1}{2} \times f4 + \delta 4$$

$$f6 : \frac{1}{3} \times f5 + \delta 5$$

Where each δ*i* is independent and identically distributed (*iid*) standard normal variable (mean 0 and variance 1) (Cai, 2009).

After raw data generation, we categorize each feature using the scheme described in Table 1.

Table 1 shows that *f1, f2*, and *f6* have two states; *f3* and *f5* have three states; and *f4* has seven states. PC structure learning technique (Spirtes et al.,2000) is applied to six categorical features for the BN's DAG generation.

To evaluate FAR, three separate testing datasets D1, D2, and D3 with dimension 1000, 2000 and 5000, respectively are generated for 100 replicates. $(D_i)^j$ Denotes the

$$j^{th}(1 \leq i \leq 3, 1 \leq j \leq 100)$$

replicate of dataset D_i. We keep the same distributional scheme as in the training data described earlier. On the other hand, to evaluate DR, three different testing datasets D4, D5, and D6 each with dimension 1000, 2000, and 5000 are generated for 100 replicates. $(D_i)^j$ again denotes the $j^{th}(4 \leq i \leq 6, 1 \leq j \leq 100$ replicate of dataset D_i. Furthermore, different distribution has been used for *f1* in each dataset, to make it different from the training data. For other features, we keep the same linearly dependent structure as described in Scheme 1.

Comparing the normal profile (i.e., the training dataset) with each of the replicates $(D_i, 1 \leq i \leq 3)$ individually, when the belief of a state in a replicate falls outside the normal range, then it is a false alarmed scenario. Hence, if α replicates out

Figure 3. False alarm rate and detection rate for all features (normal distribution)

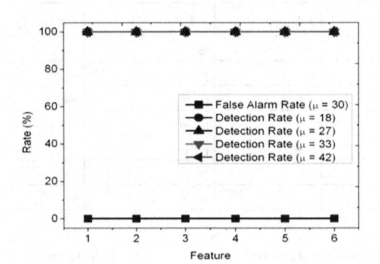

of 100 have a belief probability outside the normal range, then the false alarm rate is $\frac{\alpha}{100} = \alpha\%$; similarly, comparing the normal profile with replicates of dataset $(D_i, 4 \leq i \leq 6)$ separately, if the belief value falls inside the normal range, then miss-detection rate is $\beta\%$ leading to a detection rate of $(100 - \beta\%)$. During the testing process, at any time a single replicate is to be compared with the training sample. The FAR and DR are plotted in Figure 3 for all the six features for the training dataset of dimension 1000 and the testing dataset of dimension 5000. Similar results were obtained for other datasets.

Based on our testing environment settings mentioned before, the dataset of μ=30 is used for testing the FAR. From Figure 3, we observe the FAR of all features to be almost 0%, which indicates all belief values of all states fall into their own normal ranges. The datasets with mean μ= 18, 27, 33 and 42 are used for testing the DR. From Figure 3 we also observe that DR of all the features is almost 100%, which indicates at least 1 belief value of a state falls outside of its normal range.

Results of Figure 3 validate our BANBAD technique for anomaly detection when all the features and all their states are aggregated in our decision. Now let us assume *feature 4* to be the target feature. We explore the FAR and DR in more detail for individual states of *feature 4* that are plotted in Figures 4 and 5. The training dataset used is of 1000 dimension; similar results were obtained when normal profiles of other dimensions were used.

Threshold percentile used to bound the false alarm is below 2%. *Feature 4* has 7 states, then the lower bound of a 98% belief range is 1st percentile and the upper bound is 99th percentile. From Figure 4, we observe that the FAR of all the states of *feature 3* for dataset D1 and D2 is between 0 and 2%. For dataset D3, it is very close to 0%. Clearly, this implies that BANBAD performs as expected, i.e., one can bound the FAR to a predefined percentage and it is stable.

Figure 5 shows the detection rate for various states of *feature 4* using μ=42 and training dataset of dimension 1000 with predefined 5% bound on FAR. Recall that D4, D5, and D6 with dimension 1000, 2000, and 5000 each were designed to be anomaly. In fact, the DR is at least 95%. We can

Figure 4. False alarm rate of feature 4

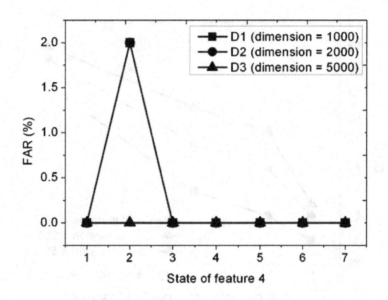

see an excellent performance for most states except state 2, which appears to show somewhat of an erratic behavior. This erratic behavior can be explained due to the way categorization of raw data in the training dataset occurs. The categorization affects the probability distribution

of a feature and DR depends on this underlying distribution. In practice, one has little control over the categorization.

However, given a categorization, one can fine-tune the threshold, by adjusting the bound on FAR. For example, if the bound for state 2 of

Figure 5. Detection rate of feature 4

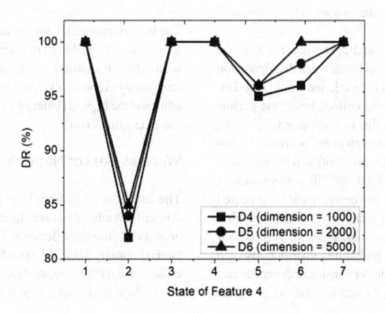

Figure 6. FAR bound versus DR for State 2 of Feature 4

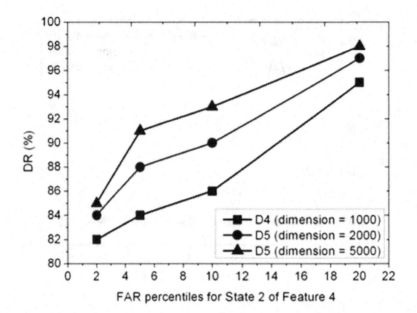

feature 4 is changed to 20% (i.e., belief values between percentiles 10 and 90 are considered normal range), the DR can be improved. Figure 6 shows the effect of varying the bound on FAR on the observed DR for state 2 of *feature 4*. Note that DR can be improved with good performance to 98%. This shows that BANBAD has the potential to detect anomaly even for a specific state of a feature, but at the expense of a potentially high FAR.

From Figures 4 and 5, we observe that the performance becomes better when the dimension is increased, from D1 to D3, and from D4 to D6; more the data we can collect, better the performance. Obviously, this is as expected.

In summary, although in the previous discussion we used normal distribution with specific μ and σ to show the FAR and DR performance of BANBAD, similar performance can be expected for other values of μ and σ or other probability distributions of raw data. We have verified our results using other probability distributions such as gamma distribution or non-linear dependencies among the features. As mentioned above, using the

threshold percentile technique applied in a manner similar to the normal distributional features, we can always bound the FAR to a predefined percentage; and by fine tuning the percentile for some specific states if necessary, we can also achieve high DR for various situations.

Using Real Dataset

The important criterion for any anomaly detection technique is to deal with real data. In this section we used raw data from two real systems, the Wireless Sensor Network (WSN) (http://db.csail.mit. edu), and the Laptop Battery Usage (LBU) (http:// traces.cs.umass.edu).

Wireless Sensor Network (WSN) Data

The dataset is taken from Intel Lab Data (http:// db.csail.mit.edu). Data is collected by 54 sensors deployed in the Intel Berkeley Research Lab between February 28th and April 5th 2004. Sensors collected data for temperature, humidity, light, and voltage once every 31 seconds.

The number of sensors used compared with the number of observed features make the collected data set a good candidate for our study. The period of 31 seconds seems to be fair enough to monitor target feature among four dependent features. For instance, the temperature and humidity can have different values during the daytime than the night. Moreover, some of these features can directly be related or affected by abnormal behavior or misuse of the network.

From this raw dataset, we select a whole month (March) of data for testing a sensor's behavior, e.g., sensor 2. Light is chosen as the target feature for anomaly detection. The data collected around midnight everyday are used for training to generate a normal profile and testing FAR, and the data collected after 8am everyday are used for testing DR.

After some raw data manipulation, we have the range [min, max) of all 4 features of WSN as shown in Table 2.

By default, we use the following categorization scheme to obtain 3 states:

Maximum value for state 1 is: $(\text{max}-\text{min}) \times 0.25 + \text{min}$.

Maximum value for state 2 is: $(\text{max}-\text{min}) \times 0.75 + \text{min}$,

Therefore, we have the categories of 4 features of WSN as shown in Table 3.

By applying BANBAD, we obtain the following results as shown in Table 4.

When we check sample #28, we find that the light value is too high which indicates that there is an anomaly around midnight; and when we check sample #19, we find that the light value is too low which indicates that there is an anomaly during the morning. Here, real dataset does demonstrate normal behavior during certain time period; therefore, we intentionally selected our target feature, light, between two different time periods, around midnight and after 8am from a sensor, for anomaly detection. From Table 4, we observe that BANBAD exhibits excellent performance, in terms of both the false alarm rate (3.45%) and the detection rate (96.55%), for the type of data

Table 2. Range of 4 Features of WSN

Temperature	Humidity	Light	Voltage
[18, 123)	[-4, 50)	[0, 626)	[2, 3)

Table 3. Categories of 4 features of WSN

Temperature	Humidity	Light	Voltage
<51.25	<9.5	<156.25	<2.25
[51.25, 96.75)	[9.5, 36.5)	[156.25, 469.5)	[2.25, 2.75)
>=96.75	>=36.5	>=469.5	>=2.75

Table 4. Anomaly sample # and performance of WSN

	FAR	DR
Anomaly sample #	28	19
	3.45%	96.55%

that is collected in the wireless sensor network, where no a prior probability distribution is forced.

Laptop Battery Usage (LBU) Data

This dataset is taken from UMASS Trace Repository (http://traces.cs.umass.edu). The data is collected for 60 laptop users to show their battery usage. From the raw dataset, six features are selected for our anomaly detection experiment. They are:

a. Battery capacity remaining (BCR)
b. Whether the machine was on AC (AC)
c. CPU utilization (CPU)
d. What was the disk space available (in MB) in the user account (DSA)
e. Whether the machine had Internet connectivity (INTERNET)
f. What was the time since there was a keyboard event (idle time) in milliseconds (IDLE).

The number of features that are observed in this dataset is more than the ones of the "Wireless Sensor Network (WSN) Data" section, and also the dependencies among these are more complex. The availability of different features can help in detecting anomalies effectively and can also provide some useful insights. For example, feature e) can help determine if the anomalous behavior occurred due to activity from outside the network or from within the network.

In this set of experiments, BANBAD is selected to test a user's normal behavior, e.g., idle time for user #59. A specific user has different idle time between different time periods. We consider feature f), *IDLE*, as our target feature. The data collected around midnight from Sunday to Thursday are used for training to generate a normal profile and testing FAR, and the data collected after 2pm from Monday to Friday are used for testing DR.

After some raw data manipulation, we have the range [*min, max*) of all 6 features of LBU as shown in Table 5.

By using the default categorization scheme defined in WSN subsection for 3 states, we have the categories of 6 features of LBU as shown in Table 6.

By applying BANBAD, we obtain the following results as shown in Table 7.

From Table 7, we observe that DR is very low. By adjusting state 2 of feature f), *IDLE*, to [1096006.6, 328801992.8), we obtain the updated results as shown in Table 8.

When we check anomaly sample #5, we find that the idle time is too small which indicates

Table 5. Range of 6 features of LBU

BCR	AC	CPU	DSA	INTERNET	IDLE
[64, 100)	[0, 1)	[0, 95.31)	[55068, 69871)	[0, 1)	[0, 438402657)

Table 6. Categories of 6 features of LBU

BCR	AC	CPU	DSA	INTERNET	IDLE
<73	<0.25	<23.83	<58768.8	<0.25	<109600664.3
[73, 91)	[0.25, 0.75)	[23.83, 71.48)	[58768.8, 66170.3)	[0.25, 0.75)	[109600664.3, 328801992.8)
>=91	>=0.75	>=71.48	>=66170.3	>=0.75	>=328801992.8

Table 7. Anomaly sample # and Performance of LBU

	FAR	DR
Anomaly sample #	N/A	1,2,4,6,7,9,10,11,12,13,16,19,20,21,22,24,25,26
	0%	30.77%

Table 8. Anomaly sample # and performance of LBU

	FAR	DR
Anomaly sample #	5	16
	3.85%	96.15%

that there is an anomaly during the midnight; and when we check anomaly sample #16, we find that the idle time is too big which indicates that there is an anomaly during the workday (Monday to Friday, after 2pm). From Table 8, we observe that we achieve good performance in terms of false alarm rate (3.85%) and detection rate (96.15%) for the target feature, idle time, after adjusting categorization, for LBU. Recall that one has little control over the categorization; therefore, it is not necessary to achieve good performance at once and a fine-tuning of threshold may be necessary. From both Table 4 and Table 8, we demonstrate that BANBAD is widely applicable under different scenarios.

CONCLUSION AND FUTURE WORK

We showed that BANBAD is an efficient anomaly detection technique based on belief networks. It has the potential to achieve high detection rates while reducing false alarm rates. BANBAD significantly contributes to the field of anomaly detection in a few ways. First, it describes a method of easily generating and maintaining a profile. It achieves both high detection rate (>= 95%) and

low false alarm rate (<= 5%) for the target feature, and false alarm rate can be bounded by certain predefined threshold. It also has the potential to function with an incomplete sample in the testing process. This function is useful in ad hoc networks, because its dynamically changing topology can result in the incomplete observations for the selected features. Moreover, BANBAD works well with real datasets of different networks, in addition to achieving good performance, it detect anomaly efficiently and accurately.

There is, obviously, potential for future work. Adaptive learning techniques could be involved to keep the normal profile updated and therefore, incorporate an ability to alarm the user when the profile is not completely reliable for further testing; Researchers can develop a distributed BANBAD algorithm (in contrast to a centralized BANBAD) to optimize resource consumption, computation and communication overhead, fault-tolerance etc. Furthermore, seasonal effect, time series techniques could be involved for users to select a time period for anomaly detection, not just from human intuition and personal experience; and feature selection techniques could be explored further under different network scenarios for anomaly detection.

ACKNOWLEDGMENT

The authors would like to thank Aakash Gupta for his contributions during the early stages of this study.

REFERENCES

Alves, R., Ferreira, P., Belo, O., & Lopes, J. (2006). Discovering telecom fraud situations through mining anomalous behavior patterns. *Proceedings of the International Conference of Knowledge Discovery and Data Mining* (SIG-KDD'06), Workshop on Data Mining for Business Applications, Philadelphia, USA.

Barnes, L. R., Schultz, D. M., Gruntfest, E. C., Hayden, M. H., & Benight, C. C. (2009). Corrigendum: False alarm rate or false alarm ratio? *Weather and Forecasting, 24*, 14-53. doi: 10.1175 / 2009WAF2222300.1

Cai, C. (2009). *Anomaly detection techniques for ad hoc network*. Unpublished doctoral dissertation, Department of Computer Science, Western Michigan University, Kalamazoo, MI, USA.

Cai, C., Ci, S., Guizani, S., & Al-Fuqaha, A. (2006). Constructing an efficient mobility profile of ad-hoc node for mobility-pattern-based anomaly detection in MANET. *Proceedings of the IEEE Global Communications Conference* (Globecom) (pp. 1-5).

Cai, C., Gupta, A., & Paul, R. (2009). BANBAD - a centralized belief-network-based anomaly detection algorithm for MANETs. *Proceedings of the IEEE Global Communications Conference* (Globecom), (pp. 1-6).

Chandola, V., Banerjee, A., & Kumar, V. (2009). Anomaly detection: A survey. *ACM Computing Surveys, 41*(3). doi:10.1145/1541880.1541882

Chatzigiannakis, V., Androulidakis, G., Pelechrinis, K., Papavassiliou, S., & Maglaris, V. (2007). Data fusion algorithms for network anomaly detection: Classification and evaluation. *Proceedings of the Third International Conference on Networking and Services* (pp. 50-57).

Chatzigiannakis, V., Papavassiliou, S., Androulidakis, G., & Maglaris, B. (2006). On the realization of a generalized data fusion and network anomaly detection framework. *Proceedings of the Fifth International Symposium on Communication Systems, Networks and Digital Signal Processing* (CSNDSP'06), Patra, Greece.

Cooper, G. F., & Herskovits, E. A. (1992). A Bayesian method for the induction of probabilistic networks from data. *Machine Learning, 9*, 309–347. doi:10.1007/BF00994110

Da Silva, A., Martins, M., Rocha, B., Loureiro, A., Ruiz, L., & Wong, H. (2005). Decentralized intrusion detection in wireless sensor networks. *Proceedings of the First ACM International Workshop on Quality of Service & Security in Wireless and Mobile Networks*.

Denning, D. E. (1987). An intrusion detection model. *IEEE Transactions on Software Engineering, SE-13*, 222–232. doi:10.1109/TSE.1987.232894

Ferreira, P., Alves, R., Belo, O., & Cortesão, L. (2006). Establishing fraud detection patterns based on signatures. *Proceedings of the Industrial Conference on Data Mining*.

Gollmann, D. (1999). *Computer security*. West Sussex, UK: John Wiley & Sons Ltd.

Heckerman, D. (1996). *A tutorial on learning with Bayesian networks. (Technical Report, MSR-TR-95-06)* (pp. 1–2). Microsoft Research.

Hilas, C. S. (2009). Designing an expert system for fraud detection in private telecommunications networks. *Expert Systems with Applications, 36*(9), 11559–11569. doi:10.1016/j.eswa.2009.03.031

Ingham, K. L., & Somayaji, A. (2007). A methodology for designing accurate anomaly detection systems. *Proceedings of the 4th international IFIP/ACM Latin American Conference on Networking*, pp. 139-143).

Intel Lab. (n.d.). *Data*. Retrieved on November 15, 2009, from http://db.csail.mit.edu/ labdata/ labdata.html

Kyriakopoulou, A. (2007). Using clustering and co-training to boost classification performance. *Proceedings of the 19th IEEE International Conference on Tools with Artificial Intelligence.*

Li, G., He, J., & Fu, Y. (2006). Key management in sensor networks. *Proceedings of the International Conference on Wireless Algorithms, Systems and Applications* (pp. 457-466).

Li, G., He, J., & Fu, Y. (2007). A group-based dynamic key management scheme in wireless sensor networks. *Proceedings of the 21st International Conference on Advanced Information Networking and Applications* (pp. 127-132).

Li, G., He, J., & Fu, Y. (2008). Group-based intrusion detection system in wireless sensor networks. *Computer Communications, 31*(18), 4324–4332. doi:10.1016/j.comcom.2008.06.020

Li, Y., & Guo, L. (2008). TCM-KNN scheme for network anomaly detection using feature-based optimizations. *Proceedings of the 2008 ACM Symposium on Applied Computing* (pp. 2103-2109).

Lidong, Z., & Zygmunt, J. H. (1999). *Securing ad hoc networks*. New York: IEEE Network, Special Issue on Network Security.

Liu, D., & Ning, P. (2003). Location-based pairwise key establishments for static sensor networks. *Proceeding of the ACM Workshop on Security in Ad Hoc and Sensor Networks* (pp. 72-82).

Liu, F., Cheng, X., & Chen, D. (2007). Insider attacker detection in wireless sensor networks. *Proceedings of the 26th IEEE International Conference on Computer Communications*, (pp. 1937–1945).

Luo, W., & Wang, X. (2004). Relations between detection rate and evolutionary generations in ENSAs: Concepts and experiments. *Neural Information Processing, 5*(3), 49.

Ma, L., Cheng, X., Liu, F., Rivera, J., & An, F. (2007). iPAK: An in-situ pairwise key bootstrapping scheme for wireless sensor networks. [TPDS]. *IEEE Transactions on Parallel and Distributed Systems, 18*(8), 1174–1184. doi:10.1109/TPDS.2007.1063

Maronna, R. A., Martin, R. D., & Yohai, V. J. (2006). *Robust statistics: Theory and methods*. West Sussex, UK: John Wiley & Sons, Ltd.

Nychis, G., Sekar, V., Andersen, D. G., Kim, H., & Zhang, H. (2008). An empirical evaluation of entropy-based traffic anomaly detection. *Proceedings of the 8th ACM SIGCOMM Conference on Internet Measurement* (pp. 151-156).

Pearl, J. (1988). *Probabilistic reasoning in intelligent systems: Network of plausible inference*. San Francisco, CA: Morgan Kaufmann Inc.

Ren, K., Lou, W., & Zhang, Y. (2006). LEDS: Providing location-aware end-to-end data security in wireless sensor networks. *Proceedings of the IEEE INFOCOM 2006*, Barcelona, Spain.

Robinson, R. W. (1977). Counting unlabeled acyclic digraphs. *Lecture Notes in Mathematics, 622*, 28–43, Berlin, Germany: Springer. doi: 10.1007/BFb0069178

Rubinstein, B. I., Nelson, B., Huang, L., Joseph, A. D., Lau, S., & Rao, S. …Tygar, J. D. (2009). Antidote: Understanding and defending against poisoning of anomaly detectors. *Proceedings of the 9th ACM SIGCOMM Conference on Internet Measurement Conference* (pp. 1-14).

Schneier, B. (2000). *Secrets & lies: Digital security in a networked world*. Canada: John Wiley & Sons Ltd.

Sekar, R., Gupta, A., Frullo, J., Shanbhag, T., Tiwari, A., Yang, H., & Zhou, S. (2002). Specification based anomaly detection: A new approach for detecting network intrusions. *Proceedings of ACM Computer and Communications Security Conference.*

Siaterlis, C., & Maglaris, B. (2005). One step ahead to multisensor data fusion for DDoS detection. *Journal of Computer Security, 13*(5), 779–806.

Spirtes, P., Glymour, C., & Scheines, R. (2000). *Causation, prediction, and search* (2nd ed.). USA: MIT Press.

Sun, B., Wu, K., Yu, F., & Leung, C. M. (2004). *Mobility-based anomaly detection in cellular mobile networks*. ACM Workshop on Wireless Security (WiSe'04), Philadelphia, PA.

Sun, B., Yu, F., Wu, K., Xiao, Y., & Leung, V. C. M. (2006). Enhancing security using mobility-based anomaly detection in cellular mobile networks. *IEEE Transactions on Vehicular Technology, 55*(3).

University of Massachusetts. (2009). *Laptop battery usage trace*. Retrieved on November 15, 2009, from http://traces.cs.umass.edu/ index.php/ Power/ Power

Witten, I. H., & Frank, E. (2005). *Data mining: Practical machine learning tools and techniques*. San Francisco, CA: Elsevier Inc.

Yang, Y., Huang, C., & Qin, Z. (2009). A network misuse detection mechanism based on traffic log. *Proceedings of the International Conference on Networks Security, Wireless Communications and Trusted Computing* (NSWCTC '09), (pp. 526–529). Wuhan, China.

Zhang, Y., & Lee, W. (2000). Intrusion detection in wireless ad hoc networks. *Proceedings of the 6th Annual Intl. Conf. on Mobile Computing and Networking* (ACM MobiCom'00), (pp. 275-283) Boston, MA.

ADDITIONAL READING

Cai, C., & Gupta, A. (2008). Mobility-pattern-based anomaly detection algorithm in mobile networks. *Proceedings of the IEEE International Conference on Communications*, (pp. 1680-1684).

Callegari, C., Giordano, S., Pagano, M., & Pepe, T. (2010). On the use of sketches and wavelet analysis for network anomaly detection. *Proceedings of the 6th International Wireless Communications and Mobile Computing Conference* (pp. 331-335), Caen, France.

Chou, T., & Chou, T. (2009). Hybrid classifier systems for intrusion detection. *Proceedings of the Seventh Annual IEEE Communications Networks and Services Research Conference* (pp. 286-291), doi: 10.1109/CNSR.2009.51.

Chou, T.-S., & Yen, K. K. (2007). Fuzzy belief k-nearest neighbors anomaly detection of user to root and remote to local attacks. *Proceedings of the 2007 IEEE Workshop on Information Assurance* (pp. 208-213).

Crosbie, M., & Spafford, G. (1995). Applying genetic programming to intrusion detection. *Working Notes for the AAAI Symposium on Genetic Programming*, (pp. 1–8), Cambridge, MA.

Das, K., Schneider, J., & Neill, D. B. (2008). Anomaly pattern detection in categorical datasets. *Proceedings of the 14th ACM International Conference of Knowledge Discovery and Data Mining* (SIGKDD'08), (pp. 169-176), ACM 978-1-60558, Las Vegas, Nevada, USA.

Dickerson, J. E., & Dickerson, J. A. (2000). Fuzzy network profiling for intrusion detection. *Proceedings of the 19th International Conference of the North American Fuzzy Information Processing Society* (NAFIPS), (pp. 301–306) Atlanta, GA.

Fantahun, Y. A., & Xuan, Z. C. (2010). Preventing black hole attack in mobile ad-hoc networks using anomaly detection. *Proceedings of the 2nd International Conference on Future Computer and Communication,* V3(pp 672-676).

Fu, H., Yuan, X., & Wang, N. (2007). Multi-agents artificial immune system (MAAIS) inspired by danger theory for anomaly detection. *Proceedings of the International Conference on Computational Intelligence and Security Workshops* (pp.570-573). doi: 10.1109/CIS.

Jamdagni, A. Tan1, Z., Nanda, P., He, X., Liu, R. P.(2010). Intrusion detection using GSAD model for HTTP traffic on web services. *Proceedings of the 6th International Wireless Communications & Mobile Computing Conference* (IWCMC), (pp.1193-1197) Caen, France.

Javitz, H. S., & Valdes, A. (1991). The SRI IDES statistical anomaly detector. *Proceedings of the 1991 IEEE Symposium on Research in Security and Privacy* (pp. 316-326).

Kirda, E., Jha, S., & Balzarotti, D. (2009). Recent advances in intrusion detection. *Proceedings of the 12th International Symposium,*(RAID 2009), Saint-Malo, France.

Kruegel, C., Mutz, D., Robertson, W., & Valeur, F. (2003). Bayesian event classification for intrusion detection. *Proceedings of the 19th Annual Computer Security Applications Conference,* Las Vegas, NV.

Mahoney, M. V., & Chan, P. K. (2002). Learning nonstationary models of normal network traffic for detecting novel attacks. *Proceedings of the International Conference on Knowledge Discovery and Data Mining* (SIGKDD), (pp. 376–385), Edmonton, Canada.

Mehdi, M. Zair, S., Anou, A. & Bensebti, M..(2007). A Bayesian networks in intrusion detection systems. *Journal of Computer Science,* 3, I(5): 259-265.

Panda1, M. & Patra, M. R.(2007). Network intrusion detection using naïve bayes. *International Journal of Computer Science and Network Security,* 7, n(12), 258-263.

Shyu, M. L., Chen, S. C., Sarinnapakorn, K., & Chang, L. (2003). A novel anomaly detection scheme based on principal component classifier. *Proceedings of the IEEE Foundations and New Directions of Data Mining Workshop,* (pp. 172–179), Melbourne, FL.

Smaha, S. E. (1988). Haystack: An intrusion detection system. *Proceedings of the Fourth IEEE Aerospace Computer Security Applications Conference,* (pp. 37–44), Orlando, FL.

Staniford, S., Hoagland, J. A., & McAlerney, J. M. (2002). Practica automated detection of stealthy portscans. *Journal of Computer Security,* 10, 105–136.

Thottan, M., & Ji, C. (1998). Proactive anomaly detection using distributed intelligent agents. *IEEE Network,* 21–27. doi:10.1109/65.730748

Tylman, W. (2008). Misuse-based intrusion detection using bayesian networks. *Proceedings of the third International Conference on Dependability of Computer Systems, IEEE,* 48, (pp., 203-210), doi:10.1109/DepCoS-RELCOMEX.

Valdes, A., & Skinner, K. (2000). *Adaptive model-based monitoring for yber ttack etection* (pp. 80–92). Toulouse, France: Recent Advances in Intrusion Detection.

Yang, L., Liu, C., Schopf, J. M., & Foster, I. (2007). Anomaly detection and diagnosis in grid environments. *Proceedings of the 2007 ACM/IEEE conference on Supercomputing* Reno, NV.

Yi, P., Jiang, Y., Zhong, Y., & Zhang, S. (2005). Distributed intrusion detection for mobile ad hoc networks. *Proceedings of the Symposium on Applications and the Internet Workshops* (SAINTW'05), (pp. 94-97).

Zhang, W., Yang, Q., & Geng, Y. (2009). A survey of anomaly detection methods in networks. *Proceedings of the International Symposium on Computer Network and Multimedia Technology (CNMT)*, (pp. 1-3), Wuhan, China.

KEY TERMS AND DEFINITIONS

Ad-Hoc Network: is an independent network that provides usually temporary peer-to-peer connectivity without relying on a complete network infrastructure, which includes one or more access points.

Anomaly Detection: refers to detecting patterns in a given data set that do not conform to an established normal behavior. The patterns detected are called anomalies and often translate to critical and actionable information in several application domains. It is sometimes also referred as *outlier detection*.

Bayesian Network: is a directed acyclic graph whose nodes represent random variables in the Bayesian sense. Edges represent conditional dependencies and unconnected nodes represent variables that are conditionally independent of each other. Each node is associated with a probability function that takes as input a particular set of values for the node's parent variables and gives the probability of the variable represented by the node.

Belief Network: is a set of nodes interconnected with arcs to form a directed acyclic graph. Each node represents a random variable, or uncertain quantity, which can take two or more possible values. The arcs signify the existence of direct influences between the linked variables, and the strength of each influence is quantified by a forward conditional probability.

Detection Rate (DR): is the number of events of interest that are recognized, as a percentage of all actual events which occur in an experimental context.

False Alarm Rate (FAR): is the number of times an event alert is issued but the event actually does not occur, expressed as a percentage. False alarm is also known as a false-positive.

Structure Learning: is the process of distinguishing structure graphs by discovering the relationships as conditional dependencies and independencies among the variables or features in data samples.

Chapter 14
Data Regulation Protocol for Source–End Mitigation of Distributed Denial of Service

Nirav Shah
Arizona State University, USA

Dijiang Huang
Arizona State University, USA

ABSTRACT

This chapter, proposes Data Regulation Protocol (DRP), a hybrid (proactive as well as reactive) solution, to achieve packet filtering at the source end to mitigate distributed denial of service (DDoS). DRP is unique in a way, as it provides target controlled traffic regulation mechanism implemented at the source gateway. A capability based model using cryptographically secure hash functions is designed for the target to identify and filter malicious traffic. DRP provides the target the choice to opt out of communication with a non-adherent source network, any time it's overloaded. The gateway of a source network is held accountable for all of the egress traffic leaving the network. This provides an incentive for a source network to ensure each of its users complies with DRP target's requirements.

INTRODUCTION

Despite a significant breadth of research, Distributed Denial of Service (DDoS) remains a huge problem even today. Highly sophisticated and automated tools such as TFN-2000, WinTrinoo, Mstream, Stacheldraht et. al. are freely available. These tools provide novice attackers the capabil-

ity to perform a really sophisticated attack. There are two basic ways of carrying out a DDoS. A semantic attack involves a master node, which exploits system vulnerabilities in the operating system and the drivers, to recruit a large set of nodes (agent machines) over a wide periphery. Most of these machines have no knowledge of their role in the attack. The attacker then carries out a well co-ordinated assault in which each of

DOI: 10.4018/978-1-60960-777-7.ch014

the agent machines simultaneously overwhelm the victim's (usually a server) resources. Another method involves source address spoofing wherein the attack is carried out by a single malicious node. It prepares a list of IP addresses belonging to nodes which may or may not exist and uses these as the source address for flooding the victim's network. A more sophisticated attack will be to use a mixed strategy where in the master node configures each agent machine with a list of IP addresses to spoof the outgoing packets. This provides the actual attacker (master node) another layer of protection and hence making it really difficult to pin-point the real attacker.

Defense against such sophistication cannot solely depend on effective filtering around the target to ensure reliable operation of the services. Besides being a bottleneck scenario such a solution cannot identify malicious traffic only on the basis of known traffic patterns. Source address spoofing along with the use of innovative traffic patterns makes target filtering completely ineffective. IP traceback methods (Stone, 2000; Duanfeng, 2004) can be used to trace the actual IP address of the actual source of the received traffic without relying on the address mentioned in the header. Besides other issues, IP traceback is a reactive solution that requires identification of an attack to employ corrective measures. This is difficult as even simple attacks such as TCP syn flooding can easily be hidden from the victim (Savage, 2001).

Egress (filtering outgoing traffic at the source gateway) filtering based solutions have been suggested for more than a decade. Active filtering at the source can effectively mitigate a score of DDoS attacks. But due to a variety of reasons, egress solutions have found no practical implementation in real world routers. The main reason is being the source network has no incentive to invest in monitoring outgoing traffic. Also even though source filtering can be effective but the target still does not decide who it communicates with. In the absence of universal implementation target will still needs a mechanism to protect itself against malicious traffic.

Capability based marking schemes using core routers have been suggested to help filters at the receiver identify malicious traffic (Anderson, 2004; Yang, 2005; Yaar, 2004). Core routers operate on the Internet backbone and are used to mark transient traffic using a value called *capability*. The traffic reaching the target filters will be marked with a set of such capabilities, each uniquely belongs to the core router in the path. The knowledge that the source traffic was first marked by this core router can definitely provide a direction for investigation. But since each of these routers directly serves a number of ISPs it cannot pin point exactly the actual source or even the ISP to which a marked traffic belongs. Another problem is that the core routers have a huge amount of collated traffic passing through. Therefore, even a simple marking scheme can lead to severe performance degradations. As such again the Autonomous system governing these routers has no incentive to implement such a solution.

Mirkovic (2002) showed it is relatively much more efficient for a source based system to monitor local malicious traffic. But passive monitoring of traffic at the source, using a predefined statistical model cannot encompass the dynamic nature of these attacks. The target still needs to decide on an acceptable level of load that it can handle. *Capabilities*, if resistant to spoofing can be used by the target to regulate incoming traffic. Therefore, there must be an efficient marking algorithm at the source which undeniably indentifies source traffic. In addition any implementation at the source end will require additional investment by the source network. Thus an incentive for the source network must be clearly established. This can be done by assigning accountability to the source network for all the outgoing traffic.

DRP proposes the use of a cryptographically secure hash function (Bellare, 2006) to develop a proactive capability model. Also these capabilities are unspoofable and efficient, in the sense that the overhead involved in marking individual packets is minimal. DRP uses a hybrid solution based on the co-operation between the gateway and the destination to mitigate malicious traffic. DRP does not assume internet wide acceptance instantly. It provides reactive measures for partial implementation to be just as effective. The incentive for source networks to adopt DRP is that, under heavy load, the filters around the target may filter out any packets not using capabilities. The filtering by the destination is fair because this is the only means by which it can identify legitimate traffic, in face of an attack.

The important characteristic illustrating the objective of DRP can be summarized as follows:

- A hybrid (proactive as well as reactive) mechanism that mandates filtering of packets at the source.
- An efficient, non-spoofable capability model which helps the destination control incoming traffic.

BACKGROUND

DDoS prevention efforts based on the location of the defense mechanism can be broadly classified into three categories. One of the most common methods is to have a set of routers surrounding the victim perform extensive filtering of incoming traffic (Keromytis, 2002; Householder, 2001; Stone, 200) Target filtering methods use a secure overlay network (Keromytis, 2002) established between the filtering routers and the victim to carry the filtered legitimate traffic. The advantage of using such a scheme is that victim has full control over these filters and as a result on the incoming traffic. But if the source address is spoofed these filters cannot sufficiently identify the actual source of these packets. As a result it is very difficult to differentiate legitimate traffic from malicious at this point. There are no currently available methods to perform IP traceback using just the destination based filters. The second type of solution uses IP traceback and requires a minimum number of core routers to participate in the

defense (Bellovin, 2000; Savage, 2001; Snoeren, 2002; Korkmaz, 2007). On detection the receiver initiates the process of tracing back the packet to the source which may require co-operation with a number of intermediate nodes which may or may not be the core routers. The effectiveness of this solution depends upon the detection time coupled with the accuracy and time to trace the source.

The third type uses Network egress/ingress filters (Ferguson, 2000; Killalea 2000) for proactive filtering of spoofed packets at the gateway of an area network. A need for Internet wide implementation at the gateway of each stub is the main reason why egress filtering has not been used. DRP develops its own version of network egress filtering which does not assume internet wide implementation. Park (2001) came up with a power law based proactive solution for filtering of malicious packet at the network gateway without the internet wide implementation requirement. The contribution is towards achieving maximum possible filtering by optimizing the selection of border gateways without assuming complete co-operation. The shift towards filtering at the border gateway cannot ensure 100% filtering as is the case in egress filtering hence establishing the need for hybrid (proactive and reactive) mechanisms.

D-ward (Mirkovic, 2002) successfully elaborates the motivation behind monitoring traffic at the source gateway, but there are some design issues. D-ward is reactive and hence depends heavily on the traffic analysis model. The model assumes that if the destination sends out acknowledgements (ack) back more often than not, it has successfully balanced the load issues. It ignores the possibility of spoofed acknowledgement sent from agent machines outside its control. Hence statistical analysis at the source cannot effectively judge the impact of congestion at the target. Further the use of multiple gateways makes the traffic analysis much more difficult. The security analysis section shows that DRP is not affected by such an attack.

Yang (2005) proposed TVA, a capability based model which enable routers to mark packets en route to the destination. If the destination identifies it as legitimate, it returns the accumulated marks to the client as a capability. The routers are also engaged in filtering traffic with invalid capabilities. A main drawback of this architecture is that capabilities are route-dependent and thus become invalid during route changes or when multipath routing is used. Further, this architecture inflicts collateral damage on legitimate traffic during ticket request floods. TVA tickets are valid for limited number of packets.

Argyraki (2005) propose AITF which uses route recording available in the IP headers as the capability to traceback the path of the attack. AITF, has no clear definition how the path is verified and when the reaction mechanism is to be triggered. Furthermore, AITF is reactive; where in the reaction time of AITF depends on how quickly it is able to establish a filter at one of the core router along the attacker's path. This can vary exponentially with the cooperating and filtering capabilities of these routers.

Yaar (2004) proposed SIFF, a system very similar to TVA, with respect to how capabilities are generated and used. SIFF capabilities are valid for a limited time; hence suffer from a overhead of renegotiating the capabilities once they expire. SIFF also assumes static network deployment, and

problems such as router failures can cause a lot of false positives. A major issue with most of the capability based solutions is that the core routers processing huge amount of traffic can provide only marginal filtering capability especially as the governing AS has no incentive to perform the additional task. There is also an absence of accountability of the traffic due to spoofing.

There has been a huge body of research on DDoS over the years. This paper has emphasized only a few of the important ones which draw parallel to the proposed solution. In summary, all of the above mentioned techniques concentrate on individual aspects of the required properties to mitigate DDoS.

DRP DESIGN DETAILS

DRP uses a variant of semi-transparent gateway firewall first introduced for prevention of TCP syn flooding by Schuba (1997). The functioning of a semi-transparent gateway can be summarized in Figure 1. The gateway sends out the ack instantly there will be no half open tcp connections at the destination. The semi-transparent gateway system illustrates the advantage of a proactive role played by the source gateway.

Figure 1. Sequence diagram for semi-transparent gateway

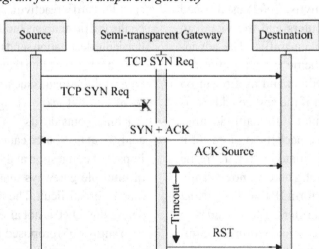

Figure 2. DRP overview

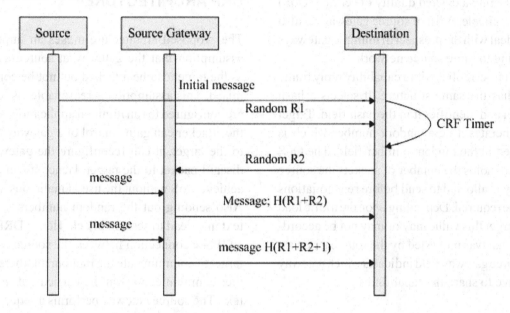

Although the above architecture is specific to TCP, the implementation of DRP allows it to be protocol independent. Figure 2 gives a conceptual overview of the DRP architecture. For a target with which capabilities are not set both the gateway and target exchange a set of random numbers. The sum of the random numbers is computed and incrementally used as an input to the hash function. The output is used as a capability for marking all packets leaving the network and with the destination address of the corresponding target.

Practical implementation of DRP does not exchange just the random numbers, but require negotiation on a number of parameters. To achieve this DRP introduces a capability request frame embedded in a UDP packet as shown in Figure 3. The first two fields indicate the addresses of the source gateway and the target. The capability request frame is used to negotiate a set of capabilities with the entire source network and not an individual client. The distribution of these capabilities among its client is left to the ISP, based on its own pricing scheme.

The first field of the capability request frame (CRF) consists of names of any 4 cryptographically secure hash implementations available with the source gateway. This field is used to negotiate a mutually available hash function. The source gateway also calculates a 128 bit random number which is appended as shown in the figure. A field

Figure 3. Capability request frame

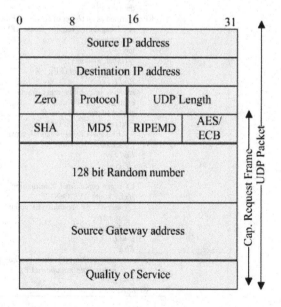

for requesting a desired quality of service (QoS) is also available. A list of source gateways is also sent to deal with the prospect of multiple gateways belonging to same source network.

The target replies with a capability reply frame which has the same structure. It selects a hash function and identifies it in the hash field. Target also generates a new random number which is appended in the random number field. The QoS field here holds the number of packets the source gateway is allowed to send before renegotiations might be required. Depending upon the traffic load at the target this value may or may not be according to what was requested by the source gateway. The source gateway field indicates which gateway may have to share the capabilities.

DRP ARCHITECTURE

The proposed architecture makes an important assumption that the gateway at source as well as the target can be attacked but not be compromised. This assumption is reasonable, as routers are configured to run minimal application. Also if the attacker can gain control of a gateway router to the target, it can reconfigure the gateway to discard packet to the target. Hence it can easily achieve DoS without the use of malicious traffic. Also sending out the random numbers in clear text may lead to session hijack. Hence DRP uses an IPSec connection between the source and the target to communicate the random numbers. Further communication can be carried out in plain text. The source gateway performs a sequence of steps, which are illustrated in Figure 4. A set of

Figure 4. Source gateway algorithm

```
                        Monitor(input: Outgoing packet P)
//for packets P leaving the network
      If (P.source != list.source)
// source of packet does not belong to this network
// if target known and source is part of the attack list.
            drop(P);
            return 0;
      End If
// secure() function check if it has already been granted a set of secure capability from
destination
// No capabilities for this particular target present.
      If (!secure (P.dest))
            send (P)                           // Send a request frame with the message with respect to
      the target
// RF is defined as an object of class capability_req_frame
            send (capability_request_frame RF);
            start_timer ();                    //To avoid reply from multiple gateway send it to them
      too.
            If (timer_expires ())
                  Retransmit (RF);
            End If
            receive (capability_reply_frame EF); // EF is defined as an object of class
            capability_rep_frame
            sum = EF.rand + RF.rand;           //pre compute capabilities
            For(i=0; i<EF.QoS; i++)
                  EF.capability[i]= EF.hash(sum);
                  EF.count =0; sum++;
            End For
      End If
      Else
            EF = get_capability ( P.destination);
            If (EF.count < EF.QoS)
                  mark(P, EF.capability[EF.count]);
                  send(p);
                  EF.count++;
            End If
            Else
                  drop(P); //drop packets exceeding QoS
                  renegotiate_capability(EF);
            End Else
      End Else
```

capabilities are pre-computed which are sequential used to mark all outgoing packet corresponding to that particular destination.

For each outgoing packet the gateway must check if the source is a client of the particular ISP. This can be performed efficiently using the gateway mask, assuming classless internet domain routing (CIDR) is used. Even in networks that use dynamic allocations (DHCP), the allocated IP addresses can still be within a particular range. Hence it should not be difficult to identify out of range IP addresses. If the packet is not from any of its clients then the gateway assumes source address spoofing and drops the packets. These packets can also be effectively filtered out at the filters surrounding the target since they will not carry any capabilities. But intermediate networks can save a lot of its own resources by filtering this unwanted traffic right as close to the source as possible.

If the packet belongs to one its clients, the *secure*() function checks if it has already negotiated a set of capability with the target. If so it attaches the next sequential capability and forwards the packet. The target also pre computes the entire list of capabilities for efficiency. An important consideration here is that the packets may not arrive sequentially at the target. Since capabilities need to be checked for each packet a careless implementation can considerably drop the system performance. The target need not search the entire list to verify a specific value. It can check values within a range of the value last received. This may not be a problem in TCP but this is an important issue for UDP traffic.

Even if the target is unknown i.e., a set of capabilities has not been assigned yet the first packet is sent without modification. The gateway then generates a CRF and sends it to a target over an IPSec connection. The use of IPSec adds an extra level security, though protocol works irrespectively due to the obscure nature of the Internet. IPSec cannot be used for the entire communication as it will make the communication slower and the

gateway will require a large number of resources to scale to so many IPSec connections.

The target is also required to perform a series of steps but these are not as extensive. On receiving a new packet without capabilities the target starts a timer. If a CRF message is received before the timer expires the target allocates memory to the gateway, generates a CRF reply message. The target needs to decide the QoS parameter in terms of the number of packets the gateway is allowed to send. The QoS parameter should be carefully set taking the current load at the target into account. For a highly trusted source the target may consider the QoS requested by the gateway. The target sends out the capability reply frame. Based on the values of the random numbers it can also compute the capabilities. These values can, therefore, be used to verify the legitimacy of an incoming packet. Thus capabilities essentially give the target a method to distinguish legitimate traffic from illegitimate. As only a fixed number of such capabilities are assigned and each can be used for a single packet only they are bound to be used up at some point. Once the limit for capabilities is reached the source gateway must repeat the process in Figure 4. Though a unilateral action from the target such as re-issuing, a new capability reply frame can just as easily avoid the renegotiation overhead that the source must go through.

If the CRF has not been received from the source gateway, a decision is required to be made by the target. The target may or may not choose to communicate with the source. Under heavy load the destination will most definitely discard all packets which do not having the assigned capabilities. Target may also add a persistent source to it blacklist. The filters around the target will be used to filter out packets with address in the blacklist. If a gateway along the path is identified to have a secure connection to the target, a request may be sent to block a particular source address. Hence DRP uses reactive measures to take care of attack from non-compliant source networks. This shows that DRP does not require all the source networks to implement DRP and is equally effective for partial implementations. Also it shows that a hybrid solution used by DRP is much more efficient compared to only proactive or reactive solutions.

Each gateway is allocated a fixed number of capabilities which are shared by all the nodes belonging to the particular network. Therefore the gateway will have to proactively ensure that each source uses only the allocated number of capabilities. Hence it is also accountable towards the normal behavior of its nodes. The network can easily design a priority based scheme for sharing of these capabilities among its users. This provides an additional incentive to the source network to pursue DRP as a viable option. This is in contrast to solutions like network egress filtering wherein the gateway has no incentive to perform the filtering task.

SECURITY ANALYSIS

The security analysis involves the evaluation of the robustness of DRP under various attack scenarios. The objective is to theoretically test the quality of a valid communication in presence of multiple attackers. The attack model makes no assumption on the capacity of the attacker. It assumes the attacker can spoof any number of packets. It also can recruit any number of agent machines to carry out a DDoS attack. It is observed that DRP is still resilient to mitigate all of the attacks.

Source Address Spoofing

If a cryptographically secure hash function is used, it is guaranteed that no outside attacker can spoof the capabilities of a compliant network. An attacker belonging to a compliant network can spoof a wide variety of IP addresses but the gateway will drop all packets outside the valid range. The attacker can also spoof IP addresses

belong to other nodes of the same network. But each network is allocated only a specific number of capabilities based on the current traffic load at the destination. Therefore only a pre allocated number of packets will be allowed to reach the target and it cannot affect the normal function of the target. As a result from the target's point of view this does not qualify as an attack. Also since the source network is controlling only a specific set of user such an attack should easily be detected by the gateway.

Distributed Attack on Target

DRP obliterates any possibility of a distributed attack from the agent machines present anywhere in the internet. Since a set of non spoofable capabilities are used, only nodes belonging compliant networks can obtains these capabilities. Also the number of these capabilities is restricted to a manageable level by the target. Under heavy load, filters surrounding the target will filter all the traffic which does not carry the required capability. As a result even if the agent machines belong to a non-compliant network DDoS cannot be achieved.

Multiple Source Gateways

A lot of the medium and high business networks have started using more than one gateway for traffic regulation. DRP unlike D-ward which is also a source end solution can easily be adapted to include this feature. Capability request frame already has a field to identify each of the source gateways to the target. A simple solution would be to divide the capabilities equally among the gateways. A virtual shared memory among gateways is already used to transfer BGP information such that each gateway has the same view of the internet. This virtual memory can be used to store capabilities so that each gateway has access to all the shared capabilities. Further research is required to design a multi-gateway fair capability allocation system for each network.

Spoofed Acknowledgements

D-ward has vulnerabilities in it statistical model for TCP traffic. It assumes that as long as it receives a sufficient number of acknowledgements from the target, the target has not been attacked. The assumption is not valid as any agent machine outside the given network can be configured to send back spoofed ack. Hence the attack easily hides the congestion issues at the target. DRP does not have to rely on acknowledge from the target to access the load pattern. This also suggests that DRP performs equally well for both UDP and TCP based traffic.

IMPLEMENTATION

A small test bed consisting of 4 nodes was created in planet-lab (Planetlab, 2010). The experiment involved creating a slice for the project which was implemented at each of the involved nodes. The processing capability of each of the planet-lab nodes can be obtained from www.planet-lab. org. The source network was implemented at the Princeton University site. Multiple threads were spawned at node 1 to simulate the behavior of agent machines in a distributed attack. The experiment involved two target nodes implemented at Arizona

State University site. The implementation was carried out in C using a GCC 4.24.2 compiler. Planet-lab was used as it provides a real testing framework for testing protocols under actual internet traffic which a simulator cannot provide.

The goal of the experiment was to compare the valid data throughput in three scenarios. 1) Under normal operation (—— line). 2) under the DDoS attack using DRP (— — line). 3) Under DDoS attack without DRP (-- line). This was done to evaluate the effectiveness of DRP under attack. The metric is data throughput. It can be observed that for a normal throughput range of 80-130Mb/s (no attack), the performance of DRP in presence of an attack is much closer to the normal behavior. The absence of DRP causes significant loss in throughput. For a higher bandwidth throughput (130-above) though since the gateway bottleneck is reached the performance of DRP suffers but it is still much better than non-DRP scenario. The attack has been simulated through a multi-threaded application on one of the nodes which spawns new threads every 5 seconds. Each of the thread acts as a new source using an incremental port number value. The restriction of a single physical source node was due to the policies of planet-lab which prohibits multi-source DoS attacks by attaching of a large numbers of nodes to a single slice. This performance is really close to normal

Figure 5. DRP performance evaluation

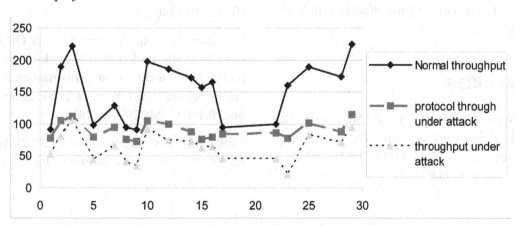

curve which represent non malicious traffic. The overhead at the source gateway to negotiate capabilities accounts for the difference. The above implementation is a simple proof of concept to confirm the conceptual claims made in this chapter.

CONCLUSION

Distributed denial of service attacks have been studied for a long time. A lot of these solutions are not practically implementable due to a variety of factors. The most important problem is that an internet wide acceptance instantly cannot be assumed. Conceptually it can be shown that the performance of DRP is not compromised even if partially implemented. Also the use of the hybrid solution by DRP allows it to mitigate the possibility of any form of attacks. DRP also establishes an incentive for the source gateway to participate in the solution by providing the destination the choice to opt out of a communication. The gateway is hence accountable to proactively regulate the traffic reaching the destination. The filtering of packets at the source end ensures that the boundaries of the attack are restricted to within the source network. It also ensures that the traffic is regulated to a specific quality of service which is defined by the target based on its current load. Hence DRP establishes an effective communication between the gateway and the target. DRP is also resistant to any sort of spoofing by the attacker to hide its own identity.

REFERENCES

Anderson, T., Roscoe, T., & Wetherall, D. (2004). Preventing Internet DoS with capabilities. *ACM SIGCOMM, 34*(1), 39–44. doi:10.1145/972374.972382

Argyraki, K., & Cheriton, D. R. (2005). *Active Internet traffic filter*. Usenix Annual Technical Conference, (pp. 135 –148).

Bellare, M. (2006). New proofs for NMAC and HMAC: Security without collision-resistance. In *Advances in cryptology – CRYPTO'06*, (LNCS 4117, pp. 602–619). Springer.

Bellovin, S. M. (2000). *ICMP traceback messages*.

CERT Coordination Center. (1996). *TCP SYN flooding and IP spoofing attacks*. Retrieved from http://www.cert.org/advisories/CA-1996-21.html

Duanfeng, S., Qin, L., Xinhui, H., & Wei, Z. (2004). *Security mechanisms for SIP-based multimedia communication* (*Vol. 1*, pp. 575–57).

Ferguson, P., & Senie, D. (2000). *Network ingress filtering: Defeating denial of service attacks that employ IP source address spoofing*. (Internet RFC 2827).

Householder, A., Manion, A., Pesante, L., & Weaver, G. M. (2001). *Managing the threat of denial-of-service attacks*. CERT @ Coordination Center, v10.0.

Keromytis, A., Misra, V., & Rubenstein, D. (2002). *SOS: Secure overlay services* (pp. 61–72). ACM SIGCOMM.

Killalea, T. (2000). *Recommended Internet service provider security services and procedures*. (RFC 3013 2000). Retrieved from http://www.ietf.org/rfc/rfc3013.txt.

Korkmaz, T., Gong, C., Sarac, K., & Dykes, S. (2007). Single packet IP traceback in AS-level partial deployment scenario. *International Journal of Security and Networks, 2*(1/2), 95–108. doi:10.1504/IJSN.2007.012828

Mirkovic, J., Prier, G., & Reiher, P. (2002). Attacking DDoS at the source. In *Proceedings of ICNP*.

Park, K., & Lee, H. (2001). On the effectiveness of route-based packet filtering for distributed DoS attack prevention in power-law Internets. In *Proceedings of ACM SIGCOMM.*

Planetlab. (2010). Retrieved from http://www.planet-lab.org/

Savage, S., Wetherall, D., Karlin, A. R., & Anderson, T. (2001). Network support for IP traceback. *IEEE/ACM Transactions on Networking, 9*(3), 226–237. doi:10.1109/90.929847

Schuba, C., Krsul, I., Kuhn, M., & Spafford, E. (1997). *Analysis of a denial of service attack on TCP.* IEEE Symposium on Security and Privacy.

Snoeren, A., Partridge, C., Sanchez, L., Jones, C., Tchakountio, F., & Schwartz, B. (2002). Single packet IP traceback. *IEEE/ACM Transactions on Networking, 10*(6), 721–734. doi:10.1109/TNET.2002.804827

Stone, R. (2000). CenterTrack: An IP overlay network for tracking DoS floods. In *Proceedings of the USENIX Security Symposium.*

Yaar, A., Perrig, A., & Song, D. (2004). *SIFF: A stateless Internet flow filter to mitigate DDoS flooding attacks.* In IEEE Symposium on Security and Privacy.

Yang, X., Wetherall, D., & Anderson, T. (2005). A DoS limiting network architecture. *ACM SIGCOMM, 35*(4), 241–252. doi:10.1145/1090191.1080120

Chapter 15
Instant Messaging Security

Zhijun Liu
The Ohio State University, USA

Guoqiang Shu
The Ohio State University, USA

David Lee
The Ohio State University, USA

ABSTRACT

Instant Messaging (IM), a popular communication system, is inevitably exposed to security attacks. With its commercial and government applications, its secure and reliable service becomes indispensable.

In this chapter, we introduce IM system and its security with an emphasis on the most damaging threats of IM spam and worm. Due to the real-time nature of IM services, the existing Internet and e-mail spam and worm defense techniques are not directly applicable to IM systems; new and effective methods are urgently needed for coping with IM network security problems.

After a review of the existing IM spam and worm defense approaches, we present our solutions for filtering IM spam and controlling IM worm, including smart worm. Based on the characteristics of IM system architecture and services, as well as worm spread patterns, we propose an analytical model with statistical branching process and provide a detailed analysis. As a result, we design new and effective defense procedures, including topology based tracing and quarantine and topology-aware throttling.

"Introduction" contains an introduction to IM system and its security threats along with a survey of various defense methods. "Instant Messaging Spam: SPIM" is on IM spam filtering. "Instant Messaging Worm" presents a mathematical model and analysis of IM worm along with its defense mechanisms.

DOI: 10.4018/978-1-60960-777-7.ch015

INTRODUCTION

Instant Messaging (IM) provides real-time communication services with presence information of the communicating parties – typically end-users (Debbabi & Rahman, 2004; Day et al., 2000; Day et al., 2002). Started as a simple chatting service, IM has become a popular communication mechanism that allows users to chat anywhere from desktop to cell phone and handheld device.

Due to its simplicity and convenience users are enjoying online chatting with different kinds of IM tools (Grinter & Palen, 2002). Popular IM systems, such as Internet Relay Chat (IRC), America Online Instant Messenger (AIM), Microsoft MSN Messenger (MSN), ICQ, Yahoo! Instant Messenger (YIM), Jabber, Google Talk, Skype and Tencent QQ, have changed the way we communicate with friends, acquaintances and business associates. Social networking providers, such as Facebook, Twitter and Myspace, often offer IM capabilities. IM service has been extended for commercial applications. Companies and government organizations are interested in using IM for communications at work places (Herbsleb et al. 2002; Scupelli et al., 2005). Many companies begin to deploy internal enterprise IM systems as a supplement of traditional E-mail communication systems to take advantage of the convenience and efficiency of IM services. Prevalent business IM systems include Google Talk, Enterprise AIM, Microsoft Office Communications Server, Yahoo Business Messenger, Jabber XCP, MSN, IBM Lotus Sametime (Jabber), and Cisco Webex Connect (Jabber).

However, as IM is gaining popularity, it is also exposed to severe security threats, which have become a major hurdle for IM to be offered as a secure and reliable communication service. Most prevalent IM systems are designed with scalability rather than security, and, consequently, IM systems are vulnerable to various security attacks, among which IM spam and IM worm are particularly damaging. With its real-time communications IM differs from other Internet applications and most existing security mechanisms, which are designed for other Internet applications such as E-mail, are inadequate for IM. For the public awareness of the threats to IM systems and for secure IM services, it is indispensible to explore existing IM attacks and investigate the corresponding defense techniques.

This chapter introduces the architectures and protocols of IM systems, describes existing threats to IM services, and discusses various defense methods with an emphasis on IM spam and worm. In more details, we discuss new defense procedures against IM spam and worm that we have developed in recent years. For effective filtering of IM spam, we design a new defense method that takes advantage of the unique infrastructure of IM systems and facilitates IM spam filtering at client and server side, as well at various IM gateways. A number of mature spam filtering techniques are also discussed and modified for IM applications. We introduce a statistical branching process for the modeling and analysis of IM worm. Stochastic variables are used for modeling user behaviors, social network knowledge, worm propagation patterns and its impact on defense mechanisms. Based on the analysis, two IM worm defense schemes are developed: 1) Topology based detection and quarantine mechanism that aims at multicast-based worms and that provides real-time worm detection and isolation by constructing the potential infection chaining graph from abnormal network events; and 2) Topology-aware throttling procedure that achieves better usability and worm containment by utilizing the clustering information of IM network topology and that effectively detects and filters worms, including smart worms.

Instant Messaging Systems

As a popular Internet communications service, IM systems enable individuals to exchange text messages and track presence information with each other in real-time. To use IM service, a user usually needs to register and login an IM server

Figure 1. IM Architecture

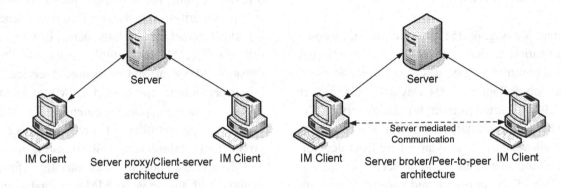

first. A user is provided with a list of buddies' IDs along with their presence information. There are two communication modes: (1) One-to-one chat when a user sends or receives messages from another user; and (2) Group chat when more than two users are engaged in exchanging messages.

There is a host of IM protocols, and most public IM services use proprietary protocols, including MSN, YIM and AIM. There have been several attempts to create a unified standard IM (Wikipedia, 2009), such as IETF's SIP (Session Initiation Protocol) and SIMPLE (SIP for Instant Messaging and Presence Leveraging Extensions), APEX (Application Exchange), Prim (Presence and Instant Messaging Protocol), the open XML-based XMPP (Extensible Messaging and Presence Protocol), and IMPS (Instant Messaging and Presence Service), yet without much success. Currently, the two most popular candidate standards for IM services are: XMPP that is a typical client-server protocol and defines an open XML-based protocol for extensible IMP application (P.Saint-Andre, 2004); and SIMPLE that is an instant messaging (IM) and presence protocol suite based on SIP, which is developed by the SIMPLE Working Group of IETF and it is viewed as the protocol of choice for 3G IP-based communication networks (B. Campbell et al., 2002).

There are two types of IM architectures with XMPP and SIMPLE as the representatives, re-

spectively. See Figure 1. The first one is based on server proxy architecture where all messages need to go through the server that forwards the messages to the intended receiver. The other is based on server broker architecture where connection requests are initiated at server but messages can be exchanged directly between peers.

1. Server Proxy/Client-Server Architecture

All the IM communications are going through the server, as in Figure 1. For instance, when Alice and Bob want to exchange messages both of them must log into a same IM server but they cannot send messages directly to each other. Instead, the messages are first sent to the server. The server then forwards the message to the intended recipient. In this case, the server acts as a proxy between the users. The advantage of this architecture is that both clients initiate connections through the server but none of them is required to accept incoming connections that a corporate firewall may block. In general, this is the default method that all major IM networks use today. Most popular IM service systems, such as IRC, MSN, YIM, AIM, Google Talk and Jabber, adopt this architecture. Note that P2P communications may also occur, for instance, audio/video chat and file transfer, in MSN and YIM.

2. Server Broke/Peer-to-Peer Architecture

In this architecture connections can be established directly between peers; the only packets that are sent to the server are those requesting the server to initiate communication between two clients. The server essentially facilitates the connection between the two clients. The server provides the clients with the connection information; the clients then directly connect to each other. For instance, if Alice wants to send a message to Bob, she sends a request to the server to initiate a session. The server then notifies Bob that Alice wishes to chat with him. If Bob agrees, he replies to the server with his contact information (typically an IP address and port number) and this information is forwarded to Alice. Then, Alice can directly connect to Bob and exchange messages without server involvement. SIMPLE is a typical P2P based server broker architecture. Another one is Skype that provides IM service based on an overlay P2P network.

Security Threats to Instant Messaging Systems

According to a report of Radicati Group (Kerner, 2005), the total number of active IM accounts reached 867 million by the end of 2005 and would increase to 1.2 billion by the end of 2009. As a matter of fact, today there are more than 2.8 billion registered IM accounts of different IM systems and more than 1.6 billion active IM users, according to an incomplete and conservative estimation of IM user database report (Wikipedia, 2009). It appears that the number of users of IM services is still growing. IM systems are no different than other Internet communication media and are inevitably targeted by various security attacks (Mannan & Oorschot, 2004; Hindocha & Chien, 2003). Most IM systems initially were designed with the prime purpose of the basic functionality and little or no effort was made to take the security

issues into serious consideration. Consequently, they are vulnerable to various security attacks and become a target for hackers (Leavitt, 2005). In this section we describe a few most significant security threats to IM systems.

Eavesdropping and Data Access

Given that most popular IM systems, such as MSN, YIM, Jabber and AIM, do not encrypt network traffic, an attacker can easily eavesdrop conversations between two IM users using a packet sniffer or similar technique. Skype and Google Talk utilize proprietary protocols to encrypt conversations. Some enterprise IM systems, such as Yahoo Business Messenger, protect IM messages with SSL encryption, however, the encrypted messages are still exposed at IM servers/gateways. Trillian, a third party IM client, applies Diffie-Hellman key exchange and Blowfish cipher and provides text message encryption for AIM accounts when Trillian clients are used in both peers (Trillian, 2000). A Diffie-Hellman protocol that is modified for IM is proposed to prevent malicious system administrator from intercepting message and applying data mining techniques to obtain private information of end users (Kikuchi et al., 2004). A different Instant Messaging Key Exchange protocol for secure IM communications is proposed and it enables private and secure communications between two users who share no authentication tokens, mediated by a server on the Internet (Mannan & Oorschot, 2006). A security design for IM based on the RSA algorithm and Triple DES algorithms is presented in (Guo et al., 2009). To enhance authentication, integrity and confidentiality of text messages exchanged, AIM clients can use a personal digital certificate. However, both users have to buy Class 2 digital certificates from VeriSign. Note that the solution with digital certificate is a safe and efficient mechanism, however, it is very expensive for IM users and it poses on end users extra burden of certificate distribution, verification, expiry, renewal and revocation. In order to provide extra protection for existing public IM systems, a number of third party IM plug-ins are developed, such as Pidgin (formerly named Gaim) that enables the use of digital certificate (Pidgin-Encryption, 2003) and MSNShell, as an MSN add-on, which provides extended services, including encryption for MSN Messenger (MSNShell). A secure IM system framework is proposed and an IM secure add-in for the MSN client is designed and implemented in (Zhang et al., 2008). A popular cryptographic protocol, Off-the-Record Messaging (OTR), which uses a combination of the AES symmetric-key algorithm, the Diffie-Hellman key exchange, and the SHA-1 hash function, is used in several 3rd party IM clients, including Adium, Climm, Pidgin and Trillian, to provide strong encryption for IM conversations (OTR, 2004). Note that both IM users need to run the same or compatible plug-ins to have protection of their conversations.

Most IM clients allow message archive at local storage. Attacks may break into the archived conversation logs. Surprisingly, at most IM client sides, user conversations are saved in a plaintext format in a predictable system location. Revelation of these messages can potentially be a very significant loss of message confidentiality for both corporate and home users. Conversation logs are usually enabled by almost all IM clients by default, and, consequently, anyone who can access the stored data is able to access to all the conversations. Apparently, for IM service security, offline message archiving should be encrypted.

Man-in-the-Middle Attack and Impersonation

Many IM systems are vulnerable to account hijacking or spoofing. An attacker can hijack a user's IM account and impersonate that user to contact other users. The typical man-in-the-middle attack can succeed in IM systems if traffic is not encrypted. Furthermore, almost all popular IM systems support storing user password in client computer to facilitate user login procedure whereas password protection is rather limited in most IM systems. Often user passwords are stored in a data file that is in plain text or has weak encryption protection. Even with encryption, if the file system is not well designed, the files can be cracked easily. In order to cope with account hijacking and man in the middle attack in IM networks, (Orebaugh, 2006) proposes an IM anomaly-based intrusion detection system based on IM authorship identification and validation. By applying character frequency analysis of IM messages for authorship identification and validation, users of an IM conversation can be identified.

Scripting Instant Messaging

Several Instant Message platforms offer scripting capabilities, which enable users to write code in Visual Basic, JavaScript, or other program languages to control various features at the client side. Most of scripting languages are lack of strong security binding with IM client. As a result, once the script is loaded, it is out of control of IM application's authentication session. This functionality, while convenient, has the vulnerability that enables the spread of computer worms, virus and blended threats. With these scripts attackers can control an IM client for malicious activities, such as stealing data files at client machine, contacting other users, sending files without owner's knowledge and involvement, changing program and system settings, and executing malicious programs.

Malicious Hyperlink and File Transfer

Malicious Hyperlink is a known threat for Internet security for a long time. An attack can construct a message containing a hyperlink to a counterfeit site, which asks victims to login with their user ID and password, therefore, the attacker can obtain user's login information. Malicious hyperlinks may lead to remote code execution as well. If a user clicks on a malicious link, the attacker can take complete control of the victim system. Since links to web pages containing malicious contents can be sent as normal IM messages, receiving and clicking a URL link within IM message may put the client machine in a dangerous status. A most effective way to protect oneself from malicious hyperlinks is not to click on them. Some IM clients, such as ICQ, have an option to accept or reject messages with hyperlinks and certain IM systems do not allow clicking any URL by IM clients.

Most IM systems provide file transfer and file sharing services. However, it also opens a door for malicious content. A good practice is not to accept any un-recognized file transfer request and always apply Anti-virus tools to scan the received files before accessing them.

Insecure Default Settings in IM Client

Improper default privacy and security settings at IM client side may introduce another security hole to attackers. For instance, certain IM clients support unattended automatic file download for user's convenience, and, consequently, attackers may use it to upload malicious payloads like worm/virus/Trajan to user's machine without owner's knowledge. Some IM clients come with default privacy and security settings, which allow anyone from the same IM service to add any users to the Buddy List, view online presence status, and send text messages and files. As a result, IM users may be attacked by unsolicited messages or file transfer requests sent via IM system. For most non-business IM systems, usually IM users do not communicate with strangers, therefore, the best practice is only allowing connections from a user's contact list. The built-in contact list actually is a handy filter to stop most of the unsolicited traffic. However, for IM business applications and customer services, setting up a Buddy List and having strict authorization for IM communication may have negative impact on business opportunities.

IM Application Integration

Popular IM systems, such as MSN, YIM and Google Talks, can be integrated with other applications, including E-mail and web services where each IM account is also an E-mail and web service account. IM features, such as contact list and presence information, are also shared with other applications. That introduces additional security vulnerability for IM services, host applications and devices; a security flaw in an IM system can affect other applications and devices and vice versa.

IM Server Vulnerabilities

So far we have discussed various types of vulnerabilities of IM clients. IM server vulnerability is also a major security concern. As the center of IM system, IM server stores all the information of registered users, sensitive data, conversation logs and personal private information. If an attacker accesses to a server, he obtains all the information, eavesdrops conversations, impersonates any user, and launches denial-of-service and other malicious attacks with little effort. Note that even when IM traffic is encrypted, an attacker with full control of an IM server can still gain access to all the encrypted traffic. Similar to other Internet-enabled software systems, IM server also has vulnerabilities that can be exploited by attackers, such as buffer overflow.

Design decisions of IM services may impact on the security of IM systems. Several popular IM servers do not limit the message sending rate, which allows users send a large amount of IM messages in a short period of time. This vulnerability is particularly severe for IM systems, which have published APIs of their services. For instance, anyone can access the open source code of Jabber server. With the source code and APIs available, attackers can easily design malicious code to launch attacks on server, such as automating a large number of account registrations, sending spam messages through IM server, and launching DoS attacks.

Denial-of-Service (DoS) Attacks on IM Client and Server

IM platforms are susceptible to Denial-of-Service (DoS) attacks in a variety of ways. Attackers may send a large volume of messages to IM servers/gateways to prevent legitimate messages from passing through IM systems. Alternatively, attackers can send a large amount of messages to a user or a group of users. By flooding the target users with unwanted messages, attackers can crash the IM client/server/gateway or make them unstable or hang. Note that when users choose to receive messages from everyone on his Buddy List, flooding with unwanted messages is particular easy. Even most IM clients support user blocking of attacker's account ID, an attacker can still crash IM systems by praying on only a few naive users who do not use the blocking capability and thus open doors for DoS message flood. Or an attacker can compromise many IM accounts and simultaneously use them to launch DoS attacks.

Firewall Tunneling

Several IM systems allow IM clients tunnel through firewalls and that introduces additional security risks. Most IM services come through well-publicized ports: 5190 for AIM, 1863 for MSN, 5050 for YIM, and 5222 for XMPP. IM clients can also exploit any open port in the firewall, including those used by other applications, such as Port 80 for Web and HTTP traffic. Consequently it becomes hard for companies to enforce security policy through firewall over the usage of public IM services. Since IM traffic can thus circumvent firewall inspection, it creates a security hole in firewalls. The situation is getting even worse when IM clients have peer-to-peer connections or establish connections through randomly negotiated ports.

Botnet

Botnet refers to a collection of compromised computers (called zombie computers) running malicious software that is usually installed via unattended or indirectly authorized downloads, through exploitation of web browser vulnerabilities, worms, Trojan horses, or backdoors under a common command-and-control infrastructure by Botmaster.

A typical botnet threat plaguing Internet is IRC bots. IRC is used by its members to manage access lists, run quizzes, or serve files over IRC channel, which is known as a "chat room". Attackers can also use IRC bots to install Trojans, which contain virus and worm, into unsuspecting Internet users' computers. Once Trojans are implanted in user's machine, they start an IRC client, connect to an IRC server, and make a bot join an IRC channel, thus allowing hackers to control the client machine via IRC channel. Such bots are particularly dangerous; they can install keystroke logging software for compromising user passwords, credit card numbers and other confidential information. Furthermore, by issuing a command to that channel, an attacker can use bots to launch Dos/DDos attacks against Internet servers. Since the attackers are hidden deeply within IRC network, such attacks are usually hard to trace.

Instant Messaging Spam

Spam of unsolicited junk messages is known to be one of the major security problems of E-mail services. Similarly, IM spam is unsolicited commercial messages sent via IM messengers. Since IM systems provide a very similar messaging service, inevitably IM services are targeted by spammers.

IM spam poses a particularly serious security threat to those IM users who choose to receive messages from everyone for business/corporate IM applications. Since IM messages are delivered in real-time and often users accept messages by default, IM spam may cause more severe damages than usual E-mail spam. Although IM spam and E-mail spam have a lot in common, due to the real-time delivery nature of IM services, most of the existing anti-spam techniques for E-mail services are not applicable for IM spam filtering.

Instant Messaging Worm

IM worm refers to malicious software program that propagates over IM networks by exploiting features and vulnerabilities of IM clients and protocols. Since IM system provides a robust communication channel between end users, virtually all IM software products maintain a list of buddies with whom the user can interact. Similar to E-mail address book, IM Buddy List can be leveraged as a hit list to spread malicious payloads, such as virus and worm, rapidly through IM networks. Different than E-mail and Internet worm, IM worm propagates through a highly available social network in nearly real-time, often resulting in much faster infection. It is worth noting that more sophisticated IM worms are launched from IM botnet that is controlled by botmaster. By infecting a large number of hosts in a short period of time, IM worms and virus can damage user data, steal sensitive information, remotely control users' computers, launch massive DoS attacks, and relay a large amount of IM spams.

Threats to Mobile IM

With the increasing use of mobile services, the interoperability between SMS (Short Messaging Service) and IM networks enables mobile users to seamlessly communicate over the Internet. Inevitably, mobile handheld devices are targeted by various viruses and malwares. By exploiting vulnerabilities of SMS/MMS (Multimedia Messaging Service) and short-range radio interfaces such as Bluetooth, mobile worm/virus is able to infect nearby devices and spread itself to other devices in the mobile network (Bose & Shin,

2006). Meanwhile, mobile handheld devices and mobile IM networks become another effective communication media for SMS/IM spams with severe economical damages due to the charge for the unexpected use of messaging services. Moreover, infected mobile IM devices integrated with advanced GPS (Global Positioning System) technology may reveal people's locations through presence information service of IM. These security issues become particularly severe when mobile IM is applied to healthcare services (Bønes et al., 2006).

Instant Messaging Spam and Worm

As discussed in the previous section, a variety of security attacks are haunting current IM services. Among them IM spam and worm are responsible for most of the severe blended attacks and they are the major threats to IM services.

IM spam, often called spim, began to hit IM services in a large scale since 2002. Between 2002 and 2003, the volume of spim was doubled with more than 500 million spim messages, and more than 8% of corporate IM messages are spim (Claburn, 2004). With the development of mobile and social network services, spammers are targeting at mobile text-messaging, web-based instant messaging, blogs and social network communities (Espiner, 2006). By 2008, an IM user gets on an average 25 spim messages per day. Since the IM messages are delivered in real-time and often users accept messages by default, IM spim is hard to filter and may cause more severe damages than E-mail spam. Similar to E-mail spam, IM spim mainly consists of commercial advertisements. According to a Radicati report, 70% of spim messages contain links to pornographic websites, around 12% convey "get rich" schemes, product sales account for 9%, and loans or finance messages consist of 5%. Although IM spim and E-mail spam have a lot in common in terms of content, they are spread quite differently, and the existing anti-spam techniques are not directly applicable to IM spim filtering.

IM worm began to hit IM services since 2001. As indicated in a report from IMlogic Threat Center, IM and P2P exploits exploded in 2005, and grew 50% each month since (Keizer, 2005), including "SoFunny@AIM", "Hello/FunnyFiles/ Choke/Annoying@MSN", in 2001, "Aphex/ Aplore@AIM" in 2002, "Bropia/Kelvir@MSN", "Velkbot@AIM/MSN/YAHOO" in 2005, "Braban@MSN", "Yhoo32.explr@YAHOO" in 2006, "Sendphotp.a@MSN", "Win32.Agent.g@MSN", "W32/Skipi.A/Pykse@SKYPE" in 2007, "Win32/ Pakabot.A/Polyglot/Pushbot.BE@MSN", "W32. Svich@YAHOO" in 2008, "W32.Yalove, F@ YAHOO", Win.32.AutoIt.g@MSN/ICQ and "Viddyho@GoogleTalk in 2009. As a result almost all popular IM systems are attacked by different kinds of worms. Along with Internet and E-mail worms, IM worm becomes another major carrier for distributing malicious payloads, such as virus, Trojan and spam. Although IM worm is quite similar to E-mail and Internet worm in terms of self-replication and propagation, IM real-time delivery and user instant response allow IM worm to propagate rapidly and make it difficult to control. For instance, a simulation performed by Symantec (Hindocha & Chien, 2003) shows that 500,000 machines can be infected with an IM worm in approximately 30 seconds. Conventional approaches for dealing with Internet and E-mail worm are not directly applicable to IM worm since they fail to capture IM worm real-time propagation characteristics.

In the following sections, we investigate in more detail IM spim and worm. We present their analysis, detection and defense mechanisms.

INSTANT MESSAGING SPAM: SPIM

After a review of E-mail and IM spam and their differences, we discuss IM spam detection and filtering. We explore the characteristics of IM spam

and present a new architecture and methods for its detection and filtering, which can be implemented and deployed at IM server, gateway or client side with the flexibility of a global system-wide and a personalized spam defense.

IM spam is often called spim and we will use this term in the description.

E-Mail Spam and IM Spim

E-mail spam and IM spim have similarities and differences. We first briefly describe their differences and then survey the prevalent spam detection and filtering techniques before presenting our approach for spim filtering.

Spam vs Spim

Although spam and spim have a lot in common, there are significant differences between them:

- IM message is relatively short and E-mail can be long with large attachments. Therefore, IM traffic is not as significant as E-mail.
- IM client usually maintains connection to IM server and the message delivery is real-time whereas e-mail does not have such requirement. Therefore, offline e-mail spam defense techniques are not applicable to spim. The challenge of defending against spim is how to effectively detect and filter spim while guaranteeing real-time communication.
- Storage consumption by spim on IM server is not of much concern as that for E-mail servers due to the small IM message size and that IM messages are usually without attachments.
- Most of E-mail spams are from SMTP open relay where spammers can take advantage of mis-configured SMTP server or compromised computer for sending a large amount of junk E-mails. In general this is

not a concern for IM. However, sophisticated spimmers can compromise IM account with malwares that harvests victim's Buddy List for spim delivery.

Given the differences between spam and spim, the existing Internet and E-mail spam defense techniques are not directly applicable to or effective for IM spim. Indeed, we may revise some of them for applying to spim detection. More importantly, we want to design new and more targeted and effective spim filters, based on the characteristics of IM systems.

Spam Detection and Filtering Techniques

We first briefly review the existing spam detection and filtering techniques, which contain a broad range of solutions:

- **Black List/White List:** A general list-based spam blocking technique eliminates spam E-mails from the Black List (known spammer addresses or malicious mail server IP addresses) and only allows E-mails from the White List.
- **Content-based filtering:**
  - **Keyword based filtering:** spots any E-mail that contains certain keywords that are commonly used in spam.
  - **Signature based filtering:** identifies spam by comparing incoming E-mail with known spam. Either fingerprint (Zhou et al., 2003) or digest (Damiani et al., 2004) can be used as the signature of spam for a comparison.
  - **Rule based Filtering:** analyzes E-mail and assigns a score to each keyword, and the total score determines whether an E-mail is a spam.
  - **Statistical filtering, also called Bayesian filtering (Sahami, 1998):** assigns frequency-based probability

distribution to words as spam indicators and aggregates single word probabilities for spam detection.
- **Response & Challenge based filtering:** It imposes constraints on sender. Whenever an E-mail is sent from an unknown person, it challenges the sender by a small image, a piece of audio or a question before the E-mail delivery.
- **Collaborative spam filtering:** Collects spam information based on user feedback.
- **Distributed P2P based approaches** (Zhou et al., 2003; Damiani et al., 2004; Metzger et al., 2003): Peer-to-peer architecture is used to collaboratively share spam information for curtailing its propagation.

Each method has its pros and cons and none of them can solve the spam problem completely. Furthermore, most of them are off-line processes, that is, they rely on the capability of examining E-mails first for making a decision and it is infeasible for IM spim analysis due to its real-time nature. We discuss it next.

IM Spim Detection and Filtering Techniques

IM spim began to haunt IM networks from the beginning of 2004, yet little effort has been made to defend against it. Prevalent spim filtering techniques include:

- Blocking incoming messages from unknown senders, based on a White List.
- Individual user blocks spimmer, based on a Black List.
- Trust/Reputation based spam detection and charging based techniques, which are specifically designed to detect SIP spams. (Rebahi et al., 2006)
- Trust/Reputation based Anti-spim: a Black List based anti-spim mechanism (Bi et al., 2008).

- Limit automatic user registration by including a registration process and an image verification test that eliminates automated registration by spimmers.
- Collaborative spim filtering by service provider and users.
- Sharing data for Anti-spim at the content and network level (Trivedi et al., 2007)
- A stateful firewall is introduced to defend against Dos and flooding attacks in SIP network (Lahmadi & Festor, 2009).

Most pubic IM services, such as MSN or YIM, only allow delivering messages to users from their Buddy List. This White List is helpful but is not an ultimate solution, since it significantly constraints IM services and is not suitable for certain business users, such as customer service representatives, who have to deal with new customers who are not on White List. Furthermore, similar to E-mail spam, this blocking method is often ineffective and can only mitigate the spim problem to some extent. More effective and specialized spim detection and filtering methods are urgently needed.

Detection and Defense Against IM Spim

In this section we present out spim detection and filtering approach. To have our discussion more focused we consider XMPP IM and study an open IM architecture where IM user allows messages from unknown users. We discuss the spim detection and defense procedures. We examine in more detail the problems of unsolicited junk IM messages – advertisement in general and DoS attacks.

An Architecture

E-mail server is on the client/user side and relays messages asynchronously. IM client side system plays a role of IM client and also message relay yet in real-time. On the other hand, IM server and gateway are global components of IM systems that E-mail system does not have and they play an essential role in message exchanges. Consequently, we can take advantage of the unique IM system architecture and deploy spim detector and filter at IM server and gateway side; it provides an effective way to guard IM system against spim and DoS attacks. Note that due to the requirement of real-time delivery of IM messages, most of the E-mail server based spam defense techniques are inappropriate for spim. However, some of them can still be revised for IM spim and installed at IM client side; it may filter certain spim in a similar way as for E-mail spam.

Based on an analysis of the characteristics of spim, we propose a hierarchical spim detection and filtering approach. For a schematic diagram, see Figure 2. It includes our new techniques: (1) Detect and filter spim based on IM message sending rate; and (2) Detection and filtering conducted at IM server and gateway. These methods are different from the existing E-mail spam detection methods and are applicable and particularly effective for IM spim. We also integrate appropriate known spam filtering techniques in the architecture with needed revision for spim, including White/Black List, challenge-response based filtering, content-based technique, and collaborative feedback-based filtering.

Server and Gateway Side Sending Rate Control

Spim attacks are usually in a form of flooding IM users with a large amount of unwanted messages, which put a heavy burden on the receiving users, IM server and gateway. Since the messages are going through the server and gateway, such attack messages can be detected and filtered at the server/gateway side. Specifically, server/gateway monitor its own traffic load and each IM user's traffic to detect and restrict abnormal users whose sending rate is greater than a certain threshold; messages from the abnormal users can be discarded effectively by the server or gateway.

Figure 2. Spim detection and filtering architecture

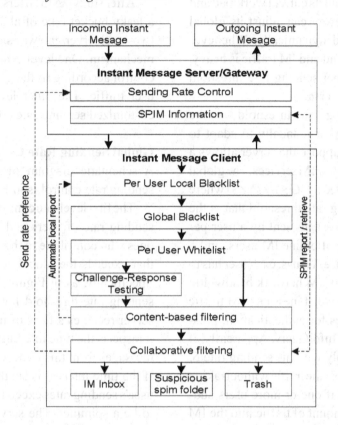

This mechanism can reduce the unexpected traffic burst in the IM network, curtail malicious users, and effectively defend IM system against spim and DoS attacks. Obviously, this effective global defense mechanism only applies to IM system with its unique system architecture; it is not applicable to E-mail system.

This sending rate control is particularly useful when a burst of messages is sent at an abnormal rate in real-time. For instance, popular IM systems, such as Jabber, MSN, YIM and AIM, support devices other than PC, such as PDAs and mobile phones, which have very limited bandwidth. Unexpected excessive IM messages can easily exhaust and disable services of such mobile devices. IM server and gateway control can effectively prevent such chaotic situation.

In addition, the capability of sending rate control by the server/gateway also provides user with personalized rate control; a user can customize a comfortable receiving/sending rate threshold collaboratively for members on his Buddy List so that he will not be overwhelmed by unexpected flood of messages.

At the server/gateway side, user traffic is monitored, measured and controlled by two thresholds: global threshold and receiver customized threshold. Server/gateway monitor the rate C of messages from a user and compares it with the global sending rate threshold G and receiver's personalized sending rate threshold P. If the sender's sending rate $C > min \{G, P\}$, his messages are discarded, and the server/gateway alerts the sender accordingly. Otherwise, the messages are forwarded. We explain this rate control scheme in detail next.

Dynamic Threshold of Global Sending Rate
The global sending rate control mechanism provides a dynamic protection for IM server/gateway

and users. By monitoring its current workload and traffic, IM server/gateway can adjust its global sending rate threshold dynamically. Whenever the total server workload and IM traffic is heavy, it can reduce the global sending rate threshold accordingly, and vice versa.

The global sending rate threshold can be adjusted automatically or manually to adapt to current traffic load. Suppose the server allows a maximum bandwidth B for IM services. The global sending rate is controlled by: $G \leq B / (N \times S)$ where G is the global sending rate threshold that is the number of allowed messages sent by a user per second, N the number of online IM users, and S the average message size. That is, each user has to observe his fair share of IM network bandwidth. Note that in addition to chat messages IM traffic also contains messages for authentication, presence information and Info/Query. Apparently, if all the IM users comply with his sending rate S, server/gateway monitors the traffic without taking any action. However, if one or more users suddenly inject a large amount of traffic into the IM network with a rate much higher than G, it will be immediately detected by the server/gateway and the involved users will be alerted or throttled with their messages discarded.

Sever/Gateway Side Sending Rate Control

The global sending rate control only considers the sending rate from a global view of an IM system. Consideration of individual IM user's behaviors leads to customized sending rate control. A normal user's usual sending rate is no more than *3* messages per second. In order to protect server from spim, client side rate control is also enforced. For instance, YIM only allows user send up to *3* messages per second. However, such sending rate control at client side provides rather weak protection because there are many third party software clients, which allow excessive spim messages easily bypass this restriction. In general, rate control for spim filtering can only be effectively executed at server/gateway side.

After studying IM users' behaviors, we design a leaky bucket type of algorithm and propose a two-level server/gateway side sending rate control mechanism. One level is an overall sending rate control according to the global system load and user traffic. The other level is individual user customized sending rate control.

Global Sending Rate Control

A schematic diagram of the two-level global sending rate control is in Figure 3.

The first level rate control estimates the overall sending rate of users and filters out suspicious ones who contribute to the majority of the traffic that exceeds the global sending rate threshold. Specifically, as in Figure 3, $r = G$ is the global sending rate threshold for each user. When the server receives a flow of messages from a user, it inspects the time interval of receiving the last h messages from this user, regardless of receivers. If the time interval is smaller than h/r, then this user's sending rates exceeds r and he is suspected to be a spimmer. The server/gateway alerts the user and discards the subsequent messages. A challenge-response then tests the sender for server/gateway to take further actions.

The goal of this overall sending rate control is to help the server/gateway identify potential spimmers and prevent their spim or DoS attacks. Note that IM broadcast may contribute to a large volume of messages and may very likely be identified as spim attack. This problem can be solved, for instance, by policing message types; only the approved users are allowed to broadcast messages at an overall higher rate.

Customized Sending Rate Control

IM users may customize message rate due to the limited bandwidth or personal preference. For this, we propose a procedure of leaky bucket type.

The leaky-bucket mechanism is used to control the rate of traffic sent out to an output link (Ferguson & Huston, 1998) so that bursty traffic can be shaped or policed to have a steady stream

Figure 3. Sever/Gateway side global sending rate control

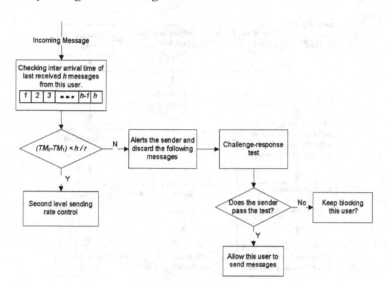

of traffic to the network at a contracted rate, as opposed to traffic with erratic bursts of low and high-volume flows.

Our revised leaky bucket approach works as follows: 1) Bucket has a specified leak rate according to the contracted sending rate; 2) Bucket has specified depth which can accommodate variations of the arriving rates and the depth of bucket imposes limit on the burst size of erratic high-volume traffic; and 3) Arriving messages to IM server/gateway are conforming if they do not overflow the bucket. The non-conforming messages are either dropped or processed differently, such as marking them for later processing or giving it a lower priority. Consequently, server/gateway can monitor traffic flows continuously to ensure that they meet the contracted sending rate. In this leaky bucket model, given bucket size $L+I$ and contracted rate $1/I$, the allowed burst size can be computed as $MBS = 1 + [\, L / (I - T)]$ where L is the burst tolerance, T is the peak cell rate of the incoming traffic, and I is the sustainable cell rate.

By applying this leaky bucket mechanism, each user is able to set up a bucket with a customized sending rate threshold for everyone on his buddy list. The contracted sending rate is customized by each user's agreement with his buddies. Only messages sent at a rate below the threshold are delivered. For all of the unknown users who are not on the buddy list, a single bucket is created and a large sending rate threshold can be chosen to constrain the potential malicious traffics. If arriving messages from a particular sender to this user overflows the bucket, the server will discard the subsequent messages and alter the sender. By enforcing appropriate sending rate threshold for all of his buddies, a user can limit the maximum allowable bursty traffic from senders and control his overall receiving rate under certain level. It prevents users, especially those who have limited bandwidth, from being overwhelmed by unexpected burst of high-volume traffic. Note that some malicious spimmers might ignore server's alert and keep sending spim messages at a high rate. In order to save the server's bandwidth and protect the server from such DoS attack, conservative protection mechanisms can be applied. For instance, the server can disable service of malicious users who send at a rate exceeding certain threshold or who have been alerted more than certain times, and only allow them login again after a while.

Figure 4. Client side spim detection and filtering

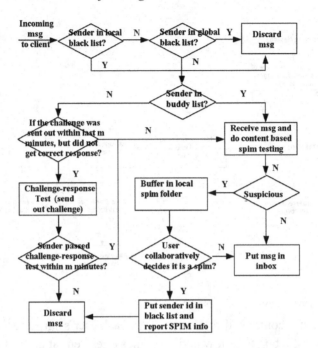

Smart spimmer may still broadcast a few messages to thousands of users to bypass our rate control. Since each receiver has a separate rate control for a sender, the spimmer's traffic might unfortunately sustain under this control mechanism. In this case, our global sending rate control mechanism that has been discussed earlier can help to stop the spimmer. Other approaches, such as limiting the number of buddies to whom a user can send messages in a short period of time, can also be used to reduce such traffic burst.

Client Side Filter Integration

At IM client side we deploy a filter pipeline that processes incoming messages, as in Figure 2. We have analyzed each filter efficiency and error rate. Among all the filters, the Black List has the fastest running speed and is produced by user feedback; it has the least error rate and is most efficient. We conduct a simple simulation by creating a Black List based on the number of the occurrences of E-mail addresses in a spim corpus. When the number

of the occurrences reaches a threshold, the sender address is added to the Black List. Experiment shows that up to 64% spims are filtered out when we set the threshold to 10. The Black List is the most efficient and effective technique to catch malicious users. Content-based filtering is more time consuming due to the semantic comparison operations, hence the precedence of challenge-response filtering can greatly reduce the load of content-based filtering, since a large amount of automatically generated messages by IM robot-spimmer can be filtered out. Consequently, at IM client side we order the filters in the IM message filtering pipeline by their efficiency and accuracy – from high to low. Analysis and experiments show that this ordering has the best performance to eliminate spim. A flowchart of the client side spim detection and filtering is in Figure 4. We now elaborate in detail the filtering process.

Black List/White List Filtering
There are two types of Black Lists: global Black List and local Black List. The global Black List

comes from the server that maintains a list of malicious users who have sent or may send unsolicited junk messages or flooding messages. Users can also customize their own local block list, based on the Black List mechanism where client side can filter out all the messages sent by users who are on the Black List. This is a commonly used method against either E-mail spam or IM spim. Only the users on the White List (Buddy List) who have been authorized can have their messages received by the receiving client side.

Challenge-Response Filtering

This approach differentiates unknown users from users on the Buddy List. Messages coming from the users on the Buddy List are accepted. All the messages from unknown users have to go through the challenge-response test first. When a message comes from an unknown user a challenge is immediately sent back to the sender with a note stating that the message will be delivered to the recipient only if the sender successfully meets a challenge. If the sender cannot complete the test within a specified small time interval, all his messages will be discarded. A challenge can be an image verification test that automated system cannot pass. This technique is also often used to limit the automated E-mail/IM user registration.

Content-Based Filtering

We further exploit content-based filers such as signature based filter, Bayesian filter and full text comparison approach, and investigate the performance of these algorithms:

1. **Fingerprint Vector Based Filtering:** The fingerprint vector based approximate text comparison algorithm (Zhou et al., 2003; Manber, 1994) is a signature based filter where messages are checked as follows. For a text string, a set of fingerprints is generated. To calculate a block text fingerprint vector, the checksums of all consecutive substrings of length L are calculated. There are ($n - L$ + 1) such substrings for a given string of n characters. Calculating checksums of all such substrings is a fast operation with a cost of $O(n)$. By sorting the set of all checksums and selecting a subset of size N with the lowest values, we can use this fingerprint vector to represent the whole text string. The number of common checksums represents the similarity of two text strings. Based on this text string similarity checking technique, we first construct a database of known spim fingerprint vectors and then check each incoming suspicious message and determine whether it is similar to any one of the spim in the database for possible filtering.

2. **Word Based Longest Common Subsequence Filtering:** Full text comparison approach is not efficient for E-mail spam detection due to the message size. However, the size of IM messages is relatively small, and we may afford full text comparison. Longest Common Subsequence (LCS) algorithm can be used. Instead of matching two texts by characters, we compute an LCS of words to decide the similarity of two messages, that is, an incoming message with one in a database of known spims. LCS-based spim detection has high fault-tolerance because it is based on full text comparison.

3. **Bayesian Filtering:** Bogofilter (Bogofilter, 2002; Graham, 2002) is a fast Bayesian spam filter. It uses Gary Robinson's geometric-mean algorithm with Fisher's modification to distinguish spam from ham. Bogofilter calculates a probability that an E-mail is spam by a statistical analysis by tokenizing the input and checking each token against a word list database that keeps track of the number of occurrences of each token in spam corpus. These numbers are used as an estimate of the probability that a message is a spam.

The criteria of a sound spim filter are low false positives and false negatives; it filters out most of the spim yet without eliminating too many legitimate IM messages. Due to IM real-time nature, low computational overhead should also be considered as another important performance metric. From our evaluations, we remark on the above content-based filters (Liu et al., 2005):

1. The fingerprint vector based algorithm works well for large message/file comparison that is uncommon in IM systems though. Note that IM message is relative short and if the size of the spim message is less than L, this algorithm fails to filter it out. However, user can customize a length L of consecutive substrings to tune the granularity for a similarity match. A length L of 50 may work well for E-mail filtering (Zhou et al., 2003). Experiments show when $L=10$ it achieves low false positives and negatives for IM message filtering. Note that the goal of using content-based filter is to filter out the unsolicited commercial advertising messages whose length are usually greater than 10.

2. Word Based Longest Common Subsequence Algorithm works well when we choose 7 as a threshold for the number of common words. The time complexity of this algorithm is comparable to the fingerprint vector based filtering algorithm.

3. Bogofilter performs well with respect to false negatives, however it causes high false positives primarily due to the small size of IM messages. Since shorter message conveys less information which can be used to distinguish ham from spam, if the message is too short, the maximum number of words of interests turns out to be the number of words contained in the message. It greatly reduces the power of Bogofilter. Therefore, it may not be appropriate for spim filtering.

Collaborative Feedback Based Filtering

Similar to E-mail spam, the collaborative user feedback based filtering is an effective mechanism to collect spim information for filtering, such as Black List or known spim database. This information can be distributed by IM server throughout IM network and help IM users filter spim messages.

Based on the content-based checking, suspicious spim messages are placed in a folder where the owner can decide whether they are spim or not and take due actions - either discard them and/or report to the server. On the other hand, a client side periodically retrieves the latest spim information from server/gateway and updates its local spim database. Note that either client sides of a communication can periodically pull spim information from server/gateway, or server/gateway can push spim information to client sides. Meanwhile server/gateway may collect and exchange spim information with each other in their service domains.

It is worth noting that 86% of E-mail users simply delete E-mail spam instead of reporting it to server (Fallows, 2003). Without the cooperation of users, the collaborative filtering is ineffective. Since forcing users to change habit is not an option, one might consider a client side option that enables client side automatic spim reporting. If messages from a sender are recognized as spim more than a certain number of times, he is automatically added to the receiving user's local Black List that is also be reported to server automatically.

INSTANT MESSAGING WORM

We now discuss another severe security threat to IM systems: IM worm. We study the main differences between Internet/E-mail worm and IM worm, and review prevalent IM worm modeling and defense techniques. We propose a statistical modeling of IM worm for an accurate analysis of its behaviors and spread patters. Based on the analysis, we further discuss various IM worm

Figure 5. IM worm propagation

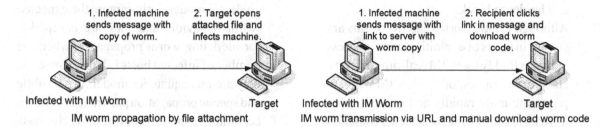

1. Infected machine sends message with copy of worm.
2. Target opens attached file and infects machine.

Infected with IM Worm — Target
IM worm propagation by file attachment

1. Infected machine sends message with link to server with worm copy
2. Recipient clicks link in message and download worm code.

Infected with IM Worm — Target
IM worm transmission via URL and manual download worm code

defense mechanisms and present two new IM worm defense procedures.

Internet/E-mail Worm and IM Worm

After a review of IM worm transport and activation, we compare it with Internet/E-mail worm along with a brief survey of the existing IM worm modeling and defense techniques.

IM Worm

IM worm propagates by malicious URLs or automatic file transfer requests with valid IM user ID, taking advantage of the target list (user Buddy List) of compromised host for connecting to online target machines.

IM worm transports itself among IM clients in two different ways, as shown in figure 5. (1) IM worm propagates via file attachment – similar to mass mailers. IM worm often sends an entire piece of worm-code along with a message that entices the recipient into opening it in a similar way as E-mail-borne mal-ware. "Bropia@MSN" is a typical example. (2) IM worm transmits via URL for manual download of worm code. This type of IM worm contains a malicious URL in a message that links to a third part server or a web server that has been created on an infected machine. "Kelvir@MSN" is an example. In both cases, once a user responds to a received worm message, that is, by opening and executing the attachment or clicking on an enclosed link, his machine will be infected and self-replicated worm

messages are immediately multicast to all or part of his online buddies.

IM worm activation can be categorized into two classes: (1) Manual Activation: It entices a user to execute a local copy of a worm code or click an enclosed link; and (2) Automatic Activation: IM worm exploits client software vulnerability and automatically opens an enclosed attachment with worm while user is viewing the message.

IM Worm vs. Internet/E-mail Worm

With the special features and transmission characteristics of IM, such as rich presence information, real-time delivery, small message size and instant user response, IM worms are quite different from Internet scanning worms and E-mail worms in terms of victim identification, infection mechanism and propagation speed:

1. Internet scanning worms usually propagate by randomly scanning IP addresses for preying target machines and they often fail due to invalid IP addresses or particular status of target systems. In contrast, IM worms do not have to scan IM networks for vulnerable targets; they propagate by sending malicious URL-embedded messages or generating automatic file transfer requests with valid IM user IDs, taking advantage of the existing target lists, IM Buddy Lists, of the compromised hosts and connecting to and infecting online target machines via

IM servers. Such attacks are more effective and harder to block.

2. Although E-mail worms and IM worms are similar in terms of exploiting users' address books or Buddy Lists, IM real-time delivery and user instant response allow IM worm to propagate more rapidly and make it more difficult to control. For instance, a simulation performed by Symantec (Hindocha & Chien, 2003) shows that 500,000 machines can be infected by an IM worm in 30 seconds.

Modeling Worm Behavior

In order to cope with IM worm attacks it is necessary to have a thorough knowledge of its behaviors and propagation patterns. An accurate model of active worms is a key for a design of effective defense mechanisms. Much work has been done on modeling worm behaviors yet none of them is specifically for IM worms:

1. Most models of worm propagation are based on the deterministic epidemic modeling of disease propagation (Zou et al., 2003; Kephart & White, 1993; Thommes & Coates, 2006). For example, (Kephart & White, 1993) presents a biological epidemiology based worm model and uses nonlinear differential equations to provide an analysis of its spread and control. A study by (Zou et al., 2003) focuses on modeling slower propagating worms such as Code Red, based on the RCS equations, incorporating the Kermack-Mckendrick model, which is an SIR model for the number of people infected with a contagious illness in a closed population over time, accounting for the removal of infectious hosts and extending it to the removal of susceptible hosts as well. Similar epidemiological model is created in (Thommes & Coates, 2006) for analyzing P2P virus. A survey of mathematical epidemic models of computer virus can be found in (Serazzi & Zanero, 2003). These epidemic models only capture the expected worm behaviors and they are acceptable for modeling worm propagation when the number of infected hosts is large. However, they are inadequate for modeling the subtle and special propagation patterns of IM worm accurately, especially during the early phase when the number of infected hosts is small.

2. Stochastic process is used for modeling worm behaviors. For instance, (Garetto et al., 2003) uses interactive Markov chains to model worm propagation in small-world topology. Apparently, it is inappropriate for modeling IM worms.

3. An interesting branching process is proposed by (Sellke et al., 2005) to model Internet worm. They provide a condition that determines whether worm will eventually die out. They also derive a probability that the total number of infected hosts will be controlled under a certain level. Their branching process based worm modeling works well for Internet/E-mail worms but often inappropriate for IM worm due to its special propagation patterns. We also use a branch process that includes timing analysis which is essential for accurately modeling IM worm and for designing effective defense methods due to its real-time nature.

IM Worm Defense Techniques

There is an enormous amount of research effort on Internet/E-mail worms, including containment-based defense (Staniford, 2003), rate-limit to slow down worm scan rate (Chen & Tang, 2004), worm quarantine (Moore et al., 2003; Zou et al., 2003), and E-mail worm modeling and defense (Zou et al., 2004). However, these worm defense techniques are not directly applicable to IM worm due to its different way of activation and propagation.

There have been research activities on IM worm defense, however, most of them are still in a preliminary stage:

1. Temporary server shutdown (Hindocha & Chien, 2003) is a solution that takes advantage of the IM centralized structure to stop IM worm-outbreak as follows. Shutdown an IM server that is under worm attack, manually analyze the worm, and build a client patch. Then enforce an update when users attempt to login the IM server again. This is not a user-friendly solution.

2. Temporarily disable online users and disconnect some critical nodes (determined by the size of contact lists). This approach may increase IM network diameter and, consequently, slow down the spread of IM worm and allow time for patching (Smith, 2005).

3. Virus throttling (Williamson & Parry, 2004) limits the rate at which a user can interact with his contacts in a way that impedes worm spread.

4. An improved virus throttling scheme (Mannan & Oorschot, 2005) limits the file transfer requests and messages with URL and challenges the sender with a file transfer request or URL message by automated public Turing tests. However, usability affected by unnecessary delay is a major concern for throttling and the solution does not take the network topology into consideration that may further facilitate the worm containment.

5. (Xie et al., 2007) proposes a framework called HoneyIM that uses decoy IM accounts in normal user Buddy Lists to detect IM worm propagation in enterprise networks. This solution highly depends on the decoy user accounts and requires involvement of IM clients.

6. (Yan et al., 2002) proposes a change-point detection technique and only focuses on worm detection based on traffic statistics.

7. An enhanced malware detection scheme based on monitoring the behavior of IM client software is proposed in (Huerta & Liu, 2008). This solution requires running a special security monitoring program in each IM client machine.

8. Content-based filtering guards against known malware in file transfers and cannot defend against malicious URL messages.

We are ready to present our algorithms for the detection and defense against IM worm, including smart worm.

Detection and Defense Against IM Worm

After presenting our statistical modeling and analysis of IM worm behaviors, we propose new and more effective defense procedures against IM worm.

Statistical Modeling and Analysis

In order to understand IM worm's behaviors and design efficient defense procedures, we propose a stochastic model for analyzing IM worm propagation, including smart worm.

Assumptions

To accurately model a broad range of IM worms we make the following assumptions, which are based on IM protocols and user behaviors:

1. IM messages can only be sent to online users;
2. Once a user responds to a worm message, that is, by opening and executing an attachment or clicking on an enclosed link, his machine is infected and self-replicated worm messages will be immediately multicast to all or part of the user's online buddies;
3. Users can be re-infected if they receive and open a same worm message again; and

4. Users can send legitimate multicast messages to their online buddies.

We model the topology of an IM network as a directed graph $G=<V, E>$ where V and E are the IM users and their connections, respectively. An edge $e=(u, v)$ in E where $u, v \in V$, denotes an outgoing connection from u to v if v is on the Buddy List of u. $N=|V|$ is the total number of users.

The spread of IM worms depends on IM users' response time λ_i, presence probability Ps_i and the probability of an IM message being opened Po_i. User response time λ_i is the time interval between the sender sending out the message and user i opening the received message. The transmission delay is ignored since it is dominated by user response time. Here λ_i may follow different distributions with small mean reflecting the real-time nature. $E[\lambda_i]$ denotes the mean user response time for user i. Presence probability Ps_i determines whether a user i is online or not ($0 \leq Ps_i \leq 1$). Opening probability Po_i is determined by user's behavior ($0 \leq Po_i \leq 1$). Furthermore, Po_i varies by the decreasing re-infection factor d_j; whenever a user receives a duplicated message, Po_i is reduced by this factor. λm_i is the inter-arrival time for user i to launch regular multicast and it may follow an exponential distribution. $E[\lambda m_i]$ denotes the mean multicast inter-arrival time for user i.

We first model the behaviors of regular worms which propagate by multicasting. A general model that includes smart worm is also provided.

Modeling IM Worm

Original branching process (Karlin & Taylor, 1975) considers a population of particles with independent random lifetimes, at the end of which each particle splits into a random number of new particles that have the same life span as the parent. Similarly, in IM worm propagation after a node receives and responds to (opens/executes) a received worm message, it is infected and multicasts the worm messages to its online neighbors. Worm propagation is only delayed by the user's

response time which plays an important role in measuring the propagation speed of IM worms. If we consider a worm multicast from an infected node as a splitting activity and take the user's response time as the lifetime, IM worm propagation process is a branching process except that the infected node remains. Therefore, IM worm propagation behavior can be modeled as a branching process with a random number of descendants. The number of descendants of an infected node is the number of its online responding buddies who choose to open the received worm messages. One difference is that in original branching process a particle splits into several particles upon its death whereas in worm propagation process infected nodes, which multicast worm messages, still stay alive in the network.

Based on this analogous branching process, we present a model for IM worm propagation. Let $N(t)$ denote the number of infected nodes at time t of a probability distribution $P_k(t) = P\{N(t)=k\}$ for $k=0,1,2....$. Let $G(s,t)$ be the probability generating function of $N(t)$, i.e., $G(s,t) = \sum_{k=0}^{\infty} P_k(t)s^k$. Assume that there is only one worm at the very beginning and we have $P_0(t) = 0$ for all $t \leq 0$, $P_1(t) = P\{N(t)=1\}=P\{T > t\} = 1- F(t)$, where T is the random variable for user response time and $F(t) = P\{T \leq t\} = \int_0^t f(\tau)d\tau$ is the cumulative distribution function of T. When a node is infected, it will multicast worm messages to a random number of buddies. A generalization of IM worm process can be modeled as follows:

$$G(s,t) = s \int_0^t h(G(s,t-\tau))f(\tau)d\tau + [1 - F(t)]s$$

where an infected host multicasts worm messages to l buddies with probability q_l, $l=0, 1, 2, ...,$ $h(s)= \sum_{l=0}^{\infty} q_l s^l$ is the corresponding generating function (Liu & Lee, 2007).

With the probability distributions for different worm spread patterns we can analyze its propagation quantitatively.

IM Worm Propagation Analysis

With the general statistical IM worm model from the previous section we analyze worm propagation speed and the impact of user response time.

1. **Worm Propagation:** Although we have the complete probability generating function for modeling IM worm propagation, it is hard to derive the probability $P_k(t)$ for arbitrary user response time distribution. Given the general probability generating function

$$G(s, t) = s \int_0^t h(G(s, t - \tau)) f(\tau) d\tau + [1 - F(t)]s,$$

we analyze the expected number of infected nodes $E[N(t)]$ that represents the worm propagation speed. In the following analysis, it is assumed that nodes can be infected repeatedly by a same worm message. Since

$$\frac{dG(s,t)}{ds}\bigg|_{s=1} = \sum_{k=1}^{\infty} k P_k(t) = m(t) = E(N(t))$$

where $m(t)$ is the expected number of infected nodes at time t, when $s=1$, $G(1, t - \tau) = \sum_{k=1}^{\infty} p_k(t - \tau) = 1$ and $h'(G(1, t - \tau)) = \sum_{l=1}^{\infty} q_l l = E[l]$ where $E[l]$ is the average number of online responding buddies. Let $d = E[l]$, we have the expected number of infected nodes at time t:

$$m(t) = \frac{dG(s,t)}{ds}\bigg|_{s=1} = 1 + d \int_0^t m(t - \tau) f(\tau) d\tau$$

In summary, the expected number of infected nodes at time $t \geq 0$ is $m(t) = 1 + d \int_0^t m(t - \tau) f(\tau) d\tau$ (1) where d is the average number of online responding

buddies and $f(t)$ is the probability distribution of user response time.

2. **User Response Time and IM Worm Propagation:** We now study the impact of user response time on IM worm propagation. We model user response time λ_i as a stochastic variable determined by user behaviors. Here λ_i may follow different distributions. We study how different distributions of user response time affect the propagation. Particularly, we are interested in analyzing worm propagation speed under the assumption of exponential distribution where users respond to received IM messages with a random time delay, that is, responding action is a Poisson process. We also compute the expected number of infected nodes $E(N(t))$ under 2nd order Erlang distribution when users periodically respond to received messages. For the following specific distributions of user response time, from (1), we have (Liu & Lee, 2007):

    a. Exponential distribution:
    $$m(t) = \frac{1}{1 - d} + \frac{e^{(d-1)\lambda t}}{1 - 1/d};$$

    b. 2nd order Erlang distribution:
    $$m(t) = \frac{1}{1 - d} + \frac{\sqrt{d} e^{(-\lambda + \lambda\sqrt{d})t}}{2\sqrt{d} - 2} + \frac{\sqrt{d} e^{(-\lambda - \lambda\sqrt{d})t}}{2\sqrt{d} + 2};$$

    c. Users periodically respond:
    $$m(t) = \frac{d^{\lambda t} - 1}{d - 1}$$

    where d is the average number of online responding buddies and λ is the average user response rate. According to the above analysis, it is clear that due to IM real-time nature and instant user response behaviors it can infect a large amount of nodes in a very short period of time.

3. **User Behaviors Follow a Poisson Process:** From the above analysis, worm propagates with the fastest speed among the three distributions, if user response time follows an exponential distribution, or, equivalently, the

time interval between user responses follows a Poisson distribution. This is a well studied topic of inter-arrival time for modeling the telephone call patterns – a popular model of human behaviors. We believe this is also true for user response that leads to the rapid worm propagation.

We now further investigate worm propagation with the assumption that user inter-response time is a Poisson process, that is, user response time follows an exponential distribution. To simplify the analysis, we assume all users have a same number of buddies de, presence probability Ps, opening probability Po, average user response delay μ_t and average multicast interval μ_T. Let $\lambda=1/\mu_t$, $\lambda_m=1/\mu_T$, $d=de\times Ps\times Po$, and $d_f=1$ where d is the average number of online responding buddies.

We have the following results on the impact of user response time on the propagation of IM worms. It is clear that user behaviors have a significant impact on the rapid worm propagation.

Proposition 1. If IM user response time interval is a Poisson process, the sequence of random variables

$$Y_n = \sum_{i=1}^{n}(T_i - \frac{1}{\lambda S_{i-1}})\ n=1, 2, \ldots$$

is a Martingale with respect to $\{(\tau_n, \zeta_n)\}$, that is,

$$E\ [Y_{n+1} \mid Y_0, Y_1, \ldots, Y_n] = Y_n$$

where T_i is the time between the $(i-1)^{th}$ and i^{th} worm multicast, S_i is the number of infected nodes in a worm population when i^{th} worm multicast occurs, and λ is the expected user response rate.

The following result shows that the number of infected nodes can be doubled in a rather short period of time and that explains why IM worms can be spread rapidly.

Proposition 2. If IM user response time interval is a Poisson process, the time to double the infected nodes is asymptotically a constant:

$$\Delta t \cong \frac{\log 2}{(d-1)\lambda}$$

where d is the average number of online responding buddies and λ is the average user response rate.

Proposition 3. If IM user response time interval is a Poisson process, worm infection events constitute a multicast tree with leveled Gamma distribution, i.e., $t_i \sim Erlang\ (i, \lambda)$, where t_i is a random variable of the time at which a user at level i is infected and launches a worm multicast.

Proposition 4. If IM user response time interval is a Poisson process, the probability that there are exactly k worm infections occurring within a time window of size W is:

$$P_k(W) = \sum_{\substack{\sum_{k+1}^k l_i=k \wedge l_0=1 \wedge \\ l_{k+1}=0 \wedge l_j \le l_{j-1} \times d}} \left(\sum_{i=1}^{k+1} C_{l_{i-1}\times d}^{l_i} \times (\frac{P_i}{P_{i-1}})^{l_i} \times (1 - \frac{P_i}{P_{i-1}})^{l_{i-1}\times d-l_i} \right)$$

that approximately follows a binomial distribution at each level where d is the average number of online responding buddies and P_i is $P(t_i \le W)$, the cumulative distribution function of Gamma distribution with degree i for a given a window of size W.

Note that in reality, for a particular worm, it will not spread forever in the network; instead, it will eventually die out either because some countermeasures are taken or because people do not open a same or similar message again. If we consider this situation in our analysis, then we have the following results. They show quantitatively how user behaviors cause IM worm being eliminated from IM networks.

Proposition 5. If a reduction factor $\theta(t)$ is taken into account, the expected number of infected nodes at time $t \ge 0$ is

$$m_\theta(t) = 1 + d \int_0^t m_\theta(t-\tau)\theta(\tau)f(\tau)d\tau \qquad (2)$$

where the reduction factor $\theta(t)$ denotes the decreasing re-infection factor, d is the average number of online responding buddies and $f(t)$ is the probability distribution function of the random variable T of user response time.

This is a classical equation, known as a renewal equation (Asmussen, 2003). According to Renewal Process Theorem, and $m_\theta(t)$ in (2) can be derived for the *proper* case ($\eta = 1$), the *defective* case ($\eta < 1$) and the *excessive* case ($\eta > 1$):

$$\lim_{t\to\infty} m_\theta(t) = \begin{cases} \dfrac{t}{d\int_0^\infty \theta(\tau)f(\tau)\tau d\tau}, & \text{if } \eta = 1 \\[3ex] \dfrac{1}{1 - d\int_0^\infty \theta(\tau)f(\tau)d\tau}, & \text{if } \eta < 1 \\[3ex] \dfrac{e^{-\beta t}}{d\int_0^\infty \theta(\tau)f(\tau)\tau e^{\beta\tau}d\tau}, & \text{if } \eta > 1 \end{cases}$$

where $\eta = d\int_0^\infty \theta(\tau)f(\tau)d\tau$ is the number of buddies infected by a single initial worm and $-\beta$ is the epidemics exponent.

The epidemics will spread or die out exponentially fast depending on whether η is larger or smaller than 1. When $\eta > 1$, $d\int_0^\infty \theta(\tau)f(\tau)e^{\beta\tau}d\tau = 1$, we have $\lim_{t\to\infty} m_\theta(t) = e^{-\beta t}$.

In summary, if IM worm sends out a worm message after Δ seconds until it finishes its infection attempts on all of its Buddies instead of a multicast, the expected number of infected nodes at time $t \geq 0$ is

$$m_\Delta(t) =$$

$$1 + d\int_0^t f(x)m_\Delta(t-x)dx - \sum_{n=2}^d \int_0^{(n-1)\Delta} f(x-(n-1)\Delta)m_\Delta(t-x)dx$$

where d is the average number of online responding buddies, $f(t)$ is the probability distribution func-

tion of the random variable T for user response time. Comparing with regular worm propagation, we have

$$m_\Delta(t) \leq m(t).$$

IM Worm Defense

IM worm modeling and analysis in the previous sections provide quantitative results on IM worm propagation patterns and speed, as well as the impact of user behaviors on the propagation. They offer guidelines for the design of the detection and defense procedures against IM worms. In order to efficiently and effectively defend against IM worm, we also need to consider its characteristics, such as its real-time nature and propagation patterns, based on social network topology.

In this section, we describe two worm defense schemes, which are specifically designed for IM worms. The first one is topology based tracing and quarantine that is capable of coping with multicast based worms. To deal with smart worms, we present the second one, that is, a topology-aware worm throttling procedure.

Topology Based Tracing and Quarantine Procedure

Since IM worms propagate more rapidly than Internet/E-mail worms (IM worms can potentially plague an entire IM network within seconds or minutes), a mechanism that can simultaneously detect and restrain it in real-time is desired. Since IM worms only propagate along the existing IM social network, the knowledge of buddies' relationships can further facilitate worm detection and defense. For instance, an observed worm multicast tree indicates the presence of IM worm. On the other hand, due to the rapid propagation speed of IM worms, it is crucial to isolate/quarantine infected machines at a very early stage of IM worm infection.

With all the above considerations we design a topology based IM worm tracing and quarantine

Figure 6. Multicast Event Tree DAG

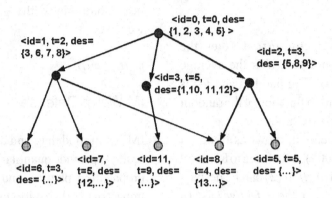

procedure that can detect worms by constructing a potential infection chaining graph from abnormal multicast events. Meanwhile we dynamically quarantine infected hosts to restrain IM worm propagation:

1. **Topology based Multicast Event Tree Tracing:** Based on an analysis of worm multicast event tree, we can use a centralized topology based multicast tracing mechanism that detects IM worms by tracing and identifying the potential worm infection chaining graph. In order to trace worm propagation, a Directed Acyclic Graph (DAG) is built. Each node in the graph represents one event triggered by a user who sends out multicast worm messages at a certain time. A multicast event is associated with its sender, a set of receivers, and a timestamp of its occurrence. An edge represents the potential infection relationship between two multicast events. An edge is added from event e_1 to event e_2 if and only if e_1 occurs earlier than e_2 and the user at e_2 belongs to the multicast destination set of event e_1. As shown in Figure 6, all nodes and edges reachable from a root node (without incoming edges) constitute a DAG. For simplicity, we still call it a multicast tree even though it is no longer a tree in general. We summarize our IM worm tracing and

quarantine procedure (see Algorithm 1). The algorithm is executed as follows:

a. *Event tree creation:* Whenever a new multicast event occurs, it is attached to all possible predecessor events in the graph. Only events within the monitoring window of length W are recorded and old events outside of the monitored window are deleted from the tree. A tree may become a forest after removing obsolete nodes along with their incidental edges.

b. *Worm diagnosis:* With the multicast event trees worms can be detected based on the depth and width of the tree. Instead of calculating the number of messages forwarded, we inspect the number of users who request multicast in the event tree within the monitoring window. If a total number of multicasts in a tree is greater than a threshold r, we conclude that a worm is detected.

c. *Worm quarantine:* If a tree that is suspicious of worm infection is identified, all users and their destinations in the event tree are blocked for a period of time and no new multicast requests are allowed. After that blocking period, the blocked users are permitted to multicast again. To further reduce the false positives,

Algorithm 1. Topology based tracing and quarantine

```
while (true)
    Receive a multicast sending request m from user i;
    e:= <id_i, tm, m.des >; //tm is timestamp, des is the recipients id set
    // Event tree creation, Treess denotes the monitoring tree set
    for (each tree_i in Trees)
        //n.tm is the timestamp of multicast event n
        for (∀ n∈tree_i: e.id_i∈n.des ∧ tm≥n.tm)
                n.children.add(e);
    if (e has not been attached to any trees)
        Trees.add(e);
    // Event tree update based on the monitoring window
    for (each tree_i in Trees)
        if (Currentime - tree_i.root.Timpstamp > W)
            tree_i.remove(tree_i.root);
            for (each subtree_j of tree_i)
                Trees.add(subtree_j);
    //Worm diagnosis and quarantine
    for (each tree_i in Trees)
            if (tree_i.size > r)
            for (all nodes in tree_i and their destination nodes)
                Block node's multicast requests for a period of length d_b;
```

users are asked for confirmation for their blocked multicasts. If users correctly confirm their multicast requests, the multicast requests are granted.

2. **Algorithm Analysis:** We now discuss the false negative and false positives of our algorithm.

   ○ **False negative.** False negative occurs when worm is present but not detected. We can derive false negative P_{fn}, which is the probability that the multicast events form a tree yet the number of nodes in the tree is less than the threshold r for identifying the presence of worm:

   $$P_{fn} = P_{k<r}(W) = \sum_{i=0}^{r-1} P_i(W)$$

   ○ **False positives.** False positive occurs when worms are reported but no worm exists. In the worst case, when no worm is present, the normal multicast events may form a multicast event tree that triggers a false alarm. The expected number of multicast event trees within a window W with r multicast nodes in the tree is:

   ○ where $M_n = \lambda_m \times W \times N \times Ps$ is the expected number of normal multicasts within W, $P'(r)$ is the probability that given a node sequence of length r, each node in the sequence can be attached to one of the previous nodes as a child in the tree, and $p=de \times Ps /N$ is the probability that one user is an online buddy of another user. Here M_n represents the storage overhead at server side. False positives also occur when normal multicast requests are incorrectly blocked since the blocking mechanism always blocks all users in the tree once a worm is detected and

$$T_{fp} = C_{M_n}^r \times P'(r) = C_{M_n}^r \times \prod_{k=1}^{r-1}\left(1 - (1-p)^k\right)$$

some normal multicasts may be incorrectly blocked. Let d_b denote the blocking delay and I_b denote the expected number of normal multicasts, which are incorrectly blocked. We have: $I_b = r \times (\text{de} \times \text{Ps}) \times (\lambda_m \times d_b)$. Note that our dynamic quarantine mechanism can only mitigate the propagation of worms but cannot stop them completely. As a result, any escaped worms may continue to propagate.

3. **An Evaluation:** To evaluate the performance of our proposed approach, we build an IM simulation framework, based on the discrete event simulation tool Peersim (Peersim), and conduct experiments on a real AIM topology (Buddyscan, 2005) with different parameters. From the experiments, clearly, without any detection mechanisms, the IM worm infected proportion expands exponentially fast and worm traffic rapidly saturates the whole network. Although the proposed approach can not completely stop worm propagation, the dynamic quarantine mechanism can slow down worm propagation speed and significantly reduce worm traffic by tracing and restricting the multicast requests. For a given threshold r, better performance can be achieved by using larger monitoring window W. To leverage the tradeoff between server overhead and worm detection performance the algorithm parameters need to be carefully configured. The algorithm analysis gives a guideline on how to choose the parameters.

Comparing to the solution presented in our previous work (Liu et al., 2006), which detects IM worm based on the first l levels in the multicast tree, this approach takes into consideration the unbalanced multicast tree that can slow down worm propagation more effectively and has negligible false negative. On the other hand, it is worth pointing out that around 7-14% normal multicasts in the simulation may be delayed by the quarantine mechanism. This can be alleviated by applying user confirmation mechanism. That is, once an IM account is suspected to be infected, further multicast requests are granted only if the user goes through a challenge-response test that automated systems cannot pass. We believe that it is essential to quarantine suspicious users provisionally and the inconvenience for the legitimate users caused by the blocking/confirmation is necessary for worm defense.

Our proposed approach is different that traditional count-based or trend-based worm detection approaches. Although these approaches are useful in worm detection and can also be utilized in IM worm defense by monitoring traffic anomaly in IM network, they are not effective in worm containment, since they are not specifically designed to deal with the real-time nature of IM worm propagation. By taking advantage of the knowledge of IM network topology and the dynamic quarantine mechanism, our approach can simultaneously detect and restrain IM worms in real-time.

Topology-Aware Worm Throttling Procedure

We now study IM worm mitigation, including smart worms. The goal is to slow down the delivery of potential worm messages without affecting regular message delivery.

Virus throttling could be a promising worm mitigation method, however, may incur notable delay for regular messages. Taking advantage of the clustering information of IM network topology, we study IM worm throttling and propose a new topology-aware throttling procedure. This method can cope with both regular multicast IM worms and also smart worms.

1. **Worm Throttling:** Virus/Worm throttling has been shown to be successful in detecting and slowing down fast scanning worms and IM worms. To limit the propagation of worms, (Williamson & Parry, 2004) introduces a general mechanism based on the observation that an IM user generally interacts with a slowly varying subset of its contacts while a worm sends messages to all online contacts. Consequently, a small working set of contacts is maintained for each user to record the recent recipients of messages sent from this user. If a new outgoing message sent to a user is not in the working set, the message is put in a delay queue. Messages in the delay queue are then sent at a slower rate. As a result, the delay for a user to respond to the worm message now becomes $\theta(t)f(t)$ where $f(t)$ is the probability density function of the user response time and $\theta(t)$ is the worm reduction factor. According to Williamson's throttling technique, a sending request for a worm message that has the destination outside the working set goes through a FIFO queue, and is processed at a rate of r messages per second. Assume that an outgoing message sending request is dropped when the queue reaches a critical length q. If the average position of the sending request in the queue is l, the average receiver's response delay probability is then determined by

$$\theta(t)f(t) = f(t \mid l) = \begin{cases} 0 & l > q \\ 0 & l \leq q \wedge l > t \times r \\ f(t - l/r) & l \leq q \wedge l \leq t \times r \end{cases}$$

where the queuing delay is taken into consideration. Since $\theta(t)f(t) < f(t)$, the worm propagation is slowed down.

2. **Topology-aware Throttling:** While the above general throttling mechanism is effective in slowing down the propagation of worm, it introduces delay for regular messages if the receiver is not in the working set. To reduce the impact of throttling on legitimate messages and achieve better usability we propose a new throttling scheme that can reduce unnecessary delays without sacrificing the goal of worm mitigation. The key is to utilize the clustering property of IM networks. There are studies on IM network topology with a conjecture that IM network is a scale-free network (Smith, 2005; Morse & Wang, 2005). IM network to a great extent reflects users' social network. A sociology research result by (Moody, 2001) shows that a topology of social network presents strong small-world characteristics and users usually constitute dense clusters with high internal connectivity and relatively low cross-cluster connectivity based on their social relationships. We believe that IM network shares the same clustering characteristics and an improved worm throttling mechanism can be derived by associating the throttle delay with "distance" between two users according to their cluster membership. In another word, we only restrain cross-cluster messages aggressively for: (1) Facilitating worm containment within cluster; and (2) Minimizing the delay of benign messages. To achieve the goal of the topology-aware worm throttling, the first step is to identify the clusters in the network.

3. **RNM and K-means Based Clustering:** A network graph $G(V, E)$ can be partitioned into K clusters, i.e.

$$V = \cup_{i=1}^{k} C_i \quad \forall i,j : i \neq j \rightarrow C_i \cap C_j = \varphi.$$

The goal of cluster identification is to minimize $Max(\rho_i)$ where $\forall i : \left| C_i \right| \geq N_0, N_0 \leq |V|/K$, and ρ_i is the ratio of total inter-cluster edges to total edges of cluster i, i.e.

Algorithm 2. Modified_RNM Algorithm

```
Each node is assigned a vector of m random numbers in [0..N_max], Y
Loop T times
```

```
    Reset each node's value(s) for Y to the mean of its neighbors, such as
```

$$Y_{im_t} = \frac{Y_{im_t} + \sum_L Y_{jm_{t-1}}}{|L|+1}$$

```
    where m indexes dimensions, I indexes nodes, t indexes the iteration
    number and L is the set of neighbor nodes.
```

$$\rho_i = \frac{\left|\{(u,v) \mid (u,v) \in E, u \in C_i, v \notin C_i\}\right|}{\left|\{(u,v) \mid (u,v) \in E, u \in C_i\}\right|}.$$

This is not a trivial task and, instead of attempting to identify the optimal clustering, we use a two phase procedure to obtain an approximate solution. First we use a modified Recursive Neighborhood Mean (RNM) algorithm (Moody, 2001) to assign multidimensional values for each node in the network, and then use the classic K-mean algorithm to extract clusters. The modified RNM algorithm summarizes the two phase procedure (see Algorithm 2). RNM algorithm is based on peer influence model and is very efficient in clustering classification. It utilizes an *m*-dimensional vector to iteratively compute and aggregate the peer influence. By iteratively pulling the values from the node's neighbors and taking their "opinions" into consideration, nodes within a cluster gradually converge. Original RNM algorithm only calculates the neighbors' mean. In our modified version we also take the current node's value into the mean computation and truncate the mean value into an integer to expedite convergence. Figure 7 shows the result of two dimensional RNM after 20 rounds of iterations for an AIM network with 4,878 nodes where the coordinate values of nodes are normalized.

Interestingly, the resulting dimensions clearly separate users into distinct regions. With RNM layout potential clusters can be identified by aggregating nodes within a same area in an *m* dimensional space. In order to identify the potential clusters for a given *m* dimensional layout, pattern recognition algorithms can be used. Given a set of *n* data points in *d*-dimensional space R_d and an integer *k,* the problem is to determine a set of *k* center points in R_d and minimize the mean square distance from each data point to its nearest center. We apply one of the simplest and fastest unsupervised learning algorithms, K-means pattern recognition algorithm (Kanungo et al., 2004), which has a time complexity of $O(nk)$. Note that K-means does not guarantee the size of the generated clusters. If a cluster's size is less than N_0, we slightly adjust K-means output and iteratively move the closest node from other clusters of size greater than N_0 to it until it reaches size N_0. To measure the quality of clustering and decide when to stop RNM algorithm we run the hybrid version of Lloyd's and Swap K-means clustering algorithm (Kanungo et al., 2004) on the RNM output for each round and inspect the average ratio ρ_i of the number of inter-cluster edges to that of total edges. Experiments show RNM algorithm converges quickly and the average ratio ρ_i reaches 90% after

Figure 7. Two Dimensional RNM Layout

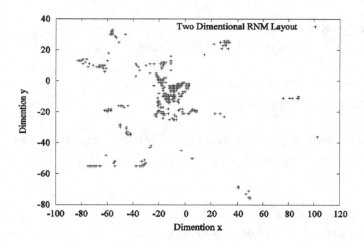

Figure 8. Clustered AIM Topology (N=4878, K=20)

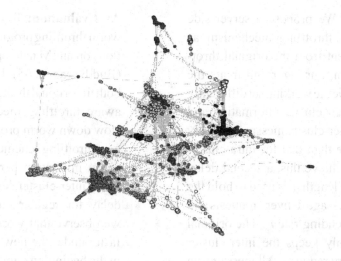

10 rounds and it does not vary too much in the subsequent rounds. In the experiment, we run RNM *20* rounds and have $N_0 = 30$, $Ave(\rho_i) = 95\%$ and $Min(\rho_i) = 83\%$. After running K-means algorithm over the two dimensional RNM layout as in Figure 7, we identify 20 clusters in the AIM network. Figure 8 is the AIM topology graph drawn with tool Pajek (Pajek, 2005) after assigning each node to a cluster. AIM user clusters are clearly identified and our conjecture of the clustering characteristics of IM network is confirmed.

4. **Clustering based Throttling Mechanism:** According to the previous analysis and experiments, IM network has strong clustering characteristics. The proportion of cross-cluster edges is determined by $1-\rho_i$, which is small compared to the proportion of inter-cluster edges. Due to the high internal connectivity a new worm will infect the nodes within a cluster rapidly. To propagate itself to other clusters a worm has to cross over the cross-cluster edges. We believe that the small number of cross-cluster edges is the keys for us to restrain worms

Algorithm 3. Clustering based throttling

```
layout = Modified_RNM(topology);
K-means(layout);        //cluster identification
while (true)
   Receive a message sending request m from user i;
   if (i∈workingset_i)   sendmsg(m);
   else
     if (Cluster(m.des) = Cluster(m.src))  //intra-cluster message
       if (queue.size + queue_c.size < q) queue.add(m);
       else drop m;
     else
     //cross-cluster message
       if (queue_c.size < q_c) queue_c.add(m);
       else  drop m;
```

within clusters. We propose a server-side topology-aware throttling mechanism as follows. Different from the original throttling mechanism, our algorithm treats the recipients outside the working set differently according to their cluster information and delay, that is, inter-cluster message delivery takes more time than that for intra-cluster messages. To achieve this, a second delay queue $queue_c$ of length q_c is used to hold the cross-cluster message delivery requests and with a slower sending rate r_c. The original delay queue only keeps the inter-cluster message delivery requests. All messages in the queues are sent out at a designated rate. The procedure is summarized in Algorithm 3. Suppose that ρ is the average ratio of the number of total inter-cluster edges to that of all the edges. Then the average receiver's response delay probability is:

$$\theta(t)f(t) = \rho\theta_{inter}(\tau)f_{inter}(\tau) + (1-\rho)\theta_{cross}(\tau)f_{cross}(\tau).$$

We can leverage the queuing delay between inter-cluster message requests and cross-cluster message requests to reduce the unnecessary delays of normal requests without hampering worm mitigation.

5. **An Evaluation:** To evaluate the proposed worm throttling protocol we conduct simulations on an IM network with AIM topology (Buddyscan, 2005). From the experiments, both the original throttling and our topology-aware throttling mechanism significantly slow down worm propagation. Further, our new throttling scheme achieves comparable worm mitigation performance with much lower inter-cluster delay, which implies less delay for regular messages. Specifically, we observe that worm propagates slightly faster under the new throttling mechanism in the beginning due to the low intra-cluster delay, but it has more effective control and slows down the worm propagation more than the original throttling mechanism due to the control enforced on the cross-cluster communications. In another word, by imposing a strict delay restriction r_c for $1 - \rho_i$ (5% - 17% in the experiment) cross-cluster communications we can significantly relax the delay restriction r for ρ_i (83% - 95% in the experiment) intra-cluster message delivery requests, thus achieving better usability and more effective containment. We also observe that parts of the traffic curves from some single runs under the new throttling

mechanism display an obvious "ladder" shape, which accounts for the almost complete IM worm containment within clusters.

CONCLUSION

While Instant Messaging (IM) is gaining popularity severe security threats are plaguing IM networks whereas most of the prevalent public IM services are offered without appropriate security measures. Research and engineering efforts are urgently needed to make IM networks reliable and secure.

For researchers and engineers, as well as IM users, this chapter offers an introduction to IM system and its security issues. Various mechanisms for its security defense are surveyed. For researchers in IM security, the second part of the chapter contains a mathematical model of IM worm and detailed analysis of its behaviors, including the smart worm that is known to be hard to deal with. Effective algorithms against IM spim and worm are presented along with simulations for evaluation.

IM is not a mature technology yet nor will it disappear soon. On the contrary, with its unique features of real-time service, presence information and open architecture for new application integrations, it will play an increasingly important role in Internet services. It is indispensable to improve its reliability and security so that it can better benefit the society.

REFERENCES

Asmussen, S. (2003). *Applied probability and queues*. Springer.

Bi, J., & Wu, J. Wu, & Zhang, W. (2008). *A trust and reputation based anti-spam method*. INFOCOM 2008. 27th Annual Joint Conference of the IEEE Computer and Communications.

Bogofilter. (2002). Retrieved from http://bogofilter.sourceforge.net/

Bønes, E., Hasvold, P., Henriksen, E., & Strandences, T. (2006). Risk analysis of information security in a mobile instant messaging and presence system for healthcare. *International Journal of Medical Informatics*.

Bose, A., Shin, K. G. (2006). *On mobile viruses exploiting messaging and Bluetooth services*. Securecomm and Workshops, 2006.

Buddyscan. (2005). *AIM status data*. Rochester Institute of Technology. Retrieved from http://lacuna.rit.edu/

Campbell, B., Rosenberg, J., Schulzrinne, H., Huitema, C., & Gurle, D. (2002). *RFC3428: Session initiation protocol extension for instant messaging*.

Chen, S. G., & Tang, Y. (2004). Slowing down Internet worms. In *Proceeding of IEEE ICDCS*, Tokyo, Japan.

Claburn, T. (2004). Spim, like spam, is on the rise. *Information Week*. Retrieved from http://www.informationweek.com/ news/ security/ showArticle.jhtml? articleID=18600413

Damiani, E., De Capitani di Vimercati, S., Paraboschi, S., & Samarati, P. (2004a). *P2P-based collaborative spam detection and filtering*. Fourth International Conference on Peer-to-Peer Computing (P2P'04).

Damiani, E., De Capitani di Vimercati, S., Paraboschi, S., & Samarati, P. (2004b). An open digest-based technique for spam d*etection*. In *Proc. of the 2004 International Workshop on Security in Parallel and Distributed Systems*.

Day, M., Aggarwal S., Mohr, G., & Vincent, J. (2000). *RFC2779: Instant messaging / presence protocol requirements*.

Day, M., Rosenberg, J., & Sugano, H. (2000). *RFC2778: A model for presence and instant messaging*.

Debbabi, M., & Rahman, M. (2004). *The war of presence and instant messaging: Right protocols and APIs.* In 1st IEEE Consumer Communications and Networking Conference, (pp. 341–346). Las Vegas, NV.

Espiner, T. (2006). *Spim, splog on the rise.* Retrieved from http://news.cnet.com/ Spim,-splog-on-the-rise/ 2100-7349_ 3-6091123.html

Fallows, D. (2003). *Spam: How it is hurting e-mail and degrading life on the Internet.* Pew Internet & American Life Project. Retrieved from http://www.pewinternet.org/ Reports/ 2003/ Spam-How-it-is-hurting-e-mail-and-degrading-life-on-the-Internet.aspx

Ferguson, P., & Huston, G. (1998). *Quality of service: Delivering QoS on the Internet and in corporate networks.* John Wiley & Sons, Inc.

Garetto, M., Gong, W. B., & Tonsley, D. (2003). *Modeling malware spreading dynamics.* INFOCOM 2003. 22nd Annual Joint Conference of the IEEE Computer and Communications.

Graham, P. (2002). *A plan for spam.* Retrieved from http://www.paulgraham.com/ spam.html

Grinter, R. E., & Palen, L. (2002). Instant messaging in teen life. *In Proceedings of the 2002 ACM Conference on Computer Supported Cooperative Work* (pp. 21–30). ACM Press.

Guo, W., Li, Z., Chen, Y., & Zhao, X. (2009). *Security design for instant messaging system based on RSA and triple DES.* In International Conference of Image Analysis and Signal Processing (IASP'09).

Herbsleb, J. D., Atkins, D. L., Boyer, D. G., Handel, M., & Finholt, T. A. (2002). Introducing instant messaging and chat in the workplace. In *Proceedings of the SIGCHI conference on Human factors in computing systems: Changing our world, changing ourselves* (pp. 171-178). Minneapolis, MN.

Hindocha, N., & Chien, E. (2003). *Malicious threats and vulnerabilities in instant messaging.* In Virus Bulletin International Conference. Symantec Security Response, Symantec Corporation.

Huerta, Y. A., & Liu, J. (2008). *Enhancing malware detection in an IM environment.* IEEE International Conference on Electro/Information Technology (EIT 2008).

Jelasity, M., Montresor, A., Jesi, G. P., & Voulgaris, S. (2003). *PeerSim: A peer-to-peer simulator.* Retrieved from http://peersim.sf.net/

Kanungo, T., Mount, D., Netanyahu, N., Piatko, C., Silverman, R., & Wu, A. (2004). A local search approximation algorithm for k-means clustering. In *Computational geometry: Theory & applications.*

Karlin, S., & Taylor, H. M. (1975). *A first course in stochastic processes* (2nd ed.). Academic Press.

Keizer, G. (2005). *IM threats growing 50% per month.* TechWeb.

Kephart, J. O., & White, S. R. (1993). Measuring and modeling computer virus prevalence. In *Proceedings of the 14th IEEE Symposium on Security and Privacy.*

Kerner, S. M. (2005). *IM accounts to number in the billions.* InternetNews.com. Retrieved from http://www.internetnews.com/ stats/ article.php/ 3521456

Kikuchi, H., Tada, M., & Nakanishi, S. (2004). *Secure instant messaging protocol preserving confidentiality against administrator.* 18th International Conference on Advanced Information Networking and Applications (AINA).

Lahmadi, A., & Festor, O. (2009). *SecSip: A stateful firewall for SIP-based networks.* FIP/IEEE International Symposium on Integrated Network Management (IM '09).

Leavitt, M. (2005). Instant messaging: A new target for hackers. *Journal of Computers, 38*(7).

Liu, Z., & Lee, D. (2007). *Coping with instant messaging worms - statistical modeling and analysis.* Local & Metropolitan Area Networks. LANMAN 2007. 15th IEEE Workshop.

Liu, Z., Lin, W., Li, N., & Lee, D. (2005). *Detecting and filtering instant messaging spam - a global and also personalized approach.* First Workshop on Secure Network Protocols (NPSec).

Liu, Z., Shu, G., Li, N., & Lee, D. (2006). *Defending against instant messaging worms.* IEEE Globecom 2006.

Manber, U. (1994). Finding similar files in a large file system. In *Proceedings of Winter USENIX Conference.*

Mannan, M., & Oorschot, P. C. van. (2006). A protocol for secure public instant messaging. *Proc. of the Financial Cryptography and Data Security* 2006.

Mannan, M., & van Oorschot, P. C. (2004). Secure public instant messaging: A survey. In *Proceedings of the 2nd Annual Conference on Privacy, Security and Trust* (PST).

Mannan, M., & van Oorschot, P. C. (2005). On instant messaging worms, analysis and countermeasures. *Proceedings ACM Workshop on Rapid Malcode* (WORM'05).

Metzger, J., Schillo, M., & Fischer, K. (2003). A multiagent-based peer-to-peer network in java for distributed spam filtering. In *Proc. of the 3rd CEEMAS*, Czech Republic.

Moody, J. (2001). Peer influence groups: Identifying dense clusters in large network. *Social Networks, 23*(4), 261–283. doi:10.1016/S0378-8733(01)00042-9

Moore, D., Shannon, C., Voelker, G. M., & Savage, S. (2003). *Internet quarantine: Requirements for containing self-propagating code.* INFOCOM 2003. 22nd IEEE International Conference on Computer Communications.

Morse, C. D., & Wang, H. (2005). *The structure of an instant messenger network and its vulnerability to malicious codes.* SIGCOMM poster.

MSNShell. (n.d.). *Personalized MSN.* Retrieved from http://www.msnshell.net/ en/ index.html

Orebaugh, A. (2006). An instant messaging intrusion detection system framework: Using character frequency analysis for authorship identification and validation. *Proceedings 2006 40th Annual IEEE International Carnahan Conferences Security Technology.*

OTR. (2004). *Off the record messaging.* Retrieved from http://www.cypherpunks.ca/otr/

Pajek. (2005). Program for large network analysis. Retrieved from http://vlado.fmf.uni-lj.si/ pub/ networks/ pajek/

Peersim. (n.d.). *Peer-to-peer simulator.* Retrieved from http://peersim.sourceforge.net/

Pidgin-Encryption. (2003). *Pidgin plugins.* Retrieved from http://pidgin-encrypt.sourceforge.net/

Rebahi, Y., Sisalem, D., & Magedanz, T. (2006). *SIP spam detection.* International Conference on Digital Telecommunications (ICDT '06).

Sahami, M., Dumais, S., Heckerman, D., & Horvitz, E. (1998). *A Bayesian approach to filtering junk e-mail, learning for text categorization.* AAAI Workshop on Learning for Text Categorization, Madison, Wisconsin.

Saint-Andre, P. (Ed.). (2004a). *RFC 3920: Extensible messaging and presence protocol (XMPP): Core.* Jabber Software Foundation.

Saint-Andre, P. (Ed.). (2004b). *RFC 3921: Extensible messaging and presence protocol (XMPP): Instant messaging and presence.* Jabber Software Foundation.

Scupelli, P., Kiesler, S., Fussell, S. R., & Chen, C. (2005). *Project view IM: A tool for juggling multiple projects and teams*. In Conference on Human Factors in Computing Systems. Portland, OR

Sellke, S., Shroff, N. B., & Bagchi, S. (2005). Modeling and automated containment of worms. In *Proceeding of International Conference on Dependable Systems and Networks* (DSN).

Serazzi, G., & Zanero, S. (2003). *Computer virus propagation models*. Tutorials of the 11th IEEE/ACM Int'l Symp. on Modeling, Analysis and Simulation of Computer and Telecom.

Smith, R. D. (2005). *Instant messaging as a scale-free network*. Retrieved from http://arxiv.org/abs/cond-mat/0206378

Staniford, S. (2003). Containment of scanning worms in enterprise networks. *Journal of Computer Security*.

Thommes, R., & Coates, M. (2006). *Epidemiological modeling of peer-to-peer viruses and pollution*. INFOCOM 2006. 25th IEEE International Conference on Computer Communications.

Trillian. (2002). *Home page*. Retrieved from http://www.trillian.im/

Trivedi, A. J., Judge, P. Q., & Krasser, S. (2007). Analyzing network and content characteristics of SPIM using honeypots. In *Proceedings of the 3rd USENIX SRUTI*, Santa Clara, CA.

Wikipedia. (2009). *Instant messaging*. Retrieved from http://en.wikipedia.org/wiki/Instant_messaging

Williamson, M., & Parry, A. (2004). *Virus throttling for instant messaging*. In Virus Bulletin Conference.

Xie, M., Wu, Z., & Wang, H. (2007). HoneyIM: Fast detection and suppression of instant messaging malware in enterprise-like networks. In *Proceedings of ACSAC'07*.

Yan, G., Xiao, Z., & Eidenbenz, S. (2008). Catching instant messaging worms with change-point detection techniques. *Proc. of the 1st Usenix Workshop on Large-Scale Exploits and Emergent Threats*.

Zhang, B., Feng, M., Xiong, H., & Hu, D. (2008). *Design and implementation of secure instant messaging system based on MSN*. In International Symposium on Computer Science and Computational Technology (ISCSCT '08).

Zhou, F., Zhuang, L., Zhao, B., Huang, A., Joseph, L., & Kubiatowicz, J. (2003). Approximate object-location and spam filtering on peer-to-peer systems. In *Proc. of the ACM/IFIP/USENIX International Middleware Conference*.

Zou, C., Gong, W. B., & Towsley, D. (2003a). Worm propagation modeling and analysis under dynamic quarantine defense. *Proc. ACM Workshop on Rapid Malcode* (WORM'03).

Zou, C., Gong, W. B., & Towsley, D. (2003b). Code red worm propagation modeling and analysis. In *Proceedings of 9th ACM Conference on Computer and Communication Security*.

Zou, C., Towsley, D., & Gong, W. (2004). E-mail worm modeling and defense. In *Proceedings of the 3rd International Conference on Computer Communications and Networks* (ICCCN).

KEY TERMS AND DEFINITIONS

Branching Process: A stochastic process that considers a population of particles with independent random lifetimes, at the end of which each particle splits into a random number of new particles that have the same life span as the parent.

Instant Messaging (IM): IM service provides messaging services, which allow communicating parties send messages in one-to-one or one-to-many fashion in real-time and also provide presence information of involved communications parties.

IM Spam (Spim): Unsolicited Commercial Messages sent via an IM messenger.

IM Worms: Malicious code that propagates over IM networks by exploiting features and vulnerabilities of IM clients and protocols.

Martingale: A stochastic process that the conditional expected value of an observation at time *t*, given all the observations up to an earlier time *s*, is equal to the observation at that earlier time *s*.

SIMPLE: SIP Instant Messaging and Presence Leveraging Extensions.

XMPP: Extensible Messaging and Presence Protocol.

Compilation of References

ACFE. (2008). *Managing the Business Risk of Fraud - A Practical Guide.* Retrieved from http://www.acfe.com/documents/managing-business-risk.pdf

Adams, C. M. (1997). *Constructing symmetric ciphers using the CAST design procedure.* Retrieved December 12, 2009, from http://cryptome.org/jya/cast.html

Agrawal, R., & Srikant, R. (2000). Privacy-preserving data mining. *Proceedings of ACM SIGMOD International Conference on Management of Data*, (pp. 439–450).

Akkaya, K., & Younis, M. (2005). A survey on routing protocols for wireless sensor networks. *Elsevir Ad Hoc Networks, 3*(3), 325–349. doi:10.1016/j.adhoc.2003.09.010

Akyildiz, I. (2002). A survey on sensor networks. *IEEE Communications Magazine*, 102–114. doi:10.1109/MCOM.2002.1024422

Al, M., & Yoshigoe, K. (2008-1, July 14-17, 2008). *A secure and energy-efficient key generation mechanism for wireless sensor networks.* Paper presented at the International Conference on Parallel and Distributed Techniques and Applications, PDPTA 2008, Las Vegas, Nevada, USA.

Al, M., & Yoshigoe, K. (2008-2). *Adaptive confidentiality mechanism for hierarchical wireless sensor networks.* Paper presented at the GLOBECOM Workshops, 2008 IEEE.

Alberts, C., & Dorofee, A. (2003). *Managing information security risks, the OCTAVE approach.* Addison-Wesley.

Ali, M., Voigt, T., & Uzmi, Z. A. (2006). *Mobility management in sensor networks.* Mobility and Scalability in Wireless Sensor Networks, San Francisco, USA, June 2006.

Al-Riyami, S. S., & Paterson, K. G. (2003). Certificateless public key cryptography. *Proceedings ASIACRYPT 2003*, (LNCS 2894), (pp.452-473). Springer-Verlag, Anjum, F. (2006). *Location dependent key management using random key predistribution in sensor networks.* ACM Workshop on Wireless Security (WiSE'06), (pp. 21-30).

Analytics, I. D. (2007). *Data breach harm analysis from ID Analytics uncovers new patterns of misuse arising from breaches of identity data.* Retrieved on November 12, 2009, from http://www.idanalytics.com/ news_and_events/20071107.html

Anderson, T., Roscoe, T., & Wetherall, D. (2004). Preventing Internet DoS with capabilities. *ACM SIGCOMM, 34*(1), 39–44. doi:10.1145/972374.972382

Andrews, L. W. (2004). *Passwords reveal your personality.* Retrieved March 13, 2007, from http://cms.psychology-today.com/ articles/pto- 20020101-000006.html

ANSI. (2010). *The financial management of cyber risk: An implementation framework for CFOs.* Retrieved from http://webstore.ansi.org/cybersecurity.aspx

Araki, T. (2007). *Efficient (k, n) threshold secret sharing schemes secure against cheating from n-1 cheaters.* Australasian Conference on Information Security and Privacy (ACISP 2007), (LNCS 4586, pp. 133-142).

Argyraki, K., & Cheriton, D. R. (2005). *Active Internet traffic filter.* Usenix Annual Technical Conference, (pp. 135 –148).

Ashok, R., & Agrawal, D. (2003). Next-generation wearable networks. *Computer*, 31–39. doi:10.1109/MC.2003.1244532

Asmussen, S. (2003). *Applied probability and queues.* Springer.

Atkins, D., Stallings, W., & Zimmermann, P. (1996). *PGP message exchange formats*.

Atkins, S. (2009). *Sam Spade download*. Retrieved February 30, 2010, from http://www.softpedia.com/get/Network-Tools/Network-Tools-Suites/Sam-Spade.shtml

Audit Report Sample. (2003). *APHIS animal care program – inspection and enforcement activities*. Retrieved May 30, 2010, from www.usda.gov/oig/webdocs/33002-03-SF.pdf

AUDIT. 507 (2009). *Auditing networks, perimeters, and systems*. Retrieved March 30, 2010, from http://www.sans.org/security-training/auditing-networks-perimeters-systems-6-mid

Baker, S., & Green, H. (2010). Social media will change your business. *BusinessWeek*. Retrieved from http://www.businessweek.com/bwdaily/dnflash/ content/feb2008/db20080219_908252.htm

Bejtlich, R. (2010). Understanding the advanced persistent threat. *Information Security Magazine*. Retrieved from http://searchsecurity.techtarget.com/ magazineCurrent/0,296884,sid14,00.html

Bellare, M. (2006). New proofs for NMAC and HMAC: Security without collision-resistance. In *Advances in cryptology – CRYPTO'06*, (LNCS 4117, pp. 602–619). Springer.

Bellovin, S. M. (2000). *ICMP traceback messages*.

Bennett, C. H., & Brassard, G. (1984). Quantum cryptography: Public key distribution and coin tossing. *IEEE International Conference on Computers, Systems, and Signal Processing*, 175. Bangalore, India: IEEE.

Bennett, C. H., & Brassard, G. (1989). The dawn of a new era for quantum cryptography: The experimental prototype is working! *Sigact News*, 78-82.

Bennett, C. H., Bessette, F., Brassard, G., Salvail, L., & Smolin, J. (1992). Experimental quantum cryptography. *Journal of Cryptology*, 3-28.

Berlin, K., Cepulis, D., Chan, R., Lowell, D., Duke, J., Jair, F., ... Vincent, P. (2009). *SMBIOS reference specification version 2.6*. Standard specification. Distributed Management Task Force, Inc.

Berman, M. (2009). Virtualization audit 101: The top 5 risks and recommendations for protecting your virtual IT. *Computer Technology Review*.

Bethencourt, J., Sahai, A., & Waters, B. (2007). Ciphertext-policy attribute-based encryption. Proceedings of IEEE Symposium on Security and Privacy.

Bi, J., & Wu, J. Wu, & Zhang, W. (2008). *A trust and reputation based anti-spam method*. INFOCOM 2008. 27th Annual Joint Conference of the IEEE Computer and Communications.

Biham, E., & Shamir, A. (1991, February). Differential cryptanlysis of DES-like cryptosystems. *Journal of Cryptology*, 3-72.

Biryukov, A. (2003). Cryptanalysis of SAFER++. *CRYPTO, 2003*, 195–211.

Blair, B., Hass, J., Hilland, J., Hines, D., & Shah, H. (2007). *Systems management architecture for mobile and desktop hardware – DASH*. White paper. Distributed Management Task Force, Inc.

Blakley, G. R. (1979). Safeguarding cryptographic keys. *Proceedings of the National Computer Conference, 48*, 313–317.

Bleichenbacher, D. (1996). *Generating ElGamal signatures without knowing the secret key. Advances in Cryptology --- EUROCRYPT~'96* (pp. 10–18). Springer-Verlag.

Blumenthal, J., Handy, M., Golatowski, F., Haase, M., & Timmermann, D. (2003). Wireless sensor networks - new challenges in software engineering. *Proceedings of ETFA '03, IEEE Conference*, 16-19 Sept. 2003, vol 1, (pp. 551- 556). ISBN: 0-7803-7937-3

Bo, S., Shrestha, D., Yan, G., & Yang, X. (2008). *Self-propagate mal-packets in wireless sensor networks: Dynamics and defense implications*. Paper presented at the Global Telecommunications Conference, 2008. IEEE GLOBECOM 2008. IEEE.

Bogofilter. (2002). Retrieved from http://bogofilter.sourceforge.net/

Bojinov, H., Bursztein, E., Lovett, E., & Boneh, D. (2009). *Embedded management interfaces: Emerging massive insecurity*. Paper presented at Blackhat 2009, Las Vegas, NV.

Bønes, E., Hasvold, P., Henriksen, E., & Strandences, T. (2006). Risk analysis of information security in a mobile instant messaging and presence system for healthcare. *International Journal of Medical Informatics*.

Bonneau, J., & Preibush, S. (2010). *The password thicket - technical and market failures in human authentication on the Web*. The Ninth Workshop on the Economics of Information Security (WEIS 2010), Cambridge, MA, June 7-8, 2010.

Bose, A., Shin, K. G. (2006). *On mobile viruses exploiting messaging and Bluetooth services*. Securecomm and Workshops, 2006.

Boukerche, A., El-Khatib, K., Xu, L., & Korba, L. (2004a). *SDAR: A secure distributed anonymous routing protocol for wireless and mobile ad hoc networks*. In 29th Annual IEEE International Conference on Local Computer Networks, 16-18 Nov. 2004, (pp. 618– 624).

Boukerche, A., El-Khatib, K., Xu, L., & Korba, L. (2004b). *Anonymity enabling scheme for wireless ad hoc networks*. In Global Telecommunications Conference Workshops. GlobeCom Workshops 2004, (pp. 136–140).

Boukerche, A., El-Khatib, K., Xu, L., & Korba, L. (2004c). *A novel solution for achieving anonymity in wireless ad hoc networks*. The 1st ACM international workshop on Performance evaluation of wireless ad hoc, sensor, and ubiquitous, October 2004.

Bouras, C., & Stamos, K. (2004). *An adaptive admission control algorithm for bandwidth brokers*. 3rd IEEE International Symposium on Network Computing and Applications (NCA04), Cambridge, MA, USA, August 30 - September 1 2004, (pp. 243–250).

Bouras, C., & Stamos, K. (2005). *Examining the benefits of a hybrid distributed architecture for bandwidth brokers*. The First IEEE International Workshop on Multimedia Systems and Networking (WMSN'05).

Bouras, C., Haniotakis, V., Primpas, D., Stamos, K., & Varvitsiotis, A. (2007). *AMPS - ANStool: Interoperability of automated tools for the provisioning of QoS services*. TERENA Networking Conference 2007, Lyngby, Denmark, 21 - 24 May 2007.

Brostoff, S., & Sasse, M. A. (2001). *Safe and sound: A safety-critical approach to security*. Position paper presented at the New Security Paradigms Workshop 2001, Cloudcroft, New Mexico.

Broustis, I., Pelechrinis, K., Syrivelis, D., Krishnamurthy, S., & Tassiulas, L. (2009). *FIJI: Fighting Implicit Jamming in 802.11 WLANs*.

Buchanan, S., & Forbes Gibb, F. (2007). The information audit: Role and scope. *International Journal of Information Management, 27*(3), 159–172. doi:10.1016/j.ijinfomgt.2007.01.002

Buddyscan. (2005). *AIM status data*. Rochester Institute of Technology. Retrieved from http://lacuna.rit.edu/

Bulman, P. (2000, October 2). *Commerce Department announces winner of global information security competition*. Retrieved December 11, 2009, from http://www.nist.gov/public_affairs/ releases/g00-176.htm

Bumpus, W., Sweitzer, J., Thompson, P., Westerinen, A., & Williams, R. (1999). *Common information model: Implementing the object model for enterprise management*. John Wiley & Sons, Inc.

Burnett, M., & Kleiman, D. (2006). *Perfect passwords. Selection, protection, authentication*. Syngress.

Burnett, S. (2001). *RSA security's official guide to cryptography*. McGraw-Hill.

Cabrera, F., & Kurt, C. (2005). *Web services architecture and its specifications: Essentials for understanding WS*. Redmond, WA: Microsoft Press.

Çakiro lu, M., & Özcerit, A. (2008). *Jamming detection mechanisms for wireless sensor networks*.

Callegati, F., Cerroni, W., & Ramilli, M. (2009). Man-in-the-middle attack to the HTTPS protocol. *IEEE Security and Privacy*, 78-81.

Campanella, M., Krzywania, R., Reijs, V., Sevasti, A., Stamos, K., Tziouvaras, C., & Wilson, D. (2006). *Bandwidth on demand services for European research and education networks*. 1st IEEE International Workshop on Bandwidth on Demand, 27 Nov 2006, San Francisco (USA).

Campbell, I. (2007). *Symbian OS communications programming* (2nd ed.). West Sussex, UK: John Wiley & Sons, Ltd.

Campbell, B., Rosenberg, J., Schulzrinne, H., Huitema, C., & Gurle, D. (2002). *RFC3428: Session initiation protocol extension for instant messaging.*

Camtepe, S. A., & Yener, B. (2007). Combinatorial design of key distribution mechanisms for wireless sensor networks. *IEEE/ACM Transactions on Networking, 15*(2), 346–358. doi:10.1109/TNET.2007.892879

Camtepe, S., et al. (2008). Key management in wireless sensor networks. In J. Lopez & J. Zhou (Eds.), *Wireless sensor network security*. IOS Press.

Canetti, R., Garay, J., Itkis, G., Micciancio, D., Naor, M., & Pinkas, B. (1999). Multicast security: A taxonomy and some efficient constructions. *Proceedings - IEEE INFOCOM, 2*, 708–716.

Carpenter, M., Liston, T., & Skoudis, E. (2007). Hiding virtualization from attackers and malware. *IEEE Security & Privacy, 5*(3), 62–65. doi:10.1109/MSP.2007.63

Castellini, M. J. (2005). *LAN switching first step* (pp. 205–215). Indianapolis, IN: Cisco Press.

Cayirci, E., & Rong, C. (2009). *Security in wireless ad hoc and sensor networks*. West Sussex, UK: John Wiley and Sons. doi:10.1002/9780470516782

CERIAS. (2009). *Unsecured economies: Protecting vital information*. Retrieved from http://www.cerias.purdue.edu/site/blog/post/ unsecured_economies_and_overly_secured_reports/

CERT Coordination Center. (1996). *TCP SYN flooding and IP spoofing attacks*. Retrieved from http://www.cert.org/ advisories/ CA-1996-21.html

CERT. *(2009)*. Insider threat research. Retrieved December 1, 2009 from http://www.cert.org/insider_threat

Chakrabarti, D., Maitra, S., & Roy, B. (2006). A key pre-distribution scheme for wireless sensor networks: Merging blocks in combinatorial design. *Journal of Information Security, 5*(2), 105–114. doi:10.1007/s10207-006-0085-4

Chan, H., Perrig, A., Przydatek, B., & Song, D. (2007). SIA: Secure information aggregation in sensor networks. *Journal of Computer Security, 15*(1), 69–102.

Chan, H., & Perrig, A. (2003). Security and privacy in sensor networks. IEEE Computer Magazine, 103-105.

Chan, H., et al. (2006). Random key predistribution schemes for sensor networks. IEEE International Conference on Communication, (pp. 2262-2267).

Chartwell. (2010). Energy library. Retrieved from http://www.energylibrary.com/index.cfm/ID/7/iNewsID/197/

Chaum, D. (1981). Untraceable electronic mail, return addresses, and digital pseudonyms. *Communications of the ACM, 24*(2), 84–88. doi:10.1145/358549.358563

Chaum, D. (1988). The dining cryptographers problem: Unconditional sender and recipient untraceability. *Journal of Cryptography, 1*(1), 65–75.

Chen, Y.-F., Chan, Y.-K., Huang, C.-C., Tsai, M.-H., & Chu, Y.-P. (2007). A multiple-level visual secret-sharing scheme without image size expansion. *Information Sciences, 177*(21), 4696–4710. doi:10.1016/j.ins.2007.05.011

Chen, Z., Ji, C., & Barford, P. (2008). *Spatial-temporal characteristics of Internet malicious sources. Proceedings of IEEE INFOCOM.* Mini-Conference.

Chen, T., & Peikari, C. (2008). Malicious software in mobile devices. In Zhang, Y., Zheng, J., & Ma, M. (Eds.), *Handbook of research on wireless security*. Hershey, PA: Idea Group Publishing. doi:10.4018/9781599048994.ch001

Chen, S. G., & Tang, Y. (2004). Slowing down Internet worms. In *Proceeding of IEEE ICDCS*, Tokyo, Japan.

Chen, Z., & Ji, C. (2007). Measuring network-aware worm spreading ability. *Proceedings of the IEEE INFOCOM 2007*, Anchorage AK.

Chengfa, L., Mao, Y., Guihai, C., & Jie, W. (2005). *An energy-efficient unequal clustering mechanism for wireless sensor networks*. Paper presented at the Mobile Adhoc and Sensor Systems Conference, 2005. IEEE International Conference on.

Cheops-ng. (n.d.). Retrieved March 30, 2010, from http://cheops-ng.sourceforge.net/

Chiou, C. H., & Chen, W. T. (1989). Secure broadcast using secure lock. *IEEE Transactions on Software Engineering, 15*(8), 929–934. doi:10.1109/32.31350

Choi, W., Shah, P., & Das, S. K. (2004). *A framework for energy-saving data gathering using two-phase clustering in wireless sensor networks.* Paper presented at The First Annual International Conference on Mobile and Ubiquitous Systems: Networking and Services, 2004. MOBIQUITOUS 2004.

Chu, H. H., Qiao, L., & Nahrstedt, K. (2002). A secure multicast protocol with copyright protection. *ACM SIGCOMM Computer Communications Review, 32*(2), 42–60. doi:10.1145/568567.568570

Chung, H.-R., & Ku, W.-C. (2008). Three weaknesses in a simple three-party key exchange protocol. *Information Science, 178*, 220–229. doi:10.1016/j.ins.2007.08.004

Ciampa, M. (2007). *CWSP guide to wireless security* (pp. 49–53). Boston, MA: Thompson Course Technology.

Ciciriello, P., Mottola, L., & Picco, G. (2007). Efficient routing from multiple sources to multiple sinks in wireless sensor networks *Wireless Sensor Networks,* 34-50.

Claburn, T. (2004). Spim, like spam, is on the rise. *Information Week.* Retrieved from http://www.informationweek.com/ news/ security/ showArticle.jhtml? articleID=18600413

Cluley, G. (2009). *Passwords used by the Conficker worm.* Retrieved from http://www.sophos.com/blogs/gc/g/ 2009/01/16/passwords-conficker-worm/

COBIT. (2010). *Official site.* Retrieved March 30, 2010, from http://www.isaca.org/Knowledge-Center/COBIT/Pages/Overview.aspx

Creeger, M. (2010). CTO roundtable - malware defense. *ACM Queue; Tomorrow's Computing Today, 8*(2), 40.

Crossbow Mica2 Motes. (2010). Retrieved from http://www.xbow.com

CSI. (2009). *CSI computer crime & security survey.* Retrieved from http://gocsi.com/survey

Cui, Y., Kobara, K., Matsuura, K., & Imai, H. (2007). *Lightweight asymmetric privacy-preserving authentication protocols secure against active attac.* Fifth Annual IEEE International Conference on Pervasive Computing and Communications Workshops, 2007, (pp. 223-228). ISBN: 0-7695-2788-4

CVE-2010-0249. (2010). Retrieved from http://web.nvd.nist.gov/view/ vuln/detail?vulnId=CVE-2010-0249

CyLab. (2010). Governance of enterprise security. Retrieved from http://www.cylab.cmu.edu/outreach/governance.html

Cymru. (2006). Cybercrime - an epidemic. *ACM Queue, 4*(9), 25-28.

Damiani, E., De Capitani di Vimercati, S., Paraboschi, S., & Samarati, P. (2004a). *P2P-based collaborative spam detection and filtering.* Fourth International Conference on Peer-to-Peer Computing (P2P'04).

Damiani, E., De Capitani di Vimercati, S., Paraboschi, S., & Samarati, P. (2004b). An open digest-based technique for spam d*etection.* In *Proc. of the 2004 International Workshop on Security in Parallel and Distributed Systems.*

Dataloss, D. B. (2010). Largest incidents. *Data Loss Database.* Retrieved from http://datalossdb.org/index/largest

Day, M., Aggarwal S., Mohr, G., & Vincent, J. (2000). *RFC2779: Instant messaging / presence protocol requirements.*

Day, M., Rosenberg, J., & Sugano, H. (2000). *RFC2778: A model for presence and instant messaging.*

Deb, B., Bhatnagar, S., & Nath, B. (2003). *Information assurance in sensor networks.* Paper presented at the 2nd ACM International Conference on Wireless sensor networks and applications.

Deb, B., Bhatnagar, S., & Nath, B. (2003). *ReInForM: Reliable information forwarding using multiple paths in sensor networks.* Paper presented at the 28th Annual IEEE International Conference on Local Computer Networks, 2003. LCN '03.

Debbabi, M., & Rahman, M. (2004). *The war of presence and instant messaging: Right protocols and APIs.* In 1st IEEE Consumer Communications and Networking Conference, (pp. 341–346). Las Vegas, NV.

Deloite. (2010). *Cyber crime - a clear and present danger.* Retrieved from http://www.deloitte.com/assets/Dcom-UnitedStates/Local%20Assets/ Documents/AERS/us_aers_Deloitte%20Cyber% 20Crime%20POV%20 Jan252010.pdf

Deng, J., Han, R., & Mishra, S. (2006). Insens: Intrusion-tolerant routing for wireless sensor networks. *Computer Communications, 29*(2), 216–230. doi:10.1016/j.comcom.2005.05.018

Deng, J., Han, R., & Mishra, S. (2005). *Countermeasures against traffic analysis attacks in wireless sensor networks.* Paper presented at the First International Conference on Security and Privacy for Emerging Areas in Communications Networks, 2005. SecureComm 2005.

Department of Defense. (1985). *Password management guideline.* Retrieved September 2004, from http://www.alw.nih.gov/Security/ FIRST/papers/password/dodpwman.txt

Deraison, R., Gula, R., & Hayton, T. (2009). *Passive vulnerability scanning introduction.* Retrieved May 13, 2010, from http://www.nessus.org

Desmedt, Y., & Holloway, R. (1997). Some recent research aspects of threshold cryptography. In *Proceedings of the 1st Intl. Information Security Workshop,* (pp. 158-173). Springer-Verlag.

Di Pietro, R., et al. (2008). Catch me (If you can): Data survival in unattended sensor networks. Proceedings of IEEE PERCOM, (pp. 185-194).

Dierks, T., & Allen, C. (1999). *The TLS protocol, version 1.0. Request for Comments RFC-2246.* Internet Engineering Task Force, Network Working Group.

Diffie, W., & Hellman, M. E. (1976). New directions in cryptography. *IEEE Transactions on Information Theory, 22,* 644–654. doi:10.1109/TIT.1976.1055638

Diffie, W., Van Oorschot, P. C., & Wiener, M. J. (1992). Authentication and authenticated key exchanges. *Designs, Codes and Cryptography, 2*(2), 107–125. doi:10.1007/BF00124891

DoE. (2002). National transmission grid study. Washington DC: US Department of Energy. Retrieved from http://www.ferc.gov/industries/electric/indus-act/transmission-grid.pdf

Douceur, J. (2002). *The sybil attack.* Paper presented at the First International Workshop on Peer-to-Peer Systems (IPTPS '02), Cambridge, MA.

Du, W., Deng, J., Han, Y. S., & Varshney, P. K. (2006). A key pre-distribution scheme for sensor networks using deployment knowledge. *IEEE Transactions on Dependable and Secure Computing, 3*(1), 62–77. doi:10.1109/TDSC.2006.2

Duanfeng, S., Qin, L., Xinhui, H., & Wei, Z. (2004). *Security mechanisms for SIP-based multimedia communication (Vol. 1,* pp. 575–57).

Dulman, S., Nieberg, T., Wu, J., & Havinga, P. (2003). *Trade-off between traffic overhead and reliability in multipath routing for wireless sensor networks.* Paper presented at the Wireless Communications and Networking, 2003. WCNC 2003. 2003 IEEE.

Edugain. (2010). Retrieved from www.edugain.org

Egorova-Forster, A., & Murphy, A. L. (2007). *Exploiting reinforcement learning for multiple sink routing in WSNs.* Paper presented at the IEEE Internatonal Conference on Mobile Adhoc and Sensor Systems, 2007. MASS 2007.

Elahi, G., Yu, E., & Zannone, N. (2009). *A modeling ontology for integrating vulnerabilities into security requirements conceptual foundations.* 28th International Conference on Conceptual Modeling, Gramado, Brazil.

Ellison, C., & Schneier, B. (2000). *Ten risks of PKI: What you're not being told about public key infrastructure.* Computer Security Journal.

Eschenauer, L., & Gligor, V. (2002). A key management scheme for distributed sensor networks. Proceedings of 9th ACM Conference on Computer and Communications Security (CCS'02), (pp. 41-47).

Espiner, T. (2006). *Spim, splog on the rise.* Retrieved from http://news.cnet.com/ Spim,-splog-on-the-rise/2100-7349_3-6091123.html

Esser, S. (2001). *IE https certificate attack.* Retrieved December 1, 2009, from http://security.e-matters.de/advisories/012001.html

Evfimievski, A. (2002). Randomization in privacy preserving data mining. *ACM SIGKDD Explorations Newsletter, 4*(2), 43–48. doi:10.1145/772862.772869

Evfimievski, A., Ramakrishnan, S., Agrawal, R., & Gehrke, J. (2002). *Privacy-preserving mining of association rules*. 8th ACM SIGKDD International Conference on Knowledge Discovery and Data Mining, (pp. 217–228). ACM Press.

Fallows, D. (2003). *Spam: How it is hurting e-mail and degrading life on the Internet*. Pew Internet & American Life Project. Retrieved from http://www.pewinternet.org/ Reports/ 2003/ Spam-How-it-is-hurting-e-mail-and-degrading-life-on-the-Internet.aspx

FBI. (2010). *Speech remarks for Steven R. Chabinsky, Deputy Assistant Director, Cyber Division, FBI*. Federal Bureau of Investigations. Retrieved from http://www.fbi.gov/pressrel/ speeches/chabinsky032310.htm

Fe3d. (2010). Received March 15, 2010, from http://nmap.org/book/zenmap-topology.html

Ferguson, P., & Huston, G. (1998). *Quality of service: Delivering QoS on the Internet and in corporate networks*. John Wiley & Sons, Inc.

Ferguson, P., & Senie, D. (2000). *Network ingress filtering: Defeating denial of service attacks that employ IP source address spoofing*. (Internet RFC 2827).

Ferraiolo, D. F., Sandhu, R., Gavrila, S., Kuhn, D. R., & Chandramouli, R. (2001). Proposed NIST standards for role-based access control. [TISSEC]. *ACM Transactions on Information and System Security*, 4(3). doi:10.1145/501978.501980

Fielding, R., Gettys, J., Mogul, J., Frystyk, H., Masinter, L., Leach, P., et al. (1999). *Hypertext Transfer Protocol -- HTTP*. Retrieved December 1, 2009, from http://www.w3.org/Protocols/ HTTP/1.1/diff-v11-Rev0

FIPS PUB 197. (2001). *Advanced encryption standard*. Federal Information Processing Standards Publications, US Department of Commerce/N.I.S.T., National Technical Information Service, 2001.

Fitzgibbon, N., & Wood, M. (2009). *Conficker.C: A technical analysis*. Sophos Labs. Retrieved from http://www.sophos.com/sophos/docs/eng/ marketing_material/conficker-analysis.pdf

Fitzi, M., Garay, J., Gollakota, S., Rangan, C. P., & Srinathan, K. (2006). *Round-optimal and efficient verifiable secret sharing*. Theory of Cryptography Conference (TCC 2006), (LNCS 3876, pp. 329-342).

Foley, S. (2009). *Security risk management using internal controls*. First ACM Workshop on Information Security Governance (WISG'09), November 13, 2009, Chicago, IL.

Franklin, M. K., & Reiter, M. K. (1997). Fair exchange with a semi-trusted party. In *Proceedings of CCS'97*.

Frigault, M., Wang, L., Singhal, A., & Jajodia, S. (2008). Measuring network security using dynamic Bayesian network. In *Proceedings of 4th ACM Workshop on Quality of Protection*, (pp. 23–30).

Frye, R., Levy, D., Routhier, S., & Wijnen, B. (2003). *Coexistence between version 1, version 2, and version 3 of the Internet-standard network management framework*. Request for Comments RFC-3584.

FS-ISAC. (2009). *FBI/FS-ISAC/NACHA joint alert - account hijacking of corporate customers: Recommendations for customer education*. Retrieved from http://www.nacha.org/c/riskTools.cfm

Fu, H., Kawamura, S., Zhang, M., & Zhang, L. (2008). Replication attack on random key pre-distribution schemes for wireless sensor networks. *Computer Communications*, 31(4), 842–857. doi:10.1016/j.comcom.2007.10.026

Furguson, N., Kelsey, J., Schneier, B., Stay, M., Wagner, D., & Whiting, D. (2000). *Improved cryptanalysis of Rijndael*. Seventh Fast Software Encryption Workshop. Springer-Vertag.

Ganesan, D., Govindan, R., Shenker, S., & Estrin, D. (2001). Highly-resilient, energy-efficient multipath routing in wireless sensor networks. *ACM SIGMOBILE Mobile Computing and Communications Review*, 5(4), 11–25. doi:10.1145/509506.509514

Garetto, M., Gong, W. B., & Tonsley, D. (2003). *Modeling malware spreading dynamics*. INFOCOM 2003. 22nd Annual Joint Conference of the IEEE Computer and Communications.

Gaubatz, G., Kaps, J., & Sunar, B. (2005). *Public key cryptography in sensor networks – revisited*. Springer Inc.

GEANT network. (2010). Retrieved from http://www.geant.net/

Geer. (2006). Playing for keeps. *ACM Queue, 4*(9), 42-48.

Georgetown University. (2009). *Information security.* Retrieved November 12, 2009, from http://security.georgetown.edu/passwords.html

Gong, L., & Wheeler, D. J. (1990). A matrix key distribution scheme. *Journal of Cryptology, 2*(1), 51–59. doi:10.1007/BF02252869

Goodin, D. (2009). A grim day for browser security at hacker contest: Safari, IE and Firefox all down for the count. *The Register*. Retrieved from http://www.theregister.co.uk/ 2009/03/19/pwn2own_day1/

Goodin, D. (2010). It's official: Adobe Reader is world's most-exploited app. *The Register*. Retrieved from http://www.theregister.co.uk/ 2010/03/09/adobe_reader_attacks/

Google. (2010). *A new approach to China.* Google Blog. Retrieved from http://googleblog.blogspot.com/2010/01/new-approach-to-china.html

Gostin, L. O. (2000). *Public health law: Power, duty, restraint* (pp. 132–134). Berkeley, CA: University of California Press.

Gragg, D. (2007). *A multi-level defense against social engineering.* SANS. Retrieved July 1, 2009, from http://www.sans.org/reading_room/ whitepapers/engineering/920.php

Graham, P. (2002). *A plan for spam*. Retrieved from http://www.paulgraham.com/ spam.html

Grilo, A., Piotrowski, K., Langendoerfer, P., & Casaca, A. (2009). A wireless sensor network architecture for homeland security epplication. In Ruiz & Garcia-Luna-Aceves (Eds.) ADHOC-NOW 2009, (pp. 397-402). Berlin/Heidelberg, Germany: Springer-Verlag.

Grinter, R. E., & Palen, L. (2002). Instant messaging in teen life. *In Proceedings of the 2002 ACM Conference on Computer Supported Cooperative Work* (pp. 21–30). ACM Press.

Grupe, F. (2003). Understanding digital signatures. *The CPA Journal, 73*(6).

Gruschka, N., & Iacono, L.-L. (2009). *Vulnerable cloud: SOAP message security validation revisited.* 2009 IEEE International Conference on Web Services (pp. 625-631).

Gruteser, M., & Grunwald, D. (2003). *Anonymous usage of location-based services through spatial and temporal cloaking.* In *Proceedings of the International Conference on Mobile Systems, Applications, and Services* (MobiSys).

Guimaraes, G., Souto, E., Sadok, D., & Kelner, J. (2005). Evaluation of security mechanisms in wireless sensor networks. *ICW, 5,* 428–433.

Guo, H., Li, Z., Mu, Y., & Zhang, X. (2008). Cryptanalysis of simple three-party key exchange protocol. *Computers & Security, 27,* 16–21. doi:10.1016/j.cose.2008.03.001

Guo, W., Li, Z., Chen, Y., & Zhao, X. (2009). *Security design for instant messaging system based on RSA and triple DES.* In International Conference of Image Analysis and Signal Processing (IASP'09).

Guttman, P. (2010). *The convergence of Internet security threats* (spam, viruses, Trojans, phishing). Retrieved July 10, 2010, from http://www.cs.auckland.ac.nz/ ~pgut001/pubs/blended.pdf

Hämäläinen, P., Kuorilehto, M., Alho, T., Hännikäinen, M., & Hämäläinen, T. D. (2006). Security in wireless sensor networks: Considerations and experiments. In *Embedded computer systems: Architectures, modeling, and simulation* (pp. 167–177). Berlin / Heidelberg, Germany: Springer. doi:10.1007/11796435_18

Hanson, et al. (2009). Body area sensor networks: Challenges and opportunities. IEEE Computer, 58-65.

Hardaker, W. (2006). *Use of SHA-256 in DNSSEC Delegation Signer (DS) Resource Records (RRs). Request for Comments RFC-4509*. Internet Engineering Task Force, Network Working Group.

Härtig, H., Hamann, C.-J., & Roitzsch, M. (2010). *The mathematics of obscurity - on the trustworthiness of open source.* The Ninth Workshop on the Economics of Information Security (WEIS 2010), Cambridge, MA, June 7-8, 2010.

He, L., & Bode, N. (2005). Network penetration testing. *EC2ND 2005, Proceedings of the First European Conference on Computer Network Defense,* (pp. 3-12). UK.

Healy, M., Newe, T., & Lewis, E. (2009). Security for wireless sensor networks: A review. IEEE Sensors Applications Symposium, New Orleans, LA.

Heien, G., & Horrer, M. (1999). *GSM networks, protocols, terminology and implementation.* Norwood, MA: Artech House Inc.

Heinzelman, W. R., Chandrakasan, A., & Balakrishnan, H. (2000). *Energy-efficient communication protocol for wireless microsensor networks.* Paper presented at the 33rd Annual Hawaii International Conference on System Sciences, 2000.

Heller, J. (1955). *Catch-22.* New York, NY: Simon and Schuster.

Hellman, M. (2004, November 22). *Oral history inverview with Martin Hellman.* Transcript, 58pp. (J. R. Yost, Interviewer).

Herbsleb, J. D., Atkins, D. L., Boyer, D. G., Handel, M., & Finholt, T. A. (2002). Introducing instant messaging and chat in the workplace. In *Proceedings of the SIGCHI conference on Human factors in computing systems: Changing our world, changing ourselves* (pp. 171-178). Minneapolis, MN.

Herley, C. (2010). *The plight of the targeted attacker in a world of scale.* The Ninth Workshop on the Economics of Information Security (WEIS 2010), Cambridge, MA, June 7-8, 2010.

Heys, H. M. (2010). *A tutorial on linear and differential cryptanalysis.* Memorial University of Newfoundland. Retrieved on July 10, 2010, from http://www.engr.mun.ca/~howard/ PAPERS/ldc_tutorial.pdf

Hills, R. (2001). Sensing for danger. *Science Technology Review.* Retrieved from http://www.llnl.gov/str/JulAug01/Hills.html

Hindocha, N., & Chien, E. (2003). *Malicious threats and vulnerabilities in instant messaging.* In Virus Bulletin International Conference. Symantec Security Response, Symantec Corporation.

Hjelmvik, E. (2008). Passive network security analysis with NetworkMiner. *Insecure Magazine, 18,* 18-21. Retrieved May 13, 2010, from http://www.net-security.org/dl/insecure/INSECURE-Mag-18.pdf

Holz, T., Marechal, S., & Raynal, F. (2006). New threats and attacks on the World Wide Web. *IEEE Security and Privacy, 4*(2), 72–75. doi:10.1109/MSP.2006.46

Householder, A., Manion, A., Pesante, L., & Weaver, G. M. (2001). *Managing the threat of denial-of-service attacks.* CERT @ Coordination Center, v10.0.

Hu, F., & Sharma, N. K. (2005). Security considerations in ad hoc sensor networks. Elsevier. *Ad Hoc Networks, 3*(1), 69–89. doi:10.1016/j.adhoc.2003.09.009

Huang, G. (2003). Casting the wireless sensor net. *Technology Review, 106*(6), 50–57.

Huang, D., Chen, Z., Guo, Y., & Lee, M. (2007). Quantum secure direct communication based on chaos with authentication. *Journal of the Physical Society of Japan.*

Huang, H., & Cao, Z. (2009). *An ID-based authenticated key exchange protocol based on bilinear Diffie-Hellman problem.* ACM Symposium on Information, Computer & Communication Security (ASIACCS'09), (pp. 333-342).

Huang, H.-F. (2009). A simple three-party password-based key exchange protocol. *International Journal of Communications and Systems.* John Wiley & Sons.

Huerta, Y. A., & Liu, J. (2008). *Enhancing malware detection in an IM environment.* IEEE International Conference on Electro/Information Technology (EIT 2008).

Hupp, M. *(2007).* Protecting patient medical records from the nosy. Retrieved on November 30, 2009 from http://www.bizjournals.com/milwaukee/ stories/2007/11/12/focus3.html?t=printable

IEEE802 Committee. (2006). Part 15.4: Wireless Medium Access Control (MAC) and Physical Layer (PHY) specifications for low-rate Wireless Personal Area Networks (WPANs).

IEEE Computer Society. (1998). IEEE standard for Information Technology–telecommunications and information exchange between systems–local and metropolitan area networks–common specifications part 3: Media Access Control (MAC).

Igure, V., & Williams, R. (2008). Taxonomies of attacks and vulnerabilities in computer systems. *IEEE Communications Surveys and Tutorials, 10*(1), 6–19. doi:10.1109/COMST.2008.4483667

Intanagonwiwat, C., Govindan, R., Estrin, D., Heidemann, J., & Silva, F. (2003). Directed diffusion for wireless sensor networking. *IEEE/ACM Transactions on Networking, 11*(1), 2–16. doi:10.1109/TNET.2002.808417

Intelegen, Inc. (2008). *Human memory*. Retrieved on December 1, 2009 from http://brain.web-us.com/memory/human_memory.htm

ISACA. (2010). *Social media - business benefits and security, governance and assurance perspectives*. ISACA. Retrieved from https://www.isaca.org/Knowledge-Center/Research/ Documents/Social-Media-Wh-Paper-26-May10-Research.pdf

ITIL. (2010). *Official site*. Retrieved March 30, 2010, from http://www.itil-officialsite.com/

ITU-T. (2003). *Security architecture for systems providing end-to-end communications*. (*Recommendation, X,* 805).

ITU-T. (2005). *ITU-T recommendation X.509: Information Technology - open systems interconnection - the directory: Public key and attribute certificate frameworks*. Retrieved December 1, 2009, from http://www.itu.int/rec/T-REC-X.509-200508-I

Jaquith, A. (2007). *Security metrics: Replacing fear, uncertainty, and doubt*. Upper Saddle River, NJ: Addison-Wesley Pearson Education.

Jelasity, M., Montresor, A., Jesi, G. P., & Voulgaris, S. (2003). *PeerSim: A peer-to-peer simulator*. Retrieved from http://peersim.sf.net/

Jeong, I. R., Kwon, J. O., & Lee, D. H. (2008). Strong ID-based key distribution. *IEICE Transactions on Communications. E91-B*(1), 306–308.

Jiang, X., Wang, X., & Xu, D. (2010). Stealthy malware detection and monitoring. [TISSEC]. *ACM Transactions on Information and System Security, 13*(2).

Jing, D., Han, R., & Mishra, S. (2004). *Intrusion tolerance and anti-traffic analysis strategies for wireless sensor networks*. Paper presented at the 2004 International Conference on Dependable Systems and Networks.

Jurik, A., & Weaver, A. (2008). Remote medical monitoring. *Computer,* 96–99. doi:10.1109/MC.2008.133

Kahn, D. (1967). *The codebreakers, the story of secret writing*. New York, NY: Scribner.

Kai, Z., Kui, R., & Wenjing, L. (2005). *Geographic on-demand disjoint multiwpath routing in wireless ad hoc networks*. Paper presented at the Military Communications Conference, 2005. MILCOM 2005. IEEE.

Kamat, P., Zhang, Y., Trappe, W., & Ozturk, C. (2004). Source-location privacy in energy constrained sensor network routing. *Proceedings of the 2004 ACM Workshop on Security of Ad Hoc and Sensor Networks* (SASN).

Kamat, P., Zhang, Y., Trappe, W., & Ozturk, C. (2005). Enhancing source location privacy in sensor network routing. *Proc. of 25th (ICDCS)*, 2005.

Kanaley, R. (2001). Login error trouble keeping track of all your sign-ons? Here's a place to keep your electronic keys, but you better remember the password. *San Jose Mercury News*, 3G.

Kang, L. (2009). *Protecting location privacy in large-scale wireless sensor networks*, IEEE International Conference on Communications, 2009, (pp. 1–6). DOI: 10.1109/ICC.2009.5199372

Kantarcioglu, M., & Clifton, C. (2004). Privacy-preserving distributed mining of association rules on horizontally partitioned data. *Knowledge and Data Engineering IEEE Transaction, 16*(9), 1026–1037. doi:10.1109/TKDE.2004.45

Kanungo, T., Mount, D., Netanyahu, N., Piatko, C., Silverman, R., & Wu, A. (2004). A local search approximation algorithm for k-means clustering. In *Computational geometry: Theory & applications*.

Kargupta, H., Datta, S., Wang, Q., & Sivakumar, K. (2003). *On the privacy preserving properties of random data perturbation techniques*. 3rd Int'l Conference on Data Mining, 2003, (pp. 99–106).

Karlin, S., & Taylor, H. M. (1975). *A first course in stochastic processes* (2nd ed.). Academic Press.

Karlof, C., & Wagner, D. (2003). *Secure routing in wireless sensor networks: Attacks and countermeasures*. Paper presented at the 2003 IEEE International Workshop on Sensor Network Protocols and Applications, 2003.

Karlof, C., et al. (2004). TinySec: A link layer security architecture for wireless sensor networks. Proceedings of 2nd International Conference on Embedded Networked Sensor Systems (SenSys '04), (pp. 162-175).

Karlof, C., Sastry, N., & Wagner, D. (2004). *TinySec: A link layer security architecture for wireless sensor networks.* Paper presented at the 2nd International Conference on Embedded networked sensor systems.

Karp, B., & Kung, H. T. (2000). *GPSR: Greedy perimeter stateless routing for wireless networks.* Paper presented at the 6th Annual International Conference on Mobile computing and networking.

Katz, J., & Lindell, Y. (2008). *Introduction to modern cryptography. Taylor & Francis Group.* LLC.

Kausar, F., & Masood, A. (2006). *A random key distribution scheme for securing wireless sensor network.* Paper presented at the Multitopic Conference, 2006. INMIC '06. IEEE.

Kavitha, T., & Sridharan, D. (2010). Security vulnerabilities in wireless sensor networks: A survey. *Journal of Information Assurance and Security, 5,* 31–44.

Keizer, G. (2005). *IM threats growing 50% per month.* TechWeb.

Keizer, G. (2010). Adobe: We know we're hackers' favorite target. *NetworkWorld.* Retrieved from http://www.networkworld.com/news/2010/060410-adobe-we-know-were-hackers.html?hpg1=bn

Kellerman, T. (2010). Cyber-threat proliferation - today's truly pervasive global epidemic. *IEEE Security & Privacy, 8*(3), 70–73. doi:10.1109/MSP.2010.94

Kephart, J. O., & White, S. R. (1993). Measuring and modeling computer virus prevalence. In *Proceedings of the 14th IEEE Symposium on Security and Privacy.*

Kerner, S. M. (2005). *IM accounts to number in the billions.* InternetNews.com. Retrieved from http://www.internetnews.com/ stats/ article.php/ 3521456

Keromytis, A., Misra, V., & Rubenstein, D. (2002). *SOS: Secure overlay services* (pp. 61–72). ACM SIGCOMM.

Kikuchi, H., Tada, M., & Nakanishi, S. (2004). *Secure instant messaging protocol preserving confidentiality against administrator.* 18th International Conference on Advanced Information Networking and Applications (AINA).

Killalea, T. (2000). *Recommended Internet service provider security services and procedures.* (RFC 3013 2000). Retrieved from http://www.ietf.org/ rfc/ rfc3013.txt.

Kim, H.-S., & Choi, J.-Y. (2009). Enhanced password-based simple three-party key exchange protocol. *Computers & Electrical Engineering, 35,* 107–114. doi:10.1016/j.compeleceng.2008.05.007

Kinalis, A., & Nikoletseas, S. (2007). *Scalable data collection protocols for wireless sensor networks with multiple mobile sinks.* Paper presented at the 40th Annual Simulation Symposium, 2007. ANSS '07.

Kocher, P. C. (1996). Timing attacks on implementations of Diffie-Hellman, RSA, DSS, and other systems. *CRYPTO '96: Proceedings of the 16th Annual International Cryptology Conference on Advances in Cryptology* (pp. 104-113). London, UK: Springer-Verlag.

Kolbitsch, C., Comparetti, P., Kruegel, C., Kirda, E., Zhou, X., & Wang, X. (2009). *Effective and efficient malware detection at the end host.* 18th Usenix Security Symposium, Montreal Canada. August 10-14, 2009.

Komerling, O., & Kuhn, M. G. (1999). Design principles for tamper resistant smartcard processors. Paper presented at USENIX Workshop on Smartcard Technology, Chicago, IL.

Kong, J., & Hong, X. (2003). *ANODR: Anonymous On Demand Routing with Untraceable Routes for Mobile Ad-hoc Networks.* The 4th ACM international symposium on Mobile ad hoc networking & computing, June 2003.

Kong, J., Ji, Z., Wang, W., Gerla, M., Bagrodia, R., & Bhargava, B. (2005). *Low-cost attacks against packet delivery, localization and time synchronization services in under-water sensor networks.*

Korkmaz, T., Gong, C., Sarac, K., & Dykes, S. (2007). Single packet IP traceback in AS-level partial deployment scenario. *International Journal of Security and Networks, 2*(1/2), 95–108. doi:10.1504/IJSN.2007.012828

Kotzanikolaou, P., Mavropodi, R., & Douligeris, C. (2005, 19-21 January). *Secure multipath routing for mobile ad hoc networks.* Paper presented at the Second Annual Conference on Wireless On-demand Network Systems and Services, 2005. WONS 2005.

Kraemer, S., Carayon, P., & Clem, J. (2009). Human and organizational factors in computer and information security: Pathways to vulnerabilities. *Computers & Security, 28*, 509–520. doi:10.1016/j.cose.2009.04.006

Krebs, B. (2010). *Krebs on security blog.* Retrieved from http://krebsonsecurity.com/2010/06/anti-virus-is-a-poor-substitute-for-common-sense/

Kroeker, K. L. (2009). The evolution of virtualization. *Communications of the ACM, 52*(3). doi:10.1145/1467247.1467253

Kumar, A., Goel, P., & Saint-Hilaire, Y. (2009). *Active platform management demystified.* Intel Press.

Kumaraguru, P., Sheng, S., Acquisti, A., Cranor, L., & Hong, J. (2010). Teaching Johnny not to fall for phish. *ACM Transactions on Internet Technology, 10*(2). doi:10.1145/1754393.1754396

Kundur, D., Luh, W., Okorafor, U. N., & Zourntos, T. (2008). Security and privacy for distributed multimedia sensor networks. *Proceedings of the IEEE, 96*(1), 112–130. doi:10.1109/JPROC.2007.909914

Lahmadi, A., & Festor, O. (2009). *SecSip: A stateful firewall for SIP-based networks.* FIP/IEEE International Symposium on Integrated Network Management (IM '09).

Lai, X., & Massey, J. L. (1991). *A proposal for a new block encryption standard.* Springer-Verlag.

Lai, Y. P., & Tai, J. H. (2007). Network security improvement with isolation implementation based on ISO-17799 standard. In *Network-based Information Systems* (pp. 69–78). Springer. doi:10.1007/978-3-540-74573-0_8

Lampson, B. (2009). Usable security: How to get it. *Communications of the ACM, 52*(11). doi:10.1145/1592761.1592773

Lawton, G. (2008). Is it finally time to worry about mobile malware. *IEEE Computer, 41*(5), 12–14.

Leavitt, M. (2005). Instant messaging: A new target for hackers. *Journal of Computers, 38*(7).

Lee, B., Woo, W.-K., Yeo, C.-K., Lim, T.-M., Lim, B.-H., He, Y., & Song, J. (2004). Secure communications between bandwidth brokers. *Operating Systems Review, 38*(1), 43–57. doi:10.1145/974104.974109

Lee, S. J., & Gerla, M. (2000). *AODV-BR: Backup routing in ad hoc networks.* Paper presented at the Wireless Communications and Networking Conference, 2000. WCNC. 2000 IEEE.

Li, M., Lou, W., & Ren, K. (2010). Data security and privacy in wireless body area networks. IEEE Wireless Communications, 51-58.

Li, T., Wu, H., Wang, X., & Bao, F. (2005). SenSec: Sensor security framework for TinyOS. Proceedings of 2nd International Workshop on Networked Sensing Systems (INSS'05), San Diego, CA.

Lindell, Y., & Pinkas, B. (2002). Privacy preserving data mining. *Journal of Cryptology, 15*(3). doi:10.1007/s00145-001-0019-2

Litan, A. (2009). *Where strong authentication fails and what you can do about it.* Gartner. Retrieved from http://www.gartner.com/DisplayDocument?ref=clientFriendlyUrl&id=1245013

Liu, F., Wu, C., & Lin, X. (2010). Some extensions on threshold visual cryptography schemes. *The Computer Journal, 53*(1), 107–119. doi:10.1093/comjnl/bxn072

Liu, D., & Ning, P. (2003). Location-based pairwise key establishments for relatively static sensor networks. Proceedings of 2003 ACM Workshop Security of Ad Hoc and sensor networks (SASN'03), Fairfax, USA.

Liu, D., Ning, P., & Du, W. (2005). Group-based key predistribution in wireless sensor networks. *Proceedings of the 4th ACM Workshop on Wireless security (WiSE'05)*, (pp. 11-20).

Liu, J., Cheng, X.-G., & Wang, X.-M. (2006). *Methods to forge ElGamal signatures and determine secret key.* 20th International Conference on Advanced Information Networking and Applications, 2006. AINA 2006 (pp. 859-862).

Liu, Z., & Lee, D. (2007). *Coping with instant messaging worms - statistical modeling and analysis.* Local & Metropolitan Area Networks. LANMAN 2007. 15th IEEE Workshop.

Liu, Z., Lin, W., Li, N., & Lee, D. (2005). *Detecting and filtering instant messaging spam - a global and also personalized approach.* First Workshop on Secure Network Protocols (NPSec).

Liu, Z., Shu, G., Li, N., & Lee, D. (2006). *Defending against instant messaging worms.* IEEE Globecom 2006.

Loh, P., & Tan, Y. (2007). A constrained multipath routing protocol for wireless sensor networks. *Embedded and Ubiquitous Computing,* 661-670.

Longley, D., Branagan, M., Caelli, W. J., & Kwok, L. F. (2008). Feasibility of automated information security compliance auditing. *Proceedings of the IFIP TC 11 23rd International Information Security Conference,* (pp. 493–507).

Lopez, J., & Zhou, J. (2008). *Wireless sensor network security.* Amsterdam, The Netherlands: IOS press.

Lopez, J., & Zhou, J. (2008). *Wireless sensor network security.* IOS Press.

Lou, W., Liu, W., & Fang, Y. (2004). *SPREAD: Enhancing data confidentiality in mobile ad hoc networks.*

Lu, R., & Cao, Z. (2007). Simple three-party key exchange protocol. *Computers & Security, 26,* 94–97. doi:10.1016/j.cose.2006.08.005

Lu, G., Krishnamachari, B., & Raghavendra, C. (2007). An adaptive energy-efficient and low-latency MAC for tree-based data gathering in sensor networks. *Wireless Communications and Mobile Computing, 7*(7), 863–876. doi:10.1002/wcm.503

Luk, M., Mezzour, G., Perrig, A., & Gligor, V. (2007). MiniSec: A secure sensor network communication architecture. IEEE International Conference on Information Processing in sensor networks (IPSN'07), Cambridge, MA.

MacLeod, C. (2007). One of today's most overlooked security threats—six ways auditors can fight it. *ISACA Journal, 5.* Retrieved from http://www.isaca.org/Journal/Past-Issues/2007/ Volume-5/Pages/JOnline-One-of-Todays-Most- Overlooked-Security-Threats-Six-Ways-Auditors-Can-Fight-It.aspx

Madden, S., Franklin, M., Hellerstein, J., & Hong, W. (2002). *Tag: A tiny aggregation service for ad-hoc sensor networks.*

Malan, D. J., et al. (2004). A public-key infrastructure for key distribution in TinyOS based on elliptic curve cryptography. Proceedings of 1st IEEE International Conference on Sensor and Ad Hoc Communication Networks (SECON'04), Santa Clara, CA.

Manber, U. (1994). Finding similar files in a large file system. In *Proceedings of Winter USENIX Conference.*

Mannan, M., & Oorschot, P. C. van. (2006). A protocol for secure public instant messaging. *Proc. of the Financial Cryptography and Data Security* 2006.

Mannan, M., & van Oorschot, P. C. (2004). Secure public instant messaging: A survey. In *Proceedings of the 2nd Annual Conference on Privacy, Security and Trust* (PST).

Mannan, M., & van Oorschot, P. C. (2005). On instant messaging worms, analysis and countermeasures. *Proceedings ACM Workshop on Rapid Malcode* (WORM'05).

Marti, S., Giuli, T., Lai, K., & Baker, M. (2000). *Mitigating routing misbehavior in mobile ad hoc networks.*

Marti-Farre, J. (2007). A note on secret sharing schemes with three homogeneous access structure. *Information Processing Letters, 102*(4), 133–137. doi:10.1016/j.ipl.2006.08.016

Mason, A. G., & Newcomb, M. J. (2001). *Cisco secure Internet security solutions.* Indianapolis, IN: Cisco Press.

Mathis, F. H. (1991). A generalized birthday problem. *SIAM Review,* 265–270. doi:10.1137/1033051

McClure, S., Scambray, J., & Kurz, G. (2009). *Hacking exposed: Network security secrets and solutions* (6th ed.). New York, NY: McGraw Hill.

McDougal, M. (2009). *Castle warrior - redefining 21st century network defense*. 5th Annual Workshop on Cyber Security and Information Intelligence Research: Cyber Security and Information Intelligence Challenges and Strategies. Oak Ridge, Tennessee, April 13-15, 2009

McGee, A. R., Vasireddy, S. R., Xie, C., Picklesimer, D. D., Chandrashekhar, U., & Richman, S. H. (2004). A framework for ensuring network security. *Bell Labs Technical Journal*, 8(4), 7–27. doi:10.1002/bltj.10083

McGlasson, L. (2010). *Account takeover: The new wrinkle - fraudsters disable email verification service in CA scam*. Retrieved from http://www.bankinfosecurity.com/ articles.php?art_id=2728

Mckinney, E. H. (1966). Generalized birthday problem. *The American Mathematical Monthly*, 385–387. doi:10.2307/2315408

McMillan, R. (2010). After Google hack, warnings pop up in SEC filings. *ComputerWorld*. Retrieved from http://www.computerworld.com/s/article/9177845/After_Google_hack_warnings_pop_up_in_SEC_filings

Meiyuan, Z. (2009). Centralized trust management for securing community networks. *Intel Technology Journal, 13*(2).

Menezes, A. J., Vanstone, S. A., & Oorschot, P. C. (1996). *Handbook of applied cryptography*. Boca Raton, FL: CRC Press, Inc.

Menezes, A., Qu, M., & Vanstone, S. (1995). *Some new key agreement protocols providing mutual implicit authentication*. Second Workshop on Selected Areas in Cryptography (SAC 95), (pp. 22-32).

Merwe, J., Dawoud, D., & McDonald, S. (2007). A survey on peer-to-peer key management for mobile ad hoc networks. *ACM Computing Surveys, 39*(1), 1–45. doi:10.1145/1216370.1216371

Metke, A. R., & Ekl, R. L. (2010). Security technology for smart Grid networks. IEEE Transactions on smart grid, 1(1), 99-107.

Metzger, J., Schillo, M., & Fischer, K. (2003). A multi-agent-based peer-to-peer network in java for distributed spam filtering. In *Proc. of the 3rd CEEMAS*, Czech Republic.

MICA2. (2010). *Crossbow MICA2 wireless measurement system data sheet*. Retrieved from http://www.xbow.com/products/Product_pdf_files/Wireless_pdf/MICA2_Datasheet.pdf

Mills, E. (2009). Cybercrime cost $1 trillion last year, study. *ZDNet*. Retrieved from http://www.zdnet.com/news/cybercrime-cost-1-trillion-last-year-study/264762

Mirkovic, J., Prier, G., & Reiher, P. (2002). Attacking DDoS at the source. In *Proceedings of ICNP*.

Moody, J. (2001). Peer influence groups: Identifying dense clusters in large network. *Social Networks, 23*(4), 261–283. doi:10.1016/S0378-8733(01)00042-9

Moore, D., Shannon, C., Voelker, G. M., & Savage, S. (2003). *Internet quarantine: Requirements for containing self-propagating code*. INFOCOM 2003. 22nd IEEE International Conference on Computer Communications.

Morse, C. D., & Wang, H. (2005). *The structure of an instant messenger network and its vulnerability to malicious codes*. SIGCOMM poster.

Mpitziopoulos, A., & Gavalas, D. (2009). An effective defensive node against jamming attacks in sensor networks. *Security and Communication Networks, 2*(2), 145–163. doi:10.1002/sec.81

MSNShell. (n.d.). *Personalized MSN*. Retrieved from http://www.msnshell.net/ en/ index.html

Muraleedharan, R., & Osadciw, L. (2006). *Jamming attack detection and countermeasures in wireless sensor network using ant system*. Orlando: SPIE Defence and Security.

Nachreiner, C. (2009). Anatomy of an ARP poisoning attack. *WatchGuard Network Security Analyst*. Retrieved March 2010 from http://www.watchguard.com/infocenter/editorial/135324.asp

Nam, J. (2007). Security weakness in a three-party pairing-based protocol for password authenticated key exchange. *Information Sciences, 177*(6), 1364–1375. doi:10.1016/j.ins.2006.09.001

National Institute of Standards and Technology (NIST). (2007). Chapter 20: Assessing and mitigating risks to a hypothetical computer system. *Special Publication 800-12 – an introduction to computer security – the NIST handbook*. Retrieved from http://csrc.nist.gov/publications/ nistpubs/800-12/800-12-html/index.html

NBS FIPS PUB 46. (1977). *Data encryption standard.* National Bureau of Standards, US Department of Commerce, 1977.

NCSA. (2009). *October 2009 NCSA / Symantec small business study.* Retrieved March 2010 from http://staysafeonline.mediaroom.com/index.php?s=43&item=51

Nessus. (n.d.). *Website.* Retrieved March 30, 2010, from http://www.nessus.org/nessus/

Newsome, J., et al. (2004). The Sybil attack in sensor networks: Analysis and defenses. Proceedings of 3rd International Symposium on Information processing in sensor networks, ACM Press.

NIST SP 800-37. (2010). *Major revisions.* Retrieved July 27, 2010, from www.onpointcorp.com/documents/NIST_SP_800-37.pdf

NIST. (1999, October 25). Data encryption standard. *FIPS PUB 46-3.*

NIST. (2010). Report to NIST on smart Grid cyber security strategy and requirements. Retrieved from http://csrc.nist.gov/publications/drafts/nistir-7628/draft-nistir-7628_2nd-public-draft.pdf

NIST-Continuous Monitoring. (2010). *Frequently asked questions.*

Nixon Peabody. (2009). *Health law alert.* Retrieved on November 15, 2009 from http://www.nixonpeabody.com/publications_detail3.asp?ID=2621

Nmap. (n.d.). *Website.* Retrieved March 30, 2010, from http://nmap.org/

NoScript. (n.d.). *JavaScript/Java/Flash blocker for a safer Firefox.* Retrieved from http://noscript.net/

NSSLabs. (2010). *Vulnerability-based protection and the Google "Operation Aurora" attack.* Retrieved from http://nsslabs.com/test-reports/NSSLabs_Vulnerability-based%20Protection-Google-EPPv14.pdf

NY-OCS. (2010). *Application security procurement language.* Office of Cyber Security, State of New York. http://www.cscic.state.ny.us/ resources/aspl.cfm

OECD, Organization for Economic and Co-operative Development. (2009). *Computer viruses and other malicious software a threat to the Internet economy.* Retrieved from http://www.oecd.org/document/16/0,3343,en_2649_34223_42276816_1_1_1_37441,00.html

Office of Privacy Commissioner. Australian Government. (n.d.). *Privacy information.* Retrieved from http://www.privacy.gov.au/index.php

Ohki, E., Harada, Y., Kawaguchi, S., et al. (2009). Information security governance framework. *WISG '09, Proceedings of the first ACM workshop on Information Security governance,* Chicago, Illinois, USA.

Orebaugh, A. (2006). An instant messaging intrusion detection system framework: Using character frequency analysis for authorship identification and validation. *Proceedings 2006 40th Annual IEEE International Carnahan Conferences Security Technology.*

Osanacek, P. (2009). *Towards security issues in ZigBee architecture.* Springer.

OTR. (2004). *Off the record messaging.* Retrieved from http://www.cypherpunks.ca/otr/

Otsuka, A., Shigetomi, R., & Imai, H. (2006). *Lightweight privacy for ubiquitous devices.* IEEE International Conference on Systems, Man and Cybernetics, 2006 (SMC '06), vol. 2, (pp. 1233-1237). ISBN: 1-4244-0099-6

Otto, C., Milenkovic, A., Sanders, C., & Jovanov, E. (2006). System architecture of a wireless body area sensor network for ubiquitous health monitoring. *Journal of Mobile Multimedia, 1*(4), 307–326.

Padmavathi, G., & Shanmugapriya, M. (2009). *A survey of attacks, security mechanisms and challenges in wireless sensor networks.*

Paggen, C., & Vyncke, E. (2007). *LAN switch security: What hackers know about your switches.* Indianapolis, IN: Cisco Press.

Pajek. (2005). Program for large network analysis. Retrieved from http://vlado.fmf.uni-lj.si/ pub/ networks/ pajek/

Park, E. C., & Blake, I. F. (2007). *Reducing communication overhead of key distribution schemes for wireless sensor networks.* Paper presented at the 16th International Conference on Computer Communications and Networks, 2007. ICCCN 2007.

Park, K., & Lee, H. (2001). On the effectiveness of route-based packet filtering for distributed DoS attack prevention in power-law Internets. In *Proceedings of ACM SIGCOMM.*

Parno, B., Perrig, A., & Gligor, V. (2005). Distributed detection of node replication attacks in sensor networks. Proceedings of IEEE Symposium on Security and Privacy, Oakland, CA.

Passerini, E., Paleari, R., & Martignoni, L. (2009). How good are malware detectors at remediating infected systems? In *Proceedings of the 6th Conference on Detection of Intrusions and Malware & Vulnerability Assessment, DIMVA,* Como, Italy, Lecture Notes in Computer Science. Springer, July 2009

Peersim. (n.d.). *Peer-to-peer simulator.* Retrieved from http://peersim.sourceforge.net/

Perez, A. (2000). *Response to ten risks of PKI.* Retrieved December 1, 2009, from http://homepage.mac.com/aramperez/ responsetenrisks.html

Perrig, A., Szewczyk, R., Tygar, J. D., Wen, V., & Culler, D. E. (2002). SPINS: Security Protocols for Sensor Networks. *Wireless Networks, 8*(5), 521–534. doi:10.1023/A:1016598314198

Perrig, A. (2002). SPINS: Security Protocols for Sensor Networks. *ACM Wireless Networks, 8*(5), 521–534. doi:10.1023/A:1016598314198

Perrig, A., Stankovic, J., & Wagner, D. (2004). Security in wireless sensor networks. *Communications of the ACM, 47*(6), 53–57. doi:10.1145/990680.990707

Perrig, A., Song, D., & Tygar, J. D. (2001). ELK: A new protocol for efficient large group key distribution. *Proceedings of the 2001 IEEE Symposium on Security and Privacy,* (p. 247).

Pfleeger, C. P., & Pfleeger, S. L. (2007). *Security in computing* (4th ed.). Prentice Hall.

Phan, R. C. W., Yau, W.-C., & Gol, B. M. (2008). Cryptanalysis of simple three-party key exchange protocol (S-3PAKE). *Information Science, 178,* 2849–2856. doi:10.1016/j.ins.2008.02.008

Phan, T., & Yao, D. F. (2009). *SelectAudit: A secure and efficient audit framework for networked virtual environments. Lecture Notes of the Institute for Computer Sciences, Social Informatics and Telecommunications Engineering LNICST 10, Collaborative Computing: Networking.* Applications and Worksharing.

Phoha, S., LaPorta, T., & Griffin, C. (2007). *Sensor network operations.* John Wiley & Sons, Inc.

Pidgin-Encryption. (2003). *Pidgin plugins.* Retrieved from http://pidgin-encrypt.sourceforge.net/

Pietro, R. D., Mancini, L. V., & Mei, A. (2006). Energy efficient node-to-node authentication and communication confidentiality in wireless sensor networks. *Wireless Networks, 12*(6), 709–721. doi:10.1007/s11276-006-6530-5

Planetlab. (2010). Retrieved from http://www.planet-lab.org/

Pond, R., Podd, J., Bunnell, J., & Henderson, R. (2000). Word association computer passwords: The effect of formulation techniques on recall and guessing rates. *Computers & Security, 19,* 645–656. doi:10.1016/S0167-4048(00)07023-1

Potter, B. (2010). Thinking operationally. *IEEE Security and Privacy, 8*(3), 54–55. doi:10.1109/MSP.2010.109

Pottie, G. J., & Kaiser, W. J. (2000). Wireless integrated network sensors. *Communications of the ACM, 43*(5), 51–58. doi:10.1145/332833.332838

Public Sector Information Sheets. (2008). *Information privacy principles.* Office of Privacy Commissioner, Australian Government.

PwC. (2010). *Protecting your business - security awareness - turning your people into your first line of defence.* Price Waterhouse Coopers. Retrieved from http://www.pwc.co.uk/eng/publications/ protecting_your_business_security_awareness.html

QBone Signaling Design Team. (2002). *Final report.* Retrieved from http://qos.internet2.edu/wg/documents-informational/ 20020709-chimento-etal-qbone-signaling/

Qubes, O. S. (2010). *The QubesOs Project*. Retrieved from http://qubes-os.org/Home.html

Rabin, M. O. (1979). *Digitalized signatures and public key function as intractable as factorizations*. Cambridge, MA: Massachusetts Institute of Technology Press.

Ranum, M., & Schneier, B. (2007). Bruce Schneier and Marcus Ranum debate the necessity of penetration tests. *Information Security Magazine.* Retrieved March 2010 from http://searchsecurity.techtarget.com/magazineFeature/ 0,296894,sid14_gci1256987_mem1,00.html

Raymond, D., Marchany, R., Brownfield, M., & Midkiff, S. (2006). *Effects of denial of sleep attacks on wireless sensor network MAC protocols.* Paper presented at the Information Assurance Workshop, 2006 IEEE.

Rebahi, Y., Sisalem, D., & Magedanz, T. (2006). *SIP spam detection*. International Conference on Digital Telecommunications (ICDT '06).

RedSeal. (2010). *FISMA, continuous monitoring and near real-time risk management, complying with the new NIST risk management framework*. Retrieved July 28, 2010, from http://www.redseal.net/documents/RedSeal_and_the_NIST_Risk_Management_Framework.pdf

Reed, M. G., Syverson, P. F., & Goldschlag, D. M. (1998). Anonymous connections and onion routing. *IEEE Journal on Selected Areas in Communications, 16*(4), 482–494. doi:10.1109/49.668972

Reiter, M. K., & Rubin, A. D. (1998). Crowds anonymity for Web transactions. *ACM Transactions on Information and System Security, 1*(1), 66–92. doi:10.1145/290163.290168

Rescorla, E. (2000). *HTTP over TLS.* Retrieved December 1, 2009, from http://www.ietf.org/rfc/rfc2818.txt

Richardson, R. (2008). *2008 CSI computer crime and security survey* (pp. 14–15). Computer Security Institute.

Rivest, R. (1992). *The MD5 message-digest algorithm*. United States: RFC Editor.

Rivest, R., Shamir, A., & Adleman, L. (1978). A method for obtaining digital signatures and public key cryptosystems. *Communications of the ACM, 21*(2), 120–126. doi:10.1145/359340.359342

Rivest, R. L. (1994). The RC5 encryption algorithm. *Proceedings of the Second International Workshop on Fast Software Encryption*, (pp. 86-96).

Rivest, R. L. (1998, August). The RC6 block cipher. *MIT Laboratory for Computer Science*.

Roman, R., Alcaraz, C., & Lopez, J. (2007). A survey of cryptographic primitives and implementations for hardware-constrained sensor network nodes. *Mobile Networks and Applications, 12*(4), 231–244. doi:10.1007/s11036-007-0024-2

Romer, K., Mattern, F., & Zurich, E. (2004). The design space of wireless sensor networks. *Wireless Communications, 11*(6), 54–61. doi:10.1109/MWC.2004.1368897

Sabbah, E., Majeed, A., Kang, K., Liu, K., & Abu-Ghazaleh, N. (2006). *An application-driven perspective on wireless sensor network security*.

SafeNet. (2009). *History.* Retrieved October 20, 2009, from http://www.safenet-inc.com/About_SafeNet/The_Company/History.aspx

Sahami, M., Dumais, S., Heckerman, D., & Horvitz, E. (1998). *A Bayesian approach to filtering junk e-mail, learning for text categorization*. AAAI Workshop on Learning for Text Categorization, Madison, Wisconsin.

Saint-Andre, P. (Ed.). (2004a). *RFC 3920: Extensible messaging and presence protocol (XMPP): Core*. Jabber Software Foundation.

Saint-Andre, P. (Ed.). (2004b). *RFC 3921: Extensible messaging and presence protocol (XMPP): Instant messaging and presence*. Jabber Software Foundation.

Sandboxie. (n.d.). *Sandbox security software for Windows*. Retrieved from www.sandboxie.com

Sander, V. (2000). *The security environment of SIBBS*. Retrieved from http://qbone.internet2.edu/bb/SIBBS-SEC.doc

SANs Institute. (n.d.). *Website.* Retrieved March 30, 2010, from http://www.sans.org

Sastry, N., & Wagner, D. (2004). Security considerations for IEEE 802.15.4 networks. ACM Workshop on Wireless Security (Wise'04), (pp. 32–42).

Savage, S., Wetherall, D., Karlin, A. R., & Anderson, T. (2001). Network support for IP traceback. *IEEE/ACM Transactions on Networking, 9*(3), 226–237. doi:10.1109/90.929847

Sayana, S. A. (2003). Approach to auditing network security. *Information Systems Control Journal, 5.*

Sayrafiezadeh, M. (1994). The birthday problem revisited. *Mathematics Magazine,* 220–223. doi:10.2307/2690615

Schmitt-Manderbach, T., Weier, H., Furst, M., Ursin, R., Tiefenbacher, F., & Scheidl, T. (2007). Experimental demonstration of free-space decoy-state quantum key distribution over 144 km. *Physical Review Letters, 98.*

Schneier, B. (1995). *Applied cryptography.* New York, NY: John Wiley & Sons, Inc.

Schneier, B. (2000). *Secrets & lies: Digital security in a networked world.* John Wiley & Sons, Inc.

Schneier, B. (1994). *Description of a new variable-length key, 64-bit block cipher (Blowfish).* Retrieved December 11, 2009, from http://www.schneier.com/paper-blowfish-fse.html

Schuba, C., Krsul, I., Kuhn, M., & Spafford, E. (1997). *Analysis of a denial of service attack on TCP.* IEEE Symposium on Security and Privacy.

Schumacher, B. (1995). Quantum coding. *Physical Review A.,* 2738–2747. doi:10.1103/PhysRevA.51.2738

Scupelli, P., Kiesler, S., Fussell, S. R., & Chen, C. (2005). *Project view IM: A tool for juggling multiple projects and teams.* In Conference on Human Factors in Computing Systems. Portland, OR

Seah, W., & Tan, H. (2006). *Multipath virtual sink architecture for wireless sensor networks in harsh environments.*

Secunia. (2008a). *2008 report.* Secunia. Retrieved from http://secunia.com/gfx/Secunia2008Report.pdf

Secunia. (2008b). *Internet security suite test October 2008.* Secunia. Retrieved from http://secunia.com/gfx/Secunia_ Exploit-vs-AV_test-Oct-2008.pdf

Secunia. (2010). *Secunia half year report 2010.* Secunia. Retrieved from http://secunia.com/gfx/pdf/Secunia_ Half_Year_Report_2010.pdf

See, C. H., Abd-Alhameed, R. A., Hu, Y. F., & Horosh-enkov, K. V. (2008). *Wireless sensor transmission range measurement within the ground level.* Paper presented at the Antennas and Propagation Conference, 2008. LAPC 2008. Loughborough.

Sellke, S., Shroff, N. B., & Bagchi, S. (2005). Modeling and automated containment of worms. In *Proceeding of International Conference on Dependable Systems and Networks* (DSN).

Serazzi, G., & Zanero, S. (2003). *Computer virus propagation models.* Tutorials of the 11th IEEE/ACM Int'l Symp. on Modeling, Analysis and Simulation of Computer and Telecom.

Shaikh, R., Lee, S., Khan, M., & Song, Y. (2006). LSec: Lightweight Security Protocol for Distributed Wireless Sensor Network. *Personal Wireless Communications,* 367-377.

Shamir, A. (1979). How to share a secret. *Communications of the ACM, 22,* 612–613. doi:10.1145/359168.359176

Shamir, A., Rivest, R. L., & Adleman, L. (1978). A method for obtaining digital signatures. *Communications of the ACM, 21*(2), 120–126. doi:10.1145/359340.359342

Shamir, A. (1984). Identity-based cryptosystems and signature schemes. *Advances in Cryptology: Proceedings of CRYPTO 84,* (LNCS 196, pp. 47-53). Springer-Verlag.

Sheldon, T. (2001). *Encyclopedia of networking and communications.* Osborne/McGraw-Hill.

Shi, E., & Perrig, A. (2004). Designing secure sensor networks. *IEEE Wireless Communications Magazine, 11*(6), 38–43. doi:10.1109/MWC.2004.1368895

Shor, P. W. (1999). Polynomial-time algorithms for prime factorization and discrete logarithms on a quantum computer. *SIAM Journal on Computing,* 303–332.

Simpson, R. L. (2002). Chicago. *Nursing Management, 33*(12), 46–48. doi:10.1097/00006247-200212000-00017

Skoudis, E., & Liston, T. (2006). *Counter hack reloaded, a step-by-step guide to computer attacks and effective defenses.* Prentice Hall.

Smith, A., & Toppel, N. (2009). *Case study - using security awareness to combat the advanced persistent threat*. 13th Colloquium for Information Systems Security Education (CISSE), June 1-3, 2009.

Smith, R. D. (2005). *Instant messaging as a scale-free network*. Retrieved from http://arxiv.org/ abs/ cond-mat/ 0206378

Snoeren, A., Partridge, C., Sanchez, L., Jones, C., Tchakountio, F., & Schwartz, B. (2002). Single packet IP traceback. *IEEE/ACM Transactions on Networking, 10*(6), 721–734. doi:10.1109/TNET.2002.804827

Solms, B. V. (2005). Information security governance: COBIT or ISO 17799 or both? *Computers & Security, 24*, 99–104. doi:10.1016/j.cose.2005.02.002

Sooyeon, K., Son, S. H., Stankovic, J. A., & Yanghee, C. (2004). Data dissemination over wireless sensor networks. *Communications Letters, IEEE, 8*(9), 561–563. doi:10.1109/LCOMM.2004.833810

Sophos. (2009a). *Security threat report: 2009*. Retrieved from http://www.sophos.com/sophos/docs/eng/ marketing_material/sophos-security-threat-report-jan-2009-na. pdf

Srinivasan, A., & Wu, J. (2007). A survey on secure localization in wireless sensor networks. In *Encyclopedia of wireless and mobile communications*.

Stajano, F., & Anderson, R. (2000). *The resurrecting duckling: Security issues for ad-hoc wireless networks.* (*LNCS, 1796,* 172–182).

Stallings, W. (2006). *Cryptography and network security: Principles and practice*. Prentice Hall.

Staniford, S. (2003). Containment of scanning worms in enterprise networks. *Journal of Computer Security*.

Steinberg, U., & Kauer, B. (2010). *NOVA-a microhypervisor-based secure virtualization architecture*. EuroSys 2010 Conference. April 13–16, 2010, Paris, France.

Sternberg, G. (2010). The psychology behind security. *ISSA Journal*, April 2010. Retrieved from http://www.issa. org/Library/Journals/2010/ April/ISSA%20Journal%20 April%202010.pdf

Stone, R. (2000). CenterTrack: An IP overlay network for tracking DoS floods. In *Proceedings of the USENIX Security Symposium*.

Stroustrup, B. (2010). What should we teach new software developers & why. *Communications of the ACM, 53*(1), 40–42. doi:10.1145/1629175.1629192

Sun, H., Hsu, S., & Chen, C. (2007). *Mobile jamming attack and its countermeasure in wireless sensor networks.*

Symantec. (2010). *Internet security threat report*. Retrieved from http://www.symantec.com/business/ theme. jsp?themeid=threatreport

Tartary, C., Pieprzyk, J., & Wang, H. (2008). Verifiable multi-secret sharing schemes for multiple threshold access structures. *International Conference on Information Security and Cryptology (Inscrypt 2007)*, (LNCS 4990, pp. 167-181).

Telenable Security. (2010). *PVS - Passive Vulnerability Scanner*. Retrieved March 30, 2010, from http://www. tenablesecurity.com/products/pvs/

The Institute of Internal Auditor (IIA). (2005). *Continuous auditing: Implications for assurance, monitoring, and risk assessment*. Retrieved July 25, 2010, from www.acl.com/ pdfs/wp_gtag_may05.pdf

Thommes, R., & Coates, M. (2006). *Epidemiological modeling of peer-to-peer viruses and pollution*. INFOCOM 2006. 25th IEEE International Conference on Computer Communications.

Thompson, S. T. (2006). Helping the Hacker? Library Information, Security, and Social Engineering. *Information Technology and Libraries, 25*(4), 222–226.

Thornburgh, T. (2004). Social engineering: The dark art. *Proceedings of the 1st Annual Conference on Information Security Curriculum Development*, Kennesaw State University, Kennesaw, GA, September 2004.

Tiny, O. S. (2010). *TinyOS is an open-source operating system designed for wireless embedded sensor networks*. Retrieved from http://www.tinyos.net

TinyOS documentation. (2010). Retrieved from http:// docs.tinyos.net

TinySec on MicaZ. (2008). Retrieved from http://www. cl.cam.ac.uk/research/security/sensornets/tinysec/

Trillian. (2002). *Home page*. Retrieved from http://www. trillian.im/

Trivedi, A. J., Judge, P. Q., & Krasser, S. (2007). Analyzing network and content characteristics of SPIM using honeypots. In *Proceedings of the 3rd USENIX SRUTI*, Santa Clara, CA.

Tulloch, M. (2006). *DHCP server security*. Retrieved March 2010 from http://www.windowsecurity.com/ articles/DHCP-Security-Part1.html

Uluagac, A., Lee, C., Beyah, R., & Copeland, J. (2008). Designing secure protocols for wireless sensor networks. In *Wireless algorithms, systems, and applications* (pp. 503-514).

Undercoffer, J., et al. (2002). Security for sensor networks. Paper presented at CADIP Research Symposium, Baltimore, MD.

UNODC. (2010). *The globalization of crime: A transnational organized crime threat assessment*. United Nations Office on Drugs and Crime, 2010. Retrieved from http://www.unodc.org/unodc/en/ data-and-analysis/ tocta-2010.html

Urushidani, S., Fukuda, K., Ji, Y., Abe, S., Koibuchi, M., Nakamura, M., et al. Shiomoto, K. (2008). *Resource allocation and provision for bandwidth/networks on demand in SINET3*. IEEE Network Operations and Management Symposium Workshops, April 2008, Salvador da Bahia, Brazil.

US Department of Health and Human Services. (2009). *Protecting the privacy of patients' health information*. Retrieved on November 12, 2009 from http://www.hhs. gov/news/facts/privacy.html

US-DOJ. (2010). *US v. Albert Gonzalez*. US Department of Justice. Retrieved from http://www.usdoj.gov/usao/nj/ press/ press/files/pdffiles/GonzIndictment.pdf

US-SEC. (2010). *Heartland payment systems reports first quarter results*. US Securities and Exchange Commission. Retrieved from http://www.sec.gov/Archives/ edgar/ data/1144354/000119312510109892/dex991.htm

Utimaco. (2009). *Health IT data breaches: No harm, no foul*. Retrieved on November 12, 2009 from http:// compliance.utimaco.com/na/tag/hitech-act

Vaidya, J., Clifton, C., & Zhu, M. (2006). *Privacy preserving data mining*. Springer. Xiong, P., Zhang, W., & Shen, F. (2008). *A novel solution for protecting privacy in ad hoc network*. International Conference on Advanced Language Processing and Web Information Technology, 2008. ALPIT '08, 23-25, (pp. 404–411).

Vasarhelyi, M. A., & Halper, F. B. (1991). The continuous audit of online systems. *Auditing: A Journal of Practice and Theory, 10*(1), 110-125.

Venkatasubramanian, K. K., & Gupta, S. K. S. (2007). Security solutions for pervasive healthcare. In Xiao, Y. (Ed.), *Security in distributed, Grid, mobile, and pervasive computing* (pp. 443–464).

Verizon. (2009). *Data breach investigations report*. Verizon Business Security Solutions. Retrieved from http://www.verizonbusiness.com/resources/ security/ reports/2009_databreach_rp.pdf

Vladimirov, A. A. (2006). *Hacking exposed Cisco Networks – Cisco security secrets and solutions*. Emeryville, CA: McGraw-Hill.

Waldvogel, M., Caronni, G., Sun, D., Weiler, N., & Plattner, B. (1999). The VersaKey framework: Versatile group key management. [Special Issue on Middleware]. *IEEE Journal on Selected Areas in Communications, 17*(9), 1614–1631. doi:10.1109/49.790485

Walters, J. (2006). Wireless sensor network security: A survey. In Xiao, Y. (Ed.), *Security in distributed, Grid, mobile, and pervasive computing*. CRC Press.

Wan, C.-Y., Eisenman, S. B., & Campbell, A. T. (2003). *CODA: Congestion detection and avoidance in sensor networks*. Paper presented at the 1st International Conference on Embedded networked sensor systems.

Wang, X., & Yu, H. (2005). *How to break MD5 and other hash functions. EUROCRYPT* (pp. 19–35). Berlin/ Heidelberg, Germany: Springer.

Wang, L., & Wu, C. (2006). *Authenticated group key agreement for multicast*. Cryptology and Network Security (CANS2006), ([]. Springer-Verlag.]. *LNCS, 4301*, 55–72.

Wang, S., Cao, Z., Choo, K.-K. R., & Wang, L. (2009). An improved identity-based key agreement protocol and its security proof. *Information Sciences*, *179*(3), 307–318. doi:10.1016/j.ins.2008.09.020

Wang, Y., Attebury, G., & Ramamurthy, B. (2006). A survey of security issues in wireless sensor networks. *IEEE Communications Surveys and Tutorials*, *8*(2), 2–23. doi:10.1109/COMST.2006.315852

Wang, Q. (2009). Dependable and secure sensor data storage with dynamic integrity assurance. *Proceedings - IEEE INFOCOM*, *09*, 954–962.

Wang, D., Li, X., & Yi, F. (2008). *Probabilistic (n, n) visual secret sharing scheme for grayscale images.* International Conference on Information Security and Cryptology (Inscrypt 2007), (LNCS 4990, pp. 192-200).

Wang, L., & Kulkarni, S. (2006). *Authentication in reprogramming of sensor networks for mote class adversaries.*

Wang, L., Singhal, A., & Jajodia, S. (2007). Toward measuring network security using attack graphs. *Proceedings of the 3rd International Workshop on Quality of Protection.*

Wang, X., Feng, D., Lai, X., & Yu, H. (2004). *Collisions for hash functions MD4, MD5, HAVAL-128 and RIPEMD.* Cryptology ePrint Archive, Report 2004/199.

Watro, R., et al. (2004). TinyPK: Securing sensor networks with public key technology. Proceedings of 2nd ACM Workshop on Security of Ad Hoc and Sensor Networks (SASN'04), Washington, D.C.

Watro, R., Kong, D., Cuti, S.-f., Gardiner, C., Lynn, C., & Kruus, P. (2004). *TinyPK: Securing sensor networks with public key technology.* Paper presented at the 2nd ACM Workshop on Security of ad hoc and sensor networks.

Westcott, R. (2007). Maximizing the ROI of a security audit. *Network Security*, (March): 8–11. doi:10.1016/S1353-4858(07)70026-0

Westervelt, R. (2008). *Exploit code released for critical VMware flaw.* Search Security. Retrieved from http://searchsecurity.techtarget.com/news/article/0,289142,sid14_gci1302293,00.html

Westervelt, R. (2010a). *For Google, DNS log analysis essential in Aurora attack investigation.* SearchSecurity. com. Retrieved from http://searchsecurity.techtarget.com/news/ article/0,289142,sid14_gci1514965,00.html

Westervelt, R. (2010b). *More firms targeted by advanced persistent threats, study finds.* SearchSecurity.com. Retrieved from http://searchsecurity.techtarget.com/news/article/0,289142,sid14_gci1516233,00.html

WhatsConnected. (n.d.). Retrieved May 15, 2010, from http://www.whatsupgold.com/products/whatsup-gold-plugins/whatsconnected/index.aspx

Wiesner, S. (1983). Conjugate coding. *SIGACT News*, 78-88.

Wi-Fi-Alliance. (2010). *Wi-Fi Alliance.* Retrieved from http://www.wi-fi.org

Wikipedia. (2009). *Instant messaging.* Retrieved from http://en.wikipedia.org/ wiki/ Instant_messaging

Wikipedia. (n.d.). *History of financial audit.* Received May 20, 2010, from http://en.wikipedia.org/wiki/Financial_audit

Wilde, G. J. S. (2001). *Target risk 2: A new psychology of safety and health.* Toronto, Canada: PDE Publications.

Williamson, M., & Parry, A. (2004). *Virus throttling for instant messaging.* In Virus Bulletin Conference.

Wilson, T. (2009). *ITRC report: Malicious attacks increased in first half of 2009.* Retrieved March 23, 2010, from http://www.darkreading.com/insiderthreat/security/privacy/showArticle.jhtml?articleID=218000187

Wojtczuk, R., & Tereshkin, A. (2009). *Ring -3 rootkits.* Paper presented at Blackhat 2009, Las Vegas, NV.

Wong, C. K., Gouda, M., & Lam, S. (2000). Secure group communications using key graphs. *IEEE/ACM Transactions on Networking*, *8*(1), 16–30. doi:10.1109/90.836475

Wood, A. D., & Stankovic, J. A. (2002). Denial of service in sensor networks. *Computer*, *35*(10), 54–62. doi:10.1109/MC.2002.1039518

Wood, A. D., & Stankovic, J. A. (2006). AMSecure: Secure link-layer communication in TinyOS for IEEE 802.15.4-based wireless sensor networks. Proceedings of 4th International Conference on Embedded Networked Sensor Systems (SenSys'06), (pp. 395-396).

Worthen, B. (2009, January 20). Card data breached, firm says. *Wall Street Journal*, 2009. Retrieved from http://online.wsj.com/article/ SB123249174099899837.html

Wright, C., Freedman, B., & Liu, D. (2008). An introduction to network audit. In *The IT regulatory and standards compliance handbook* (pp. 195–227). Syngress. doi:10.1016/B978-1-59749-266-9.00009-6

WS-Security Specification. (2010). *Library specification*. Retrieved from http://www.ibm.com/developerworks/library/specification/ws-secure/

Xiao, Y., Rayi, V. K., Sun, B., Du, X., Hu, F., & Galloway, M. (2007). A survey of key management schemes in wireless sensor networks. *Computer Communications, 30*(11-12), 2314–2341. doi:10.1016/j.comcom.2007.04.009

Xiaoyan, H., Pu, W., Jiejun, K., Qunwei, Z., & jun, L. (2005). *Effective probabilistic approach protecting sensor traffic*. Paper presented at the Military Communications Conference, 2005. MILCOM 2005. IEEE.

Xie, M., Wu, Z., & Wang, H. (2007). HoneyIM: Fast detection and suppression of instant messaging malware in enterprise-like networks. In *Proceedings of ACSAC '07*.

Xprobe2. (2010). Received March 30, 2010, from http://xprobe.sourceforge.net/

Xu, J., & Zha, X. (2007). Secret sharing schemes with general access structure based on MSPs. *The Journal of Communication, 2*(1), 52–55.

Xu, W., Trappe, W., Zhang, Y., & Wood, T. (2005). *The feasibility of launching and detecting jamming attacks in wireless networks*.

Xue, Q., & Ganz, A. (2009). Runtime security composition for sensor networks (secure sense). IEEE 58th Vehicular Technology Conference (VTC'03), (pp. 2976-2980).

Xun, Z., Yu, L., & Hong Ge, M. (2006). *Node-disjointness-based multipath routing for mobile wireless ad hoc networks*. Paper presented at the Information and Communication Technologies, 2006. ICTTA '06.

Yaar, A., Perrig, A., & Song, D. (2004). *SIFF: A stateless Internet flow filter to mitigate DDoS flooding attacks*. In IEEE Symposium on Security and Privacy.

Yan, G., Xiao, Z., & Eidenbenz, S. (2008). Catching instant messaging worms with change-point detection techniques. *Proc. of the 1st Usenix Workshop on Large-Scale Exploits and Emergent Threats*.

Yanchao, Z., Wei, L., Wenjing, L., & Yuguang, F. (2006). Location-based compromise-tolerant security mechanisms for wireless sensor networks. *IEEE Journal on Selected Areas in Communications, 24*(2), 247–260. doi:10.1109/JSAC.2005.861382

Yang, C.-N., & Chen, T.-S. (2006). Reduce shadow size in aspect ratio invariant visual secret sharing schemes using a square block-wise operation. *Pattern Recognition, 39*(7), 1300–1314. doi:10.1016/j.patcog.2006.01.013

Yang, G. Z. (Ed.). (2006). *Body sensor networks*. Springer-Verlag. doi:10.1007/1-84628-484-8

Yang, X., Wetherall, D., & Anderson, T. (2005). A DoS limiting network architecture. *ACM SIGCOMM, 35*(4), 241–252. doi:10.1145/1090191.1080120

Yang, Y., et al. (2007). A survey on technologies for implementing sensor networks for power delivery systems. Proceedings of IEEE Power Engineering Society General Meeting, (pp. 1-8).

Yang, Z., Zhon, S., & Wright, R. N. (2005). Privacy-preserving classification of customer data without loss of accuracy. *Proceedings of the Fifth SIAM International Conference on Data Mining*, Newport Beach, CA, April 21-23, 2005.

Yao, A. C. (1986). *How to generate and exchange secrets*. 27th IEEE Symposium on Foundations of Computer Science, 1986, (pp. 162–167).

Yao, J., & Wen, G. (2008). *Protecting classification privacy data aggregation in wireless sensor networks*. 4th International Conference on Wireless Communications, Networking and Mobile Computing, 2008. WiCOM '08, 12-14 Oct. 2008 (pp. 1–5). DOI 10.1109/WiCom.2008.951

Ye, F., Zhong, G., Lu, S., & Zhang, L. (2005). GRAdient broadcast: A robust data delivery protocol for large scale sensor networks. *Wireless Networks, 11*(3), 285–298. doi:10.1007/s11276-005-6612-9

Ye, F., Luo, H., Cheng, J., Lu, S., & Zhang, L. (2002). *A two-tier data dissemination model for large-scale wireless sensor networks*. Paper presented at the 8th Annual International Conference on Mobile computing and networking.

Yi, X. (2004). Identity-based fault-tolerant conference key agreement. *IEEE Transactions on Dependable and Secure Computing, 1*(3), 170–178. doi:10.1109/TDSC.2004.31

Yi, X., & Zhang, Y. (2007). Privacy-preserving distributed association rule mining via semi-trusted mixer. *Data & Knowledge Engineering, 63*(2). doi:10.1016/j.datak.2007.04.001

Yi, X., & Zhang, Y. (2009). Privacy-preserving naive Bayes classification on distributed data via semi-trusted mixers. *Information Systems, 34*(3), 371–380.

Yibin, L., & Midkiff, S. F. (2005). *Multipath Fresnel zone routing for wireless ad hoc networks*. Paper presented at the 2005 IEEE Wireless Communications and Networking Conference.

Yick, J. (2008). Wireless sensor network survey. *Elsevier Computer Networks, 52*(12), 2292–2330. doi:10.1016/j.comnet.2008.04.002

Younis, M., Ghumman, K., & Eltoweissy, M. (2006). Location-aware combinatorial key management scheme for clustered sensor networks. *IEEE Transactions on Parallel and Distributed Systems, 17*(8), 865–882. doi:10.1109/TPDS.2006.106

Yu, Z., & Guan, Y. (2008). A key management scheme using deployment knowledge for wireless sensor networks. *IEEE Transactions on Parallel and Distributed Systems, 19*(10), 1411–1425. doi:10.1109/TPDS.2008.23

Yu, Y., Govindan, R., & Estrin, D. (2001). *Geographical and energy aware routing: A recursive data dissemination protocol for wireless sensor networks*. (UCLA Computer Science Department Technical Report, UCLA-CSD TR-01-0023).

Zalewski, M. (n.d.). *p0f*. Retrieved from http://lcamtuf.coredump.cx/p0f.shtml

Zeng, W. G. (2002). A secure fault-tolerant conference key agreement protocol. *IEEE Transactions on Computers, 51*(4), 373–379. doi:10.1109/12.995447

Zetter, K. (2008). Revealed: The Internet's biggest security hole. *Wired Magazine*. Retrieved March 2010 from http://www.wired.com/threatlevel/2008/ 08/revealed-the-in/

Zetter, K. (2010). Google hack attack was ultra sophisticated, new details show. *Wired*. Retrieved from http://www.wired.com/threatlevel/ 2010/01/operation-aurora/

Zhang, B., Feng, M., Xiong, H., & Hu, D. (2008). *Design and implementation of secure instant messaging system based on MSN*. In International Symposium on Computer Science and Computational Technology (ISCSCT '08).

Zhang, J., Fang, D., & Liu, L. (2009). Intelligent content filtering model for network security audit system. *Proceedings of Second International Workshop on Knowledge Discovery and Data Mining*, (pp. 546-548).

Zhou, Y., & Fang, Y. (2008). *Securing wireless sensor networks: A survey* (pp. 6–28). IEEE Communications Surveys & Tutorials.

Zhou, F., Zhuang, L., Zhao, B., Huang, A., Joseph, L., & Kubiatowicz, J. (2003). Approximate object-location and spam filtering on peer-to-peer systems. In *Proc. of the ACM/IFIP/USENIX International Middleware Conference*.

Zhu, B., Wan, Z., Kankanhalli, M. S., Bao, F., & Deng, R. H. (2004). *Anonymous secure routing in mobile ad-hoc networks*. The 29th Annual IEEE International Conference on Local Computer Networks, Nov. 2004, (pp. 102–108).

Zhu, S., et al. (2003). LEAP: Efficient security mechanism for large scale distributed sensor networks. Proceedings of 10th ACM Conference on Computer and Communications Security (CCS'03), (pp. 62-72).

Zhu, S., Setia, S., & Jajodia, S. (2003). *LEAP: Efficient security mechanisms for large-scale distributed sensor networks*. Paper presented at the ACM CCS.

ZigBee. (2010). *ZigBee Alliance webpage*. Retrieved from http://www.zigbee.org

Zimmerman, P. (1991). *Phil's pretty good privacy*. Retrieved December 1, 2009, from ftp://ftp.pgpi.org/pub/pgp/2.x/doc/pgpdoc1.txt

Znaidi, W., Minier, M., & Babau, J. (2008). *An ontology for attacks in wireless sensor networks*.

Zou, C., Gong, W. B., & Towsley, D. (2003a). Worm propagation modeling and analysis under dynamic quarantine defense. *Proc. ACM Workshop on Rapid Malcode (WORM'03)*.

Zou, C., Gong, W. B., & Towsley, D. (2003b). Code red worm propagation modeling and analysis. In *Proceedings of 9th ACM Conference on Computer and Communication Security*.

Zou, C., Towsley, D., & Gong, W. (2004). E-mail worm modeling and defense. In *Proceedings of the 3rd International Conference on Computer Communications and Networks* (ICCCN).

About the Contributors

Dulal C. Kar is currently an Associate Professor in the Department of Computing Sciences at Texas A&M University – Corpus Christi, Texas. Previously, he was a faculty in the Department of Computer Science at Virginia Polytechnic Institute and State University, Virginia; Mountain State University, West Virginia; and Bangladesh University of Engineering and Technology, Bangladesh. He received the B.Sc.Engg. and the M.Sc.Engg. degrees from Bangladesh University of Engineering and Technology, Dhaka, Bangladesh and the MS and the Ph.D. degrees from North Dakota State University, Fargo, North Dakota. He is in the editorial board of the International Journal of Distance Education Technologies published by IGI Global. His research interests include wireless sensor networks, signal and image processing algorithms, network architecture and performance measurement, network and information security, information retrieval, and educational technology. He has published over fifty refereed journal and conference articles in those areas. His research works have been supported by various grants from NSF, DoD, NASA, and Cisco Systems.

Mahbubur Rahman Syed is currently a professor of Information Systems and Technology at Minnesota State University, Mankato (MSU), USA. He has about 30 years of experience in teaching, in industry, in research, and in academic leadership in the field of computer science, engineering, and Information Technology/Systems. Earlier, he worked in the Electrical and Computer Engineering Department at the North Dakota State University in USA, in the School of Computing and Information Technology at Monash University in Australia, in the Department of Computer Science and Engineering at Bangladesh University of Engineering and Technology (BUET) in Bangladesh, and in Ganz Electric Works in Hungary. He was a founding member of the Department of Computer Science and Engineering at BUET and served as Head of this Department during 1986-92. He served as the General Secretary of Bangladesh Computer Society and also as the General Secretary of BUET Teacher's Association. He received the UNESCO/ROSTSCA' 85 award for South and Central Asia region in the field of Informatics and Computer Applications in Scientific Research. He won several other awards. He has co-edited several books in the area of e-commerce, software agents, distance education, multimedia systems, and networking. He has more than 100 papers published in journals and conference proceedings. He has been serving in different roles such as co-editor-in chief, as associate editors, in editorial review committees, and as member of review board in several international journals. Dr. Syed has been involved in international professional activities including organizing conferences and serving as conference and program committee chair.

* * *

Rajeev Agrawal is an Assistant Professor at North Carolina A&T State University. He received his PhD from Wayne State University on "Narrowing down the Semantic Gap between Content and Context in Image Retrieval." His paper 'Image Clustering using Multimodal Keywords' was selected as the best paper in International Conference on Semantics and Digital Media Technology (SAMT 2006). He has published about 30 papers and 4 book chapters. His current research interests are in personal privacy and security, anomaly detection, and improving image clustering and retrieval performance. Earlier he worked at HP Inc. as Senior Business Analyst for healthcare and transportation industry. While working at HP, he received the best performance award for his work on American Airlines project.

Aftab Ahmad (D.Sc. 1992, George Washington University) is Associate Professor in Computer Science Department at Norfolk State University (NSU). At NSU, he has taught courses on Data Communications, Wireless Networking, 3D Computer Graphics, Computer Organization, Computer Architecture, Programming in C++, and Scientific Visualization. He has been a visiting professor in Royal Institute of Technology (KTH) and Gwangju Institute of Science and Technology (GIST). Dr. Ahmad has published extensively in wireless networking and data communications areas. His publications include several journal and conference papers and two books. Dr. Ahmad is a senior member of the IEEE and a member of the ACM. He is the General Chair of the 14th Symposium on Communications and Networking (Boston, April 2011). He has been on the review panels of NSF, NDSEG, and NASA. In the past, he has chaired Wireless QoS Symposium and has been on the editorial board of the Int'l Journal of Communications Systems. He co-edited a special issue of Int'l Journal on Semantic Computing on Wearable Communications and the Int'l Journal of Communications Systems. Dr. Ahmad lives in Virginia Beach with his wife Mahmooda and son Aftab Sani Ahmad.

Murat Al received his B.S. degree in Electrical Engineering and M.S. degree in Computer Technology and Telecommunication from the University of Applied Sciences in Darmstadt, Germany, in 2001 and 2005, respectively. Currently, he is completing his Ph.D. degree in Applied Science with emphasis on Applied Computing at the University of Arkansas at Little Rock (UALR). Since 2006, has been working as an instructor and researcher in the Department of Computer Science of UALR, and is a member of ACM. His current research interests include the analysis and design of wireless sensor networks, computer and network security, and information security.

Jiang Bian is the Technical Team Lead of the research program at the Information Technology of University of Arkansas for Medical Sciences. He received his M.S. in Computer Science from University of Arkansas at Little Rock (UALR) in 2007 and is currently seeking a Ph.D. in Applied Computing, also at UALR. As a researcher, his interests focus in the computer operating systems and network security areas with an emphasis on encryption, authentication, and secure system architectures. Mr. Bian's dissertation focus is the design and implementation of a platform independent secure distributed file system called Jigsaw Distributed File System (JigDFS), which facilitates long term storage of large data archives where security and privacy is critical. At the medical school, Mr. Bian has a leading role in architecting and implementing large-scale Clinical Trial Management Systems, where data quality and security are critical aspects of ongoing research efforts.

Christos Bouras obtained his Diploma and Ph.D. from the Computer Science and Engineering Department of Patras University (Greece). He is currently a professor in the above department. He is also a scientific advisor of Research Unit 6 in Research Academic Computer Technology Institute (CTI), Patras, Greece. His research interests include analysis of performance of networking and computer systems, computer networks and protocols, telematics and new services, QoS and pricing for networks and services, e – learning, networked virtual environments, and WWW issues. He has extended professional experience in design and analysis of networks, protocols, telematics, and new services. He has published 300 papers in various well-known refereed conferences and journals. He is a co-author of eight books in Greek. He has been a PC member and referee in various international journals and conferences.

Chaoli Cai received his Ph.D. in Computer Science from the Western Michigan University in 2009. Before that, he earned his B.S. in Computer Science from the Shanghai Jiao Tong University Shanghai, China in 2000. Dr. Cai has worked as a Network Administrator and has experience in network and database analysis, design, and administration. His current areas of interest are in network security, machine learning, data mining, and artificial intelligence. He has published several papers in these areas.

J. Ken Corley II, Ph.D., is an Assistant Professor in the Department of Computer Information Systems in John A. Walker College of Business at Appalachian State University, North Carolina. He has been employed as an art director at Augusta Sportswear, a member of an in-house marketing group at Kennametal IPG, and general manager of Beaed Corporation. Ken is particularly interested in Human-Computer Interactions, e-commerce, e-learning, Internet technologies/middleware, Supply Chain Management, security, and international computing issues.

Ajay Gupta is a Professor of Computer Science at Western Michigan University. From 1998 to 2002, he was the Chairman of the Computer Science Department at Western Michigan University. Dr. Gupta received his Ph.D. in Computer Science from Purdue University in 1989, his M.S. in Mathematics and Statistics from the University of Cincinnati in 1984, and his B.E. (Honors) in Electrical and Electronics Engineering from the Birla Institute of Technology and Sciences, Pilani, India in 1982. Dr. Gupta's research interests include sensor systems, cloud computing, mobile computing, Web technologies, computer networks, evolutionary computation, scientific computing, and design and analysis of parallel and distributed algorithms. He has published numerous technical papers and book chapters in refereed conferences and journals in these areas. A paper he co-authored, "Adaptive Integration Using Evolutionary Strategies," won the Best Paper award in the International Conference on High Performance Computing in 1996. Another paper he co-authored, "Lightweight Intrusion Detection for Sensor Networks," received Honorable mention at the CERIAS Information Security Symposium in 2006. He also holds joint copyright for the parallel and distributed automatic numerical integration software package, ParInt 1.1. He is a senior member of the IEEE and member of the IEEE Computer Society, the IEEE Communications Society, the ASEE and the ACM.

Bruce Hartpence has been faculty within RIT's Networking, Security and Systems Administration department for the past 12 years. Having completed a successful tour in the United States Naval nuclear power program and after working in industry at Mobil Chemical, he now teaches wired and wireless communication within the Golisano College of Communication and Information Sciences. He has developed many courses including Wireless Security, Network Troubleshooting and VoIP Security/QoS. Mr. Hartpence has several papers on related topics with a current interest in the intersection of wireless, real time data, and security. His latest project is a collaboration with industry to build a secure, wireless communication network for the transfer of driver and telemetry data for trucks.

Dijiang Huang received his Bachelor of Science degree in Telecommunications from Beijing University of Posts & Telecommunications in 1995. He received his Master of Science and PhD degrees from University of Missouri-Kansas City in 2001 and 2004, respectively. Both majored in Computer Science and Telecommunications. He joined Computer Science and Engineering department at ASU in 2005 as an assistant professor. His current research interests are in two areas. *Security and privacy*: cryptography, key management, authentication protocol, attack analysis, privacy preserving, and attack resilient network design. *Computer system and networking*: cloud computing, network protocols design, and mobile communication. Dr. Huang's research is supported by NSF, ONR, AFRL, and Consortium of Embedded System (CES). He is a recipient of ONR Young Investigator Award 2010.

Md. Golam Kaosar is a Ph.D. student at the School of Engineering and Science, Victoria University, Australia. Before he started his Ph.D., he used to work as an engineer at Research Institute (RI) in King Fahd University of Petroleum and Minerals (KFUPM), Saudi Arabia. Before that, he got his MS in Computer Engineering and BSc in Computer Science and Engineering from KFUPM, and Bangladesh University of Engineering and Technology (BUET), Bangladesh in the years 2006 and 2001, respectively. As a young researcher, he has a good research background. He has published number of reputable journal and conference papers. His area of research includes, but is not limited to: privacy preserving data mining, ubiquitous computing, security and cryptography, ad-hoc sensor networks, mobile and wireless networks, network protocols, et cetera.

David Lee. Having received a Master's and a Ph.D. degree in Computer Science from Columbia University in 1986, he joined AT&T, and became Vice President of Bell Labs Research in 1999, responsible for the creation of Bell Labs Research China in Beijing, 2000-2004. He joined The Ohio State University as Ohio Board of Regents Distinguished Professor in 2004. He is an IEEE Fellow, and has won the best paper awards of IFIP International Conference PSTV-FORTE'2000 and IFIP International Conference TestCom'2005. He has six US patents and more than 120 publications in referenced journals and conference. He is a Senior Editor of IEEE Journal on Selected Areas in Communications and serves at the editorial board Journal of Law and Policy for the Information Society.

Zhijun Liu was born in China. He graduated from University of Science and Technology of China with a B.S. in Computer Sciences in 1999. In 2002, he obtained an M.E. degree in Computer Sciences from Institute of Software, Chinese Academy of Sciences. In 2006, he received a M.S. degree from the Department of Computer Science and Engineering, The Ohio State University, and became a Ph.D. candidate in Computer Sciences. At the end of 2007, he joined Cisco System, Inc. Currently, he is a Software Engineer and working in Security Technology BU of Cisco. He is a TPC Member of IEEE ICC and GLOBECOM from 2006-2010. Over the years, his research and working areas include: Information System security and management, distributed system, instant messaging worm/spam, intruder detection system, and Firewall security technology.

Salvador Mandujano is with the Security Center of Excellence at Intel Corporation in Hillsboro, Oregon, where he is responsible for security analysis and vulnerability discovery for a number of Intel vPro and Centrino Pro platform technologies. He has published numerous papers in the areas of information security, privacy, and artificial intelligence, and has done research with academic groups such as the Purdue University CERIAS computer security center and the Department of Computer Science at Cornell University. He holds a Ph.D. from Instituto Tecnologico y de Estudios Superiores de Monterrey, a M.Sc. degree from Purdue University, a B.Sc. from Universidad Nacional Autonoma de Mexico, as well the CISSP and CEH information security certifications. His current security projects involve low-power CPUs and system-on-chip products.

Douglas B. May, Ph.D., is an Associate Professor in the Department of Computer Information Systems in John A. Walker College of Business at Appalachian State University in Boone, North Carolina. He served as the Director of Academic Computing Services for Appalachian State University from 1995 to 2006. Dr. May is particularly interested in programming languages, database, Internet technologies/middleware, Human-Computer Interactions, security, and international computing issues.

B. Dawn Medlin is the Chair of the Department of Computer Information Systems and the Director of the Center for Advanced Research on Emerging Technologies, John A. Walker College of Business, at Appalachian State University in Boone, North Carolina. Her teaching and research activities have mainly been in the area of security, healthcare informatics, and e-commerce. She has published in journals such as The Journal of Information Systems Security, Information Systems Security, International Journal of Electronic Marketing and Retailing, and the International Journal of Healthcare Information Systems and Informatics. Additionally, she has taught at the Université d'Angers and Addis Ababa University in Ethiopia.

Sumita Mishra joined RIT in 2007 and is an Assistant Professor in the Networking, Security and Systems Administration department. She has a doctorate in Electrical Engineering with concentration in wireless communications and networking. As a part of her Ph.D. thesis (funded in part by National Science Foundation), she developed an analytical framework for comparing different locating schemes in cellular networks. For the past 10 years, she has been working in the areas of security, performance, and mobility management for cellular, sensor, and ad hoc networks. As the manager of the Embedded Wireless Division of CompSys Technologies Inc., Amherst, NY, Dr. Mishra was actively involved for several years in technology development in the areas of ad hoc and sensor network security. She has published papers in IEEE journals and conferences such as MILCOM, WCNC, GLOBECOM and VTC. Her current research involves security for smart Grid networks.

Yin Pan is an associate professor in the Department of Networking, Security and Systems Administration at RIT. She received her Ph.D. in Systems Science and M.S. degree in Computer Science in 1997 from Binghamton University. Dr. Pan holds four US patents in areas of network Quality of Services, Voice over IP and Artificial Intelligence. Since 2004, Dr. Pan has been actively involved in the network security area, especially in IT security audits and computer forensics. Her current research involves information security auditing, social networking security, and computer forensics. She has published many papers in these fields. Dr. Pan is a certified steganography investigator. She also held the GIAC Systems and Network Auditor (GSNA) Certificate and Advanced Windows Forensics Tool Kit Certificate.

Rajib Paul is an Assistant Professor in the Department of Statistics at the Western Michigan University. Dr. Paul received his PhD degree in Statistics from the Ohio State University in 2008 under the guidance of Dr. Mark Berliner. Prior to that, Dr. Paul received his B. Sc. degree in Statistics from Calcutta University, India, followed by an M. Sc. degree from the Indian Institute of Technology, Kanpur, India.

Reed Petty has been continuously active in the commercial transportation industry for more than 30 years, working both as a developer and in leadership roles managing global IT infrastructures. His encryption related contributions to the Linux kernel have been cited in the kernel credits since 1999. Mr. Petty is also a contributing developer to Hercules virtualization effort which implements IBM mainframe architectures in software. He is the author of the AWSSL family of virtualization utilities. Mr. Petty studied computer science and Information Science as undergraduate at the University of Utah and John Brown University. Subsequently, he has received an M.B.A. and is now seeking a Ph.D. in Applied Science with an emphasis in Information Quality at the University of Arkansas at Little Rock.

Remzi Seker received his Ph.D. degree in Computer Engineering from the University of Alabama at Birmingham in December 2002. His research areas are security and safety-critical computer systems. Dr. Seker, as a researcher, focuses on protection mechanisms from the asymmetric threats that arise from rapid, yet necessary use of technology. He is co-author of one of the very first papers that was published on mobile phishing and possible techniques for preventing it. Aside from professional research and scholarly efforts, Dr. Seker participates in variety of activities to increase public awareness on information assurance and security. Dr. Seker is currently an Associate Professor in the Computer Science Department at the University of Arkansas at Little Rock.

Nirav Shah was a graduate student in the Computer Science department at Arizona State University and is currently working as a Software Engineer at Intel Corporation. He has been working on developing network security and routing protocols for the past 3+ years. He specializes in denial of service prevention techniques. He has been working towards building a set of best practices for secure implementation of open source cloud computing systems.

Guoqiang Shu received his Ph.D degree in computer science from Department of Computer Science and Engineering, The Ohio State University in 2008. His research interest includes network protocols, network security, and formal method. He received M.E. and B.S. degree from Chinese Academy of Sciences and Peking University in 2003 and 2000, respectively. He currently works as a Member of Technical Staff for VMware, Inc. in Palo Alto, USA. Guoqiang Shu is a Senior Member of IEEE.

Kostas Stamos obtained his Diploma, Master Degree, and Ph.D. from the Computer Engineering and Informatics Department of Patras University (Greece). He has worked for the Networking Technologies Sector of CTI, Research Unit 6 of CTI and the Greek Research and Education Network (Grnet). He is also teaching at the Computer Engineering and Informatics Department at the University of Patras, and at the Technological Educational Institute of Patras. He has published seven articles in journals and 28 papers in well-known refereed conferences. He is also co-author of two technical books, several encyclopaedia articles and of a Global Grid Forum (GGF) standard document.

Christophe Veltsos (CISSP, CISA, CIPP) regularly teaches Information Security and Information Warfare classes in the Department of Information Systems & Technology at Minnesota State University. Christophe has presented on information security topics at the local, regional, and national level, including at major security conferences like RSA. Beyond the classroom, Christophe is also very active in the security community, engaging with community groups and business leaders, as well as IT and security professionals. From 2007 to 2010, he served as President of the Mankato Chapter of the Information Systems Security Association (ISSA). In 2009 and 2010, he contributed to the work of the privacy subgroup of the NIST Smart Grid Interoperability Panel Cyber Security Working Group (SGIP-CSWG). Christophe holds a Ph.D. from the University of Louisiana at Lafayette and is a member of many information security and privacy related organizations. Both faculty and practitioner, Dr. Veltsos maintains the DrInfoSec.com blog.

Chuan-Kun Wu, BSc. 1985, MSc. 1988, PhD Engin. 1994. Since January 1988, he was teaching at Xidian University. He was promoted by Xidian University to a Lecturer in 1990, an associate professor in 1992, and a full professor in 1995. In September 1995, he became a postdoctoral research fellow at QUT in Australia, then from 1997 a research fellow at UWS, and from 2000 a Lecturer in the Department of Computer Science, Australian National University. He has got many awards while he was in China, including China Government Special Subsidy, awarded in 1993. As a co-founder, he has served as a program committee chair for 2001, 2002, and 2003 International Workshop on Cryptology and Network Security (CANS), and is an associate editor of IEEE Communications Letters, a member of the editorial board of International Journal of Network Security, a senior member of IEEE since 2000.

Xun Yi is an Associate Professor with School of Engineering and Science, Victoria University, Australia. Before joining Victoria University, he was an Assistant Professor with School of Information Science, Japan Advanced Institute of Science and Technology (JAIST), Japan, and an Assistant Professor with School of Electrical and Electronic Engineering, Nanyang Technological University (NTU), Singapore. Currently, he is visiting the Department of Risk Engineering, University of Tsukuba in Japan as an Associate Professor. He obtained a Ph.D. degree in Engineering from Xidian University in 1995. His research interests include applied cryptography, privacy-preserving data mining, computer and network security, mobile and wireless communication security, and intelligent agent technology. He has published about 100 research papers in international journals, such as IEEE Trans. Knowledge and Data Engineering, IEEE Trans. Wireless Communication, IEEE Trans. Dependable and Secure Computing, IEEE Trans. Circuit and Systems, IEEE Trans. Vehicular Technologies, IEEE Communication Letters, and conference proceedings. He is a member of Editorial Reviewer Board for International Journal of Electronic Commerce in Organization. He has ever undertaken program committee members for about 20 international conferences. He is leading an Australia Research Council (ARC) Discovery Project on Privacy Protection in Distributed Data Mining.

Kenji Yoshigoe received his Ph.D. degree in Computer Science and Engineering from the College of Engineering at the University of South Florida in 2004, and is currently an Associate Professor of Computer Science at the University of Arkansas at Little Rock (UALR). His research interest is on computer networks. He is currently investigating the scalability, reliability, and security of systems including high-performance computing (HPC) cluster, high-speed packet switches, and wireless sensor networks (WSNs). He is the founder of the WSN Lab and the HPC facility at UALR, and is a principle investigator (PI) and Co-PI for various National Science Foundation-funded projects. He has published widely in leading computer networks conferences and journals, and serves as a chair and a committee member in many symposia and conferences. He is a member of the ACM and IEEE.

Bo Yuan holds a Ph.D. degree in System Sciences from Binghamton University (SUNY), an M.S. degree in Applied Mathematics, and a B.S. in Mathematics from Shanghai Normal University. He has authored and coauthored multiple books and many research papers in the areas of computational intelligence and network security. Recently, Dr. Yuan's main interests are in the areas of wired and wireless network security, and more specifically, in network covert channels. Dr. Yuan is also working on creating a search engine for mathematical formulas.

Index

X

Z